Data Acquisition

edited by

Dr. Michele Vadursi

Data Acquisition

Edited by Dr. Michele Vadursi

Republished by InTech

Janeza Trdine 9, 51000 Rijeka, Croatia

Publishing Process Manager Jelena Marusic

Technical Editor Goran Bajac

Cover Designer Martina Sirotic

Additional hard copies can be obtained from orders@intechopen.com

Data Acquisition, Edited by Dr. Michele Vadursi
p. cm.
ISBN 978-953-307-193-0

Meet the editor

Associate Professor of Electrical and Electronic Measurements. Teacher of Electronic and Biomedical Measurement courses (Degree in Computer Engineering, Biomedical and Telecommunications) and Measurements and Electrical Safety (Master's Degree in Management Engineering). Graduated with honors in Telecommunications Engineering in 2002 at the University of Naples Federico II, in 2005 he obtained the title of Doctor of Research in Electrical Engineering (Electric and Electronic Measurements Sector) at the same University. In 2006 he became Researcher in Electrical and Electronic Measurements at the Faculty of Engineering of the University of Naples "Parthenope". His main research interests concern the definition and implementation of innovative measurement methods, based on numerical processing algorithms, for diagnostics and verification of the performance of telecommunications systems and equipment, and the definition of measurement methodologies for problems. coexistence of wireless communication systems. In 2009 he received the IET Communications Premium Award for best work published in the journal IET Communications.

Contents

Preface

The book is intended to be a collection of contributions providing a bird's eye view of some relevant multidisciplinary applications of data acquisition. While assuming that the reader is familiar with the basics of sampling theory and analog-to-digital conversion, the attention is focused on applied research and industrial applications of data acquisition. Even in the few cases when theoretical issues are investigated, the goal is making the theory comprehensible to a wide, application-oriented, audience.

In detail, the first chapter examines the effects of noise on the performance of data acquisition systems, and the performance improvements achievable thanks to dithering and averaging techniques. The second chapter presents some practical solutions for the acquisition of band-pass signals. The following chapters deal with distributed data acquisition systems, wireless sensor networks, and data acquisition systems architectures: they address synchronization, design and performance evaluation issues. Finally, a series of chapters present some multidisciplinary applications of data acquisition for sensing and on-line monitoring, ranging from energy and power systems to biomedical system, from nuclear and particle physics to magnetic shields characterization.

Editor

Dr. Michele Vadursi
University of Naples "Parthenope"
Department of Technologies
Naples, Italy

1

Noise, Averaging, and Dithering in Data Acquisition Systems

Filippo Attivissimo and Nicola Giaquinto[1]
Dipartimento di Elettrotecnica ed Elettronica
Politecnico di Bari,
Italia

1. Introduction

In any data acquisition system (DAS) many error effects, both of systematic nature (e.g. nonlinearity) and of random nature (e.g. electronic noise) are simultaneously present. While systematic errors are a comparatively stable characteristic of a DAS, random errors may be smaller or larger in different situations, and it is important to understand how they degrade the overall performance of the system. It is even more important to understand that random errors can be actually used to *improve* the fidelity of the acquisition, i.e. the technique of dithering. This possibility is due to the inherent presence in any DAS of a particular kind of error: the quantization error.

Quantization is a basically simple operation and it is easily understood at an elementary level. However, evaluating its effects on signals, with or without the simultaneous presence of other errors, requires quite complex mathematics, usually not mastered by engineers and even by researchers without a specific interest in the topic. Due to the complexity of the subject (an excellent reference book is [WK08]), misunderstandings and mistakes are common when dealing with noise in DAS. For example, it is true that averaging a particular number of samples is convenient to reduce the noise, but it is easy to disregard the fact that it is useless to increase the number of samples beyond a certain limit (contrary to what happens in analogue measurements). In the same way, even if introducing noise in a DAS may be desirable and effective, and is expressly a feature in commercial DAS (e.g. [Nat97], [Nat07]), few users are aware of how the appropriate level of noise (and other parameters) can be chosen.

The present chapter deals with the topic of performance degradation/improvement in a DAS, deriving by the presence (wanted or unwanted) of noise, and by averaging or filtering the output samples. The aim is making the theory understandable and usable by a wide audience, using ideas and mathematics as simple as possible. Proper reference, when needed, is made to works with rigorous mathematical demonstration of the derived results. The chapter covers only the case of perfectly linear DAS, with no (or negligible) nonlinearity errors. The more general case of nonlinear DAS with noise is a subject for a possible future expanded version of the chapter.

---

[1] corresponding author: http://dee.poliba.it/DEE/Giaquinto.html

2. Effective number of bits

If $x(t)$ is the analogue input of a DAS and y_n are the output samples, the evaluation of the overall acquisition fidelity takes into account, customarily, only transformations involving the *shape* of $x(t)$. Therefore, the fidelity evaluation excludes:

- linear transformations in the amplitude of the signal (due to fixed gain and offset errors);
- linear transformations in the time of the signal (due to a fixed trigger delay and a fixed error in sampling frequency).

Formally, this means that one has to identify four constants a, b, c, d so that, if t_n are the nominal (ideal) sampling instants, the *scaled* input samples

$$x_n^s = a + b \cdot x(c + d \cdot t_n) \tag{1}$$

have minimum distance, in the least squares (LS) sense, from the output samples y_n ($\sum_n (y_n - x_n^s)^2 = \min$.)

In practical DAS testing, $x(t)$ is often a large sinusoidal signal, i.e. a sinusoid stimulating at least 90% of the full-scale range (FSR) of the acquisition channel (as specified in [IEE94], Clause 3.1.29). Identifying the four constants a, b, c, d means to determine with the LS method the four parameters $C, V, \omega_x, \varphi_x$ in the expression

$$x_n^s = C + V \cos(\omega_x t_n + \varphi_x) . \tag{2}$$

After determining x_n^s, a logical fidelity measure is the mean squared error (MSE)

$$\sigma_e^2 = \overline{(y_n - x_n^s)^2} = \overline{e_n^2} . \tag{3}$$

The MSE, however, is an absolute number lacking an immediately clear meaning. It is preferred, therefore, to express the value of MSE in terms of *effective number of bits* (ENOB), defined by the formula

$$b_e = b - \frac{1}{2}\log_2 \frac{\sigma_e^2}{\sigma_q^2} \tag{4}$$

where

$$\sigma_q^2 = Q^2 / 12 \tag{5}$$

is the MSE of an ideal sampler/quantizer with the same resolution of the DAS. It is obvious that in an actual DAS, which has additional errors besides quantization, it is always true that $\sigma_e^2 > \sigma_q^2$ and therefore $b_e < b$.

The meaning of the ENOB definition (4) is better understood by considering a conventional input signal with uniform distribution in the whole FSR of the converter, e.g. a triangular signal (or a ramp, a sawtooth, etc.). The FSR has amplitude

$$x_{fs} = 2^b \cdot Q \tag{6}$$

and therefore the full-scale triangular signal has power (without considering a possible dc component)

$$\sigma_x^2 = \frac{x_{fs}^2}{12} \tag{7}$$

For an ideal quantizer, the resolution b may be expressed in terms of the logarithm of the ratio between the power of the full-scale triangular signal σ_x^2 and the power of the ideal quantization error σ_q^2, i.e.

$$\frac{1}{2}\log_2 \frac{\sigma_x^2}{\sigma_q^2} = \frac{1}{2}\log_2 \frac{x_{fs}^2}{Q^2} = \frac{1}{2}\log_2 2^{2b} = b \tag{8}$$

For an actual DAS, the same ratio, with the actual MSE σ_e^2 instead of the ideal one σ_q^2, yields the ENOB:

$$\frac{1}{2}\log_2 \frac{\sigma_x^2}{\sigma_e^2} = \frac{1}{2}\log_2 \frac{\sigma_x^2}{\sigma_q^2} - \frac{1}{2}\log_2 \frac{\sigma_e^2}{\sigma_q^2} = b - \frac{1}{2}\log_2 \frac{\sigma_e^2}{\sigma_q^2} = b_e \tag{9}$$

Therefore, expression (4) of the ENOB gives the resolution of an ideal quantizer with the same MSE of the actual DAS (although the result is in general a non-integer number of bits). It is worth to highlight that, if $10\log_{10}$ is substituted to $(1/2)\log_2$ in (8), the ideal dynamic range $DR = 6.02 \cdot b$ of the DAS is obtained, and in the same way the quantity $6.02 \cdot b_e$ may be considered a measure of actual dynamic range (although this is not a standardized definition).

The given definition of ENOB, like the MSE σ_e^2, depends on the actual signal $x(t)$ used to stimulate the input of the DAS. The normal practical choice, which has become a standard, is a sinusoidal signal smaller than the FSR, but larger than 90% of the FSR itself ("large sinusoid"). The main reason for choosing the sinusoid is that the difference between the actually generated signal and its ideal mathematical expression must be a negligible quantity with respect to the error introduced by the DAS itself. This is technologically much more feasible for the sinusoid then for any other waveform. The large sinusoid, on the other hand, has its drawbacks, in practice and in theory.

1. Under a practical point of view, the large sinusoid does not cover exactly the whole range of the DAS, nor it stimulates uniformly the covered range. Therefore, nonlinearity errors near the border of the scale weigh less then errors near the centre, and the errors outside the range of the signal are not accounted for at all [GT97].
2. Under a theoretical point of view, in an ideal quantizer the sinusoid does not produce a MSE exactly equal to $\sigma_q^2 = Q^2/12$ [WK08]. Besides, there is a logical inconsistency in evaluating the MSE produced by a sinusoidal signal, and comparing it with the power of a uniformly distributed signal, as the ENOB definition (8) requires.

Because of the aforementioned problems, a perfectly linear ramp or a triangular signal are also used when possible. When the sinusoidal signal is the only feasible choice, a good suggestion (first given and developed in [GT97], and confirmed in [KB05]) is to stimulate the DAS with some overdrive, since in this way the signal laying in the FSR is almost uniformly distributed. As a matter of fact, in this way the ENOB evaluation is practically insensitive to small variations in the amplitude and offset of the stimulus sinusoid (contrary to what happens without overdrive), and the evaluation is much more consistent with the results obtained by different tests (e.g. the histogram test of nonlinearity, which uses a sinusoid with overdrive [IEE00]). The issue of practical ENOB testing, however, is not further addressed here.

In this chapter, mainly to avoid theoretical inconsistencies (point 2 above), the stimulus signal $x(t)$ is always assumed to be uniformly distributed in the FSR of the DAS. Since dynamic effects (like e.g. dynamic nonlinearity, sampling jitter, etc.) are not examined in the chapter and not included in the mathematical analysis and in the simulations, the frequency of the input is inessential. If one wants to obtain practical measurements in good accordance with the theory developed in the chapter, a sinusoidal signal with some overdrive must be used. Using a large sinusoidal signal leads to similar results, but with meaningful differences.

Another convention followed in this chapter is that the quantization step is assumed to be $Q = 1$. This is equivalent to express in LSB units all the quantities with the same physical dimension of Q (voltages), and simplifies many equations and notations. For example, since $\sigma_q = Q/\sqrt{12} = 1/\sqrt{12}$, ENOB may be expressed by

$$b_e = b - \frac{1}{2}\log_2 12\sigma_e^2 \tag{10}$$

provided that Q=1, or, equivalenty, that σ_e is expressed in LSB units. Under this condition, all the equations in the chapter can be used without modifications.

3. Perfectly linear DAS with noise and no averaging

The case of perfectly linear DAS with noise and no averaging is elementary but is also preliminary to the analysis of more complete and complex cases.

In an actual DAS there are many sources of noise, but the overall effect can be seen (and is quantified by manufacturers) as a single noise generator with power σ_n^2 at the input of the system. If the DAS has negligible nonlinearity, it can be represented by the very simple equivalent model in Fig. 1.

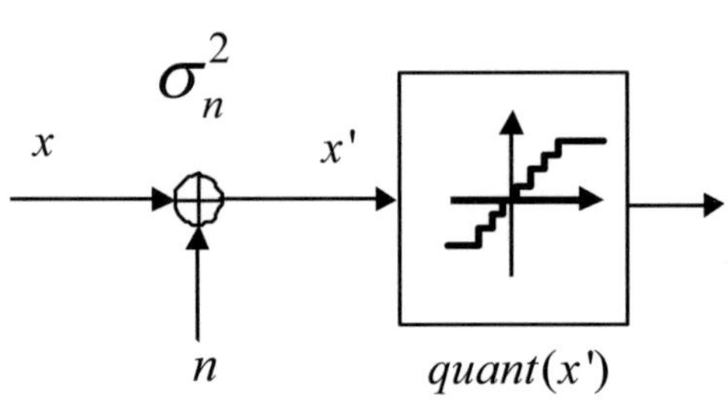

Fig. 1. Equivalent model of linear DAS with noise.

The ideal quantizer adds, of course, a quantization error $e_q(x')$, which is a function of the input $x' = x + n$. For a fixed input signal, and in particular for a full-scale triangular signal, the quantization error has a fixed power. Consequently, the model in Fig. 1 can be substituted by the fully additive model of Fig. 2 (a typical operation in quantization theory). Under broad conditions on the quantized signal x', quantization theory assures that quantization error is: (i) uniformly distributed in $[-Q/2, Q/2]$ and therefore zero-mean with power equal to $\sigma_q^2 = Q^2/12$; (ii) white; (iii) uncorrelated with the input. It can be proven (the more general proof is probably the one given in [SO05]) that n and e_q are uncorrelated, too, and therefore the overall MSE of the DAS is:

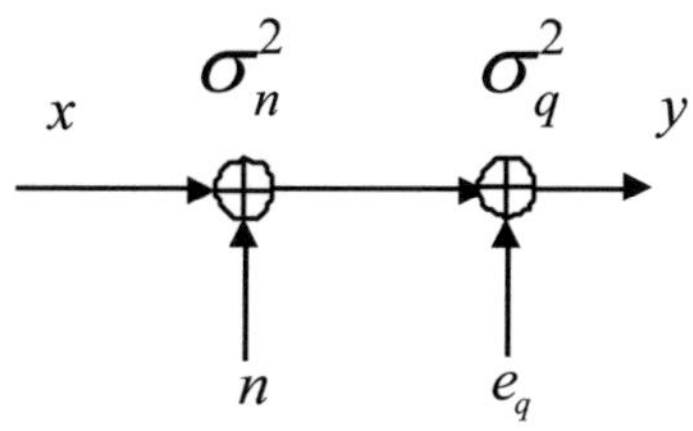

Fig. 2. Additive model equivalent to that in Fig.1.

$$\sigma_e^2 = \sigma_n^2 + \sigma_q^2 . \tag{10}$$

Taking into account the normalization convention ($Q = 1$), the term in (10) becomes $12\sigma_e^2 = 1 + 12\sigma_n^2$, and therefore in this elementary case the ENOB of the DAS is:

$$b_e = b - \frac{1}{2}\log_2\left(1 + 12\sigma_n^2\right) \tag{11}$$

A simple numerical simulation (performed for b in the range 8÷16 bits) confirms the formula (Fig. 3). It is interesting to note the formal similarity of the law of the performance degradation $\Delta b = -(1/2)\log_2(1 + 12\sigma_n^2)$ with that of a first-order low-pass filter, with a cut-off frequency equal to the pure root mean square (rms) quantization error, $\sigma_q = Q/\sqrt{12} \cong 0.289$ LSB. At the cut-off ($\sigma_n = \sigma_q$) the ENOB is half a bit below the nominal resolution b. After the cut-off, the ENOB decreases with a rate of 1 bit/octave, or 3.32 bit/decade, equivalent to a decrease in the dynamic range of 6.02 dB/octave or 20 dB/decade.

4. Perfectly linear DAS with noise and averaging: an important case of non-subtractive dithering

4.1 Oversampling and averaging

When the performance of a measurement system is degraded by noise, the obvious method to increase accuracy is some form of averaging.
The simple non-weighted averaging is the well-known optimal method to estimate an unknown constant signal buried in white Gaussian noise (WGN). When the signal is not constant, averaging is advantageously substituted by other filtering techniques, ranging from simple low-pass or band-pass filtering to adaptive filtering, etc. The basic principle is, however, the same: to obtain each output sample by a (weighted) average of many samples of the input, in order to reduce the acquisition error. This is the principle of *oversampling*, i.e. trading bandwidth (and possibly sampling frequency) for accuracy, e.g. in terms of ENOB.

As a side note, it must be highlighted that oversampling is implemented by design in a wide class of analog-to-digital converters (sigma-delta converters, etc.), used in commercial DAS [Nat05]. This chapter does not deal with this "hard" oversampling which involves built-in hardware to improve performance, e.g. in the form of embedded feedback loops. The chapter deals, instead, with the "soft" oversampling implemented by the user in the form of output processing when there is unwanted noise, and an abundance of acquired samples with respect to the signal bandwidth. Soft oversampling does not include the implementation of feedback loops, or similar techniques.

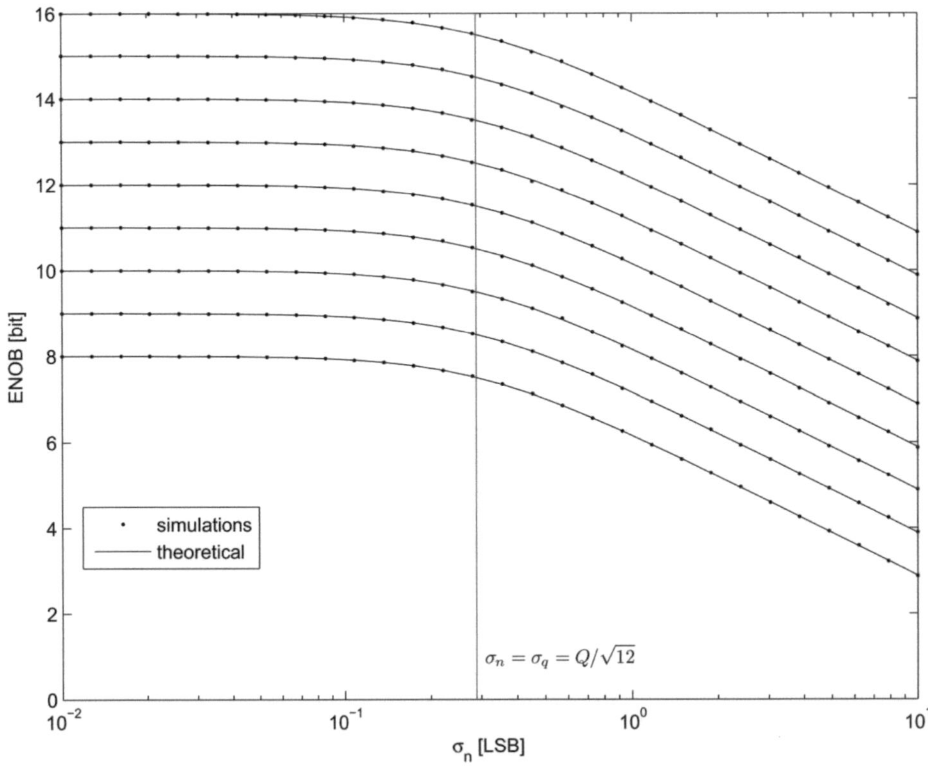

Fig. 3. ENOB of perfectly linear DAS (with resolution in the range 8÷16 bits) affected by input noise (with rms value in the range 0÷10 LSB). Numerical simulations are compared with theoretical equations. The "cut-off" at $\sigma_n = Q / \sqrt{12} = 0.289$ LSB is highlighted.

In the rest of the chapter, attention will be focused on the case of simple (non-weighted) averaging of many output samples of a DAS, when the input is an unknown constant with additive WGN.

Like for the hypothesis of uniformly distributed signal for ENOB evaluation, the choice of the case is primarily justified by theoretical convenience. In this way the problem is mathematically treatable and accurate closed-form equations are derivable. Besides, the analysis and the results provide a good understanding, useful for more general cases, of the interaction between the signal-dependent errors introduced by quantization, and the signal-independent errors introduced by noise.

In practice, the case of WGN is by far the most common, and it is easy to repeat the analysis for other kinds of noise (non-Gaussian and/or non-white). Also the hypothesis of constant signal is verified in many practical cases, e.g. when the sampling frequency is very high with respect to the variations of the input, when a sample-and-hold is used to acquire many samples with "frozen" signal, or when there is a repetitive sampling of many periods of a periodic signal. It is also not too difficult to extend the analysis to specific cases of linear filtering applied to a non-constant signal.

4.2 Dithering

Besides being present as an unwanted disturbing signal, WGN can be purposely added to the input of a DAS in order to improve the final accuracy. This is a particular case of the well-known technique of *dithering*, which is a main error-correction method among those available for DAS [BDR05]. The basic idea is that, since there is no way to remove or reduce the error introduced by quantization when the input is perfectly constant, random variations in the input are beneficial for error-correction. Indeed, the addition of a random signal to the input randomizes the quantization error which, in turn, can be removed (or reduced) by averaging.

Subtractive dithering in DAS consists in adding a dither signal to the input, and subtracting it from the output before possible further processing [Sch64]. Subtractive dithering inherently requires accurate knowledge of the signal added to the input (or specific hardware to measure it) and is therefore more difficult and expensive to implement.

Non-subtractive dithering, instead, implies averaging/filtering the output without previous subtraction of the dither added at the input. This technique is much easier to implement with respect to subtractive dithering, and has been studied quite deeply in a number of theoretical works (see, e.g. [WLVW00], and the bibliography in [WK08]). Even easier is to use simple WGN as a dither signal, since this noise is (almost always) already present at the input of DAS, and may be easily incremented if necessary. This very common kind of dithering may be called "white Gaussian non-subtractive dither" (WGND). Averaging the output of a linear DAS with WGN is therefore also a particular but very common and important case of non-subtractive dithering, the WGND (Fig. 4).

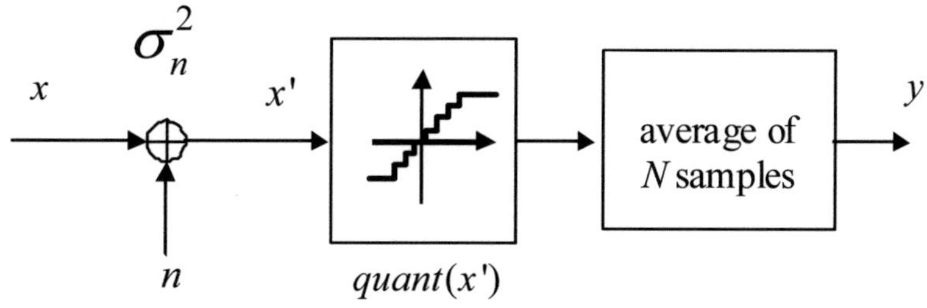

Fig. 4. Basic scheme of operation of WGND applied to a perfectly linear quantizer.

For the sake of completeness, it must be clarified that dithering consists in general in purposely altering the signal at the input of a system (the technique is not limited to data acquisition), in order to improve the performance of the system itself. In the field of data acquisition, besides adding an external signal, other kinds of dithering are possible and used, aiming at different performance improvements. For example, an effective anti-aliasing filter can be obtained, without increasing the sampling rate and without introducing

physical filters, by a proper randomization of the sampling instants. Amplitude and time dithering may be combined efficiently [AH98]. Of course random errors in sampling instants can be also an undesired effects, and in this case they are studied with specific mathematical models [AD09]. These techniques, dealing with errors in sampling instants and other kinds of alterations of the input signal, are not within the scope of this chapter.
The scheme reported in Fig. 4 has been deeply examined in the context of quantization theory using the typical, quite complex mathematical tools of the theory. The analysis reported here is probably the simpler and most direct way to understand the actual benefits given by WGND, and in general by averaging/filtering in presence of noise at the input of the DAS. The analysis is centred on the determination of the attainable ENOB in given conditions.

5. Averaging infinite output samples

The analysis starts considering the average of *infinite output samples* in the scheme of Fig. 4. Averaging infinite samples transforms the system, which includes random contributions, in a purely deterministic one. The input-output relationship of the system is the convolution of the ideal quantization function $\mathrm{quant}(x)$ with the probability density function (pdf) of the dither, i.e. with the zero-mean Gaussian density

$$\varphi(x,\mu,\sigma)=\frac{1}{\sigma\sqrt{2\pi}}e^{-\frac{1}{2}\left(\frac{x-\mu}{\sigma}\right)^2} \tag{12}$$

with $\mu=0$ and $\sigma=\sigma_n$. The result of the convolution is a nonlinear function which is actually a smoothed quantization, or a *dithered quantization* $y=\mathrm{quantd}(x)$. The system in Fig. 4 is transformed in that represented in Fig. 5.

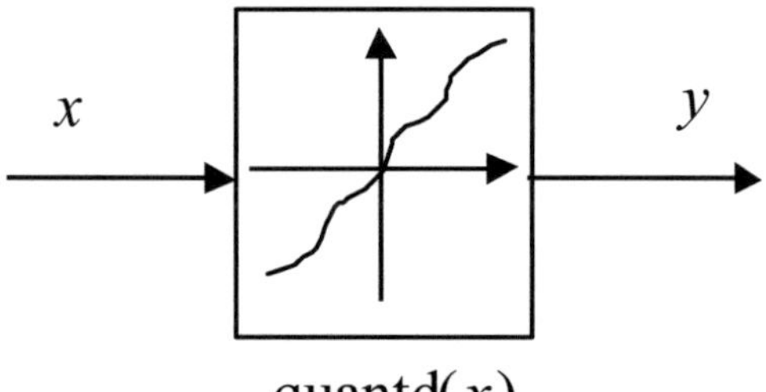

Fig. 5. Representation of a nonlinear system equivalent to a perfectly linear DAS with WGN at the input and averaging of infinite samples at the output.

The error introduced by the dithered quantization, $e_{qd}(x)=\mathrm{quantd}(x)-x$, may be directly obtained by the convolution

$$e_{qd}(x)=e_q(x)*\varphi(x)=\frac{1}{\sigma_n\sqrt{2\pi}}\int_{-\infty}^{+\infty}e^{-\frac{1}{2}\left(\frac{\xi}{\sigma_n}\right)^2}\cdot e_q(x-\xi)d\xi\,, \tag{13}$$

where $e_q(x)$ is the ideal quantization error $\mathrm{quant}(x)-x$ (Fig. 6).

For a fixed input signal, and in particular for a full-scale triangular signal, the system in Fig. 5 may be represented also as an additive error (the dithered quantization error) with a fixed power σ_{qd}^2 (Fig. 7). This additive model is perfectly analogous to that used for the ideal quantization error.

The rms error σ_{qd} introduced by dithered quantization may be evaluated by means of a numerical integration of the square of the smooth curve in Fig. 6, weighted with the distribution of the input signal. For the case of triangular uniformly distributed signal, there is no weighting:

$$\sigma_{qd}^2 = \frac{1}{Q}\int_{-Q/2}^{Q/2} e_{qd}^2(x)dx \,. \tag{14}$$

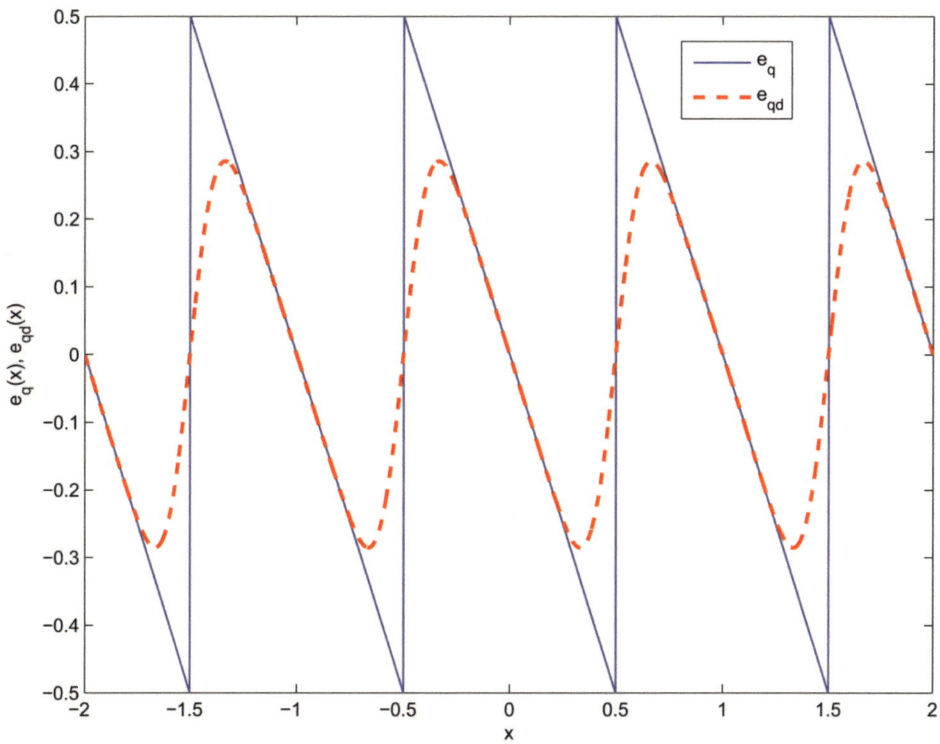

Fig. 6. Ideal quantization error $e_q(x)$ and dithered quantization error $e_{qd}(x)$ (for the case $\sigma_n = 0.1$ LSB).

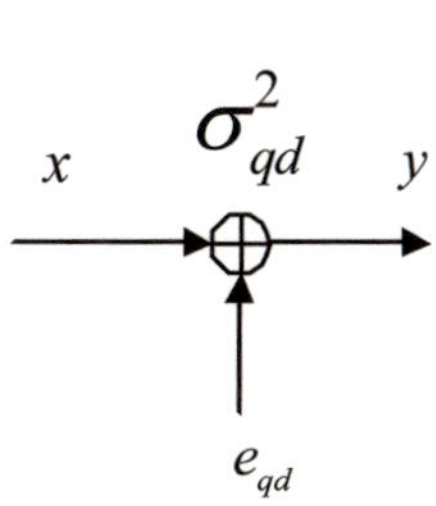

Fig. 7. Additive model of the dithered quantization of Fig. 5.

(If $e_q(x)$ is substituted to $e_{qd}(x)$, the result is trivially $\sigma_q^2 = Q^2/12$.) Of course the result of integration (14) with integrand given by (13) depends only on the standard deviation σ_n of the input Gaussian noise:

$$\sigma_{qd} = g(\sigma_n)\,. \tag{15}$$

This function can be easily evaluated numerically. The result is reported in Fig. 8, and the values in a few points are reported in Tab. 1.
The result shows that σ_{qd} becomes practically negligible at $\sigma_n \cong 0.5$ LSB : more precisely, at $\sigma_n = 0.5$ LSB the dithered quantization error σ_{qd} is about $1.6 \cdot 10^{-3}$ LSB (Fig. 9). This means that $\sigma_n \cong 0.5$ LSB achieves an *almost* complete randomization of the quantization error (i.e., $e_{qd}(x) \cong 0$ for every x). A *perfectly* complete randomization, however, is theoretically achieved only for an infinite σ_n. The randomized quantization error is removed by averaging a sufficiently high (theoretically, infinite) number of samples.

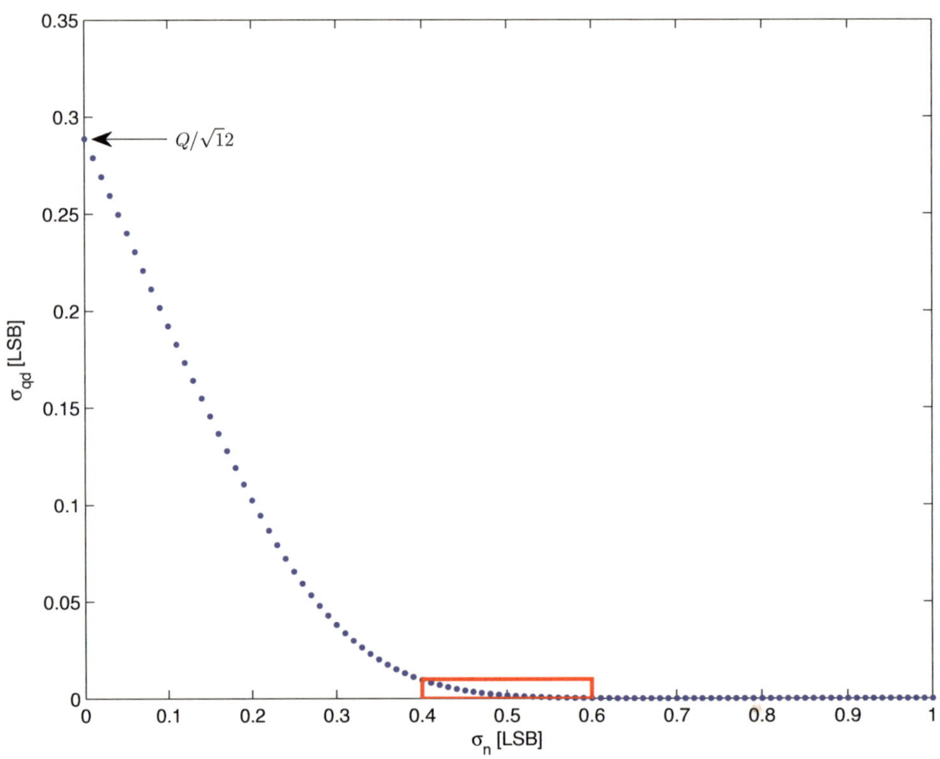

Fig. 8. Rms dithered quantization error, σ_{qd}, as a function of the rms input Gaussian noise, σ_n. For $\sigma_n = 0$ the dithered quantization error becomes pure quantization error with standard deviation $\sigma_q = Q/\sqrt{12}$. A zoom of the curve in the rectangle is represented in Fig. 9.

σ_n	σ_{qd}
0	0.2887
0.1	0.1921
0.2	0.1023
0.3	0.0381
0.4	0.0096
0.5	0.0016

Tab. 1. Some points of the function $\sigma_{qd} = g(\sigma_n)$ (both in LSB units).

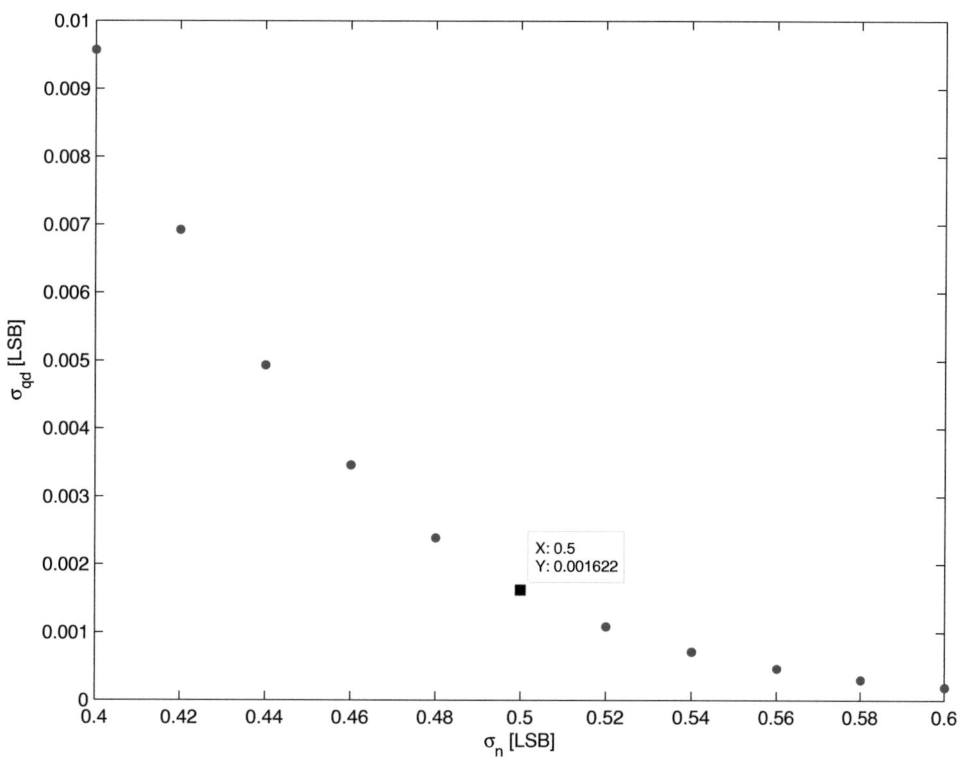

Fig. 9. Zoom of the curve in Fig. 8 in the neighbourhood of $\sigma_n = 0.5$ LSB .

It is worth to recall that according to well-known results of quantization theory [Sch64], [WK08], a perfectly complete randomization of the quantization error is possible with a proper pdf of the input noise, and there are infinite pdfs that lead to such a perfect result. For example, a uniformly distributed noise in $[-Q/2, Q/2]$ yields exactly $e_{qd}(x) \equiv 0$ and therefore $\sigma_{qd} = 0$. However, implementing a uniformly distributed noise with exact amplitude is unpractical; besides, it can be shown that the performance of a uniformly distributed dither, contrary to that of a Gaussian dither, is quite poor if there are nonlinearity errors in the quantization [WK08].

The result depicted in Figs. 8-9 suggests that if one wants to improve the resolution using WGND, the ideal choice is a standard deviation $\sigma_n \cong 0.5$ LSB . This is indeed a typical choice of manufacturers who implement WGND in their DAS [Nat97],[Nat07]. However, even if the hypothesis of perfectly linear DAS is fulfilled, the ideal choice depends actually on the number of averaged samples, as shown in the next Section.
An exact closed-form expression for the function $g(\cdot)$ represented in Fig. 8 is not available. In [CP94] a series expansion of $e_{qd}(x)$ is derived using typical methods of quantization theory; then, the series is truncated at its first term, squared and integrated. An asymptotic approximation of $g(\cdot)$, usable for high enough σ_n , is derived:

$$g(\sigma_n) \cong \frac{1}{\sqrt{2} \cdot \pi} \cdot e^{-2\pi^2\sigma_n^2} . \tag{16}$$

This expression is implicit in [CP94], and written out explicitly in [SO05]; in both papers, it is recommended for $\sigma_n > 0.3$ LSB . For some computations, like those presented in the next Section, an accurate evaluation of $g(\cdot)$ is needed also for σ_n near to zero. This can be achieved with empirical approximate formulae.
The simpler approximation, which makes use of (16), is:

$$g(\sigma_n) \cong g_1(\sigma_n) = \begin{cases} \dfrac{1}{\sqrt{12}} - \sigma_n & \text{for } \sigma_n \le 0.11 \text{ LSB} \\ \dfrac{1}{\sqrt{2} \cdot \pi} \cdot e^{-2\pi^2\sigma_n^2} & \text{for } \sigma_n > 0.11 \text{ LSB} \end{cases} \tag{17}$$

(the threshold 0.11 LSB achieves a nearly optimal approximation of $g(\cdot)$ for this formula). A more accurate, even if less elegant approximation, is given by the expression (a refinement of that proposed in [AGS08]):

$$g(\sigma_n) \cong g_2(\sigma_n) = k \frac{\varphi(\sigma_n, \mu_1, \sigma_1)}{\Phi(\sigma_n, \mu_2, \sigma_2)} . \tag{18}$$

where $\varphi(x,\mu,\sigma)$ is the Gaussian pdf (12), and $\Phi(x,\mu,\sigma) = \int_{-\infty}^{x} \varphi(x',\mu,\sigma)dx'$ is the Gaussian cumulative distribution function. The five parameters $k, \mu_1, \sigma_1, \mu_2, \sigma_2$, are determined by a nonlinear LS fitting and have the values:

$$k = 0.0774;\ \mu_1 = 0.0190;\ \sigma_1 = 0.1543;\ \mu_2 = -0.0587;\ \sigma_2 = 0.1201 . \tag{19}$$

Both the approximations are quite good (Fig. 10): in the range $\sigma_n \in [0,1]$ LSB , $g_1(x)$ approximates $g(x)$ with a maximum error of $4 \cdot 10^{-3}$ LSB, while the error introduced by $g_2(x)$ is 20 times lower ($2.1 \cdot 10^{-4}$ LSB). It is to be remarked that the asymptotic expression (16) is usable for σ_n as low as 0.11 LSB, and the condition $\sigma_n > 0.3$ is a bit too pessimistic.

6. Averaging a finite number of output samples

In practice, only a finite number of samples may be averaged. In order to evaluate the resulting ENOB it is convenient to derive a system equivalent to the noisy quantizer in

Fig. 1. Since the averaging is at the output, and not at the input, the signal-dependent and the signal-independent error contributions must be in reversed order. For the particular case of averaging infinite samples, the new equivalent system must reduce to that in Fig. 5. Therefore, the system is bound to have the form represented in Fig. 11.
The contribution e_{qr} is a random error with standard deviation σ_{qr}, which takes into account the effect of the noise as seen *at the output*. As the error e_{qd} is not removed at all by averaging, so e_{qr} is completely removed by infinite averaging. The analysis of the system requires the introduction of the usual additive model of the deterministic error, obtaining the system in Fig. 12.

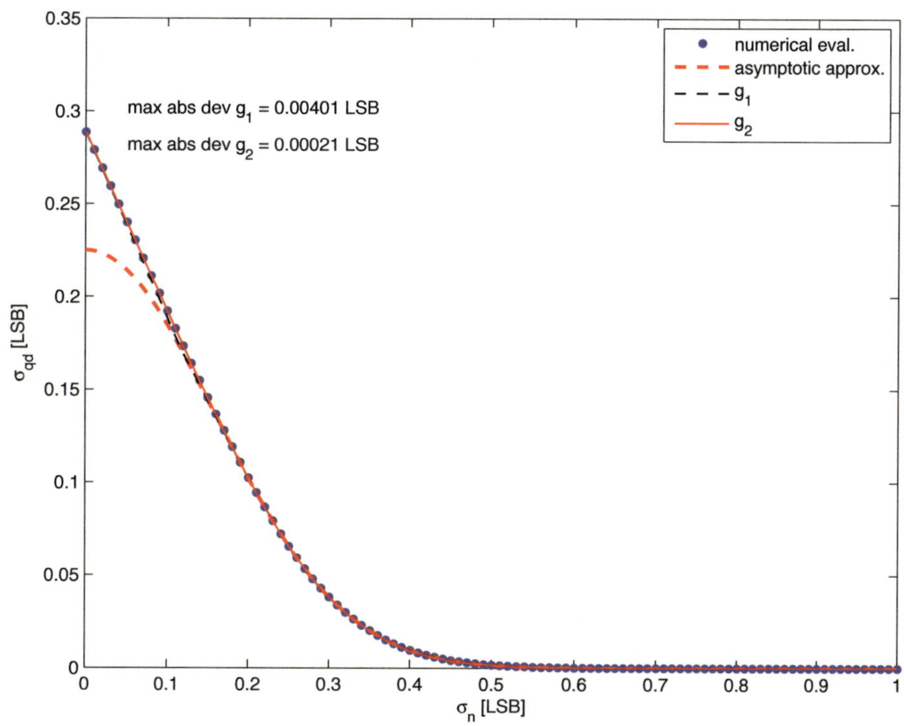

Fig. 10. Comparison between the numerically evaluated points of the function $g(\cdot)$, the asymptotic expression (16), and the approximations $g_1(\cdot)$ and $g_2(\cdot)$.

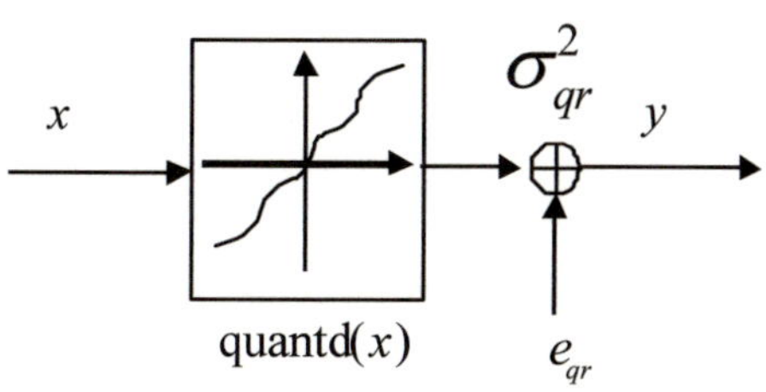

Fig. 11. Equivalent representation of the noisy quantization in Fig. 1.

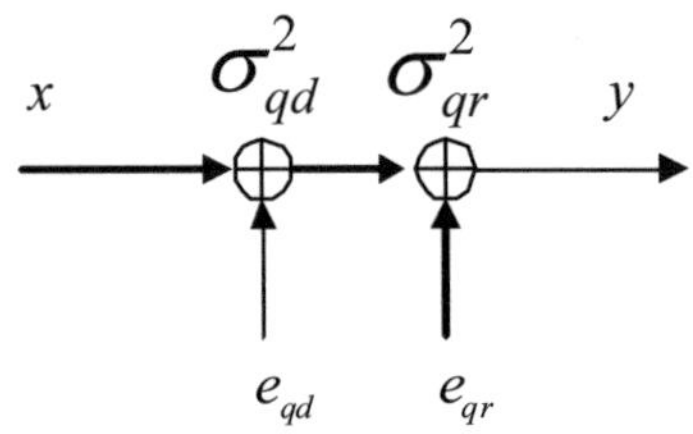

Fig. 12. Equivalent representation of the noisy quantization for a fixed input signal. The input signal determines the parameter σ^2_{qd} and σ^2_{qr}.

For a full-scale uniformly distributed input signal, the standard deviation σ_{qd} is given by the function $g(\sigma_n)$ represented in Fig. 8 and approximated by expressions (16) and (18). As regards the determination of the standard deviation σ_{qr}, even if a formal analysis of the problem is quite complicated, it can be proven [SO05] that e_{qr} is white and uncorrelated with e_{qd}. This can be seen as a direct consequence of the equivalence of the system with that in Fig. 2, where the input noise n is white and uncorrelated with the deterministic error e_q. From the uncorrelation between e_{qr} and e_{qd} and the equivalence of the systems in Figs. 12 and 2 follows that

$$\sigma_n^2 + \sigma_q^2 = \sigma_{qd}^2 + \sigma_{qr}^2 \tag{20}$$

and therefore

$$\sigma_{qr}^2 = \sigma_n^2 + \sigma_q^2 - \sigma_{qd}^2 = \sigma_n^2 + \sigma_q^2 - g^2(\sigma_n)\,. \tag{21}$$

As a particular case, by assuming $\sigma_{qd} \cong 0$ (a condition achieved exactly only for $\sigma_n = +\infty$, and approximately for $\sigma_n \cong 0.5\ \text{LSB}$) the random output error has variance

$$\sigma_{qr}^2 = \sigma_n^2 + \sigma_q^2 = \sigma_e^2\,, \tag{22}$$

i.e. the acquisition error is purely random.
Now, by substituting the system of Fig. 12 in the noise + quantization cascade of Fig. 4, it is easy to compute the MSE σ_e^2, and therefore the ENOB, obtained by averaging N samples (Fig. 13).

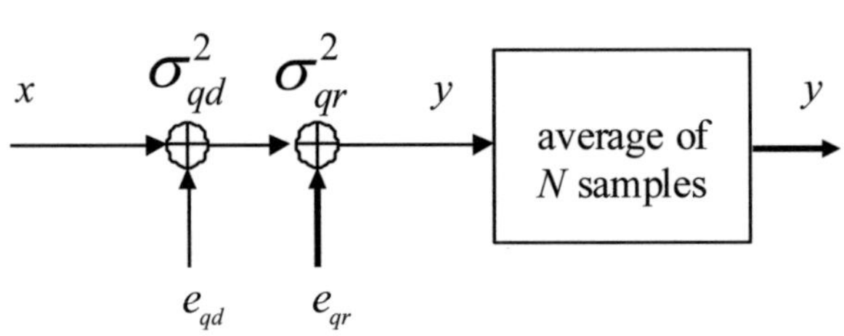

Fig. 13. Equivalent representation of the WGND applied to a linear quantizer.

The ENOB of the system, from the uncorrelation between e_{qd} and e_{qr}, and the whiteness of e_{qr}, is

$$b_e = b - \frac{1}{2}\log_2 12\sigma_e^2 = b - \frac{1}{2}\log_2 12\left(\sigma_{qd}^2 + \frac{\sigma_{qr}^2}{N}\right) \tag{23}$$

This expression is first derived in [AGS04] (and re-published in [AGS08]), and recovered in the broader work [SO05]. An explicit expression of ENOB in terms of the rms input noise σ_n may be written in a simple approximate form or in exact form. The approximate formula is derived by assuming $\sigma_{qd} \cong 0$ and $\sigma_{qr}^2 \cong \sigma_n^2 + \sigma_q^2 = \sigma_n^2 + 1/12 = \sigma_e^2$:

$$b_e \cong b - \frac{1}{2}\log_2\left(1 + 12\cdot\sigma_n^2\right) + \frac{1}{2}\log_2 N\,. \tag{24}$$

The exact formula is derived by substituting $\sigma_{qd} = g(\sigma_n)$:

$$b_e = b - \frac{1}{2}\log_2\left(12g^2(\sigma_n) + \frac{1 + 12[\sigma_n^2 - g^2(\sigma_n)]}{N}\right). \tag{25}$$

Figs. 14-16 show the result of numerical simulations of an 8-bit quantizer with various levels of input WGN (ranging from 0.05 to 0.5 LSB), and Fig. 17 shows the result of an analogous simulation for a 12-bit quantizer. Simulations results are compared with both expressions (24) and (25). In (25), the approximate function $g_1(\cdot)$ has been used (slightly better agreement with simulations is obtained using $g_2(\cdot)$; this is especially true for the case in Fig. 17.) Simulations basically demonstrate that (25) is able to predict with great accuracy the ENOB of a perfectly linear DAS with input noise and output averaging. A number of interesting and important facts follow from the validity of (25), and they are well illustrated by the curves in the figures.

1. For a given σ_n, the maximum (asymptotic) increase of performance is given by (Fig. 18):

$$\Delta b = -\log_2\sqrt{12} - \log_2 g(\sigma_n) \tag{26}$$

   An accurate evaluation of (26) for low σ_n can be obtained by using the approximation $g_2(\cdot)$ given by (18) (values in Tab. 2). The approximation $g_1(\cdot)$ given by (17) is also usable, obtaining an extension of the formula given in [CP94]:

$$\Delta b \cong \begin{cases} -\log_2(1 - \sqrt{12}\sigma_n) & \text{for } \sigma_n \le 0.11 \text{ LSB} \\ \log_2\dfrac{\pi}{\sqrt{6}} + 2\pi^2\sigma_n^2\cdot\log_2 e & \text{for } \sigma_n > 0.11 \text{ LSB} \end{cases} \tag{27}$$

   The unbounded increase predicted by approximation (24) is untrue.

2. The usability of (24) depends on the actual number N of averaged samples, and not simply on σ_n. Under this viewpoint it is quite inaccurate to say that $\sigma_n \cong 0.5$ is the right value to obtain an approximately full randomization of the quantization error. For example, $\sigma_n = 0.3$ LSB is not too low for the validity of (24), provided that $N < 32$. On the other hand, $\sigma_n = 0.5$ LSB is not sufficient to use (24), if $N > 2^{15}$.

3. As a consequence, if one wants to add some WGN to increase performance by averaging, the choice is dictated by the number of samples that may be averaged. This is clearly suggested by the intersecting continuous lines in Fig. 18, and better illustrated by Fig. 19, in which ENOB is plotted as a function of σ_n for fixed N. It is clear, for example, that for $N = 4$ it is convenient $\sigma_n \approx 0.2$ LSB, etc. Quite surprisingly, the very frequent choice $\sigma_n = 0.5$ is optimal only for N of the order of 2^{13}.

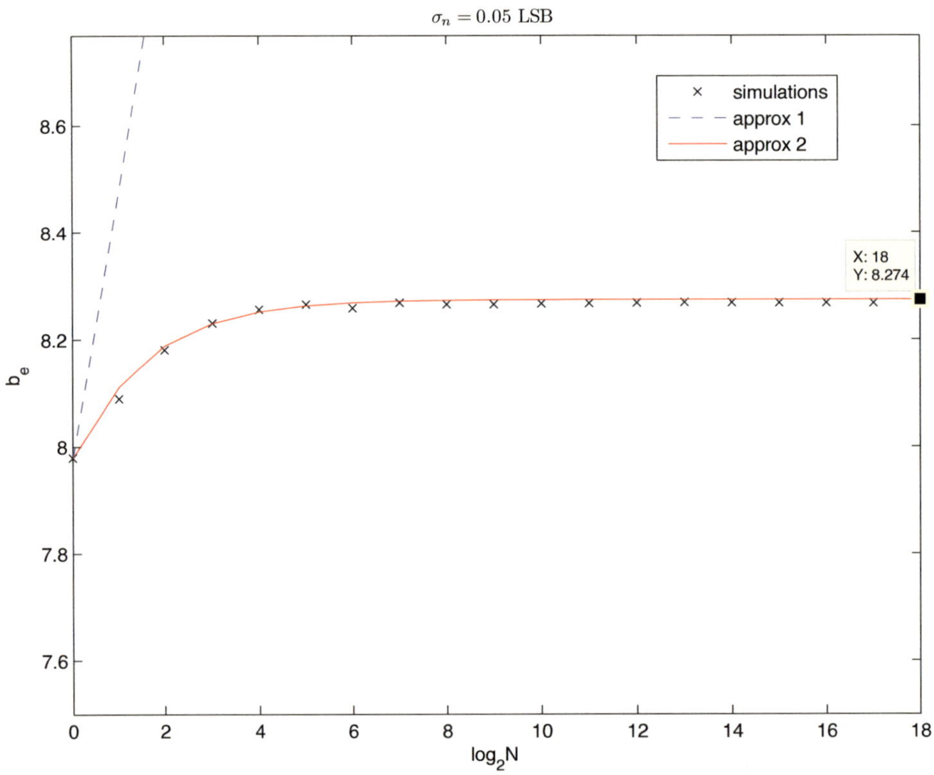

Fig. 14. ENOB of an 8-bit linear DAS with input WGN ($\sigma_n = 0.05$ LSB), as a function of the number N of the averaged samples.

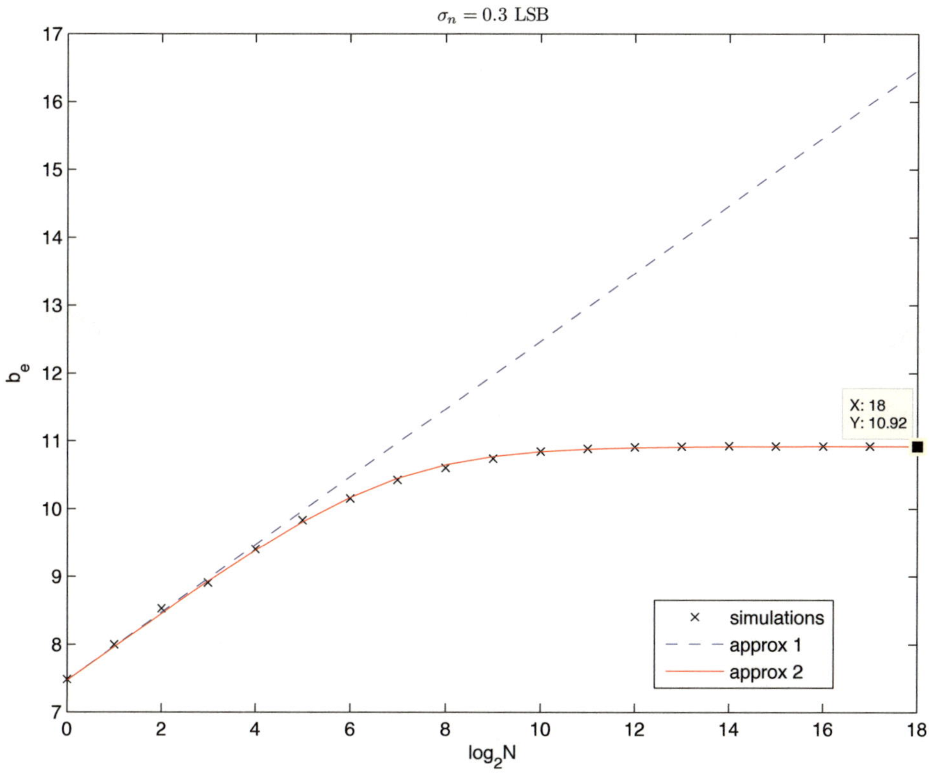

Fig. 15. ENOB of an 8-bit linear DAS with input WGN ($\sigma_n = 0.3$ LSB), as a function of the number N of the averaged samples.

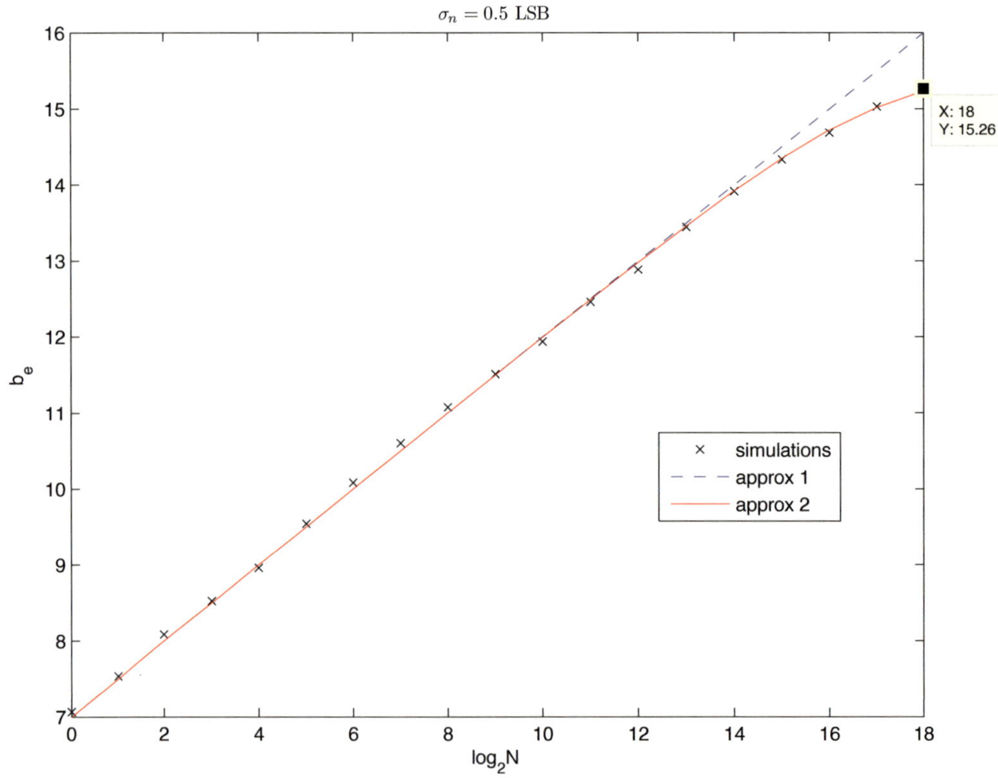

Fig. 16. ENOB of an 8-bit linear DAS with input WGN ($\sigma_n = 0.5$ LSB), as a function of the number N of the averaged samples.

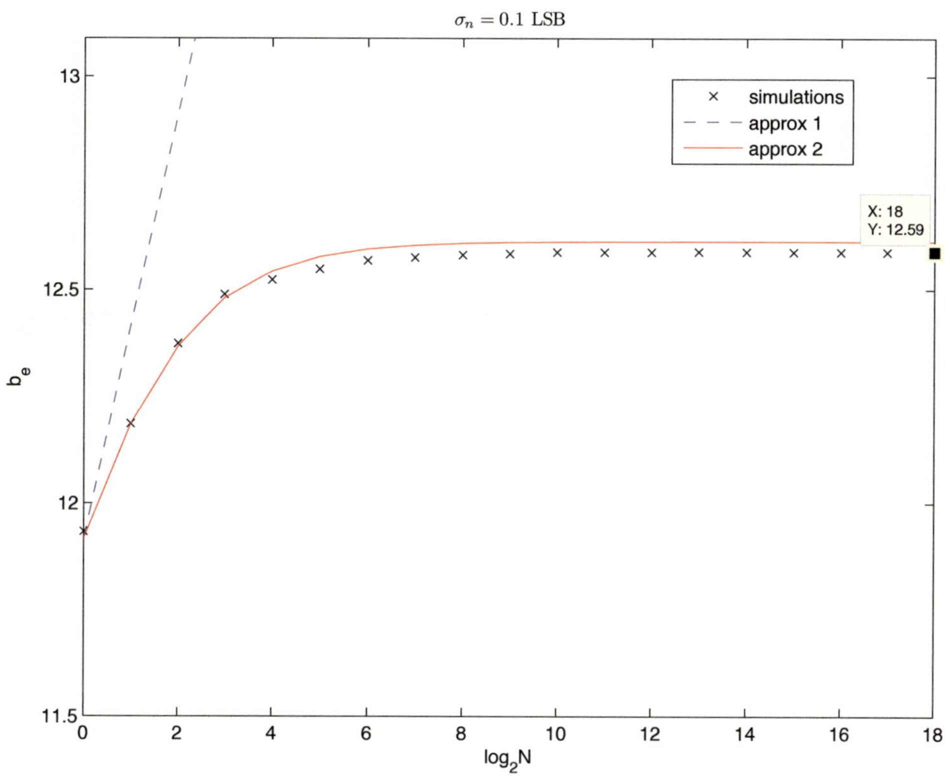

Fig. 17. ENOB of a 12-bit linear DAS with input WGN ($\sigma_n = 0.1$ LSB), as a function of the number N of the averaged samples.

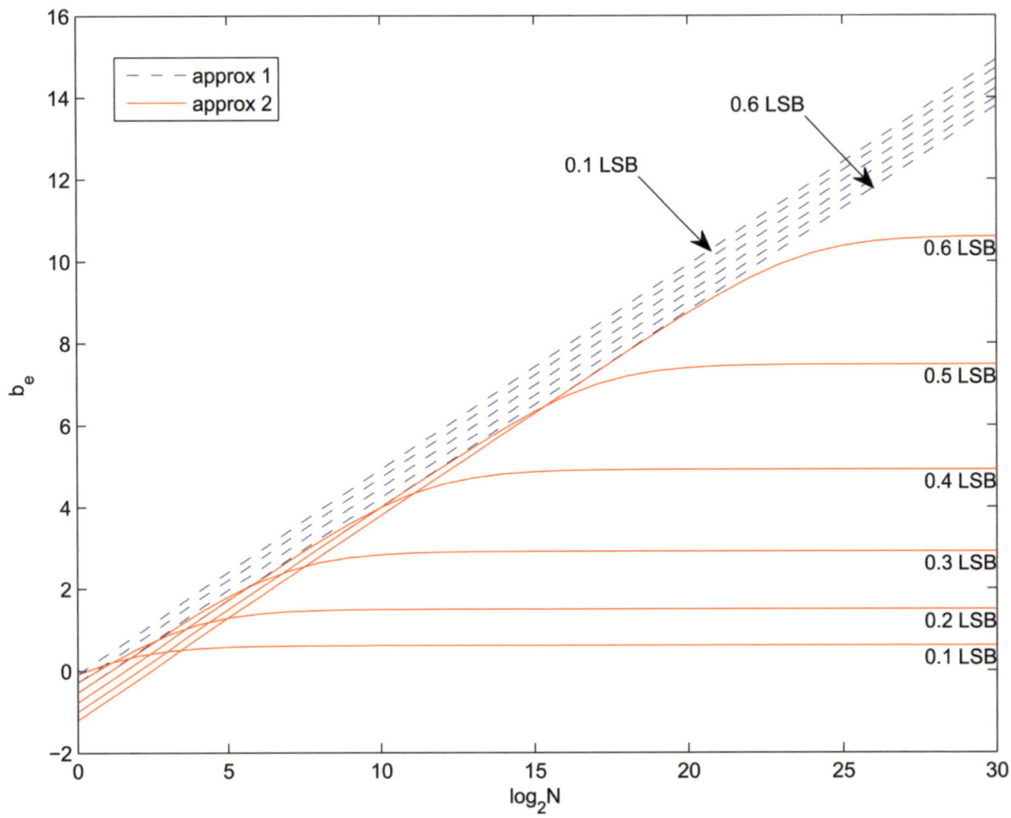

Fig. 18. Variation in the ENOB (with respect to the nominal resolution b) as a function of the number N of the averaged samples, for different values of input WGN ($\sigma_n = 0.1, 0.2, 0.3,$ $0.4, 0.5, 0.6$ LSB). The figure compares the approximation given by (24) (approx. 1) with expression (25), in which the approximation (17) of $g(\cdot)$ is used (approx. 2).

σ_n [LSB]	Δb [bit]
0	0
0.1	0.59
0.2	1.50
0.3	2.92
0.4	4.92
0.5	7.48

Tab. 2. Maximum (asymptotic) increase of ENOB attainable by averaging, for given levels σ_n of input WGN.

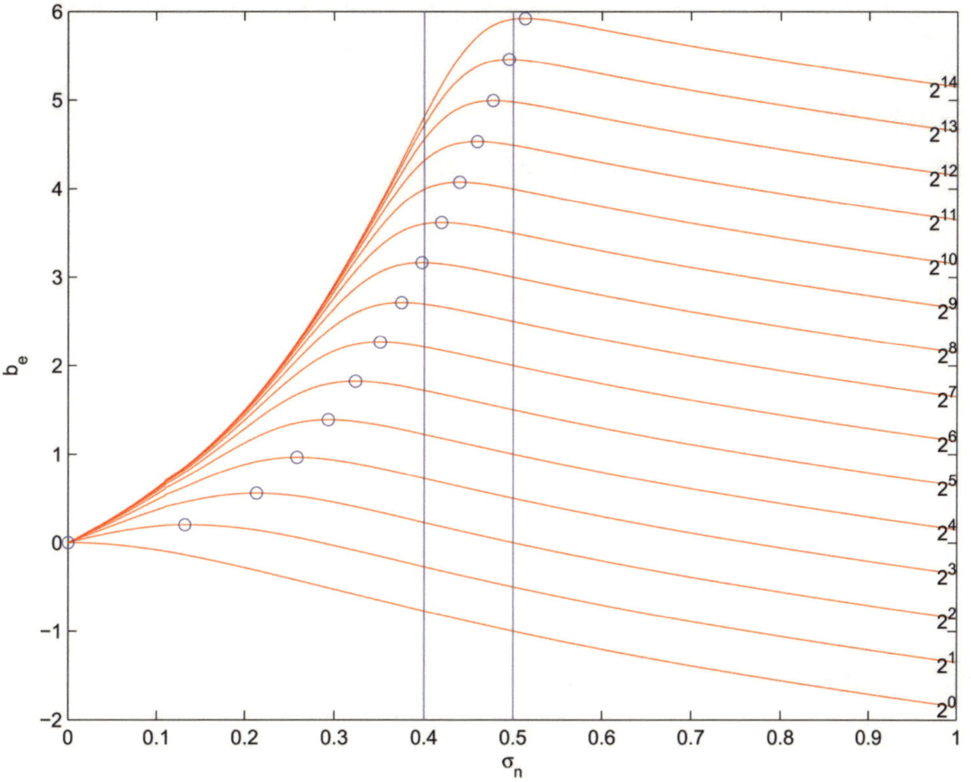

Fig. 19. ENOB increase as a function of the input noise σ_n, for fixed values of the number N of averaged samples. The maxima of the curves, and the typical values $\sigma_n = 0.4$ LSB and $\sigma_n = 0.5$ LSB are highlighted.

7. Conclusions

The chapter examines the overall effect, in terms of effective resolution, of input noise and output averaging in linear DAS. The analysis applies to both the cases of unwanted system noise, and of noise purposely added to increase the performance (non-subtractive dithering). After a brief discussion of the ENOB figure of merit, the equations to determine the ENOB in various situations are derived and validated by simulations. The results clarify the nature of the acquisition error in presence of noise - in terms of "dithered quantization error" e_{qd} and "randomized quantization error" e_{qr} - and can be used, for example, to choose the optimal level of input noise in a non-subtractive dithering scheme. The choice is demonstrated to be non-trivial, even if quite simple with the use of the proper equations. In particular, the very common choice $\sigma_n = 0.5$ LSB is demonstrated to be suboptimal in most practical cases.

A very important warning is that the presented analysis is limited to the case of perfectly linear DAS, and is not applicable in the common case of meaningful nonlinearity error affecting the DAS. The case of non-subtractive dithering in nonlinear DAS can be analyzed with means similar to those presented in this chapter. In particular, the optimal levels of noise for nonlinear DAS are considerably higher than those derived for linear DAS [AGLS07]. This is, however, the subject of a possible future extended version of the chapter.

8. Acknowledgements

The authors wish to thank prof. Mario Savino for helpful discussions and suggestions.

9. References

[AD09] L. Angrisani and M. D'Arco. Modeling timing jitter effects in digital-to-analog converters. *IEEE Trans. Instrum. Meas.*, 58(2):330–336, 2009.

[AGLS07] F. Attivissimo, N. Giaquinto, A. M. L. Lanzolla, and M. Savino. Effects of midpoint linearization and nonsubtractive dithering in A/D converters. *Measurement*, 40(5):537–544, June 2007.

[AGS04] F. Attivissimo, N. Giaquinto, and M. Savino. Uncertainty evaluation in dithered A/D converters. In *Proc. of IMEKO TC7 Symposium*, pages 121–124, St. Petersburg, Russia, June 2004.

[AGS08] F. Attivissimo, N. Giaquinto, and M. Savino. Uncertainty evaluation in dithered ADC-based instruments. *Measurement*, 41(4):364–370, May 2008.

[AH98] O. Aumala and J. Holub. Dithering design for measurement of slowly varying signals. *Measurement*, 23(4):271–276, June 1998.

[BDR05] E. Balestrieri, P. Daponte, and S. Rapuano. A state of the art on ADC error compensation methods. *IEEE Trans. Instrum. Meas.*, 54(4):1388–1394, 2005.

[CP94] P. Carbone and D. Petri. Effect of additive dither on the resolution of ideal quantizers. *IEEE Trans. Instrum. Meas.*, 43(3):389 –396, June 1994.

[GT97] N. Giaquinto and A. Trotta. Fast and accurate ADC testing via an enhanced sine wave fitting algorithm. *IEEE Trans. Instrum. Meas.*, 46(4):1020–1025, August 1997.

[IEE94] IEEE Standards Board. *IEEE Standard 1057 for Digitizing Waveform Recorders*. IEEE Press, New York, NY, December 1994.

[IEE00] IEEE Standards Board. *IEEE Standard 1241 for Terminology and Test Methods for Analog-to-Digital Converters*. IEEE Press, New York, NY, December 2000.

[KB05] I. Kollár and J. J. Blair. Improved determination of the best fitting sine wave in ADC testing. *IEEE Trans. Instrum. Meas.*, 54:1978–1983, October 2005.

[Nat97] National Instruments, Inc. *PCI-1200 User Manual*, January 1997.

[Nat05] National Instruments, Inc. *PXI-5922 Data Sheet*, 2005.

[Nat07] National Instruments, Inc. *DAQ E-Series User Manual*, February 2007.

[Sch64] L. Schuchman. Dither signals and their effect on quantization noise. *IEEE Trans. Comm. Tech.*, 12(4):162–165, December 1964.

[SO05] R. Skartlien and L. Oyehaug. Quantization error and resolution in ensemble averaged data with noise. *IEEE Trans. Instrum. Meas.*, 54(3):1303 - 1312, June 2005.

[WK08] B. Widrow and I. Kollár. *Quantization Noise: Roundoff Error in Digital Computation, Signal Processing, Control, and Communications*. Cambridge University Press, Cambridge, UK, 2008.

[WLVW00] R. A. Wannamaker, S. P. Lipshitz, J. Vanderkooy, and J. N. Wright. A theory of nonsubtractive dither. *IEEE Trans. Signal Process.*, 48(2):499–516, 2000.

2

Bandpass Sampling for Data Acquisition Systems

Leopoldo Angrisani[1] and Michele Vadursi[2]
[1]*University of Naples Federico II, Department of Computer Science and Control Systems*
[2]*University of Naples "Parthenope", Department of Technologies*
Italy

1. Introduction

A number of modern measurement instruments employed in different application fields consist of an analogue front-end, a data acquisition section, and a processing section. A key role is played by the data acquisition section, which is mandated to the digitization of the input signal, according to a specific sample rate (Corcoran, 1999).

The choice of the sample rate is connected to the optimal use of the resources of the data acquisition system (DAS). This is particularly true for modern communication systems, which operate at very high frequencies. The higher the sample rate, in fact, the shorter the observation interval and, consequently, the worse the frequency resolution allowed by the DAS memory buffer. So, the sample rate has to be chosen high enough to avoid aliasing, but at the same time, an unnecessarily high sample rate does not allow for an optimal exploitation of the DAS resources.

As well known, the sample rate must be correctly chosen to avoid aliasing, which can seriously affect the accuracy of measurement results. The sampling theorem, in fact, affirms that a band-limited signal can be alias-free sampled at a rate f_s greater than twice its highest frequency f_{max} (Shannon, 1949).

As regards bandpass signals, which are characterized by a low ratio of bandwidth to carrier frequency and are peculiar to many digital communication systems, a much less strict condition applies. In particular, bandpass signals can be alias-free sampled at a rate f_s greater than twice their bandwidth B (Kohlenberg, 1953). It is worth noting, however, that this is only a necessary condition. It is indeed possible to alias-free sample bandpass signals at a rate fs much lower than $2f_{max}$, but such rate has to be chosen very carefully; it has been shown in (Brown, 1980; Vaughan et al., 1991; De Paula & Pieper, 1992; Tseng, 2002) that aliasing can occur if fs is chosen outside certain ranges. Moreover, particular attention has to be paid, as bandpass sampling can imply a degradation of the signal-to-noise ratio (Vaughan et al., 1991). Some recent papers have also focused on frequency shifting induced by bandpass sampling in more detail (Angrisani et al. 2004; Diez et al., 2005), providing analytical relations for establishing the final central frequency of the discrete-time signal, which digital receivers need to know (Akos et al., 1999) and determining the minimum admissible value of fs that is submultiple of a fixed sample rate (Betta et al., 2009).

Sampling a bandpass signal at a rate lower than twice its highest frequency f_{max} is referred to as bandpass sampling. Bandpass sampling is relevant in several fields of application, such as optics (Gaskell, 1978), communications (Waters & Jarrett, 1982), radar (Jackson & Matthewson, 1986) and sonar investigations (Grace & Pitt, 1968). It is also the core of the receiver of software-defined radio (SDR) systems (Akos et al., 1999; Latiri et al., 2006).

Although the theory of bandpass sampling is now well-established and the choice of sample rate is very important for processing and measurement, at the current state of the art it seems that digital instruments that automatically select the best f_s, on the basis of specific optimization strategies, are not available on the market. A possible criterion for choosing the optimal value of f_s within the admissible alias-free ranges was introduced some years ago (Angrisani et al., 2004). An iterative algorithm was proposed, which selects the minimum alias-free sample rate that places the spectral replica at the normalized frequency requested by the user. The algorithm, however, cannot be profitably applied to any DAS. Two conditions have, in fact, to be met: (*i*) the sample rate can be set with unlimited resolution, and (*ii*) the sample clock has to be very stable. Failing to comply with such ideal conditions may result in an undesired and unpredictable frequency shifting and possible aliasing.

More recently, a comprehensive analysis of the effects that the sample clock instability and the time-base finite resolution have on the optimal sample rate and, consequently, on the central frequency of the spectral replicas was developed (Angrisani & Vadursi, 2008). On the basis of its outcomes, the authors also presented an automatic method for selecting the optimal value of f_s, according to the aforementioned criterion.

The method includes both sample clock accuracy and time-base resolution among input parameters, and is suitable for practical applications on any DAS, no matter its sample clock characteristics. Specifically, the method provides the minimum f_s that locates the spectrum of the discrete-time signal at the normalized central frequency required by the user, given the signal bandwidth B, a possible guard band B_g, and original carrier frequency f_c. Information on the possible deviation from expected central frequency, as an effect of DAS non-idealities, is also made available. In fact, the proposed method is extremely practical, since (i) it can be profitably applied no matter what the time-base resolution of the DAS is, and (ii) it takes into account the instability of the sample clock to face unpredictable frequency shifting and the consequent possible uncontrolled aliasing.

A number of tests are carried out to assess the performance of the method in correctly locating the spectral replica at the desired central frequency, while granting no superposition of the replicas. Some tests are, in particular, mandated to highlight the effects of DAS non-idealities on the frequency shifting and consequent unexpected aliasing.

This chapter is organized as follows. The theory of bandpass sampling will be presented in Section 2, along with analytical relations for establishing the final central frequency of the discrete-time signal and details and explicative figures on the frequency shifting resulting from the bandpass sampling and on the effects of the sample rate choice in terms of possible aliasing. Section 2 also presents the analysis of the effects that the sample clock instability and the time-base finite resolution which was first introduced in (Angrisani & Vadursi, 2008). Section 3 presents the proposed algorithm for the automatic selection of the sample rate given the user's input, and shows the results of experiments conducted on real signals.

2. Analysis of the effects of bandpass sampling with a non-ideal data acquisition system

Let $s(t)$ be a generic bandpass signal, characterized by a bandwidth B and a central frequency f_c. As well known, the spectrum of the discrete-time version of $s(t)$ consists of an infinite set of replicas of the spectrum of $s(t)$, centered at frequencies

$$f_{\lambda,\nu} = \lambda f_c + \nu f_s \tag{1}$$

where $\nu \in \mathbf{Z}$ and $\lambda \in \{-1;1\}$.
The situation is depicted in Fig.1 with regard to positive frequencies of magnitude spectrum.

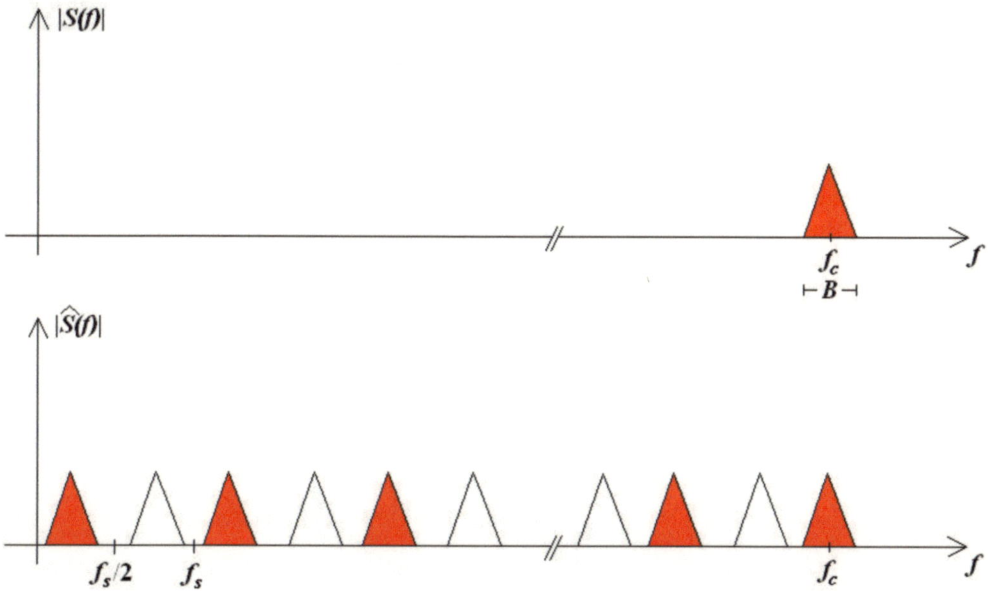

Fig. 1. Typical amplitude spectrum of (a) a bandpass signal s(t) and (b) its sampled version; f_s is the sample rate. Only the positive portion of the frequency axis is considered.

Replicas of the 'positive' spectrum (red triangles in Fig.1) are centered at $f_{1,\nu}$, whereas those peculiar to the 'negative' one (white triangles in Fig.1) are centered at $f_{-1,\nu}$. It can be shown that only two replicas are centered in the interval $[0, f_s]$, respectively at frequencies

$$f_{\lambda 1,\nu 1} = f_c \bmod f_s \tag{2}$$

and

$$f_{\lambda 2,\nu 2} = f_s - (f_c \bmod f_s) \tag{3}$$

where mod denotes the modulo operation. The condition to be met in order to avoid aliasing is

$$\frac{B+B_g}{2} < f^* < \frac{f_s-(B+B_g)}{2} \tag{4}$$

where f^* is the minimum $f_{\lambda 1,\nu 1}$ and $f_{\lambda 2,\nu 2}$. Inequality (4) implies the following condition on ($f_c \bmod f_s$):

$$f_c \bmod f_s \in \left(\frac{B+B_g}{2}, \frac{f_s-(B+B_g)}{2}\right) \cup \left(\frac{f_s+B+B_g}{2}, f_s-\frac{B}{2}\right) \tag{5}$$

The algorithm proposed in (Angrisani et al., 2004) allows the choice of the normalized frequency f^*/f_s , granting a minimum guard band between adjacent replicas, and gives in output the ideal sample rate f_s. However, the problem is not solved yet. In fact, the operative condition provided in (Angrisani et al., 2004) has to cope with the characteristics of an actual DAS. First of all, the sample rate cannot be imposed with arbitrary resolution, but it has to be approximated according to the resolution of the time-base of the DAS. Moreover, the time-base instability makes actual sample rate unpredictable. By the light of this, the actual value of the sample rate given by the DAS could be different from the ideal one in such a way that alias-free sampling could not be guaranteed anymore.

Given the nature of bandpass sampling, simply increasing f_s is not advisable (Vaughan et al., 1991), but an appropriate model is rather needed. Taking into account that: (i) the nominal sample rate, f_s^{nom}, that the user can set on the DAS, differs from f_s of a deterministic quantity ε and (ii) the actual sample rate, f_s' , i.e. the rate at which the DAS actually samples the input signal, is random due to the time-base instability, the following model results:

$$f_s' = f_s^{nom}(1+\chi) = (f_s+\varepsilon)(1+\chi) \tag{6}$$

with

$$|\chi| < \chi_M \tag{6a}$$

$$\varepsilon < \Delta f/2 \tag{6b}$$

where Δf is the resolution and χ_M is the clock accuracy expressed in relative terms, as commonly given in the specifications of the DAS on the market. The actual sample rate f_s' thus differs from the expected value by the quantity

$$\Delta f_s = \chi f_s + (1+\chi)\,\varepsilon \tag{7}$$

which depends on the output value of the algorithm, f_s.

As alias-free sampling is a strict priority, the model will be specialized in the following letting χ coincide with its maximum value χ_M. Let us separately analyze the two cases $f^* = f_{\lambda 1,\nu 1}$, with a replica of the positive spectrum centered in f^*, and $f^* = f_{\lambda 2,\nu 2}$, with a replica of the negative spectrum centered in f^*.

2.1 Replica of the positive spectrum in (0, $f_s/2$)

This happens when $\lambda = 1$ and $\nu=-\lfloor f_c/f_s \rfloor$, that is the integer part of f_c/f_s. According to (6), the actual value of f^* is

$$f^{*\prime} = f_c + \nu f'_s = f_c + \nu\,(f_s + \varepsilon)(1+\chi) \tag{8}$$

and (4), evaluated for the actual values of f_s and f^*, yields

$$\frac{B+B_g}{2} + g_1(\varepsilon,\chi) < f^* < \frac{f_s - B + B_g}{2} + g_2(\varepsilon,\chi) \tag{9}$$

where

$$g_1(\varepsilon,\chi) = -\nu\left[\chi f_s + \varepsilon(1+\chi)\right] \tag{10}$$

$$g_2(\varepsilon,\chi)=\left(\frac{1}{2}-\nu\right)\left[\chi f_s+\varepsilon(1+\chi)\right]. \tag{11}$$

To find the pair $\{\varepsilon, \chi\}$ that maximizes $g_1(\varepsilon, \chi)$ in the domain $\mathcal{D} = [-\Delta f/2, \Delta f/2] \times [\chi_M, \chi_M]$ let us first null the partial derivatives of g_1 with respect to variables ε and χ:

$$\begin{cases} -\nu(1+\chi)=0 \\ -\nu(f_s+\varepsilon)=0 \end{cases}. \tag{12}$$

The system (12) has no solutions in actual situations. Similarly, it can be shown that the restriction of the function to the borders does not have local maxima. The maximum has therefore to be searched among the vertices of the rectangle representing the domain. Table 1 enlists the coordinates of the vertices along with the related values assumed by the function.

As $\nu < 0$, g_1 assumes its maximum in the point C, and the left side of (9) is maximized by

Vertex	*Coordinates*	*Value of g_1*
A	$\left(-\frac{\Delta f}{2},-\chi_M\right)$	$-\nu\left[-\chi_M f_s-\frac{\Delta f}{2}(1-\chi_M)\right]$
B	$\left(-\frac{\Delta f}{2},\chi_M\right)$	$-\nu\left[\chi_M f_s-\frac{\Delta f}{2}(1+\chi_M)\right]$
C	$\left(\frac{\Delta f}{2},\chi_M\right)$	$-\nu\left[\chi_M f_s+\frac{\Delta f}{2}(1+\chi_M)\right]$
D	$\left(\frac{\Delta f}{2},-\chi_M\right)$	$-\nu\left[-\chi_M f_s+\frac{\Delta f}{2}(1-\chi_M)\right]$

Table 1. Values assumed by $g_1(\varepsilon, \chi)$ in the vertices of its domain $\mathcal{D}$.

$$\frac{B+B_g}{2}-\nu\left[\chi_M f_s+\frac{\Delta f}{2}(1+\chi_M)\right]. \tag{13}$$

With regard to the right side of (9), it can be similarly shown that $g_2(\varepsilon, \chi)$ assumes its minimum on one of the vertices of the domain $\mathcal{D}$. The four alternatives are enlisted in Table 2. Being $\nu < 0$, the vertex C can be discarded, because g_2(C) is sum of all positive terms. Moreover, as $\chi_M (f_s - \Delta f/2) > 0$, $g_2(A) < g_2(B)$. Finally, posing $g_2(A) < g_2(D)$ implies $-\Delta f (1 - \chi_M) < 0$, which is always true in actual situations.

In conclusion, g_2 assumes its minimum in A, and the right side of (9) is minimized by

$$\frac{\left(f_s-\frac{\Delta f}{2}\right)(1-\chi_M)-(B+B_g)}{2}+\nu\left[\chi_M f_s+\frac{\Delta f(1-\chi_M)}{2}\right]. \tag{14}$$

According to (13) and (14), in the most restrictive case the condition (9) can be rewritten as

$$\begin{cases} f^* < \dfrac{\left(f_s - \dfrac{\Delta f}{2}\right)(1-\chi_M) - \left(B + B_g\right)}{2} + \nu\left[\chi_M f_s + \dfrac{\Delta f(1-\chi_M)}{2}\right] \\ f^* > \dfrac{B+B_g}{2} - \nu\left[\chi_M f_s + \dfrac{\Delta f}{2}(1+\chi_M)\right] \end{cases}. \tag{15}$$

Vertex	*Coordinates*	*Value of g_1*
A	$\left(-\dfrac{\Delta f}{2}, -\chi_M\right)$	$\left(\dfrac{1}{2}-\nu\right)\left[-\chi_M f_s - \dfrac{\Delta f}{2}(1-\chi_M)\right]$
B	$\left(-\dfrac{\Delta f}{2}, \chi_M\right)$	$\left(\dfrac{1}{2}-\nu\right)\left[\chi_M f_s - \dfrac{\Delta f}{2}(1+\chi_M)\right]$
C	$\left(\dfrac{\Delta f}{2}, \chi_M\right)$	$\left(\dfrac{1}{2}-\nu\right)\left[\chi_M f_s + \dfrac{\Delta f}{2}(1+\chi_M)\right]$
D	$\left(\dfrac{\Delta f}{2}, -\chi_M\right)$	$\left(\dfrac{1}{2}-\nu\right)\left[-\chi_M f_s + \dfrac{\Delta f}{2}(1-\chi_M)\right]$

Table 2. Values assumed by $g_2(\varepsilon, \chi)$ in the vertices of its domain $\mathcal{D}$.

2.1 Replica of the negative spectrum in (0, $f_s/2$)

This is the case when $\lambda = -1$ and $\nu = \lceil f_c/f_s \rceil > 0$, that is the nearest greater integer of f_c/f_s. According to (6), the actual value of f^* is

$$f^{*\prime} = -f_c + \nu f'_s = -f_c + \nu\,(f_s + \varepsilon)\,(1+\chi) \tag{16}$$

and (4), evaluated for the actual values of f_s and f^*, yields the same expression as in (9).
As already stated, the function g_1 assumes its maximum in one of the vertices of $\mathcal{D}$. A comparison of the values enlisted in Table 1 permits to affirm that the maximum is assumed in A, and the left side of (8) is maximized by

$$\frac{B+B_g}{2} - \nu\left[-\chi_M f_s - \frac{\Delta f}{2}(1-\chi_M)\right]. \tag{17}$$

Similarly, it is easy to show through pairwise comparisons that the function g_2 assumes its minimum in the point C, and the right side of (8) is maximized by

$$\frac{\left(f_s + \dfrac{\Delta f}{2}\right)(1+\chi_M) - \left(B + B_g\right)}{2} - \nu\left[\chi_M f_s + \frac{\Delta f}{2}(1+\chi_M)\right]. \tag{18}$$

According to (17) and (18), in the most restrictive case, the condition (9) can be rewritten as

$$\begin{cases} f^* < \dfrac{\left(f_s + \dfrac{\Delta f}{2}\right)(1+\chi_M) - (B+B_g)}{2} - \nu\left[\chi_M f_s + \dfrac{\Delta f(1+\chi_M)}{2}\right] \\ f^* > \dfrac{B+B_g}{2} + \nu\left[\chi_M f_s + \dfrac{\Delta f}{2}(1-\chi_M)\right] \end{cases}. \tag{19}$$

In conclusion, time-base resolution and time-base instability are responsible for a shifting of the replica included in $[0, f_s/2]$ from its expected central frequency f^*, and can consequently introduce unexpected aliasing, depending on the values of Δf and χ_M.

3. Optimal selection of the sample rate

The sample rate can be chosen within an infinite set of values, its choice having direct consequences on spectral location of replicas. The idea underlying the method proposed in (Angrisani & Vadursi, 2008) is to let the user choose where to place the replica characterized by the lowest central frequency and, consequently, automatically determine the lowest f_s that satisfies the choice, thus guaranteeing an optimal use of DAS resources. In particular, the main advantages consist in the optimization of DAS vertical resolution and memory resources, given the observation interval. On the basis of the results presented in Section 2, a method for the automatic selection of the DAS sample rate is hereinafter proposed. Two different implementations of the method are, in particular, given. The first proves appropriate when the sample clock is characterized by a constant resolution, as it happens when the DAS accepts an external sample clock. The second is addressed to variable sample clock resolution, which characterizes the cases when no external sample clock is either allowed or available and the DAS can vary its sample rate according to a specific rule.

3.1 Data acquisition systems with constant sample clock resolution

As it is evident from relation 1 and Fig. 1, replicas are not equally spaced on the frequency axis, and one and only one replica comes out to be centered in $(0, f_s/2)$. The first implementation allows the choice of the normalized frequency f^*/f_s. Specifically, the user can choose f^* in terms of a fraction of f_s:

$$f^* = f_s / p \;, \qquad p > 2. \tag{20}$$

Moreover, the user can input a value for the minimum guard band between adjacent replicas. By substituting (20) into systems (15) and (19), it is possible to derive the conditions on f_s that must be respected in order to avoid aliasing. Such conditions are expressed as

$$\begin{cases} f_s > \dfrac{p}{1-p|\nu|\chi_M}\left[\dfrac{B+B_g}{2} + |\nu|\dfrac{\Delta f}{2}(1+\chi_M)\right] \\ f^* > p\dfrac{B+B_g+\Delta f\left(|\nu|+\dfrac{1}{2}\right)(1-\chi_M)}{-2+p(1-\chi_M)-2p|\nu|\chi_M} \end{cases} \tag{21}$$

when $\lambda = 1$ (positive replica), and as

$$\begin{cases} f_s > \dfrac{p}{1-p|\nu|\chi_M}\left[\dfrac{B+B_g}{2}+|\nu|\dfrac{\Delta f}{2}(1-\chi_M)\right] \\ f^* > p\dfrac{B+B_g+\Delta f\left(|\nu|-\dfrac{1}{2}\right)(1+\chi_M)}{-2+p(1+\chi_M)-2p|\nu|\chi_M} \end{cases} \tag{22}$$

when $\lambda = -1$ (negative replica).

Once the user has entered the desired value of p, the algorithm provides the lowest f_s that verifies (20) and (21) (or (20) and (22), if $\lambda = -1$), given the bandwidth and the central frequency of the input signal, and the desired guard band between two adjacent replicas, B_g.

Let us impose $f^* = f_s / p$ in (1), and solve the equation with regard to f_s; the equation can be solved when either $\lambda = 1$ and $\nu \leq 0$, or $\lambda = -1$ and $\nu \geq 1$.

In such cases the solution is

$$f_s = \frac{\lambda\, p}{1-\nu\, p} f_c \,. \tag{23}$$

The set of possible values for $(1-\nu p)\backslash\lambda\, p$, arranged in increasing order, is

$$\left\{\frac{p-1}{p}, \frac{p+1}{p}, \frac{2p-1}{p}, \frac{2p+1}{p}, \ldots, \frac{n\,p-1}{p}, \frac{n\,p+1}{p}, \ldots\right\}. \tag{24}$$

The algorithm iteratively explores the set of solutions in (24), starting from the highest value for f_s, and halts when the current f_s does not respect either of the alias-free conditions (21) or (22) anymore. The last value of f_s which is compliant with the alias-free conditions is the lowest sample rate that provides the desired positioning of replicas and guarantees the minimum required guard band.

3.2 Data acquisition systems with variable sample clock resolution

When the resolution of the sample clock is variable, besides the inputs described in the previous case, the user is also required to give the set of possible sample rates allowed by the DAS. Since DAS's generally vary their sample rate according to the common 1:2:5 rule, i.e.

$$f_s \in \{\ldots, 10\ MHz, 20\ MHz, 50\ MHz, 100\ MHz, \ldots\} \tag{25}$$

a different approach is followed to find out the optimal value of f_s. In such a case, the set of possible values for f_s is, in fact, limited.

Due to the coarse-grained distribution of allowed values for f_s, the value of ε in (6) can be significantly too large, and induce intolerably large deviations from the expected value of f^*. Therefore, the adoption of the iterative algorithm described above would be meaningless, whereas an exhaustive approach should be preferred. Specifically, for each allowed value of f_s greater than twice the bandwidth of the signal, the corresponding value of f^* is calculated and the alias-free condition is checked.

In particular, only the effects of sample clock instability are taken into account, since the allowed values of f_s are given in input by the user; ε is therefore equal to 0. Then, the user can select the preferred sample rate, on the basis of the corresponding values of f^* and of the frequency resolution (equal to f_s/N, N being the number of acquired samples).

4. Examples

The analytical results described in Section 2 show that taking into account finite time-base resolution and clock accuracy produces a modification of the values of the two thresholds given by (4). The new thresholds are given in (15) and (19).
Before giving details of the performance assessment of the proposed method, some application examples are proposed in order to evaluate how the optimal sample rate is affected by the new thresholds, how different the effects of finite time-base resolution and clock accuracy on the modification of the optimal sample rate are, and how aliasing is introduced when finite time-base resolution and clock accuracy are not properly considered.

4.1 First example

The case described hereinafter gives quantitative evidence of the modification introduced in the thresholds and, consequently, in the optimal sample rate, when finite time-base resolution and clock accuracy are included among input parameters. Let us consider a bandpass signal characterized by a bandwidth $B = 3.84$ MHz and a carrier frequency $f_c = 500$ MHz, and let us suppose that the values of B_g and p chosen by the user are equal to 0 and 3, respectively. Ignoring the effects of ε and χ would lead to an optimal sample rate, f_s, equal to 11.538461 MHz (Angrisani et al., 2004). On the contrary, when $\chi_M = 3.54 \cdot 10^{-4}$ and $\Delta f = 10$ Hz are taken into consideration, the optimal sample rate is 12.60504 MHz, which implies an increase of more than 9%. Let us go through the steps of the algorithm implementing the proposed method to evaluate how such modification is determined. Table 3 shows all the solutions of (23), that is all the sample rates meeting user's requirements, included between the aforementioned 11.538461 MHz and the suggested 12.60504 MHz, which is the optimal sample rate according to the new method. For each sample rate, Table 3 (*i*) states whether a positive ($\lambda = 1$) or negative ($\lambda = -1$) replica is located in the frequency range $[0, f_s/2]$, (*ii*) gives the values of the thresholds $f_{1,old}$ and $f_{2,old}$, calculated according to (4) and utilized in (Angrisani et al., 2004), and (*iii*) provides the thresholds f_1 and f_2, calculated according to the new conditions (15) and (19). Looking at the table, the

f_s [MHz]	λ	f^* [MHz]	$f_{1,old}$ [MHz]	$f_{2,old}$ [MHz]	f_1 [MHz]	f_2 [MHz]
11.53846	1	3.84615	1.92000	3.84923	2.09585	3.67133
11.71875	-1	3.90625	1.92000	3.93938	2.09859	3.76285
11.81102	1	3.93700	1.92000	3.98551	2.09581	3.80760
12.00000	-1	4.00000	1.92000	4.08000	2.09862	3.90350
12.09677	1	4.03225	1.92000	4.12839	2.09577	3.95046
12.29508	-1	4.09836	1.92000	4.22754	2.09865	4.05106
12.39669	1	4.13223	1.92000	4.27835	2.09573	4.10041
12.60504	-1	4.20168	1.92000	4.38252	2.09868	4.20606

Table 3. Thresholds calculated according to the proposed method and that presented in (Angrisani et al., 2004). The signal under test is characterized by a bandwidth $B = 3.84$ MHz and a carrier frequency $f_c = 500$ MHz. Time-base resolution is 10 Hz and sample clock accuracy is $3.54 \cdot 10^{-4}$. The chosen value of p is equal to 10.

effects of finite time-base resolution and sample clock instability on the location of spectral replicas can be quantitatively evaluated; the critical threshold comes out to be the upper threshold f_2. In detail, if the signal is sampled at a rate equal to 11.538461 MHz, the replica is placed at a central frequency f^* equal to 3.84615 MHz, which meets the alias-free condition (4). As a consequence of the modification of the upper threshold from $f_{2,old}$ = 3.84923 MHz to f_2 = 3.67133 MHz, the value of 11.538461 MHz does not guarantee alias-free sampling anymore and has to be discarded. The same happens with successive solutions of (23): they all fail to fall within the new thresholds. The set of possible solutions of (23) has to be explored until 12.60504 MHz, which represents the minimum alias-free sample rate, is reached.

4.2 Second example

Let us consider a bandpass signal characterized by a bandwidth B = 140 kHz and a carrier frequency f_c = 595.121 MHz. Let us suppose that values of B_g and p chosen by the user are equal, respectively, to 0 and 10. The method in (Angrisani et al., 2004) would give an optimal sample rate, f_s, equal to 700.060 kHz. Table 4 gives the values of the optimal sample rate provided by the proposed method for different values of Δf ({1, 10, 100} Hz) and χ_M (between 10^{-8} and $3.54 \cdot 10^{-4}$). As expected, they are all greater than $f_{s,old}$ = 700.060 kHz. What is notable, they range from 704.369 kHz (when Δf = 1 Hz and $\chi_M = 10^{-8}$), which is within 1% from $f_{s,old}$, to 2.9158 MHz (when Δf = 100 Hz and $\chi_M = 3.54 \cdot 10^{-4}$), which represents an increase of more than 300%! Fig.2 permits to evaluate the different roles played by finite time-base resolution and clock accuracy in modifying the optimal sample rate with respect to that furnished by the method in (Angrisani et al., 2004). It shows the optimal sample rate versus clock accuracy, for different values of Δf. For lower values of χ_M, the most significant increase of f_s with respect to $f_{s,old}$ is mainly due to the resolution Δf and the curves are practically horizontal. As accuracy worsens (χ_M increases), the vertical difference among the three curves reduces, and becomes practically negligible for $\chi_M = 3.54 \cdot 10^{-4}$.
So, neither resolution nor accuracy can be said to prevail in determining the optimal sample rate.

χ_M \ Δf	*100 Hz*	*10 Hz*	*1 Hz*
10^{-8}	998.3	740.29	704.369
10^{-6}	1003.4	745.85	710.253
$5.47 \cdot 10^{-6}$	1024.1	770.78	736.445
10^{-5}	1045.7	797.64	763.857
10^{-4}	1494.9	1319.26	1299.107
$3.54 \cdot 10^{-4}$	2915.8	2819.14	2819.143

Table 4. Optimal sample rate, expressed in kilohertz, for a bandpass signal characterized by a bandwidth B = 140 kHz and a carrier frequency f_c = 595.121 MHz, as a function of different values of time-base resolution and clock accuracy. The value of p has been chosen equal to 10.

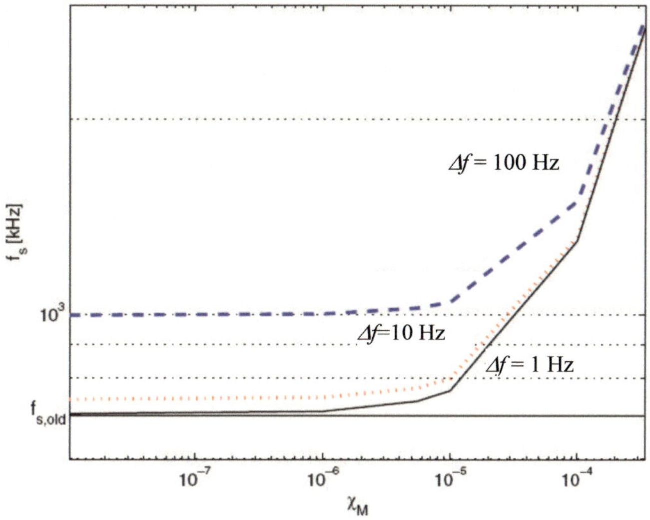

Fig. 2. Optimal sample rate versus clock accuracy, for different values of Δf. The bandpass signal under test has a bandwidth B = 140 kHz and a carrier frequency f_c = 595.121 MHz. The value chosen for p is 10.

4.3 Third example

This example refers to an experimental test conducted by means of the measurement station described in Section 5. Let us suppose that an external source, with a resolution Δf equal to 100 Hz, is utilized as DAS sample clock. The signal under test is a QAM (Quadrature Amplitude Modulation) signal, with bandwidth equal to 140 kHz and carrier frequency equal to 595.121 Hz. The value of p is chosen equal to 10. If the lowest alias-free sample rate that allows to place the lowest frequency replica at the normalized frequency $1/p$ was obtained through the application of an algorithm that does not take into account the finite resolution of the external source, a value of f_s equal to 700.060 kHz would be found, and the expected central frequency of the sampled signal would be 70.000 kHz. Rounding it to the nearest multiple of Δf would result in an actual sample rate of 700.1 kHz. As an effect of the rounding, the actual central frequency of the sampled signal would be 36.0 kHz, which means introducing unexpected, yet not negligible, aliasing. Fig. 3 shows the evolution versus time of the I baseband component measured from the sampled signal, referred to as I_{dem}, and the corresponding original one, assumed as reference, and referred as I. Similarly, Fig. 4 shows the evolution versus time of the Q baseband component measured from the sampled signal, and referred to as Q_{dem}, and the corresponding original one, assumed as reference, and simply as Q. The difference between the measured and reference signals, which is evident from the figures, is responsible for high values of the indexes ΔI (equal to 51%) and ΔQ (equal to 52%), defined in Section 5. On the contrary, an algorithm based on the analysis conducted in Section 2, which takes into account both finite time-base resolution and clock accuracy ($\chi_M = 3.54 \cdot 10^{-4}$, in this example), would produce a sample rate f_s = 2.9158 MHz, with a central frequency f^* = 297.8 kHz. No aliasing would occur, as Fig. 5 and Fig. 6 show, as the measured and the reference components are very close to each other. Values of ΔI and ΔQ lower than 5% are experienced.

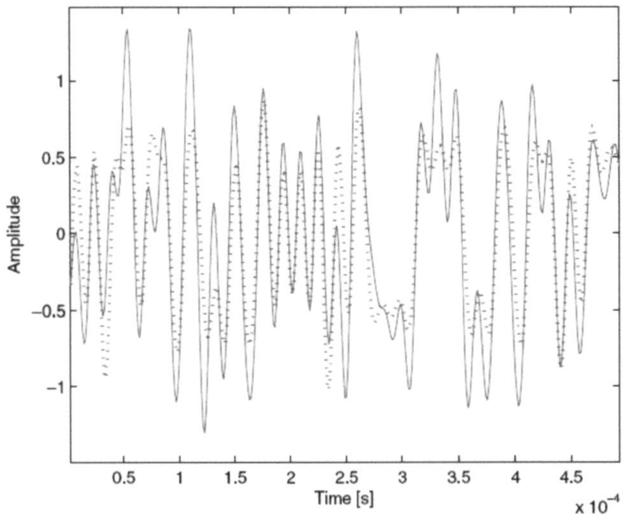

Fig. 3. Evolution versus time of measured I_{dem} (continuous line) and reference I (dotted line) with aliasing.

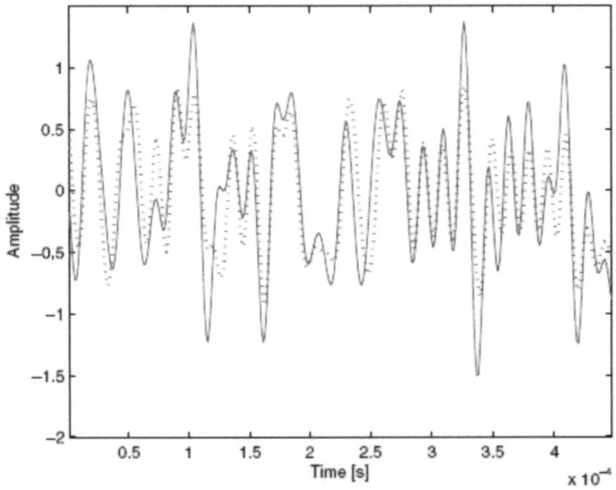

Fig. 4. Evolution versus time of measured Q_{dem} (continuous line) and reference Q (dotted line) with aliasing.

5. Performance assessment

A wide experimental activity has been carried out on laboratory signals to assess the performance of the two implementations of the method.

5.1 Measurement station

Fig. 7 shows the measurement station. The station consists of (*i*) a processing and control unit, namely a personal computer, (*ii*) a digital RF signal generator (250 kHz-3 GHz output frequency range) with arbitrary waveform generation (AWG) capability (14 bit vertical resolution, 1MSample memory depth, 40 MHz maximum generation frequency), (*iii*) a DAS (8 bit, 1 GHz bandwidth, 8 GS/s maximum sample rate, 8 MS memory depth) and (iv) a synthesized signal generator (0.26-1030 MHz output frequency range), acting as external clock source; they are all interconnected by means of a IEEE-488 standard interface bus.

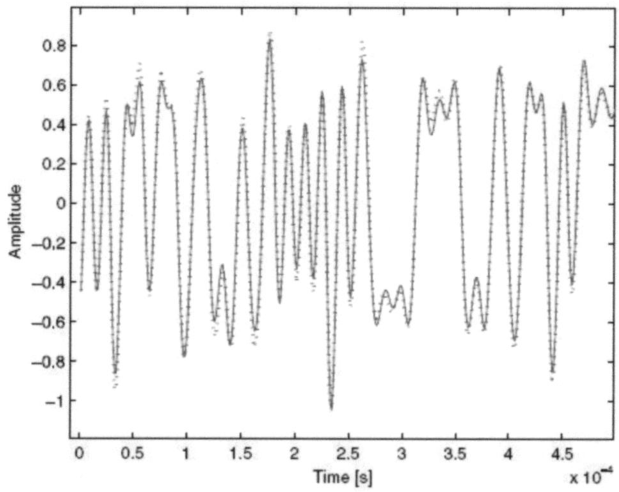

Fig. 5. Evolution versus time of measured I_{dem} (continuous line) and reference I (dotted line) without aliasing.

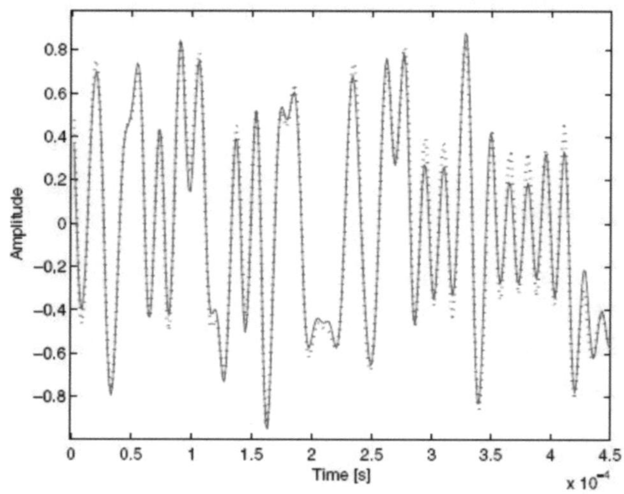

Fig. 6. Evolution versus time of measured Q_{dem} (continuous line) and reference Q (dotted line) without aliasing.

5.2 Test signals

A variety of digitally modulated signals have been taken into consideration, including M-PSK (M-ary Phase Shift Keying) and M-QAM (M-ary QAM) signals. Test signals have been characterized by carrier frequency and bandwidth included, respectively, in the range 100 MHz-700 MHz and 100 kHz-5 MHz.

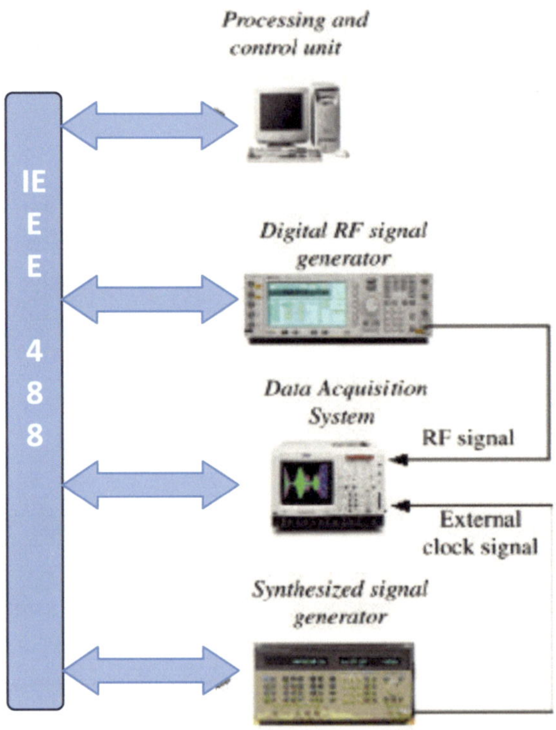

Fig. 7. Measurement station.

5.3 Measurement procedure

Experimental tests have been carried out according to the following procedure: 1) the digital RF signal generator produces a bandpass RF signal, characterized by known bandwidth and carrier frequency; 2) given the specified central frequency f^* and guard band B_g, the proposed method provides the optimal sample rate f_s; 3) in the case of external sample clock, the synthesized signal generator is commanded to output a sinusoidal signal characterized by a frequency value equal to f_s, otherwise the value of f_s is imposed as DAS sample rate; 4) the DAS digitizes the RF signal at a sample rate equal to f_s; 5) the processing and control unit retrieves the acquired samples from the DAS, through the IEEE-488 interface bus.

A two-domain approach has been used. The digitized signal has, in fact, been analyzed in the frequency and modulation domains to verify the concurrence of its actual central frequency with its expected value. With regard to frequency-domain, the difference between the actual and nominal central frequency, Δf^*, has been evaluated. In detail, the acquired samples have suitably been processed to estimate the power spectrum of the analyzed signal (Angrisani et al., 2003). Taking advantage of spectrum symmetry, the actual carrier frequency has been measured as the threshold frequency that splits up the signal power in halves (Agilent Technologies, 2002). Concerning the modulation-domain, the digitized signal has gone through a straightforward I/Q demodulator, and tuned on the expected value of f^*, in order to gain the baseband components I_{dem} and Q_{dem}. I_{dem} and Q_{dem} have then been compared to the baseband components I and Q acquired from the auxiliary analog outputs of the digital RF generator and assumed as reference, in order to calculate the following indexes

$$\Delta I = \frac{1}{N}\sum_{i=1}^{N}\left|\frac{I_{dem}(i)-I(i)}{I(i)}\right| \times 100\% \qquad (26)$$

$$\Delta Q = \frac{1}{N}\sum_{i=1}^{N}\left|\frac{Q_{dem}(i)-Q(i)}{Q(i)}\right| \times 100\% \, . \qquad (27)$$

Moreover, EVM (Error Vector Magnitude), which is a key indicator for modulation quality assessment, has been evaluated. EVM bears traces of possible causes of signal impairments (Angrisani et al., 2005); its value, in particular, gets worse upon the increasing of the deviation of the central frequency increases from its expected value.

5.4 Results

With regard to frequency-domain analysis, Table 5 enlists the results obtained in the tests conducted on a QAM signal characterized by a bandwidth B = 3.84 MHz and a carrier frequency f_c = 500 MHz. Results are expressed in terms of percentage difference Δf^* between actual and expected central frequency of the replica, for different values of p, B_g, and Δf. Values of Δf^* lower than 1% prove the good performance of the method. Similar outcomes have been experienced with the other test signals taken into consideration.

Concerning modulation-domain analysis, the values of ΔI, ΔQ, and EVM, in percentage relative terms, have been, on average, equal to 3.5%. Considering that the demodulator utilized in the experiments is not optimized, the achieved results are extremely encouraging and prove the capability of the method in correctly placing the spectral replica at the desired frequency.

6. Conclusions

The chapter has presented a comprehensive method for automatically selecting the sample rate to be adopted by a DAS when dealing with bandpass signals. The method stems from a thorough analysis of the effects of sample clock instability and clock accuracy on the location on the frequency axis of spectral replicas of the sampled signal, and allows an automatic selection of the sample rate, in accordance to user's *desiderata,* given in terms of spectral location of the replicas and minimum guard band between replicas. Two alternative implementations have been presented, which refer to constant and variable time-base resolution of the DAS. The former can be applied when the DAS accepts an external clock source, whereas the latter is designed to work with the internal clock of the DAS that follows the common 1:2:5 rule.

		B_g [MHz]	f_s [MHz]	f^* [MHz]	Δf^* [%]
$p = 3$	$\Delta f = 10$ Hz	0	12.60504	4.20160	0.10
		1.16	16.30435	5.43485	0.12
		3.84	24.19355	8.06455	0.12
	$\Delta f = 100$ Hz	0	12.6050	4.2000	0.15
		1.16	16.3043	5.4333	0.20
		3.84	24.1935	8.0635	0.20
$p = 4$	$\Delta f = 10$ Hz	0	8.43882	2.10970	0.09
		1.16	10.81081	2.70274	0.19
		3.84	16.26016	4.06496	0.19
	$\Delta f = 100$ Hz	0	8.4388	2.1108	0.27
		1.16	10.8108	2.7032	0.33
		3.84	16.2602	4.0662	0.25
$p = 8$	$\Delta f = 10$ Hz	0	17.16738	2.14598	0.21
		1.16	21.62162	2.70274	0.18
		3.84	33.05785	4.13225	0.24
	$\Delta f = 100$ Hz	0	17.1674	2.1454	0.25
		1.16	21.6216	2.7032	0.25
		3.84	33.0579	4.1315	0.39

Table 5. Frequency-domain results related to a QAM signal with bandwidth $B = 3.84$ MHz and a carrier frequency $f_c = 500$ MHz. Sample clock accuracy is $3.54 \cdot 10^{-4}$.

Several experiments, carried out on digitally modulated signals, have assessed the performance of the proposed methods through a two-domain approach. Results have shown that the difference between actual and expected value of the central frequency of the sampled signal is very low ($\Delta f^* \leq 1.0\%$). Moreover, the baseband I and Q components have been reconstructed on the basis of the expected value of the central frequency. Thealues of ΔI, ΔQ, and EVM have, in fact, been on average lower than few percents.

7. References

Agilent Technologies (2002). Testing and troubleshooting digital RF communications transmitter designs. *Application Note 1313 Agilent Technologies Literature No.5968-3578E.*

Akos, D. Stockmaster, M. Tsui, J. & Caschera, J. (1999). Direct bandpass sampling of multiple distinct RF signals. *IEEE Trans. on Communications.* Vol.47, No. 7, (July 1999), pp.983-988.

Angrisani, L. D'Apuzzo, M. & D'Arco, M. (2003). A new method for power measurements in digital wireless communication systems. *IEEE Trans. Instrum. Meas..* Vol.52. pp. 1097-1106.

Angrisani, L. D'Arco, M. Schiano Lo Moriello, R. & Vadursi, M. (2004). Optimal sampling strategies for bandpass measurement signals, *Proc. of the IMEKO TC-4 Interational Symposium on Measurements for Research and Industry Applications.* pp. 343-348, September 2004.

Angrisani, L. D'Arco, M. & Vadursi, M. (2005). Error vector-based measurement method for radiofrequency digital transmitter troubleshooting. *IEEE Trans. Instrum. Meas..* Vol.54. pp. 1381-1387.

Angrisani, L. & Vadursi, M. (2008). On the optimal sampling of bandpass measurement signals through data acquisition systems. *IOP Meas. Sci. Technol.* Vol.19, (April 2008) 1-9.

Betta, G. Capriglione, D. Ferrigno, L & Miele, G. (2009). New algorithms for the optimal selection of the bandpass sampling rate in measurement instrumentation, *Proc. of XIX IMEKO World Congress*, pp. 485–490, September 2009.

Brown, J.L. (1980). First-order sampling of bandpass signals - A new approach. *IEEE Trans. on Information Theory*, Vol. 26, No. 5, (Sept. 1980), 613-615.

Corcora, J.J. (1999). Analog-to-Digital Converters, In: *Electronic Instrument Handbook,* C. F. Coombs (Ed.), Chapter 6, McGraw-Hill Professional, New York City, NY, USA..

Coulson, A.J. Vaughan, R.G. & Poletti, M.A. Frequency-Shifting Using Bandpass Sampling. *IEEE Trans. on Signal Processing*. Vol.42. No.6. pp.1556-1559.

De Paula, A. & Pieper, R.J. (1995). A more complete analysis for subnyquist bandpass sampling, *Proceedings of the 24th Southeastern Symp. on System Theory and the 3rd Annual Symp. on Communic., Signal Processing, Expert Systems, and ASIC VLSI Design,* March 1992.

Diez, R.J. Corteggiano, F. & Lima, R.A. (2005). Frequency mapping in uniform bandpass sampling, *Proceedings of the 24th Southeastern Symp. on System Theory and the 3rd Annual Symp. on Communic., Signal Processing, Expert Systems, and ASIC VLSI Design,* March 1992.

Gaskell, J. D. (1978). *Linear systems, Fourier transforms and optics.* Wiley. New York City, NY, USA.

Grace, O.D. & Pitt, S.D. (1968). Quadrature sampling of high frequency waveforms. *J. Acoustic Soc. Am.,* Vol. 44, pp. 1432-1436.

Jackson, M.C. & Matthewson, P. (1986). Digital processing of bandpass signals, *GEC J. Res.,* Vol. 4, No.1, 1986.

Kohlenberg, A. (1953). Exact interpolation of band-limited functions, *J. Appl. Phys.,* Vol. 24, 1432–1436.

Latiri, A. Joet, L. Desgreys, P. & Loumeau, P. (2006). A reconfigurable RF sampling receiver for multistandard applications. *Comptes Rendus Physique,* Vol. 7, No. 7, September 2006, pp. 785-793.

Ronggang, Q. Coakley, F.P. & Evans, B.G. (1996). Practical considerations for bandpass sampling. *Electronic Letters*. Vol.32. No. 20. Pp.1861-1862.

Shannon, C. (1949). Communication in the presence of noise, *Proc. IRE,* Vol. 37, 10–21.

Tseng, C.H. (2002). Bandpass sampling criteria for nonlinear systems. *IEEE Trans. on Signal Processing*, Vol. 50, No. 3, (March 2002).

Vaughan, R.G.; Scott, N.L.; White,D.R. (1991). The theory of bandpass sampling, *IEEE Trans. Signal Proc.*, Vol.39, No.9, (Sept. 1991) 1973-1984, ISSN

Waters, M. W.; Jarrett, B.R. (1982). Bandpass signal sampling and coherent detection, *IEEE Trans. Aerosp. Electron. Syst.*, Vol. AES-18, No. 4, (Nov. 1982).

3

Clock Synchronization of Distributed, Real-Time, Industrial Data Acquisition Systems

Alessandra Flammini and Paolo Ferrari
University of Brescia, Dept. of Information Engineering
Italy

1. Introduction

In distributed data acquisition systems for industrial applications, the synchronization of the time references of the nodes is essential to guarantee the right real-time behaviour of the system. All the modern distributed automation plants require a clock synchronization mechanism.

The use of distributed architectures in industrial applications based on networks has many benefits, including high system flexibility and scalability. However, this enhancement does not come for free; basically, a high-performance network communication among the nodes is needed and the data exchange across the network requires more complex management software than centralized systems (Felser, 2005). Moreover, a key point in all distributed data acquisition systems is the synchronization of the time reference among the nodes (Eidson & Lee, 2003). A typical automation plant is composed by several distributed nodes, controllers, sensors and actuators that need to sample and control the system in a time coordinated fashion. Considering the real-time applications for data-acquisition, the clock synchronization of the time reference across the network is essential in order to support:

- Data fusion of the measures obtained using distributed data acquisition system and sensors (Proft, 2007).
- Distribute signal processing which takes the "time" into account.
- Coordination of the actions across a distributed set of actuators if a control action has to be taken.
- Optimization of the transmission bandwidth in the network, thanks to channel medium access control such as TDMA (Time Division Multiple Access), for both wired and wireless systems (Ueda & Yakoh, 2004).

The scientific community has proposed several types of synchronization algorithms: some of them are dedicated to wired networks, with different kind of complexity and accuracy; others are specifically dedicated to satisfy the requirements of wireless networks. The aim of this chapter is the definition of basic concepts in the field of clock synchronization in order to better understand the typical applications of clock synchronization techniques to industrial data acquisition systems.

This chapter is organized as follows. A brief introduction to essential notions regarding the time keeping and clock performance metrics is provided in Section 2 and 3. Clock synchronization for distributed data acquisition systems are discussed in Section 4. Real examples of synchronized data acquisition systems for industrial applications are presented in Section 5 for wired systems and in Section 6 for wireless systems.

2. Clocks and time: a brief introduction

A clock can be considered as composed essentially by two parts. The first part is an oscillating device used to determining the length of the second or other time interval: in other words, the clock frequency. Usually, in a common application, a quartz crystal oscillator is used to provide the reference oscillation to an electronic circuit. On the contrary, in an atomic clock, the oscillation of an electromagnetic signal associated with a quantum transition between two energy levels in an atom has been chosen as reference. The second part is a counter, called also adder or accumulator, that keeps track of the number of seconds or oscillator cycles that have occurred.

In theory, if a clock is set perfectly and it has a perfect frequency, it keeps the correct time indefinitely. In practice the clock cannot be set perfectly because of random and systematic variations which are present in any oscillator. Moreover, the clock frequency may change from ideal due to environmental changes.

The quality of a clock can be described by means of four measures:

- frequency accuracy;
- frequency stability;
- time accuracy;
- time stability.

The frequency of a clock is how well it can realize the defined length of the second. A commonly-used measure is the normalized frequency departure y(t); since it is calculated as the change in the time error of a clock divided by the elapsed time t between two measurements, it is time-dependent and dimensionless. The frequency stability indicates the change in frequency between two periods of time. The time accuracy means how well a clock agrees with the Coordinated Universal Time (UTC). The time accuracy is an important quality for distributed data-acquisition systems, since it is an indicator of the consistency of time in several places (spatially distributed). Time stability is related both with frequency stability and with time accuracy, especially in distributed systems. For instance, a clock of a data acquisition system can lose exactly half a second per month: its time accuracy worsens half a second per month from the initial setting, but it has perfect frequency stability, and hence perfect time predictability. Generally speaking if the time or frequency errors of the clocks may be estimated and compensated, the performance of a distributed acquisition system based on that clock can be improved.

Besides the qualities of a clock, two other definitions are fundamental for the time keeping of distributed data acquisition systems: synchronization and syntonization. They are needed for the development of the methods and theories that rule distributed systems.

Synchronization: the times of distributed clocks are synchronized if their readings are the same after taking into account the reference frame delay along the distribution system (e.g. a network). Synchronization needs to be specified to within some level of uncertainty, sometimes referred as "synchronization accuracy".

Syntonization: the rates, or frequencies, of clocks are syntonized if the rates are the same after taking into account the reference frame corrections. Syntonization needs to be specified to within some level of uncertainty.

3. Methods and measurements for clock characterization

An ideal clock has an error in each frequency measurement that is random and uncorrelated with any of the previous errors. On the other hand, since the time of a clock results from adding or integrating the frequency of an oscillator, the time errors are also integrated. The time error, x_i, for each clock adds all the independent frequency errors. The x_i follows the so called random-walk process. The time error at any point in time correlates with the past because it is an accumulation of all the previous errors. Because of the random-walk phenomena, the standard deviation of the time error of a clock is unbounded also in the ideal case. If v is the frequency of the oscillator, the frequency departure is defined as the normalized derivative of the frequency

$$y(t) = \frac{\partial \upsilon}{\upsilon} \tag{1}$$

The time error x(t) can be expressed in function of its frequency offset:

$$x(t) = \int_0^t y(t')dt' \tag{2}$$

The standard deviation is not recommended to measure the frequency instability because the long-term frequency behaviour of most clocks tends to walk off, and so the standard deviation appears unbounded. The recommended measures for the instability, both from IEEE and ITU, are described in the following (Hackmand & Sullivan, 1996; Sullivan et al., 1990). Three sequential time error measurements of a clock, x_n, x_{n+1}, and x_{n+2}, spaced by a measurement interval τ must be considered. The normalized frequency departure averaged over the n to n+1 interval is given by

$$y_n = \frac{(x_{n+1} - x_n)}{\tau} \tag{3}$$

or in terms of finite difference notation

$$y_n = \frac{\Delta x_n}{\tau} \tag{4}$$

In the same way the average frequency departure for the next interval may be written

$$y_{n+1} = \frac{\Delta x_{n+1}}{\tau} \tag{5}$$

The instability in this clock for its frequency, averaged over the first τ interval to the next τ can be represented by the change in frequency:

$$\Delta y_n = y_{n+1} - y_n = \frac{\Delta^2 x_n}{\tau} \tag{6}$$

The sum of the squares of these second differences (6) for n from 1 to N-2, where N is the number of time error measurements in a series for a particular clock, divided by 2(N-2), is an estimate of the two-sample variance, $\sigma_y^2(\tau)$, also called Allan variance (AVAR) (Allan 1987). AVAR can be written as follow:

$$\sigma_y^2(\tau) = \frac{1}{2\tau^2}\left\langle \left(\Delta^2 x\right)^2 \right\rangle = \frac{1}{2}\left\langle \left(\Delta y\right)^2 \right\rangle \tag{7}$$

where the notation "<>" stands for an infinite time average. The average of the second difference is taken over the entire data length, hence the best confidence on the estimate is obtained for long data record. Allan variance is used as a measure of frequency stability in precision oscillators. The advantage of this variance over the classical variance is that it converges for most of the commonly encountered kinds of noise, whereas the classical variance does not always converge to a finite value.

Several different types of noise are used to model the time and frequency noise which is present in any real system: white-noise time or phase modulation (PM); flicker or 1/f PM; random-walk FM; flicker-noise or 1/f FM; and white-noise (random and uncorrelated) frequency modulation (FM). The classical variance is non convergent both for flicker-noise (or 1/f FM) and for random-walk FM noise types, whereas the AVAR is convergent for all the types of noise. Moreover the type and level of noise can be inferred observing the dependence of the variance changing the averaging time τ; the only exception are the white-noise PM and flicker-noise PM, that have similar dependence to τ.

In order to remove the ambiguity just mentioned for AVAR, the modified two-sample variance, MVAR, is introduced in (Howe, 1995). In equation (7), three time-error readings form the second difference, $\Delta^2 x_i = x_{i+2} - 2x_{i+1} + x_i$. Replacing the three time-error values with three time-error averages (over adjacent windows of duration τ), then the MVAR is obtained. Its equation is:

$$Mod.\sigma_y^2(\tau) = \frac{1}{2\tau^2}\left\langle \left(\Delta^2 \overline{x}\right)^2 \right\rangle \tag{8}$$

where the bar notation for x means the average over a windows of duration τ.

In addition to these estimates a new variance measure has been introduced for characterization of network performance. The new time variance, TVAR, takes into account both variance of measurement noise and variance of time and frequency transfer. TVAR can be written as follows:

$$\sigma_x^2(\tau) = \frac{\tau^2}{3} Mod.\sigma_y^2(\tau) = \frac{1}{6}\left\langle \left(\Delta^2 \overline{x}\right)^2 \right\rangle \tag{9}$$

where the 6 in the denominator normalizes TVAR in order to be equal to the classical variance on the time residuals in the case of classical white noise PM.

The three time domain variances are very useful in order to specify the uncertainty in time and frequency metrology for characterizing the stochastic or random processes in clocks (oscillators, and so on). However, in real cases, the systematic effects may limit the performance of clocks, oscillators and time/frequency transfer. As a result, the specification of uncertainty has to consider both the systematic and the random effects; hence they are usually combined as the square root of the sum of the squares.

In precision oscillators often occurs frequency drift, a typical systematic error. Frequency drift occurs, for example, in all crystal oscillators. The time error caused by frequency drift is given by ½ Dt^2, where t is the time since the clock is both synchronized and syntonized and D = y(t)/t is the amount of the frequency drift. This time error is called the time-interval error (TIE). Frequency drift affects the previous measures with the following relation:

$$\sigma_y(\tau) = Mod.\sigma_y(\tau) = \frac{D\tau}{\sqrt{2}} \tag{10}$$

If τ is the time since synchronization and syntonization, the TIE≈1.2 $\sigma_x(\tau)$ because of frequency drift. The time interval error in a network can be adjusted varying the synchronization interval.

4. Clock synchronization for real-time distributed systems

The clocks of devices belonging to distributed data acquisition system can differ after some amount of time (even the clocks are initially set accurately) because of the clock drift due both to the different rate of local oscillators and to environmental perturbations.

If a synchronization algorithm is employed in the system to compensate the time error, two main sources of error remains; the information about the time of a clock degrades due both to the drifts of the clocks (as before) and to the uncertainty of the delay that the messages carrying the time take to travel along the distributed network. The drift of the clock usually is more influent than the message delays in the case the time-carrying communication is infrequent; with the decrease of the frequency of communication, the uncertainty due to the clock drift increases, while the uncertainty due to the message delays remains constant. A trivial solution may be the decrease of the synchronization interval, but any clock synchronization schemes require the time information obtained through the communication to be processed. The computation power and the memory required by the synchronization algorithms must increase with the increase of communication data exchanges. This means a trade-off between the computational power and the accuracy must be achieved.

The synchronization of the clocks in a network where the time is provided outside the network is known as external; the synchronization is external even if the source of the common system time is either a node in the network or not. The external synchronization requires consistency within the network and in respect to the externally provided system time. The internal synchronization is the synchronization shared only among the clocks inside the network, without a predetermined master time.

The synchronization can have a global scope, if the clock synchronization is required in all the nodes of the network or a limited scope if it is required in a subset of nodes only.

There are algorithms in which the network nodes exchange synchronization messages without interruption and the time synchronization is continuous. On the contrary, other applications require"on-demand synchronization"; if no synchronization is needed, the communication can be reduced. There are two types of on-demand synchronization: event-triggered on-demand synchronization, used when a node needs a synchronized clock only immediately after the event happened; the time-triggered on-demand synchronization is used for collecting data from several nodes at a given time. Since there is no trigger event, the nodes of the network has to be synchronized at a given time and maintain the synchronization at least until the data acquisition takes place. Such a behaviour can be obtained using the "immediate synchronization", where nodes receive the command to take

a sample and time-stamp it, or the "anticipated synchronization", where the order is to take the sample in a future time. The anticipated synchronization is mandatory when the transfer of command and time cannot be simultaneous to all the involved nodes. Note that the minimum synchronization accuracy required by the anticipated synchronization is related to the time that elapses between the synchronization instant and the programmed event.
A good synchronization algorithm for data acquisition systems must estimate both the clock rate (syntonization, as explained before) and the offset from the reference time. Offset estimation is sufficient for data fusion operations, while syntonization is required if time intervals have to be measured.
Last, time synchronization can be achieved in two different ways. The clocks can be forced to have the "same" time at any given moment or each clock has it own time but can transform the timescales of the other clocks. Equal results can be obtained using the two approaches: the first approach requires the same amount of communication across the network, whereas the latter require a huge computational and memory overhead. The time information are exchanged between clocks specifying either a time instant or a time intervals; additional information about the quality of the synchronization (time uncertainty) may be also provided.

4.1 Clock synchronization over packet-switched, wired networks

Several solutions have been proposed in order to synchronize the drift of the local clocks in a distributed system: some of them use dedicated hardware, such as GPS receiver, atomic clock or synchronization signals (e.g. 1-PPS - 1 pulse per second), to compensate drift of local clock. Unfortunately these approaches require a separate network for time distribution, which means extra costs and reduced reliability of the whole system. The most attracting clock synchronization solutions for distributed data acquisition system for industrial applications are the algorithms that can also be used in packet-switched networks, like Ethernet.
The most diffused communication protocols are NTP ("Network Time Protocol") (IETF RFC1305, 1992) and IEEE 1588 PTP ("Precision Time Protocol") (IEEE1588, 2002; IEEE1588V2, 2008). Both solutions have advantages and disadvantages for data acquisition applications that should be balanced by the analysis of the application requests (timing performance) and constraints (cost and development time). In some applications the requested synchronization accuracy is below 1 μs. Typical cases are: electrical and industrial automation; control systems; and distributed measurement applications for time referenced data acquisition, also known as timestamping of events. In such situations, the reference hi-performance system against which the other solutions are compared is the use of a GPS receiver for each device to be synchronized. GPS can guarantee a high level of accuracy (≈100 ns) but has the disadvantage of the antenna cabling and placing (especially in an industrial environment or with indoor application). On the other hand, the use of the same network that connects the devices and transports process data also for transmitting the time information is the clever solution.
The Network Time Protocol (NTP) was developed starting in 1985 by the University of Delaware and it is based on UDP transport protocol. NTP implements the Marzullo algorithm (Marzullo, 1984) that gives an optimal value elaborating set of estimates and their confidence intervals. The synchronization accuracy that is usually obtained using NTP (with Internet applications) is on the order of few ms, even if in more controlled scenario (like

local area networks and ideal conditions) NTP can achieve an accuracy as low as few μs. NTP synchronizes the local clock to UTC, even if it can be used also to distribute any time scale on private sub-networks (uncommon). A simplified version of NTP is the Simple Network Time Protocol (SNTP) used by simpler devices and application thanks to the lower computational power required.

The NTP protocol clock sources are hierarchically organized into levels called stratum, and identified by numbers. The stratum indicates the distance of that clock from the reference clock. The top level has the number 0; devices belonging to this stratum are the servers for the stratum 1 devices and so on. Usually, the nodes of a given stratum (e.g. 2) query several servers of the parent stratum (e.g. 1) because the NTP algorithm can extract the best data samples. Querying clock belonging to the same stratum is also possible to improve time accuracy. NTP theoretically supports up to 256 strata, depending on the protocol version. The NTP time has a 64 bit representation, 32 bit for the seconds and 32 bit for the fractional part of the second.

NTP uses a client-server synchronization model. The synchronization transaction is initiated by the client that asks a time server. Making the request, the client stores the originate timestamp of the transmitted packet. A server that receives this packet stores the receive timestamp and gives it back into the response packet sent to the client. When the client receives the reply, it logs the receive time to estimate the travelling time of the packet. The propagation time (delay) is estimated to be half of the total delay minus the remote (server) processing time, assuming a symmetrical communication delay. The same time differences can be used for the estimation of the time offset between client and server. The estimate of the current time is more accurate if the round trip time is short and symmetric.

The time obtained from the estimation must be validated using a set of "sanity checks" before being used at the application. Usually several exchanges are necessary to reach a valid time estimate. Usually a quite long time (up to few minutes) may be required for NTP convergence. Each NTP server continuously updates an estimate of the quality of its reference clocks together with statistics about its own behaviour.

IEEE 1588 PTP (Precision Time Protocol) is a time synchronization protocol developed for distributed measurement and control systems. It is designed in order to provide synchronization to systems that require an accuracy higher than NTP. This protocol allows obtaining a sub-microsecond accuracy if:

- oscillator stability and accuracy has to be such that a second measured by any of the clocks is within ±0.01% of SI second;
- the timestamps have to be taken as close as possible to the hardware;
- the network must support multicast transmission;
- the communication paths have to be symmetric;
- each clock has to be accurately described by well-defined properties.

PTP is an external synchronization protocol in which all clocks in the network are synchronized to the time of a single clock, the grandmaster clock. The clock that provides the time to a sub-network is called master clock whereas the others are called slave clocks. PTP achieves time synchronization in two steps: first, the clocks in the network are organized into a master-slaves hierarchy, and then the nodes start to exchange timestamped messages between master and slave clocks.

Each clock participating in an IEEE 1588 synchronization is described using several properties, such as its stratum, identifier, and variance. The stratum represents the

synchronization capabilities of the clock to UTC by means of protocols other than PTP (such as NTP or GPS). The identifier represents the accuracy of synchronization to UTC. The variance gives the stability and noise properties of the local oscillator.
During the first step of the protocol, each clock broadcasts its properties to the other clocks in its time domain. These information are used by the Best Master Clock (BMC) algorithm which is running independently in any nodes, and is used in order to determine the best clock of the current time domain. The best clock becomes the master whereas the rest become slave clocks. The BMC algorithm arranges the local network in a clear master-slaves hierarchy as shown in Fig. 1 An ordinary clock interfaces with only one broadcast domain and can act as a master or slave in the domain. On the other hand, boundary clock interfaces with more than one broadcast domain but acts as a slave in only one of the domains, and as master in the others.

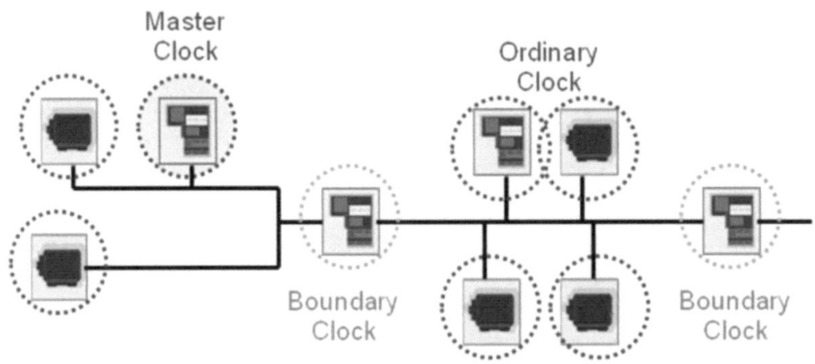

Fig. 1. The clocks hierarchy in a IEEE 1588 synchronization network.

IEEE 1588 provides for five types of messages: Sync, Follow_Up, Delay_Req, Delay_Resp, and Management messages. Sync and Follow_Up messages are transmitted by the master clock so the slaves can calculate their time offset from the master time. The Follow Up message is used to transport the timestamp of the preceding Sync message. The Delay_Req message is transmitted by a slave clock in order to estimate the one way delay due to the communication channel. The Delay_Resp message is transmitted by the master clock in response to the Delay_Req message; it contains the time in which the Delay_Req message has been received from the master. The management messages are used to configure and manage the clocks.
IEEE 1588 protocol specifies two message models for synchronization: a "two steps" model and a "one step" model. The exchange of messages is shown in Fig. 2. The grandmaster clock is an ordinary clock that acts as a master clock in the sub-network. In the two steps model, the master sends a Sync message to all the slave clocks in the time domain every sync period. The time in which the Sync message has been sent, Tm1, is transported to the slave clocks in a following Follow Up message. When a slave clock receives the Sync message, it timestamps the time of reception Ts1, according to its local clock. In the same way, the slave clock sends a Delay_Req message to its master and registers the time of transmission, Ts2. The master responds with a Delay_Resp message that contains the time in which the Delay_Req message has been received, Tm2.
The one step model for the exchange of the messages is similar except that the Sync message carries the transmission timestamp in order to eliminate the need of the Follow Up message. The phase offset of the slave clock from the master is called offset_from_master, and the one-way delay (one_way_delay) due to the communication path is symmetric. These two parameters can be calculated as:

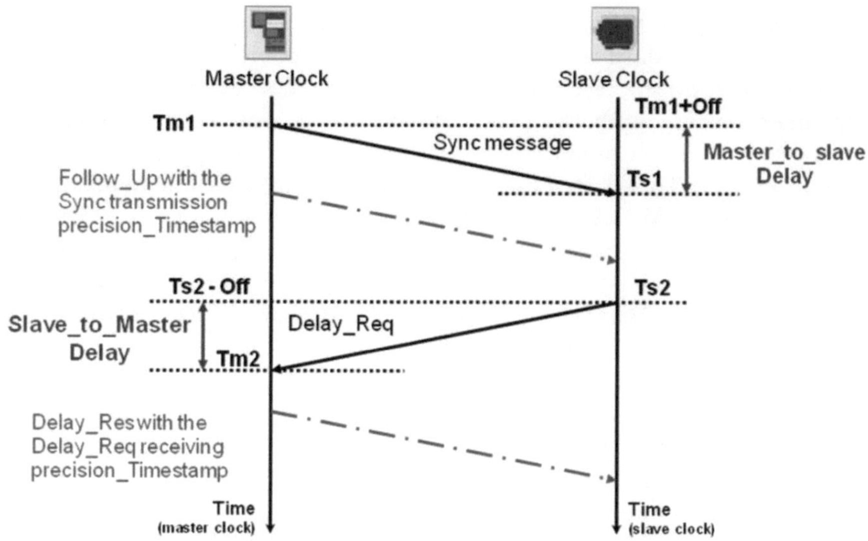

Fig. 2. The exchange of messages in IEEE 1588 protocol.

$$one\_way\_delay = \frac{\{(T_{s1} - T_{m1}) + (T_{m2} - T_{s2})\}}{2} \tag{11}$$

$$offset\_from\_master = (T_{s1} - T_{m1}) - one\_way\_delay \tag{12}$$

where (Ts1-Tm1) is the master-to-slave delay (m2sDelay), and (Tm2-Ts2) is the slave-to-master delay (s2mDelay). So the equations (11) and (12) can be written respectively as:

$$one\_way\_delay = \frac{\{\text{ m2sDelay} + \text{s2mDelay}\}}{2} \tag{13}$$

$$offset\_from\_master = (\text{m2sDelay}) - one\_way\_delay \tag{14}$$

The minimum time interval between two Syncs is one second. The time information is transported using two fields of 32 bits each: seconds and nanoseconds since 00:00:00 of the 1st January 1970.

The estimate of the one_way_delay in the calculation of the offset is very important in order to obtain a high precision synchronization. The protocol does not specify how use the offset to correct local the clock. The different implementations use different approaches. The open source daemon PTPd (Corell et al., 2005) uses a simple PI controller to modify the system clock of LINUX based slaves/master, using the filtered measured data obtained exchanging messaging. On the other hand, more complex solutions, such as (Giorgi & Narduzzi, 2009), use a Kalman filter to update the local clock; these solutions try to keep into account the effects of huge network traffics and complex topologies on the synchronization accuracy.

The application of IEEE 1588 protocol to fields different from the control and measurement environment (such as telecommunications and hi-end data acquisition systems) triggered the revision of the standard. In March 2008 an updated version of the standard has been approved; this version of the protocol is known as IEEE 1588 Version 2. This version introduces in the PTP standard several improvements in order to adapt the synchronization protocol to different application scenarios. Unfortunately this new version of the standard is not directly interoperable with the previous version. A new class of devices has been introduces, the so called transparent clocks. A transparent clock is used to connect together two links of a network. This device has been introduced into PTP architecture in order to prevent error accumulation in cascaded topologies using the boundary clocks defined in PTP Version 1. Boundary clocks employ a servo loop to recover the clock on the slave port, and then the recovered clock is used by the other PTP master ports. The cascade of multiple boundary clocks within a network can degrade clock accuracy of the system because of the cumulative effect of multiple servo loops. The quality of the crystal oscillator used in a boundary clock can also impact the accuracy of the PTP clocks in the system. On the other hand, the transparent clocks are used to update and append a timing correction field into PTP payload. The correction field is updated with a value that represents the "residence time" of the message to pass through the transparent clock. In this way each switch appears as a wire because does not alter the time calculation for packets passing through them. The correction field accumulates the value of the residence times of all the cascaded transparent clocks between Master and Slave. The other devices, ordinary and boundary clocks, take into account the value of the correction field in their calculations. In this way the jitter is reduced and the accuracy and stability of the clocks can be increased. Two kinds of transparent clocks are provided from the standard: the end-to-end (E2E) and the peer-to-peer (P2P) transparent clock. In the P2P transparent clocks each port of the node computes the peer link path delay with its link partner on another P2P node. The link path delay calculation is obtained through newly defined V2 messages: PDelay_Req, PDelay_Resp, and PDelay_Resp_Follow_Up. P2P transparent clocks add the link path delay time estimated into the value in the correction field (in addition to the residence time of the message). P2P transparent clocks can work only with nodes (including ordinary and boundary clocks) that support the peer delay function.

The size of sync messages has been reduced in order to improve the efficiency of the protocol, reducing the synchronization information transmitted each sync period. The structure of the Sync messages has been modified and it is incompatible with previous version. In order to increase the precision that can be obtained using the PTP, the length of the timestamp field has been increased. In this way a sub-nanosecond accuracy can be obtained. The PTP messages can also be directly carried by layer 2 messages (such as Ethernet), reducing bandwidth occupied by PTP protocol. The synchronization interval can be dynamically changed during the synchronization, and the sync rate can be faster (more than 1000 time per second) than previous one.

The application of PTP in different environment other than the measurement applications requires the addition of several features to enhance the "strength" of the protocol. In particular the PTP2008, supports fault tolerant architecture that is needed in order to ensure that no single network element failure can cause clocks to fail in their synchronization. In a system with redundant grandmasters, the redundant grandmaster must be able to detect failure of the first grandmaster, and the ordinary clocks must be able to switch from one grandmaster to another without incurring in an unacceptable frequency or phase jumps. Fault tolerance is critical in telecom applications and many data acquisition applications, where safety and reliability are required (De Dominicis et al., 2010a).

4.2 Clock synchronization over wireless networks

In the last years, wireless networks are becoming very popular. The high flexibility of wireless solutions allows the creation of innovative data acquisition systems to monitor a great number of quantities. Moreover, the data logging over a wide area can be done by means of wireless distributed data acquisition systems. Generally speaking, a wireless distributed data acquisition system is composed by a large number, often variable, of autonomous nodes distributed in the environment. Usually, the devices used to develop a wireless network should be: low-cost; ruggedized; low power; smart and with high computational power. For instance IEEE802.15.4 devices can satisfy large part of these requests and they are widely used to implement wireless distributed acquisition applications.

Besides helping in data fusion of measures, the synchronization of wireless network is useful both for reducing the power consumption of each node and for improving the medium access control. For instance the synchronized node can transmit/receive during its time slot, while it remains in low power idle the rest of the time.

The traditional protocols cannot be used because of: the low energy available in the nodes; limited storage capabilities; and limited communication capabilities. Synchronization algorithms for wired networks require the exchange of a large amount of messages, and the continuous listening of synchronization messages. Moreover, the number of active nodes and the network topology of a wireless network may vary frequently and unpredictably. For instance, such situations can lead to unstable estimation of the end to end delay of a message.

For all these reasons, in the last years special synchronization protocols have been developed. With respect to wired networks, the number of wireless synchronization protocols is quite high. In the following, a very short overview of the most important synchronization algorithms that can be used for wireless distributed data acquisition systems is provided.

Timestamp Synchronization (TSS) (Römer, 2001) provides an on-demand, internal synchronization scheme. The clocks run without synchronization and the event timestamps are valid within the node that generated them. If timestamped data are sent to another node a timescale transformation occurs in the receiver (multiple hops imply multiple transformations). The timestamp transformation is obtained subtracting the age of the data from its time of arrival. The age is the time elapsed since its creation. The age of a timestamp consists of two components: the time the timestamp stays in the nodes along the path, and the total amount of time needed to transfer the timestamp from node to node. The first component is measured in the local unsynchronized timescale, while the second component is estimated using the round-trip time of the message and its acknowledgment. Using such a bidirectional message exchange, the receiver can estimate upper bound and lower bound of the timestamp age. Moreover, the parameter "maximum clock drift" is used for time intervals trasformation between the node timescales. The synchronization information is added to acknowledge messages, hence no additional synchronization messages are needed. A first initialization message is required to start the round trip measurement.

Reference Broadcast Synchronization (RBS) (Elson et al., 2002) is aimed to provide the synchronization in an entire network. There is a beacon node that broadcasts synchronization messages. Any client that receives the beacon exchanges its receiving times with other clients. A linear regression is used to estimate the relative offsets and rate differences between clients. The local timescale can be transformed in another timescale using offset and rate differences. The network is clustered in case of multihop systems; each cluster has a separate beacon. Gateways can participate in two or more clusters spreading the time reference across the entire network. In any case, acquired data are timestamped using the local clock and the timestamps are then transformed in the timescale of the receiver node.

Timing-sync Protocol for Sensor Networks (TPSN) (Ganeriwal et al., 2003) is specifically designed for the synchronization of a sensor network, but can be applied to wireless distributed data acquisition as well. As first step, a node is elected as the synchronization master and the construction of a spanning tree (with the master at the root) is started. As second step, the nodes synchronize to their respective parent following the tree structure; a round-trip synchronization is used. The synchronization action is repeated cyclically; the start is given by the root that broadcasts a synchronization-request message to its children. Even if the nodes can receive the messages of their parent, they start the synchronization only after the parent concludes its synchronization process. The master election and the tree construction must be repeated in case of topology changes.

Interval-Based Synchronization (IBS) has been proposed in (Marzullo & Owicki, 1983). After an external synchronization of the network the nodes maintain an estimate of the lower and upper bound on the current time. Meanwhile the time advances, each node varies its estimated bounds according the drift bounds of its local clock. If a communication between two nodes occurs, the bounds are exchanged and combined by choosing the larger lower and the smaller upper bound. Improvements to IBS must be obtained keeping trace of the time history of each node. Clearly this solution becomes inapplicable when the size of the network increases.

Time Diffusion Synchronization Protocol (TDP) is a synchronization algorithm that uses a set of master nodes (Su & Akyildiz, 2005). If the master nodes have access to a global time, external synchronization can be obtained. Each master node broadcasts a request message containing its current time and all the receivers send back a reply message. By means of the round-trip measurements, each master node can calculate the average message delay and its standard deviation. This information is then sent back to all the receivers that also collect data from all the leaders. This procedure is now repeated by the receivers that assume the role of "diffused leaders" for (more) remote nodes in the network. The diffusion is stopped when a preset number of hops from the masters is reached. At the end of the diffusion all nodes receive from master the time h_m of the initial leader, the accumulated message delay Δ_m, and the accumulated standard deviation σ_m. The clock estimate is computed as

$$H=\Sigma m \, \omega_m (h_m+ \Delta_m) \quad (15)$$

where the weights ω_m are inversely proportional to the standard deviation σ_m. The entire synchronization can be repeated several times before the convergence to a common time can be obtained.

Most of these algorithms have been applied to IEEE802.15.4-based solutions and the synchronization accuracy is on the order of 1 ms. For this reason, the research continuously investigate new timestamping or synchronization mechanisms as in (De Dominicis, 2010b).

5. Synchronized wired system for data acquisition

The application of distributed data acquisition systems to industrial manufacture for in-process measuring is mainly realized by means of wired networks. The collected data are generally used for the adjusting of production parameters in order to constantly improve the overall quality of the products. A typical example is given in (Ferrari et al., 2008a) where the case of a modern tool machine which is equipped with dozens of sensors, is discussed.

The use of Ethernet as communication system for the realization of industrial grade, distributed data acquisition systems is driven by the same reasons that makes it common in the consumer market: speed and cost. However, high-speed and low-cost are not enough to match requirements of high-end industrial systems with deterministic real-time behaviour. For this reason International Electrical Committee (IEC) published the new standards (IEC 61784-2, 2007; IEC 61158, 2007) about Real-Time Ethernet (RTE) in order to offer determinism over standard Ethernet. Since the sharing of a common time reference is very important in RTE networks, suitable synchronization methods are used to constantly update time in all the network nodes. The clock synchronization is a need for reducing the uncertainty in case the information is derived from the combination of data taken in different points of the systems. Several synchronization techniques have been developed for RTE, but the most accepted is the IEEE1588-PTP discussed in the previous Section.

Starting form previous experiences on RTE (Depari et al., 2008) and adapting the architecture described in (Ferrari et al., 2008b), an implementation of a distributed, synchronized data acquisition system is proposed.

The proposed distributed data acquisition system is composed of a "network of probes" designed to simultaneously log data in different places, as shown in Fig. 3. The proposed probe must log physical input signals using the same timestamping reference; for instance, if an event causes the signals of two probes to change, the proposed system can measure the delay between the effective change of the inputs. An arbitrary number of probes can be placed in the field, and all the captured data are transmitted to the Data Acquisition Station, together with their timestamp. A network, called "data logging network", has been created to convey logging data and timestamping. A strict clock synchronization among probes is required in order to compare the timestamps of different probes. The proposed probe has two main ways to achieve synchronization: the use of 1-PPS sources (e.g. GPS) or the network synchronization based on IEEE1588, which is distributed over the data logging network. The proposed architecture uses single chip FPGA-based probes and the Data Aquisition Station is a PC.

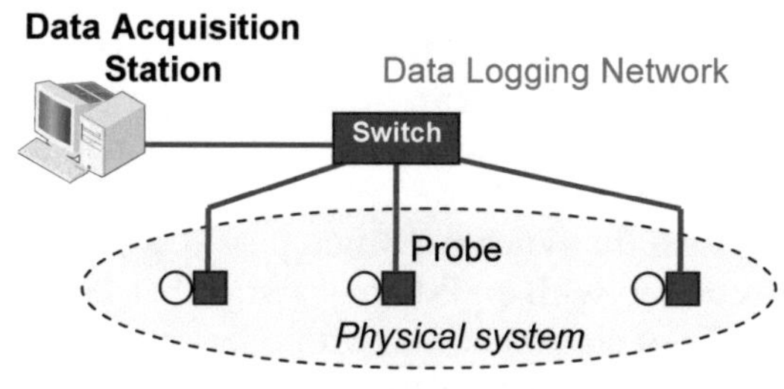

Fig. 3. Distributed data acquisition system based on a network of probes.

In order to prove the feasibility of the proposed solution, two probes of the distributed data acquisition system have been built. The probe prototypes have been implemented with a EP2S60F672C3 Stratix II FPGA (60k LE) mounted on an Altera NIOS development kits. Further features of the the NIOS board are: 1MB of static RAM, 16MB of SDRAM and 16 MB of Flash memory; two serial RS232 interfaces; a 10/100BaseT interface complete with PHY

and MAC. The program for the FPGA is stored in the Flash and during the initialization it is bootstrapped to internal RAM. The external SRAM can be used to temporary store data samples. The Ethernet MAC on-board has been disabled since it is not suitable for the hi-speed timestamping needed for low synchronization accuracy. Consequently, an expansion board has been designed to provide adequate Ethernet interface. A 1000BaseT port (Port M) has been realized with a Marvell chip (88E1111) using the GMII (Gigabit Medium Independent Interface) who is capable to transfer 8 bits at 125 MHz. The proposed probe implementation occupies a small part of the available FPGA resources. The complete system resides in less than 9% of the FPGA ALUT (the basic block of Altera Stratix) and 7% of the FPGA RAM.
The scope of the experimental characterization is the evaluation of the capability of the system to assign timestamps to events. In order to compare the results with the best synchronization techniques available for distributed systems, an external signal (1-PPSin) from a pulse generator (cables of equal length) is used as the time reference, according to Fig. 4.

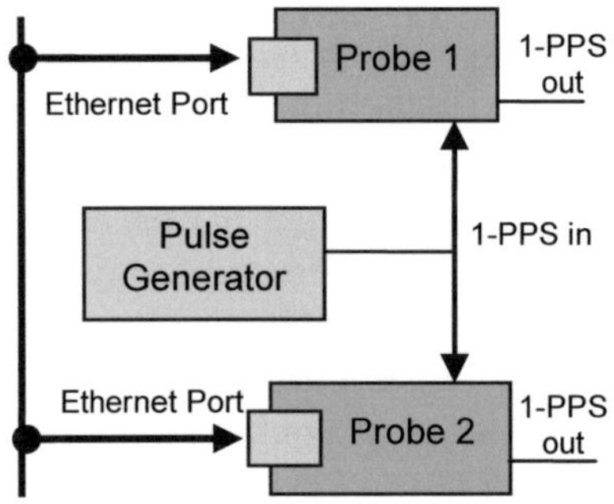

Fig. 4 Experimental setup.

A point-to-point wired synchronization isused as the reference case: the probes must track this 1-PPSin signal for compensating the local time variation and generating an output signal (1-PPSout). Offset between the output signals 1-PPSout of the two probes is always below 100 ns (standard deviation is 16 ns over a period of 10 hours), as shown in Table 1. Clearly, the reference case with the synchronization among probes performed by 1-PPS signal is not suitable for an industrial environment due to extra cabling.
Thus, IEEE1588 PTP is used to synchronize the probes. The PTP master (Probe 1) transmits Sync messages every 1 s to Probe 2 by a cross-cable, in order to evaluate best performance achieved by a PTP-based solution. Table 1 shows that the maximum deviation between probes slightly increases with respect to the reference case. As generally occurs the performance further decrease if the synchronization period is set to 2 s. Moreover, a test case where the cross-cable is replaced with an Ethernet switch has been realized. The maximum deviation between the 1-PPSout signals of the two probes increases to about 350 ns and the standard deviation on the order of 100 ns. This value is independent from the logging traffic over the data acquisition network; even if both probes are logging full-rate traffic (64bytes-long frames @ 100Mbit/s in one direction) this value practically does not change. In conclusion, timestamping performance in distributed data logging systems are greatly affected by synchronization among probes; for this reason, in order to achieve best performance, a great care must be taken with the choice of the switch and of the synchronization period.

Synchronization method	Sync interval (s)	Offset error (ns)		
		Ave.	Std. dev.	Max.
1-PPS signal	1	23	18	89
PTP, cross-cable	1	13	39	146
PTP, cross-cable	2	9	52	215
PTP, switch	2	11	91	344
PTP, switch, loaded	2	18	97	348

Table 1. Offset error between two probes timestamping the same event.

6. Synchronized wireless data acquisition: the Sun SPOT devices

Wireless Data-Acquisition Networks are used in a great number of applications. Unfortunately the long time required for creating the program code is one the main problem that limits the diffusion of this technology in commercial applications. In order to meet the strict requests of distributed wireless application, such as power optimization, specific operative systems (TinyOS), and programming languages have been largely used. Recently, the SunSPOT platform introduces the Java language and high level programming environment also in the field of wireless data-acquisition. The goal of this section is to evaluate the synchronization capabilities of an example of synchronized data acquisition nodes based on SunSPOT devices (Li at al, 2008).

The Sun SPOT devices are composed by two parts, the eSPOT main board (processor board) and the eDEMO board (sensor board). The first one is equipped with an Atmel AT91RM9200 32-bit processor with a 180 MHz clock. The memory of the system is a multichip Spansion MCP S71PL032J40 and consists of a 4 MB flash and 512 kbyte of SRAM memory. It should be highlighted that the most diffused platforms for distributed wireless applications (e.g. MICAz from CrossBow or XBEE from Digidevice) are based on 8-bit microcontroller with few kbytes of memory. The e SPOT board is powered through an USB connection or an on-board rechargeable Lithium-ion battery (3.7V 720mAh). The main board provides also the communication part, through the CC2420, a IEEE802.15.4 transceiver from Texas Instruments. The eDEMO is a sensor board equipped with several useful sensors, such as: light sensor, temperature sensor and tri-axial accelerometer; it is interfaced to the main board through an SPI slave.

The powerful hardware requires a lot of power and the Sun SPOTs firmware try to optimize the power consumption by means of three operating states:

- RUN, when at least an application thread is working and all the hardware peripherals are active. The eSPOT consumption is about 70-120 mA and the sensor board drains up to 400mA.
- IDLE/Shallow sleep, when there are no active threads. ARM9 clock and the radio are off. System wake up by means of interrupts whose latency to return into RUN state is very small. The power consumption is 24-46 mA.
- Deep Sleep, when IDLE last more than 2 seconds. The power consumption is 32µA. The processor wakes up from deep-sleep is by hardware interrupts within 10 ms.

An 8 bit Atmel Atmega88 processor is used to wake up the processor from the Deep Sleep mode and to manage the power of the main board. It should be highlighted that power

consumption is about one order of magnitude greater than the one of 8-bit microcontrollers used in traditional low-level programming platforms, but the good performance of the processor decreases the time the node must be in RUN state. The low-power transceiver CC2420 drains in the receiving phase 20mA, and 18mA during the transmission phase.
The device operating system is the Squawk JVM, a java written Java Virtual Machine (JVM) for devices with low hardware resources, based on Java Micro Edition. In Table 2, the memory occupancy of the software libraries has been reported. The JVM and the library use less than a third of the overall flash memory and less than 20% of the RAM memory.

Software Library	Static Memory Occupancy (kByte)
JVM	149
CLDC Lib	363
SunSPOT API	156

Table 2. Memory required by the software libraries.

The structure of the software platform of a SunSPOT is described in the following. The Squawk JVM is divided in two parts, the suite creator and an on-device JVM (split VM architecture). The first, executed on a separate host, makes several optimizations on the java byte code in order to obtain the so called squawk byte code (file suite) that can be interpreted and executed directly by the JVM implemented on the SunSPOT device. The latter offers also several services of a OS. It provides resources and interrupt management, scheduling of threads and the boot loader. Another important feature of Squawk JVM is the Application isolation mechanism. Each application is handled like an object and this allows to execute several applications at the same time. The Squawk JVM implementation is compliant with the CLDC 1.1 ("Connected Limited Device Configuration") and the APIs of the device are compliant with the profile IMP 1.0 ("Information Mobile Profile"). On the top of the software architecture there are several libraries (SunSPOT API) used to provide (to the application) the access to specific hardware resources, such as radio transceiver and sensors.
The accuracy of synchronization algorithms used in Wireless Data-Acquisition Network relies on the identification of receiving and transmitting time (timestamp) of the specific synchronization frames sent by the master clock. Therefore the evaluation of synchronization performance implies the identification and quantification of the jitter sources on timestamping. Usually the commercial transceivers provide a SFD ("Start of Frame") signal used by the controller to identify the transmission or the reception time of a frame at the physical layer. The transceiver CC2420, has a standard deviation of 100 ns related to SFD identification. Unfortunately the Sun SPOT platform introduces several other sources of jitter at higher levels (Flammini et al., 2010). The java real-time library (RTSJ) is not implemented in the SunSPOT system and the time resolution provided by the JVM is 1 ms, limiting the real-time and synchronization performance. The use of the Java timer implies that timestamps accuracy is lower than with traditional low-level programming platforms (C or Assembly), where a resolution of 1 μs can be achieved.
A very good improvement can be obtained if the timer/counter (TC) of the processor is used. The TC has a resolution better than 1 μs; it is accessible as Spot.getInstance().getAT91_TC(0). The SFD hardware line, which comes from the transceiver, activates every time the transceiver detects a Start_Of_Frame in an incoming or an outgoing frame. The line is connected to the microprocessor that can be programmed to

capture the value of the TC in correspondence on a rising edge of SFD line. The recorded value (RegA) can be read later using an API calling. A very accurate timestamping, both for transmission and for reception, can be obtained; it is limited only by the resolution of the timer of the microprocessor. In the following experiments, the clock of the TC is set to 1.87MHz and the time resolution is 0.5346µs.

An experimental setup has been deployed in order to identify and quantify each source of timestamp jitter and, hence, evaluate synchronization performance. The test system is composed by three SunSPOTs: a traffic generator ("TX1"), used to generate the 802.15.4 frame following a predefined scheme (sync interval, data length, etc.); and two receivers ("RX1" and "RX2"), that receive and timestamp the frames. The received frames and their related timestamps are then collected and transmitted to a PC for an off-line analysis. Using this set-up is possible to obtain and compare the timestamps, both on the transmitting and receiving side. Several timestamp values, taken at different levels (physical and application) have been caught, both on the receiving and transmitting side, in order to identify and quantify each source of uncertainty that can affect the synchronization. The timestamp values are:

- RXCnt: The value the processor counter TC as "captured" when a frame is received.
- RXIRQ: Time in which the IRQ routine for the reception of a frame is called. Its resolutions is 1 ms.
- RXApp: Time in which the frame from the IRQ routine reach the application level. This timestamp enables to identify the delay and the jitter introduced by the JVM and the software application. The resolution is 1 ms.
- TXCnt: The value the processor counter TC as "captured" when a frame is transmitted.

As first test, the repeatability of the transmission interval of synchronization frame has been analyzed. Several tests have been made, changing the transmission interval ("TXInt") and with different application load. Table 3 shows the measures on transmission interval, i.e. the difference between two consecutive TXCnt timestamps. As expected, the application load heavily affects the behaviour of the system apart from the nominal transmission interval; the standard deviation in both cases increases of an order of magnitude. Fig. 5 compares the distribution of transmission interval jitter (50 samples, nominal transmission interval of 1 s) with and without application load. A huge application load (software operation on objects) delays the transmission of several ms, because of the Garbage Collector operation, though this affects less than 10% of the test frames. The synchronization algorithms usually use the receiving time of a synch message sent by a clock master in order to update the local clock. In the experimental setup the clocks of the Rx nodes have no relation and for this reason the timestamps related to the same receiving frame cannot be directly compared.

In order to evaluate the jitter between the reception timestamps of the two receivers at application level, the difference between the corresponding interval reception (i.e. difference between consecutive RXApp timestamps) has been measured. The test has been made with different transmission intervals ("TxInt") and in several load conditions (with or without operation on objects). Table 4 reports the results. The resolution of RXApp timestamp is only 1 ms, but in any case the application load heavily affects the timestamp accuracy. The Fig. 6 highlights the effect of the load on the distribution of the jitter of receiving interval. For this reason, the accuracy obtained from a synchronization algorithm that uses RXApp timestamp should be on the order of some ms.

TXInt(s)	Load	Mean(μs)	Dev.std(μs)	Max(μs)
0.5	No load	499989	49	269
	With Load	499633	8093	64661
1	No load	999982	40	208
	With Load	999319	4825	34561

Table 3. Transmission Interval of Sun Spot transmitter (100 tests).

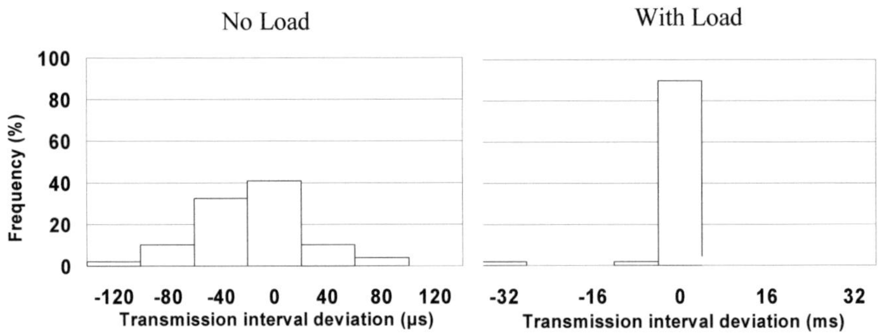

Fig. 5. Distribution of Sun SPOT transmission interval deviation.

Tx Int (s)	Load	Mean (ms)	Std. Dev.(ms)
0.5	No load	1	0.5
	With Load	5	2
1	No load	1	0.2
	With Load	5	1.5

Table. 4. Receiving Interval Deviation of SunSpot using the JVM timer (100 tests).

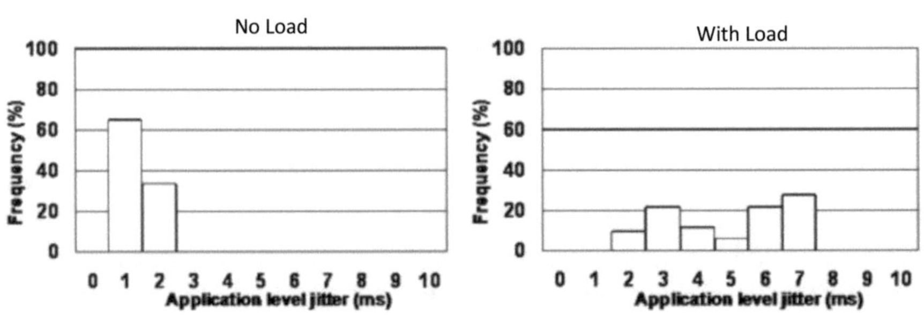

Fig. 6. Distribution of the Receiving Interval Deviation using the JVM timer at application level.

In the second experiment the difference between corresponding interval receptions using the processor timer has been measured (i.e. difference between consecutive RXCnt timestamps). The results are shown in Table 5 and in Fig. 7. The statistics about the Receiving Interval, obtained with the processor timer, demonstrates as an higher resolution timestamp is useful to identify and to estimate several sources that affect the

synchronization. The mean value is mainly due to the frequency drift of the respective board oscillators; it increases with the increasing of the transmission interval ("Tx Int") during the different tests. This parameters usually is estimated and compensated by a synchronization algorithms. On the other side the standard deviation, mainly due to the jitter of the SFD signal, cannot be compensated.
In conclusion, the microcontroller timers have to be used in order to improve the synchronization accuracy which is otherwise affected by the SunSPOT system architecture. Using the SFD signal provided by the 802.15.4 transceiver to catch the timer value during the transmission and reception of a frame can improve the overall performance. The timestamp resolution is less than 1 μs (below the jitter of the transceiver) and the synchronization accuracy that can be obtained is on the order of few μs, equal to the best results which are obtained on traditional, low-level programming platforms. This means that the analyzed platform is suitable for Wireless Data-Acquisition Network in industrial applications.

TxInt(s)	Load	Mean(μs)	Std. Dev.(μs)	Max(μs)
0.5	No load	1.2	0.4	1
	With Load	1.4	0.4	1.6
1	No load	2.3	0.4	1.6
	With Load	2.7	0.4	1

Table 5. Receiving Interval Deviation of SunSpot using the processor counter (100 tests).

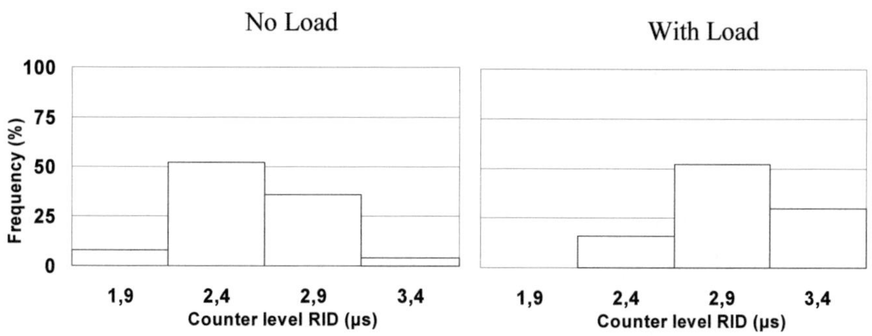

Fig. 7. Distribution of Receiving Interval Deviation (RID) measured at counter level.

7. Conclusions

The chapter presented the basic concepts regarding the clock synchronization of distributed systems, paying a special attention to the applications of data acquisition in the industrial field. Essential notions of time keeping science have been given in order to define the performance metrics necessary for the evaluation of the clock synchronization algorithms. The clock synchronization for distributed data acquisition system has been discussed in details for both wired and wireless implementation. Many synchronization algorithms have been presented and compared. Last, two real case examples of synchronized data acquisition systems for industrial applications have been presented in order to show the applicability and the advantages of clock synchronization. In the wired case, the application

uses one of the most diffused and accepted protocol for clock synchronization over a packet-switched network: the IEEE1588 protocol. In the wireless case, a new and promising platform for wireless data acquisition networks has been introduced and its clock synchronization performance has been evaluated.
The results of both the real cases confirm that the clock synchronization by means of the same network that is used to collect the logged data, can improve the performance and the versatility of a distributed data acquisition system.

8. Acknowledgment

Authors would like to thank Ing. Stefano Rinaldi, PhD, for the useful preliminary discussions.

9. References

Allan D.W. (1987)."Should the Classical Variance Be Used as a Basic Measure in Standards Metrology?", *IEEE Trans. on Instrumentation and Measurement,* Vol. 36, pp. 646-654, 1987

Correll K., Barendt N., Branicky M. (2005) "Design Considerations for Software Only Implementations of the IEEE 1588 Precision Time Protocol", in Proc. of *Conference on IEEE-1588 Standard for a Precision Clock Synchronization Protocol for Networked Measurement and Control System,* pp. 1-6, 2005.

De Dominicis C. M., Ferrari P., Flammini A., Rinaldi S., Quarantelli M. (2010a). "Integration of Existing IEC61850-based SAS within new High-Availability Architectures", *2010 First IEEE International Workshop on Applied Measurements for Power Systems,* Aachen, Germany, September 22-24, 2010, pp. 12-17.

De Dominicis C. M., Ferrari P., Flammini A., Sisinni E. (2010b). " Wireless Sensors Exploiting IEEE802.15.4a for Precise Timestamping ", *International Symposium on Precision Clock Synchronization for Measurement, Control and Communication, 2010. ISPCS 2010,* Portsmuth, USA, September 29- October 1, 2010, pp. 48-54. Best Paper Award

Depari A., Ferrari P., Flammini A., Marioli D., Taroni A.(2008). "A New Instrument for Real-Time Ethernet Performance Measurement", *IEEE Trans. Instrumentation and Measurement,* January, 2008, Vol. 57, N. 1, pp. 121-127.

Eidson J.C., Lee K. (2003). "Sharing a common sense of time", *Instrumentation & Measurement Magazine, IEEE,* Volume 6, Issue 1, March 2003 Pages: 26 - 32

Elson J., Girod L., Estrin D. (2002). "Fine-grained network time synchronization using reference broadcasts". In Proc. of *Fifth Symposium on Operating Systems Design and Implementation (OSDI 2002),* December 2002.

Felser M. (2005). "Real-Time Ethernet - Industry Prospective", in *Proc. of IEEE,* Volume: 93, Issue: 6, 2005, pp. 1118-1129

Ferrari P., Flammini A., Marioli D., Taroni A. (2008a). "IEEE 1588-Based Synchronization System for a Displacement Sensor Network", *IEEE Trans. Instrumentation and Measurement,* February, 2008, Vol. 57, N. 2, pp. 254-260.

Ferrari P., Flammini A., Marioli D., Taroni A. (2008b). "A Distributed Instrument for Performance Analysis of Real-Time Ethernet Networks", *IEEE Transactions on Industrial Informatics*, Vol. 4, No. 1, 2008, pp. 16-25.

Flammini A., Rinaldi S., Casalegno F., Telhan O. (2010). "Improving performance of a Java-based platform for Wireless Sensor Network applications", *2010 IEEE Instrumentation and Measurement Technology Conference (I2MTC)*, Austin, TX, USA, May 3-6, 2010, pp. 1618-1623.

Ganeriwal S., Kumar R., Srivastava M. B. (2003). “Timing-sync protocol for sensor networks”. In Proc. Of *First ACM Conference on Embedded Networked Sensor Systems (SenSys)*, November 2003.

Giorgi G., Narduzzi C. (2009). “Performance analysis of Kalman filter-based clock synchronization in IEEE 1588 networks”, in Proc. of *IEEE Int. Symposium on Precision Clock Synchronization for Measurement, Control and Communication (ISPCS09)*, Brescia, Italy, pp. 6-12 Oct. 2009.

Hackmand C., Sullivan D. B. (1996). “Time and Frequency Measurement”, *American Association of Physics Teachers*, 1996.

Howe D. (1995). “An Extension of the Allan Variance with Increased Confidence at Long Term”, in *Proc. 1995 IEEE international Frequency Control Symposium*, USA, pp. 321-329, 1995.

IEC 61158 family Ed. 2 (2007). “Industrial Communication Networks - Fieldbus specification”, IEC, 2007.

IEC 61784-2 Ed. 1. (2007). “Industrial communication networks - Profiles - Part 2: Additional fieldbus profiles for real-time networks based on ISO/IEC 8802-3”, IEC, 2007.

IEEE std.1588. (2002). “Standard for a precision clock synchronization protocol for networked measurement and control system”, *IEEE*, 2002.

IEEE std.1588. (2008), “Standard for a Precision Clock Synchronization Protocol for Networked Measurement and Control Systems”, *IEEE*, Mar 2008.

IETF RFC 1305 (1992) “Network Time Protocol, Specification, Implementation and Analysis ”, *IETF*, 1992.

Li C. McKerrow P.J., Lu Q., (2008). “Developing Real-time Applications with Java Based Sun SPOT”, in proc. of the *2008 Australasian Conference on Robotics & Automation*, Canberra, 3-5 December 2008.

Marzullo K.A., Owicki S. (1983). “Maintaining the time in a distributed system”. In Proc. Of *Second annual ACM symposium on Principles of distributed computing*, pp 295–305. ACM Press, 1983.

Marzullo K.A. (1984). “Maintaining the Time in a Distributed System: An Example of a Loosely-Coupled Distributed Service”. Ph.D. dissertation, *Stanford University, Department of Electrical Engineering*, Feb. 1984.

Proft C. (2007). “The power of LXI instrumentation – use cases and performances”, *Autotestcon 2007*, pp.482-489, 2007.

Römer K. (2001).” Time synchronization in ad hoc networks”. In Proc. of *ACM Symposium on Mobile Ad-Hoc Networking and Computing*, October 2001.

Su W, Akyildiz I. F. (2005). “Time-diffusion synchronization protocol for sensor networks”. *IEEE/ACM Transactions on Networking*, Vol. 13 , Issue 2, pp. 384–397, April 2005.

Sullivan D.B., Allan D.W., Howe D., and Walls F.L. (1990). "Characterization of Clocks and Oscillators", *NIST Tech Note 1337*, 1990.

Ueda K., Yakoh T. (2004). "Development of time division switching hub for synchronous TDMA", *IEEE WFCS2004 International Workshop on Factory Communication Systems*, Sept. 2004, pp. 45 – 50

4

Real Time Data Acquisition in Wireless Sensor Networks

Mujdat Soyturk[1], Halil Cicibas[2] and Omer Unal[2]
[1]*Istanbul Technical University*
[2]*Turkish Naval Academy*
Turkey

1. Introduction

Implementation of low cost sensor nodes in recent years allow sensor nodes to be applicable in many different areas e.g. environment monitoring, homeland security and disaster relief operations. One major contribution is their high demand on data acquisition. Real-time data acquisition is more challenging and promising issue in these application areas. There are many approaches and solutions proposed for real-time data acquisition in the literature. In this chapter, we focus on real-time data acquisition in wireless sensor networks.

Wireless Sensor Networks (WSNs) consist of many tiny wireless sensors which operate in an environment in order to collect data for a specific mission. In most type of WSNs, once sensor nodes are deployed, thereafter no additional actions are employed. In a typical WSN, data is gathered from the environment by sensor nodes, aggregated in intermediate nodes and then transmitted to a base station. Because all these operations are executed by sensor nodes with limited power in a wireless media; reliable communication, power efficiency and network survivability issues are among critical concerns. WSNs are different from traditional networks because of their inherent characteristics. The specific properties of these networks pose various challenges such as energy consumption, limited bandwidth, and low storage. In the following sections we will introduce these constraints in detail.

WSNs can be used in a wide range of application areas. Networks e.g. composed of video and audio sensors can be used to provide monitoring and surveillance systems or can be used to enhance the existing ones. Some critical areas for homeland security, such as borders, gulfs, strait entrances and port approach waters, are subject to enemy infiltration in crisis and in wartime. Using an instantly deployable network composed of sensor nodes in these operation areas would be a good solution to increase the probability of detecting a penetration in a cost effective and efficient way than the conventional ones. Some applications, e.g. military operations, introduce additional requirements on sensor and ad-hoc networks such as reliability and operating in real-time. Limited battery life of the nodes requires efficient energy consumption techniques which challenge real-time and reliability requirements.

There are many routing approaches to provide either or both of the objectives of reducing the end-to-end delay and providing the reliability. However, most of these routing approaches challenge with other aspects such as energy-efficiency, long-lifetime and low-cost expect of the system. Energy aware protocols in the literature generally use multi-hop paths to use energy more efficiently. However, increase in number of hops between the source and the destination nodes bears some issues that must be considered (Monaco et al, 2006) (Du et al, 2006). First of all, nodes close to the sink deplete their energies quickly; leaving the sink unreachable and forcing the system into off-state (Yuan et al, 2007). Secondly, increase in the hop-number cause more nodes to buffer the packet on-the-route, causing a processing overhead and delay at in-between nodes. Processing overhead and buffer fill-up may cause packets to be dropped. On the other hand, delay at nodes may prevent to fulfill the real-time requirements of the system (Monaco et al, 2006). As the network size grows, the length of the constructed paths will increase, causing the problem described above more challenging. New routing techniques which provide reliability and real-time response to sensor readings in energy efficient way are always required in Wireless Sensor and Ad Hoc Networks.

Mobility is the other major concern that hardens the problem. Mobility of nodes degrades the performance of the system, making the problem more challenging and impractical. Mobility introduces additional overhead, increases complexity and makes the conventional routing algorithms fail. Therefore, novel and special algorithms are required for mobile environments.

In this study we introduce and discuss some proposed MAC protocols, routing protocols and aggregation techniques which address real-time needs in literature. Then we present two applications for real-time data acquisition using WSN. The structure of this chapter is as follows. In Section 2, we define real time data acquisition and relevant constraints. Real time communication issues are also discussed in this section. MAC layer and network layer protocols are presented in Section 3 and Section 4, respectively. In Section 5, aggregation techniques are stated. We give two sample Real-Time WSN applications in Section 6.

2. Real-time data acquisition

Real-time data acquisition can be stated as collecting, processing and transmitting data in predetermined latency boundaries. It mainly includes sampling, MAC layer operations, network layer routing, data aggregation and some additional processes.

Real-time data acquisition is a mandatory issue which must be considered in some WSN applications. This application may be a surveillance system, a temperature detector (He et al, 2006)(Lu et al, 2005), fire monitoring or intruder tracking system. Thus, the sensor data will be valid only within limited time duration (Felemban et al, 2005).

Real-time QoS is classified into two categories: hard real-time and soft real-time. In hard real-time, end-to-end delay boundaries are described as deterministic values. Latency in a message's delivery higher than this value will be a failure. However in soft real-time, a probabilistic latency value is used and some delay delay is tolerable (Li et al, 2007). The delay metric in every process stage determines the latency issues in algorithms and approaches. So in order to design a real-time WSN system, each process stage should be well designed.

2.1 Real time data acquisition constraints in WSN

In [Akyildiz et al, 2002], constraints in WSN are classified as sensor node constraints and networking constraints. These constraints also affect the real time data acquisition. In the Section 2.2, we present relations between real time data acquisition and these constraints.

2.1.1 Sensor node constraints

These constraints are mostly hardware related. The capabilities and constraints of a sensor node's hardware affect the latency. These constraints are listed as follows:

Limited Memory and Storage Space: The data size is important in guaranteeing real time data acquisition because sensor nodes are small devices and they have limited storage spaces, memories and processors. For example, there must be sufficient memory space and processor in order to aggregate data. If this process is executed by non-sufficient memory nodes, this may increase delay.

Energy Limitation: Energy is consumed during both computation and communication processes within a node. Energy limitation is one major constraint that affects the capabilities of sensor nodes extremely. Optimal solutions must be determined in order to transmit real-time data while consuming low communication power. Energy consumption in aggregation process is another critical issue.

Environmental Limitations: Sensor nodes have to struggle with many environmental difficulties such as physical obstacles, node terminations, unpredictable errors that avoid functioning of nodes, or communication interferences

2.1.2 Networking constraints

In addition to hardware-related constraints, real-time data acquisition in WSNs is affected by network-related constraints.

Communication Constraints: In order to provide a real time communication scheme between nodes, some preventive actions have to be taken. The relevant subjects of communication constraints are: [Akyildiz et al, 2002].

- Unreliable communication
- Bandwidth limitation
- Frequent routing changes
- Channel error rate

Additional Limitations: Most WSNs are deployed for specific reasons or objectives. This emerges new constraints specific to the applied area.

- Node mobility
- Intermittent connectivity
- Isolated subgroups
- Population density

In order to guarantee real time requirements all these constraints must be considered.

2.2 Real-time communications in WSNs

In this section we define the communication issues in MAC protocols, routing protocols and data aggregation process. We try to emphasize how these affect real time communication.

High utilization of bandwidth, reducing collisions, low latency, dynamic and fast operation of medium access control mechanism, fairness along with ensuring energy efficiency are among major concerns for a WSN's performance. A MAC algorithm must also achieve fairness, where every node should be allowed to transmit its data by considering efficiency and urgency.

A MAC protocol may adopt a distributed or a centralized approach. A distributed MAC protocol, where each sensor node determines its cycle behavior, is simple and easy-to-implement. This approach, however, is susceptible to collisions that reduce bandwidth utilizations and efficiency. The other type of MAC protocol, that is the centralized one, provides easy medium access management, simple synchronization, and low packet losses due to the frequency differences. However, such a protocol has some drawbacks; relatively short lifetime of cluster-head nodes, registration requirements, and additional energy consumption of mobile nodes when registering to a new cluster-head. MAC layer collisions increase end-to-end latency, jitter, and time-outs. Retransmitted packets cause overheads and underutilize the limited bandwidth. In Section 3 we define more issues, related with MAC layer protocols.

The performance of a MAC algorithm affects the network layer routing algorithm. While MAC layer decides which node will use the medium to transmit, network layer decides the next node to transmit. Routing decision directly affects end-to-end latency, congestion and bandwidth utilization. A routing protocol includes discovery of neighborhood, selection of next forwarding node, traffic load balancing and congestion handling processes. For a real-time system, all the issues mentioned must be provided with minimum jitter in a given time limitation. We detail network layer routing protocols in Section 5.

Another key concern in WSN communication is data aggregation, in which sensed data is combined into a single message and then, transmitted to a base station (Heinzelman et al., 2000) by sensors. The goal of data aggregation is to reduce the communication load which directly affects the efficiency of MAC protocol and network layer routing in a WSN. Such an operation must be organized in a systematic way because data aggregation increases latency and energy consumption. In adaptation of an aggregation technique, causative latency and energy consumption should be considered.

3. Medium access in WSNs

Wireless communications use a shared medium. This means that in a signal range, in one period of time, only one instance can send data. It is the MAC protocol's duty to transmit frames over this medium. Because of the limitations of power and network lifetime, the medium access process is harder due to the low-duty cycles of the nodes within a WSN.

Designing a good MAC protocol requires taking several parameters into consideration. Energy efficiency, scalability, adaptability, reliability, throughput, utilization of bandwidth, and latency are among these. We focus on, first, energy consumption issue, and then, low latency data delivery issue which is required for real-time applications. We present the energy wastage reasons in MAC protocols, and then discuss the proposed MAC protocols from the real-time communication view, and lastly present a comparison table of the protocols.

3.1 Reasons of energy waste

The most energy wastage sources in MAC protocols for WSNs are (Demirkol et al, 2006) defined as follows. The first one is *collisions*, when a node receives more two or more packets simultaneously. The retransmission of the collided packets increases the energy consumption. The second one is *idle-listening*. This occurs when a node listens an idle channel to receive traffic. The third one is *overhearing*, that means a sensor node receives packets that are destined for other nodes. The fourth one is control packet *overheads*. These packets are required to control the access to the channel. The fifth one is *over-emitting*. This occurs when a message is transmitted to a destination node which is not ready to receive. Additionally, transition between cycles of sleep, idle, receive and transmit also increases energy consumption. All these factors must be paid attention for designing an energy efficient protocol.

Another issue for reducing the energy consumption is that MAC protocols have a policy for duty cycles and switching off the radio. Basic protocols use a *fixed duty cycle*, and some others implement *adaptive duty cycle*, in which they adapt to changes in traffic over time and place (Langendoen, 2007).

3.2 IEEE 802.11

It is the standard for WLANs. It provides low latency and high throughput, but due to idle listening, its energy consumption is high. Therefore this protocol cannot be used for WSNs (Ye at al, 2001).

3.3 Real time MAC approaches

In WSNs, bandwidth utilization, channel access delay and energy consumption parameters are mainly determined by the MAC protocol. Considering a layered protocol stack, routing in the network layer determines the end-to-end or multi-hop delay, as the MAC layer settles single-hop or channel access delay. There are also cross-layer approaches developed in the literature for an optimized communication (Li et al, 2007) as discussed in Section 3.4.

I-EDF: (Caccamo et al., 2002) Implicit Prioritized Access Protocol (I-EDF) guarantees a HRT delay, using cellular backbone network. It offers collision-free communication via its mixed TDMA and FDMA scheme. It assures high throughput even in high loads.

Dual-Mode MAC Protocol: (Watteyne et al., 2006) supports HRT which adapts a linear network with identical nodes. In order to achieve a collision-free communication, it uses TDMA for global synchronization and a mixed FDMA-TMA scheme is adopted. Energy-efficiency is also aimed in this protocol.

DMAC: (Lu et al., 2004) was proposed for unidirectional data gathering trees. It balances the nodes' active/sleep cycles due to their depths on tree, thus eliminates the sleep delay, and incessant traffic forwarding is achieved. It is shown that DMAC is both energy efficient and low-delay bounded.

SIFT: (Jamieson et al., 2003) SIFT is designed for event-driven applications. To select a slot within the slotted contention window, a probability distribution function is used. It is efficient in terms of latency when many nodes want to send packets, however related energy consumption is a trade-off. Also, it introduces idle-listening and overhearing.

DSMAC: (Lin et al, 2004) Dynamic Sensor MAC has dynamic duty cycle property in addition to S-MAC (Ye et al.,2004). Decreasing the latency is the primary goal. Nodes have a SYNC period where sleep cycles are shortened when needed. It has better latency than S-MAC.

DB-MAC: (Bacco et al., 2004) It is a contention-based protocol aimed for reducing the delay in hierarchically structured applications. It employs a prioritized access mechanism and therefore reduces energy consumption and delay.

Z-MAC: (Rhee et al., 2005) It applies dynamic shift between SDMA and TDMA. It is topology-aware and performs well when there is high contention.

PEDAMACS: (Ergen & Varaiya, 2006) It has high powered access points which can be reached by one hop. They gather topology information and apply a scheduling algorithm. Bounded delay as well as energy efficiency is guaranteed.

A comparison of the afore mentioned MAC protocols is given in Table 1 to identify their QoS support and major differences.

Protocol Name	MAC Type	Latency/ RT Type	Energy Efficiency	Centralized/ Distributed	Scalability
*S-MAC	CSMA/CA	best effort	high	Distributed	good
*T-MAC	CSMA/CA	best effort	high	Distributed	good
*B-MAC	CSMA/CA	best effort	high	Distributed	good
I-EDF	FDMA-TDMA	HRT	NA	Centralized	moderate
Dual Mode MAC	FDMA-TDMA	HRT	NA	Centralized	moderate
D-MAC	contention-based	Best effort	Moderate	Distributed	good
DBMAC	contention-based	Best effort	High	Distributed	good
Z-MAC	CSMA-TDMA	Best effort	High	Hybrid	moderate
PEDEMACS	TDMA	HRT	High	Centralized	low
IEEE 802.15.4	Slotted CSMA/CA, GTS	Best effort / HRT	Moderate	Distributed	good
SIFT	CSMA/CA	Very low latency	Low	Distributed	
DSMAC	CSMA	Low latency	High	Distributed	good

Table 1. A comparison of MAC Protocols. "*" notated ones are non-real-time protocols.

3.4 Cross-layer solutions

There are some designs in the literature that aim to achieve real time parameters in a cross layer approach. This enables a higher layer to communicate with lower distant layers.

RAP: (Lu et al., 2002) Discussed in section 4.2.

MERLIN: (Ruzzelli et al., 2006) This protocol aims both low latency and energy efficiency, that combines MAC and routing protocols and applies a hybrid CSMA TDMA scheme. A schedule table is used to relay packets, in which the network is seperated into time regions with respect to hop numbers to the sink node.

VigilNet: (He et al., 2006) It is developed for real time target detection and tracking in a large area. It adapts multi path diffusion tree. Energy consumption is aimed as well. This application is detailed in section 6.1.

In summary, the parameters of a layer in the communication stack are reported to the next layer up. Coordination among lower and upper layers is made possible. There are two methods for a cross-layer design. The first one is to enhance the effectiveness of the protocol based on the parameters in other layers. The second one is to unite the related protocols in a single part. While this may allow a closer communication with all protocols, the connection is hard to distinguish. Also, the merged component's functionality can be very complicated. So it is preferable to allow transparency between the layers (Li et al, 2007).

4. Real time routing protocols in WSNs

Though the MAC layer can deliver packets considering real time needs, its effect remains local. Real-time requirements for end-to-end connections (or communication) should be satisfied. Routing protocols are those that should have ability to satisfy end-to-end real-time requirements (He et al., 2003). They are provided as either deterministic or probabilistic delay guarantee (Li et al., 2007).

4.1 Real time routing protocols design issues

End-to-end delay is mainly affected by the applied routing scheme. Therefore, some design issues must be considered in the design of routing protocols. These issues are well summarized in (Akyıldız et al., 2002) and (Al-Karaki & Kamal, 2004) as follows:

Energy consumption: Sensor node lifetime shows a strong dependence on the battery lifetime (Heinzelman et al., 2000). Each sensor in a WSN can act as a relay unit, hence energy consumption become as an important issue. If energy consumption is not managed properly, some node's batteries may exhaust. These malfunctioning nodes can cause topological changes and might require rerouting of packets and reorganization of the network (Al-Karaki & Kamal, 2004). It is to note that reorganization and rerouting processes increase the end-to-end-delay.

Data Reporting Model: This issue affects the delivering latency of a data packet. The data delivering method can be categorized as either time-driven, event-driven, query-driven, and hybrid (Al-Karaki & Kamal, 2004). Event-driven and time-driven (with low period) approaches can be considered in real time routing protocols.

Fault Tolerance: Some sensor nodes may fail because of internal or external reasons such as power exhaustion or environmental factors. In addition to MAC layer, the routing protocols have to find new forwarding choices in order to relay the data timely or in a low latency bound (Al-Karaki & Kamal, 2004). So while designing a real time routing protocol fault tolerance techniques must be determined.

Scalability: With the increase of the network size, the management would become more complicated. A real time routing protocol should be scalable enough to respond to events in the environment timely (Al-Karaki & Kamal, 2004). In order to relay a delay-constraint data time-synchronization techniques may be while coordinating a huge network.

Network Dynamics: It is to note that a network is a dynamic form which can adjust themselves according to environmental factors and needs. For example the location of nodes or the amount of data can change in time. These changes may cause some delay while transmitting a data. The real time routing protocol must consider such as network dynamics.

Transmission Media: This part is discussed in Section 3.

Quality of Service: In addition to bounded latency some routing protocols have to concern other QoS metrics such as accuracy or long network lifetime. Hence real time routing protocols are required to capture these requirements.

These issues are not the only ones which can be used to distinguish the routing protocols. But they are the mandatory ones. While designing a routing protocol which addresses real time or latency, these issues must be concerned in all steps.

4.2 Real time routing protocols

A number of real time routing protocols are proposed for WSNs in literature. We can list key real time routing protocols as follows:

RAP is the first routing protocol (Lu et al., 2002) which addresses real time requirements using a cross-layer design. In RAP each packet is given a prioritization level called as requested velocity and this parameter of each packet is determined locally. It is assumed in protocol, the routing layer is aware of physical geography.

SPEED (He et al., 2003) can be considered as a benchmark real time routing protocol among others. It affords three types of real-time communication services as real-time unicast, real-time area-multicast and real-time area-anycast. SPEED bases on a stateless non-deterministic geographic forwarding routing protocol which enables to find a next hop that is closer to the destination with its location aware structure.

Another real time routing protocol is MMSPEED (Felemban et al., 2005) which can be stated as an extension of SPEED. It is designed to provide a timeliness and reliable routing schema as an approach between the network and the MAC layers. The main difference of MMSPEED from SPEED is supporting different delivery velocities and levels of reliability.

A real-time power-aware routing (RPAR) protocol (Chipara et al., 2006) is proposed to adapt the transmission power and routing decision mechanisms dynamically. RPAR differs from the above protocols via the following features:

- Trade-off between energy consumption and communication delay
- A novel approach to handle lossy links
- Neighborhood management mechanism

Pothuri et al proposes an energy efficient delay-constrained heuristic solution (Pothuri, 2006) which is based on estimating of end-to-end delay. It is to note that the proposed algorithm is well suitable for small scale WSN applications.

Cheng et al introduce a novel real time routing protocol (Cheng et al., 2006) in which all path's end-to-end delay requirements are determined. In the proposed study each sensor node can decide its forwarding node due to the value of the links requirements. So it is not necessary to calculate the sum of each link's delay along the path. Hence the proposed algorithm differ from with its reduced overhead and simplified route discovery mechanism.

Directional Geographical Real-Time Routing (DGR) protocol's goal is to find a solution for real time video streaming while taking into consideration a number of resource and performance constraints (Chen et al., 2007). It proposes a novel multipath routing schema which regards forward error correction (FEC) coding.

Real Time Load Distributed Routing Protocol (RTLD) (Ali et al., 2008) aims link reliability and packet velocity through one-hop while providing energy efficiency in real time communication. In RTLD, the forwarding node is determined via optimal values of velocity, called PRR and the remaining power. It differs from other real time routing protocols with its feature which utilize the remaining power parameter to select the forwarding candidate node.

Soyturk and Altilar introduce a novel real time data acquisition approach (Soyturk&Altilar, 2008) which can also be used for rapidly deployable Mission-Critical Wireless Sensor Networks. It is based on the real-time routing algorithm, namely Stateless Weighted

Routing (SWR) algorithm. Data is carried over multiple paths simultaneously to provide reliability and to provide time limitations. It is a completely stateless routing approach that nodes do not need any topology knowledge for routing. Algorithm is simple and efficient which reduces the complexity at nodes and hence provides low-cost architecture.
In the proposed approach the routing tables are not hold in nodes thus they don't know their neighbors' information. The routing decision is made due to weight values of nodes. These values are calculated from geographical position and some QoS parameters, as shown in Equation (1);

$$\text{weight of node } i\,,\quad w_i = location_i + parameters_i + parameters_{network} \tag{1}$$

These weight values of nodes are depend on remaining power or else. This technique reduces delay, energy consumption and processing requirement. The existing packet header and QoS fields in SWR are depicted in Fig. 1.

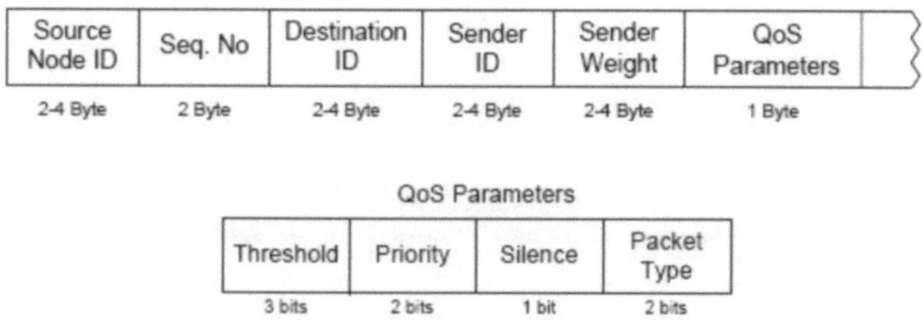

Fig. 1. Simple packet header and its QoS fields (Soyturk&Altilar, 2008)

Basically the SWR works as follows (Soyturk&Altilar, 2006): The source node determines the weight value of packet and adjusts this value into the packet then broadcast it. When an intermediate node receives packet, it compares the packet's weight value and its own weight value. If its weight value is smaller than the transmitting node's weight value and the destination's weight value (that is *0* for sink), it rebroadcasts the packet, otherwise drops the packet.
The proposed algorithm (Soyturk & Altilar, 2006):

- provides scalability since neither routing tables nor beaconing is used.
- simplifies the routing process by designing an appropriate algorithm which utilizes a weight metric.
- decreases calculations, delay, and resource requirements (such as processor and memory) at nodes since a weight metric is used instead of time consuming operations on routing tables.
- decreases energy consumption by;
    - not beaconing,
    - considering the remaining energy levels at nodes,
    - limiting the number of relaying nodes.
- provides reliability by exploiting multiple paths and recovering from voids.
- executes routing process completely in the network layer, independent of the MAC layer underneath.

The key contribution of SWR is eliminating the communication overhead and energy consumption produced in topology learning approaches. SWR utilizes resources allowing data flow over multiple paths rather than prior topology learning and path construction. Simulations prove that SWR is scalable in both large and mobile networks.

4.3 Comparison of routing protocols in WSN

We compare routing protocols stated above according to basic criteria (1-7) and functional criteria (8-11) in Table 2. This comparison is based on the issues defined in the chapter. No additional experiments or simulation is made to evaluate them. We do not include (Chen et al., 2007) and (Pothuri,2006) to comparison list because the stated criteria of them are not enough to fill the table and not fully correspond our criteria.

5. Real time data aggregation in WSN

5.1 Delay considerations for real-time data aggregation

In WSN, nodes sense and transmit data to the base station or a sink node. Base station or the sink node has to perform data collecting in a systematic way while considering constraints in WSN. Among collected data, there needs to be some correlation and combining processes in order to achieve high quality information delivery. This can be accomplished by data aggregation. Data aggregation is defined as *"the process of gathering the data from multiple sensors in order to eliminate redundant transmission and provide united and meaningful information to the base station"* (Rajagopalan & Varshney, 2006). The main goal of data aggregation is to enhance network lifetime by reducing transmission power consumption in addition to increase the quality of delivered information.

If we figure out data aggregation in a tree based approach, which is shown in Fig. 2, E aggregates packets of B and A.

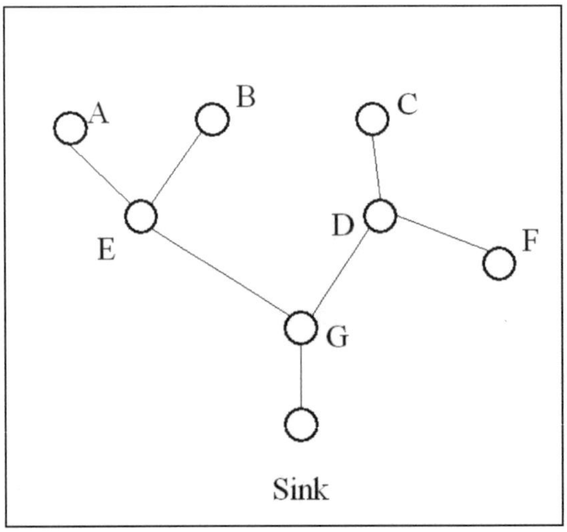

Fig. 2. An example of data aggregation (Heinzelman et al., 2000)

No	Criteria	RAP	SPEED	MM-SPEED	RPAR	RTLD	(Soyturk & Altilar, 2006)	(Cheng et al.,2006)
1.	**Control packet overhead**	Moderate	Moderate	Low	Low	Low	Low	Low
2.	**Energy Consumptio n**	N.M.	Moderate	N.M.	Moderate	Low	Low	Low
3.	**Reliability**	N.M.	N.M.	Moderate	N.M.	High	High	N.M.
4.	Algorithm Complexity	N.M.	Moderate	High	N.M.	N.M.	Low	N.M.
5.	**Void avoidance/ recovery**	N.M.	Yes	Yes	Yes	N.M.	Yes	No
6.	**Scalability**	Large Scale and High Density	Medium scale and high density networks	Large scale and high density networks	Large Scale Networks	N.M.	Large Scale, High Density, and Mission-Critical	N.M.
7.	**Node Discovery Methodology**	Nodes are aware of physical geography	Beacon exchange mechanism	Via periodic location update packets	On-demand neigborhood management	Via invoke packet	Nodes do not need to know their neighbors	Via reply messages to broadcasting

N.M. : This feature is *not mentioned* in protocol

Table 2. Comparison of Delay-Constraint Routing Protocols in WSNs

No	Criteria	RAP	SPEED	MM-SPEED	RPAR	RTLD	(Soyturk&Altilar, 2006)	(Cheng et al.,2006)
8.	**Forwarding node selection criteria**	Select node, has the shortest geographic distance	Select node, meets with packet delay requirements	Select node set, meets with packet's speed level	Select the most energy-efficient node, meets the packet's required velocity.	Select node set, meets with the delay requirements and remaining power	Packet is broadcasted to nodes. Nodes that have the higher weight value that packet's value rebroadcast.	Due to the value of the links requirements (CED)
9.	**Real-time achiving methodology**	Prioritize due to velocity of packets	Select node, has the min delay parameter	Multiple packet delivery approach	Via Dynamic velocity assignment policy	Select appropriate node due to end-to-end delay with the best PRR value and remaining power	Via packet classification due to QoS metrics	Via constructed Equivalent Delay Concept
10.	**Energy Consumption Reducing Strategy**	N.M.	Via stateless non-deterministic geographic forwarding	N.M.	Adapts variable transmission power.	Adapting transceiver states	Via threshold field and nodes don't consume energy to discover its neighbors	Reduced route discovery process.
11.	**Location Awareness Strategy**	Via GPS or other location services	Via beacon packets	Via GPS or other location services	Via GPS or other location services	Via pre-determined neighbor nodes	Via GPS or other location services	N.M.

N.M. : This feature is *not mentioned* in protocol

Table 2. Comparison of Delay-Constraint Routing Protocols in WSNs (continued).

In (Krishnamachari et al., 2002) two methods of data aggregation are defined: optimal aggregation and suboptimal aggregation. In optimal aggregation, all the sources send a single packet to the same receiver through an aggregation tree. In the suboptimal aggregation, sources send packets to different destinations which are determined by distance or greedy approaches.

The design of data aggregation schema affects delay parameters. For example, if sensor nodes whose packets will be aggregated are in different distances to the sink node, the receiving times of packets to the sink node may vary. In Fig. 3, A is the aggregator node. If E and B transmit simultaneously, the arriving times of E's packet and B's packet will be different. It is to note that the aggregation process in an aggregator node increases delay (Krishnamachari et al., 2002).

According to these considerations, trade-off between delay and energy consumption become an important issue while designing an aggregation schema. Also, the delay tolerance of the application is an important factor, affects the optimality of the data aggregation method (Zhu et al., 2005). So delay boundaries must be determined for achieving maximum energy efficient structure (Zhu et al., 2005).

There exists such data aggregation methods, focus on energy efficiency, network lifetime and data accuracy in literature. In the following subsection we present the basic functionality of the delay constraint data aggregation algorithms due to their introduced features.

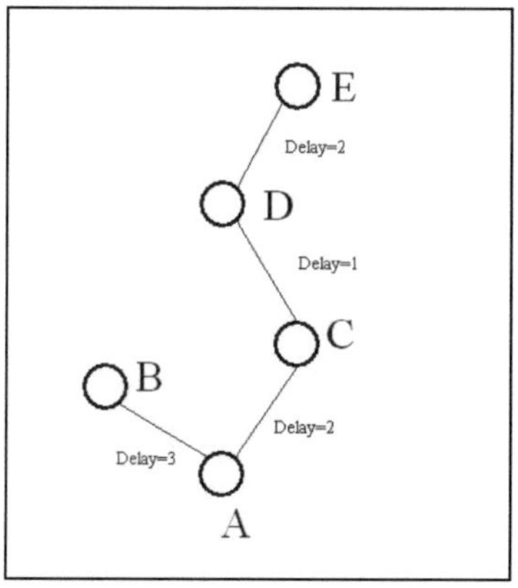

Fig. 3. Distance and delay interaction (Krishnamachari et al., 2002)

5.2 Delay constraint data aggregation algorithms

In literature, a number of data aggregation methods are proposed which address latency, reliability and energy consumption issues. In this section we mention data aggregation methods whose features meet real time requirements while considering other issues.

We start with Upadhyayula et al's (2003) study which proposes a CDMA/TDMA based algorithm that constructs a tree and schedules its nodes for collision-free transmission. The aim of the proposed study is to establish a network which requires fast and reliable data aggregation by considering energy efficiency.

In the proposed study the increase of parallel data transmissions reduce the latency. Hence required delay boundaries are achieved via constructed balanced tree.

Yu et al. (2006) proposed a delay-constraint data aggregation schema which addresses packet scheduling in a general tree structure while considering a real time latency constraint.
Yu et al. (2006) indicate that "the transmission energy does not monotonically decrease as the transmission time increases - the transmission energy may increase when the transmission time exceeds some threshold value" Also a model is introduced which describes the tradeoff between energy and latency. The energy-latency trade-off function w(τ) is described as follows (Yu et al., 2006):

$$w(\tau) = [C \cdot (2^{\frac{s}{\tau \cdot R}} - 1) + F] \cdot \tau \cdot R \tag{2}$$

Also the energy-latency function curve for long range and short range communication is figured as follows:

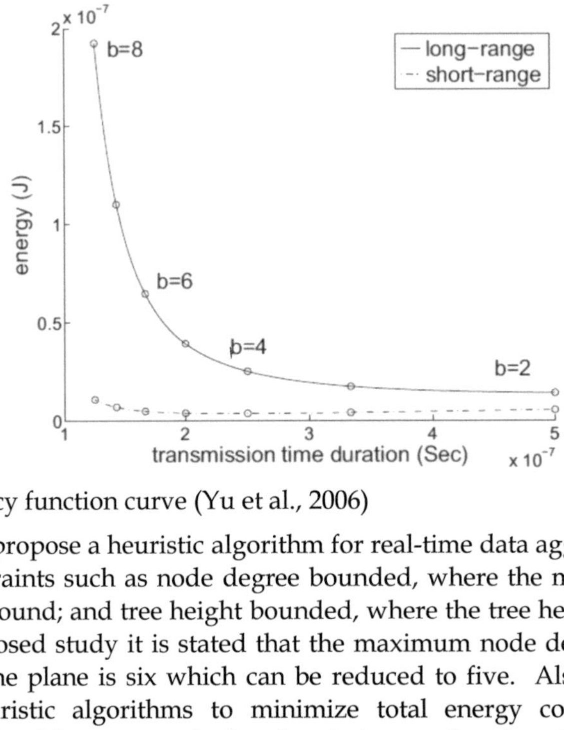

Fig. 4. Energy-latency function curve (Yu et al., 2006)

Cheng et al. (2006) propose a heuristic algorithm for real-time data aggregation. The authors consider two constraints such as node degree bounded, where the maximum node degree shall not exceed a bound; and tree height bounded, where the tree height shall not exceed a bound. In the proposed study it is stated that the maximum node degree of the Minimum Spanning Tree in the plane is six which can be reduced to five. Also Cheng et al., (2006) propose three heuristic algorithms to minimize total energy cost under the latency constraint. These algorithms are node first heuristic, tree first heuristic and hop bounded heuristic. More details about these algorithms are stated in Cheng et al. (2006).
Akkaya et al. (2005) propose an efficient aggregation method for delay-constrained data. The proposed study investigates the problem of efficient in-network data aggregation of delay-constrained traffic in wireless sensor networks. Authors consider both real time and non-real time data while designing the proposed method. Real-time data are generated and relayed to the gateway in response to delay-sensitive queries.
There is a real time queue at each relay node for the incoming packets of these multiple flows which is described in Fig.5 (Akkaya et al., 2005). The purpose of having a different queue is to enhance storage capacity of a sensor node and to generate real time flows depending on the number of active real time source sensors.

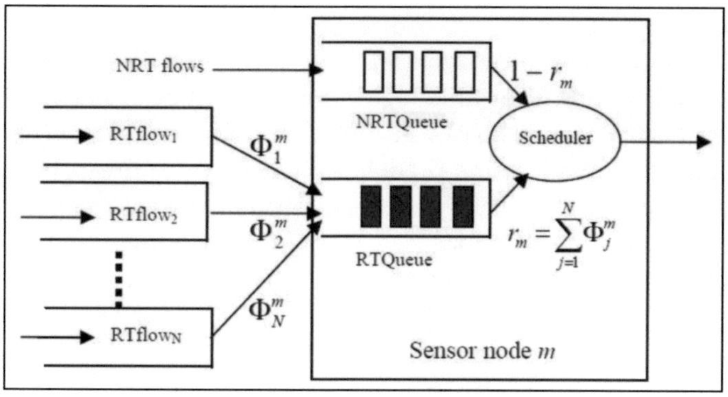

Fig. 5. Queuing model on sensors (Akkaya & Younis, 2004)

We have compared the delay-constraint data aggregation methods, stated above according to tree construction and energy-latency trade-off approaches.
A comparasion of these techniques are depicted in Table 3.

	Data Gathering Tree Construction	**How manage energy-latency trade-off**
(Upadhyayula et al., 2003)	Propose a CDMA/TDMA based algorithm which adds new nodes to the least weight branch.	Constructing a balanced tree. Establishing parent-child relationship with other nodes.
(Yu et al., 2006)	-	Rate adaptation techniques and non-monotonic energy model.
(Cheng et al., 2006)	Construct a degree bounded and height bounded tree via proposed algorithms	Use in order to obtain a Establish a spanning tree by heuristic algorithms. In the tree all nodes are no more than H hops away from the root.
(Akkaya et al., 2005)	It uses the Shortest Path Tree heuristic in order to build an initial aggregation tree.	A Weighted Fair Queuing based mechanism for packet scheduling is employed at each node.

Table 3. Real time latency data aggregation methodology

6. Real-time WSN applications

Applying the developed RT WSN methods over real-world applications shows their quality, applicability, and good or bad sides. Also, discussing such applications enables people to understand the structure of the methods more clearly. We examine design issues of Real Time WSN first, and then present some of the latest RT-WSN applications in industrial and academic field. In previous studies, researchers have classified WSN applications according to usage areas such as medical, military or community-related but it will be more useful to classify them according to their functionalities. We group applications as following:

- Surveillance applications
- Status monitoring
- Localization

- Motion monitoring

Design issues differ for each of these areas; however, real time parameters are the key issues for each group of applications. Real time requirements must be maintained while providing other requirements such as energy consumption and accuracy. Providing real time guarantee is conducted by using some predetermined deadline times, being probabilistic or deterministic. Deadline times must be short enough that the reaction taken by the system will be efficient. In most applications we examined, deadline times are divided into subdeadlines for each subprocess. We make a general list of subprocesses having subdeadlines:

- Initial Activation
- Sensing
- Wake-up
- Media Access
- Transmission
- Routing
- Aggregation
- Base Process

Most of these subprocesses exist in large scale networks, but small scale networks may not have all of them.

In these applications sensors may be mobile or fixed, and make a wireless communication with each other via single-hop or multi-hop. Sensors close to each other form a group, where each group communicates with other groups or base station by its cluster head. The base station is a device which coordinates the groups, compiles the data sent from them, and it has more enhanced resources compared to the nodes. The communication between the base station and cluster heads is generally single-hop, however in some applications it may be multi-hop. The base station relays the meaningful data it gathered to a main server or an end user via some media such as wired, satellite, 802.11 WLAN links.

There are numerous real time applications using WSNs. In this section, in order to support the real time issues stated previously, we limit our application examples in two. One sample application is a large scale network and the other is relatively small scale one that are both examples of latest Real-Time WSNs.

6.1 Sample application: Vigilnet - real time target tracking with WSN

The developed application in (He et al., 2006) detects fast moving targets in real time while considering energy consumption and accuracy. The system design is implemented due to the pre-determined latency boundaries. It is stated that for environment surveillance the rate of event occurrence is low, so the sensor nodes wait in idle state most of their lifetime. The sentry nodes wake up other nodes in the presence of critical events. If a target enters the area nodes in idle state are waken up and start to monitor and sample. All the sensors transit their data to a group leader which is responsible for aggregation, periodically. After the aggregation process group leaders report the event to the nearest base. It is to note that the communications between group members and group leader is one-hop, so the capabilities of group members are equal. After receiving event information to the base station, data is correlated by logical methods. The authors state some challenges while designing such a network. These design challenges are:

- *Selection of sentry nodes* and *determining its duty cycle* according to probability of event occurrence. This issue affects the coverage ratio of the whole area.
- *Minimizing the actuation delay*. The sufficient timeliness must be achieved in order to detect fast targets.
- *Designing fast detection algorithms*. It is to note that detection is a discrete event. The total data in these events must be met with a threshold value in order to decide an occurrence as an event. If detection delay is reduced, the detection confidence will increase simultaneously.
- *Designing effective wake-up services*. Nodes in 1% are awake and 99% are in idle state. If any transmission is received from sentry nodes in this tiny wake-up period, non-sentry nodes activate and start to monitor. If the tiny wake-up periods become longer, the activation time of node becomes minimal but energy consumption is increased.
- *Determining the degree of aggregation (DOA)*. As mentioned before, more aggregation process increases the level of accuracy but introduces additional energy consumption.
- *Classification of information*: In order to achieve a meaningful data, it is necessary to collect these data from many sources. For example, to determine a car's speed, the number of sources reporting must be at least 3. However collecting information from many sources causes some delay.

As a summary, (He et al., 2006) presents a complex real time sensing network design, where timeliness is guaranteed by sub-deadlines. This can be considered as a good example that figures out the trade-offs in design processes.

6.2 Sample application: real-time monitoring of hurricane winds with WSN

This application proposed in (Otero et al., 2009) is deployed in relatively medium scale. It remotely monitors the effects of hurricane winds on man-made structures like house or a factory (Otero et al., 2009) using wireless sensor network. The system architecture is illustrated in Fig. 6.

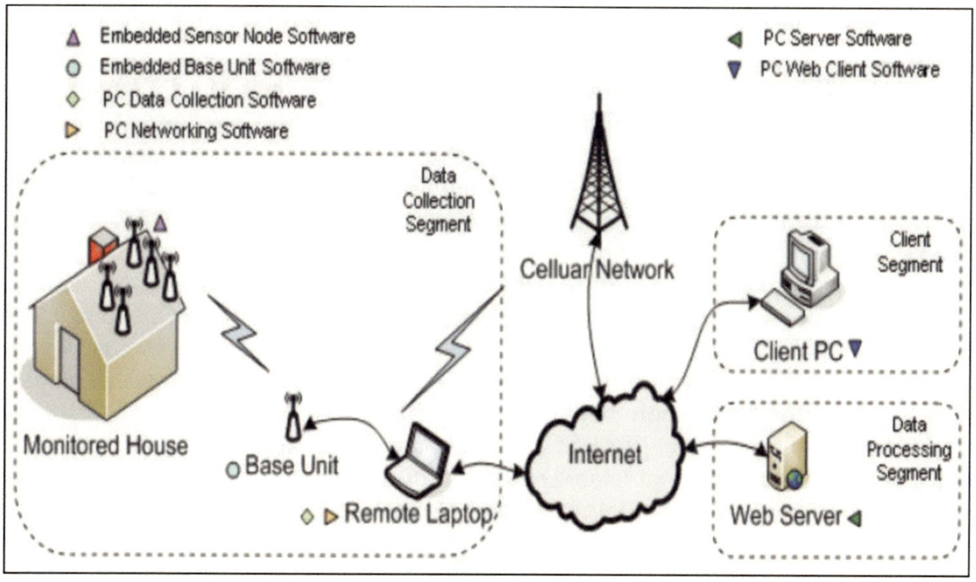

Fig. 6. System Architecture (Otero et al., 2009)

In (Otero et al., 2009), the real time requirements are not mentioned in numerical limits like in (He et al., 2006), but stated as 'near-real time'. In order to increase the communication performance between monitored house and remote laptop, the sampling node and transmission efficiency are considered as (Otero et al., 2009):

- Sampling rate must be at least 10 samples/second for pressure measurements.
- Nodes must transmit at least 5 MB of collected data to the remote site in every 5 minutes interval.

As mentioned above a time driven reporting schema is used. Basically system works as follows:

Data, collected by sensor nodes, are transmitted to a base station. This transmission is hold in one-hop and all the sensors have similar capabilities. Also the transmission of remote sensor nodes is managed by base station. A scheduling algorithm is used to assign internal transmission slots to remote sensor nodes (Otero et al., 2009). Nodes can only transmit their data in their active slots.

The key design issues stated in (Otero et al., 2009) are:

- Determining appropriate timing mechanisms between sensor nodes.
- Determining number of sensor nodes. It is to note that the density of nodes affects the timing problem.
- Developing or selecting appropriate compression algorithms. In this application, data is zipped rather than aggregated.

As a conclusion, this application uses a single-hop transmission, where due to the small deployment area and less number of nodes, zipping is used instead of aggregation in order to establish a simple architecture.

7. Conclusion

Data required for applications can be provided in several ways and with different methods. These methods constitute the data acquisition phase of these applications. Real-time data acquisition differs from usual data acquisition due to goals behind it and applied provision methods. While the usual (non-real time) data is used to make strategic level decisions, real-time data supports to make tactical decisions. Consumer of the real-time data, hence, should be supplied in a timely manner to fulfill consumer requirements. Time interval for real-time may change with respect to application needs either in terms of microseconds, milliseconds, seconds, or minutes. It should be fast enough to preserve the essential information associated with the event. Real time data is then processed immediately in order to make a decision or to make a reaction.

In this chapter, we overview real-time data acquisition in Wireless Sensor Networks. We present the approaches proposed in the literature and their primary positive and negative aspects. As described in the chapter, real-time data acquisition involves operations on multiple layers in the communication architecture. It becomes a complex task to manage in such a wireless communication network. Constraints and features peculiar to sensor networks harden the problem. We underline the key points and aspects in such a multi-tasking environment and present related studies in the literature.

While the medium access is mandatory issue that must be solved locally in real-time, end-to-end communication requirements drive the limits and shape the approaches to become efficient and applicable in WSN. We present the performance issues and factoring parameters for real-time data acquisition in WSN. Of the approaches that aim to solve one communication task, e.g. medium access or routing, we also present comparisons of them. These comparisons provide a snapshot view of the protocols and derive conclusions on how new approaches should be. Of the routing protocols, Stateless Weighted Routing (SWR) is one key protocol that aims to solve multiple objectives and problem in WSN. With respect to other protocols, SWR is the easiest and the simplest one to implement. It has many advantages and is superlative compared to other similar protocols.

While aggregation approaches are needed to reduce communication overhead, to provide efficient bandwidth usage, and to provide higher quality data, these approaches introduce delay. Moreover, aggregation is a complex task to be handled in identical tiny sensor nodes. Aggregation at more powerful nodes (with additional ability and higher resources) is more attractive solution.

There are applications that use real-time data aggregation via Wireless Sensor Networks. Of these, we present two and give design strategies of them. By increased demand on sensor applications, applications that use real-time data aggregation via WSN will increase in near future.

8. References

Akkaya K. and M. Younis, (2004) "Energy-aware routing of time-constrained traffic in wireless sensor networks," *in the International Journal of Communication Systems, Special Issue on Service Differentiation and QoS in Ad Hoc Networks*, 2004

Akkaya K., M. Younis, and M. Youssef, (2005) "Efficient aggregation for delay-constrained data in wireless sensor networks", *The Proceedings of Internet Compatible QoS in Ad Hoc Wireless Networks*, 2005.

Akyildiz I. F., W. Su , Y. Sankarasubramaniam , E. Cayirci, (2002) "Wireless sensor networks: a survey", *Computer Networks: The International Journal of Computer and Telecommunications Networking*, v.38 n.4, p.393-422, 15 March 2002

Ali A., LA Latiff, MA Sarijari, N. Fisal," (2008) Real- time Routing in Wireless Sensor Networks", *The 28th International Conference on Distributed Computing Systems Workshops*, 2008, pp 114- 119.

Al-Karaki JN, AE Kamal, (2004) "Routing techniques in wireless sensor networks: a survey", *IEEE Wireless Communications*, 2008

Annamalai V., S. K. Gupta and L. Schwiebert. (2003) On Tree-Based Convergecasting in Wireless Sensor Networks. *IEEE Wireless Communications and Networking Conference 2003*, New Orleans.

Bacco, G.D., T. Melodia and F. Cuomo, (2004) "A MAC protocol for delay-bounded applications in wireless sensor networks" *Proc. Med-Hoc-Net.* pp. 208-220.

Caccamo, M., L.Y. Zhang, L. Sha and G. Buttazzo, (2002) "An implicit prioritized access protocol for wireless sensor networks", *Proc. 23rd IEEE RTSS.* pp. 39-48.

Chen M, Leung VCM,Mao S, Yuan Y. (2007) Directional geographical routing for real-time video communications in wireless sensor networks. *Elsevier Computer Communications* 2007.

Cheng H, Q Liu, X Jia (2006) "Heuristic Algorithms for Real-time Data Aggregation in Wireless Sensor Networks", *IWCMC'06*, July 3-6, 2006, Vancouver, British Columbia, Canada.

Cheng W, L Yuan, Z Yang, X Du, (2006), "A Real-time Routing Protocol with Constrained Equivalent Delay in Sensor Networks", *Proceedings of the 11th IEEE Symposium on Computers and Communications (ISCC'06)*

Chenyang Lu , Brian M. Blum , Tarek F. Abdelzaher , John A. Stankovic , Tian He, (2002) RAP: A Real-Time Communication Architecture for Large-Scale Wireless Sensor Networks, *Proceedings of the Eighth IEEE Real-Time and Embedded Technology and Applications Symposium (RTAS'02),* p.55, September 25-27, 2002

Chipara O., Z. He, G. Xing, Q. Chen, X. Wang, C. Lu, J. Stankovic, and T. Abdelzaher. (2006) Real-time Power Aware Routing in Wireless Sensor Networks. *In IWQOS*, June 2006

Chipcon. CC2420 low power radio transceiver, http://www.chipcon.com.

Chlamtac I. and S. Kutten. (1987) Tree-based Broadcasting in Multihop Radio Networks. *IEEE Transactions on Computers* Vol. C-36, No. 10, Oct 1987.

Demirkol I, C Ersoy, F Alagoz, "MAC protocols for wireless sensor networks: a survey", (2006*) IEEE Communications Magazine.*

Du H. X. Hu, X. Jia, "Energy Efficient Routing And Scheduling For Real-Time Data Aggregation In WSNs", *Computer Communications*, vol.29 (2006) 3527–3535

Felemban E., C.-G. Lee, E. Ekici, R. Boder, and S. Vural, (2005) "Probabilistic QoS Guarantee in Reliability and Timeliness Domains in Wireless Sensor Networks," in *Proceedings of IEEE INFOCOM* 2005, Miami, FL, USA.

Ergen, S.C. and P. Varaiya (2006). PEDAMACS: power efficient and delay aware medium access protocol for sensor networks. *IEEE Trans. Mobile Comput.* 5(7), 920-930.

Francomme, J., G. Mercier and T. Val (2006).A simple method for guaranteed deadline of periodic messages in 802.15.4 cluster cells for control automation applications. In: *Proc.IEEE ETFA*. pp. 270-277.

He T., J. Stankovic, C. Lu, T. Abdelzaher, (2003) SPEED: A real-time routing protocol for sensor networks, in: *Proc. IEEE Int. Conf. on Distributed Computing Systems (ICDCS)*, Rhode Island, USA, May 2003, pp. 46–55.

He T., P. A. Vicaire, T. Yan, L. Luo, L. Gu, G. Zhou, R. Stoleru, Q. Cao, J. A. Stankovic, and T. Abdelzaher, (2006) "Achieving real-time target tracking using wireless sensor networks." in *RTAS'06*.

He, T., L. Gu, L. Luo, T. Yan, J. Stankovic, T. Abdelzaher and S. Son (2006b). An overview of data aggregation architecture for real-time tracking with sensor networks. In: *Proc. IEEE RTAS*. pp. 55-66.

Heinzelman W., A. Chandrakasan, and H. Balakrishnan, (2000), "Energy -Efficient Communication Protocol for Wireless Microsensor Networks," *In Proceedings of the Hawaii Conference on System Sciences*, Jan. 2000.

Heinzelman W., A. Chandrakasan, and H. Balakrishnan, (2000), Energy-Efficient Communication Protocol for Wireless Sensor Networks, *Proceeding of the Hawaii International Conference System Sciences*, Hawaii, USA, January 2000.

Hu Y, N Yu, X Jia, (2006) "Energy efficient real-time data aggregation in wireless sensor networks " *IWCMC'06*, July 3–6, 2006, Vancouver, British Columbia, Canada.

IEEE Std 802.15.4 (2006). Part 15.4: Wireless medium access (MAC) and physical layer (PHY) specifications for low-rate wireless personal area networks (WPANs). *IEEE-SA*.

Jamieson K., H. Balakrishnan, and Y. C. Tay, (2003) "Sift: A MAC Protocol for Event-Driven Wireless Sensor Networks," MIT Laboratory for Computer Science, *Tech. Rep.* 894, May 2003

Kim T.H. and S. Choi (2006). Priority-based delay mitigation for event-monitoring IEEE 802.15.4 LR-WPANs. *IEEE Commun. Letters* 10(3), 213-215.

Koubaa A., M. Alves, B. Nefzi and Y. Q. Song (2006). Improving the IEEE 802.15.4 slotted CSMA/CA MAC for time-critical events in wireless sensor networks. In: *Proc. Workshop Real-Time Networks.* pp. 270-277.

Krishnamachari L, D Estrin, S Wicker, (2002), "Impact of Data Aggregation in Wireless Sensor Networks", *Distributed Computing Systems Workshops,* 2002

Langendoen K, Medium access control in wireless sensor networks. In H. Wu and Y. Pan, editors, (2007) *Medium Access Control in Wireless Networks,* Volume II: Practice and Standards. Nova Science Publishers, Inc.

Li, Y.J.; Chen, C.S.; Song, Y.-Q.; Wang, Z. (2007) Real-time QoS support in wireless sensor networks: a survey. In *Proc of 7th IFAC Int Conf on Fieldbuses & Networks in Industrial & Embedded Systems (FeT'07),* Toulouse, France.

Lin P., C. Qiao, and X. Wang, (2004) "Medium access control with a dynamic duty cycle for sensor networks", *IEEE Wireless Communications and Networking Conference,* Volume: 3, Pages: 1534 - 1539, 21-25 March 2004.

Lu C., G. Xing, O. Chipara, C.-L. Fok, and S. Bhattacharya, (2005) "A spatiotemporal query service for mobile users in sensor networks," in *ICDCS '05.*

Lu C., B.M. Blum, T.F. Abdelzaher, J.A. Stankovic and T. He (2002). RAP: a real-time communication architecture for large-scale wireless sensor networks. In: *Proc. IEEE RTAS.* pp. 55-66.

Lu G., B. Krishnamachari and C.S. Raghavendra, (2004) "An adaptive energy-efficient and low-latency MAC for data gathering in wireless sensor networks" *Proc. Int. Parallel Distrib. Process. Symp.* pp. 224-231.

Monaco U., et.al. "Understanding Optimal Data Gathering In the Energy and Latency Domains of A Wireless Sensor Network", *Computer Networks,* vol. 50 (2006) 3564–3584

Otero Carlos E., Antonio Velazquez, Ivica Kostanic, Chelakara Subramanian, Jean-Paul Pinelli,(2009) "Real-Time Monitoring of Hurricane Winds using Wireless and Sensor Technology", *Journ. of Comp*

Raghunathan V., C. Schurgers, S. Park, and M. B. Srivastava, (2002) "Energyaware wireless microsensor networks," *IEEE Signal Processing Mag.,* vol. 19, no. 2, pp. 40–50, Mar. 2002.

Rajagopalan R, PK Varshney, (2006) "Data aggregation techniques in sensor networks: A survey", *IEEE Communications Surveys & Tutorials,* 2006

Rhee I., A. Warrier, M. Aia and J. Min, (2005) "Z-MAC: a hybrid MAC for wireless sensor networks". *Proc. ACM Sensys.* pp. 90-101.

Ruzzelli A.G., G.M.P. O'Hare, M.J. O'Grady and R. Tynan (2006). MERLIN: a synergetic integration of MAC and routing protocol for distributed sensor networks. In: *Proc. IEEE SECON.* pp. 266-275.

Soyturk M., D.T. Altilar, (2008) Reliable Real-Time Data Acquisition for Rapidly Deployable Mission-Critical Wireless Sensor Networks, *IEEE INFOCOM 2008.*

Soyturk M., T.Altilar. (2006) "Source-Initiated Geographical Data Flow for Wireless Ad Hoc and Sensor Networks", *IEEE WAMICON'06*

Upadhyayula S, V Annamalai, SKS Gupta (2003) "A low-latency and energy-efficient algorithm for convergecast in wireless sensor networks "- *IEEE GLOBECOM* 2003

Watteyne T., I. Auge-Blum and S. Ubeda, (2006) "Dual-mode real-time MAC protocol for wireless sensor networks: a validation/simulation approach", *Proc. InterSen.*

Wu J., P. Havinga, S. Dulman and T. Nieberg (2004). Eyes source routing protocol for wireless sensor networks. In: *Proc. EWSN.*

Ye Wei, John Heidemann, Deborah Estrin (2001) "An Energy-Efficient MAC protocol for Wireless Sensor Networks", *USC/ISITECHNICAL REPORT* ISI-TR-543, SEPTEMBER 2001.

Yu Y, VK Prasanna, B Krishnamachari, (2006), "Energy minimization for real-time data gathering in wireless sensor networks" *IEEE Transactions on Wireless Communications,* Vol. 5, No. 11, November 2006

Yuan L., W. Cheng, X. Du. "An Energy-Efficient Real-Time Routing Protocol For Sensor Networks", *Computer Communications,* vol.30 (2007) 2274–2283

Zhu Y., K. Sundaresan, and R. Sivakumar.(2005) Practical limits on achievable energy improvements and useable delay tolerance in correlation aware data gathering in wireless sensor networks. In *Proc. of SECON,* 2005

5

Practical Considerations for Designing a Remotely Distributed Data Acquisition System

Gregory Mitchell and Marvin Conn
United States Army Research Laboratory
United States of America

1. Introduction

As government and commercial entities continue moving towards a condition based maintenance approach for logistics, the need for automated data acquisition becomes vital to success. For the duration of this document data acquisition is defined as the means by which raw facts are gathered for transmission, evaluation, and analysis (Pengxiang et al., 2004). Condition based maintenance is an advanced maintenance management mode, which helps avoid disrepair or excessive repair due to periodic maintenance, reduces maintenance cost, and also improves equipment reliability and availability. The analysis of critical system data minimizes the vulnerabilities of monitored systems, maximizes system availability, and concurrently produces a proactive logistics enterprise. This chapter discusses the design and implementation details of an adaptable automated data acquisition system (DAS) comprising several automated data acquisition nodes. Ideally, a versatile DAS design should have the capabilities to acquire and transmit data on key system test points in electronic or mechanical systems as well as provide the capacity for onboard data storage.

In many cases, a DAS will be embedded within a mechanical platform, electrical platform, or in an environment that is hazardous to humans; thereby disallowing direct human interaction with the DAS. In such remote applications, automation is particularly important because by definition human control of the system is either extremely limited or completely removed from the scenario. Here, automation means the mechanical or electrical control of a standalone apparatus or system using devices that take the place of human intervention. An automated DAS offers many advantages over manual and semi-automated acquisition techniques. Automated systems provide an accurate data recording mechanism that eliminates human error in the acquisition process. Automation also provides the ability to report data payloads in real time, whereas manual and semi-automated processes only allow data access after the fact.

The crucial features of a successful DAS will be data payload accessibility, automation, and an optimized means of transmission. The key issues for automation are the type of data to be collected, timing and frequency of data sampling, and the amount of onboard processing needed at the local level (Volponi et al., 2004). The type of data directly impacts not only the types of sensors needed but also the timing and frequency of the data sampling rate. Data types that require a high sampling rate or continuous sampling to identify key features of the data set will need some form of onboard processing to reduce the bit density of the

payload to be transmitted. For applications with discrete or low sampling rates this may not be an issue. This chapter will address various situations that apply to both types of data sets. Payload accessibility and means of transmission are intertwined because often the transmission medium is what grants external access to an embedded DAS.
Benefits of embedding an automated DAS include continuous user awareness of platform operational status and a reduction of maintenance costs by facilitating condition based maintenance as opposed to a fixed time based maintenance schedule. Automating the DAS means that diagnostics sensors can run continuously and discretely with functionality remaining transparent to the user.
Within this chapter, a specific DAS design will be used as a case study to highlight how the issues associated with each of the design features manifest themselves in the design process as well as to highlight the tradeoffs that are made in addressing these issues. This case study will illustrate the effects of said tradeoffs on both the design of the hardware and development of the control software. Finally, the results of a demonstration of the wireless DAS embedded within a platform will be reviewed. Performance will be evaluated for use on electrical fuses within a remotely operated weapons platform and on mechanical bearings for use in ground vehicles. This chapter compares experimental vibration data for mechanical bearing degradation collected by the automated DAS to data collected by an off-the-shelf DAS. The comparison characterizes the accuracy of the automated DAS method as compared with other proven laboratory methods. This will be especially important in demonstrating how each of the choices used to optimize the tradeoffs associated with the DAS will affect the ability to successfully and efficiently perform the operations for which it was designed.

2. System design concept

This DAS design concept focuses on having one or more embedded wireless sensor nodes (WSNs) that take measurements on key system test points within the platform of interest. The end WSN can acquire and store sensor data to its local memory or stream data in real time through the master WSN, which acts as a router to a control station (CS). The CS may be a computer, laptop, or other display device. The overall DAS architecture is illustrated in figure 1. The CS remotely configures and queries a WSN for status updates and data payloads. The combination of multiple WSNs and a single CS make up a comprehensive DAS. The WSN supports multiple mediums of communications such as wireless, inter-integrated circuit (I2C), and universal serial bus (USB) connections, which provide reasonable flexibility to operate even in environments that are not condusive to wireless communication. The general operating concept of this design is that an operator establishes a remote connection to each WSN either wirelessly or serially through the CS. The user then issues configuration commands to each WSN, and once the operator has configured and activated the WSN network the DAS operates autonomously.
Once the general design architecture is complete, the sensors required for the WSN to operate within the application platform must be defined. The application for this case study encompasses monitoring four separate circuit cards located in separate compartments which control the azimuth rotation, elevation, video unit, and actuator of a remotely activated weapon system. In each compartment, the requirements were to monitor temperature on a Polymer Positive Temperature Coefficient (PPTC) resettable fuse, temperature on a pulse modulator integrated circuit (IC), main power supply voltage and current, and the three-

axis vibration characteristics of the four circuit cards. These requirements resulted in the final WSN design comprising the following sensors: three thermocouple sensors, one voltage sensor, one current sensor, one external three-axis accelerometer, and one onboard accelerometer to determine WSN orientation.

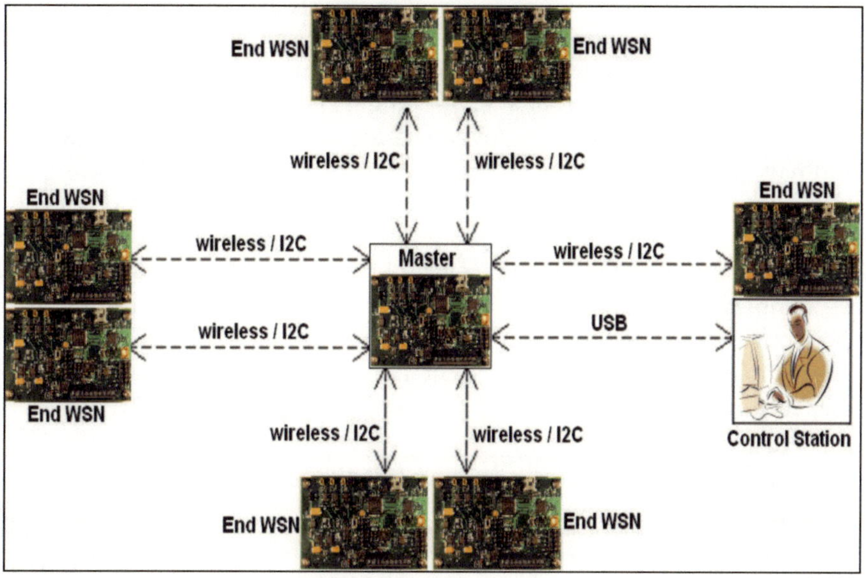

Fig. 1. Overall network configuration of the DAS.

2.1 Data acquisition design decisions

A round robin technique was used in the DAS for simplicity of implementation. If during acquisition, the WSN is configured to sample from the external tri-axis accelerometer and also from the voltage sensor, a block of samples from each input would be sampled and then stored to memory. This cycle would continue until a stop command is issued from the CS. In the present release of the firmware, a maximum of 512 samples could be acquired. The reason for the simplicity of this implementation becomes apparent when considering the following discussion.

What follows is meant to illustrate the complexities that would need to be addressed in the implementation of a more sophisticated data acquisition scheme. A more ambitious requirement might be to simultaneously sample all sensors while simultaneously storing the data to the secure digital (SD) memory card without a time break in the sampling. The storage rate to the memory card would have to support the sum of the maximum sampling rates of all sensors. This would require use of the microcontroller unit's (MCU) internal direct memory access (DMA) and require multiplexing between two memory buffers for each sensor during acquisition and storage. Key design considerations would be the clock rate, maximum sampling rates, contention between input/output (I/O) ports, random access memory (RAM) of the MCU, SD card memory size, and I/O bit rates. Since the MCU controls all of these functions, a clear understanding of the acquisition requirements is necessary to avoid overtaxing the capabilities of the MCU.

In extending this complexity to the sensor of the WSN for this case study, the following assumptions can be made with respect to possible sensor sampling requirements. The thermocouples require 2-byte words per sample at data rates of 1 hertz (Hz) or less. The external three-axis accelerometer requires 2-byte sample words on each axis with a maximum sample rate of about 8 kilohertz (KHz) per axis. The onboard three-axis accelerometer with max output data rate of 400 Hz for each axis requires 2 bytes per sample. The current and voltage sensors will be assumed to sample at an 8 KHz rate with 2 bytes per sample. Table 1 summarizes this discussion.

Several points can be made regarding the different sensors used in the WSN. First, the MCU would have to time share its internal analog-to-digital converter (ADC) across the external accelerometer, the current sensor, the voltage sensor, and the onboard accelerometer. The MCU would have to manage switching across these sensors while maintaining the desired sampling rates for each. As noted in table 1, all sensors do not have the same sampling rate, and other applications would conceivably require using sampling rates different from those in table 1. The MCU would have to initiate samples taken on the thermocouples, and these sensors are sampled using external ADCs which are controlled via the serial peripheral interface (SPI) bus. Writing acquired data to the SD memory card also requires the use of the SPI bus. The complexity of such an implementation soon becomes apparent, and one has to consider that such a configuration may not be possible with a single MCU.

Sensor Type	Bytes Per Sample	Required Sample Rate (Hz)	Data Rate KB/s	Measurement Device
M3000 axis-x	2	8000	16	ADCMSP430
M3000 axis-y	2	8000	16	ADCMSP430
M3000 axis-z	2	8000	16	ADCMSP430
CSA-V1	2	8000	16	ADCMSP430
Voltage TP	2	8000	16	ADCMSP430
LIS302DL axis-x	2	400	0.8	ADCMSP430
LIS302DL axis-y	2	400	0.8	ADCMSP430
LIS302DL axis-z	2	400	0.8	ADCMSP430
K-Thermocouple 1	2	1	0.02	ADS1240
K-Thermocouple 2	2	1	0.02	ADS1240
K-Thermocouple 3	2	1	0.02	ADS1240
		Required Storage Data Rate	82.5	

Table 1. Overview of different sensors used in the WSN where the M3000 is an external accelerometer, CSA-V1 is a current sensor, Voltage TP is a voltage sensor, LIS302DL is an onboard accelerometer, and K-Thermocouple is a temperature sensor.

2.2 WSN hardware design

This section gives a more detailed description of the design process for the WSN to be embedded on a platform. Figure 2 shows the WSN with all external sensors connected to the onboard hardware. The dimensions are 4.0 x 2.125 inches, and these were designed to match up exactly to the dimensions of the four circuit cards to be monitored. Also, because the type of application drives the number and type of sensors in the WSN design, the size limitations of the design are application specific in some respects. In all DAS designs, tradeoffs have to be made between performance, types of sensors needed, and size of the WSN. The MCU selected for the WSN is the Texas Instruments (TI) MSP40F2619 which has 128 kilobytes (KB) of flash memory and 4 KB of RAM. The memory was adequate for this application, but the small size of RAM limited the number of continuous samples during acquisitions. In this application, the RAM space had a general allocation of approximately 1024 bytes for sensor sampling and the remaining 3072 bytes for general firmware logic. This limited the contiguous block sample size to 2 bytes per sample, resulting in 512 samples per acquisition block. The small RAM size could be a problem for applications that require larger data acquisition blocks.

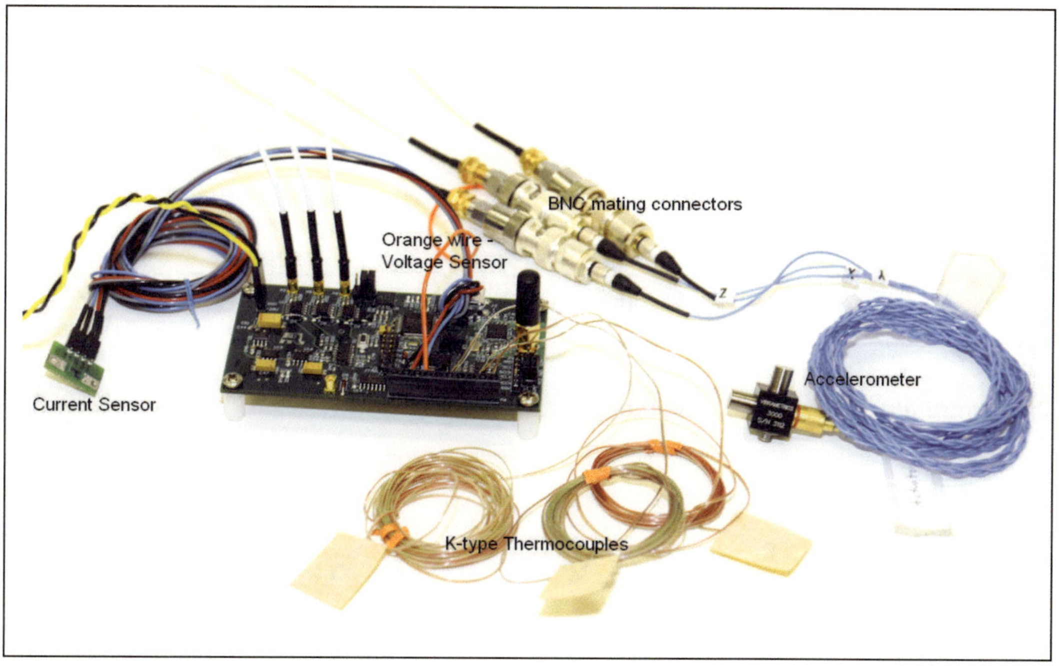

Fig. 2. WSN with all external sensors connected.

The WSN is powered by a 28 volt power connector. Although the onboard hardware of the WSN board is low-power and the MCU can run off of a 3.3 volt DC power supply, the 28 volt power connector was designed to allow the WSN to harvest from the 28 volts supplied by the platform. Also, the external three-axis accelerometer requires a power source which is derived from this 28 volt platform power supply. Onboard the WSN, the 28 volt supply is regulated down to 24 and 3.3 volts respectively and distributed to the circuit components. The power regulation for the 3.3 volt supply will be discussed in further detail in section 2.3. There are three miniature coax-M connectors, a separate connector for each axis, to connect the Model 3000 (M3000) external accelerometer as depicted in figure 2.

2.3 Power distribution details

Figure 3 shows the power regulation circuitry for the WSN powered by 28 volts supplied at the P3 power connector with positive voltage on pin 2 and GND on pin 1. An L78L24 power regulator chip regulates the voltage to 24 volts, which is used to power the external accelerometer circuitry. The LM9076MBA-3.3 power regulator chip is used to generate 3.3

volts from the power source, and powers the MCU as well as other low-power IC chips in the design. The LM9076BMA-5.0 power regulator chip uses the 28 volts to generate 5 volts, which is used for debugging purposes to power a green LED to indicate the power is on. The MCU and most peripherals in the WSN design require 3.3 volts or less.

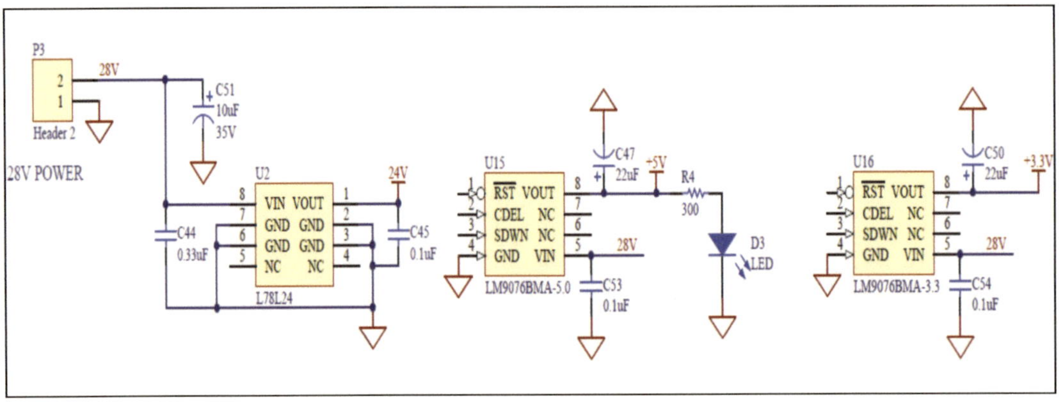

Fig. 3. Layout of circuitry to regulate the 28 volt DC power input to 3.3 volts for MCU operation.

2.4 Secure digital multimedia memory card design

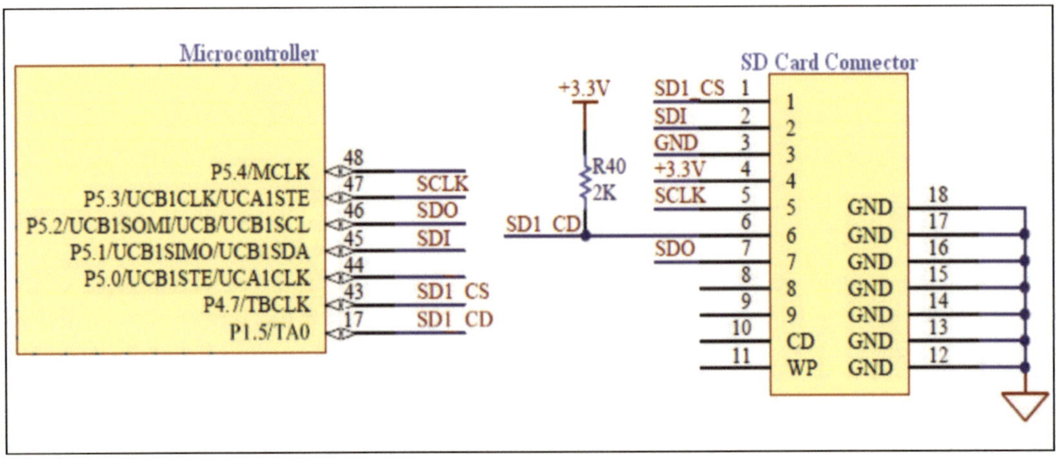

Fig. 4. Layout of digital SPI bus communication interface between the MCU and SD/MMC.

The schematic of the SPI protocol for digital communication bewteen the removeable SD memory card and the MCU is shown in figure 4. On pin 6, a 2 kilo-ohm (KΩ) pull-up resistor is used to detect when the memory card is inserted into the SD memory card connector. Inserting the memory card into the connector causes the chip detecting the voltage level on the SD1_CD line to be pulled to ground. The MCU firmware is programmed to detect ground level to confirm SD card insertion. The serial data input is connected to pin 2, serial data output is connected to pin 7, and the serial clock SCLK is connected to pin 5 of the SD memory card.

2.5 MCU clock use and distribution design

MSP430 Clock	Peripheral	Speed	Clock Source	Comments
MCLK	MSP430F2169	8 MHz or 16 MHz	XT2 crystal	A central processing unit (CPU) clock. Preferred to run at 8 MHz to maximize data processing, data transfers, storage rate, and communications.
MCLK or ADC12OSC	ADC12	8 MHz, 16 MHz, or 5 MHz with ADC12OSC	XT2 crystal	The actual rates affect sample and hold. Setup times are defined by the ADC12 registers. Review these carefully in the MCU documentation. This clock rate is not the same as the sample rate of ADC12. The ADC12 sample rate is dictated by sample and hold setup times and the Timer A1 interrupt rate as used in the firmware.
SMCLK	Timer A1	1 MHz	MSP430 F2169 internal DCO	Timer A1 is used for the overall sampling rate of ADC12, taking into consideration setup/hold/conversion times as discussed above.
SMCLK	UART	1 MHz	MSP430 F2169 internal DCO	The UART requires a fixed rate clock to get a 115,200-baud rate. The MCU and user interface are presently hardwired to a 115,200 baud rate.
SMCLK	ADS1240	1 MHz	MSP430F2169 internal DCO	The ADS1240 clock rate cannot be greater than 4 MHz; however, this clock can be locked at the lower 1 MHZ rate because sampling occurs at a low clock rate. Specifications indicate that the ADS1240 clock minimum is 1 MHz.
SMCLK	I2C	1 MHz	MSP430 F2169 internal DCO	Clock source selection is done in the I2C master initialization driver. It is presently set to SMCLK, which is set to 1 MHz on the DCO.

Table 2. Overview of the MCU clocks and their corresponding clock sources where MCLK is generated by an external XT2 crystal, and SMCLK is generated by the internal digital controlled oscillator (DCO).

This section describes the use of the internal MCU clocks and the clock source, defining which peripherals use which clocks and the desired clock rate settings of each. Given the difference in clock speeds for the various peripherals, it is important to keep in mind the settings of these clocks and their sources. Care must be taken in the firmware to manage these clock rates. Table 2 is presented to make the developer aware of the need to pay close attention to the clock settings and how they impact the system. The clock settings are primarily dictated by how fast data moves in the DAS, clock specifications of the peripheral devices, and system power requirements. Here ADC12 is an ADC internal to the MCU, Timer A1 is an internal MCU timer, UART is the universal asyncronous transmitter/receiver (UART), ADS1260 is an external ADC, and all clock rates are in megahertz (MHz).

3. Communication mediums

Payload accessibility is crucial to a fully functional DAS, and making reliable decisions requires large amounts of data. Due to bandwidth limitations the primary issues with data acquisition have already transitioned from storage to the buffering and distribution of the data. The three ways in which the WSN boards can communicate are wireless, I2C, and USB. A user can issue commands to the WSN via a graphical user interface (GUI) to configure the WSN, retrieve status updates, or stream sensor data via any one of these communication mediums. The manner in which these mediums are used or configured is strictly a matter of how the firmware is written. The TI CC2420 2.4 gigahertz (GHz) chip is the transceiver which provides the wireless communication capability of the WSNs. An I2C bus connection was available to link multiple WSNs together for serial communication of data between one another. The USB provides an ability to connect the WSN directly into a laptop or desktop computer. By incorporating all three communications interfaces the WSN achieves the flexibility to operate in a wider variety of environments and meet potential high bandwidth requirements that could not be achieved simply with a wireless communication medium.

Since the WSN is designed to operate in a networked configuration, a method was required to identify each board uniquely. A three-port jumper is used to set the WSN local node address. The jumpers allow addresses from 0 through 7, providing a maximum of eight possible WSNs in the network. In other applications, a maximum of 65,536 WSNs could be supported by either increasing the number of jumpers to 16 or using some other means of control in the firmware.

3.1 I2C design details

The I2C protocol is a wired, serial communications interface standard. Data is transferred on the serial data line (SDA) and synchronization is maintained by the serial clock (SCL). Each WSN can act as either an I2C end node or an I2C master on the communication bus in the current implementation.

In figure 5, the I2C bus header P8 is used to interconnect two or more WSNs on the I2C bus. The SDA, SCL, and ground pins must be interconnected using the P8 connector. On each WSN all SDAs must be connected together, all SCLs must be connected together, and all grounds must be connected together. Furthermore, the master WSN has the two pull-up resistor, R13 and R12, jumpers installed to pull the SDA and SCL lines high. On the master WSN there is a closed jumper connecting pins 1 and 2 and a closed jumper connecting pins 3 and 4 on P12. All end WSNs do not have the P12 jumpers closed. Figure 5 shows that the MCU pins P3.1 and P3.2 are used to control the SDA and SCL signals respectively.

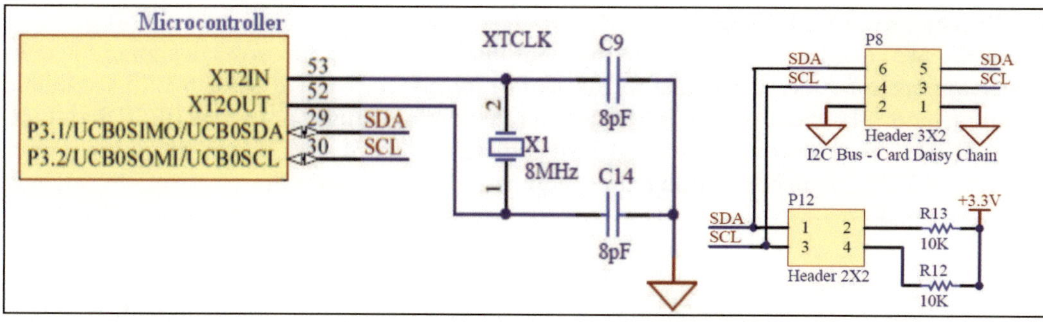

Fig. 5. Layout of the serial I2C communication interface to the MCU.

3.2 USB design details

Figure 6 shows the interface connections of the URXD0 and UTXD0 control lines to the MCU. Figure 7 shows the schematic of the USB interface design, which uses the CP2102 USB to UART bridge chip. The present implementation does not implement any hardware handshaking which may be of interest in future designs. A USB connector at J2 in figure 7 provides the communications interface between the master WSN and the CS.

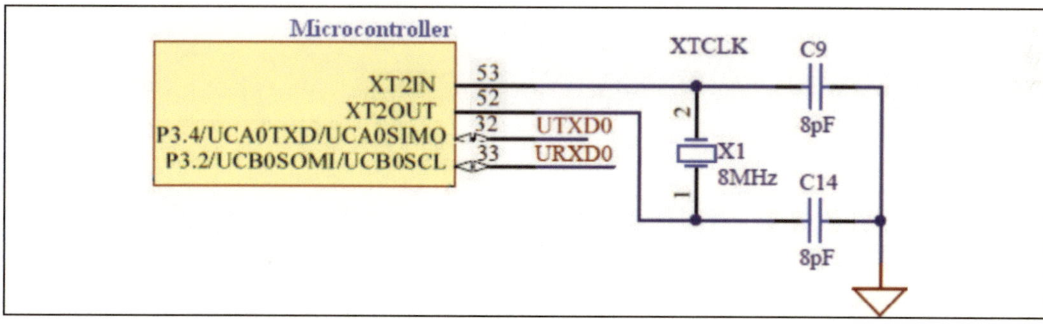

Fig. 6. Layout of the serial USB communication interface to the MCU.

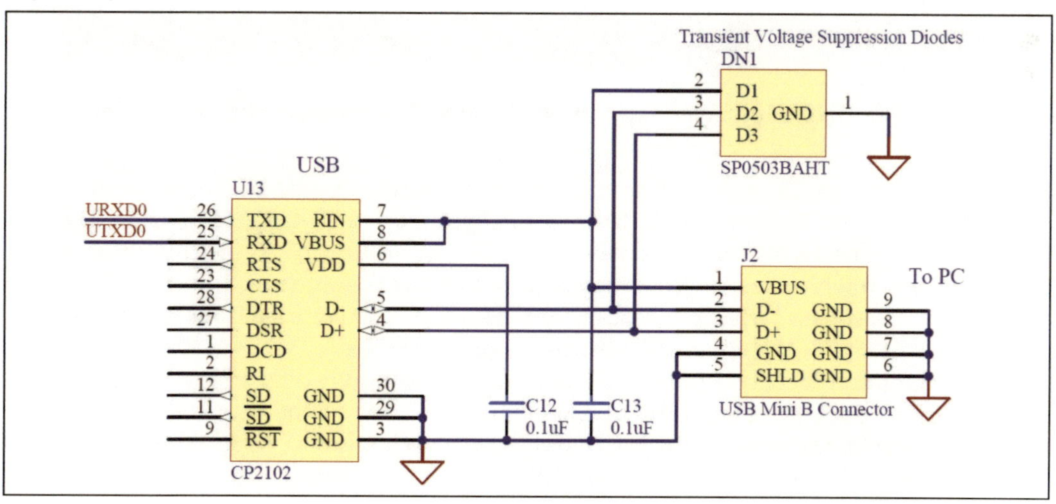

Fig. 7. Layout between the external USB connector and USB to UART bridge chip.

3.3 Wireless front end design

The TI CC2420 is a 2.4-GHz IEEE 802.15.4 compliant wireless transceiver designed for low-power applications meant for use in low-data rate networks. The IEEE 802.15.4 wireless communication standard is ideal for low-data rate wireless sensor networks (IEEE Standard, 2003). Sixteen communication channels are available, each of which supports a maximum data rate of 250 kilobits per second (Kbps) and has 5 MHz bandwidth.

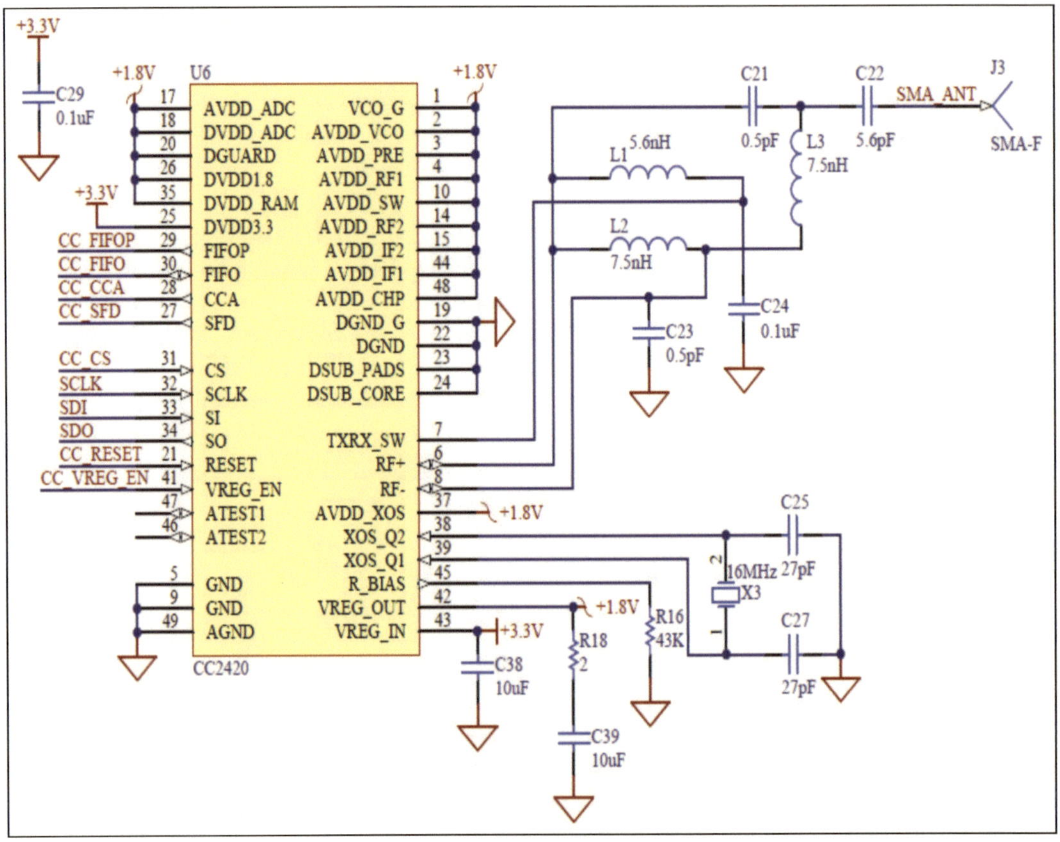

Fig. 8. Typical CC2420 transceiver application circuit with discrete balun for single-ended operation.

The transceiver has 33 two-byte configuration registers, 15 one-byte command strobe registers, a 128-byte transmit (TX) RAM, a 128-byte receive (RX) RAM, and an 112-byte security RAM. The TX and RX RAM can be accessed by address or accessed through two 1-byte registers, in which case the memory acts as first-in-first-out (FIFO) buffers. This case study does not address writing or reading any data from the security RAM and the system does not access the TX and RX RAM as memory, only as FIFOs.

Digital communication between the MCU and transceiver occurs over a four-wire SPI bus. It is necessary to track the FIFO, FIFOP, SFD, and CCA pins of the transceiver to monitor communication status between the MCU and transceiver registers. In addition to using the SPI pins, it is also necessary to drive the VREG_EN and RF_RESET pins during transceiver operation. VREG_EN is used to wake up the transceiver from an idle state and RF_RESET will reset the configuration registers of the transceiver to default status.

The transceiver hardware includes a digital direct sequence spread spectrum baseband modem providing a spreading gain of 9 dB and built in support for packet handling, data buffering, burst transmissions, data encryption, data authentication, clear channel assessment, link quality indication, and packet timing information. The external circuitry for the CC2420 transceiver used in the WSN is shown in figure 8.

For this application, the 250 Kbps rate was not a significant problem because high data sampling rates were not needed. In future applications, a higher wireless data rate and increased channel bandwidth may become necessary. This would facilitate using a different transceiver than the one described here or may even require the development of a custom wireless front end as the application warrants.

One issue encountered with the selected transceiver chip is that is does not support a full duplex transceiver capability. This means that it does not transmit and receive data packets simultaneously. During the development of the wireless firmware for the WSN, we decided that when streaming large amounts of data it was ok to occasionally drop a random packet. Although the transceiver chip included automatic reception acknowledgements, this feature introduces additional lag in node-to-node communication, and this lag only increases in the case of dropped packets. Significant development time was needed to debug and reduce the number of dropped packets via implementation in the firmware. The firmware implementation will be further dicussed in section 4.1.

3.4 Wireless networking capabilities

A star network topology was used for inter-node communications. The primary disadvantage of a star topology is the high dependence of the system on the functioning of the master WSN. While the failure of an end WSN only results in the isolation of a single node, the failure of the master WSN renders the network inoperable and immediately isolates all nodes. The performance and scalability of the network also depend on the capabilities of the master WSN. Network size is limited by the number of connections that can be made to the master WSN, and performance for the entire network is capped by its throughput. For much larger networks, a mesh network solution with ad-hoc capabilities may be advisable. An automatically reconfigurable network would be much more robust in the presence of failed routing WSNs, and allow for multiple access points to the DAS CS. This topology would eliminate the network's dependence on the functionality of a single master WSN.

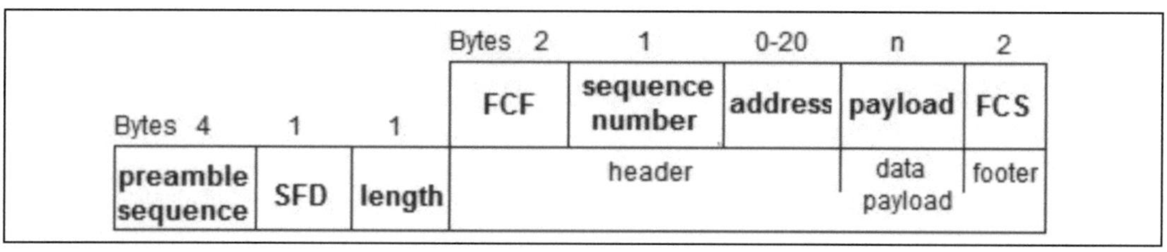

Fig. 9. Data packet structure used in wireless WSN-to-WSN communications based on the IEEE 802.15.4 standard.

Figure 9 shows the IEEE 802.15.4 data packet structure for wireless communications used in the DAS comprised of the media access control (MAC) and physical (PHY) layers (IEEE Standard, 2003). The structure of this data packet is what determines the order in which bytes are written and read from the transceiver FIFOs as well as the decoding of data payloads within the firmware.

The frame control field (FCF), data sequence number, and frame check sequence (FCS) are all defined by the firmware controlling the microcontroller. The FCF contains information such as whether automatic packet acknowledgements, data encryption, and what mode is in use. The FCF is generated based on the contents of various registers. The sequence number simply keeps track of the TX and RX sequence of data packets between WSN addresses, which is important when monitoring dropped packets or using automatic acknowledgements. A 2-byte FCS follows the last payload byte, which is calculated over the header, payload, and footer as indicated in figure 9. This field is automatically generated and verified by the hardware when the AUTOCRC control bit is set in the MODEMCTRL0 control register field of the transceiver. If the FCS check indicates that a data packet is corrupted, then the firmware disregards the entire packet.

The addressing information and data payload are both variable lengths. In the WSN, the addressing information consists of 6 bytes: two each for the network identifier (ID), destination node address, and source node address. The rest of the data packet is made up of the data payload. This payload may consist of inter-node messages, user requests, or simply sensor data being transmitted between network nodes. As defined for the application, the largest acceptable data payload for a wireless transmission packet is 111 bytes; however, all 111 bytes do not have to be used. The format of the data payload is the same for both wireless and I2C data payload streams.

4. Firmware system level design

This section describes the firmware design of the WSN in general terms. With the message driven paradigm, a single master WSN (client) and multiple end WSNs (servers) topology is used in the form of a star network as shown in figure 1. The master is typically connected to the CS via a USB port. The CS runs the system command and control GUI. Through the GUI, the user can issue commands to the master WSN to configure the master itself and/or all of the end WSNs in the system. The master WSN serves as the connection point or router between the CS and all end WSNs in the DAS; therefore, the master WSN acts as a communications broker in this architecture.

The master WSN can issue commands such as making status or data requests, and can send configuration commands to each end WSN. Each master and end WSN pair has a unique 3-bit address identification number that is configured by setting the appropriate jumpers on each WSN, which is then recognized by the hardware. The 3-bit address limits the number of nodes in the DAS to eight for this application, but with minimal design change the number of nodes in the system can be increased to whatever is required up to 65,536. The master WSN must always be connected to the CS and its address identification number must always be set to zero (000). The end WSN addresses must be set to settings from 1 through 7 (001–111). To avoid communication conflicts in the network, care must be taken to ensure the address identification numbers of each WSN is unique. These node address settings are used by the USB to universal synchronous/asynchronous receiver/transmitter (USART), wireless, and I2C communication mediums in the system.

The primary function of the master WSN is to transmit configuration and status commands between the CS and end WSNs as well as stream data from the end WSNs to the CS. The primary task of the end WSNs is to acquire data from the sensors based on their configuration settings and stream any requested information back to the CS. Although the master and end WSNs conceptually have different tasks, they both run the same firmware and are populated with the same hardware. Also, at the application programming interface (API) level, whether a master or an end WSN, the same type of message processing operations are performed. This design decision was made to simplify firmware development; therefore, only one copy of firmware is required for programming all the nodes within the DAS. The WSN address identification jumpers dictate if a WSN behaves as a master or an end node within the network.

The network is designed so that only the master WSN issues master-type WSN commands to the end WSNs, but a master WSN can also issue end-type WSN commands because it looks like an end WSN to the CS GUI interface. The end WSNs only issue end-type WSN commands, and in most cases, an end WSN responds to commands sent to them from the master WSN. An end WSN can also generate error messages if it detects a system error.

4.1 Communication network design considerations and limitations

Each WSN has a USB connector used to allow a user to issue commands to the DAS through the CS GUI if necessary. This means that connecting a CS to the master WSN via the USB interface gives the user remote access to all WSNs in the DAS. However, connecting a CS into the USB of an end WSN only gives the user access to control the individual WSN to which the CS is physically connected. The DAS communication hierarchy is implemented in this manner to limit the communication firmware design complexity. A more functional network realization might allow a CS to connect to any end WSN via USB and establish that WSN as the master via firmware implementation. This functionality will be much easier to achieve if implementing a real time operating system (RTOS) in the firmware.

The interrupt handler of the MCU must process interrupts for multiple communications channels. Interrupt flag registers must then be monitored to determine the actual source of the interrupt to process the interrupts correctly. This process increases the complexity of software integration between differing communication mediums.

4.2 Message bus architecture

Figure 10 shows the general mechanism for inter-node communication within the DAS. Although this example shows communications from the GUI to one end WSN via the I2C medium, this mechanism is used to communicate with all WSNs in the system and over the wireless medium as well. Each message sent on the message bus must have a message header. The message header defines the originating source of the message, the destination of the message, and the gateway or router to be used to pass the message from source to destination. The source, destination, and gateway are all defined by two parameters: medium and address. When a WSN initiates communication on the message bus, it must fill in this header information correctly for the message to be sent to the proper destination and for a potential reply message to be initiated. In the example shown in figure 10, the GUI sends a message to WSN 001, and WSN 001 sends a message back to the GUI. This process is performed using the following 4 steps:

Step 1. The message from the GUI always moves across the UART (USB) connection. The GUI configures the source medium as UART and the source address as GUI. The GUI node also fills in the destination medium as I2C and destination address as WSN 001. In the present system, the gateway is always configured to be the master

WSN (address 000) and the communication medium in this example is configured as I2C. The GUI sends a message with this header information to the master WSN, which is always the gateway.

Step 2. Once the master WSN receives the message sent from the GUI in step 1, its job is to determine if the message is for the master WSN or if the message should be forwarded to a destination WSN. If the message is intended for the master WSN, the master WSN processes the message according to the command set. In this example, however, the master WSN is required to forward the message to destination WSN 001 across the I2C bus as indicated by the destination setting configured by the GUI. So the master WSN forwards the message out to the I2C bus to WSN 001 with the original information unmodified.

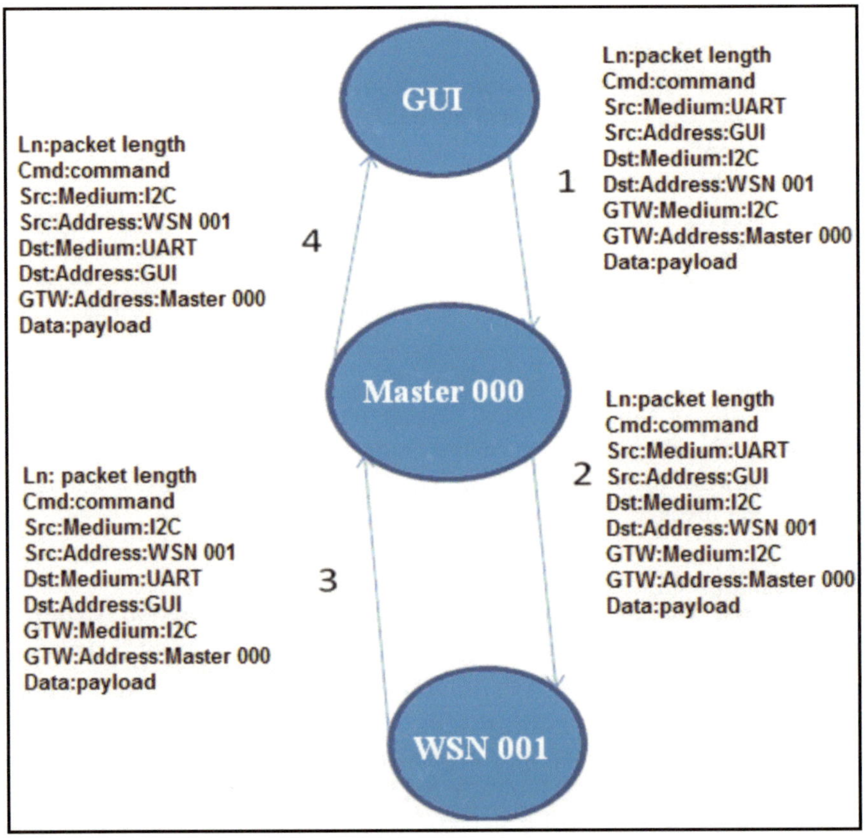

Fig. 10. Example of GUI-to-WSN communication via the I2C medium in the DAS using the master WSN as a gateway.

Step 3. WSN 001 receives the message and processes the message according to the command set. If WSN 001 is required to reply back to the GUI then the header information determines where to send the reply. In this example, WSN 001 sets the source medium as I2C based on the medium dictated in the message header and the source medium as WSN 001. WSN 001 sets the destination medium to be the UART based on the source medium dictated by the received message header. Using the same medium guarantees that the message will get back to the GUI since it is communicating on the same communication channel. Since this is an end WSN, it uses the gateway and address information to send a message back to the GUI. In this example, WSN 001 sends a message using the gateway medium as I2C and the gateway address as Master 000.

Step 4. Upon receiving the message from WSN 001, the master WSN again determines if the message is for itself (and processes it if it is) or forwards the message onto the destination address. In this case, the master WSN forwards the message unchanged to the GUI using the destination medium UART and address GUI as defined in the message header.

4.3 Communication message format

What follows is pseudo code of what the actual message formats are in the firmware. All data types are little-endian, which is derived from the MCU architecture. Every message sent or received in the network is communicated in the form of one or more message packets. The number of packets must form a complete message as defined in the *msgPacket* data structure. The *msgPacket* structure consists of a message header data type followed by an optional data payload. The packet *msgHeader* has several fields defined below:

```
typedef struct
{
        msgHeader hdr; //variable containing all information in msgHeader struct
        char *data; //[MAX_MSG_DATA_LENGTH_BYTES];
} msgPacket;

typedef struct
{
        unsigned char haa; //header information
        unsigned char h55; //header information
        unsigned short ln; //length field
        unsigned short cmd; //command field
        unsigned char totalPackets; //number of packets requiring assembly
        unsigned char packetNumber; // sequence number
        ChannelType src; //source address
        ChannelType dst; //destination address
        ChannelType gtwy; //gateway address
}msgHeader;
```

The first 2 bytes of the header contain the hexadecimal synchronization codes 0xaa and 0x55 which are used for data packet integrity checks. These values are always checked on the reception of a packet, and if they are not there then the complete packet is ignored. This check is done as a means to detect dropped or invalid data packets. The length field is used to determine the length of the complete packet including the byte lengths of the packet header and the data payload. Although the length field is a 2-byte unsigned short integer, the maximum value of length is restricted to less than the value of *MAX_PACKET_LENGTH_BYTES*. The command field is a 2-byte short integer that defines the command transmitted by the message. The valid values of the command field are defined by the enumerated type *PdCommandSet*.

The data payload is optional because some messages do not have a data payload, only a command. Each message packet size is limited to the size of the message header plus the size of the maximum allowed data payload. The design defines the maximum data payload to be *MAX_MSG_DATA_LENGTH_BYTES*. The maximum size of the data payload is dictated by various aspects of the hardware, such as the available RAM memory of the MCU or the largest byte size a message can send through a given communications medium.

The total packet field defines the total number of packets that make up a complete message. Reception of multiple message packets requires their reassembly before processing occurs. The packet number field defines the sequence number of the packet received. The source field defines the source node address and communication medium. This information allows the receiver of a message to reply back to the originator. The destination field is the destination WSN address and communication medium. The gateway field is always the master WSN address and communication medium.

For the network to operate properly, a critical point to consider in this design is that all WSNs communicating in the DAS must adhere to the same message command structure. All nodes must be programmed with the same command tables for proper command processing. If the command table on the GUI software is updated, all WSNs in the network must be reprogrammed with the same command table as the GUI. Conversely, if the command table on the WSN is modified then the GUI command tables must be updated to the same values.

A complete message is made up of multiple packets. The maximum number of packets for a complete message is defined by the *totalPackets* field, which is limited to a maximum number of 255 packets per message. Furthermore, the maximum number of bytes allowed per data payload is defined by *MAX_MSG_DATA_LENGTH_BYTES*, which is set to 80 bytes. This setting implies that the total data length of a complete message in the network can be no greater than 80 × 255 = 20,400 bytes. These values can be adjusted depending on the need of the DAS, but these restrictions are driven primarily by the limited RAM of the MCU. If messages greater than 20,400 bytes are required, there are several options available. One could design a higher level message structure that could be imposed on the interpretation of the data, use a bigger data size for *totalPackets*, or consider using a MCU with a larger RAM that would allow increasing the data payload size.

As a design rule, an end WSN should not be sent messages of sizes greater than one packet because they only need to receive commands and not large data streams. In contrast, an end WSN must be able to send messages composed of multiple packets when sending data streams whose payload spans multiple packets.

4.4 Digital communications via the serial peripheral interface

The digital interface between the MCU and transceiver allows the MCU to configure the transceiver registers, read and write buffered data, and read back transceiver status information. This communication is provided by a digital 4-wire SPI bus. Figure 11 illustrates the SPI interface between the transceiver and MCU. The CC_CS, SDI, SDO, and SCLK pins comprise the 4-pin SPI bus while the CC_FIFO, CC_FIFOP, CC_CCA, and CC_SFD pins allow the software to monitor the status of the TXFIFO and RXFIFO as well as the start of frame delimiter and clear channel assessment pins.

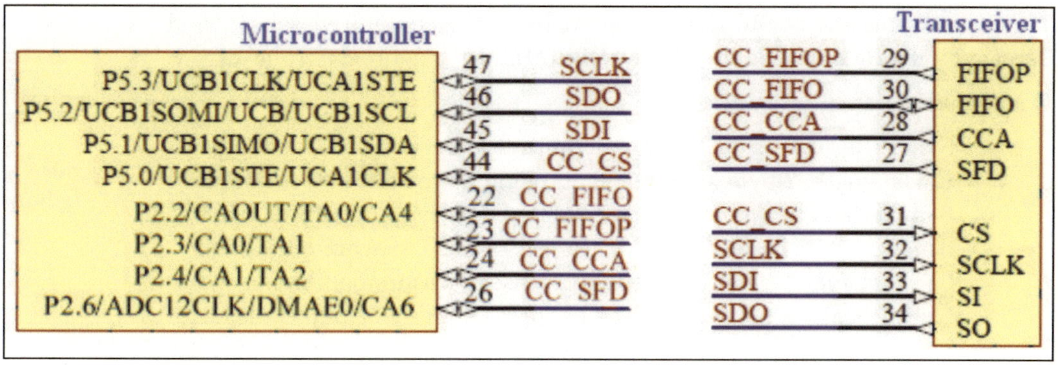

Fig. 11. Layout of the SPI interface between the transceiver and microcontroller.

4.5 Secure digital multimedia card data storage

This section documents the general data storage format on the SD memory card. The biggest storage sizes of memory cards used in this case study is 2 gigabytes (GB); however, larger cards can be used. For easy access to the data stored on the card, a file allocation table (FAT32) file system was used on the memory card. Although this has major advantages, a key disadvantage of FAT32 is that the I/O speeds are not as fast as using raw file I/O.

Because of some limitations of the FAT32 driver used, empty directories for each sensor type were created on the SD memory card using a bat script file before inserting the removable SD memory card into the WSN memory card slot. In a complete FAT32 firmware library, creating directories directly on the WSN should be possible.

When a WSN is configured to archive data, it creates bin files for each sensor type if they do not already exist. If the data file already exists when a WSN attempts to store a data set, the data is automatically appended to the file. This is done to preserve previous acquisitions. Which sensor data is stored during acquisitions depends on how the WSN has been configured through the CS GUI.

Each data file has a well-defined data storage format. Each sample set of data for each sensor is written to the file as a block of data. The data is stored as sequential sets of data blocks that consist of the data block header, followed by the raw sensor data. The data storage structure of the file is as follows, *M* is the maximum number of data blocks in the file:

Block1:

DataBlockHeader;
DataBlock;

Block2:

DataBlockHeader;
DataBlock;

.

.

.

BlockM:

DataBlockHeader;
DataBlock;

The *DataBlock* is the actual data acquired from the configured sensor, and its context is defined by the *DataBlockHeader*. The *DataBlockHeader* is defined as follows:

DataBlockHeader:

SyncPattern_aa_55h: 2-byte syncronization pattern for data integrity.
BlockLength: 2-byte length field allowing up to 65 KB block length.
SampleRateHz: 4-byte unsigned integer denoting the sample rate in Hz.
Sensor: 1-byte field identifying the sensor used to acquire the data.
SampleUnits: 1-byte field denoting sensor measurement units.
SampleScaleFactor: 4-byte float integer that gives the data scale factor.
NumSamples: 2-byte field denoting the number of samples in the data block.
EpochTimeStamp: 4-byte time stamp denoting when the data was acquired.

This design approach focused primarily on the flexibility of storage, not on storage speed or efficiency. There are cases where the data block overhead is a significant portion of the data block. As an example, when measurements are taken on a thermocouple, single point measurements are typically taken over periods of seconds, minutes, or greater time periods due to the nature of slow temperature changes. This is also due to the slow sample rate of the ADCs attached to the thermocouples. For every 2-byte thermocouple measurement taken, there is an overhead of 20 bytes for the data block header that amounts to 90% of the data block. In a second example, the current sensor might take 512 2-bytes samples per block. This would lead to a header overhead of 2% of the data block. The developer needs to be aware of the overhead tradeoffs and be open to exploring some other approach to a data storage format that may offer better storage efficiency if necessary.

Another point of interest relates to the required accuracy of the time stamp applied to the data block header. The timestamp represents the time at which a data block's acquisition began. For this case study, a one second time resolution was suitable, but different applications may require a more accurate resolution. Knowing this in advance will drive requirements on the hardware design of the WSN.

The addition of a file header providing additional information about the acquired data may be required depending on the nature of the data. For example, an American Standard Code for Information Interchange (ASCII) text block describing the nature of the measurement and identifying which WSN address acquired the data would address the possibility of switching memory cards from one WSN to another.

5. Performance and functionality

5.1 Fault simulator and test setup

To verify the capabilities of the WSN, accelerometer data was collected using a machinery fault simulator from Spectra Quest. This simulator provided a platform to generate vibration signatures for mechanical bearings of different sizes rotating at different frequencies. Data was collected using the WSN and stored on the SD memory card. The data on the memory card was analyzed and compared to data collected using an eDAQ Lite Laboratory DAS made by Somat, Inc. Both the WSN and eDAQ Lite measured the data using a Vibra-Metrics Model 3000 miniature tri-axial accelerometer capable of sensing ±500 G's.

5.2 WSN machinery fault simulator test results

Frequency responses of the data for both systems were analyzed using an averaged Fourier Transform of the raw data. The data was normalized using the root mean squared (RMS) value and the DC bias was subtracted out before applying the Fourier Transform. Normalizing the raw data by the RMS value suppresses the noise within the signal and minimizes any contribution such noise would have on the vibration signature.

Due to data block size limitations on the WSN, data was acquired using multiple 512 sample blocks of non-continuous data. The eDAQ Lite DAS was able to stream continuous data without the 512 block sample size limitation. To account for this discrepancy in the systems, individual Fourier Transforms were applied to 80 randomly selected data blocks of the eDAQ Lite data, each containing 512 data points. The magnitudes of the Fourier Transform of each individual data block were averaged to produce the frequency responses.

Figure 12 shows the vibration signatures computed from the data collected from the test setup. These frequency responses represent the vibration signatures for one of the three axes

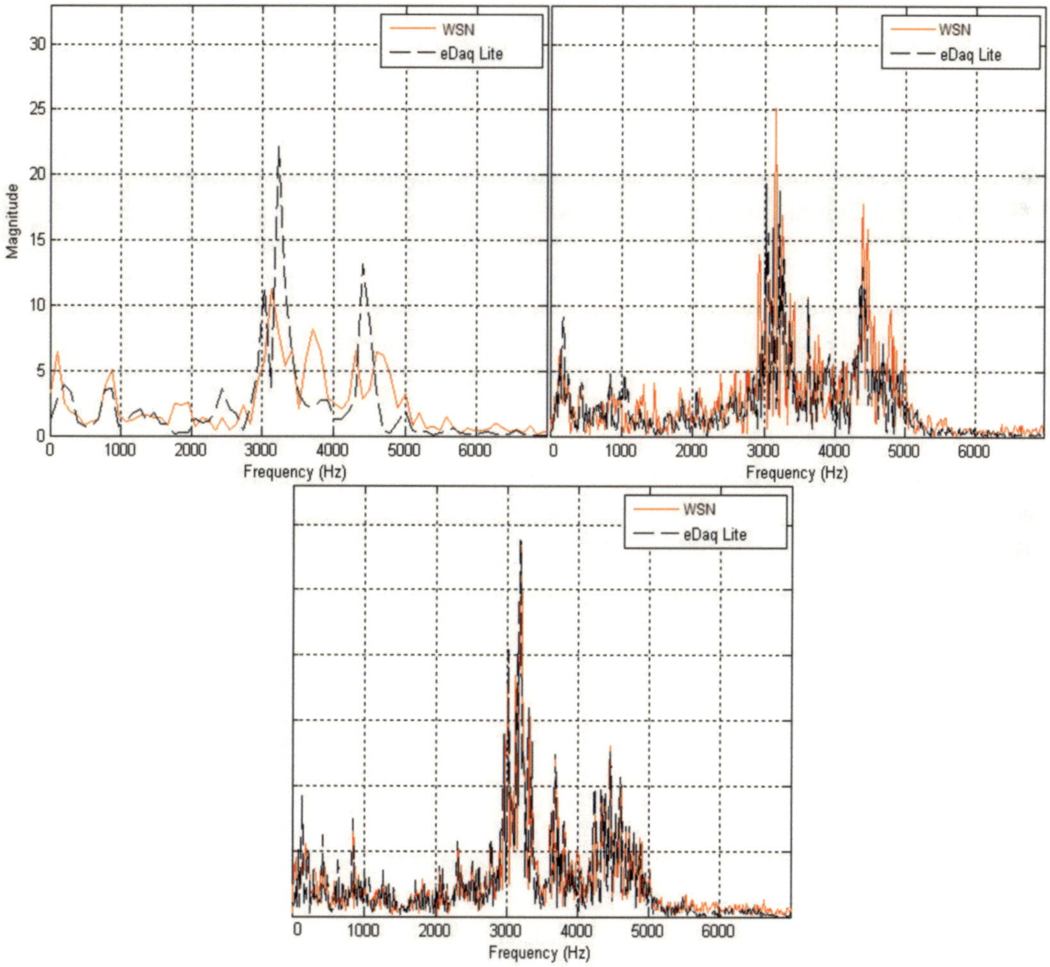

Fig. 12. Overlaid vibration signatures for the WSN and eDAQ Lite DAS computed using the averaged Fourier Transform of 10, 40, and 80 data blocks of 512 samples each.

Peak	Freq 1 (Hz)	Freq 2 (Hz)	Difference (Hz)	Mag1	Mag 2	Difference
1	146.8	146.8	0	4.44	4.05	0.39
2	440.3	440.3	0	3.01	2.52	0.49
3	831.7	831.7	0	3.11	2.93	0.17
4	2348.0	2348.0	0	2.83	2.48	0.35
5	2593.0	2593.0	0	2.70	3.27	0.56
6	3033.0	3033.0	0	11.38	11.15	0.23
7	3229.0	3229.0	0	10.30	10.70	0.40
8	3718.0	3718.0	0	5.17	5.20	0.04
9	4452.0	4452.0	0	7.09	6.39	0.70
10	4795.0	4795.0	0	4.51	5.24	0.73
11	5528.0	5528.0	0	0.70	0.85	0.15

Table 3. Vibration signature data comparison between the WSN DAS and EDAQ Lite DAS based on the vibration signature using 80 data blocks.

for a healthy bearing. An important point made by this figure is how data between the two collection systems compares as more 512 sample data blocks are incorporated into the Fourier Transform calculation. Figure 12a, 12b, and 12c shows the vibration signature using 10, 40, and 80 data blocks respectively. As expected there is higher resolution in the Fourier Transform as more data points are included in the calculation, but the accuracy between the two data collection systems also improves as the resolution improves. This improvement follows a law of diminishing returns, and an important consideration is the optimal amount of data to collect to provide the necessary resolution without over sampling.

Because data was collected with the two different systems for two separate runs with the same setup parameters, minor differences in the measured results are expected. This data corresponds to data collected on the y-axis of the tri-axial accelerometer. Data collection was performed for both systems in two separate runs on the machinery fault simulator with identical setups at a data sampling rate of 50 KHz. The frequency of rotation for the bearings was 45 Hz. The data was displayed in multiples of the gravitational constant in units of m/s^2. Differences in the magnitude can possibly be attributed to differing noise levels in the two systems or to gain errors in the ADC data acquisition circuitry. However, differences in the magnitude of the raw data did not affect the frequency components of the signal. Table 3 shows that numerical magnitude comparisons for significant peaks of the vibration signatures produced by the two data acquisition systems exhibit a close correlation. The average magnitude differences between the WSN and eDAQ Lite data are less than 10%. This comparison is based on the data calculated using 80 data blocks of 512 samples each.

5.3 Application platform demonstration

The application platform is a gun mounted on a remotely controlled swivel with multiple cameras that allow operators to remain inside the relative safety of an armored vehicle. This section provides an overview of the demonstration of an embedded DAS based on the WSN. The primary purpose of this trial was to demonstrate real-time data collection and wireless communication capabilities of the WSNs as well as to demonstrate the capability to detect changes in the functionality of the monitored components. In this proof of principle demonstration, multiple WSNs were integrated into separate cavities of the platform, with a master WSN connected to the CS. The end WSNs were remotely configured to monitor the control circuit cards in the platform using the CS command and control GUI. The WSNs monitored the accelerometer, voltage, temperature, and current data from each of the test points within the platform while the platform remained fully operational.

Figure 13 shows a WSN wired into the platform elevation control cavity and mounted directly on top of the circuit card to be monitored. The circuit card is already secured to the side of the inner chassis of the cavity, and the WSN is mounted directly above the circuit card to allow access to the fuse underneath, which is not visible in the figure. The WSN was designed to connect to several external sensors so that they can be routed to various test points and provide the ability to monitor multiple areas from a central location. In order to ensure wireless functionality within a closed chassis, the antenna is attached to the outside of the platform and connected to the WSN via a 50 Ω coaxial cable. The external antenna is shown on the outside of the closed chassis in figure 14.

The WSN was wired to monitor the temperature of a resettable fuse using thermocouple 1, the temperature of the L-chip using thermocouple 2, the main power voltage level using a voltage test point sensor, and the main power current using a current test point sensor. Figure 14 shows a WSN module wired into the sealed platform sensor unit motor/actuator cavity. The cavity was sealed to demonstrate that the WSN could be completely integrated into the platform system. A hole was drilled into the cavity to allow the wireless antenna to be installed on the external surface for communications back to the master WSN and CS which was a laptop computer.

Fig. 13. WSN installed on the elevation control circuit card which can be partly seen underneath.

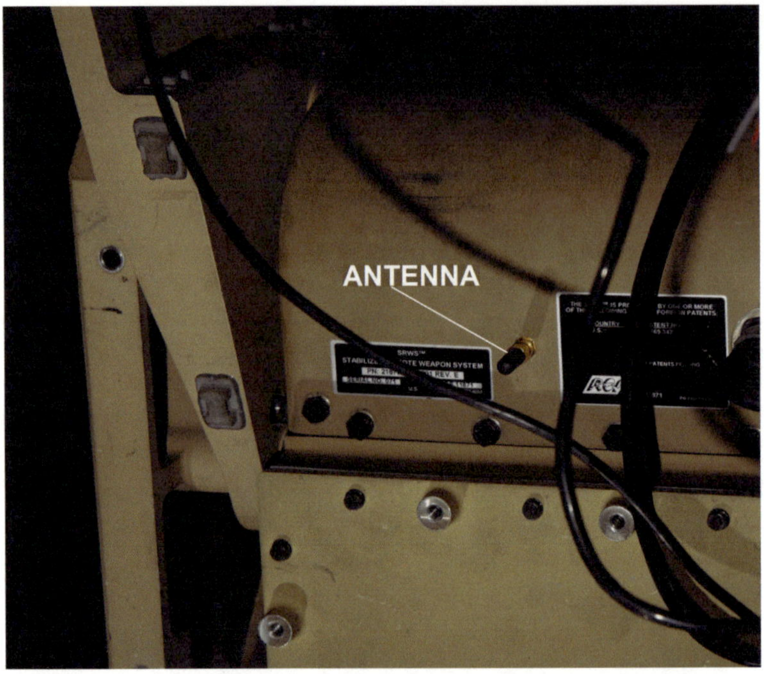

Fig. 14. External WSN antenna mounted on the outside of the closed chassis.

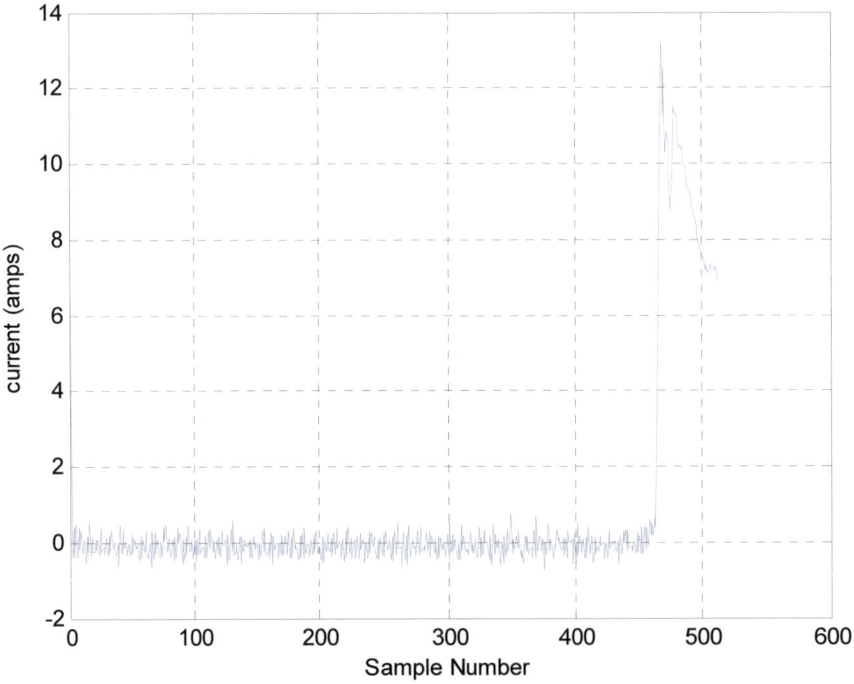

Fig. 15. Current data collected across the fuse during operation of the platform.

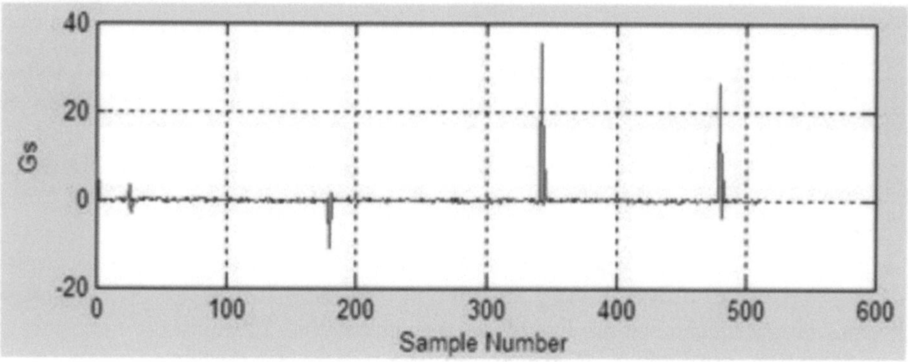

Fig. 16. Shock data collected on the outer chassis during operation of the platform.

Current, voltage, temperature, and shock data was collected as the platform was operated using the joystick interface employed in the field. Figure 15 shows current data and figure 16 shows accelerometer data that was collected as the joystick was used to alter the azimuth rotation and elevation of the platform. This data was wirelessly streamed from the WSN and displayed on the GUI for visual observation and analysis. During normal operation the current fluctuates at less than 1A peak-to-peak, but when the joystick operator overdrives the elevation circuit by pushing the elevation of the gun past its specified level, a sharp spike in current measured across the fuse occurs. In figure 15, this sharp spike is directly followed by a sloping off of the current level, which indicates that as the fuse cools down and its resistance increases, the current measured across the fuse decreases. This depiction of the fuse functionality, as interpreted from the changes in current data, verifies that the automated data collection and transmission system accurately reflects measurements that would be expected from previous methods of data collection.

6. Conclusion

A WSN design for an automated DAS that can be utilized for various applications in electrical and mechanical systems has been presented. Vibration signatures for healthy bearings were calculated from data acquired by the WSN and compared to those based on data acquired by the eDAQ Lite bench top DAS. The results of these experiments show that the RFID performs accurate data measurements that allow for reproduction of known results through data analysis.

The design includes multiple sensors and communication interfaces to allow it to be customized to various platforms with minimal redesign effort needed. The effectiveness of such an approach was demonstrated on a platform by monitoring key test points within the system. Collected data provided an accurate analysis of the successful operation of an embedded electrical fuse. The greatest advantage of such an automated approach is the fact that this method of embedded data collection is as accurate as laboratory methods and can be transitioned to future and presently fielded platforms.

Future development efforts should involve enhancing the WSN by adding onboard digital signal processing hardware and algorithms, and in making the architecture more scalable and robust. In addition, efforts should focus on the development of firmware to support more sophisticated networking architectures such as self healing and ad-hoc networks.

7. References

(2003). IEEE Standard for Information technology—Telecommunications and information exchange between systems—Local and metropolitan area networks Specific requirements, Part 15.4: Wireless Medium Access Control (MAC) and Physical Layer (PHY) Specifications for Low-Rate Wireless Personal Area Networks (LR-WPANs), *IEEE Computer Society*, The Institute of Electrical and Electronics Engineers, Inc., New York, 2003.

Pengxiang, B.; Jun, X.; Hongyun, Z. (2005). Practice and Strategy for Condition Based Maintenance of Power Supply Equipment, *Proceedings of IEEE/PES Transmission and Distribution Conference and Exhibition: Asia and Pacific*, 2005.

Volponi, Allan J.; Brotherton, Tom; Luppold, Robert & Simon, Donald L. (2004). Development of an Information Fusion System for Engine Diagnostics and Health Management, *NASA/TM-2004-212924, ARL-TR-3127*, February 2004.

6

Portable Embedded Sensing System using 32 Bit Single Board Computer

R. Badlishah Ahmad, Wan Muhamad Azmi Mamat
Universiti Malaysia Perllis
Malaysia

1. Introduction

Data acquisition is the process of bringing a real-world signal, such as a voltage, into the computer, for processing, analysis, storage or other data manipulation (Rongen, n.d.). Generally, Data Acquisition Systems (DAS) are used to electronically monitor or gather data from the external physical environment (Ng, 1994). DAS normally consists of three elements: acquisition hardware, input and storage/display unit. The acquisition hardware plays a vital role in influencing the performance of DAS. Most of the previous research has used Personal Computer (PC) as the acquisition hardware. The trend was then changed from standard PC to high speed PC to provide better performance in terms of data processing and data transferring. The embedded processor board has become a new alternative platform for DAS application. Several embedded processor board used as acquisition hardware are microcontroller, Field Programmable Gate Array (FPGA), Digital Signal Processor (DSP) and Single Board Computer (SBC). The microcontroller is the most popular platform for small and simple application because of its low cost. Some developments use FPGA as Data Acquisition Unit (DAU). FPGA allows modification of internal logic circuitry without touching hardware component. The DSP board is mostly used in applications that handle real-time computation process. The other current trend on embedded technology application is the Single Board Computer (SBC). One major advantage of using an SBC is that it can handle multitasking processes since it run with a modular Operating System (OS). The development can be done using high level language such as C, Java and Perl which are widely used, flexible and have a lot of support from the open source community. However, the key to select a suitable processor board depends on the purpose of its application so that the optimum functionality can be used according to its specifications.

2. Embedded-based DAS

In the early days of DAS, the Personal Computer (PC) is a main choice to operate as acquisition hardware (Omata, 1992; Rangnekar, 1995). Data is collected from the input using serial communication. This medium needs both input and data logger connected to serial or parallel port. Martin, S. (1990) stated that a major limitation of desktop computers in data acquisition and control application is the fact that it were designed for in office automation. He also mentioned that the desktop computer often does not meet the real-time requirement of high performance data acquisition and control. The use of the PC in DAS has several restrictions. It is normally installed in the laboratory or at a fixed place. Hence, it is not portable to handle different situation such as real-time outdoor testing. A sample may change due to varying time and conditions and this will influence the measured result if the measurement is not done in real-time. The embedded-based DAS is therefore a promising solution towards a portable DAS within a small scale hardware system.

The advancement in electronic and Integrated Circuit (IC) technology development has spawned a new platform in DAS. The DAS is changing from PC-based to embedded system application based. The embedded system is normally designed so as to minimize size, power consumption and cooling requirements (James, 2000). In these systems, hard disks are frequently replaced by ROM-based device which provide storage for all software including the operating system. An embedded controller is a mixture of control hardware and software to perform specific task. The embedded controller can handle many tasks depending to the software embedded within it. The processor board is an important component in industrial application. It handles most of the system processes such as retrieving data and controlling the systems. The advancement of recent electronic and fabrication technology has led to widespread utilization of tiny processors to manage complicated and complex tasks. Microcontroller, Digital Signal Processor (DSP) and Field Programmable Gate Array (FPGA) are examples of popular embedded based acquisition hardware currently in use. Microcontrollers use serial communication, while DSP, FPGA and SBC might include faster communication method such as Universal Serial Bus (USB) and Ethernet.

Microcontroller is one of the early embedded-based acquisition hardware used in DAS. The DAS microcontroller based is very popular previously and is still being used because of its low cost (Hansen, 2004; Riley, 2006; Misal, 2007). Many applications are using microcontrollers as control units for simple system and small applications. The trend in embedded based DAS is changing towards a more advanced and powerful processor board. The Field Programmable Gate Array (FPGA) is a semiconductor device that can be configured by the customer or designer after manufacture. It has an internal logic blocks or digital electronic gates to perform complex combination functions. FPGA has become a popular DAU since it allows modification and simulation of logic circuitry without hardware modification (Laymon, 2003). The Digital Signal Processer (DSP) is a specialized microprocessor designed for digital signal processing generally in real-time computing. DSP board are widely used in applications such as audio signal processing, video compression, speech recognition and image manipulation. According to Eyre and Bier (2000), the latest DSP processor board functions with a faster clock cycle, has more instruction set and have wider data buses to enable more data to be processed. The DSP board is also chosen as a processor board to handle real-time computation with mean acquisition rate around micro second (μs) (Alderighi et al., 2002).

3. Single board computer

The early microcomputer uses backplane that is attached with several circuit modules such as Central Processor Unit (CPU), memory, serial port and peripherals. The idea of SBC is to combine all those parts in a single board without backplane. Robert A. Burckle (n.d.) from WinSystems in his article 'The Evolution of Single Board Computers' states that the first SBCs were proprietary designs needed to satisfy a specific application. That statement is precisely true and fulfills the standard of embedded systems definition. Table 2.1 outlines several SBCs from various manufacturers with CPU architecture, form factor and its features. Only a few examples are taken from original sources (Baxter, 2001), and with different table view.

Manufacturer/ SBC (model)	CPU Architecture/ Form Factor	Features
Motorola/ MVME5100	PowerPC/ VMEbus	750/7400 Altivec, dual-PCI mezzanine card sites, up to 1GB ECC SDRAM, dual Ethernet ports, two serial ports, up to 16MB Flash
Zynx/ ZX4500	PowerPC/ CompactPCI	24 10/100 Ethernet ports, two Gigabit Ethernet ports, PMC/PPMC slot for additional I/O and an expansion processor, fully hot-swap compliant
Ampro/ Little Board/P5x	x86/ EBX	PC/104-plus expandable PCI/ISA bus, P5x supports up to 256MB DRAM with bootable Compact Flash socket and 10/100Base-T Ethernet, USB, IrDA, KB, floppy, IDE, serial and parallel I/O, also supports C&T 69000-series PCI LCD/CRT controller with PanelLink, LVDS and NTSC options
WinSystems	x86/ PC/104	133MHz 586DX with up to 72MB Flash disk, CRT/LCD display video controller, Ethernet, IDE and floppy disk controllers, serial, parallel and keyboard
Bright Star/ mediaEngine	StrongARM/ 5.2"x5.3"	8-64MB SDRAM at 100MHz, 1-20MB Flash, Type II Compact Flash socket, Type I/II/II PCMCIA socket, 10Base-T Ethernet, three serial ports, V.90 modem, LCD panel controller, USB slave interface
Intel/ Assabet	StrongARM/ 2.5"x5"	64-256MB of TSOP SDRAM, 64-128MB onboard socketed Flash, integrated LCD support, Bluetooth, GSM digital radio, audio in and out, built-in TV encoder supporting S-video, NTSC, PAL and RGB formats, IrDA port, soft-modem support

Table 1. Embedded Linux SBCs (Baxter, 2001)

Generally the SBC is a complete computer built on a single Printed Circuit Board (PCB). It has all important elements similar to the standard computer including processor, memory and Input Output (I/O). Certain peripheral are also available within SBC including serial port, parallel port and USB port. The Ethernet port, wireless network socket, audio line in and VGA port may customize as well that are sometimes custom-built to perform specific tasks. Otherwise it does not come with default display unit and input hardware. The most

important feature of the SBC is it can run modular OS. The Z80-based "Big Board" (1980) was probably the first such SBC that was capable of running a commercial disk operating system (LinuxDevices, n.d.).
Most SBC boards use commercial off-the-shelf (COTS) processor. This helps reducing development time and dependencies on technical staff to develop dedicated processor board from scratch. The SBC processor board is suitable for use in critical and complex applications to develop a systems model or handle an analysis before running the real system such as in a flight simulator (Peters, 2007). SBCs are often integrated into dedicated equipment which is used, for example, in industrial or medical monitoring applications (James, 2000). The use of embedded systems is reasonably low cost and small physical size promising the most effective solution. It is not only suitable for portable system but also significantly improving the capabilities of the instrument (Perera, 2001). Zabolotny et al. (2003) has replaced the VME (Versa Module Eurocard bus) controller with embedded PC for TESLA cavity controller and simulator DAS. The replacement was made to enhance functionality in terms of bits and register manipulation, data processing operation and to increase efficiency of data acquisition and control and enhancing data transfer.

4. System overview

Hardware design gives an overview of the physical interaction among the devices of the system. Hardware components of the DAS are shown in Fig. 1 below. SBC acts as an acquisition hardware that acquires data from sensors. A signal conditioning circuit is used for high output impedance sensor, to match the built-in ADC on the SBC board. The developed DAS based on SBC is named Portable Embedded Sensing System (PESS). PESS is developed with an integration of SBC, matrix keypad, LCD panel and sensors. The matrix keypad functions as an input device and information data is displayed using LCD panel. Fig. 2 outlines the PESS system architecture which consists of hardware and software.

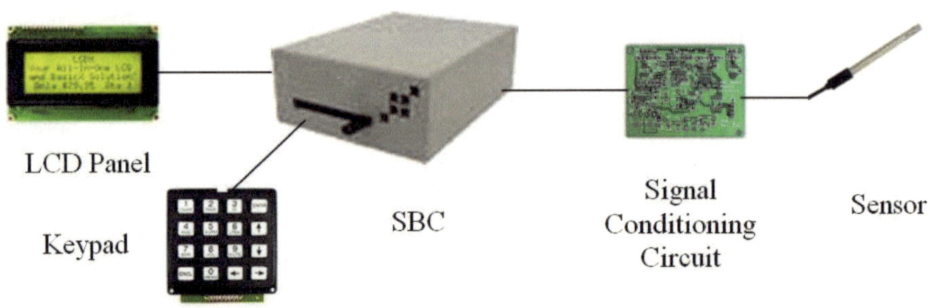

Fig. 1. PESS hardware design

The PESS system has several limitations in terms of storage capacity and data view space. Compact Flash (CF) is used as storage devices which functions as a hard disk for the SBC. The data that can be stored on the CF is up to 4GB. Due to the limitation of CF storage device, PESS is not suitable for applications that require large storage capacity.

4.1 Embedded acquisition hardware: TS-5500 SBC

Technologic System offers semi-custom and off-the-shelf Single Board Computers (SBC). The product from Technologic Systems available in two different architectures which are ARM and X86.

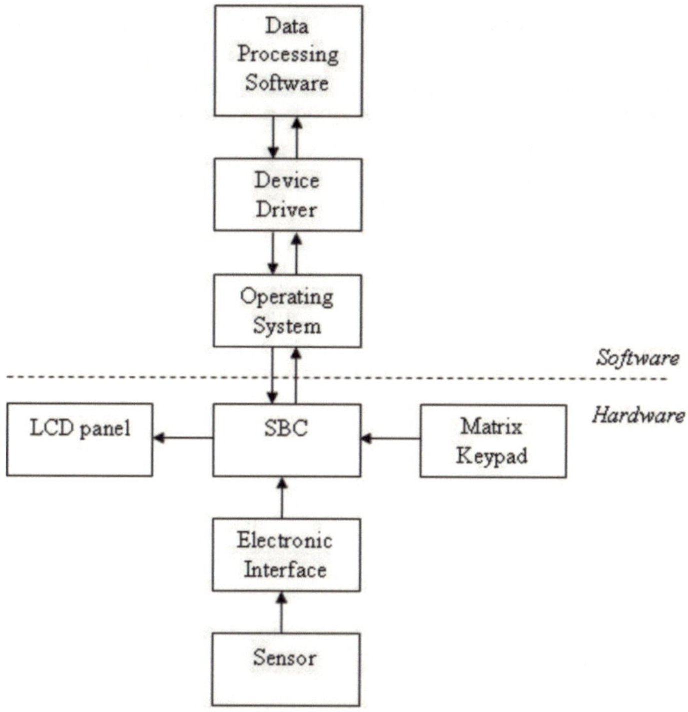

Fig. 2. PESS system's architecture

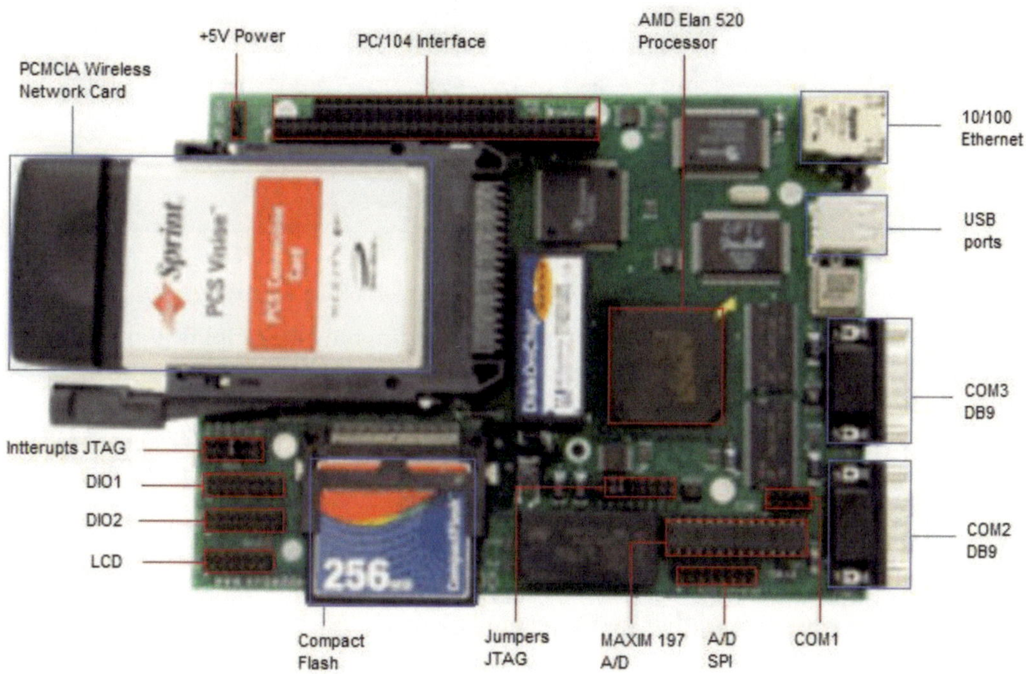

Fig. 3. TS-5500 Single Board Computer

For ARM SBCs, they can be identified with TS-7000 number series. There are four series for ARM SBCs which are TS-7200 series, TS-7300 series, TS-7400 series and TS-7800 series. The X86 SBCs is available in two series which are TS-3000 and TS-5000. The X86 SBCs have slower CPU compared to ARM SBCs. The TS-3000 series run Intel 386 CPU with 33 MHz and has small memory which is 8 MB. The TS-5000 series run 133 MHz AMD Elan 520 CPU and has 32 MB of memory. The TS-5000 series is manufactured with wireless network interface. Fig. 3 show the TS-5500 SBC main board.

TS-5500 SBC from Technologic Systems has been used by many developers in various fields including robotic, web server application and data acquisition and control system. In 2003, Hoopes, David, Norman and Helps presented the development of autonomous mobile robot based on TS-5500 SBC. The other example of robotic design and development based on TS-5500 SBC was built by Al-Beik, Meryash and Orsan.

4.2 Sensor interfacing

Two types of analog sensors are used which are temperature sensor and ion selective electrode. LM35DZ temperature sensor from National Semiconductor is a simple analog sensor used in this research where it's measurement is not using a signal conditioning circuit. Copper (Cu^{2+}) ion selective electrode from Sensor Systems are used with a reference electrode for high impedance output sensor type. Fig. 4(a) and 4(b) show the Copper ion selective electrode and reference electrode respectively.

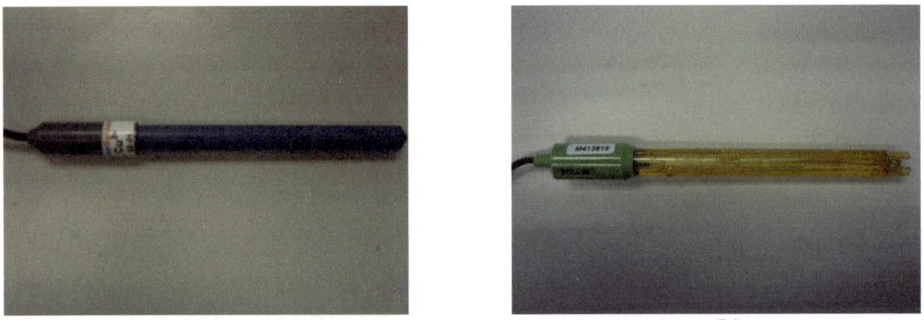

(a) (b)

Fig. 4. a) Copper ion-selective electrode b) Ion-selective reference electrode

The most frequently processes performed in signal conditioning are amplification, buffering, signal conversion, linearization and filtering (Ismail, 1998). ADC normally can read analog inputs that have low output impedance. If the input impedance of the sensor is high, the ADC reading is unstable and not reliable. Typically the glasses electrodes such as pH probes or gas concentration probes are of this type (Microlink, n.d.). Therefore a signal conditioning circuit has to be integrated with a high output impedance sensor (*Application notes 270*, 2000). This can be done by attaching to a voltage follower as a buffer element to match the impedance. In this research, the signal conditioning circuit built has two stages circuit. The first stage functions as a buffer unit which will decrease the input impedance from analog input. The second stage is a filter that removes the noise signal. The OPA2111 (*OPA2111*, 1993) operational amplifier is used within the signal conditioning circuit. The OPA2111 has high internal resistance of 10^{13} Ω for differential mode and 10^{14} Ω for common-mode. The signal conditioning circuit used is shown in Fig. 5.

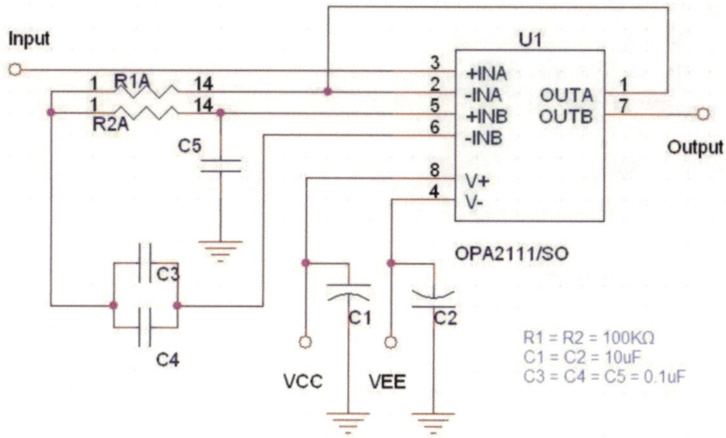

Fig. 5. Signal conditioning circuit

4.3 Input/Output of PESS system

The 4x4 16 button matrix keypad is used as input device for the system developed. The keypad is manufactured by ACT Components, Inc with physical size 4.7"W x 1.7"H x 0.4"T. A nine (9) pin input is used to connect between matrix keypad with device or processor board using serial cable. The 24x2 alphanumeric LCD panel is use as display for this system. The LCD is manufactured by Lumex Inc with physical size of 118mm x 36mm x 12.7mm. It connected to processor board using 9 inputs serial cable.

(a) (b)

Fig. 6. a) 4x4 matrix keypad b) 24x2 alphanumeric LCD panel

4.4 Embedded OS: TSLinux

Technologic Systems provides two free OSes which are developed by their research team: Linux and DOS. These OSes are developed to be used with their product only. However, many other OSes can also be used with TS products such as uC/OS-II, eRTOS, microCommander modular Human-Machine Interface (HMI), MicroDigital SMX modular and QNX Embedded Real Time OS. TSLinux is chose to run on SBC in this research. TSLinux is a PC compatible embedded Linux distribution built from open source. There is a tailored Linux kernel for each TS SBC, along with completed driver support for the hardware. The kernel source is also provided to end users to enable custom changes and development.

Several TSLinux features as follows:

- Glibc version 2.2.5
- Kernel version 2.4.18 and 2.4.23
- Apache web server with PHP
- Telnet server and client
- FTP server and client
- BASH, ASH, minicom, vi, busybox, tinylogin

5. Software development

Two software modules developed in the PESS system which are the Analog Input Preprocessing and Data Presentation. The Analog Input Preprocessing module involves data acquiring from sensor, converting analog input to digital output and calculating converted output to human readable value. A C code named *sensor* to cope all those processes is developed. Data Presentation module in PESS system is handled by a program named *Interactive System*. An *Interactive System* provides current sensor' readings and the information of the system such as disk (CF) usage and memory capacity status. Fig. 7 show the interaction between both software modules which running concurrently. *Sensor* program processing the analog inputs and store converted data into shared memory, meanwhile those current data available on shared memory can be accessed via *Interactive System* program.

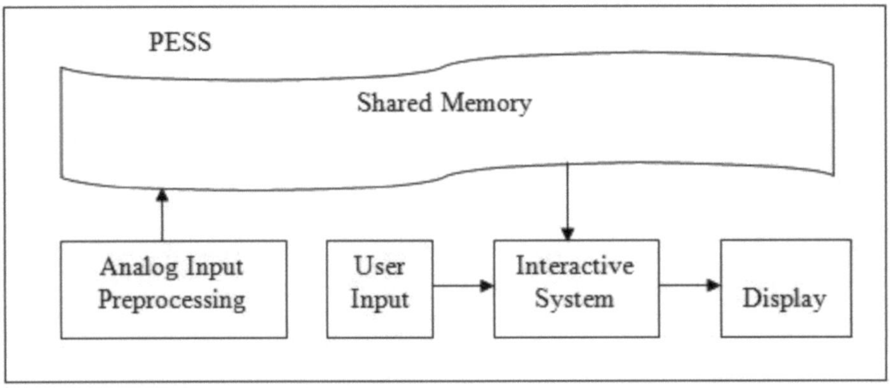

Fig. 7. Software architecture of PESS system

5.1 Analog input preprocessing

Signals from analog sensors must be converted to digital signals before electronic device can read them. The conversion from analog input to digital output is done using the ADC. The digital outputs which are in binary format is then calculated into human readable value in decimal value and presented in Volt parameter. The TS-5500 supports an eight-channel, 12-bit ADC capable of 60000 samples per second. Each channel is independently software programmable for a variety of analog input ranges: -10V to +10V, -5V to +5V, 0V to +10V and 0V to +5V. The ADC control register, the Hex 196 setting is outlined by Fig. 8 below. The IO address is read from right to left starting with 0. The settings are based on a bipolar mode with 5V output range for all channels.

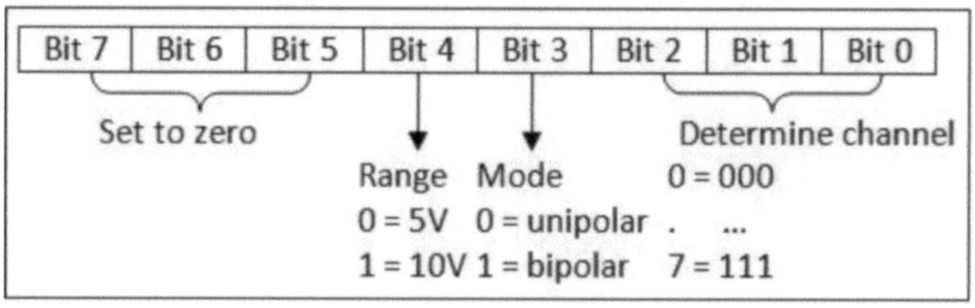

Fig. 8. ADC control register

The processes of Analog Input Preprocessing can be divided into four stages: initialization, bit checking, reading and storing. At the initialization stage, the permission to access ADC IO register must be set. Three registers are involved in accessing the ADC I/O address which are, Hex 195, Hex 196 and Hex 197. The digital output of an analog input is available after the ADC has completely converted the input within 11µs. The End of Conversion (EOC) status can be checked at bit 0 of register Hex 195. The conversion is completed if the bit 0 of Hex 195 indicates '0'. The digital output of the converted analog input is available at Hex 196 and Hex 197. 8 bits of them is available at Hex 196 which called as the lower 8 bits or LSB. The other 4 bits is available at Hex 197 which called as the upper 4 bits or MSB.

Analog Input Preprocessing algorithm

Step 1 : Initialize the IO permission of ADC
Step 2 : Create and attach shared memory file descriptor
Step 3 : Set up ADC control registers
Step 4 : Check End Of Conversion (EOC) signal
  4.1 If EOC signal HIGH (1)
    Go to Step 4 until EOC signal LOW (0)
Step 5 : Determine input mode
  : Check sign bit
Step 4 : Read all (12) digital output (LSB and MSB)
Step 5 : If input mode negative
  5.1 Perform two's compliment
Step 6: Convert binary value (digital output) to decimal value
Step 7: Store converted reading into shared memory
Step 8: End

Fig. 9. Analog Input Preprocessing algorithm

5.2 Data presentation

The *Interactive System* provides important information about the PESS system. The main goal of the *Interactive System* is to display current sensors' readings upon requested by the user. It also provides other information of the system (PESS) such as disk usage and memory status which viewed at the LCD panel. Another feature included in *Interactive System* is a control process. This process is to enable user to restart or shutdown the PESS for maintenance purposes. The matrix keypad functions as an input device that handles menu selection in the *Interactive System*. Fig. 10 outlines the main flow chart of the *Interactive System*.

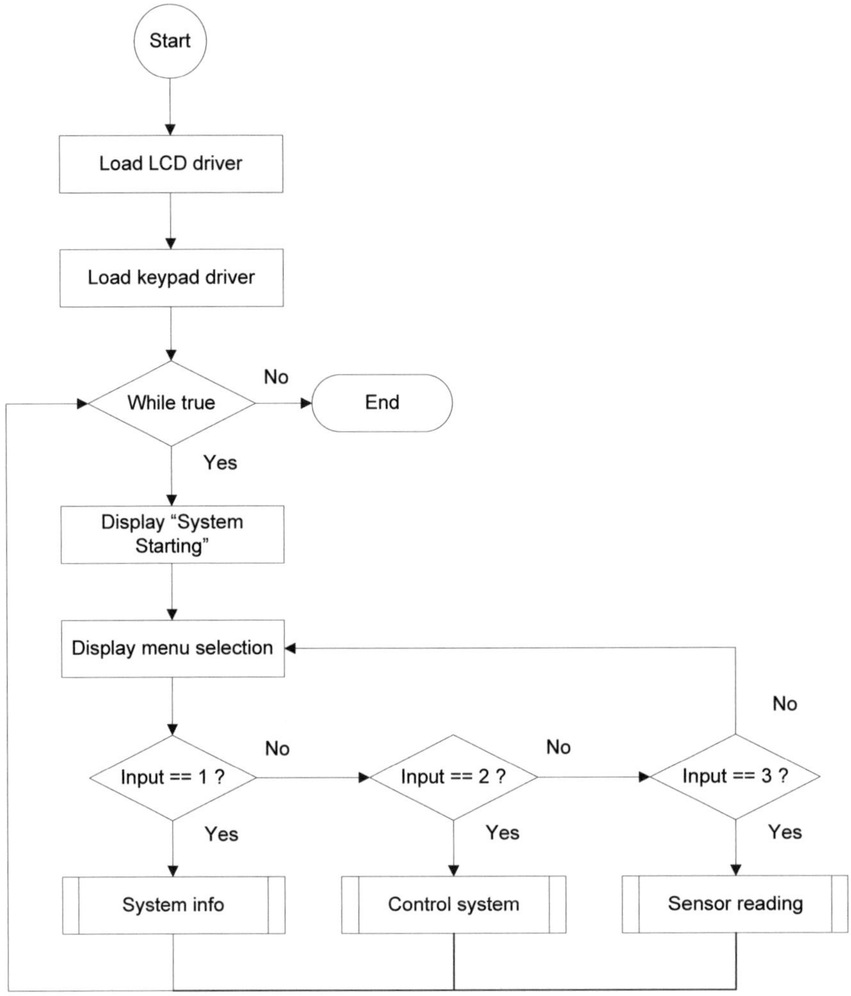

Fig. 10. *Interactive System* flowchart

Three options are provided: to check current sensors' readings, to check systems' information or to control the system. Three subroutines are created to handle those processes which are *system info*, *control system* and *sensor reading* as outlined by Fig. 10 above. Actually the processes of these three subroutines are carried out by combining the binary C code and shell scripts. Shell scripts retrieve current sensors' readings which are processed by the *sensor* program, and manipulate Linux commands to retrieve system information and control the system. The binary C code grabs the data given by the shell script codes and displays them.

6. PESS implementation

Standard method to gain the result of environment parameters such as water and air quality is using laboratory experiment. The laboratory experiment is not suitable for long period testing work such as in monitoring process. The alternatives method can resolve that limitation. The US Environment Protection Agency (EPA) define alternatives method as any method but has been demonstrated in specific cases to produce results adequate for compliance monitoring (Quevauviller, 2006).

The alternatives method leads to real-time data sampling which can produce instant output result for *in situ* deployment. It also provides easier usage with advance electronic devices in a compact size but can perform multitasks excellently. The handheld instrument usage is one of the alternatives methods such as using Data Acquisition (DAQ) device. The DAQ device such as SBC offers variety of peripherals to make it function as a standalone system. Meanwhile the ion specific electrodes is also been used in many application with handheld instrument. For example, non-invasive chemical sensor arrays provide a suitable technique for *in situ* monitoring (Bourgeois, 2003). Many researches use specific ion selective electrode or sensor array for detection of target environmental substance or gases (Carotta, 2000; Becker, 2000; Wilson, 2001; Lee, 2001).

The measurement of the LM35DZ temperature sensor is done without connecting the signal conditioning circuit. The LM35DZ sensors are only given a power supply and grounding. The sensor' outputs are connected directly to ADC port of SBC during measurement. Fig. 11 shows the experimental setup to acquire ion selective electrode's reading. Three parts involve here are: (1) SBC, (2) Sensors (electrodes) and (3) Signal conditioning circuit. While the red arrows marks from point A and B are the input and output from signal conditioning circuit respectively. Sensor reading' results are presented in next section.

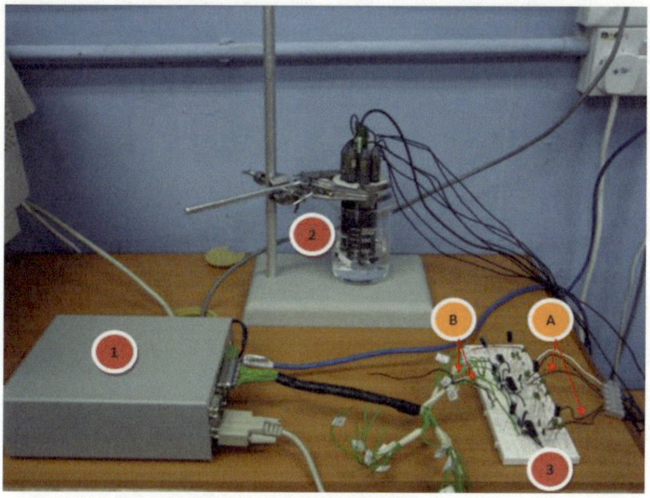

Fig. 11. Experimental setup of ion-selective electrodes

The programs called *sensor* and *Interactive System* are developed to handle all processes involved in Analog Input Preprocessing and Data Presentation modules respectively. Both modules are running separately but have a relationship in terms of data sharing. Fig. 12 outlines the state diagram for PESS system and the running processes listing. The current running process on PESS system including *sensor* and *Interactive System* as underlined in figure below. Analog Input Preprocessing module acquires data from sensors and storing converted data in a shared memory at PESS. These processes are repeated again with new inputs after certain time interval. While the *Interactive System* retrieve those converted data from shared memory and view it at LCD panel.

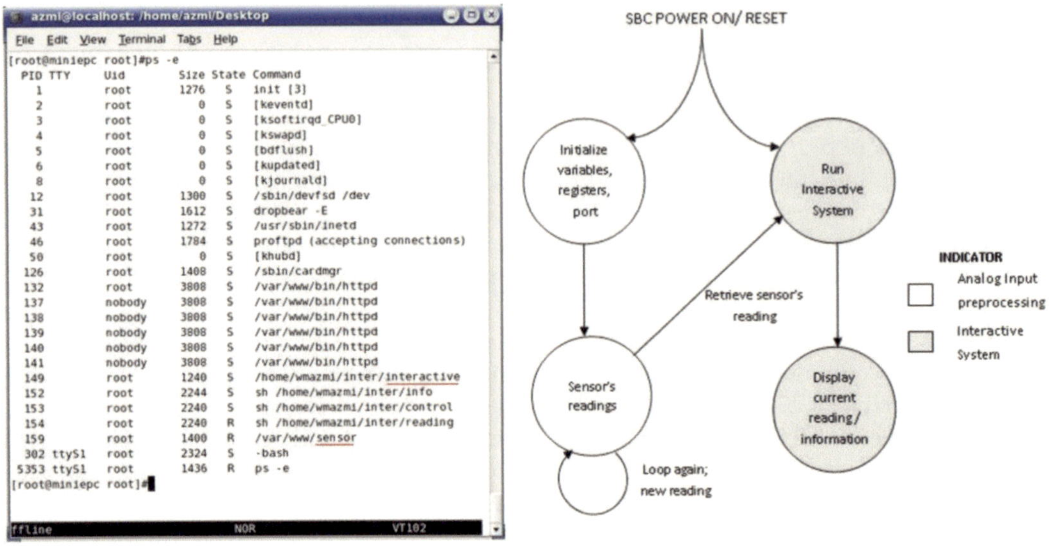

Fig. 12. PESS state diagram and running process listing

Four processes (programs) are set up to automatically start during the boot up program. The processes are: inserting the matrix keypad driver module; running *sensor* process; running the scripts (*info.sh*, *reading.sh* and *control.sh*) of *Interactive System*; and running the *Interactive System* program itself. These processes are underlined in Fig. 13. This procedure can be done by configuring how process will start up at */etc/init.d* directory.

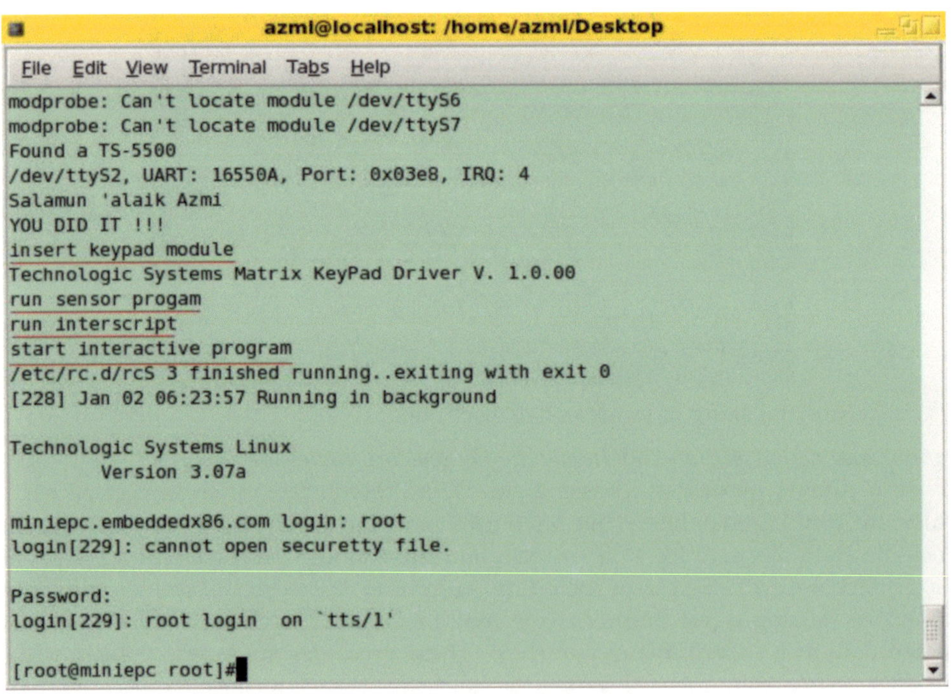

Fig. 13. Start processes automatically during system boot up

The integration between the SBC, the matrix keypad and the alphanumeric LCD display is to create an *Interactive System* for a standalone system. Fig. 14(a) shows the components that are connected to allocated ports. A serial ribbon cable is used to connect the matrix keypad and LCD panel to pin ports on SBC. Fig. 14(b) and Fig. 14(c) show the menu selection of *Interactive System* and current sensor' readings respectively.

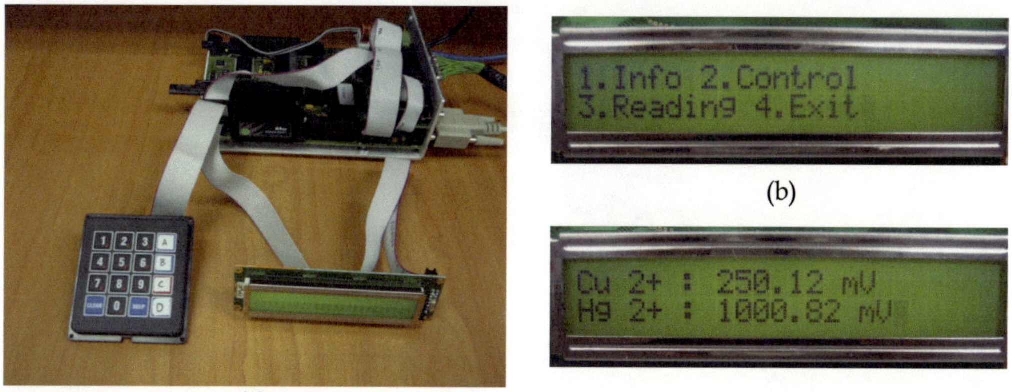

(a) (b) (c)

Fig. 14. a) Hardware used in *Interactive System* b) *Interactive System* menu selection c) Example of current sensor' readings

7. Result and discussion

Bit error is the value of an encoded bit that has been changed due to a transmission problem such as noise in the line and which is then interpreted incorrectly. Commonly notated as bit error ratio (BER), the ratio of the number of failed bits to the total number of bits calculated. The number of bits in the ADC determines the resolution of the data acquisition system. The resolution of an ADC is defined as follow (*Principle of Data Acquisition and Conversion*, 1994);

$$\text{Resolution} = \text{One LSB} = \frac{V_{FSR}}{2^n} \quad (1)$$

Where V_{FSR} is a full scale input voltage range and n is the number of bits.
The ADC is set up to read all eight analog channels using bipolar mode within 5V range. Therefore the total output range is 10V which are from -5V to +5V. The step resolution of digital output is calculated as below;

$$n = 12$$

$$V_{FSR} = 10\text{V} \ (-5\text{ V to } +5\text{ V})$$

$$\text{Resolution} = \frac{10\text{ V}}{2^{12}} = 2.44\ mV$$

Analog input reading verification is the important part in PESS development as it will ensure that the sensor' readings is correct and reliable. Verification testing of analog input reading is carried out by checking the output of each ADC channels. DC power supply is used as input to ADC and tapped manually to every channel. In a single reading, only one channel is given 1.0 V input while the rest is given 0 V using ground signal of SBC. The first

1.0 V input is given to channel 7, then to channel 6 until the last channel, channel 0. Fig. 15 shows the input from DC power supply while Fig. 16 show the result of analog input reading verification testing. From Fig. 15, the input from DC power supply is 1.002V as displayed by digital multimeter.

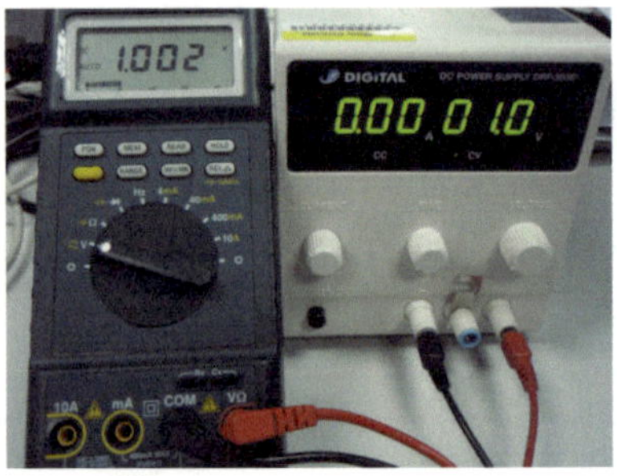

Fig. 15. Input from DC power supply

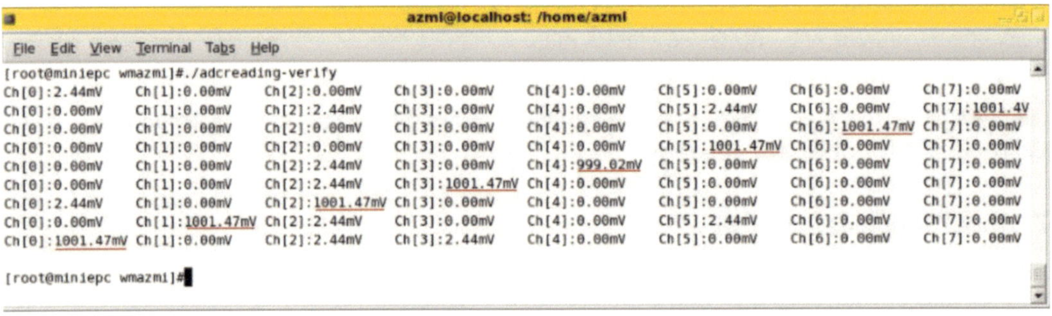

```
azml@localhost: /home/azml
File Edit View Terminal Tabs Help
[root@miniepc wmazmi]#./adcreading-verify
Ch[0]:2.44mV     Ch[1]:0.00mV     Ch[2]:0.00mV     Ch[3]:0.00mV     Ch[4]:0.00mV     Ch[5]:0.00mV     Ch[6]:0.00mV     Ch[7]:0.00mV
Ch[0]:0.00mV     Ch[1]:0.00mV     Ch[2]:2.44mV     Ch[3]:0.00mV     Ch[4]:0.00mV     Ch[5]:2.44mV     Ch[6]:0.00mV     Ch[7]:1001.4V
Ch[0]:0.00mV     Ch[1]:0.00mV     Ch[2]:0.00mV     Ch[3]:0.00mV     Ch[4]:0.00mV     Ch[5]:0.00mV     Ch[6]:1001.47mV  Ch[7]:0.00mV
Ch[0]:0.00mV     Ch[1]:0.00mV     Ch[2]:0.00mV     Ch[3]:0.00mV     Ch[4]:0.00mV     Ch[5]:1001.47mV  Ch[6]:0.00mV     Ch[7]:0.00mV
Ch[0]:0.00mV     Ch[1]:0.00mV     Ch[2]:2.44mV     Ch[3]:0.00mV     Ch[4]:999.02mV   Ch[5]:0.00mV     Ch[6]:0.00mV     Ch[7]:0.00mV
Ch[0]:0.00mV     Ch[1]:0.00mV     Ch[2]:2.44mV     Ch[3]:1001.47mV  Ch[4]:0.00mV     Ch[5]:0.00mV     Ch[6]:0.00mV     Ch[7]:0.00mV
Ch[0]:2.44mV     Ch[1]:0.00mV     Ch[2]:1001.47mV  Ch[3]:0.00mV     Ch[4]:0.00mV     Ch[5]:0.00mV     Ch[6]:0.00mV     Ch[7]:0.00mV
Ch[0]:0.00mV     Ch[1]:1001.47mV  Ch[2]:2.44mV     Ch[3]:0.00mV     Ch[4]:0.00mV     Ch[5]:2.44mV     Ch[6]:0.00mV     Ch[7]:0.00mV
Ch[0]:1001.47mV  Ch[1]:0.00mV     Ch[2]:2.44mV     Ch[3]:2.44mV     Ch[4]:0.00mV     Ch[5]:0.00mV     Ch[6]:0.00mV     Ch[7]:0.00mV

[root@miniepc wmazmi]#
```

Fig. 16. Analog input reading verification output

Every channel is given 0 V input for first reading as shown in first line in Fig. 16. The error recorded in first line reading is 2.44 mV which is given by channel 1 which equals to 1 step resolution. Then 1.0 V input is given to channel 7 as shown by the second reading and for other channels the input given is 0V. The reading is presented in 2 floating point. From Fig. 16, the readings recorded are 1001.47 mV and 999.02 mV for channels that was given 1.0 V input. The reading variants are 0.53 mV and 2.98 mV respectively. From the results above, the analog input reading has small error which are 1 and 2 step resolutions so that the readings is considered reliable.

The readings of temperature sensor at room temperature is around 1110 mV and 1120 mV as shown by line 1 until line 5 in Fig. 17 below. Heat was forced to the temperature sensor using a lighter (fire) for a few seconds. The readings are increased at the moment the heating process as shown by line 6 until line 10 in Fig. 17.

A measurement of ion-selective electrodes is carried out to observe their output reading reliability. The reading of ion-selective electrodes are considered reliable if their readings are stable and do not fluctuate. The Copper electrode is tested with Copper standard solution which has been produced by mixing sterile water and Copper liquid. In this research, five different standard solution densities are used: 10 ppm, 20 ppm, 30 ppm, 40 ppm and 50 ppm. Firstly, the Copper sensor is tested using 10 ppm standard solution. The Copper ion-selective electrode together with the reference electrode are immersed in 10 ppm Copper standard solution. Measurement is started five minutes after those electrodes immersed. The measurement is repeated for 20 ppm of Copper standard solution. These steps are repeated until the standard solution reaches 50 ppm. Fig. 18 shows the reading of Copper ion-selective electrode. From the graphs, the readings are decrease with higher standard solution density for each case.

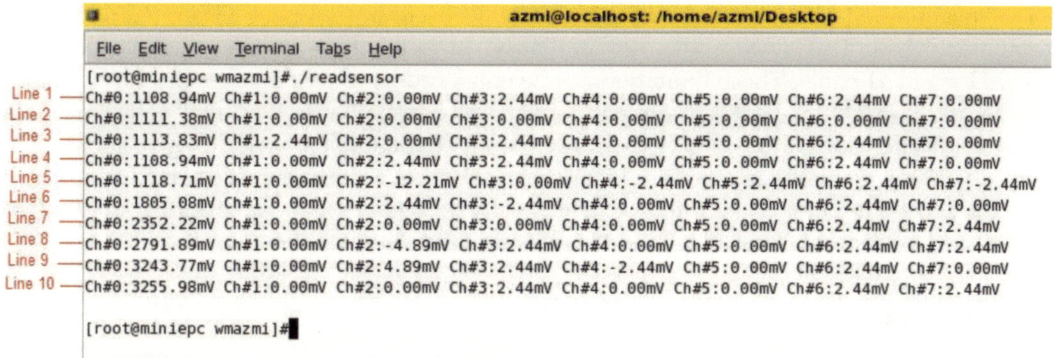

Fig. 17. LM35DZ temperature sensor readings

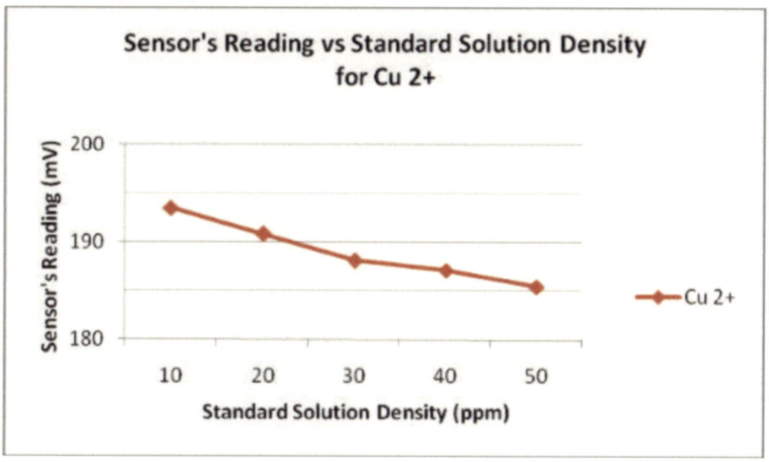

Fig. 18. Copper sensor's reading versus standard solution density

8. Conclusion

Data Acquisition System (DAS) is one of common system currently applied in industrial application such as automation control, alert system and monitoring system. The advancement of electronic technology has led to tremendous applications using embedded systems. Embedded based application has led to portable and small form factor system with medium or high speed processor. In this research, a DAS has been developed using a 32bit Single Board Computer (SBC). The developed DAS is an integration of SBC, matrix keypad and LCD display and named as Portable Embedded Sensing System (PESS). PESS can be used as a data logger for a short term data collection which can provide immediate results for portable works either for indoor or outdoor experiment.

Two software modules developed in PESS systems which are Analog Input Preprocessing and Data Presentation. The processes involved in Analog Input Preprocessing are acquiring analog sensor's input, converting analog signal to digital signal and calculating digital output to human readable values. These processes are done by a program named *sensor*. An *Interactive System* handles input given by user via matrix keypad and output to the LCD display for Data Presentation modules.
PESS has limited data storage capacity since it used a Compact Flash (CF) to store temporary data. This system also has limitation in term of visualization where data are viewed via LCD panel. These limitation can be enhanced by extending the PESS system into a network based DAS. PESS system can be used as Sensor Node (SN) that collecting data from fields and sending the collected data to the server that able in providing larger storage capacity. The user interface can be developed to provide interactive data presentation which can be access remotely via internet. The network based DAS is normally applied in monitoring system especially for long period and scheduled activities.

9. References

Al-Beik, H., Meryash, N. & Orsan, I. A. (2005). *Detect, Verify, Locate, Build (DVLB) Rover.* Project Report, Worcester Polytechnic Institute.

Alderighi, M., Anzalone, O., Bartolucci, M., Cardella, G., Cavallaro, S., De Filippo, E., et al. (2002). CHIMERA data acquisition and computational system using DSP-based VME modules. *IEEE Transactions on Nuclear Science, 49*(2), 432-436.

Application Notes 270. (2000). *Analog-Signal Data Acquisition in Industrial Systems.* Retrieved April 14, 2006 from http://pdfserv.maxim-ic.com/en/an/AN270.pdf

Baxter, M. (2001). Embedded Linux SBCs. *Linux Journal.* Retrieved March 23, 2006 from http://www.linuxjournal.com/files/linuxjournal.com/linuxjournal/articles/047/4726/4726t1.html

Becker, T., Mühlberger, S., Braunmühl C. Bosch-v., Müller, G., Ziemann, T & Hechtenberg, K. V. (2000). Air pollution monitoring using tin-oxide-based microreactor system, *Sensors and Actuators B: Chemical, 69*(1-2), 108-119

Bourgeois, W., Romain, A-C, Nicolas, J. & Stuetz, R. M. (2003). The use of sensor array for environmental monitoring: interests and limitations. *Journal of Environmental Monitoring, 5*, 852-860.

Burckle, R. A., (n.d.). *The Evolution of Single Board Computers.* Retrieved Jun 30, 2006 from http://www.winsystems.com/whitepapers/SBC_Evolution.pdf

Carotta, M. C., Martinelli, G., Crema, L., Gallana, M., Merli, M., Ghiotti, G et al. (2000). Array of thick film sensors for atmospheric pollutant monitoring, *Sensors and Actuators B: Chemical, 68*(1-3), 1-8.

Eyre, J. & Bier, J. (2000). The evolution of DSP processors. *IEEE Signal Processing Magazine, 17*(2), 43-51.

Hansen, S., Jordan, T., Kiper, T., Claes, D., Snow, G., Berns, H., Burnett, T. H., Gran, R. & Wilkes, R. J. (2004). Low-cost data acquisition card for school-network cosmic ray detectors. *IEEE Transaction on Nuclear Science, 51*(3), 926-930.

Hoopes, D., Davis, T., Norman, K. & Helps, R. (2003). An Autonomous Mobile Robot Development for Teaching a Graduate Level Mechatronics Course. *Proceedings of*

33rd ASEE/IEEE Frontiers in Education Conference, F4E-17-F4E22. Retrieved March 23, 2006 http://cyber.felk.cvut.cz/gerstner/reports/GL128.pdf

Ismail, Y. (1998). *Data Acquisition System with Embedded Digital Signal Processor for Instrumentation/Control Applications (Design and Implementation).* Degree Thesis, Universiti Islam Malaysia.

James, K. (2000). *PC Interfacing and Data Acquisition Techniques for Measurement, Instrumentation and Control.* Oxford: Newnes.

Laymon, C. M., Miyaoka, R. S., Park, B. K. & Lewellen, T. K. (2003). Simplified FPGA-based data acquisition system for PET. *IEEE Transactions on Nuclear Science, 50*(5), 1483-1486.

Lee, D-D. & Lee, D-S. (2001). Environmental gas sensors, *IEEE Sensors Journal, 1*(3), 214-224.

LinuxDevices (n.d.). *A Linux-oriented Intro to Embeddable Single Board Computers.* Retrieved March 23, 2006 from http://www.linuxdevices.com/articles/AT6449817972.html

Martin, S. (1990). PC-based Data Acquisition in an Industrial Environment. *IEE Colloquium on PC-Based Instrumentation,* 2/1 – 2/3.

Microlink. (n.d.) *Technical Notes: Data Acquisition Techniques.* Retrieved May 13, 2006 from http://www.microlink.co.uk/dataaq.html

Misal, C. S. & Conrad, J.M. (2007). Designing a pH data acquisition and logging device using an inexpensive microcontroller. *IEEE Proceedings SoutheastCon,* 217-220.

Ng, K. Y. (1994). *General Purpose Data Acquisition and Process Control System.* Degree Thesis, Universiti Malaya.

Omata, K., Fujita, Y., Yoshikawa, N., Sekiguchi, M. & Shida, Y. (1992). A Data Acquisition System based on a Personal Computer. *IEEE Transaction on Nuclear Science, 39*(2), 143-147.

OPA2111 (1993). *Dual Low noise precision difet operational amplifier.* Retrieved April 14, 2006 from http://www.datasheetcatalog.org/datasheet/BurrBrown/mXsrqyy.pdf

Perera, A., Gutierrez-Osuna, R., & Marco, S. (2001). IPNOSE: A Portable Electronic Nose Based on Embedded Technology for Intensive Computation and Time Dependent Signal Processing. *Proceeding of the 8th Intl. Symp. On Olfaction an Electronic Nose,* 1-6.

Peters, B., Wardrop, A., Lahti, D., Herzog, H., O'Connor, T., & DeCoursey, R. (2007). Flight SEU Performance of the Single Board Computer (SBC) Utilizing Hardware Voted Commercial PowerPC Processors On-board the CALIPSO Satellite. *IEEE Radiation Effects Data Workshop 2007, 0,* 16-25.

Quevauviller, P, Thomas, O. & Beken, A. V-D. (2006). *Wastewater Quality Monitoring and Treatment.* West Sussex, England: Wiley.

Rangnekar, S., Nema, R. K. & Raman, P. (1995). PC based data acquisition and monitoring system for synchronous machines. *IEEE/IAS International Conference on Industrial Automation and Control,* 195-197.

Riley, T. C., Endreny, T. A. & Halfman, J. D. (2006). Monitoring soil moisture and water table height with a low-cost data logger. *Computers & Geosciences, 32*(1), 135-140.

Rongen, H. (n.d.). *Introduction to PC-Based Data Acquisition Systems.* Retrieved October 23, 2006 from http://www.fz-juelich.de/zel/datapool/page/160/DAQ.pdf

Wilson, D. M., Hoyt, S., Janata, J., Booksh, K. & Obando, L. (2001). Chemical sensor for portable, handheld field instruments, *IEEE Sensors Journal, 1*(4), 256-274.

Zabolotny, W. M., Roszkowski, P., Kierzkowski, K., Pozniak, K., Romaniuk, R. & Simrock, S. (2003). *Distributed Embedded PC Based Control and Data Acquisition System for TESLA Cavity Controller and Simulator*. Retrieved March 16, 2007 from http://tesla.desy.de/new_pages/TESLA_Reports/2003/pdf_files/tesla2003-34.pdf

7

Microcontroller-based Data Acquisition Device for Process Control and Monitoring Applications

Vladimír Vašek, Petr Dostálek and Jan Dolinay
Tomas Bata University in Zlín
Czech Republic

1. Introduction

Process measurement is one of the most important tasks in the whole control system. It is determined by the fact that control accuracy is fully dependent on how preciously measuring chain works. Present-day there is available number of devices performing data acquisition tasks - standard cards for PCI or ISA bus which are suitable for standard personal computers and its industrial versions and modules for industrial automation usually equipped with RS485, CAN and other interfaces. Independent category is formed by smart sensors incorporating sensor, converter to unified signal and data acquisition device in one embedded system with very compact dimensions and low power consumption. They have number of advantageous features such as automatic diagnostic and calibration, high accuracy and immunity against electromagnetic interference due to short signal paths. On the other hand lower operating temperature range reduces their usage to laboratory applications, automotive and aircraft industry where compact dimensions and low weight are crucial. Quite often occurred situations when it is necessary to measure data in terrain where it is not possible to use standard computer equipped with DAQ card. In these cases laptop computer equipped with portable data acquisition device may be very advantageous. On the market are available devices equipped with USB 2.0 connectivity which can fully functionally substitute PCI cards. But they are not able to work without connected computer which must continually control all DAQ operations. Therefore it is not possible to use them in applications where is required long-term monitoring and archiving process quantities in distant areas without access to mains power.

This contribution proposes design of multi-channel portable data acquisition device based on low cost general-purpose 8-bit microcontroller Freescale 68HC908GP32, which was developed in our department mainly for control and monitoring educational laboratory models. First part deals with hardware design of the DAQ device with focus on description of operation of individual functional blocks. After that follows description of internal software (firmware) based on real-time operating system RTMON for HC08, which was developed on our department especially for microcontroller-based embedded systems with CPU08 main processor core. Next chapters discuss DAQ device software support in form of program libraries for MS Visual C++, Control Web and Matlab/Simulink development environments, which can significantly improve development time of new process control or monitoring applications. And finally last part deals with verification of the developed DAQ device with control of selected laboratory model.

2. Data acquisition device hardware design

2.1 Hardware overview

Hardware design of the DAQ device is fully adopted to support 16 analog inputs with 12-bit resolution, 8 digital inputs and outputs and one analog output with 12-bit resolution with stress on low power consumption enabling long operation when battery supply is used. The core of the DAQ device is 8-bit general purpose Motorola microcontroller 68HC908GP32 with Von-Neumann architecture which is fully up-ward compatible with the 68HC05 family. On the chip are integrated timer interface with input capture and output compare functions, 8-channel analog-to-digital converter with 8-bit resolution, up to 33 general-purpose I/O pins, clock generator module with PLL, serial communication interface and serial peripheral interface. M68HC908GP32 has implemented several protective and security functions such as low-voltage inhibit which monitors power supply voltage, computer operates properly (COP) counter and FLASH memory protection mechanism preventing unauthorized reading of the user's program. Internal RAM memory has capacity of 512B and FLASH memory 32 KB. Internal clock frequency can be 8 MHz at 5 V operating voltage or 4 MHz at 3 V operating voltage. Microcontroller also supports wait and stop low-power modes (Freescale, 2008)

Central processor unit CPU08 which is the main part of M68HC908GP32 microcontroller is fully object code compatible with M68HC05. This feature allows easy code migration to new architecture providing high speed, low power and better processing capabilities.

Central processor unit features can be summarized in the following points:

- 8 MHz bus speed at 5 V, 4 MHz bus speed at 3 V
- 16-bit stack pointer with new stack manipulation instructions
- 16-bit index register with index register instructions
- 78 new instructions
- Memory to memory moves without using the accumulator
- 16 addressing modes including stack relative
- 64 Kbytes program/data memory space
- Fully static low-voltage/low-power design (Freescale, 2006)

Analog-to-digital conversion is performed by the A/D converter Linear Technology LTC1298. It is micro power, 2-channel, 12-bit switched-capacitor successive approximation sampling A/D converter which can operate on 5 V to 9 V power supplies. Communication with microcontrollers is handled by 3-wire synchronous serial interface. It typically draws only 250µA of supply current during conversion and only 1nA in power down mode in which enters after each conversion (Linear Technology, 1994).

Digital-to-analog circuit utilizes 12-bit D/A converter Burr-Brown DAC7611 with internal 2.435V reference and high speed rail-to-rail amplifier. It requires a single 5 V supply. Power consumption is only 2.5 mW at 5 V. Build-in synchronous serial interface is compatible with variety of digital signal processors and microcontrollers (Burr-Brown, 1998).

2.2 Circuits design

Electronic circuits of the data acquisition device can be divided into the seven main functional blocks as depicted in the Fig.1: analog-to-digital converter with analog multiplexer circuits, microcontroller circuits, digital-to-analog converter and amplifier circuits, digital I/O driver circuits, serial communication interface RS232 and finally power supply circuits.

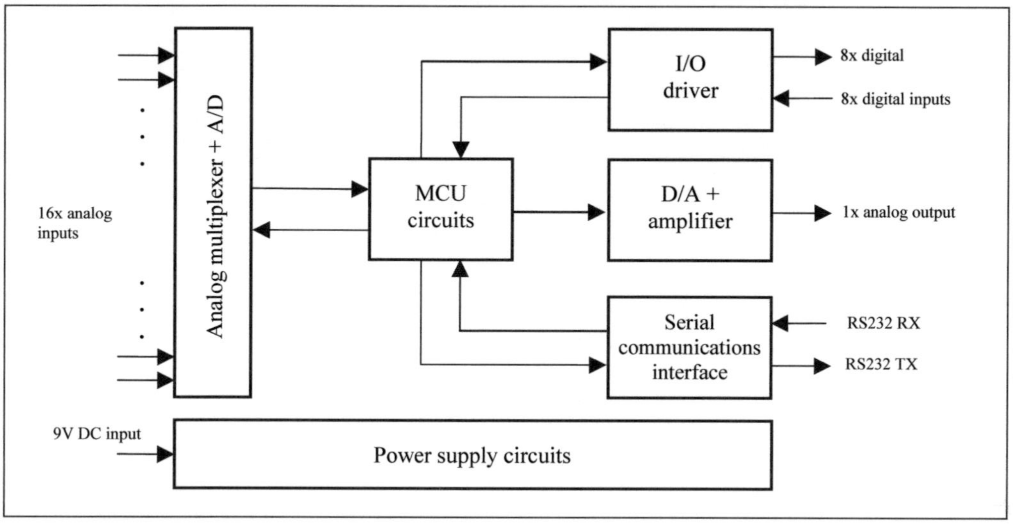

Fig. 1. Block diagram of the DAQ device

MCU circuits (Fig.2) incorporate all electronics circuits needed for correct function of the microcontroller M68HC908. They consists of Pierce crystal oscillator with output frequency of 32.768 kHz connected to OSC1 and OSC2 pins of the MCU and filter network (parts R3, C3, C4) needed by internal phase-locked loop circuit (PLL) allowing programmable selection of output frequency. Reset (RST) and interrupt request (IRQ) pins are permanently connected through pull-up resistors R4 and R5 to high level, because their function is not in data acquisition device used. Reset of the MCU is automatically generated after power on by internal circuits of the microcontroller. Output frequency of the Pierce oscillator is by internal PLL circuit increased to 32 MHz resulting in internal bus clock frequency of 8 MHz which is used as reference frequency of the CPU and most internal peripherals. Ports PTA and PTB are completely dedicated for digital input and output functions except pin PTB0/AD0 which is used in its alternative function as input of analog-to-digital converter for monitoring of accumulator battery voltage. Low voltage condition occurs when supply voltage drops below 6.5 V. So voltage of the one NiMH accumulator in the battery drops to 1.08 V indicating that approximately 80 - 90 % of its capacity is discharged. Correct DAQ device operation is guaranteed at minimum voltage of 5.5 V. Pin PTD3 is connected to the LED diode indicating status of the device. PTD0 to PTD2 pins provides binary selection of active input analog channel, PTC0 to PTC4 pins perform synchronous serial communication with A/D and D/A converters.

Digital input / output driver circuit (Fig.3) has two important functions. Firstly, it protects microcontroller inputs from electrostatic discharge which may occur during handling and connecting DAQ device to the measured object and secondly, it boosts output current from microcontroller pins and protects them against overload or short-circuits. It uses two non inverting 3-state high-speed octal bus buffers 74HC244 with 35mA maximum current output capability per pin.

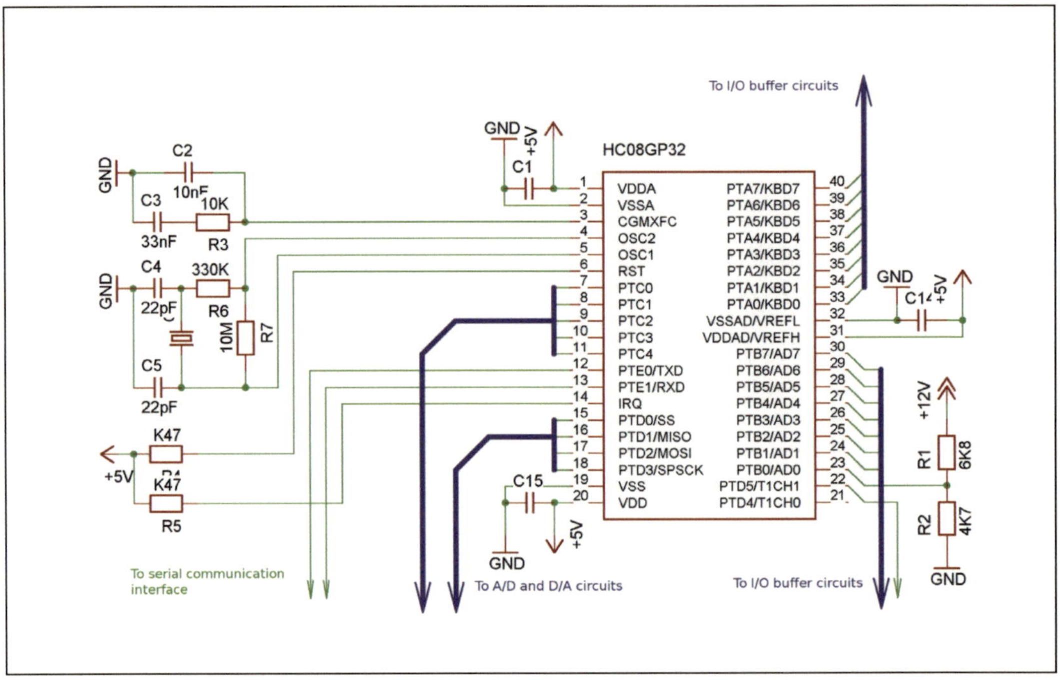

Fig. 2. Microcontroller circuits schematics.

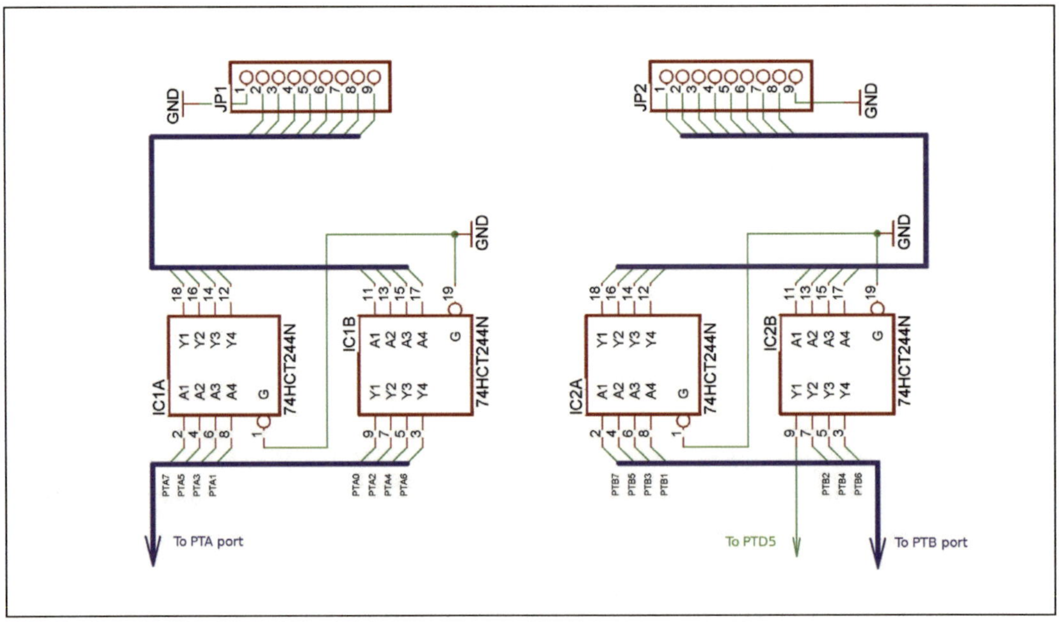

Fig. 3. Digital input/output buffer schematics.

Analog multiplexer, A/D and D/A converter circuits schematics is depicted in the Fig.4. Measured analog voltage signals 0 - 10 V first enters the input dividers performing signal conditioning to voltage range of 0 - 5 V to meet specifications of analog-to-digital converter.

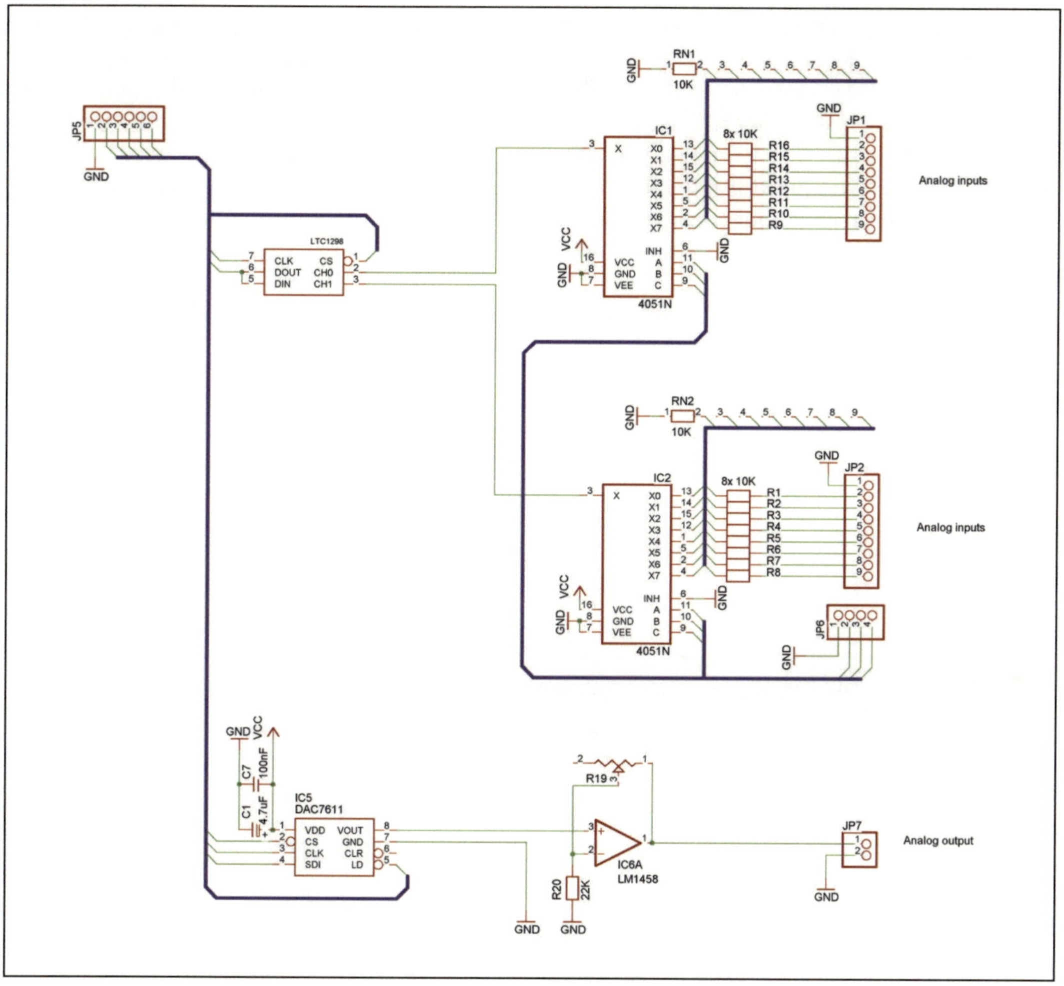

Fig. 4. Analog multiplexer, A/D and D/A converter circuits schematics.

After that they are switched by two 8-channel high-speed analog multiplexers 74HC4051 to the two input analog channels CH0 and CH1 of 12-bit A/D converter LTC1298. Input channel pair selection is realized by MCU pins PTD0, PTD1 and PTD2. Microcontroller communicates with A/D converter using pins PTC1 (data clock), PTC2 (serial data in/out) and PTC4 (chip select). One conversion is done after 16 clock signal periods resulting in maximum of 12.5 kHz sampling rate at clock frequency of 200 kHz.

Analog output circuits are based on digital-to-analog converter DAC7611 with 12-bit resolution. It is controlled by MCU pins PTC0 (chip select), PTC1 (data clock), PTC2 (serial data in) and PTC3 (load/strobe). One D/A conversion takes place after 12 clock periods, output settling time is 7μs to 1 LSB. At the converter output is connected operational amplifier MC1458 in non-inverting configuration amplifying output D/A voltage to the standard range of 0 - 10 V. Exact output range can be adjusted by variable resistor R19.

Data acquisition device contains three independent power supplies. Digital parts (MCU circuits, input/output driver, serial communications interface and D/A converter) are supplied by circuit depicted in the Fig.5. It uses low-drop 5V/1A regulator LM2940 in manufacturer's recommended wiring enabling correct operation with input voltage down to 5.5 V. Input of the supply is protected against overloading or polarity reversing by fast acting fuse. Analog-to-digital converter is supplied from high-precision voltage reference LM336-Z5.0 which is connected to adjustable current source LM334. Output voltage can be adjusted to the exact 5 V value by variable resistor R18 (Fig.6). Analog output amplifier is supplied by DC-DC converter ICL7662 providing positive and negative voltages for analog output operational amplifier from single supply.

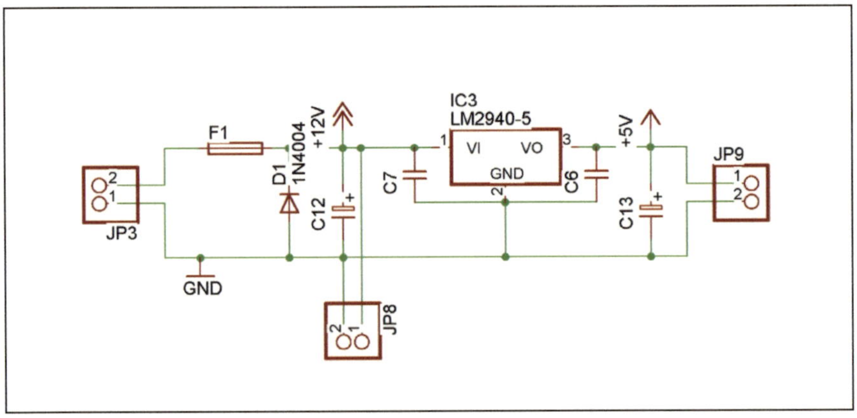

Fig. 5. Power supply for digital circuits schematic

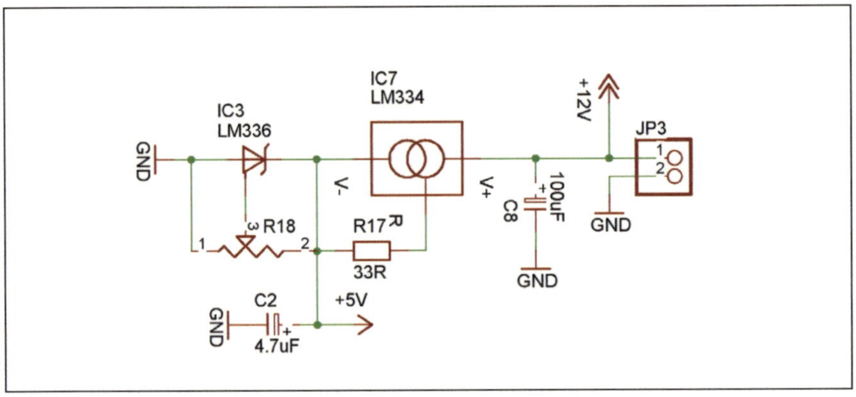

Fig. 6. Power supply for A/D converter schematics

Serial communications interface utilizes standard TTL to RS232 and RS232 to TTL converter MAX232 in manufacturer's reference wiring (Fig. 7). It is connected to microcontroller via pins PTE0/TxD and PTE1/RxD to serial communications module.

Data acquisition device is realized on two printed circuit boards (PCB), which are connected together using single row pin headers. First PCB (Fig.8 – left picture) contains mainly digital circuits - microcontroller, input / output drivers and serial communications interface. It also carries main +5V power supply equipped with low-drop voltage regulator. While second PCB (Fig.8 - right picture) incorporates all analog signal processing circuits - analog-to-digital and digital-to-analog converter, output amplifier, analog multiplexers, DC-DC converter and finally reference voltage source for A/D converter. Device features are summarized in Table 1.

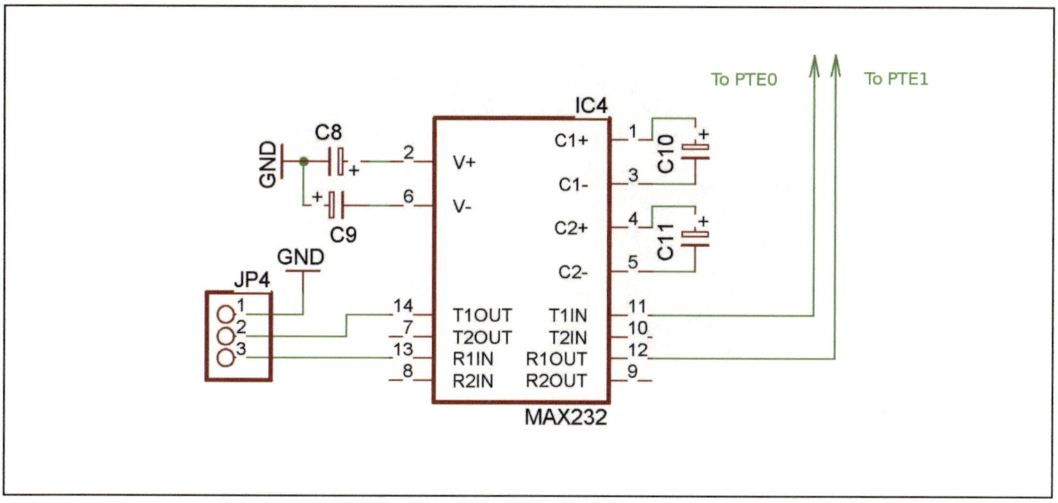

Fig. 7. Serial communication interface schematics

Fig. 8. Finalized DAQ device printed circuit boards

Digital inputs	8 channels, TTL compatible
Digital outputs	8 channels, TTL compatible
Analog inputs	16 channels, 12 bits resolution, input range 0 - 10 V
Analog outputs	1 channel, 12 bits resolution, output range 0 - 10 V
Supply voltage	6.5 to 9V DC
Communication	RS232 interface, 57600 Bd, 8-bit data, 1 start bit, 1 stop bit

Table 1. Technical parameters of the DAQ device

Fig. 9. Photograph of the prototype DAQ unit

3. DAQ device firmware design

DAQ device internal software is based on real-time operating system RTMON for HC08, which was developed on our department especially for microcontroller-based embedded systems with CPU08 main processor core. So software is formed of RTMON core and individual processes which perform all necessary tasks. Each process activity is controlled by operating system core on the basis of process priority and other information stored in the task descriptor. Structure of the DAQ device firmware is depicted in the Fig. 10. There are 4 main processes and 1 interrupt handling routine. RTMON core and program processes functions are described in chapters 4.1 and 4.2.

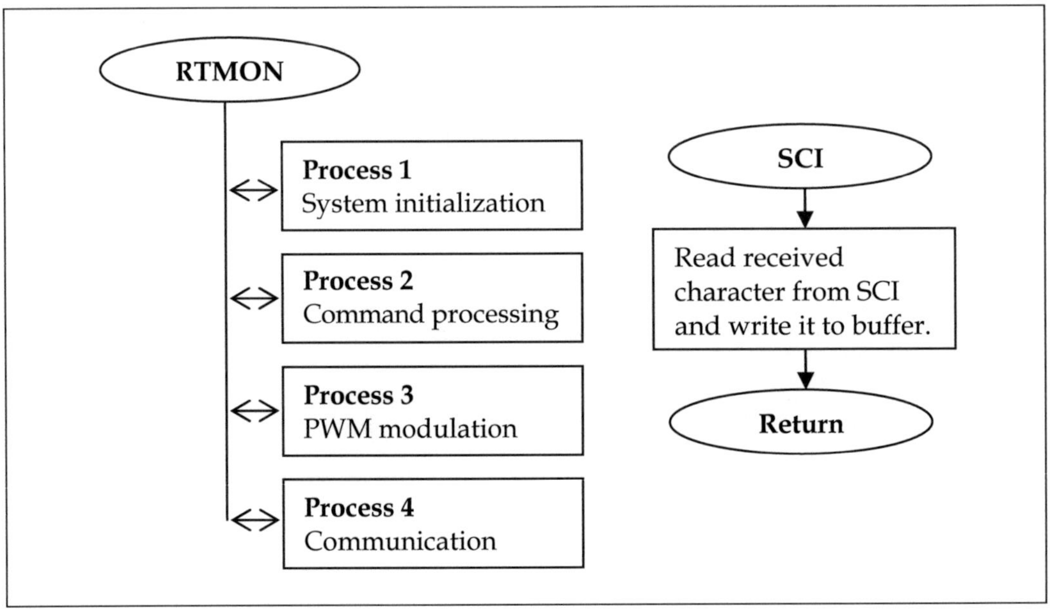

Fig. 10. Internal software structure

3.1 Real-time operating system RTMON

RTMON is preemptive multitasking operating system which is simplified to great extend to allow easy use for programmers. It is written in C language with the exception of small platform-specific code written in assembler. The scheduler assigns time slices to processes based on their priority. The priority is integer in the range 1 to 254. Priority 0 is the highest and is reserved for the RTMON initialization process and priority 255 is the lowest and is reserved for the idle process (called dummy in RTMON).

RTMON allows execution of two different types of processes (tasks): normal processes which execute only once (such process typically contains infinite loop) and periodical process which is started automatically by RTMON with given period. These periodical processes are useful for many applications, for example, in discrete controllers which need to periodically sample the input signal and update the outputs.

For the sake of simplicity of both the implementation and usage, several restrictions are applied. First, the RAM memory for processes and their stacks is statically allocated for the maximal number of processes as defined in configuration file. In the user program, it is not possible to use this memory even if there are fewer processes defined. In case more RAM is needed for the user program, the maximum number of tasks and/or stack-pool size can be changed in configuration file and the RTMON library must be rebuild.

The priority of each task must be unique, so that in each moment one task (the one with highest priority) can be selected and executed on the CPU. The scheduler does not support cyclical switching of several processes with the same priority on the CPU in round-robin fashion; it simply chooses the task with highest priority from the list of tasks which are ready to run. Processes can be created on the fly, but it is not possible to free and reuse memory of a process. No more than the maximal number of processes can be created, even if some processes were previously deleted.

These restrictions, however, do not present any big problem for most applications and allow for small kernel code size and ease of use.

There are only two objects (data structures) which RTMON contains: process (task) and queue. The queues are buffers for transferring data between processes. It would more properly be called mailboxes in our implementation as each queue can contain only 1 message. Several queues can be created, each containing a message (data buffer) of certain size. The size can be specified when creating the queue and is limited by the total size of RAM reserved for all buffers of all the queues (queue pool size). Processes can read and write data to the queue and wait for the queue to become empty or to become full. This allows for use of the queue also as a synchronization object (semaphore).

The RTMON uses timer interrupt which occurs at certain period (e.g. 10 ms) to periodically execute the scheduler, which decides which process will run in the next time slice. The timer interrupt routine is implemented in assembly language. It first stores CPU registers onto the stack and then calls RTMON kernel, which is a C function. The kernel then finds the process with highest priority which is in ready-to-run state and switches the context, so that the code of this process is executed after return from the interrupt service routine. If no process is ready to run, then a special dummy process is executed. This dummy process is contained within RTMON code and does nothing.

The following basic operations can be performed with a process in RTMON. Each operation corresponds to a function in the RTMON library which user program can call:

- create process
- start process

- stop process
- delay process
- continue process execution
- abort (delete) process

For queues there are the following functions:

- create queue (specify size)
- write to a queue with/without waiting
- read from a queue with/without waiting

There are also two functions for controlling the RTMON core:

- initialize RTMON
- end RTMON operation

The RTMON system is used as a precompiled library accompanied by a header file. This simplifies the organization of the project and the build process. User enables RTMON usage in his program by including the header file (rtmon.h) in his source and adding the library to his project.

3.2 Processes functions description

Process 1 is highest priority process which performs DAQ device initialization after power up or reset. It sets all digital outputs to low state (logic 0), setups serial communications interface to communication speed of 57600 Bd, 8-bit data frame, 1 start bit and 1 stop bit, sets analog output to 0 V and finally initializes all necessary data structures. Because of its highest priority no other processes can be switched by OS core into the "run" state. After all initializations are done, process suspends itself.

Process 2 performs all tasks related to command interpretation and execution. It waits for complete command string in the receiver buffer which is handled by serial communication interface (SCI) interrupt routine. This interrupt routine is automatically called when SCI receive one character from the higher-level control system (personal computer or programmable logic controller, for example). When command is completely received in the buffer, process will decode it and executes required action.

Process 3 is periodically activated process performing pulse-width modulation (PWM) on all 8 digital output channels when it is demanded. Its priority is set to higher level than process 2 and process 4 because the PWM is time critical function sensitive to accurate timing. Its resolution is 8-bit allows setting 256 different duty cycles at output. Period of the PWM signal is set to 1000 ms which is optimal value for many controlled systems with higher time constants (heating elements, for example).

Process 4 provides communication via RS232 serial interface with supervisory system. It generates responses to all commands regarding to defined communication protocol include error processing. It has defined lowest priority among of all processes.

3.3 Communication protocol

In order to achieve compatibility with many software platforms, universal ASCII-based communication protocol was chosen. Very advantageous is the possibility to send all implemented commands using generic terminal program that is included in most operating systems. Each command can be divided up to five parts depending on concrete function implementation. Communication starts with character "~" then must follow command name with fixed length of two characters (for example "AO" means set analog output).

After it is the first command parameter with length of one character (channel index) next character is space followed by second parameter (value). Command must be terminated by CRLF sequence.

Command:

~	A	O	0	_	4	.	2	5	CR	LF

- set analog output channel 0 to 4.25 V

Response:

~	A	O	0	=	4	.	2	5	CR	LF

- notification that AO0 was successfully set to 4.25 V

Fig. 11. Communication protocol example

4. Software support

Although communication protocol is very simple and easy to understand it is more comfortable in a control application to call functions which can automatically generate commands for the data acquisition device and consequently process its response. Application developer then does not need to know exact communication protocol and do not need to program it. This simplification results in faster program development and reduction of debugging time. For the portable data acquisition device there were created supporting program libraries for Visual C++, Control Web 5 and Matlab 6.5 (and higher versions with serial port object support) software environments.

4.1 Support libraries for visual C and Matlab

Created libraries incorporate all functions implemented in the device including error processing. For device testing and diagnosis, a DAQ test utility was created. This program can test all functions of the DAQ device and may be very helpful for testing wire connections to the monitored or controlled system. Main window of diagnostic utility is depicted in the Fig.12. Left part of the window "Analog inputs readings" contains 16 edit boxes indicating current voltage levels presented in the analog inputs. Its value is periodically updated with the period of 500 ms. "Digital inputs readings" fields show same information but for digital inputs (only two states 0 and 1). In the window part "Digital output setting" are 8 buttons enabling changing the state of the each digital output. And finally last control "Analog output setting" providing slider for setting the output voltage level on analog output channel.

Matlab 6.5 library has the same functions implemented with only one difference – in place of device handle is a serial port object. Each function is available in separate m-file, so it is very simple to modify them by the user. In the Table 2 are listed all implemented library functions for Visual C++ software environment. Matlab 6.5 library includes similar functions with only one difference – in place of device handle is a serial port object.

Function	Description
HANDLE **Open_device** (const char*)	Opens device connected to specified serial port ("COM1", "COM2", …) and returns device handle.
int **Close_device** (HANDLE h)	Closes device with specified handle.
int **Set_digital_out** (HANDLE h, int output, float value)	Sets specified digital channel (0 to 7) to desired logical value (0 or 1). When floating point value in the range (0; 1) is specified, PWM modulation is activated.
int **Set_digital_out_B** (HANDLE h, int value)	Sets digital channels to value (0 to 255). For example value of 100 sets digital outputs to state 01100100.
int **Set_analog_out** (HANDLE h, int output, float value)	Sets analog output on specified channel to desired value in volts (0 to 10V). Function accepts values in floating-point format.

Table 2. Implemented library functions for Visual C++

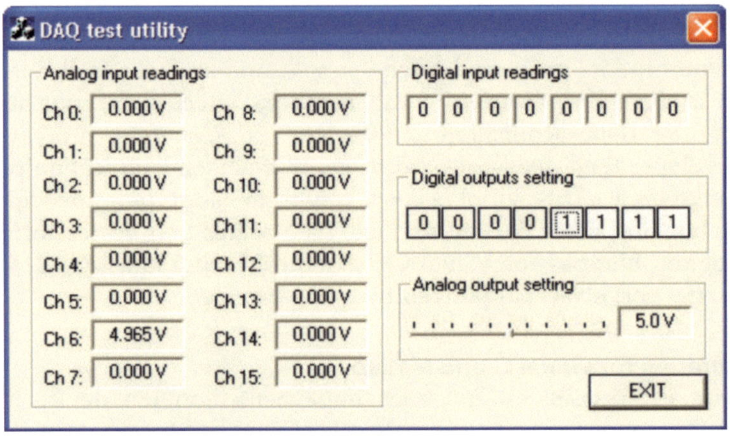

Fig. 12. Main window of the DAQ device test utility

4.2 Driver support for Control Web

Control Web is Rapid Application Development system developed by Moravian Instruments which is suitable for process visualization and real-time control, HMI applications, technological information systems and other applications.

Application design in Control Web 5 is very fast and comfortable due to integrated development environment, which supports more possibilities how to create new application. The basic idea is to build in graphical editor basic components to the larger block, which can gradually form whole system. Each component can be configured in sheet editor enabling transparent parameter settings. Because resulting code is saved in text form and then compiled there is in parallel also a text editor available. Each component can be selected from instruments palette organizing them in subcategories - for example system instruments, flat instruments and so on. Selected category can be expanded if it is possible to

next sub trees. Another type of the object in Control Web is data element. Each data element represents location in system memory, which can save value of the measured quantity, for example (Moravian Instruments, 2005).
Control Web is in standard installation equipped with several drivers which can be divided to two main categories - for demonstration and testing purposes (Virtual Driver, Model driver, Simulation Driver, Simulating Driver) and general drivers for use in real applications (DDE Client Driver, ASCDRV5 driver, TCP/IP driver). Device driver is independent component in a form of dynamically linked library with standardized interface. During development of the Control Web system gradually originated three versions of the interface. Basic interface was defined for Control Web version 3 and must be implemented in every driver. Newer interface version 4 was created with Control Web 2000 and finally newest version 5 was defined for Control Web 5. Backward compatibility is guaranteed by implementation of the basic interface in all higher versions of the interface.
Control Web communicates with driver using channels, which must be defined in the driver map file (file with extension dmf). Each channel is defined by number, direction (input, output) and data type (real, boolean, string, and others). Driver configuration is stored in the parametric text file (extension par) containing specific information for correct driver initialization. All parameters can be easily viewed and modified using "Driver inspector".
On the basis of requirements of the driver interface version 3 a device driver for portable data acquisition device was created. It supports all available hardware functions - there are 16 input real channels, 8 boolean input and output channels and one real output channel. For verification of the correct function of the driver and DAQ device test application was created. It enables to manually set output channels and in 500 ms period reads all input channels. Main window of the test application is in Fig.13.

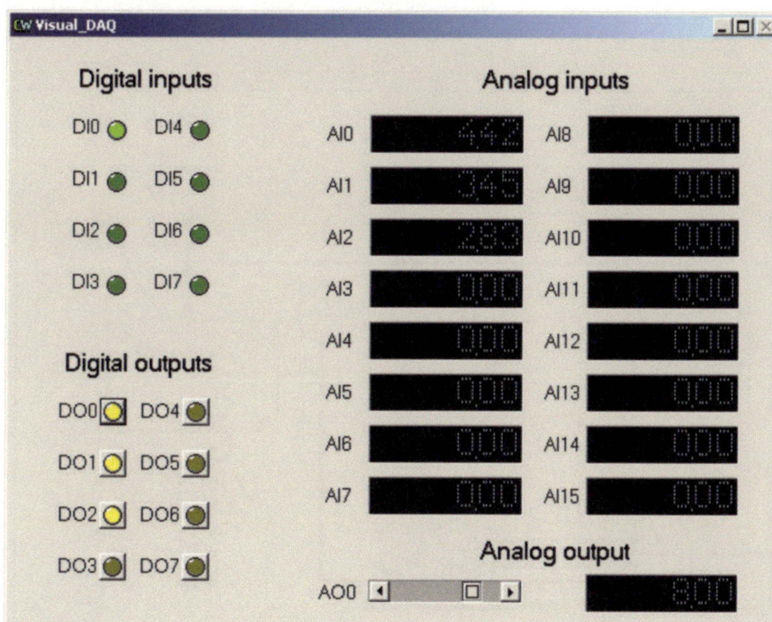

Fig. 13. DAQ test utility for Control Web

5. Verification and results

Designed device was tested on laboratory model of heating plant system with three temperature measurement channels with unified analog outputs 0 – 10 V and two digital input channels for heating element and auxiliary cooling fan control. Main cooling fan and circulation pump speed are controlled by analog inputs 0 – 10 V. DAQ is connected with standard personal computer via serial communications interface.

5.1 Heating plant model with time delay

Time delay systems are represented in many practical applications. Primarily it is in systems where matter is transferred along a certain path with a certain speed. An example of such systems is a belt conveyor apparatus, pipelines for transferring heat, dispensing systems used in chemical industry, etc. From the educational point of view it therefore appears to be useful to acquaint students with a laboratory model of this type of a system.

Educational heating-system model with time delay developed at our institute is based on the principle of transferring heat from source through a piping system using heat transferring media to heat-consuming appliance. The heat transferring fluid is transported using a continuously controllable DC pump 6 into a flow-heater 1 with 750W heat power. The temperature of the liquid leaving the heater is measured using a platinum thermometer T1. Warmed liquid then comes into a thermal insulated coil 2 which is composed of a 15m pipeline. Here a transport delay between 50 and 200 seconds originates depending on the pump speed. Heat exchanger 3 represents a heat-consuming appliance by releasing the thermal energy from the heat transferring fluid to the ambient air. The heat consumption can be set using two fans 4, 5 with adjustable speed. The temperature of the fluid entering and leaving the heat exchanger is measured by thermometers T2 and T3. Expansion tank 7 compensates for the thermal expansion effect of water. Schematic of the model is depicted in Fig.14, its photograph in Fig.15.

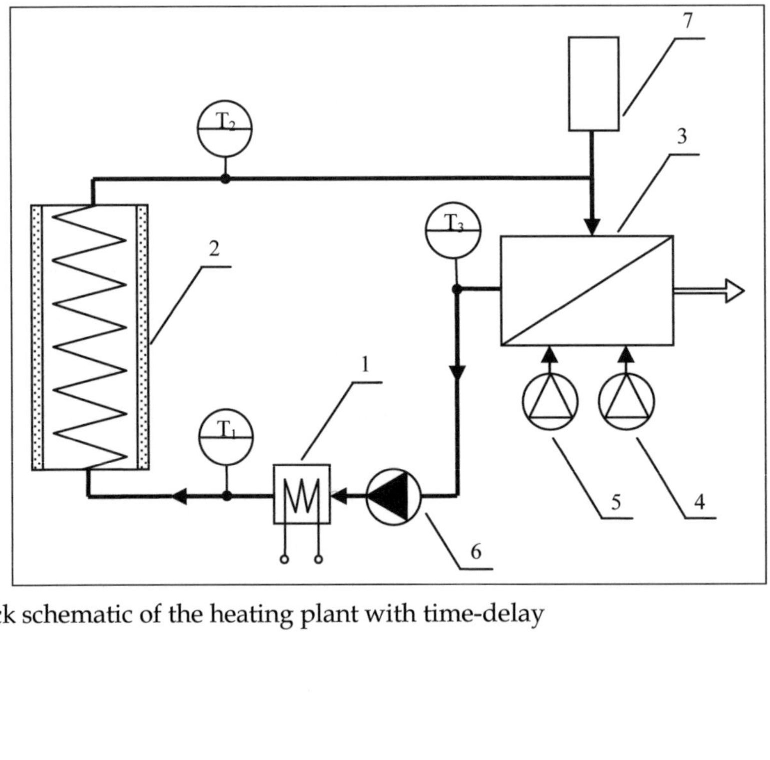

Fig. 14. Block schematic of the heating plant with time-delay

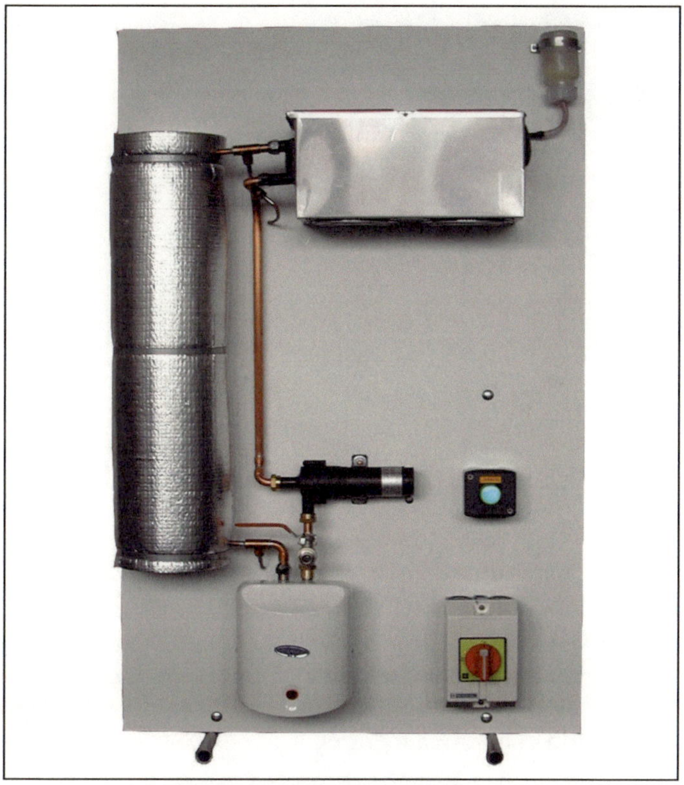

Fig. 15. Educational heating plant model with time-delay

5.2 Model control application for Control Web

Main window of the developed control application in Control Web 5 software environment is depicted in Fig.16. The left part of the window contains simplified technology schematic with two control components for pump speed and demanded temperature setting. Pump speed can be set in the range from 0 to 100 % where 0 % means minimum allowable speed (it can not be completely stopped due to possible heater damage). Demanded temperature range is limited to maximum of 85 centigrade.

The right part of the window visualizes all monitored values - temperatures in 3 important parts of the model, controller actuating signal and demanded temperature value. All these values are stored in graph with history of 1000 values.

5.3 Model control application for Matlab 6.5

All the tasks related to control and monitoring of the time delay model are served by control software with graphical user interface running in Matlab 6.5 environment. The software supports step response measurement of the system, control of the selected controlled variable using PS, PSD and general linear controller with disturbance introduction possibility. To allow quick restoring of the time-delay model to initial conditions before next measurement, cooling function was implemented. All measured data are automatically saved to the workspace in the matrix form and to the user definable text file with format suitable for import to spreadsheet processor.

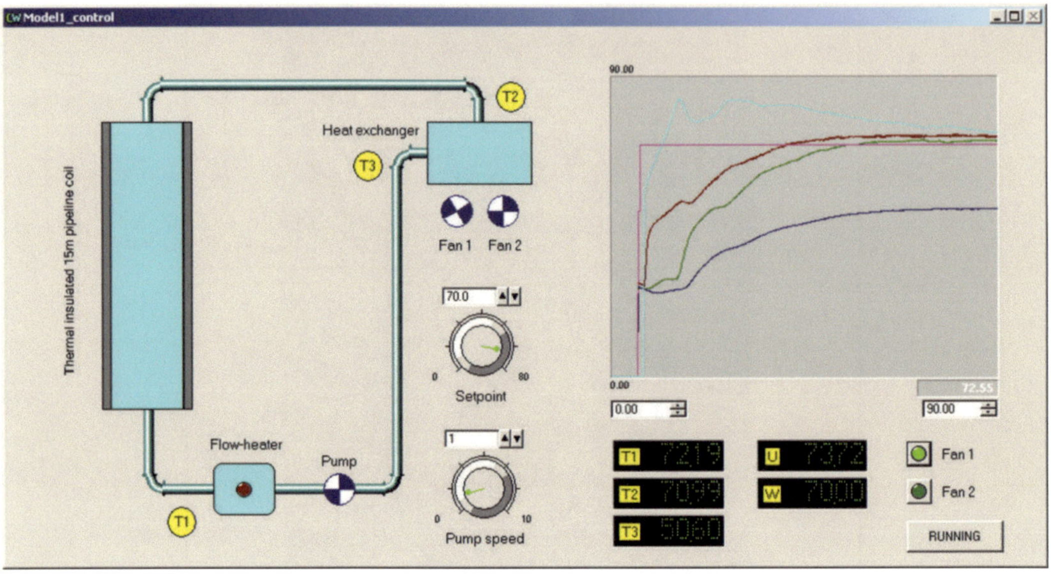

Fig. 16. Heating plant model control application for Control Web 5

After the program is executed by writing command "hmodel" in the command window of the Matlab 6.5 environment the main window depicted in the Fig.17 will appear. The window is divided into two parts - upper part is dedicated to displaying all measured system variables in the form of auto-scale graph.

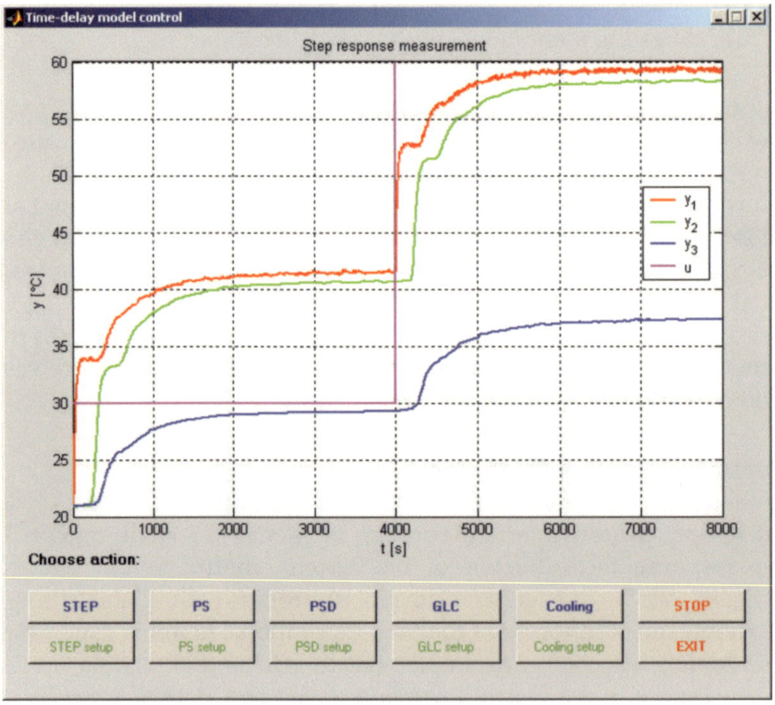

Fig. 17. Heating plant model control application for Matlab 6.5

Below the graph is situated block of buttons for selecting desired program action. These are divided into three categories depending on their function. Buttons with blue labels are used to startup program module which is performing each measurement - for example button "STEP" will initiate measurement of the step response. Green labeled buttons are intended to setup each program module. Button "STOP" interrupts current measurement with saving all measured data to file and workspace as well. Reaction to the stop command is not instantaneous - it can take up to one sampling period of the current measurement. When ALT+F4 key combination or close button is pressed during measurement, all actuating signals are immediately reset and application is closed without data saving.
Pressing "EXIT" button will close the program with resetting all actuating signals to zero values. During measurement all buttons except "STOP" button are disabled in order to prevent unwanted interference to the running experiment.
All measurements during program verification were passed in the following conditions: distilled water as heat transfer medium, pump speed at minimum (maximum time delay), fan 1 on, fan 2 at minimum speed and channel index was set to 2 (temperature before heat exchanger). Step response of the time delay model is depicted in Fig.18. It was measured with actuating signal change from 10 % to 60 % of the maximum value.

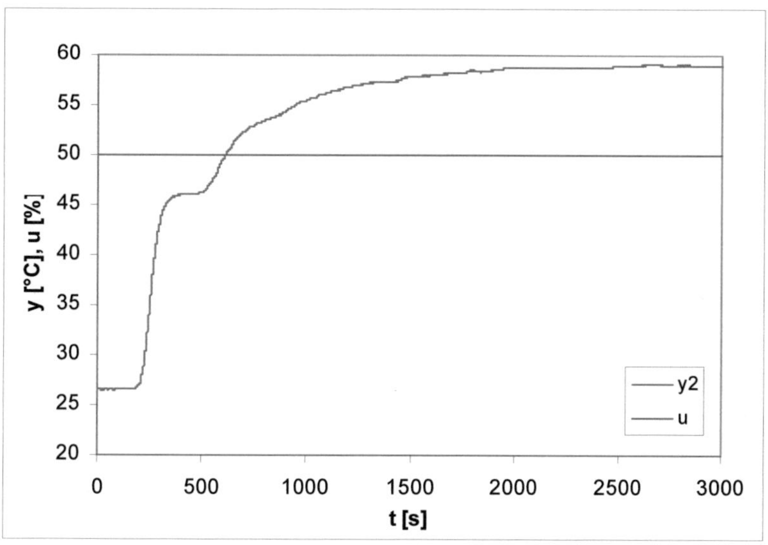

Fig. 18. Measured step response of heating plant model

System was identified with first order transfer function with time-delay (1) (Fig.19). Approximated first order transfer function with time-delay was used for PS controller design with inversion dynamics method published in (Vítečková, 2000). Parameters α and β was chosen for 5% relative overshoot of the controlled variable. Final PS controller parameters for sampling period of 10 s are: $q_0 = 1.15$, $q_1 = -1.11$.

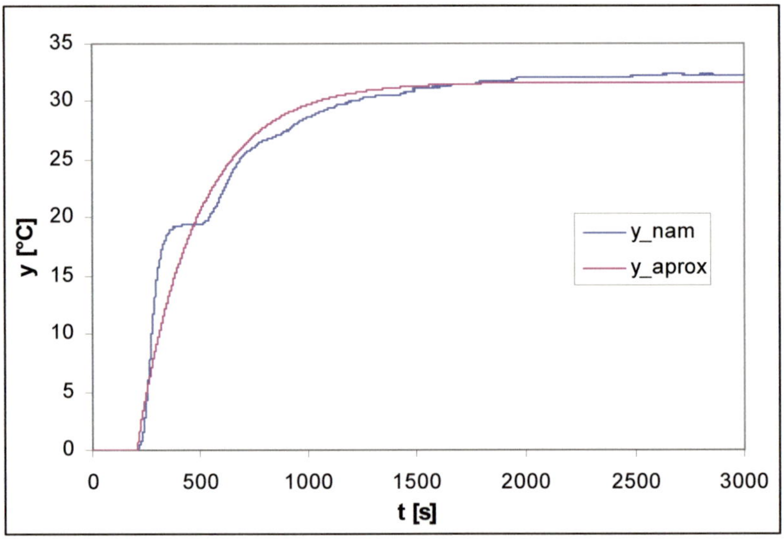

Fig. 19. Step response approximation with first order transfer function with time-delay

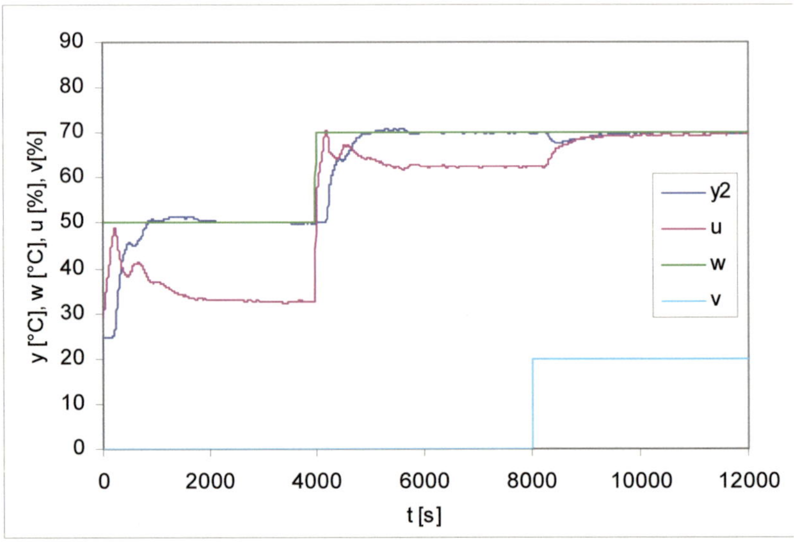

Fig. 20. PS controller control process

$$G(s) = \frac{k}{Ts+1} \cdot e^{-T_D s} = \frac{0.646}{290s+1} \cdot e^{-200s} \tag{1}$$

Resulting control process achieved with PS controller with set point values set to 50 °C at time 0 s and 70 °C at time 4000 s is in Fig.20.

6. Conclusion

The contribution deals with portable data acquisition unit which was developed at our department for control and monitoring related tasks. The device is designed with respect to possible battery operation enabling measurement in areas where power source is not available. It provides sixteen analog inputs with 12-bit A/D conversion resolution with input voltage range 0 – 10 V, eight TTL compatible digital inputs and outputs protected against electrostatic discharge and overloading and one analog output channel equipped with 12-bit D/A converter with output amplifier providing standard voltage output 0 – 10V. Communication with supervision system is realized via standard RS232 asynchronous serial interface which makes DAQ device fully platform independent. It uses universal ASCII-based communication protocol which can be easily successfully implemented in many control and monitoring software environments.
In order to improve development of new software applications with this device a support program libraries for Matlab/Simulink, Visual C++ and Control Web 5 were created. For research and educational purposes control software with graphical user interface running in Matlab 6.5 environment was developed. It supports step response measurement of the system, control of the selected controlled variable using PS, PSD and general linear controller with disturbance introduction possibility.

7. Acknowledgments

The work was performed with financial support of research project MSM7088352102. This support is very gratefully acknowledged.

8. References

Burr-Brown. (1998). *DAC7611: 12-Bit Serial Input Digital-to-Analog Converter* [online]. 1st edition. Tucson : Burr-Brown, [cit. 2010-01-10]. Available from WWW: <http:// www.burr-brown.com/>.

Freescale. (2008). *M68HC08 Microcontrollers: MC68HC908GP32 Data Sheet* [online]. 1st edition. Chandler : Freescale Semiconductor, [cit. 2010-01-22]. Available from WWW: < http://www.freescale.com/>.

Freescale. (2006). *M68HC08 Microcontrollers: CPU08 Central Processor Unit Reference Manual* [online]. 1st edition. Chandler: Freescale Semiconductor, [cit. 2010-01-20]. Available from WWW: < http://www.freescale.com/>.

Linear Technology. (1994). *LTC1286/LTC1298 Micropower Sampling 12-Bit A/D Converters* [online]. 1st edition. Milpitas: Linear Technology Corporation, [cit. 2010-01-10]. Available from WWW: < http://www.linear.com/>.

Moravian Instruments. (2005). *Control Web 5 software documentation* [online]. 1st edition. Zlín: Moravian Instruments, [cit. 2010-01-15]. Available from WWW: < http://www.mii.cz/>.

Vítečková M. (2000). *Controller tunning by method of inverse dynamics*. Ostrava: VŠB – Technical University of Ostrava, 56p. ISBN 80-7078-628-0.

8

Java in the Loop of Data Acquisition Systems

Pedro Mestre[1], Carlos Serodio[1], João Matias[2],
João Monteiro[3] and Carlos Couto[3]
[1]*Centre for the Research and Technology of Agro-Environment and Biological Sciences, University of Trás-os-Montes and Alto Douro*
[2]*Centre for the Mathematics, University of Trás-os-Montes and Alto Douro*
[3]*Industrial Electronics Department, University of Minho*
Portugal

1. Introduction

Modern Distributed Data Acquisition Systems consist of many different components. Those components can be made by different manufacturers, be based on different hardware platforms, running different software or firmware applications and implement by different hardware/software system developers.

This component variety makes distributed systems to be heterogeneous at two levels: at executable code level, due to the fact that the binary code of a platform might be incompatible with other platforms; at data level, because different platforms might have different ways to represent, store and deal with data.

To overcome issues raised by this platform heterogeneity it can be used a Virtual Machine technology, a Middleware technology or both technologies together. Virtual Machines present to the programmer a homogeneous development platform, therefore the programmer does not need to concern about the final platform where the application will be used. Middleware offers the tools for programmers to develop distributed applications without concerning about details of objects' communications.

Java is one of the most used Virtual Machine technologies and it has support for different platforms. Its support goes from desktop computers to mobile phones. A key point of this technology is its support for many different Operating Systems such as Microsoft Windows family, Solaris, Linux and Mac OS. Java also supports the most used Middleware technologies, allowing the implementation of distributed data acquisition systems compatible with components made with other development tools.

Based on the latest trends in consumer electronics and industrial applications using WSN (Wireless Sensor Network), smart sensors and embedded systems, we can conclude that future nodes must become smarter, cheaper and smaller.

So, the major challenge is to produce smart sensing devices which have very low resources. Besides that, also the reduction of both the development time and costs are needed. Considering this, two approaches can be used: in the first, hardware resources are made accessible, e.g. connecting them over TCP/IP, putting these devices at the distance of *a click;* the second is to give to bus-level devices some characteristics that until now are mainly found in the traditional computing systems. The second approach is based on the application of "write once, run anywhere and any time" Java concept. However, it must be taken in consideration that bus-level devices, like sensor nodes, have several constraints regarding the lack of resources, particularly memory issues.

In this chapter the use of Java Technology is proposed. Not only in desktop applications where it is traditionally used, but also on the other system components. Java can be used not only at the higher layers, on data acquisition software applications where data is gathered, processed and stored, but also in device drivers that do the interface between applications and data communication systems used for data acquisition, such as wireless communications and fieldbuses. To implement the concepts presented in this chapter, IEEE802.15.4 for wireless communications and CAN (Controller Area Network) as fieldbus technology were used, for proof of concept purposes.

Java can even be used in networked distributed nodes where data are collected. Not only in state-of-the-art embedded systems but also in low-resource devices, such as 8-bit microcontrollers with a few kilobyte of memory and low clock speed. For such systems it is presented a solution based on a dedicated Java Virtual Machine, embedded in a 8-bit microcontroller, which acts as its Operating System.

Authors do not intend to present a replacement for JDDAC (Java Distributed Data Acquisition and Control), (Engel et al., 2006), which is a platform to build Java-based data acquisition systems and sensor networks. In fact, some of the aims of the present work are similar, even though it is not an API (Application Programming Interface) or a Framework, JDDAC can be fitted in some of the layers of the model presented in this chapter.

2. Java technology and platform heterogeneity

A completely homogeneous platform where all the system components have the same characteristics is not possible to achieve. Even if a newly deployed distributed system is made of homogeneous components, sooner or later, the elements that make part of it will start to be different from each other, as new devices are added. Those devices might not have all the same characteristics in what concerns to processor architecture, processing power, memory amount and communications technologies.

Being a technology which supports multiple computation platforms, Java is one of the solutions to take in account when the subject is the platform heterogeneity. It is based on a Virtual Machine, the Java Virtual Machine (JVM), which has support for the most used computing platforms. The use of Virtual Machines to overcome problems related with platform heterogeneity has more than 30 years (Gough, 2005), with the definition of a Virtual Machine able to run code generated from PASCAL, the P-Code.

When Virtual Machines are used the programmer works without the need to concern about the target processor or operating system. There is no need to know any detail about the real platforms used in the system. This gives the ability to develop applications targeted for currently available and future architectures and devices.

Besides offering a homogeneous execution environment, Java technology offers different kind of support according to the characteristics of the used devices and the type of service to be implemented.

2.1 Java solutions

From the most traditional computing platforms such as Personal Computers, to embedded systems, passing by interactive television applications, PDA (Personal Digital Assistant) and mobile phones, Java supports a large number of different types of computing platforms. Java support for the traditional computing platforms is offered through two different solutions (Sun, 2003):

- Java EE (Java Platform, Enterprise Edition) for enterprise applications and servers;
- Java SE (Java Platform, Standard Edition) for desktop applications and servers.

For use in consumer electronics devices, and for embedded servers and applications as well, Java support for the existing technologies is offered by the following solutions:

- Java ME (Java Platform, Micro Edition), for use in PDAs, Mobile Phones and specific embedded applications;
- Java Card, for applications with Smart Cards;
- Java TV, to be used in Iterative Television applications;
- JES (Java Embedded Server), for embedded applications.

The use of Java is a step to achieve a system with homogeneous components. Although each type of node, in distributed data acquisition systems, has a different type of Java support, they all have a similar behaviour. Their applications are based on a similar API (Application Programming Interface), use the same programming language, share a "virtual processor" that uses the same bytecodes, and represent and store data the same way.

It is possible to build distributed systems where the nodes are compatible at data and executable code levels. This means that nodes can share data without concerning about its representation and, executable code can be shared by the nodes.

Using Java in all system components of the distributed system, besides hiding from the programmer the "real" platform and supporting data mobility, also code mobility is possible. This code mobility can be explicit by downloading code from a server and then execute it or, code can be embedded in method invocations. Java applications can call remote code in other JVMs and, when doing this remote code invocation, they can send as input parameters or receive as return values of the called methods, data or objects (which are made of code and data). Code can dynamically be sent between networked nodes. This dynamic code mobility is a key point in this technology.

2.2 Integrating Java with other technologies

Not all applications used in distributed system are developed using Java. This leads to the need of finding a solutions that enable the Java components to communicate with other applications. This can be done using Middleware Technologies.

Middleware technologies work as an abstraction layer to the programmer. Its objective is to hide system implementation details, offering a uniform view of the network and the Operating Systems (Sun & Blatecky, 2004). It supports communications between distributed software components and copes with the problems related with the platform heterogeneity (Mattern & Sturm, 2003). For each platform that makes part of the distributed system, an implementation of the middleware technology must exist.

From the programmer's point of view, middleware offers the needed abstraction for the programmer not having to concern about low-level issues of the deployment platform and the communications protocols used in the distributed system. It offers transparency to the network. Independently of protocols and platforms used to deploy and develop the different components, the programmer sees a uniform system.

Programmers only need to concern about the coding of their applications and with the interfaces made available by the programming language to access the functions offered by the middleware layer. All the issues related with the transport of requests and responses between objects in a distributed system, are dealt by the middleware layer. Also details about discovering remote services and their interfaces are dealt by it.

Java Technology, besides supporting Java-centric middleware technologies, also has support for other widely adopted middleware technologies, enabling applications developed with this platform to communicate with applications developed using other tools. From the list of middleware technologies supported by Java Web Services, which use the same technology that is used on the Web, is one of the most adopted.

2.2.1 Web services

Created to be applied in de development of distributed systems that operate over the Internet, the aim of Web Services is to have a technology that is independent of the programming paradigms, languages and technologies. They represent a return to the old client/server model (Coulouris et al., 2005) on which both peers are functionality specialized.

Message exchanges between client and server are made using SOAP (Simple Object Access Protocol) and the transport of these messages is typically done using the HTTP (Hypertext Transfer Protocol) protocol. However, other protocols can be used to transport it.

SOAP defines how information must be formatted in XML (Extensible Markup Language) for information exchange between the elements that are part of the distributed system (Mitra & Lafon, 2007).

The use of XML presents several advantages when compared with binary formats to transport data, for example it can be interpreted by humans making the debug process more easy. XML also helps in the cross platform compatibility, enabling the definition of structured documents that can be interpreted by most platforms. However, to transport the same information, XML has a higher overhead and it needs more processor and memory resources to be decoded, when compared with binary formats.

As for any other technology that allows a client to remotely use services, clients need to know which methods are available on the server, i.e., client needs to know the server remote interface, which describes the methods available on the server. This description is called WSDL (Web Service Definition Language).

Independently of their programming language (Java, C++, C#, etc) and running platform, applications can communicate with each other over the network. This is thus a middleware technology to be taken in account when communication between heterogeneous networked elements is needed.

3. Generic model for Java based data acquisition

A model for Networked Data Acquisition Systems, based on Java Technology and its remote code invocation features, is presented in Fig 1. Besides distributed data acquisition devices, e.g. smart sensors spread in the field, it also supports Distributed Device Drivers and remote Data Acquisition Applications.

This model has the following four layers:

- Device Layer – Where the data acquisition devices are located. These devices can be connected directly to a computer or through a data communications network (e.g. a filedbus, WSN technology);

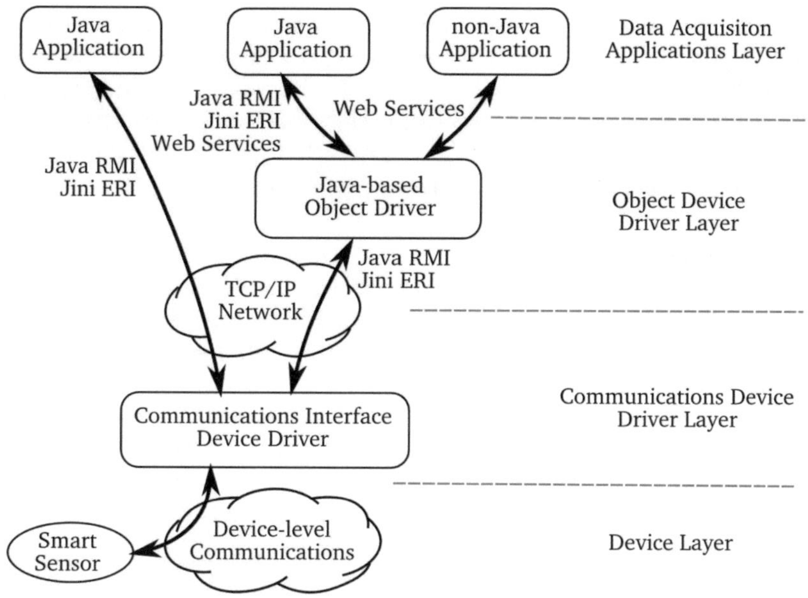

Fig. 1. Generic model for Java-based networked data acquisition systems.

- Communications Device Driver Layer – This layer is responsible for the interface with the data acquisition devices. It sends messages from the upper layers to devices and *vice versa;*
- Object Device Driver Layer – For higher level interfacing with applications. For each smart sensor, an object driver can exist in this layer;
- Data Acquisition Applications Layer – Where the final consumers for the data from the sensors are located.

A common philosophy in this model is the fact that all elements can be spread over the network. From the lower layers (device level) to the upper layer (applications level), nodes can be anywhere in the network, as long as they have network connectivity and there is a possible route between them.

3.1 Data acquisition applications layer

Applications can consume data from two sources, depending the degree of knowledge they have about the target device. If an application knows how to communicate with the hardware, i.e., it knows the low-level protocol used by the device, it can interface directly with the data communications device driver. When the application does not know such details or, a higher level of abstraction is needed, then applications can communicate with the corresponding Object Device Driver that routes information requests and responses between information source and consumer.

These two approaches for device interfacing give two different abstraction levels, to be used in two different situations. One for direct communications with the field devices and the other to gather data from the sensors. When accessing the Object Device Driver, independently of the network technology used by the field-level device, applications should be able to interface in the same way sensors that have the same function. For example, a temperature sensor should have the same software interface either when using CAN or IEEE802.15.4 wireless communications.

In the Applications Layer, two types of software applications might exist: Java-based applications and non-Java applications. These two types of applications communicate with the Java-based Object Driver, using Web Services. In the case of Java applications also Java RMI (Remote Method Invocation) and Jini ERI (Extensible Remote Invocation) are available. Java applications can also use Java RMI or Jini ERI to communicate directly with the Communication Device Driver, bypassing the Object Driver.

3.2 Object device driver layer

Applications do not have to know how to communicate with the real device, where data is actually being acquired. Remote sensors are modelled as objects according to their functions and, hardware devices can be modelled as several different objects. One object per acquisition function that it has.

Requests for data are made by applications to the Object Driver, which forwards the data requests to the real device, using the lower layer services. When the device answers, it sends the responses back to the applications. These communications between the Object Driver and the Communications Device Driver are made using Java RMI and Jini ERI, since these two elements are implemented in Java.

3.3 Communications device driver layer

For communications with the real device, the Object Device Driver Layer and some Java applications must use the lower level driver, the Communications Interface Device Driver. This driver is to be used only by components that understand both the Layer 2 and high level protocols used by devices.

While the Object Driver works mainly in a request/response way, using the traditional client/server model, the low-level device driver works in asynchronous mode. The driver is stateless and does not know the meaning of messages exchanged between applications and devices. Therefore it cannot track connections. So, the driver is unable to know if new data is expected or even if data will arrive from remote nodes. Data exchange sequence depends on the network technology, time needed by the remote node to process data and on the higher level protocols used by devices.

3.4 Device layer

In the lowest layer, devices capture data consumed by the applications in the upper layer. These acquisition devices can be directly connected to a computer or can be connected to a data acquisition network, such as a fieldbus or WSN technology. Devices communicate, through the Communications Interface Device Driver, with the Object Driver or the Applications. They do not communicate with the Communications Interface Device Driver, which only transports data and does not know its meaning.

Implementation of the high level communications protocol used to exchange information with the remote data acquisition devices must be done either in the Object Driver Layer or in the Application Layer.

4. Java device drivers

When new hardware is added to a computer or to a networked environment it is needed to install a device driver to handle communications between applications, Operating System and the device. This leads to the need of multiple versions for the device driver, one for each supported platform. If the device driver is built using a Virtual Machine Technology supported by multiple Operating Systems, such as Java, one version of the driver can be used by several different platforms.

Based on the model above presented in section 3, two different concepts and philosophies of device drivers are presented:

- Low-level Communications Device Driver, used for direct interface with the communications hardware. Although it can be used by any application, this driver is intended to be used by the next driver type;
- High level Object Driver, used by applications to access data from objects available on the network. In the context of data acquisition, an object is any source of data, e.g. a smart sensor.

The first belongs to the Communications Device Driver Layer and the second to the Object Device Driver Interface Layer. These two drivers implement two different low-level communications protocols:

- Low-level communications between the Java device driver and the communications hardware, dealt by the Low-level device driver;
- Low-level communications between the Object Driver (and some applications) and the remote data acquisition devices.

4.1 Low-level communications device driver

Low-level interfacing with the device driver involves the use of multiple technologies: native code for basic hardware level communications; Java to implement the core of the device driver; Java-based middleware technology enabling communications between the device driver and the remote object drivers and applications. The layered model for this device driver is presented in Fig. 2.

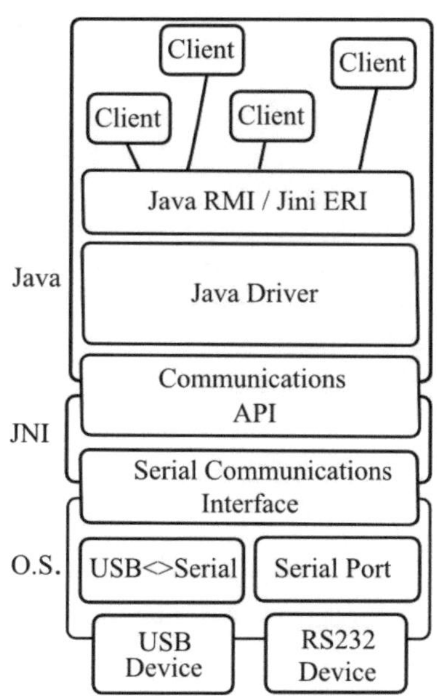

Fig. 2. Low-level Java-based device driver layered model

This device driver model has the following four layers:

- Hardware Layer, where the communication hardware interfaces can be found;
- Operating System Layer, where platform serial drivers are;
- Java Native Interface Layer, which makes the bridge between the Java world and the Operating System;
- Java Layer, where the core of the device driver for the communications protocol is implemented.

4.1.1 Hardware layer

This is a hardware only layer, responsible for the physical connection between the communications hardware (Network Interface Card) and the host computer that will share this hardware with the other components of the distributed data acquisition system.
For this layer two of the industry adopted solutions for communications with devices are used: serial port (RS-232 compatible) and serial port emulation over USB (Universal Serial Bus).
Although in the implementation presented in this chapter the device driver is serial port centric, it can be adapted to other type of hardware. Whenever it is possible to communicate with the hardware using JNI (Java Native Interface), then this device driver concepts can also be used.

4.1.2 Operating system layer

This is a platform dependent layer since it relies on the existence of a native device driver to deal with the low-level communications between the Operating System and the serial or USB port. This is the first software layer and it is implemented in native code.
The Operating System Layer does not need to know how to communicate with the Network Interface Card, it only needs to know how to send and receive data from the serial port. Independently of the type of interface used in the Hardware Layer (RS-232 or USB), it presents to the Java Native Interface Layer a generic serial port. Hardware isolation is then another of its features.

4.1.3 Java native interface layer

Interfacing between the Java core of the device driver (implemented in the upper layer) and the Operating System Layer is done by the Java Native Interface Layer. It is implemented in the platform native code and Java code, using JNI.
Although this layer is platform dependent, the used API for communications with the serial port, the Java Communications API, has implementations for many platforms: officially by Orcale for the Linux and Solaris platforms and by a third party for Linux, Solaris, MacOS and Microsoft Windows[1].

4.1.4 Java layer

This is the core of the low-level Java device driver, where the low-level communications protocol used to interface the network interface hardware is implemented. Completely implemented in Java, this is the first system independent layer of the device driver. For

[1] The gnu.io library, an implementation of the Java Communicatons API that can be found at http://rxtx.org/

communications between the driver and the remote client applications, this layer supports both Java RMI and Jini ERI.
Being the core of the device driver, this layer is network technology dependent. It must know the low-level protocol used in the acquisition network and provide to applications the correct remote interface. It is also network hardware dependent, since it must know how to communicate with the hardware.
Traditionally device drivers and applications must be executed in the same computing device to which the network interface card is connected. In the presented solution, by using Java RMI and Jini ERI, it is possible for applications to be located in a remote computer. Devices can then be remotely accessed by applications and the device can be shared by multiple distributed applications. Since the used technologies rely on the TCP/IP protocol suite, applications and drivers can be locate anywhere in the Internet. However it must be taken in account that connections over the Internet might have a high latency. Real time requirements of applications must then be considered.
In the present work two types of communications protocols were used. One wired (CAN) and another wireless (IEEE802.15.4). Nevertheless these two protocols were used in the tests, concepts presented here can be applied to other protocols.

4.2 Interface between applications and the low-level device drivers

Interfacing between applications and device drivers must be done using well defined Interfaces. The driver must allow applications to send messages to the devices and, when a message arrives the driver must deliver it to all applications that need that information. Driver and applications use the client/server model.
Since this part of the network interfacing operates at the Data Link Layer of the OSI (Open System Interconnection) model, decision about to which application send the information must be done based on this layer addressing scheme, or equivalent concept, of the used technology. For this to be possible, applications must be able to register the interest on receiving certain frames.
Applications must also be able to asynchronously receive the frames from the device driver. This is done by using a call back mechanism, on which the device driver calls remote methods implemented by the application. Client and server switch roles.
When an application sends frames and when it registers its interest on receiving some types of frames, the driver acts as the server and the applications as the client. When a message arrives to the device driver, the application acts as the server and the device driver acts as the client.
Besides the definition of object interfaces, used for communication between driver and applications, also the inter-process communication method(s) must be specified. The technology must be wide accepted and allow clients to be running remotely, not only in the same computer where the driver is installed. Since this part of the device driver and the applications that use it (object driver) are implemented in Java, two of the Java inter-process communication technologies are used: Java RMI and Jini ERI.
Java RMI is a very popular inter-process communication for Java-based distributed applications and it is part of the standard distribution of Java since the version 1.1 of JDK (Java Development Kit). It has multiple implementations, besides the original JRMP (Java Remote Method Protocol) (Newmarch, 2006), implemented based on TCP/IP. However those implementations have different programming interfaces, having thus a lack of technology abstraction.

A solution for this issue is presented by Jini Technology, which itself was built on top of Java RMI. This solution is called Jini ERI (Extensible Remote Invocation). One of its main characteristics is the possibility of the programmer to access each layer of an RMI call and allowing the service deployer to decide at runtime (not hard-coded in the applications) the most suitable implementation for those layers for a specific deployment scenario (Sommer, 2003).
Providing support for Jini ERI allows the use of modern Jini-enabled systems, which benefit with its Plug-and-Work features. On the other hand, support for Java RMI allows the integration of legacy systems, without support for Jini, or modern systems where Jini is not installed. For testing and proof of concept purposes, low-level device drivers for CAN fieldbus and IEEE802.15.4 were implemented.

4.2.1 Interfacing the CAN bus

Controller Area Network is a fieldbus designed for the automotive industry but with application in many other areas related with data acquisition and control. It does not use the traditional Layer 2 protocol addressing scheme. Instead of source and destination addresses, CAN uses the concept of message significance. Each message has its own meaning and is received and interpreted by all nodes to which it may concern.
For applications to be able to communicate with the device driver, a well defined interface must exist. Independently of the technology type used by the CAN interface card to connect to the host computer, its Java device driver must implement the `CANDriverInterface` shown in Fig. 3.

<<interface>> **CANDriverInterface**
Attributes
Operations
public void readCANMessage( )
public void sendCANMessage(int ID, byte RTR, byte DLC, int data[0..8])
public void sendCAMMessage(Port msg)
public boolean receivedCANMessage( )
public void register(CANNotificationInterface object, int CANid)
public void register(CANNotificationInterface object)
public void remove(CANNotificationInterface object)
public void remove(CANNotificationInterface object, int CANid)

Fig. 3. CAN Driver Interface definition, which must be implemented by all drivers.

Applications can send CAN message using the `sendCANMessage` method, either specifying the CAN message parameters, according to the CAN specifications (Robert Bosch GmbH, 1991), or by sending an object of the type `CANMessage` which represents the CAN message (Fig 4). This class has four fields, representing each field of a CAN message: CAN Identifier (ID); Remote Transmission Request bit (RTR); Data Length Code (DLC); the message data (data), if any.
When a message, coming from the bus arrives to the driver, it will try to deliver it to all message consumers. For an application to register itself as a consumer for arriving CAN messages, it must call the `register` method. If an application wants to receive all CAN

messages, then it must call it without specifying the message ID. Otherwise it must call the other `register` method specifying the ID of the message it wants to receive. The other parameter of these methods is the *stub* of the client application.
If an applications wants to stop receiving some or all CAN messages, then they need to unregister themselves from the device driver using one if the `remove` methods.
For an application to be able to consume CAN messages, it must implement the `NotificationInterface` (Fig. 4). This Interface defines a single method (`notify`) used by the CAN driver to send a received message to its consumer.

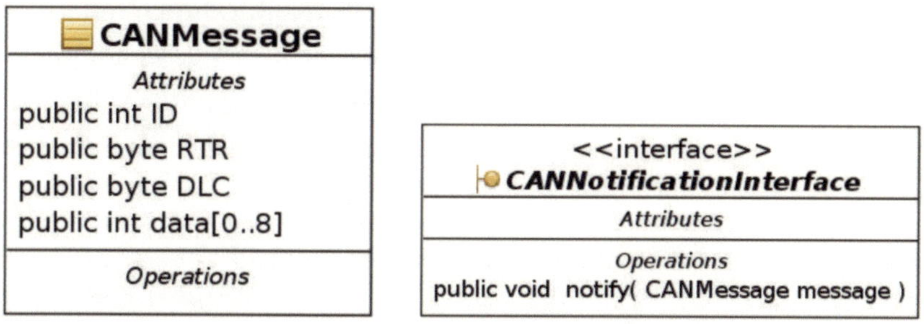

(a) CAN Message (b) CAN Notification Interface

Fig. 4. Definition of the CAN Message Class (a) and the Notification Interface that applications must implement to be able to receive CAN messages from the driver (b).

Only applications that implement this Interface can be notified, by the device driver, when a new message is received by the communications hardware. These notifications are made using the call-back mechanism of Java RMI or Jini JERI.

4.2.2 Interfacing IEEE802.15.4

Similarly to CAN interfacing, the IEEE802.15.4 device driver needs to implement an interface known by the clients, presented in Fig. 5. This interface defines the `sendFrame` method that accepts an IEEE802.15.4 Frame (Fig. 6) as input parameter.

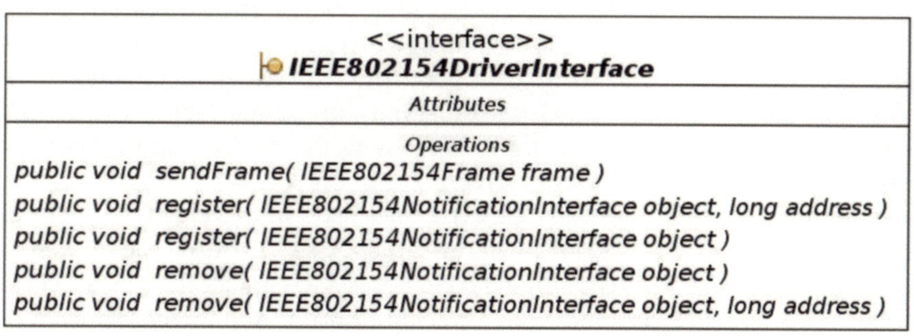

Fig. 5. IEEE802.15.4 Driver Interface which must be implemented by all drivers.

It also has methods for clients to register themselves as consumers of all frames or frames with a specific source MAC (Medium Access Control) address, received by the driver coming from the wireless interface, the `register` methods. With the opposite meaning, also two `remove` methods are defined.

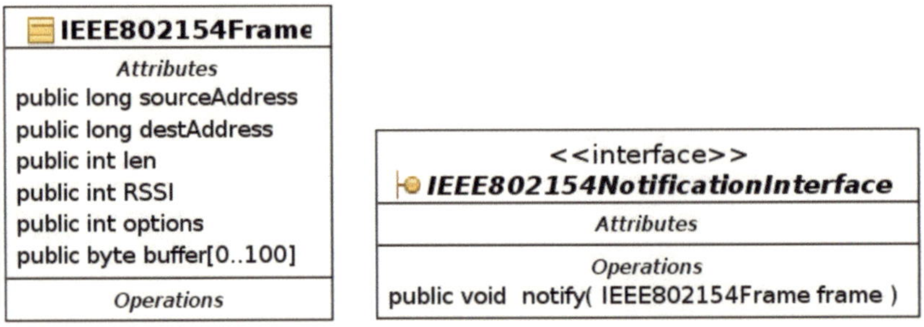

(a) IEEE802.15.4 Frame (b) IEEE802.15.4Notification Interface

Fig. 6. Definition of the IEEE802.15.4 Message Class (a) and the Notification Interface that applications must implement to be able to receive frames from the driver (b).

The fields of the class which represents the IEEE 802.15.4 Frames were define according to the IEEE802.15.4 specifications (IEEE, 2006). It contains the destination MAC address field (`destAddress`), to be used only when sending frames since the source address of the frames is automatically set by the hardware. Therefore the field `srcAdrress` is to be used in the received frames to determine the sender, and the `RSSI` (Received Signal Strength Indicator) to indicate the RSSI value of the received frame.

To be used in both sending and receiving operations, there are the `data` and the `len` fields used for data buffering and to indicate the data length of the frame (received or to be sent) respectively.

As for the CAN bus, for applications to be notified by the driver when a new fame arrives, they must implement the `IEEE802154NotificationInterface`, presented in Fig. 6.

4.3 High level object interfacing

High level interfacing with the system is the preferable entry point for applications and, it should be in this layer that final consumers gather data from the sensors. It is also this layer that is responsible for communications with the non-Java applications, since this layer besides supporting Jini JERI and Java RMI also supports Web Services. Although only these middleware technologies were included in the current implementation, integration of other middleware technologies can be made, as long as it is supported by Java. For communications between this layer and the lower level layer, the Java based middleware technologies are used. Each data source in acquisition network (e.g. sensors) which are available for applications through this layer must have an object device driver. Applications using this layer do not know how to communicate with the device and therefore cannot use the lower level Communications Device Driver.

Fig. 7 shows an example of an interface defined for a sensor, in this case a temperature sensor. The object driver for the specific sensor must implement this interface. The implementation of Object Driver for the sensor must contain the code needed to contact the real sensor hardware, using the sensor low-level communications protocol (through the lower layer device driver), obtain the sensor reading and return the value to the caller application.

The interface presented in the Fig. 7 is implemented by one of the device drivers used in an example, shown in section 6, where a non-Java applications, implemented using LabView, gathers data from a wireless temperature sensor. In that example, the application does not know where the real device is nor how to communicate with the hardware. It uses a Web Service made available by the Object Driver.

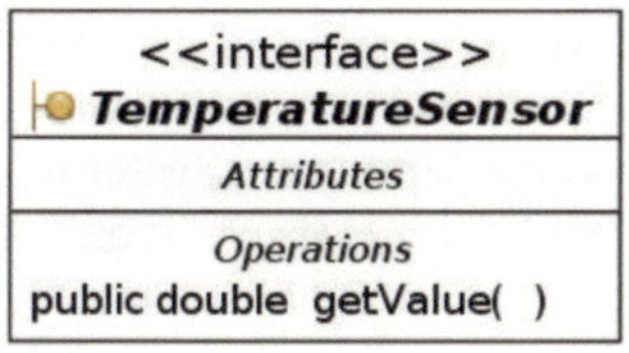

Fig. 7. Temperature Sensor Interface.

5. Java in embedded devices

Devices that belong to the Device Layer, of the above presented model, typically execute their applications using native code. One step that can help to achieve device homogeneity, even at the field level, is the ability of running Java on this type of devices. For this to be possible Java support must be provided by an embedded JVM.
Java in embedded systems has been subject of several projects. Its implementation has been based on FPGA (Field-Programmable Gate Array) and on microcontrollers (Hardin, 2001; Ito et al., 2001; Pfeffer & Ungerer, 2004). One of this embedded systems that runs Java was presented by Sun Microsystems, the Sun SPOT (Sun, 2005) which runs on a 32bit microcontroller with 256Kbyte of RAM and 2Mbyte of FLASH.
It is however possible to run embedded Java in low resources microcontrollers, such as the 80C592, a 8051 based microcontroller (Serodio et al., 2001) or PIC18F2680 (Serôdio et al., 2007), both 8-bit microcontrollers. Obviously that these implementations of the JVM are optimized for data acquisition tasks, so some details of a full JVM are not implemented on them.

5.1 Embedded Java implementations

Levis (Levis & Culler, 2002) and Rosenblum (Rosenblum & Garfinkel, 2005) proposed a definition for the JVM that includes the traditional approach, on which Virtual Machines are focused on hardware virtualization, intermediate program representation or bytecode interpretation. This means that the development of JVM is frequently specific or dedicate to the application target. It is easy understood that at the bus or sensor-level, the JVM must be re-designed, making it lighter, for it to be supported by devices with poor and constrained resources.
The Virtual Machine focused on hardware virtualization can run as an Operating System and its application, which means, works as a Monitor Program. The virtualization based on byte-code interpretation works like an application on top of a Operating System. Applications developed for that Virtual Machine abstraction can run independent of the platform Operating System. Besides this, Virtual Machines can also provide code safety, for example the JVM applications are executed in a sandbox.
From the literature related with JVM development and implementation we encounter essentially two major classification groups: JVM which works as an Operating System and JVM which acts as a Class of Middleware. The classification method chosen are based in the following issues: memory footprint (code and data (ROM and RAM)), execution method, execution model and specific application domain.
Although Maté (Levis & Culler, 2002) is considered the first JVM for sensors, authors in (Serodio et al., 1999) have proposed a thin and dedicated JVM solution for 8-bit microcontrollers. This JVM was developed essentially to perform Data Acquisition and PID

control tasks applied to agricultural environments. This JVM evolved to a new solution with some features of distributed applications with the incorporation of Jini proxies (Serodio et al., 2001). These solutions belong to the Operating System Level group.
From literature and considering only the WSN universe with poor resources, it could be incorporated in this group other solutions like: MagnetOS (Barr et al., 2002) a JVM solution for distributed WSN which have support for remote call based on RMI; Squawk (Simon et al., 2006) solution, which is a full JVM implementation with no needs of OS; TinyVM and LeJOS solution from SourgeForce which support threads and dynamic linking.
In the Middleware Level Virtual Machine it can be highlighted the following initiatives: Maté (Levis & Culler, 2002) expressly developed to be applied to sensor nodes with poor resources; Scylla (Stanley-Marbell & Iftode, 2000) assumed as the first Virtual Machine developed for mobile tiny devices; SensorWare (Boulis et al., 2003) middleware to develop Virtual Machine for Wireless ad-hoc sensor networks (WASNs); DAVIM (Michiels et al., 2006) based on Mate in which the instruction set is grouped on libraries; VM* (Koshy & Pandey, 2005) framework to develop JVM for WSNs.

5.2 An implementation for 8-bit microcontrollers

Fig. 8 shows the block diagram of a JVM implemented on a PIC18F2680, a 8-bit controller from Microchip, which has 64Kbytes of FLASH memory, used to store the JVM itself, 4Kbytes of RAM, used to save all dynamic data needed by the Java applications and by the JVM and, 1Kbyte of EEPROM, used to store the `.class` file of the Java application to execute. This JVM was implemented using C programming language.

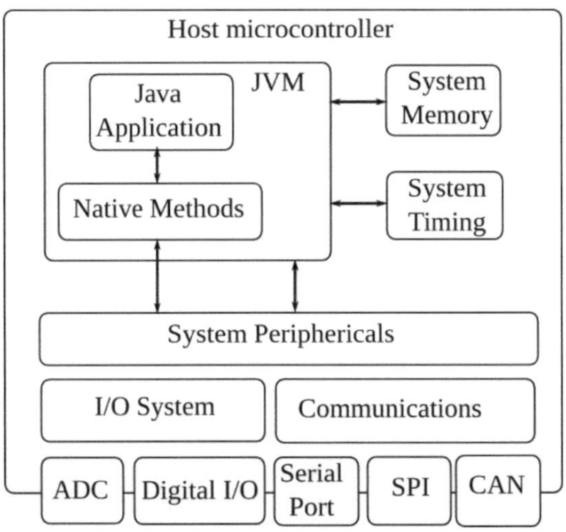

Fig. 8. Embedded Java Virtual Machine diagram block.

This system does not have an Operating System, instead the JVM running on the microcontroller acts as its Operating System. It can execute Java applications previously stored in the system FLASH memory or, it can download Java applications from the network and then execute them. Also the management of data memory used by the Java stacks and for application execution is done by the JVM.
Interaction with system peripherals is another responsibility of the JVM, either upon applications request through the implemented native methods, which includes data

acquisition from the ADC (Analogue to Digital Converter) and bit read/set of digital I/O (Input/Output), or for its own needs (timing, memory and communications).
On this prototype, communications with the outside world are made using the system console and via network interface. The system console sends its information through the microcontroller serial port and network communications are made using the microcontroller CAN interface. While console support exists in Java and therefore it was only needed to send data to the serial port in the implementation, CAN on the other hand is not supported in the standard Java distribution.
It was needed to add to the JVM and extra API to support this JVM additional functionalities of networking and data acquisition. Figure 9 shows the Java classes related with data acquisition added to the JVM API.

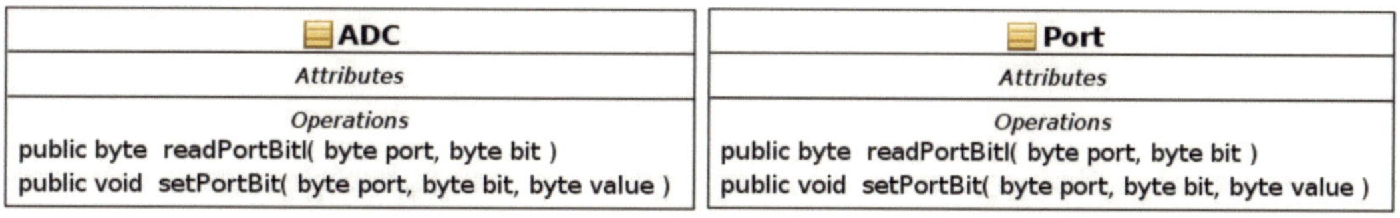

(a) ADC Class (b) Port Class

Fig. 9. ADC and Port classes added to API of the implemented JVM.

The ADC class has a single method used to read a channel of the microcontroller's ADC. To read the state of a single bit from a digital input pin, the Port class has the `readPortBit` and to set its value the `setPortBit` method is available. This last method is useful in actuation tasks or when it is needed to power on a sensor prior to data acquisition.
It is expected for a JVM running on a low-resource microcontroller to have worse performance than native code. To assess this performance difference in data acquisition tasks, some benchmarking tests were made to our JVM, running with a clock speed of 16MHz. Results of these test, which included reading values from the ADC and an digital input pin, are presented in Table 1. In the table are shown the results obtained using Java and native code to do the same tasks.

Operation	Java Code	Native Code	Speed
Read an input bit	368,00μs	1,70μs	210,29 ×
ADC reading,$v_{in} = V_{DD}$	4,54ms	4,22ms	1,08 ×
ADC reading ,$v_{in} = V_{SS}$	3,74ms	3,44ms	1,09 ×

Table 1. Time needed by the embedded JVM to do data acquisition tasks.

As expected the execution time of Java applications is higher than the time needed by native code to do the same task. These differences are highly noticed when reading a single bit from an input port of the microcontroller, however when reading the ADC this difference is only around 8 to 9%. It is then possible to use it on data acquisition task without much performance loss.
To be noticed that when a reading is made from the ADC, several samples are actually taken and then filtered. This procedure is made in native the code and, it is called by native code application and by the JVM, when a call to the `readADC` method is made.

6. Testing scenarios

Is this section a set of three data acquisition tests, made using the above presented concepts, are described and the achieved results are shown. These tests involved the acquisition of data from remote sensors, using Java and non-Java applications. As non-Java application used for testing, the well known LabView from National Instruments was used. While the Java applications use both the low-level and the high level device-drivers, communicating with them using Jini ERI or Java RMI, the LabView application used Web Services to interface the high-level object driver.

The set of three tests includes:

- Room temperature monitoring with a wireless sensor. To gather data from the sensor, using Web Services, a LabView application was used;
- Temperature control of a miniature greenhouse model, using two sensors and one actuator connected to a Java-based embedded system;
- Rotation speed control of a DC (Direct Current) shunt motor, using a Java based application.

In the last two tests, besides data acquisition, also actuation tasks are made. For this no changes needed to be made in the concepts, models and reference implementations presented in the previous sections.

6.1 Room temperaure monitorization with LabView

In this first test, the temperature acquisition of a room was made, over a period of 24 hours, using a LabView Applications. In Fig. 10 the scenario set-up used for this experiment is presented. The main objective of this experiment is to demonstrate the interoperability between the two different types of drivers and, the interoperability between Java and non-Java components.

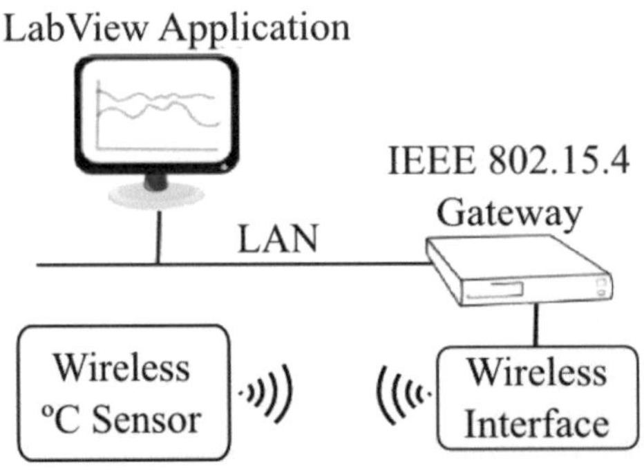

Fig. 10. Testing scenario used to monitor the air temperature using a wireless sensor.

A wireless sensor, based on a PIC18F2620 microcontroller from Microchip using, using IEEE 802.15.4 as wireless communications protocol, transmits its data to a wireless interface card. This card, based on an XBee IEEE802.15.4 transceiver, is connected to a computer where the two device drivers above presented are running: the IEEE 802.15.4 network interface device driver and the temperature sensor object driver.

On a remote computer, connected to the LAN (Local Area Network), there is a LabView application that collects data from the wireless sensor. This application communicates with the object driver using Web Services. On Fig. 11 a screen-shot of this application is presented, showing the plot of data gathered over a period of 24 hours, with a sampling period of 5 minutes.

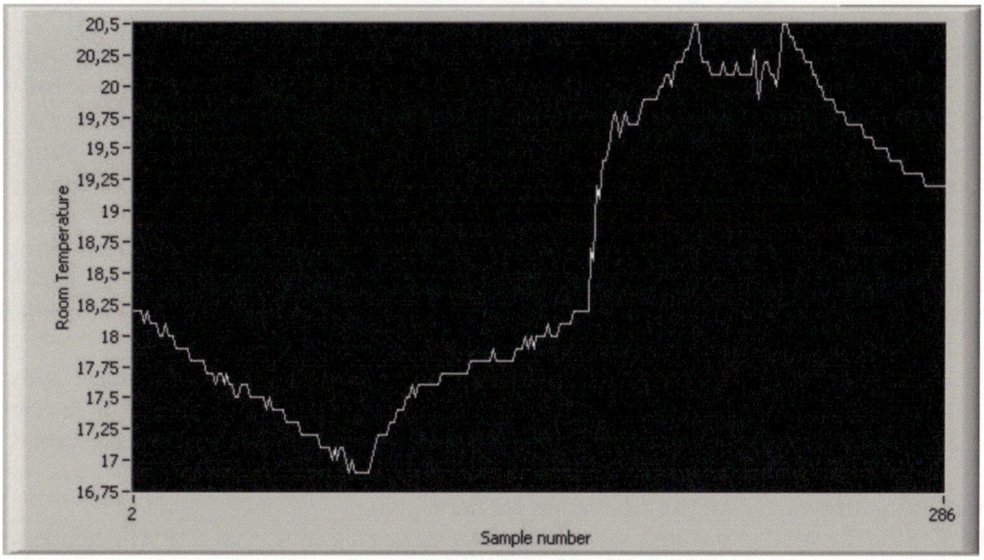

Fig. 11. Temperature acquisition from a wireless sensor using LabView.

6.2 Temperature control of a greenhouse model

This test consisted in the temperature control of a greenhouse model, using the scenario presented in Fig. 12. The objective it to control the temperature of the greenhouse, testing the proposed system in data acquisition and actuation tasks using embedded Java and the Java-based low-level device driver.

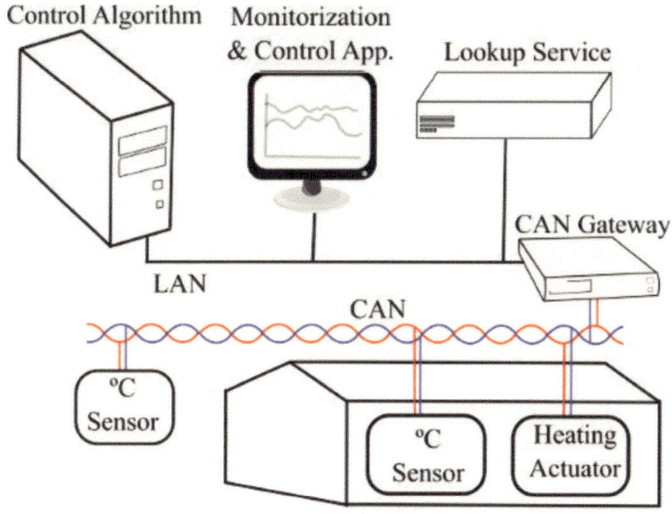

Fig. 12. Testing scenario used to control and monitor a greenhouse air temperature.

In this example two analogue temperature sensors with voltage output (LM35DZ) were plugged to two acquisition boards which were connected to a CAN bus. These boards are based on the 8-bit microcontroller PIC18F2680 and were running the embedded Java Virtual Machine. Another microcontroller-based board, also connected to the CAN bus, was used to control the heating system of the greenhouse.

A CAN gateway, running the low-level CAN device driver, is connected to the CAN bus and to the Local Area Network used in the tests. For this test, communications between applications and the CAN driver are made using Jini JERI, so a Lookup Locator Service also exists in the network. This server is used by the driver to register itself as a Jini service and by the data acquisition application to locate the services on the network.

Acquisition of temperature is made by a Java application, running on a computer connected to the Local Area Network. This application uses directly the low-level CAN driver, sending and receiving CAN message objects. The purpose of this application is to collect data from the temperature sensors (inside and outside the greenhouse) and decide if it is needed to turn on the heating inside the greenhouse.

To assess the need for heating, the Monitorization and Control Application uses an additional service connected to the network. This service, the Control Algorithm Service, is also a Jini Service that registers itself in the local Jini Lookup Locator Service. When the Monitorization and Control Application starts-up it searches, in the Lookup Locator, for the CAN device driver and Control Algorithm services.

After finding the needed services, the applications starts collecting data from the temperature sensors, sends the current temperature and set-point to the control algorithm. The control algorithm computes its output and sends it to the Monitorization and Control Application. Based on this value it regulates the energy amount to send to the heating system.

As control algorithm a P.I.D. (Proportional-Integrative-Derivative) was used to control the temperature inside the greenhouse model. In Fig 13 two plots corresponding to the temperature inside and outside the greenhouse are presented. In this test a set-point of 22°C was used and the sampling period was 1 minute.

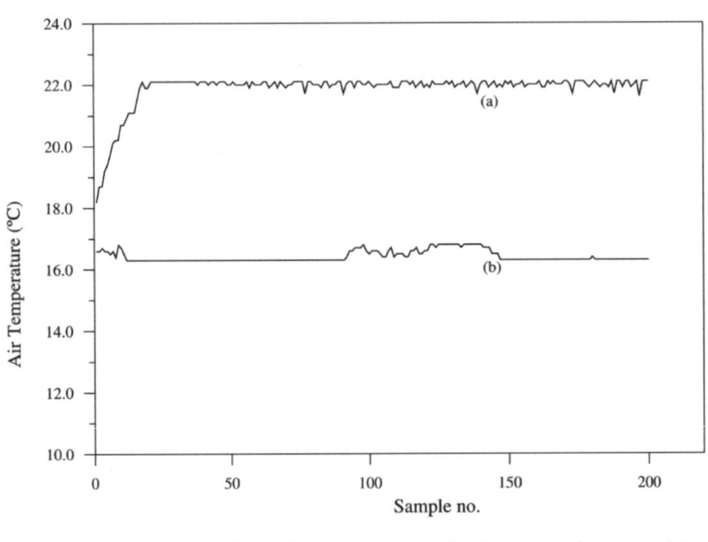

Fig. 13. P.I.D. temperature control of a miniature model of a greenhouse: a) temperature inside the greenhouse; b) temperature outside the greenhouse.

6.3 Speed control of a DC shunt motor

This last test consisted in controlling the rotation speed of a DC shunt motor, using a remote Java application. This application reads the motor speed from a sensor connected to the motor and controls its speed sending control messages to a power actuator. The scenario used to do the speed control is presented in Fig. 14.

The objective of this test is to show that with Java-based systems, it is possible to do tasks where a fast response time and low latency are needed. Speed control of a DC motor is only an example of such tasks.

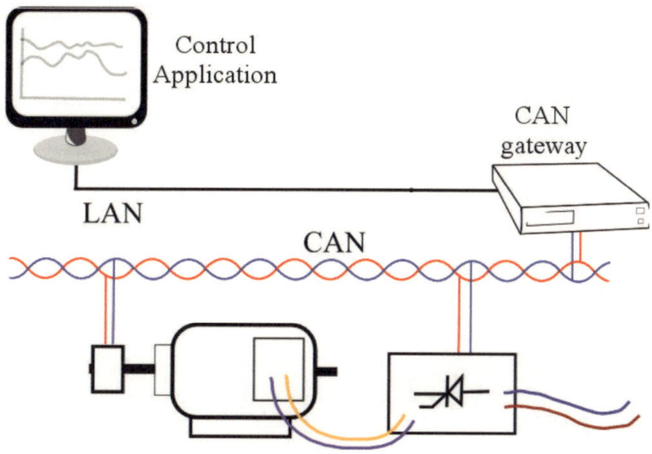

Fig. 14. Scenario used to control the speed of a DC motor.

A digital tachograph, coupled to the motor, is connected to the CAN bus, through which it sends readings of the motor rotation speed. It sends rotation speed values at a fixed rate of 5 samples per second. To be noticed that this sampling interval of 200*ms* was limited by the tachograph used in the tests, not by any constraint imposed by Java, the CAN bus speed or any other system component.

Connected to the same CAN bus there is also a controlled AC-DC converter. The output of this controller, which is remotely controlled, applies to the armature of the DC motor a variable voltage and therefore can be used to change its rotation speed.

In the scenario it also exists a computer to which the CAN interface card is connect and where the Java Device Driver is running and, in the same LAN segment, also a Java application to do the P.I.D. control of the DC motor rotation speed is running. Although this P.I.D. controller is on the same LAN segment, it is possible to connect it remotely, using the Internet, and despite the network latency it is possible to control the motor rotation speed (Silva et al., 2008).

Readings from the tachograph are sent asynchronously, i.e., when a new reading is available in the sensor it is broadcast to the CAN bus. Since the control application uses Java RMI to communicate with the device driver, it receives the speed value through the call-back mechanism. Based on the reading and the set-point, it computes the output of the P.I.D. controller and sends back to the actuator the value of the voltage to apply to the motor armature. The rotation speed of the motor is then corrected. Results from an experiment are presented in the plot of Fig. 15.

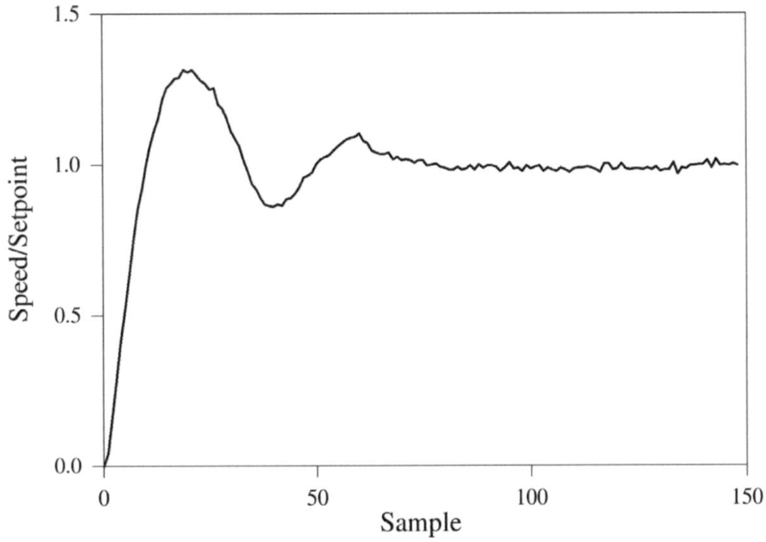

Fig. 15. P.I.D. Controll of the DC shunt motor rotation speed.

7. Conclusion

Example applications presented above demonstrate the feasibility and robustness of Java based systems for data acquisition in distributed environments, and, although Java is the core technology of the system, other execution environments can be integrated. This integration is made using a middleware technology. Being one of the most used middleware technologies, Web Services were adopted in the current implementation.

Besides these applications, authors have also been using the presented approach to Distributed Data Acquisition Systems in other work areas. Some examples of those applications include:

- DC-Motor speed control, using Matlab (Silva et al., 2008);
- Filling level gathering of recycle bins, using IEEE802.15.4;
- Wireless signal attenuation acquisition for wireless propagation studies, using IEEE802.15.4;
- Vegetation Growth detection.

The use of Java has proven to be reliable and very useful, allowing several different platforms to be used in the applications mentioned above. With this approach the examples presented in section 6 were implemented without having to concern about the target platforms. Applications and device drivers used in the testing scenarios were executed under Linux and Microsoft Windows family Operating Systems without any compatibility or performance issues.

Although Java is the preferable platform to develop the system components, and in fact it is presented as the core technology, applications developed using other tools can also be integrated in the proposed architecture. A non-Java application that interacted with the device driver using Web Services, implemented using LabView, was presented. Being a widely adopted middleware technology, Web Services allow to span the number of different platforms that can communicate with our system.

When using LabView a small wrapper application was used to convert communications between LabView and the Java-based Web Service. This wrapper was needed due to the fact that LabView does not communicate directly with Java Web Services, so a small application was developed in C# to cope with the problem. By doing this it is also shown that applications written in other programming languages, such as C#, can interact with the Object Device Driver.

At desktop and device driver levels applications have no noticeable constraints, while Java in microcontrollers can be limited by type of application (process time constants) and type of microcontroller used. In the tests made in silvopastoral and agricultural environments allowed to conclude that Java can be used in microcontrollers for this type of application without any performance constraint.

Although IEEE802.15.4 and CAN where used in our implementations, the concepts presented here can be used to implement driver to other communications technologies.

Integration of JDDAC in the layers of the proposed model and the use of IEEE 1451 are some the possibilities for future research in this project. This integration has as objective to span its compatibility, interoperability and openness levels, so desirable in a distributed data and control acquisition system.

Although tests made using a DC motor were successful, the response time of the system could not be warranted. So, another interesting future research field is the inclusion of Java Real-Time System (Sun, 2010) to deal with time critical situations. This will make the driver more reliable for systems with real time requirements.

8. References

Barr, R., Bicket, J. C., Dantas, D. S., Du, B., Kim, T. W. D., Zhou, B. & Sirer, E. G. (2002). On the need for system-level support for ad hoc and sensor networks, *ACM SIGOPS Operating Systems Review* 36(2): 1–5.

Boulis, A., Han, C.-C. & Srivastava, M. B. (2003). Design and implementation of a framework for efficient and programmable sensor networks, *MobiSys '03 - 1st International Conference on Mobile Systems, Applications and Services*, pp. 187–200.

Coulouris, G., Dollimore, J. & Kindberg, T. (2005). *Distributed Systems: Concepts and Design*, International Computer Science, 4 edn, Addison-Wesley.

Engel, G., Liu, J. & Purdy, G. (2006). *Java Distributed Data Acquisition and Control - User's Guide*, Agilent Technologies.

Gough, J. (2005). Virtual Machines, Managed Code and Component Technology, *Proceedings of the 2005 Australian Software Engineering Conference (ASWEC'05).*

Hardin, D. S. (2001). Crafting a Java virtual machine in silicon, *IEEE Instrumentation & Measurement Magazine* 4(1): 54–56.

IEEE (2006). *IEEE standard 802.15.4 – Wireless Medium Access Control (MAC) and Physical Layer (PHY) Specifications for Low-Rate Wireless Personal Area Networks (LR-WPANs).*

Ito, S. A., Carri, L. & Jacobi, R. P. (2001). Making java work for microcontroller applications, *IEEE Design & Test of Computers* 18(5): 100–110.

Koshy, J. & Pandey, R. (2005). Vm*: Synthesizing scalable runtime environments for sensor networks, *Sensys - 3rd International Conference on Embedded Networked Sensor Systems*, pp. 243–254.

Levis, P. & Culler, D. (2002). Mate: A tiny virtual machine for sensor networks, *In International Conference on Architectural Support for Programming Languages and Operating Systems)*, pp. 85–95.

Mattern, F. & Sturm, P. (2003). From distributed systems to ubiquitous computing - the state of the art, trends, and prospects of future networked systems, *in* K. Irmscher & K.-P. Fähnrich (eds), *Proc. KIVS 2003*, Springer-Verlag, pp. 3–25.

Michiels, S., Horré, W., Joosen, W. & Verbaeten, P. (2006). Davim: a dynamically adaptable virtual machine for sensor networks, *MidSens '06 - Proceedings of the international workshop on Middleware for sensor networks*, pp. 7–12.

Mitra, N. & Lafon, E. Y. (2007). *SOAP Version 1.2 Part 0: Primer*, W3C Recommendation. URL: http://www.w3.org/TR/soap12-part0/

Newmarch, J. (2006). *Foundations of Jini 2 Programming*, APress.

Pfeffer, M. & Ungerer, T. (2004). Dynamic real-time reconfiguration on a multithreaded java-microcontroller, *Proceedings of Seventh IEEE International Symposium on Object-Oriented Real-Time Distributed Computing*, pp. 86–92.

Robert Bosch GmbH (ed.) (1991). *CAN Specification*.

Rosenblum, M. & Garfinkel, T. (2005). Virtual machine monitors: Current technology and future trends, *Computer* 38: 39–47.

Serôdio, C. M., Silva, P. M. M. A. & Monteiro, J. L. (2007). A Java Virtual Machine for Smart Sensors and Actuators, *Proceedings of 2007 IEEE International Symposium on Industrial Electronics (ISIE'07)*, Centro Cultural and Centro Social Caixanova - Vigo, Spain, pp. 1514–1519.

Serodio, C., Silva, P., Couto, C. & Monteiro, J. (1999). Embedded java in agricultural control systems, *IECON '99 - The 25th Annual Conference of the IEEE Industrial Electronics Society*, Vol. 2, pp. 716–721.

Serodio, C., Silva, P., Couto, C. & Monteiro, J. (2001). Embedded java to enable jini facilities in agricultural networked systems, *IECON '01 - The 27th Annual Conference of the IEEE Industrial Electronics Society*, Vol. 1, pp. 255–260.

Silva, P., Serôdio, C. & Monteiro, J. (2008). A java-based controller area network device driver for utilization in data acquisition and actuation systems, *ISIE 2008 - IEEE International Symposium on Industrial Electronics, 2008*, pp. 1855–1860.

Simon, D., Cifuentes, C., Cleal, D., Daniels, J. & White, D. (2006). JavaTM on the bare metal of wireless sensor devices: the squawk java virtual machine, *VEE '06: Proceedings of the 2nd international conference on Virtual execution environments*, pp. 78–88.

Sommer, F. (2003). *Call on extensible RMI: An introduction to* JERI. URL: JavaWorld, Online - http://www.javaworld.com/javaworld/jw-12-2003/jw-1219-jiniology.html

Stanley-Marbell, P. & Iftode, L. (2000). Scylla: A smart virtual machine for mobile embedded systems, *WMCSA2000 - 3rd IEEE Workshop on Mobile Computing Systems and Applications*, pp. 41–50.

Sun (2003). *Java Technology Concept Map*. URL: http://java.sun.com/developer/onlineTraining/ new2java/javamap/

Sun (2005). *Sun SPOT System: Turning Vision into Reality*. URL: http://labs.oracle.com/spotlight/SunSPOTSJune30.pdf

Sun (2010). *Sun Java Real-Time System*. URL: http://java.sun.com/javase/technologies/realtime/rts/

Sun, X.-H. & Blatecky, A. R. (2004). Middleware: the key to next generation computing, *Journal of Parallel and Distributed Computing* 64(6): 689 - 691. YJPDC Special Issue on Middleware.

9

Minimum Data Acquisition Time for Prediction of Periodical Variable Structure System

Branislav Dobrucký, Mariana Marčoková and Michal Pokorný

University of Zilina
Slovak Republic

1. Introduction

The term of data acquisition can be meant as 'long-term' acquisition of integral data (maximum-, average-, and root-mean-square values) sampled in order of hundred milliseconds up to seconds. Another meaning is 'on-line' data acquisition for real time control with data sampled in hundred microseconds. The goal of this work is to obtain (determine) necessary sample of acquisited data at shortest minimum time. The chapter of the work deals with specific utilisation of data acquisition for identification and prediction of transient behaviour of power electronic systems.

Transients in dynamic systems are originated by changes of energetic state of state variables of accumulation elements (in electrical systems: chokes' currents and capacitors' voltages). Their duration is of non-zero time in every case, as the instant change of energetic state of accumulation elements would require infinite power. Duration of transients is theoretically infinite, except the cases when the transient phenomenon does not occur in the system at all (connection of inductive load at the instant of time equal to current phase angle in steady state). Time behaviour of state variables in linear systems is given by actual values of all elements in the system. **State variables time behaviour and thus also system response in inverter systems depends as well on sequence of switching elements operation.** Later on, the paper analyses systems with periodically variable structure (e.g. in Fig. 1).

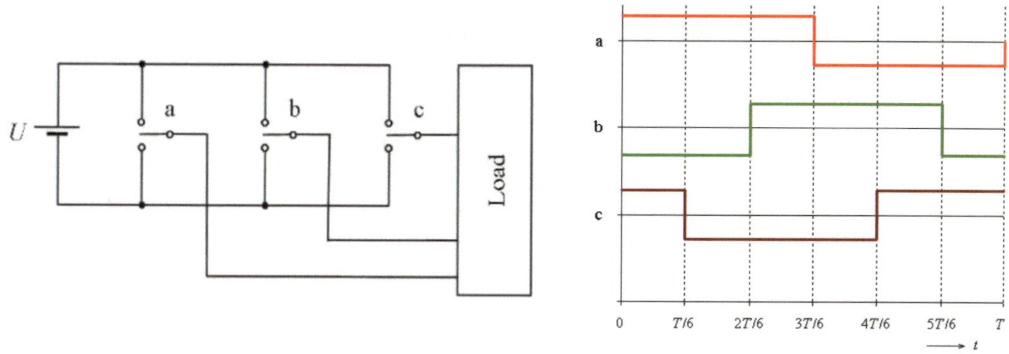

(a) (b)

Fig. 1. Three-phase inverter system as periodically variable structure (simplified model (a) and sequence of switching (b))

It is known that state variables can reach values during transients that are even multiple of their nominal values. That is one of the reasons why it is useful and desirable to know and predict these values in advance, using appropriate mathematic apparatus.
Majority of published papers dealing with discrete representation of desired quantities for transients' analysis at given time interval use methods based on sequentional insertion of values gained in preceeding interval ([Dahlquist & Bjork, 1974, Cigree, 2007, etc.]). Thus these values have to be known in advance. To speed up computation, the calculations are frequently performed in Gauss plane in orthogonal coordinates (α, β) using linear orthogonal Park-Clarke transform ([Jardan & Devan, 1969, Solik et al., 1990]). Method of prediction of the transient solution of periodical variable structure presented in the chapter is explained for the systems under periodic non-harmonic supply. It allows determination of values of desired quantities in any time instant and in any time interval, having only knowledge of situation during the first $1/2m$-th of the time period where m is number of phases.

2. Methods for steady-state and transient behaviour determination

It is useful to accomplish description of linear dynamic system in state space in the form

$$\frac{\mathrm{d}}{\mathrm{d}t}(\boldsymbol{x}(t)) = \boldsymbol{A}\cdot\boldsymbol{x}(t) + \boldsymbol{B}\cdot\boldsymbol{u}(t) \tag{1}$$

where:
$x(t)$ is the vector of state variables,
$\boldsymbol{A}, \boldsymbol{B}$ matrices of system elements,
$u(t)$ input vector of exciting functions
and also for other analysed variables in the form

$$\boldsymbol{y}(t) = \boldsymbol{C}\cdot\boldsymbol{x}(t) + \sum_{i=0}^{r}\left[\boldsymbol{D}\cdot\boldsymbol{u}^{(i)}(t)\right] \tag{2}$$

where:
$y(t)$ is the vector of output variables,
$\boldsymbol{C}, \boldsymbol{D}$ system matrices,
r highest order of derivatives of the input vector (providing the derivatives exist).
The solution for state variables can be analytical one, accomplished in time domain, e.g. using constant variation method or using convolution theorem, or numerical ([Dahlquist et al, 1974]), using time discretisation of (1)

$$\boldsymbol{x}_{\mathrm{n}+1} = \boldsymbol{F}_{\mathrm{n}}\cdot\boldsymbol{x}_{\mathrm{n}} + \boldsymbol{G}_{\mathrm{n}}\cdot\boldsymbol{u}_{\mathrm{n}} \tag{3}$$

There are a number of methods to accomplish above mentioned task; they are sufficiently explained in the literature. The only remark can be pointed out: for non-linear system with time constants of various orders (stiff system) the discretisation methods of higher orders are characterised by non-permissible residual errors; thus the methods can only be used for equations up to the second order [Dahlquist & Bjork, 1974]. The advantage is to have matrices $\boldsymbol{F}_{\mathrm{n}}$ and $\boldsymbol{G}_{\mathrm{n}}$ stationary ones – they do not have to be calculated in each computational step. Non-stationary matrixes' elements can be transferred into the input vectors of exciting functions as fictitious exciting ones. Repeated calculations of matrixes $\boldsymbol{F}_{\mathrm{n}}$ and $\boldsymbol{G}_{\mathrm{n}}$ is then necessary in case of changes of integration step only. It is more convenient to use methods for discretisation where state transient matrix exp(*A*.*t*) can be expressed in semi-symbolic form using numerical technique [Mann, 1982]. Unlike the expansion of the matrix into Taylor series these methods need a (numerical) calculation of characteristic numbers and their feature is the calculation with negligible residual errors.

So, if the linear system is under investigation, its behaviour during transients can be predicted. This is not possible or sufficient for linearised systems with periodically variable structure.

Although the use of numerical solution methods and computer simulation is very convenient, some disadvantages have to be noticed:

- system behaviour nor local extremes of analysed behaviours can not be determined in advance,
- the calculation can not be accomplished in arbitrary time instant as the final values of the variables from the previous time interval have to be known,
- the calculations have to be performed since the beginning of the change up to the steady state,
- very small integration step has to be employed taking numerical (non-)stability into account; it means the step of about 10^{-6} s for the stiff systems with determinant of very low value.

It follows that system solution for desired time interval lasts for a relatively long time. The whole calculation has to be repeated for many times for system parameters changes and for the optimisation processes. This could be unsuitable when time is an important aspect. That is why a method eliminating mentioned disadvantages using simple mathematics is introduced in the following sections.

2.1 Analytical method of a transient component separation under periodic non-harmonic supply

Linear dynamic systems responses can also be decomposed into transient and steady-state components of a solution [Mayer et al., 1978, Mann, 1982]

$$\boldsymbol{x}(t) = \boldsymbol{x}_{\mathrm{p}}(t) + \boldsymbol{x}_{\mathrm{u}}(t) \tag{4}$$

The transient component of the response in absolutely stable systems is, according to the assumptions, fading out for increasing time. For invariable input $\boldsymbol{u}(t) = u\mathrm{k}$ there is no difficulty in calculating a steady-state value of a state response as a limit case of equation (8) solution for $t = \infty$.

$$\boldsymbol{x}_{\mathrm{u}}(t) = \lim_{t\to\infty}\left\{\exp(\boldsymbol{A}\cdot t)\cdot\boldsymbol{x}_0(t) + \int_0^t \exp[\boldsymbol{A}\cdot(t-\tau)]\cdot d\tau\cdot\boldsymbol{B}\cdot\boldsymbol{u}_{\mathrm{k}}\right\} \tag{5}$$

For steady state component of state response $x_{\mathrm{T}}(t)$ with the period of T the following must be valid for any t

$$\boldsymbol{x}_{\mathrm{T}}(t) = \boldsymbol{x}_{\mathrm{T}}(t+T) = \exp(\boldsymbol{A}\cdot t)\cdot\boldsymbol{x}_{\mathrm{T}}(t) + \int_t^{t+T}\exp[\boldsymbol{A}\cdot(t+T-\tau)]\cdot\boldsymbol{B}\cdot\boldsymbol{u}_{\mathrm{T}}(\tau)\cdot d\tau \tag{6}$$

Steady-state component for one period is then obtained from overall solution

$$\mathbf{x}_{Tu}(t) = \mathbf{x}_T(t) - \mathbf{x}_p(t) \qquad (7)$$

Time behaviour in the subsequent time periods is obtained by summing transient and steady-state components of state response.
But, if it is possible to accomplish a separation of transient component from the total result, an opposite technique can be applied: steady state component is to be acquired from the waveform of overall solution for one time-period with transient component subtracted. Investigation can be conveniently performed in Laplace s-domain [Beerends et al, 2003]. If Laplace transform is used, the state response in s-domain will be

$$\mathbf{X}(s) = \frac{\mathbf{U}_T(s)}{1-\exp(-sT)} \cdot \frac{K(s)}{H(s)} \qquad (6)$$

where:
$\boldsymbol{X}(s)$ is the Laplace image of state vector,
$K(s)$, $H(s)$ polynomials of nominator and denominator, respectively,
$\boldsymbol{U}(s)$ is the Laplace image of input vector of exciting functions.
General solution in time domain is

$$\mathbf{x}(t) = \mathcal{L}^{-1}\left\{\frac{K(s)}{H(s)}\right\} = \mathcal{L}^{-1}\left\{\frac{a_n \cdot s^n + \dots a_0 \cdot s^0}{b_n \cdot s^n + \dots b_0 \cdot s^0}\right\} \qquad (7)$$

Transient component of the solution will be obtained by inverse Laplace transform of the following equation

$$\mathbf{x}_p(t) = \frac{K(0)}{H(0)} + \sum_{k=1}^{n}\left[\frac{\mathbf{u}_T(t)}{1-\exp(-sT)} \cdot \frac{K(\lambda_k)}{\lambda_k \cdot H'(\lambda_k)} \cdot \exp(\lambda_k \cdot t)\right] \qquad (8)$$

where:
λ_k are roots (poles) of denominator.
As the transient component can be separated from the overall solution, the solution is similar to the solution of D.C. circuits and there is no need to determine initial conditions at the beginning of each time period. Note: The state response can only be calculated for a half-period in A.C. symmetrical systems; then

$$\mathbf{U}(s) = \frac{\mathbf{U}_T(s)}{1+\exp\left(-s \cdot \frac{T}{2}\right)} \qquad (9)$$

The time-shape of transient components need not be a monotonously decreasing one (as can be expected). It is relative to the order of the investigated system as well as to the time-shape of the input exciting function.
Usually, it is difficult to formulate periodical function $\boldsymbol{u}_T(t)$ in the form suitable for integration. In this case the system solution using Z-transform is more convenient.

2.2 System with periodic variable structure modelling using Z-transform

The following equation can be written when Z-transform is applied to difference discrete state model (3)

$$z \cdot \boldsymbol{X}^*(z) = \boldsymbol{F}^*_{(\mathrm{T/2m})} \cdot \boldsymbol{X}^*(z) + \boldsymbol{G}^*_{(\mathrm{T/2m})} \cdot \boldsymbol{U}^*(z) \tag{10}$$

so the required **Z**-transform of state vector in z-domain is

$$\boldsymbol{X}^*(z) = \left[z \cdot \boldsymbol{E}^* - \boldsymbol{F}^*_{(\mathrm{T/2m})}\right]^{-1} \cdot \boldsymbol{G}^*_{(\mathrm{T/2m})} \cdot \boldsymbol{U}^*(z) = \frac{\mathrm{K}(z)}{\mathrm{H}(z)} \tag{11}$$

Solving this equation (11) an image of system in dynamic state behaviour is obtained. Some problems can occur in formulation of transform exciting function $\boldsymbol{U}^*(z)$ with $n.T/2m$ periodicity (an example for rectangular impulse functions is shown later on, in Section 3 and 4).
Solution – transition to the time domain – can be accomplished analytically by evaluating zeros of characteristic polynomial and by Laurent transform [Moravcik, 2002]

$$\boldsymbol{x}(t) = \mathcal{Z}^{-1}\left\{\frac{\mathrm{K}(z)}{\mathrm{H}(z)}\right\} = \mathcal{Z}^{-1}\left\{\frac{a_n \cdot z^n + \ldots a_0 \cdot z^0}{b_n \cdot z^n + \ldots b_0 \cdot z^0}\right\} \tag{12}$$

Using finite value theorem system's steady state is obtained, i.e. steady state values of the curves in discrete time instants $n.T/2m$, what is purely numerical operation, easily executable by computer

$$\boldsymbol{x}_{\mathrm{ust}}\left(\frac{T}{2 \cdot m}\right) = \lim_{z \to 1}\left\{(z-1)\left[z \cdot \boldsymbol{E}^* - \boldsymbol{F}^*_{(\mathrm{T/2m})}\right]^{-1} \cdot \boldsymbol{G}^*_{(\mathrm{T/2m})} \cdot \boldsymbol{U}^*(z)\right\} \tag{13}$$

Input exciting voltages can be expressed as switching pulse function which are simply obtained from the voltages [Dobrucky *et al.*, 2007, 2009a], e.g. for output three-phase voltage of the inverter (Fig. 2)

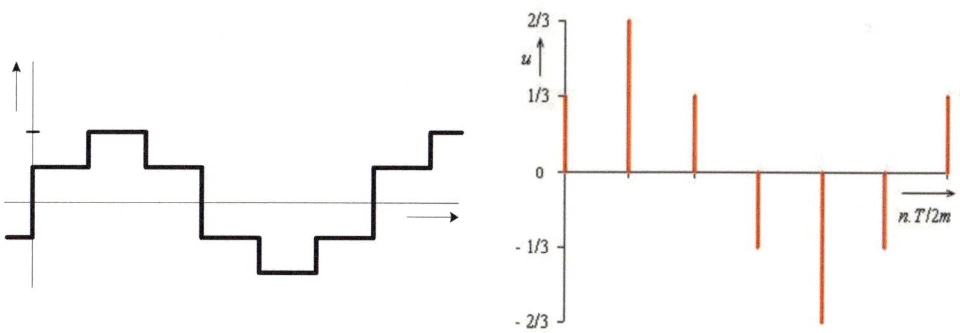

(a) (b)

Fig. 2. Three-phase voltage of the inverter (a) and corresponding switching function (b)

where three-phase voltage of the inverter can be expressed as

$$u\ (t) = \frac{2}{3} \cdot \sin\left(\mathrm{int}\left(6.f.t\right)\frac{\pi}{3} + \frac{\pi}{6}\right) \cdot U \tag{14}$$

or as switching function

$$u\ (n) = \frac{2}{3} \cdot \sin\left(\frac{n \cdot \pi}{3} + \frac{\pi}{6}\right) \cdot U \tag{15}$$

and finally as image in z-domain

$$U(z) = \frac{U}{3} \cdot \frac{z^3 + z^2 + z}{z^3 + 1} = \frac{U}{3} \cdot \frac{z \cdot (z+1)}{z^2 - z + 1} \tag{16}$$

3. Minimum necessary data sample acquisition

The question is: How much data acquisition and for how long acquisition time? It depends on symmetry of input exciting function of the system.

3.1 Determined periodical exciting function (supply voltage) and linear constant load system (with any symmetry)

Principal system response is depicted in Fig. 3

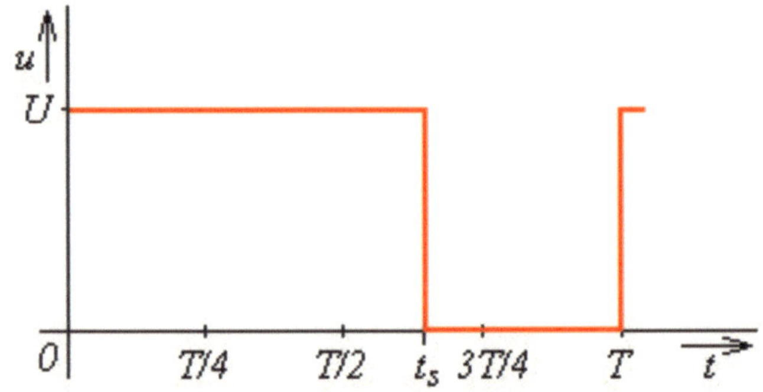

Fig. 3. Periodical non-harmonic voltage (red) without symmetry

In such a case one need one time period for acqusited data with sampling interval Δt given by Shannon-Kotelnikov theorem. Practically sampling interval should be less than 1 el. degree. Then number of samples is 360-720 as decimal number or 512-1024 expressed as binary number.

3.2 Determined periodical exciting function (supply voltage) and linear constant load system with *T*/2 symmetry

Contrary to the previous case one need one half of time period for acqusited data with sampling interval Δt given by Shannon-Kotelnikov theorem. Practically sampling interval should be less than 1 el. degree. Then number of samples is 180-360 as decimal number or 256-512 expressed as binary number.
Principal system response is depicted in Fig. 4.

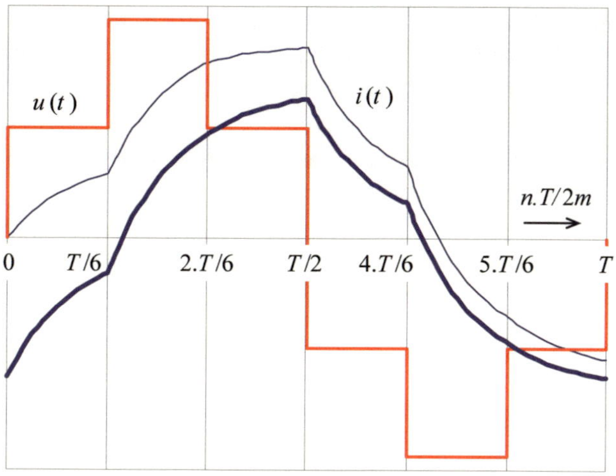

Fig. 4. Periodical non-harmonic voltage with $T/2$ symmetry (red) and current response under R-L load in steady (dark blue)- and transient (light blue) states

3.3 Determined periodical exciting function (supply voltage) and linear constant load system with *T*/6 (*T*/4) symmetry using Park-Clarke transform

System response is depicted in Fig. 5a for three-phase and Fig. 5b for single-phase system.

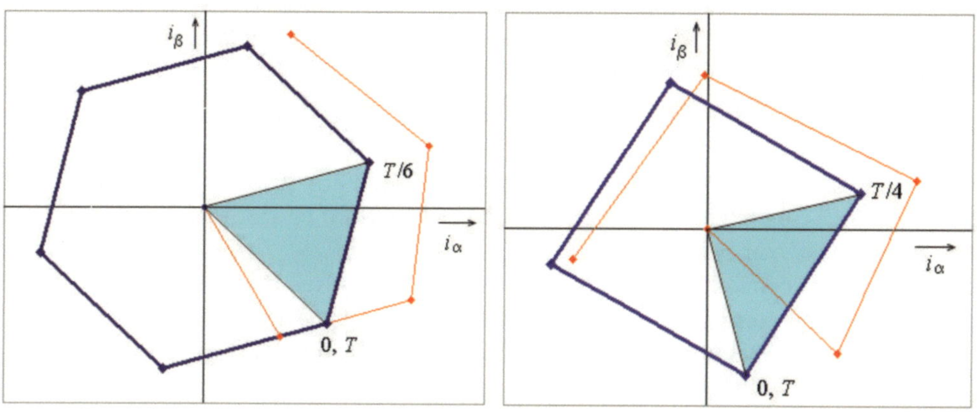

Fig. 5. Transient (red)- and steady-state (blue) current response under R-L load using Park-Clarke transform with $T/6$ ($T/4$) symmetry

In such a case of symmetrical three-phase system the system response is presented by sixth-side symmetry. Then one need one sixth of time period for acqusited data with sampling interval Δt given by Shannon-Kotelnikov theorem. Practically sampling interval should be less than 1 el. degree. Then number of samples is 60-120 as decimal number or 64-128 expressed as binary number.

In the case of symmetrical single-phase system the system response is presented by four-side symmetry [Burger et al, 2001, Dobrucky et al, 2009]. Then one need one fourth of time period for acqusited data with sampling interval Δt given by Shannon-Kotelnikov theorem. Practically sampling interval should be better than 1 el. degree. Then number of samples is 90-180 as decimal number or 128-256 expressed as binary number. Important note: Although the acquisition time is short the data should be aquisited in both channels alpha- and beta.

3.4 Determined periodical exciting function (supply voltage) and linear constant load system with *T*/6 (*T*/4) symmetry using z-transform

Principal system responses for three-phase system are depicted in Fig. 6a and for single-phase in Fig. 6b, respectively.

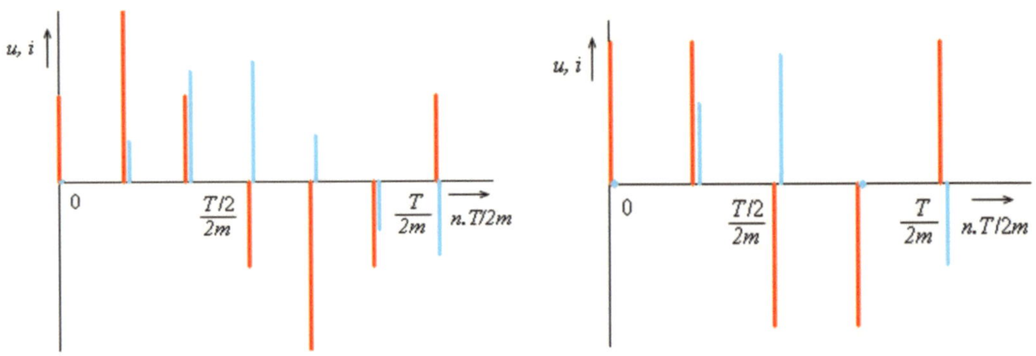

Fig. 6. Voltage (red)- and transient current response (blue) switching functions with $T/6$ ($T/4$) symmetry under *R-L* load using *z*-transform

In such a case of symmetrical three-phase system the system response is presented by sixth-side symmetry. Then one need one sixth of time period for acqusited data with sampling interval Δt given by Shannon-Kotelnikov theorem. Practically sampling interval should be better less 1 el. degree. Then number of samples is 60-120 as decimal number or 64-128 expressed as binary number.

In the case of symmetrical single-phase system the system response is presented by four-side symmetry. Then one need one fourth of time period for acqusited data with sampling interval Δt given by Shannon-Kotelnikov theorem. Practically sampling interval should be less than 1 el. degree. Then number of samples is 90-180 as decimal number or 128-256 expressed as binary number.

Note: It is sufficiently to collect the data in one channel (one phase).

3.5 Determined periodical exciting function (supply voltage) and linear constant load system with *T*/2*m* symmetry using z-transform

System response is depicted in Fig. 7.

The wanted wave-form is possible to obtain from carried out data using polynomial interpolation (e.g. [Cigre, 2007, Prikopova et al, 2007). In such a case theoretically is possible to calculate requested functions in T/6 or T/4 from three measured point of Δt. However, the calculation will be paid by rather inaccuracy due to uncertainty of the measurement for such a short time.

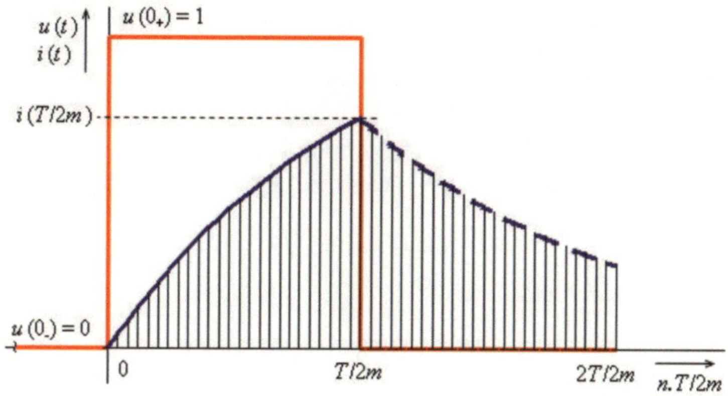

Fig. 7. Transient current response on voltage pulse with $T/2m$ symmetry under *R-L* load

4. Modelling of transients of the systems

4.1 Modelling of current response of three-phase system with *R-L* constant load and *T*/6 symmetry using z-transform

Let's consider exciting switching function of the system in α,β- coordinates

$$u_\alpha(n) = \frac{2}{3}\cdot\sin\left(\frac{n\cdot\pi}{3}+\frac{\pi}{6}\right)\cdot U \tag{18a}$$

$$u_\beta(n) = \frac{-2}{3}\cdot\cos\left(\frac{n\cdot\pi}{3}+\frac{\pi}{6}\right)\cdot U \tag{18b}$$

where n is n-th multiply of $T/2m$ symmetry term (for 3-phase system equal $T/6$).
The current responses in α,β- coordinates are given as

$$i_\alpha(n+1) = f_{T/6}\cdot i_\alpha(n) + g_{T/6}\cdot u_\alpha(n) \tag{19a}$$

$$i_\beta(n+1) = f_{T/6}\cdot i_\beta(n) + g_{T/6}\cdot u_\beta(n) \tag{19b}$$

where $f_{T/6}$ and $g_{T/6}$ terms are actual values of state-variables i.e. currents at the time instant $t=T/6$, Fig. 8, which can be obtained by means of data acquisition or by calculation.

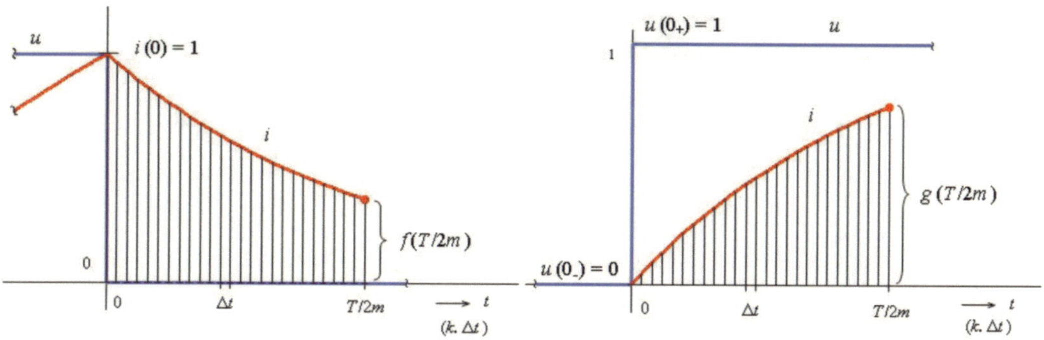

Fig. 8 Definition of the $f_{T/6}$ and $g_{T/6}$ terms for current in α- or β- time coordinates

Knowing these $f_{T/6}$ and $g_{T/6}$ terms one can calculate transient state using iterative method on relations for the currents (19a) and (19b), respectively. For non-iterative analytical solution is very useful to use *z*- and inverse *z*-transform consequently.

4.2 Determination of *f*(*T*/2*m*) and *g*(*T*/2*m*) by calculation

By substitution of $f(\Delta t) = 1 + \Delta t \cdot \mathbf{A}$ and $g(\Delta t) = \Delta t \cdot \mathbf{B}$ one obtains

$$i(\Delta t) = f(\Delta t) \cdot i(0) + g(\Delta t) \cdot u(0) \tag{20}$$

Based on full mathematical induction

$$i(k+1) = f(\Delta t) \cdot i(k) + g(\Delta t) \cdot u(k) \tag{21}$$

Note: $f(\Delta t)$ and $g(\Delta t)$ are the values of the functions in the instant of time $t = 1.\Delta t$, so, now it is possible to calculate above equation for k from $k = 0$ up to $k = \dfrac{T/2m}{\Delta t}$ having initial values $i(0) = 0$ and $u(0) = 1$.

Using transformation of equation (21) into z-domain

$$z \cdot I(z) = f(\Delta t) \cdot I(z) + g(\Delta t) \cdot U(z) + z \cdot I(0) \tag{22a}$$

$$I(z) = \frac{g(\Delta t)}{z - f(\Delta t)} \cdot U(z) + \frac{z}{z - f(\Delta t)} \cdot I(0) \tag{22b}$$

Supposing $u(k)$ to be constant then

$$I(z) = U(0) \cdot \frac{g(\Delta t)}{z - f(\Delta t)} \cdot \frac{z}{z-1} + I(0) \cdot \frac{z}{z - f(\Delta t)} \tag{23}$$

Thus solution for $i(k)$ will be

$$i(k) = u(0) \cdot g(\Delta t) \cdot \sum_{i=0}^{1} \left[\frac{1}{\left(z_i - f(\Delta t)\right) \cdot (z_i - 1)} \cdot z_i^k \right] + i(0) \cdot f^k(\Delta t) =$$

$$= i(k) = u(0) \cdot \frac{g(\Delta t)}{1 - f(\Delta t)} \cdot \left[1^k + f^k(\Delta t) \right] + i(0) \cdot f^k(\Delta t) \tag{24}$$

Note: It is needful to choose the integration step short enough, e.g. 1 electrical degree, regarding to numerical stability conditions [Mann, 1982].

So, if we put $u(0)$=0 and $k = \dfrac{T/2m}{\Delta t}$ we get $f(T/2m)$ directly

$$f(T/2m) = 0 + i(0) \cdot f^{\frac{T/2m}{\Delta t}}(\Delta t) \tag{25}$$

If we put $k = \dfrac{T/2m}{\Delta t}$ and $i(0) = 0$ we get $g(T/2m)$ directly (see Fig. 8)

$$g(T/2m) = u(0) \cdot \frac{g(\Delta t)}{1 - f(\Delta t)} \cdot \left[1^{\frac{T/2m}{\Delta t}} - f^{\frac{T/2m}{\Delta t}}(\Delta t) \right] + 0 \tag{26}$$

4.3 Determination of *f*(*T*/2*m*) and *g*(*T*/2*m*) by calculation

Using *z*-transform on difference equations (19a), (19b) we can obtain the image of α-component of output voltage in z-plain

$$U(z)=\frac{U}{3}\cdot\frac{z^3+z^2+z}{z^3+1}=\frac{U}{3}\cdot\frac{z\cdot(z+1)}{z^2-z+1} \tag{27}$$

Then, the image of α-component of output current in z-plain is

$$I(z)=\frac{U}{3}\cdot g_{T/6}\cdot\frac{z\cdot(z+1)}{(z-f_{T/6})\cdot(z^2-z+1)} \tag{28}$$

The final notation for α-current of the 3-phase system gained by inverse transformation $I(z)\rightarrow i(nT/2m)$

$$i(n)=\frac{1}{3\cdot R}\cdot g(T/6)\cdot\frac{1+f(T/6)}{f^2(T/6)-f(T/6)+1}\cdot\left[f^n(T/6)+\sqrt{3}\cdot\frac{1-f(T/6)}{1+f(T/6)}\cdot\sin\left(\frac{n\cdot\pi}{3}\right)-\cos\left(\frac{n\cdot\pi}{3}\right)\right]\cdot u(n) \tag{29}$$

Calculation of time-waveform in the interval between successive values n.T/2m and (n+1).T/2m

We can calculate by successive setting *k* into Eq. (21) starting from

$$i(k)=i(n.T/2m)\text{ for } k=0 \text{ up to } k=\frac{T/2m}{\Delta t}. \tag{30}$$

Also, we can use absolute form of the series (24) with $i(0) = i(n.T/2m)$, and $u(0) = u(n.T/2m)$. When there is a need to know the values in arbitrary time instant within given time interval

$$i(n,k)=u(n)\cdot\frac{g(\Delta t)}{1-f(\Delta t)}\cdot\left[1^k-f^k(\Delta t)\right]+i(n)\cdot f^k(\Delta t) \tag{31}$$

4.4 Modelling of current response of single-phase system with *R-L* constant load and *T*/4 symmetry using z-transform

Let's consider exciting switching function of the system in α,β- coordinates

$$u_\alpha(n)=\sqrt{2}\cdot\sin\left(\frac{n\cdot\pi}{2}+\frac{\pi}{4}\right)\cdot U \tag{32a}$$

$$u_\beta(n)=-\sqrt{2}\cdot\cos\left(\frac{n\cdot\pi}{2}+\frac{\pi}{4}\right)\cdot U \tag{32a}$$

where *n* is *n*-th multiply of $T/2m$ symmetry term (for single-phase system equal $T/4$).
The current responses in α,β- coordinates are given as

$$i_\alpha(n+1)=f_{T/4}\cdot i_\alpha(n)+g_{T/4}\cdot u_\alpha(n) \tag{33a}$$

$$i_\beta(n+1)=f_{T/4}\cdot i_\beta(n)+g_{T/4}\cdot u_\beta(n) \tag{33b}$$

where $f_{T/4}$ and $g_{T/4}$ terms are actual values of state-variables i.e. currents at the time instant $t=T/4$.
Using z-transformation on voltage equations one can get

$$U_{\alpha}(z)=U\cdot\frac{z\cdot(z+1)}{z^2+1} \tag{34a}$$

$$U_{\beta}(z)=-U\cdot\frac{z\cdot(z+1)}{z^2+1} \tag{34b}$$

Using transformation of equation (21) into z-domain

$$I_{\alpha}(z)=\frac{g_{T/4}}{z-f_{T/4}}.U_{\alpha}(z) \tag{35a}$$

$$I_{\beta}(z)=\frac{g_{T/4}}{z-f_{T/4}}.U_{\beta}(z) \tag{35b}$$

The final notation for α-current of the single-phase system gained by inverse transformation $I(z)\rightarrow i(nT/2m)$

$$I_{\alpha}(n)=\frac{U}{R}g_{T/4}\frac{f_{T/4}+1}{f^2_{T/4}+1}.f^n{}_{T/4}1+\frac{1-f_{T/4}}{1+f_{T/4}}\sin\left(n\frac{\pi}{2}\right)-\cos\left(n\frac{\pi}{2}\right) \tag{36}$$

5. Simulation experiments using acquisited data

Schematic diagram for three- and single phase connection, Fig. 9.

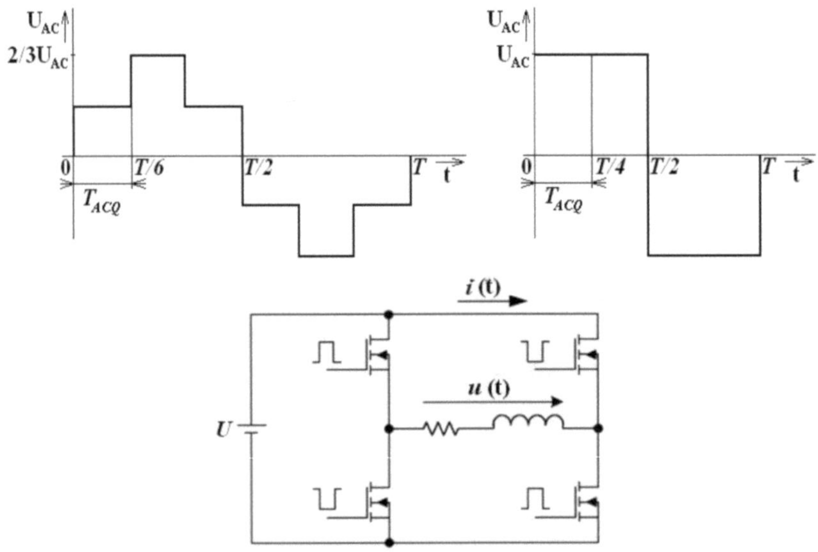

Fig. 9. Schematic diagram for three- and single phase output voltages and real connection for measurement

Equivalent circuit diagram of measured circuit is presented in Fig. 10.

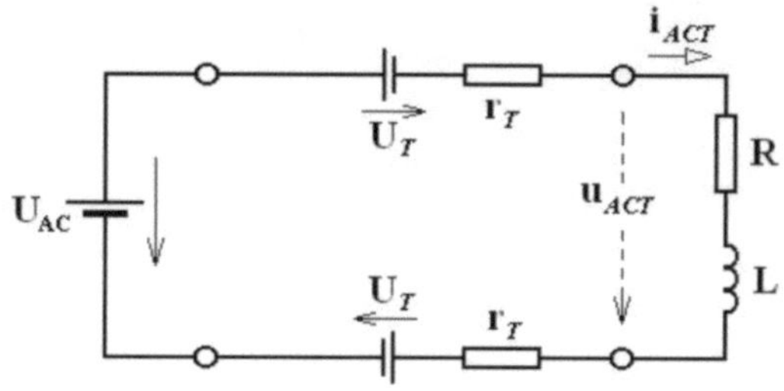

Fig. 10. Equivalent circuit diagram of measured circuit

Actual real data will be differ from calculated ones:

- other parameters, transient resistors, contact potentials, threshold voltages of the switches,
- parameters non-linearities,
- different switching due to switches inertials.

Tables of actual real values of the quantities u_{ACT} and i_{ACT} is shown bellow; Tab. 1 for determination of $g_{T/6}$ and $g_{T/4}$ terms, Tab. 2 for determination of $f_{T/6}$ and $f_{T/4}$ terms.

n	u_{ACT}	i_{ACT}	Δi
0	100,000	0,000	0,000
10	97,448	5,266	0,137
20	96,465	10,144	0,371
30	95,553	14,669	0,682
40	94,706	18,871	1,054
50	93,919	22,778	1,474
60	93,187	**26,415**	1,931
70	92,504	29,804	2,414
80	91,868	32,964	2,917
90	91,274	**35,913**	3,433

Tab. 1. Real acquisited data for determination of $g_{T/6}$ and $g_{T/4}$ terms

n	i_{ACT}
0	100,000
30	84,648
60	**71,653**
90	**60,653**

Tab. 2 Real acquisited data for determination of $f_{T/6}$ and $f_{T/4}$ terms

Actual carried-out date for simulation experiments are as following:

$f_{T/6}$ = 1,65 $f_{T/4}$t= 60,65

$g_{T/6}$ = 26,41 $g_{T/4}$t= 35,91

Time dependences of actual $u_{ACT}(t)$ and $i_{ACT}(t)$ are depicted in Fig. 10.

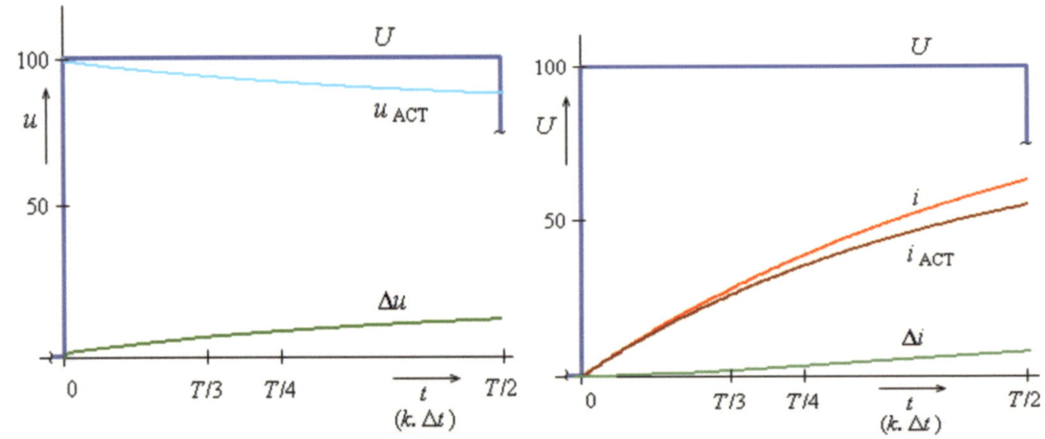

Fig. 10. Graphical comparison of actual real- and idealized calculated data of

Actually, each voltage (and/or current)-pulse should be practically shorter as idealized one from the mathematical point of view due to requested blanking time (or dead-time) $T_{\square}$ i.e. time-space between successive switched electronic switches [Mohan *et al.*, 2003]. This is fixed set between tenths of microseconds up to microseconds, so for high switching frequencies its effect will be stronger, Fig. 11.

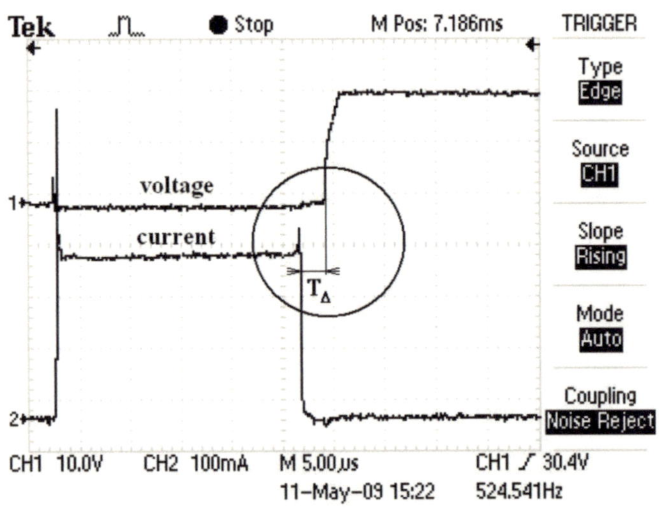

Fig. 11. Real measured blanking time at pulse width of 25 µs

Since both the complementing switches are off during blanking time, the voltage during that interval depends on the direction of the current. By averaging over one time period of the switching frequency ($f_s = 1/T_s$), the average value during T_s of the idealized waveform minus the actual waveform is

$$\Delta = +2T\Delta/T_s.U \quad \text{for} \quad i>0, \quad \text{and}$$

$$\Delta = -2T\Delta/T_s.U \quad \text{for} \quad i<0$$

The distortion in $u(t)$ at the current zero-crossing results in low order harmonics such as 3rd, 5th, 7th , and so on of fundamental frequency in the inverter output, that make it higher the total harmonic distortion of output quantities.
Simulation experiments will done with real actual data $f_{T/6}$, $f_{T/4}$ and $g_{T/6}$, $g_{T/4}$ using relation (29) and (36), respectively.
Carried-out results of three-phase system (Eq. 29) are shown in Fig. 12a,b both in complex and time domain.

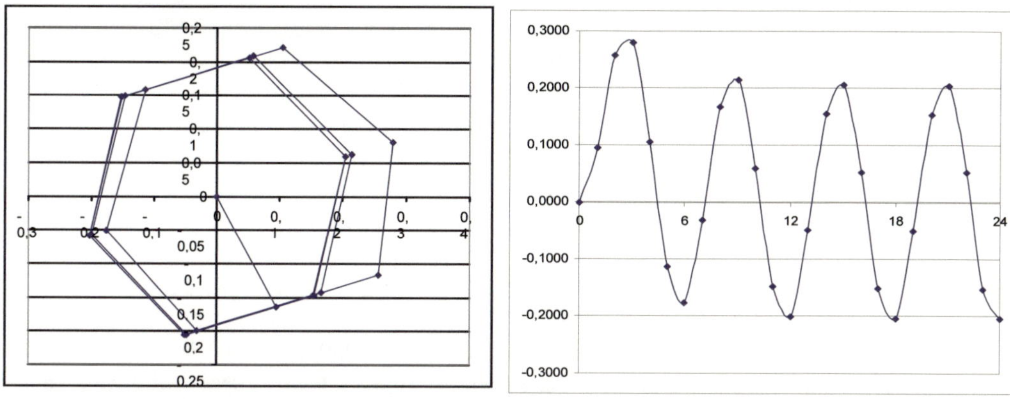

Fig. 12. a,b Trajectories of 3-phase system quantities in complex (left) and time domain (right)

Carried-out results of single-phase system (Eq. 36) are depicted in Fig. 13a,b both in complex and time domain.

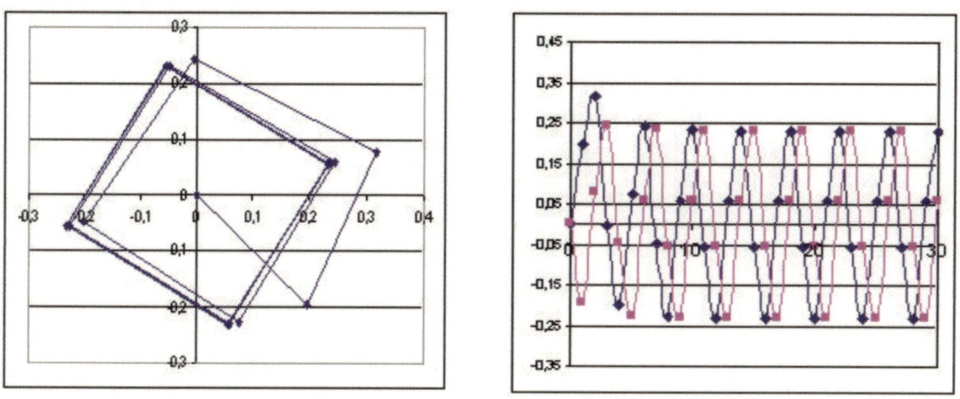

Fig. 13. a,b Trajectories of output voltage in complex (left) and time domain (right)

6. Evaluation and conclusion

A new method is introduced, which allows predicting and calculating behaviour of the system during dynamic states as e.g. switching on/off, load changes, etc. from the data obtained for one $2m$-th of time period. If impulse exciting function can be expressed with higher periodicity, e.g. nT/12, nT/18 etc., prediction of transients can be accomplished from the data gained even in shorter time interval, i.e. T/12, T/18 etc., respectively. Information about these transient states is needful for precise dimensioning of system's elements and for fair and reliable operation of the system.

7. References

Beerends, R.J., Morsche, H.G., van den Berg, J.C. & van de Vrie, E.M. (2003). *Fourier and Laplace Transforms,* Cambridge University Pres, Cambridge.

Burger, B. & Engler, A. (2001). Fast signal conditioning in single phase systems. *Proc. of 9th European Conference on Power Electronics and Applications,* pp. CD-ROM, ISBN 90-75815-06-9, Graz (AT), August 2001

CIGRE Working Group (2007). *C4.601 Modeling and Dynamic Behavior of Wind Generation Relates to Power System Control and Dynamic Performance,* CIGRE, August 2007,

Dahlquist, G. & Bjork, A. (1974). *Numerical Methods,* Prentice-Hall, New York, USA

Dobrucky, B., Pokorny M. & Benova, M. (2009a). *Interaction of Renewable Energy Sources and Power Supply Network,* in book Renewable Energy, In-Teh Publisher, ISBN 978-953-7619-52-7, Vukovar (CR), pp. 197-210

Dobrucky, B., Benova, M. & Pokorny M. (2009b). Using Virtual Two Phase Theory for Instantaneous Single-Phase Power System Demonstration. *Electrical Review / Przeglad Elektrotechniczny* (PL), Vol. 85, No. 1, Jan. 2009, pp. 174-178, ISSN 0033-2097

Dobrucky, B., Marcokova, M., Pokorny, M. & Sul, R. (2008). Using Orhogonal and Disrete Transforms for Single-Phase PES Transients – A New Approach. *Proc. of IASTED MIC'08 Int'l Conf. on Modelling, Identification, and Control,* pp. CD-ROM, Innsbruck (AT), Feb. 2008

Dobrucky, B., Marcokova, M., Pokorny, M. & Sul, R. (2007). Prediction of Periodical Variable Structure System Behaviour Using Minimum Data Acquisition Time. *Proc. of IASTED MIC'07 Int'l Conf. on Modelling, Identification, and Control,* pp. CD-ROM, Innsbruck (AT), Feb. 2007

Jardan, R.K. & Dewan, B.S. (1969). General Analysis of Three-Phase Inverters, *IEEE Transactions on Industry and General Applications, IGA-5*(6), pp. 672-679.

Mann, H. (1982). Semi-Symbolic Approach to Analysis of Linear Dynamic Systems (in Czech), *Electrical Review 71(11),* pp. 30-38

Mayer, D., Ryjacek, Z. & Ulrych, B. (1978). Analytical Solutions of Transient Phenomena of Complex Linear Electrical Circuits (in Czech). *Horizons of Electrotechnics, Vol. 67, No.* 3, pp.137-145.

Mohan, N., Undeland, T.M., Robbins, W.P. (2003). *Power Electronics: Converters, App-lications, and Design*. John Wiley & Sons, Inc., 3. Edition, 2003, ISBN 0-471-42908-2.

Moravcik, J. (2002). *Mathematical Analysis 3* (in Slovak), Alfa Publisher, Bratislava.

Prikopova, A., Hargas, L., Koniar, D. (2007). Generation of the values of the polynomial function. In: Advances in electrical and electronic engineering, Vol. 6, ZU Zilina (SK), No. 3, pp. 117-120

Solik, I., Vittek, J. & Dobrucky, B. (1990). Time-Optimal Analysis of Characteristic Values of Periodical Waveforms in Complex Domain, *Journal of Modelling, Simulation & Control, AMSE Press 28*(3), 1990, pp. 49-64.

Zhujkov, V.Ja., Korotejev, I.E. & Sutchik, V.E. (1981). Algorithm for Analysis of Electrical Circuits with Variable Structure (in Russian). *Elektritchestvo,* (3), 1981, pp.35-39.

10

Wind Farms Sensorial Data Acquisition and Processing

Inácio Fonseca[1], J. Torres Farinha[1] and F. Maciel Barbosa[2]
[1]*Institute Polytechnic of Coimbra*
[2]*Engineering Faculty of Porto University & INESC Porto*
Portugal

1. Introduction

In this chapter is introduced the issues involved in the Wind Farms Sensorial Data Acquisition and Processing. This chapter is organized in five sub chapters summarized afterwards. The first sub chapter is the introduction. The second sub chapter makes an overview of a wind maintenance system, describing in detail the software related to the acquisition system, the information system and other software. This sub chapter explains also the operation of the acquisition system, including algorithms, hardware and firmware details. The third sub chapter deals with algorithms that manage the results of a methodology presented in the second sub chapter, with the objective to illustrate the operation of the system. The penultimate sub chapter will present results including simulation and real operation of the system, data details for clock synchronization protocols with improved changes, acquisition time and a SVM (Support Vector Machines) classifier applied to sensorial wind data. Finally we will make the chapter conclusions and present the references used in this chapter.

The contribution of this chapter is in the design of the architecture proposed with emphasis for synchronous data acquisition in different geographic points. An improvement for PTP (Precision Time Protocol) is included to achieve fast time convergence in the initial phase of a clock synchronization setup. The control and setup of acquisition timings also play an important role in the system behaviour. This chapter also includes different alternatives for this subject.

Given the current energy framework and global climate change, the emphasis on renewable energy has grown a lot. One of the most important renewable energies is from wind that has given great contribution for this new paradigm. There are, however, many aspects that must be considered and are related to its framework as an energy environmentally friendly. This growth in wind farms has the effect of the increase in diversity of the type of equipment in wind turbines. Moreover, the average life of each wind generator and readiness of this kind of technology means that there is a legacy of equipments for different ages and maintenance needs.

An information system for maintenance, called SMIT (Terology Integrated Modular System) is used as a general base to manage the assets and for the strategic lines to the evolution of

maintenance management, which incorporates on-condition maintenance modules, and the support to the research and development done around this theme.
The use of open source software in many institutions and organizations is increasing. However, a balance should be considered between the software cost and the costs of its technical support and reliability. This way had shown to be a good option to integrate with SMIT, not only as the base for wind generators but as the base technology to other applications.
The SMIT system is based on a TCP/IP network, using a *Linux* server running a *PostgreSQL* database and *Apache* Web Server with PHP, and *Octave* and *R* software for numerical analysis. This maintenance system for wind systems uses also special low cost hardware for data acquisition on floor level. The hardware uses a distributed TCP/IP network to synchronize SMIT server master clock through Precision Time Protocol. The development of maintenance management models for multiple wind equipments is important, and will allow countries to be more competitive in a growth market. For on-condition monitoring, the algorithms are based on Support Vector Machines and time series analysis running under *Octave* and *R* open source software's.
A wind turbine is a complex system with several components changing constantly and supporting strong forces. By consequence, it can experience many problems, such as vibrations, electrical failures and many other kinds of faults (Joseph & Gutowski; 2008; Caselitz & Giebhardt; 2002; Hameed et al.; 2009; Scheffer & Girdhar; 2004; Durstewitz et al.; 2005). Additionally, wind farms are usually far from cities and from companies that support their maintenance. Technical assistance is expensive and the combination of on-condition maintenance with the best practices of operational research to minimize distance costs is extremely important. The main objective is to implement a maintenance plan using on-condition maintenance through on-line data instrumentation, acoustic techniques, vibration techniques (Fonseca et al.; 2009, 2008), infrared images, stress measurement, zero crossing current analysis and artificial intelligence, in a coherent and synergetic way. Another strategic objective of this work is to build the entirely system with open source and low cost hardware (MicroChip; 2010; Opensource; 2010). The reliability of actual microcontrollers and open source software is of great importance for market acceptance.

2. Wind maintenance system

2.1 Global overview

Fig. 1 gives an idea of the system design that consists of a server (SMIT), connected by TCP/IP connectivity to an Ethernet-CAN gateway. The data acquisition devices are interconnected in the CAN (Controller Area Network).
The SMIT system uses a Linux Server running *Apache* Web Server and PostgreSQL database (Open-source; 2010). This module/software is responsible for saving information in a structured way. Network connections can be made by fiber optics, UTP cables, Wireless, Satellite link or HSDPA/GSM technologies.
Data acquisition can be done using special low cost hardware made for this project, based on microcontrollers with special firmware. The methodology adopted relies on the use of low cost components and devices, to create a data acquisition system over IP networks. The basic idea consists on distributing a master clock among different field equipments, to ensure the synchronous acquisition of the different data collection points. The SNTP (Simple Network Time Protocol) (Group; 2010) and PTP protocols (PTP; 2010) are used to implement

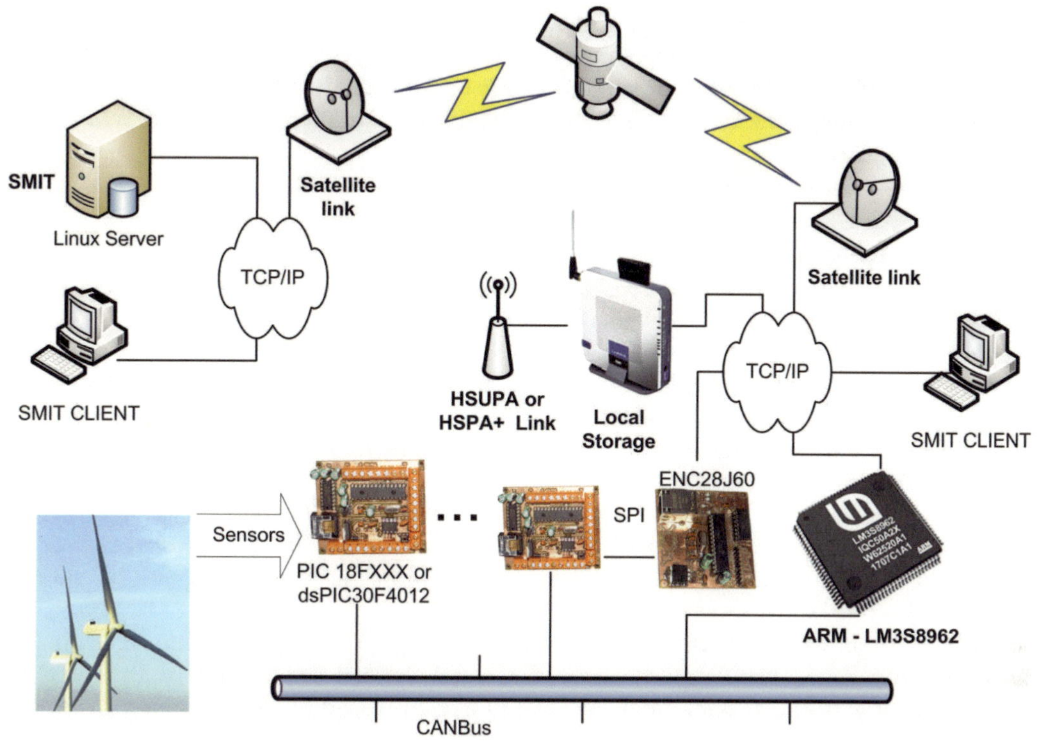

Fig. 1. An Integrated System for Maintenance of Wind Systems (Fonseca; 2010).

a set of control techniques in order to achieve clock synchronization. The basic structure of the system uses data collecting devices connected through a CAN network. One of the devices, with CAN and Ethernet connectivity, coveys the acquired information and relays it into the SMIT server. Simultaneously, this master node controls the data acquisition sequence, as well as the clock synchronization with the SMIT server. The integration of the developed hardware and software modules implies the data flow from the acquisition nodes to the server, which sends time references to the master device, including the reference clock signal. SMIT server uses a TCP/IP server for reception of data from acquisition points, using UDP (User Datagram Protocol) with acknowledgement.
Fig. 2 shows the flow information between different components.

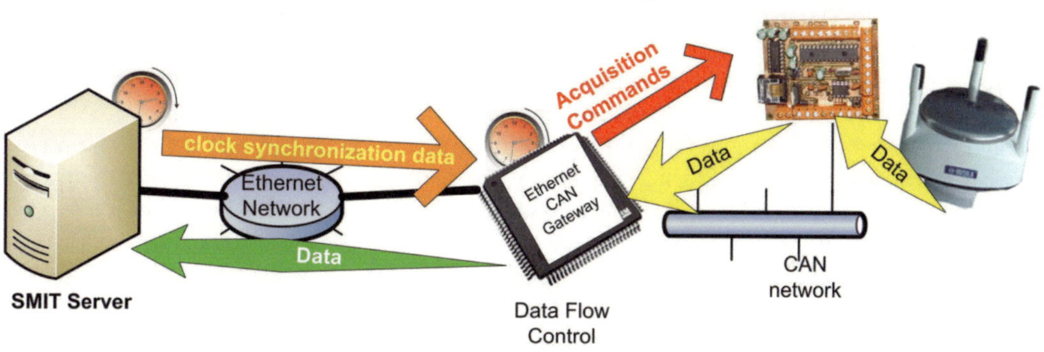

Fig. 2. Information flow between different SMIT's components (Fonseca; 2010).

The SMIT can also incorporate any hardware with IPv4 connectivity. Tests were performed with USB 6251 National Instruments Acquisition board (Hardware and Software; 2010), using LabView 8.5 and Beckhoff BC9100 (Wago & Beckhoff; 2010). These two tests addresses the industrial equipment usually used in some instrumentation systems of wind farms (Hameed et al.; 2010).
The SMIT server runs the SNTPD or the PTPD.

2.2 Software technology

The SMIT is supported by *Slackware Linux* distribution (Open-source; 2010), version 13.0 or 12.1.
The PostgreSQL has many features, for example, stored procedures are able to be written in PL/pgSQL, as native language and optional by third party, PL/PHP, PL/R, etc. SMIT uses PL/pgSQL to implement database procedures, where the main logic of the program is located. SMIT's database uses 149 tables and 156 PL/pgSQL stored procedures. *PostgreSQL* version is 8.2.3 and 7.4.16.
For remote access it is used an *Apache* Server running PHP, versions 2.2.4 and 5.2.1, respectively. Some parts of the maintenance system are available by web browser for maintenance intervention requests and information exchange by web services (Technologies; 2010).
The SMIT's users can interact with the system using a Windows interface developed in Delphi version 7 and print reports through Crystal Reports version 9.0 or PHP enabled reports both stored in a special database table in a compressed format, allowing easily new reports uploading.
The system is able to perform automatic installation of new versions in Windows systems. System administration problems with passwords are implemented using CPAU (Joeware; 2010). This is an independent software command line tool for starting processes in an alternate security context, enabling software installation, without problems with the Windows Administrator password.
In the security field, the database has been changed to protect the knowledge through encryption at the stored procedures level, configuration files and database storage. A special tool has been developed to translate a SQL database definition file to encrypt/decrypt the PL/pgSQL procedures, using lex and bison Unix utilities while the encryption algorithm is self made by the authors. All the connections to the database are made using SSL sockets, implemented through OpenSSL (Hardware and Software; 2010). The PHP distribution has been also patched to permit encryption of PHP files and storage in the SMIT Linux Server.
For numerical data processing, the SMIT integrates the Octave distribution version 3.0.3 and version 2.8.0 of R (Eaton and Gentleman; 2010)]. By default, the SMIT incorporates some algorithms (described in the next sections).
Finally, as described above, the system can be integrated with third party software via web services technology (Technologies; 2010), using any language supporting this technology.
Fig. 3 shows the type of relationship between SMIT server and SMIT client in terms of TCP ports and the type of information exchanged.

2.3 Hardware

The low cost acquisition system presented here includes PIC18F2685, ENC28J60 for Ethernet connectivity, a dsPIC30F4012 for high speed acquisition (MicroChip; 2010), a board using

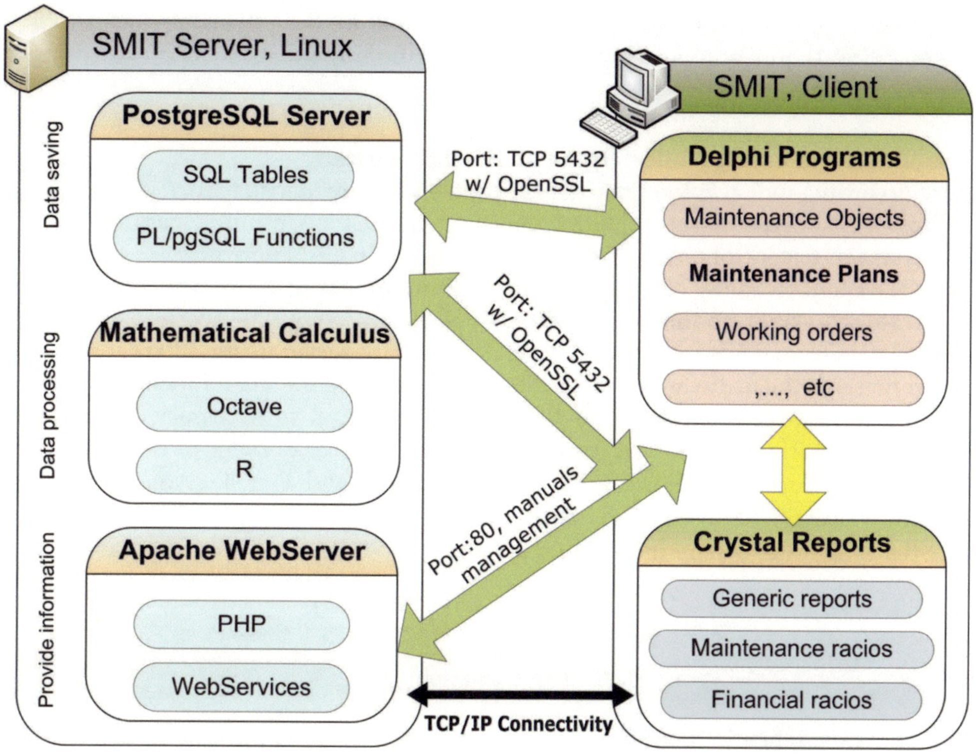

Fig. 3. Relational Diagram, SMIT Server *versus* SMIT Client (Fonseca; 2010).

Microchip digital potentiometers to implement a Butterworth low pass filter of 4th order with cut-off frequency between 100 Hz and 50 kHz and two cascade amplifiers with gain range: between 0.1 and 10. The frequency and gain are programmed by software using Programmable Gain Amplifier (PGA) and, finally, a board based on the Luminary microcontroller LM3S8962 (Luminary; 2010), an ARM-Cortex-M3 architecture with support for Ethernet packet time stamping in hardware, with two interfaces Ethernet at a 10/100 Mbps full/half duplex and a CAN 2.0 was built. All the programming tools for this microcontroller has been constructed based on GNU GCC toolchain for ARM-Cortex-M3 version 4.3.3, Binutils 2.19.1 and newlib-1.17.0 under Gygwin. This is the most expensive component of the system; however, it is priced by 12 Eur/unit and, in addition, an operational board runs with few elements. This board will be a gateway between the traffic from the CAN network and the Ethernet network (Fig. 2). Special interfaces for industrial sensors are also addressed to be used. Discrete analog signals and switching signals can be acquired. Analog signals, current and voltage are acceptable, if compatible with industrial standard 4-20mA current loop and 0-10V voltage. PIC software uses Microchip TCP Stack (MicroChip; 2010) and ARM uses lwip TCP Stack (Dunkels; 2003).

Relating to Fig. 2, the following blocks must be considered from hardware point of view:

- **Ethernet-CAN gateway** - Two systems can be used: ARM-Cortex-M3, LM3S8962, runs PTP client for clock synchronization; PIC18F2685+ENC28J60 running SNTP client for clock synchronization;
- **Acquisition points (slaves)** - PIC18F2685 for low velocity acquisition and dsPIC30F4012 for high speed acquisition connected in CAN network. ARM-Cortex- M3,

LM3S8962 and PIC18F2685+ENC28J60 connected in the Ethernet network if high demanding acquisition is required. Signal conditioning must be done according to the sensors used.

2.4 Execution and configuration of the acquisition system

In short, according to Fig. 2, the Ethernet-CAN gateway is responsible for:

1. Collect CAN network setup parameters and acquisition timings/periods table from SMIT server, to control acquisition points connected in CAN network;
2. Run PTP client receiving clock synchronization information;
3. Generate acquisition commands for acquisition points in CAN network;
4. Collect data from CAN network relaying it with SMIT server using Ethernet network.

Fig. 11, represents the firmware flow for this device showing the main functions described. For the acquisition commands to be temporally precise, it is necessary to measure the propagation time in the CAN bus, depending on the number of bytes of the CAN message sent. This procedure can be made on-line or off-line, and Fig. 4 gives an idea of the measuring process. The CAN acquisition message sent by the gateway to ask slaves to acquire data should be sent at (Figs. 4 and 5):

$$time_{propagation} = \frac{T_1 + T_2 + T_3}{2} \approx \frac{T_1 + 0 + T_1}{2} = T_1 \qquad (1)$$
$$t = time_{requested} - time_{propagation}$$

The CAN slaves, while in setup mode, will auto-baud the communication velocity until a valid CAN message is received. After this stage they will start the normal cycle, waiting for a message asking for an acquisition and forwarding packets for measuring CAN propagation delay time, or receiving messages for firmware upload.

Fig. 5 shows examples of real data measured in the system, to compute how must time previous to the acquisition commands should be sent to the CAN bus by the Ethernet-Can gateway. Fig. 6 shows the precise time when messages are sent to acquire. In this case (one message with one byte to send), the CAN message should be sent 310 μs earlier. Absolute error is about 2,5 μs which gives a relative error of 0,8.

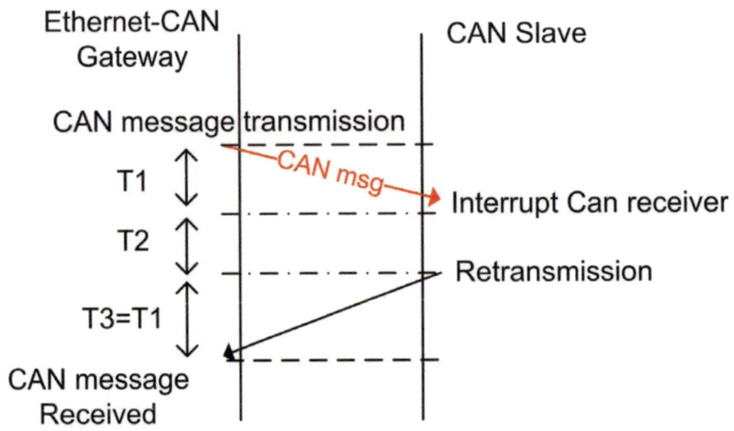

Fig. 4. Measuring delay in the CAN bus transmission media (Fonseca; 2010).

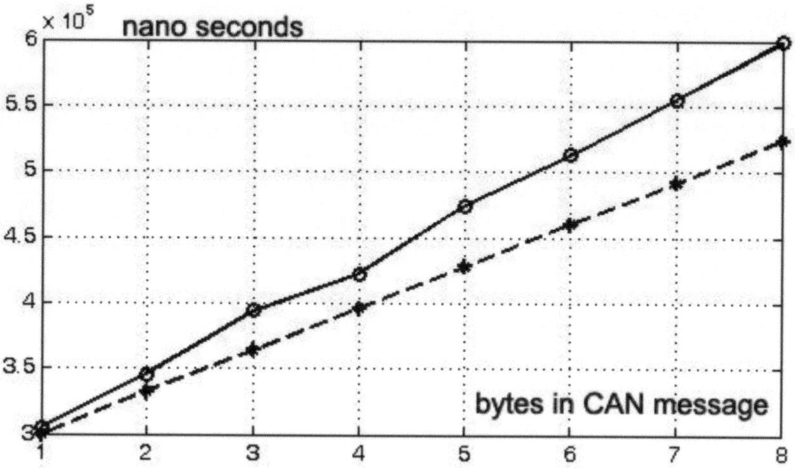

Fig. 5. Dash: Theoretical travel time (nano seconds) for transmitting extended CAN messages with 1 byte to 8 bytes of length. Solid: The delay time measured in the real system between Ethernet - CAN gateway and one CAN Slave (Fonseca; 2010).

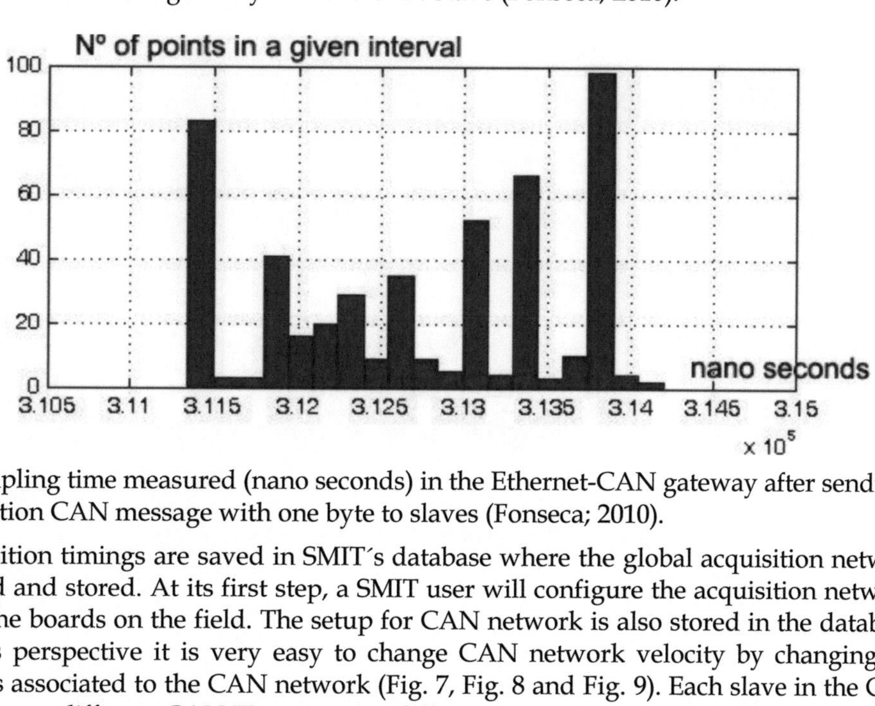

Fig. 6. Sampling time measured (nano seconds) in the Ethernet-CAN gateway after sending the acquisition CAN message with one byte to slaves (Fonseca; 2010).

The acquisition timings are saved in SMIT´s database where the global acquisition network is designed and stored. At its first step, a SMIT user will configure the acquisition network, choosing the boards on the field. The setup for CAN network is also stored in the database. Under this perspective it is very easy to change CAN network velocity by changing the parameters associated to the CAN network (Fig. 7, Fig. 8 and Fig. 9). Each slave in the CAN bus will have a different CAN ID, to receive different messages. The CAN ID for each card is always a multiple of 2. This limits the number of slaves in the CAN bus, but always lets to send a message that addresses all slaves, with acquisition instants coincident in time. At the second step, the information related to frequency sampling is indicated, and also the temporal interval like the starting and final acquisition date. These parameters are downloaded by the gateway board from SMIT server to control the sampling rate in the CAN bus, generating control signals for the I/O boards, as described.

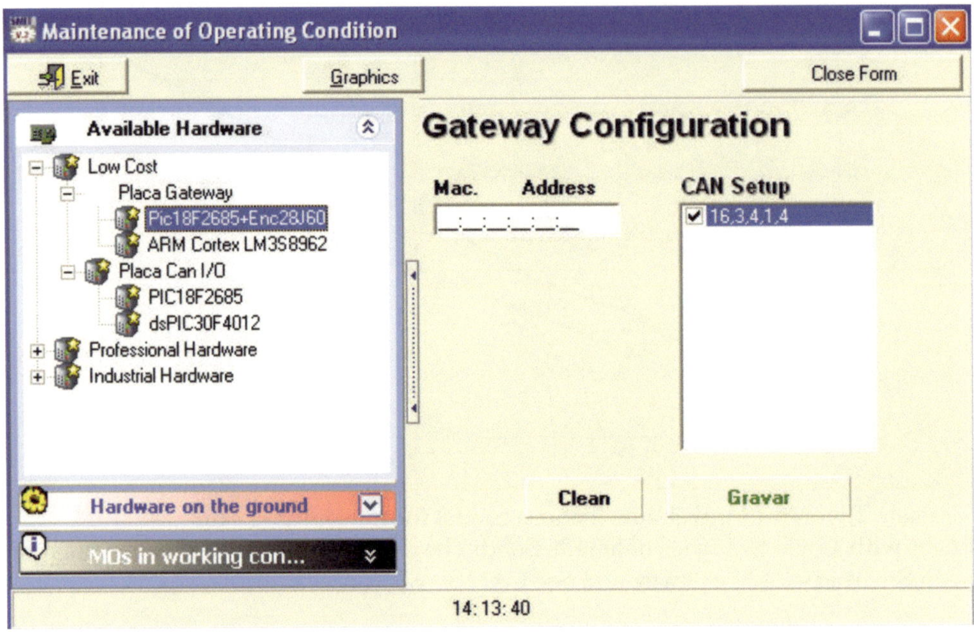

Fig. 7. Choosing hardware - in low cost mode a gateway is always needed as also as an I/O CAN board (Fonseca; 2010).

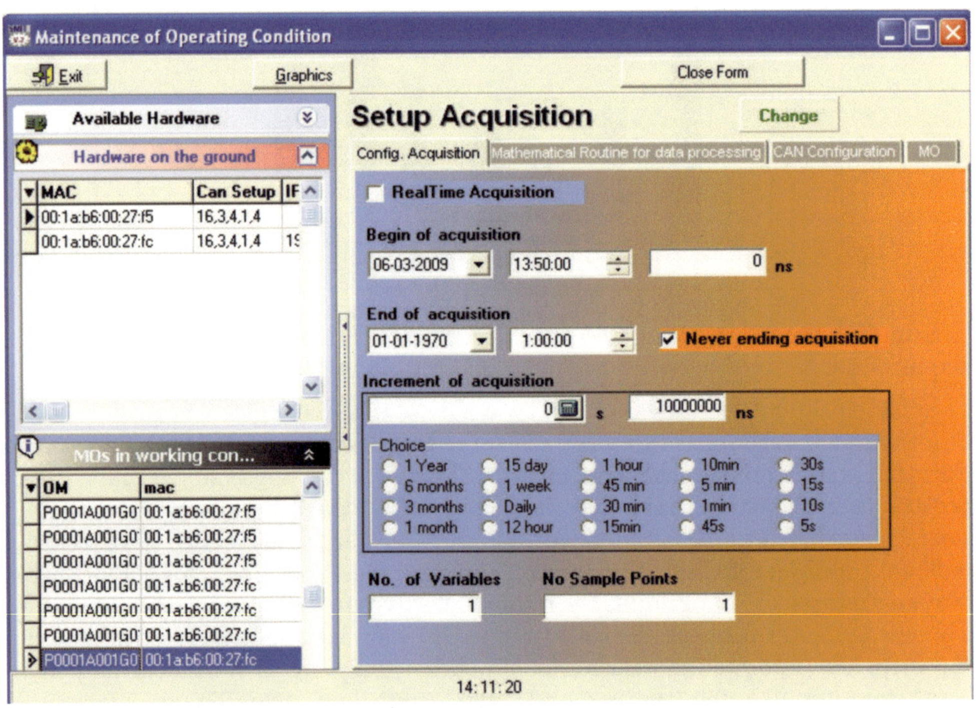

Fig. 8. Programming the acquisition temporization for each low cost I/O board in the SMIT´s on-condition module (Fonseca; 2010).

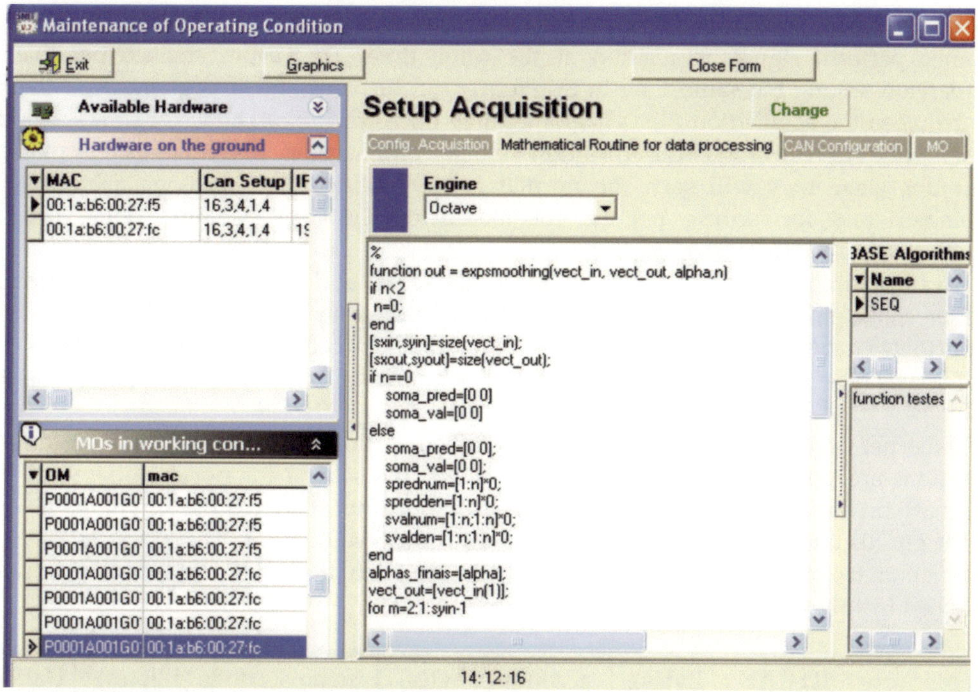

Fig. 9. Octave script using time series algorithms, for numerical data analysis (Fonseca; 2010).

2.5 Acquisition system operation

Acquisition timings are stored in SMIT's database, as also as the acquisition network topology. SMIT's user must configure the acquisition network topology, choosing the hardware that he wants to put on the ground (Fig. 7). The gateway board will use DHCP protocol to acquire an IP number, and receives the CAN setup parameters from the SMIT's database. This feature allows the user to change operation speed of the CAN industrial network in a simple way, altering the parameters stored in the database, as can be seen in Fig. 7. In the second step, the information related to frequency sampling is indicated, and also the temporal interval like the starting and final acquisition date (Fig. 8). These parameters are important to the gateway board. After this setup, the gateway will control the acquisition nodes (I/O boards), by sending acquisition commands to the CAN bus.

Fig. 2 shows a broad outline of how information flows through the system. The CAN-gateway is responsible by collecting data from acquisition modules connected to the CAN network. As can be seen, there are three types of information that can flow: a) information of clock synchronization in the Ethernet network; b) data acquired in the CAN network and then forwarded through the Ethernet network to the SMIT server using UDP packets with acknowledgment; c) acquisition timings sent by acquisition command messages to the industrial CAN network. The CAN bus devices are restricted to the global acquisition rate. If the number of nodes together generate data with a flow rate higher than the CAN network speed, the nodes must be divided by different CAN networks. Another goal is to synchronize the acquisition boards through time propagation from the SMIT server to PIC micro-controllers in the CAN bus using SNTP or PTP running in a cooperative way in the Ethernet-CAN gateway (Group; 2010; PTP; 2010).

Under this feature it is possible to ensure that different devices placed in different wind turbines perform signal acquisition at the same time. This aspect makes possible the comparison among the same data in different wind turbines and it is guaranteed that the gap between the acquisition times is less than 40 micro-seconds. The CAN slaves, in setup mode, will auto-baud the communication velocity until a valid CAN message is received. After this stage they will start the normal cycle, waiting for a message asking for an acquisition and forwarding packets for measuring CAN propagation delay time, or receiving messages from firmware.

Fig. 10 shows the information flow between SMIT server and an Ethernet-CAN gateway. In order to make possible the communication it was created on the server SMIT a UDP server on port 9945, responsible for managing all communications between the two systems. This UDP server tells to the gateways, the SMIT IP, acquisition tables and also collects the field data.

The Ethernet-CAN gateway operation is described in flowchart of Fig. 11. Two different operations are presented, one for setup mode and the second for normal operation. This flowchart presents the Gateway behaviour. Another important feature of the gateway is how it guards and relays the data information to the SMIT server. The gateway saves the information from the CAN nodes in a FIFO. For each node, the information saved is described in Table 1.

Msg size	ID CAN (4 bytes)	seconds (4 bytes)	nano-seconds (4 bytes)	Data

Table 1. Data Message saved on Gateway FIFO, for each CAN node.

If real time is required for any node, the data received from the CAN bus by gateway is not saved in its internal FIFO, but relayed to SMIT server immediately.

When the size of the FIFO reaches the maximum permissible limit of a UDP packet, the data is packed and transmitted to SMIT server. If the FIFO has not received any information in the last two minutes, the stored information is sent to the SMIT server, leaving the FIFO empty.

Each device generates the information described in Table 1, after several devices have sent their data, the FIFO will contain the information organized according to Table 2.

Equipment 1	...	Equipment n

Table 2. Information saved in the FIFO, collected from the acquisition nodes.

2.6 Synchronous data acquisition using PTP

PTP protocol works in the following way: each slave synchronizes with the RTC of the master through a set of specific messages (Sync, Delay Request, Follow Up and Delay Response). Sync messages are sent at a periodic rate of $T_{Sync} = 2\ seconds$ (Fig. 12) (PTP; 2010; Luminary; 2010; Correll & Barendt; 2006).

The master clock (SMIT) is described by two variables, seconds and nanoseconds, i.e., Ms: Mns. Each clock cycle, the nanoseconds variable is incremented and normalized to the seconds variable. The slave (Ethernet-CAN gateway), a microcontroller operating at a frequency rate of f_{no} =40Mhz (clock period $T_{no} = 25ns$), needs to keep two variables Ns:Nns in absolute synchronization with Ms:Mns variables. The maintenance of these variables is

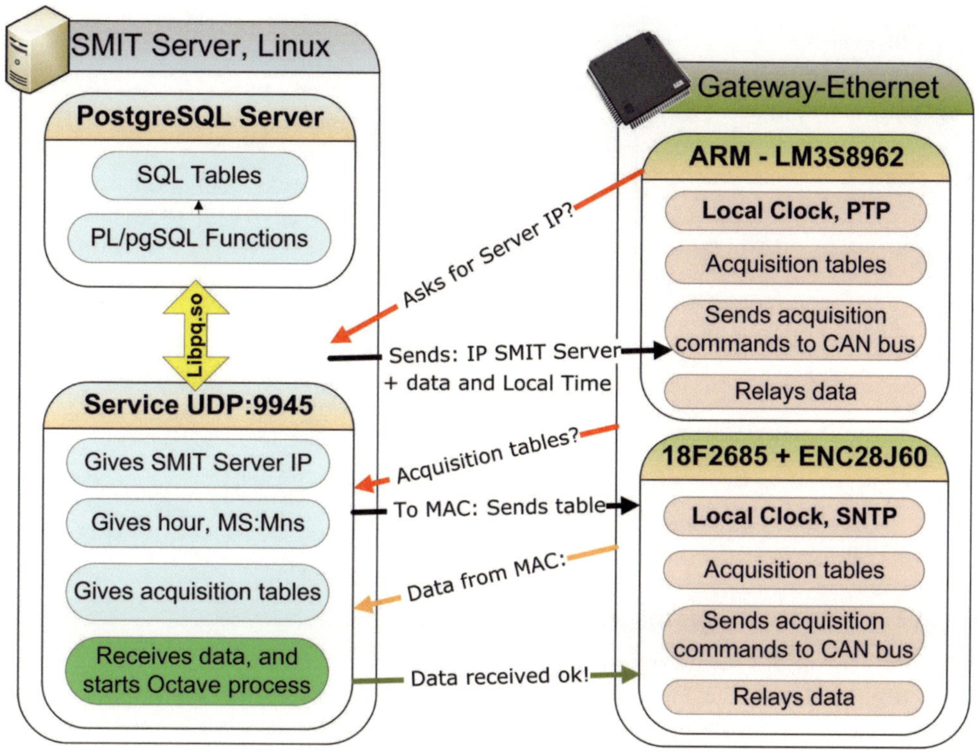

Fig. 10. Relational Diagram. SMIT server Gateway (Fonseca; 2010).

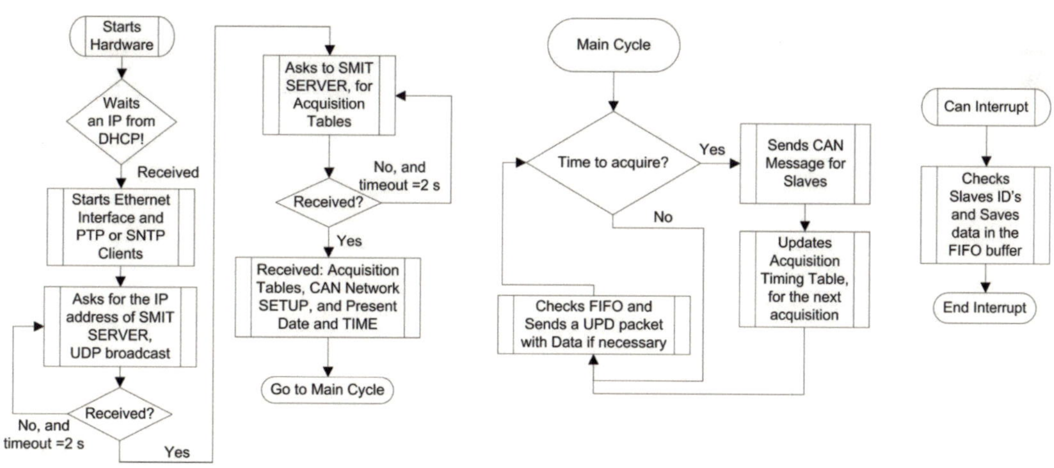

Fig. 11. Left: Ethernet-CAN gateway in setup mode. Right: Normal operation for acquisition control and data relaying (Fonseca; 2010).

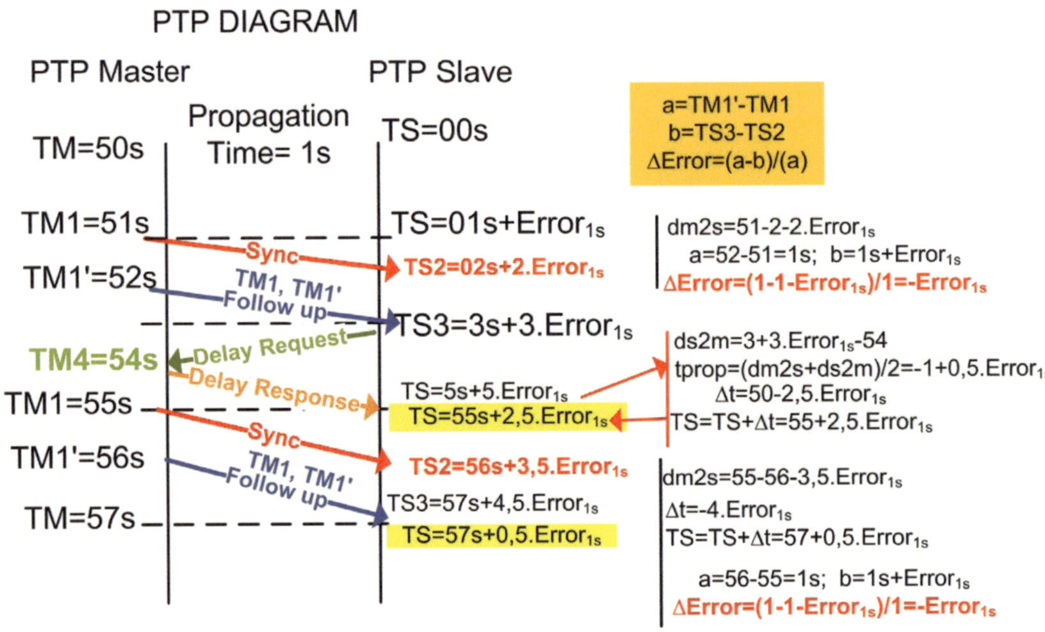

Fig. 12. PTP normal messages diagram (Fonseca; 2010).

usually done through Tick Interrupt System with a period of 10ms that is an adequate value for this timing. Thus, the value of Ns:Nns is incremented by 10 ms (10.000.000ns). In microcontrollers, when this interruption occur, it is necessary to plan a hardware counter (CNT_TICK), as described, with the value CNT_TICK_MAX = 400.000 = 10ms/25ns. The counter starts at zero and counts up until the limit (400,000), generating an interruption (to carry out maintenance on Ns:Nns), and restarting at zero again. To determine the correct time it is necessary to read the value of CNT_TICK and add it to the variables Ns:Nns. The theoretical accuracy of this system will be, in the limit, of the order of 25ns, whose value is impossible because it is the execution time of an instruction. Assuming differences in the frequency of oscillation of both clocks, which is perfectly acceptable with reference to the sender, without loss of generality the model of this differential can be designed and the clock error of the receiver defined by:

$$T_{no} = 25.T_m + \Delta T_{no} = 25ns + \Delta T_{no} \tag{2}$$

For a ΔT_{no} positive it means that the period of the slave is higher than the master. As a consequence, it will have an increase slowly over time, i.e. introduces a negative error in counting the clock given by:

$$\begin{aligned} Error_{10ms} &= -CNT\_TICK\_MAX.\Delta T_{no} \\ Error_{1s} &= 100.Error_{10ms} \end{aligned} \tag{3}$$

As the master frequency is Tm = 1ns that means: $\Delta T_{no} = T_{no} - 25.T_m$. From this description, it is clear that is necessary to require $\Delta T_{no} \rightarrow 0$ and change the value CNT_TICK_MAX. This control is not more than a software PLL function. The parameter CNT_TICK_MAX should be controlled and modified when calculating the error Δt in the reception of Follow Up

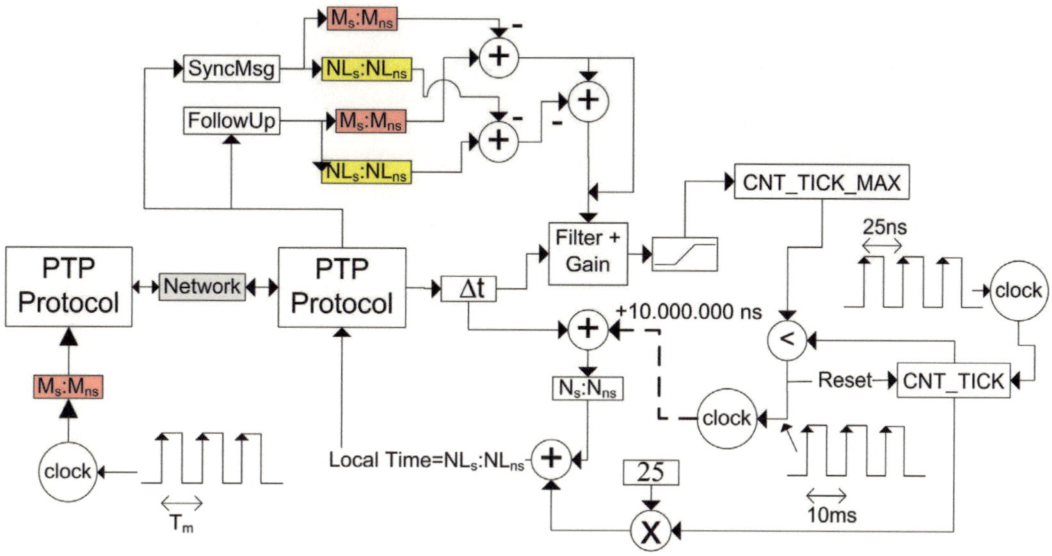

Fig. 13. Diagram to update local Slave clock with SMIT Master clock, using PTP protocol (Fonseca; 2010).

messages (if not send a Delay Request message) or at the reception of Delay Response messages, or both. This update of the base period of System Tick Interruption is directly related to the PLL operation. One additional note refers that the value of CNT_TICK_MAX has the following limits: it cannot be negative nor exceed the maximum allowable size of the microcontroller register. This means applying a threshold to the value calculated before it is reflected in the CNT_TICK_MAX parameter.

Experiences have also been made with two modifications in the PTP protocol, in particular changing the messages Sync and Follow Up to include the value of the master clock time (Fig. 12). Fig. 13 shows a block diagram of the text described, for the modifications made to PTP master software. The result shows a faster initial convergence due to decreased of initial error, but in subsequent periods is normal.

3. Relevant algorithms for wind turbine maintenance

In the literature many authors are working on this subject (Caselitz and Giebhardt; 2002; Durstewitz et al.; 2005; Hameed et al.; 2010). The data acquired from wind acquisition systems usually presents irregular values.

In this section will be presented two methodologies: the first one, a SVM classifier and the second one, prediction of the deterioration of operating conditions of the equipment by time series.

3.1 SVM classification

The data acquired from wind acquisition systems, usually presents irregular values. The system (on-condition classifiers) have to be very accurate, otherwise, a false error condition would be triggered. For example, when the wind break system is activated it is expected that the power curve differs from the relation published by the manufacturer; however, the inner axis rotation versus active power should maintain the relation, because the break will only change the rotation speed and not the relation between rotation speed and produced power. The same arguments are valid for the *pitch* system.

The first algorithm used for detecting an uncharacteristic operation will use Support Vector Machines (SVM) classifiers (Cauwenberghs & Poggio; 2000; Suykens et al.; 2002; Kecman; 2001; Zhizheng & YouFu; 2009). The goal is to decide if data measured by the sensors shall be processed in detail or just stored. If the SVM classifier indicates an anomalous situation, a detailed processing will be performed related to the sensors already installed. The SVM classifier uses $\vec{x}_{wind-turbine}$, based on equation 4, using RBF as kernel mapping function.

$$\vec{x}_{wind-turbine} = \begin{bmatrix} Wind\ Velocity \\ Wind\ Direction - Nacelle\ Direction \\ Rotor\ Shaft\ Speed \\ Generator\ Shaft\ Speed \\ Active\ Power \\ Break\ System\ State \\ Pitch\ Angle \end{bmatrix} \tag{4}$$

Due to the unavailability of measuring some of these variables, including alignment of the nacelle, the angle of the rotor blades and condition of the brake rotor, two alternatives can be used based on two vectors for classification (to determine what the best) given by equations 5 and 6

$$\vec{x}_{wind-turbine} = \begin{bmatrix} Wind\ Velocity \\ Active\ Power \end{bmatrix} \tag{5}$$

or

$$\vec{x}_{wind-turbine} = \begin{bmatrix} Rotor\ Shaft\ Speed \\ Generator\ Shaft\ Speed \\ Active\ Power \end{bmatrix} \tag{6}$$

The change described above facilitates the analysis and application of the classifier, resulting in the reduction of detectable abnormal situations. As a corollary of this assertion, for example, it is not possible to determine if the brake system works properly.

Taking in account the goal, it is only necessary to use a classifier with two states, damaged or in good operation, built on the power curve of the experimental wind turbine. Of course, there is the need to allocate a tolerance, ie, the power curve is given by a "band" as can be seen in Fig. 14. Within the two curves the equipment is still considered in "proper operation".

One suggestion for future developments might go through considering various parts of the operating condition, namely, good condition, reasonable condition, almost damaged and broken, thus making a smoother transition between areas of good functioning and malfunctioning. The problem lies in defining the transition rates between different states of damage.

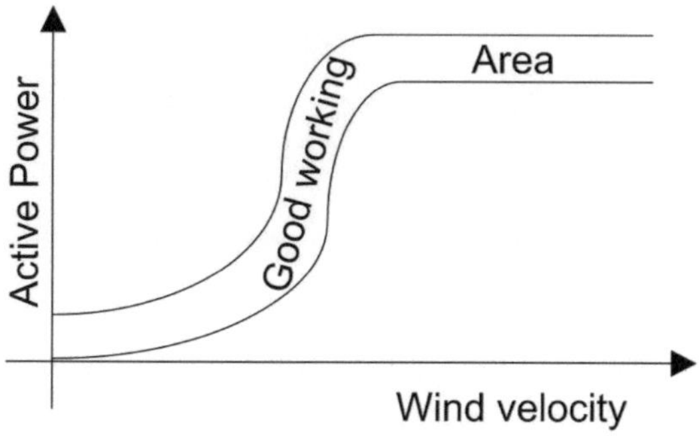

Fig. 14. Power Curve Area considered in proper operation (equation 5) (Fonseca; 2010).

3.2 Degradation curve estimation using time series

The condition of any equipment can be described using indicative variables, including the evolution of its values. A trend analysis, together with a specification of allowable limits for these parameters will permit to infer the evolution of the degradation of equipment operation. Thus an appropriate methodology is to use time series to analyze the evolution of these parameters using prediction.

Another purely statistical hypothesis would be through the Weibull distribution to characterize the reliability of equipment, supported by the calculation of probability of failure. However, this approach goes beyond the scope of this chapter because it requires a history with a considerable temporal dimension, whose data is not available.

The algorithm to forecast the degradation curve uses time series analysis techniques.

The quality of forecasting will be measured by the following error indicators: MSE (Mean Squared Error), TIC (Theil Inequality Coefficient), STD (Standard Deviation), and MAE (Mean Absolute Error).

Several methods, based on time series, were used to estimate the curve of degradation of equipment. These methods can be applied to various characteristics, such as temperature, pressure, etc.. The methods were ARRSE (Adaptive-Response-Rate Single Exponential Smoothing), ES (Exponential Smoothing), HW (Holt-Winters or Double Exponential Smoothing), HWSas (Holt-Winters with Seasonality), ESMSE (Exponential Smoothing, proposed method), ARMA (Autoregressive Moving Average), SVR-RBF (Support Vector Regression with RBF Kernels), SVR-LIN (Support Vector Regression with Linear Kernels) (details on (Fonseca et al.; 2009)). All this methods are of scientific value-added. In particular, the "exponential smoothing" modified to adapt the parameter α. The basic method of Exponential Smoothing is driven by the following equation:

$$\hat{y}[k] = \alpha . y[k] + (1 - \alpha) . \hat{y}[k-1] \tag{7}$$

The value for α can be obtained minimizing the MSE, conducting to a non-linear optimization problem, usually solved by the Levenberg-Marquardt algorithm.

It is possible to continuously update α value (results will be labeled with ESMSE) and introducing an estimation of α with an implicit error, considering that the old forecasting values are independent of α; equation 8 represents the update. However, we will use the mean of equation 8 with the equation 8 substituting $\hat{y}\,[i-1] = y[i-1]$ (MSE minimization).

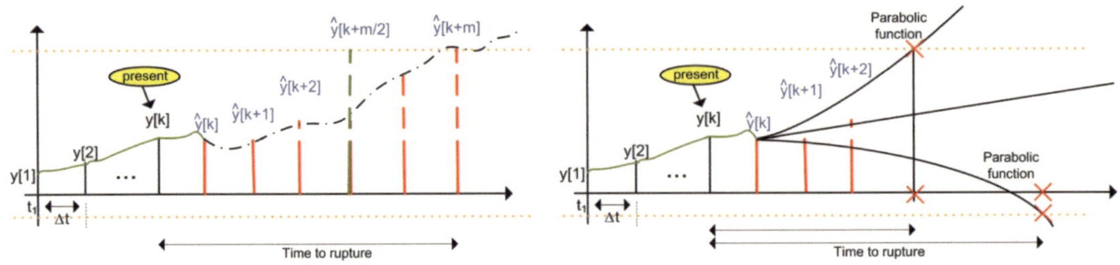

Fig. 15. Left: Prediction to rupture using time series prediction with m steps. Right: Using steps 1 to 3 with parabolic interpolation (Fonseca; 2010).

$$\alpha = \frac{\sum_{i=n}^{k}\left(y[i+1]-\hat{y}[i-1]\right).\left(y[i]-\hat{y}[i-1]\right)}{\sum_{i=n}^{k}\left(y[i]-\hat{y}[i-1]\right)^{2}}, n \geq 2 \quad (8)$$

Fig. 15 presents two methodologies to determine the time until rupture. Both techniques use upper and lower limits, indicating the area of good functioning. At left, the technique uses the prediction until m steps ahead, while the technique on the right shows an alternative based on interpolation. As the number of points to predict (between 1 to 3) is lower, the reliability of prediction increases.

4. Experimental results

This section presents experimental results based on the system described in the previous sections.

4.1 SVM classification

In section 3.1 was exposed a method, from a macroscopic point of view, to determine the operational status of a wind turbine. The methodology presented here uses values of several variables, which are subject to a classification of state (good / bad service). This section presents the results of this methodology that has been validated with real data from a wind turbine from north of Portugal.

Figs. 16 and 17 present the classification power curve according to the equations 5 and 6.

The first case, Fig. 16, uses the relationship between wind speed and produced power, which does not have into account the limitations imposed by the activation of the wind turbine brakes or by the *pitch* angle of the rotor blades. Even a malfunction, the ratio normally used does not take, as a consequence, an incorrect classification of the good points of functioning as a moment of breakdown.

The second case, Fig. 17, uses the rotor shaft velocity *versus* active power produced. This relationship includes the influences of either the pitch angle of the rotor blades or brake, or the power limitations set by the operator. As can be seen, there are many points that violate the relationship of the power curve but, in this case, are classified as good points of operation due no violation of the relationship in which they are classified (this is the best method for the data available).

In the case of wind turbine n. 8 (Fig. 16) can also be seen that the power curve seems to work orderly in operations of 1100, 800, 550 and 220 kW. Although, there is no indication about the moments and the respective reasons in which the power production is restricted.

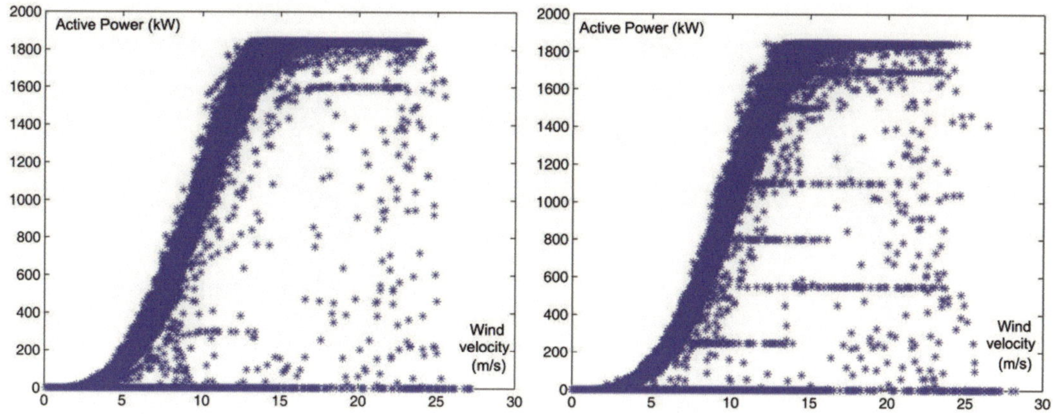

(a) Power Curve. Left: wind turbine n. 3; right: wind turbine n. 8;

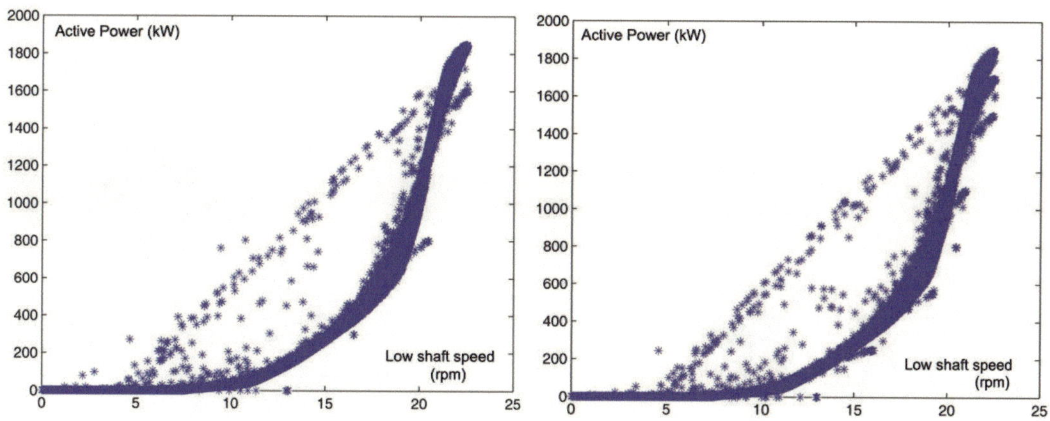

(b) Active power *versus* low shaft velocity;

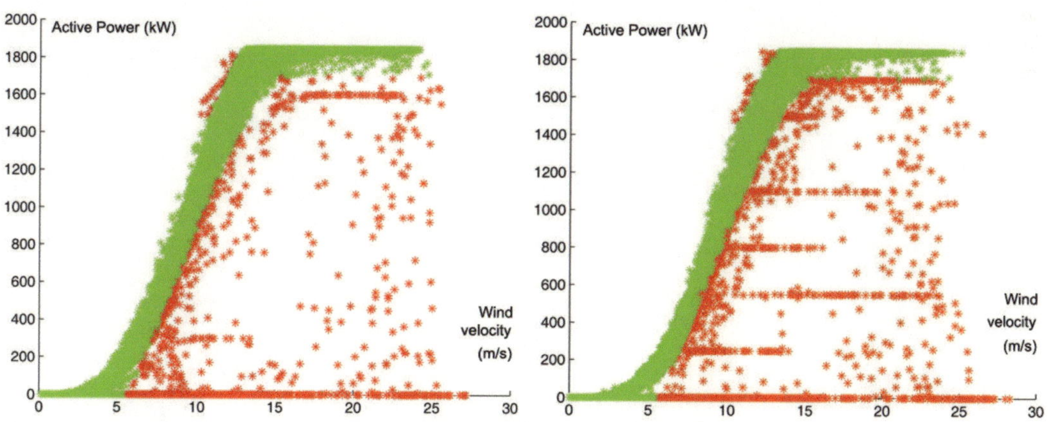

(c) SVM classification for Power curve;

Fig. 16. SVM classification of a wind farm, according to equation 5. Red: breakdown. Green: good operation (Fonseca; 2010).

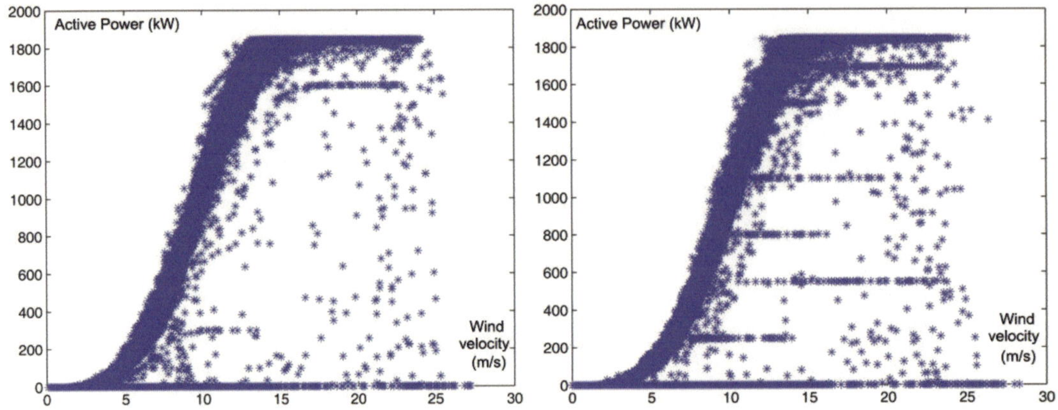

(a) Power curve. Left: Wind turbine n. 3; right: wind turbine n. 8;

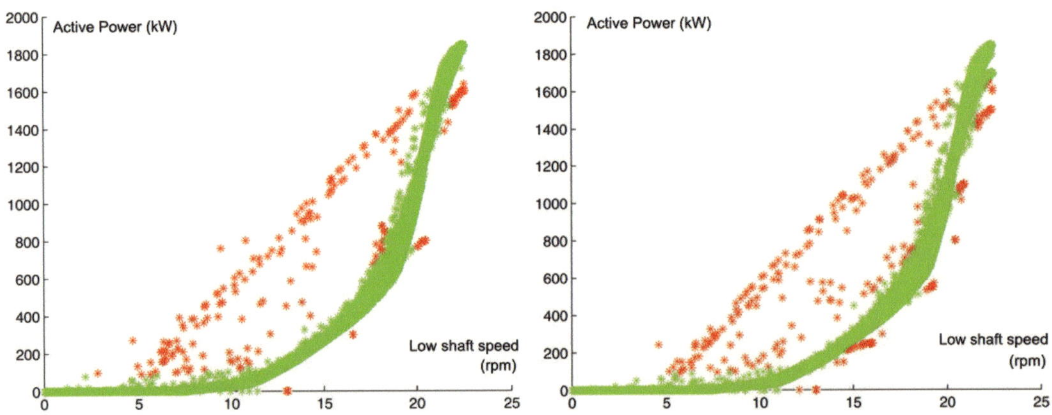

(b) SVM classification for Active power *versus* low shaft speed;

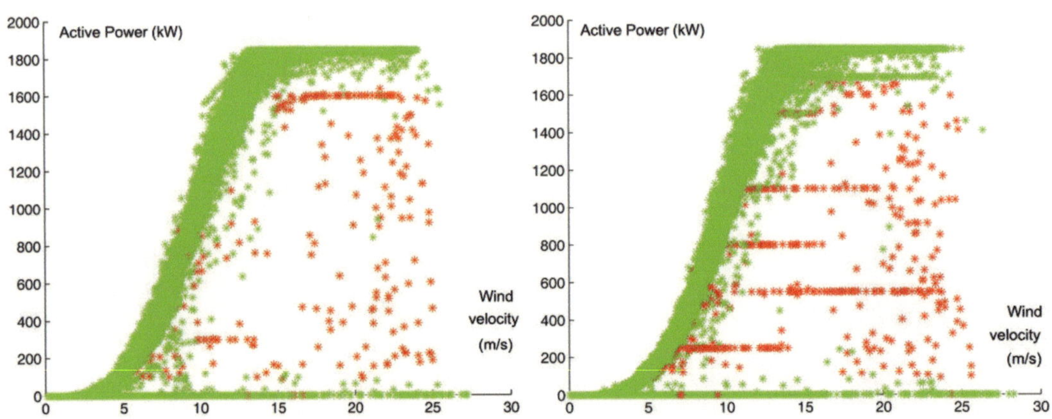

(c) SVM classification of Fig. 17(b) transposed to the power curve;

Fig. 17. SVM classification of a wind farm, according to equation 6. Red: breakdown. Green: good operation (Fonseca; 2010).

Additionally, the second method classifies identically to the first. To overcome this problem it is necessary to "relax" restrictions on the right graph of Fig. 17(b). The data indicated belongs to a wind farm in which there is not relevant information to determine surely to what situation applies.

4.2 PTP synchronization

This section presents results for PTP Synchronization. Experiences have also been made with two modifications in the PTP protocol, in particular changing the messages Sync and Follow Up to include the value of the master clock time. Fig. 12 shows a block diagram of the text described, for the modifications made to PTP master software. The results show a faster initial convergence due to the decrease of initial error, but in subsequent periods is normal.

Matlab simulation and experimental setup has been used to collect results, and the experimental work confirms theoretical simulation. The error update of CNT_TICK_MAX used in experiments is based on the mean of last two error samples, times 0.6. A 90000 threshold has been applied on this error.

Fig. 18 outline the simulation through large seconds. It can be observed the convergence of the clocks and, after 50 timing messages, at the end, a maximum deviation of 50 ns exists. In this experiment it was considered two decimal accuracy places in parameter CNT_TICK_MAX; its final value was estimated at 434782.61 for a real value of 434782.608696. At the end, the clock slave was late 8 ns. Delay Request messages are sent randomly between 2 and 30 TSync. The same simulation, changing the precision of the parameter CNT_TICK_MAX to zero decimal places, gives a final estimation of 434783.0. The clock slave was, after simulation, late in 1783 ns. The final error was about 4000ns.

Fig. 19 shows the simulation results for two decimal precision places on CNT_TICK_MAX (similar to Experience 1), but the Slave only sends one Delay Request message at the beginning. The result is a constant absolute error in the difference between clocks. The precision is equal to experience 1, i.e., about 50 ns; CNT_TICK_MAX was 434782.61. Fig. 20 shows a real experiment after long seconds.

4.3 Time series

According to the above in section 3.2, this section presents the results obtained with different forecasting methods based on time series analysis. The methods were validated with simulated time series and a Mackey-Glass series (one of the references when studying this problem) (Teo et al.; 2001).

Fig. 21 shows the simulation results for the methods. The sign chosen to develop the tests has Gaussian noise and is described mathematically by:

$$S(t) = \begin{cases} t * 0.2 + gaussian\_noise * 0.5, \; if \; t \leq 200 \\ 0 + gaussian\_noise * 0.8, \; if \; 200 < t \leq 400 \\ t * 0.2 + gaussian\_noise * 0.8, \; if \; 400 < t \leq 500 \\ t * 0.6 + gaussian\_noise * 0.6, \; if \; 500 < t \leq 600 \\ t * 0.4 + gaussian\_noise * 0.5, \; if \; 600 < t \leq 800 \\ t^2 * 0.004 + gaussian\_noise * 0.5, \; if \; 800 < t \leq 1000 \end{cases} \tag{9}$$

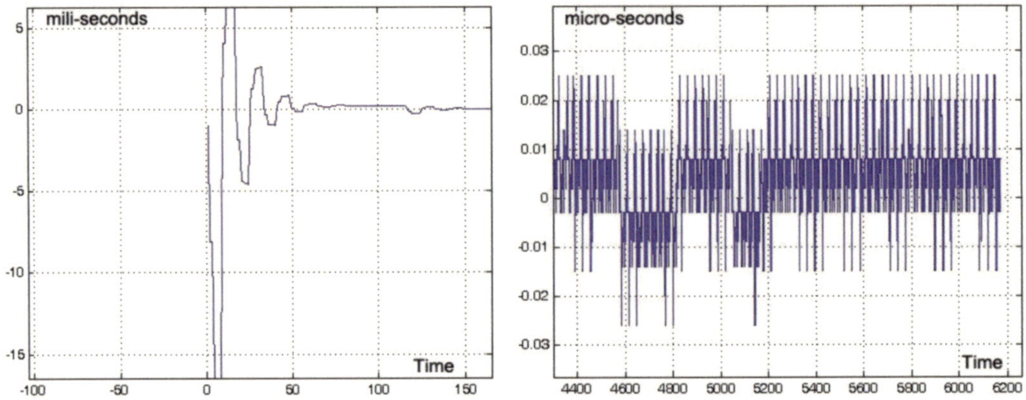

Fig. 18. Experience 1: Difference between the Master and Slave clocks (microseconds). Left: initial moments. Right: final instant (Fonseca; 2010).

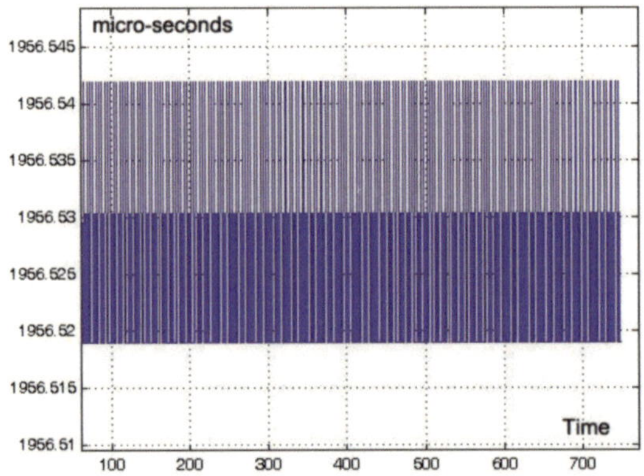

Fig. 19. Experience 2: Difference between Master and Slave clocks (Fonseca; 2010).

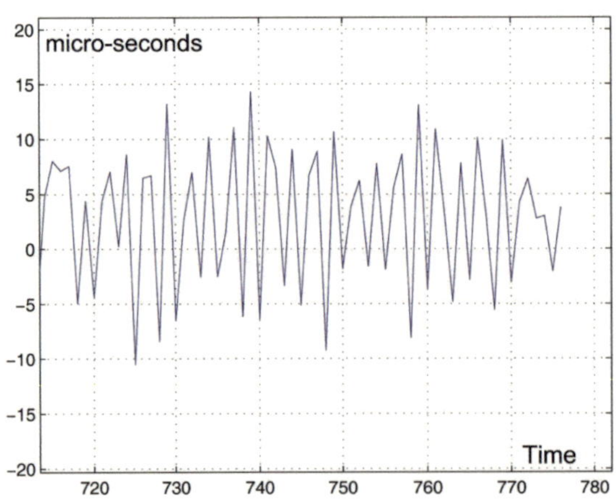

Fig. 20. Experience 3: Difference between Master and Slave clocks (microseconds), at final position, for a real system, using an ASUS Switch (Fonseca; 2010).

Alg. \ Mtr.	MSE	TIC	STD	MAE
ARRSE	17.2324	0.0486	4.1416	1.0677
ES(0.5)	20.4305	0.0531	4.5070	1.3335
HW	20.3014	0.0527	4.5005	1.1765
HWSAS	23.2613	0.0564	4.8172	1.9004
ESMSE(0.5,0)	15.6385	0.0466	3.9500	0.9850
ESMSE(0.5,5)	18.9677	0.0514	4.3471	1.1795
ARMA(2,2)	30.4376	0.0644	5.5143	1.2391
SVR-RBF	83.9986	0.1094	9.0960	3.5345
SVR-LIN	61.0381	0.0905	7.7881	1.5086

Alg. \ Mtr.	MSE	TIC	STD	MAE
ARRSE	1.3644	0.0087	0.8202	0.9596
ES(0.5)	3.7066	0.0186	2.1118	1.7807
HW	3.0305	0.0155	1.8419	1.2670
HWSAS	12.1969	0.0278	3.6379	3.2466
ESMSE(0.5,0)	1.2975	0.0084	0.8116	0.9121
ESMSE(0.5,5)	1.9957	0.0131	1.4572	1.2820
ARMA(2,2)	1.6631	0.0095	0.8083	1.0895
SVR-RBF	86.6412	0.0913	11.5840	6.5191
SVR-LIN	2.6590	0.0612	8.3743	1.5896

Table 3. Prediction results for the series of Fig. 21. Left: overall results, right: results of the range 800-1000.

The signal purpose is to simulate the divergence of certain parameter values out of the indicated tolerance, checking how the behaviour of different algorithms is.

The parameters used in each algorithm were as follows: ARRSE(0.5,0.2); ES(0.5); HW(0.5,0.2); HWSAS(0.5,0.2, 0.2,200); ESMSE(0.5,0); ARMA(2,2); SVR-RBF(30,10) and SVR-LIN(30,10) (Fonseca et al.; 2009).

From analysis of Table 3, it appears that the ESMSE method presents the best results in most of the metrics considered, to predict the values of the next instant. However, the method does not maintain the best performance in the case of prediction of values in time later in the future and is also accompanied by most methods.

Fig. 22 shows, at left, the variation of α, when using all past samples to recalculate according to equation 8. On the right we have the same variation of α, but considering only the error of the last five samples. The interpretation of the results is simple: in the first case the α reflects the total historical errors, and when there is a high prediction error, undergoes a great change, whose influence is decisive for its value; in the other case, with a "history" of five samples, the α varies more dynamically to compensate recent errors.

In a second simulation, from a reference series, uses a signal called differential equation of Mackey-Glass, whose time series is obtained after incorporating differential equation:

$$\frac{dx(t)}{dt} = \frac{A.x(t-\tau)}{1+x^{C}(t-\tau)} - B.x(t) \qquad (10)$$

In experiments described in the literature (Teo et al.; 2001), is used A = 0.2, B = 0.1, C = 10, τ=17 and, as initial conditions, $x(0)$ =1.2 and $x(-\tau)$ =0 to $0 \le t < \tau$ together with the Runge-Kutta method of fourth order with unit step, to calculate the series values. This differential equation was used at first-hand for analysis of blood concentration and analysis of patients with leukaemia (Teo et al.; 2001).

Fig. 23 and Table 4 present the results obtained by different methods outlined. The results of two experiences, forecasting of $\hat{y}[k]$ and $\hat{y}[k+2]$ are shown. There is deterioration in the quality of the forecasts with the increment of the steps to the future. However, in this case, unlike the previous series, the ESMSE method shows better performance for higher values to forecast the future.

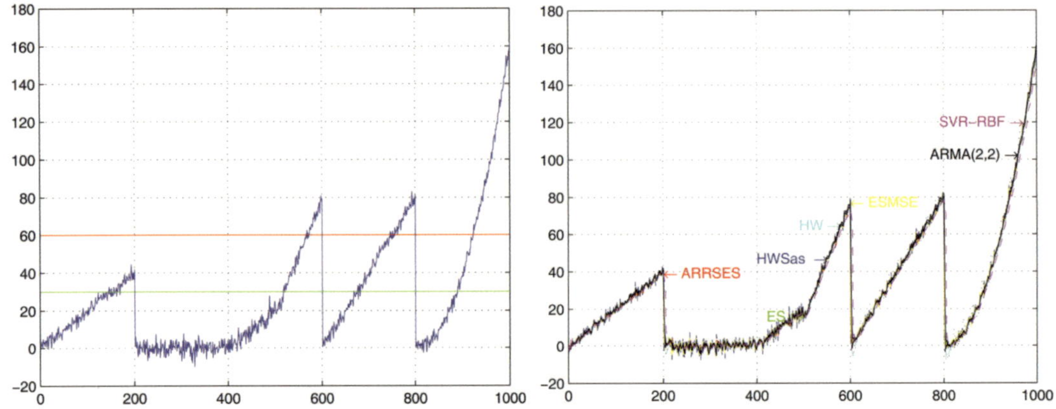

(a) Left: original signal.Right: graph of the performance of various methods;

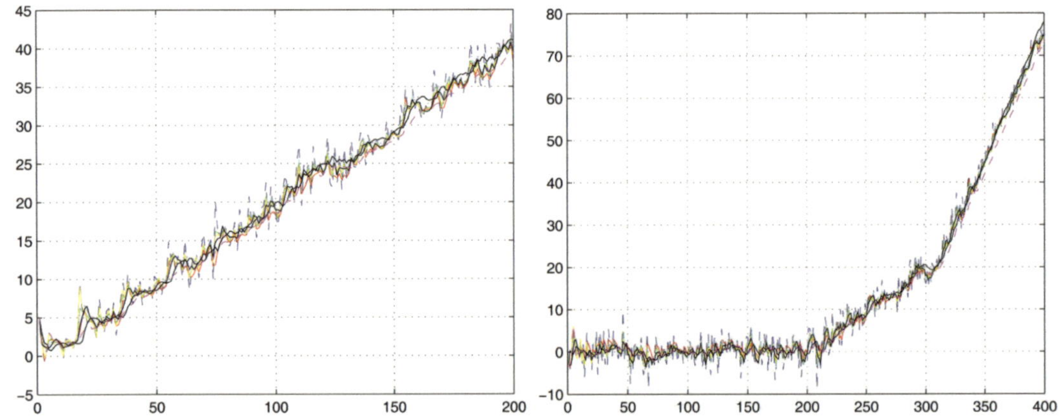

(b) Performance on the time period 0-200 (left) and 200-600 (right);

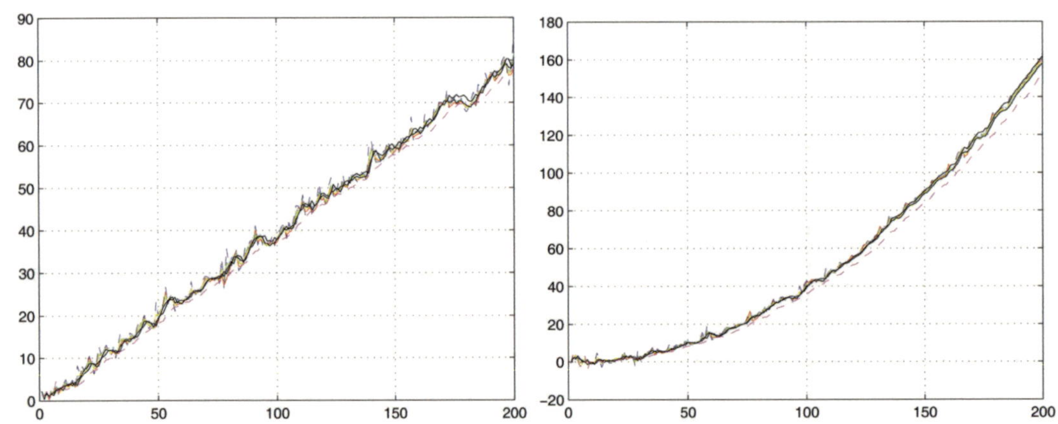

(c) Performance on the time period 600-800 (left) and 800-1000 (right);

Fig. 21. Comparative study of different methods (Fonseca; 2010).

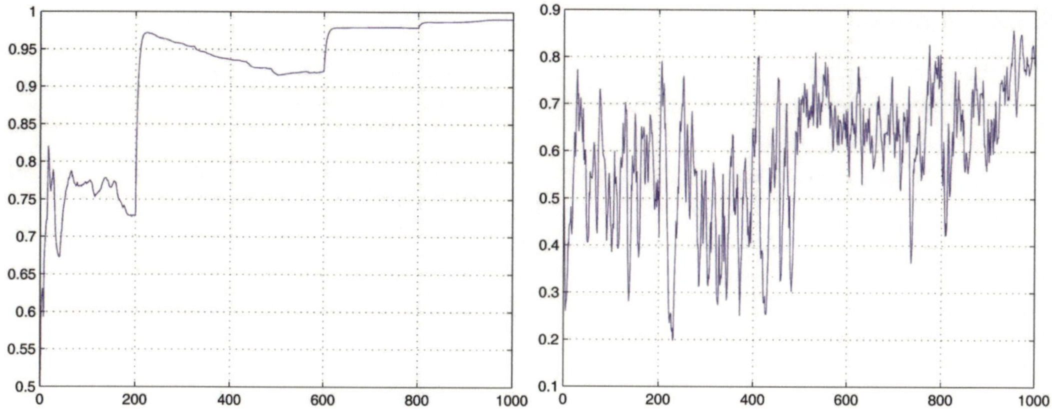

Fig. 22. Left: ESMSE(0.5,0), right: ESMSE(0.5,5). Variation of α for the prediction of the series $\hat{y}[k] \approx y[k+1]$ of Fig. 21 whose performance is in Table 3 (Fonseca; 2010).

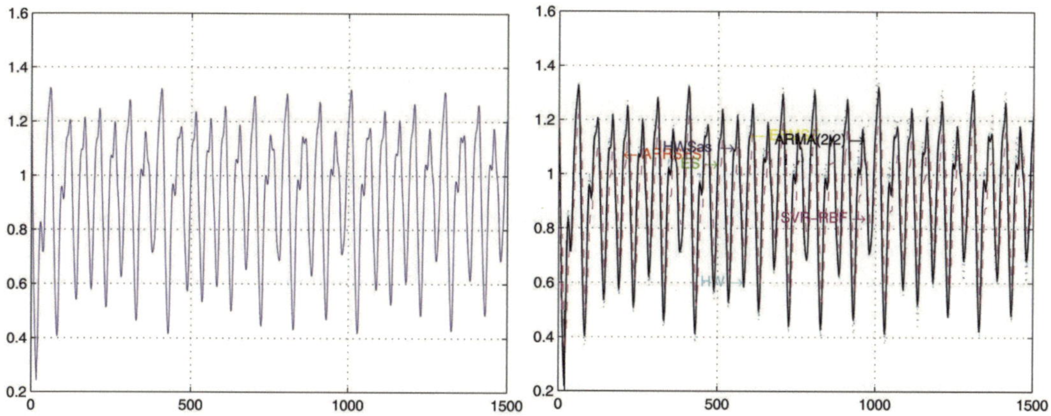

Fig. 23. Results of time series algorithms applied to the series *Mackey-Glass*: forecast $\hat{y}[k] \approx y[k+1]$ (Fonseca; 2010).

Mtr. / Alg.	MSE	TIC	STD	MAE
ARRSE	0.0025	0.0261	0.0496	0.0376
ES(0.5)	0.0041	0.0339	0.0646	0.0543
HW	0.0029	0.0285	0.0544	0.0434
HWSAS	0.0037	0.0321	0.0612	0.0496
ESMSE(0.5,0)	0.0015	0.0202	0.0385	0.0320
ESMSE(0.5,5)	0.0014	0.0198	0.0378	0.0315
ARMA(2,2)	0.0012	0.0185	0.0353	0.0290
SVR-RBF	0.0300	0.0922	0.1724	0.1537
SVR-LIN	0.0104	0.0540	0.1017	0.0928

Mtr. / Alg.	MSE	TIC	STD	MAE
ARRSE	0.0049	0.0368	0.0701	0.0482
ES(0.5)	0.0055	0.0392	0.0747	0.0614
HW	0.0052	0.0378	0.0721	0.0564
HWSAS	0.0151	0.0645	0.1234	0.0996
ESMSE(0.5,0)	0.0026	0.0272	0.0519	0.0412
ESMSE(0.5,5)	0.0026	0.0270	0.0516	0.0407
ARMA(2,2)	0.0035	0.0313	0.0594	0.0433
SVR-RBF	0.0470	0.1155	0.2161	0.1903
SVR-LIN	0.0183	0.0713	0.1353	0.1137

Table 4. Prediction results for the *Mackey-Glass* series. Left: forecast to $\hat{y}[k] \approx y[k+1]$; right: forecast to $\hat{y}[k+2] \approx y[k+3]$.

5. Conclusions

This chapter described a wind maintenance system with all the components, from software to hardware, in which the main objective is to lower maintenance costs through on-condition maintenance based on on-line data acquisition, and the use of open-source software and low cost hardware. An acquisition synchronization system was also presented using PTP hardware with time stamping facility and the related control system. Finally were briefly presented two algorithms to perform on-condition monitoring based on SVM and Time Series Analysis. One proposed method for time series analysis was modified. The ESMSE method is suitable to use on degradation estimation and to be used also on microcontrollers too.

6. References

Caselitz, P. and Giebhardt, J. (2002). Advanced condition monitoring for wind energy converters, *Proc. European Wind Energy Conference, Nice, France.*

Cauwenberghs, G. and Poggio, T. (2000). Incremental and decremental support vector machine learning, *NIPS*, pp. 409–415.

Correll, K. and Barendt, N. (2006). Design considerations for software only implementations of the IEEE 1588 precision time protocol, *In Conference on IEEE 1588 Standard for a Precision Clock Synchronization Protocol for Networked Measurement and Control Systems.*

Dunkels, A. (2003). Full tcp/ip for 8-bit architectures, lwip - light-weight ip implementation, *In Proceedings of the first international conference on mobile applications, systems and services (MOBISYS 2003).*

Durstewitz, M., Hahn, B. and Rohrig, K. (2005). *Advanced Maintenance and Repair for Offshore wind farms using fault prediction and Condition Monitoring Techniques,* E.U. final report of project NNE5/2001/710,
http://www.iset.uni-kassel.de/osmr/.

Eaton, J. W. and Gentleman, R. (2010). Octave and R, *Scientific open-source software.* www.gnu.org/software/octave/ and
www.r-project.org/.

Fonseca, I. (2010). *Maintenance of Wind turbines using IP networks (Phd Thesis in Portuguese),* Porto University,
http://www.fe.up.pt.

Fonseca, I., Farinha, J. T. and Barbosa, F. M. (2008). A computer system for predictive maintenance of wind generators, *Proceedings of the 12th WSEAS International Conference on COMPUTERS*, WSEAS, Heraklion, Greece, pp. 928–933.

Fonseca, I., Farinha, J. T. and Barbosa, F. P. M. (2009). On-condition maintenance for wind turbines, *IEEE Bucharest Power Tech Conference.*

Group, N. W. (2010). SNTP, *Simple Network Time Protocol.*
www.cis.udel.edu/~mills/ database/rfc/rfc4330.txt.

Hameed, Z., Ahn, S. and Cho, Y. (2010). Practical aspects of a condition monitoring system for a wind turbine with emphasis on its design, system architecture, testing and installation, *Renewable Energy* 35(5): 879 – 894.

Hameed, Z., Hong, Y., Cho, Y., Ahn, S. and Song, C. (2009). Condition monitoring and fault detection of wind turbines and related algorithms: A review, *Renewable and Sustainable Energy Reviews* 13(1): 1 – 39.

Hardware and Software (2010). Open-source software and commercial hardware, *National, Vaisala, Codegear, OpenSSL.*
ni.com;
vaisala.com;
codegear.com;
openssl.org;.

Joeware (2010). Program for context switching, *CPAU.*
www.joeware.net/freetools/ tools/cpau/index.htm.

Joseph, F. and Gutowski, T. (2008). TurbSim: Reliability-based wind turbine simulator, *IEEE International Symposium on Electronics and the Environment, San Francisco USA.* http://web.mit.edu/ebm/www/Publications/Joe%20Foley% 20IEEE%202008.pdf.

Kecman, V. (2001). *Learning and Soft Computing,* MIT Press, Cambridge.
http://mitpress.mit.edu/catalog/item/default.asp?ttype=2&tid=3720.

Luminary, C. (2010). ARM cortex processors, *Micro-controllers.*
www.luminarymicro.com.

MicroChip (2010). Micro-controllers, *Microchip Technology Inc.*
http://www.microchip. com.

Open-source (2010). Open-source software, *Slackware, FreeBSD, PostgreSQL, Apache and PHP.*
www.slackware.com;
www.freebsd.org;
www.postgresql.org;
www. apache.org;
www.php.net.

PTP (2010). National Institute of Standards and Technology, *Precision Time Protocol.*
http: //ieee1588.nist.gov/, and an implementation of PTPD in
http://ptpd. sourceforge.net/.

Scheffer, C. and Girdhar, P. (2004). *Practical Machinery Vibration Analysis and Predictive Maintenance,* Elsevier,
http://www.elsevier.com/wps/find/bookdescription.editors/702923/
description#description.

Suykens, J., Gestel, T. V., Brabanter, J. D., Moor, B. D. and Vandewalle, J. (2002). *Least Squares Support Vector Machines,* World Scientific Publishing Co., England. http://books.google.pt/books?id=g8wEimyEmrUC&printsec=
frontcover&source=gbs_v2_summary_r&cad=0#v=onepage&q&f=false.

Technologies, Z. (2010). Php-webservices, *PHP manual pages.*
http://www.php.net/ manual/en/refs.webservice.php.

Teo, K. K.,Wang, L. and Lin, Z. (2001). Wavelet packet multi-layer perceptron for chaotic time series prediction: Effects of weight initialization school of electrical and electronic engineering, *Springer-Verlag Berlin Heidelberg LNCS 2074,* pp. 310–317.

Wago and Beckhoff (2010). Programmable logic controller, *Automation companies*. http:// www.wago.us/; http://www.beckhoff.com/.

Zhizheng, L. and YouFu, L. (2009). Incremental support vector machine learning in the primal and applications, *Neurocomput.* 72(10-12): 2249–2258.

11

Data Acquisition System for the PICASSO Experiment

Jean-Pierre Martin and Nikolai Starinski
for the PICASSO Collaboration
University of Montreal
Canada

1. Introduction

Several key astronomical observations indicate that the Universe contains a special type of matter - Dark Matter (DM). Physics research groups look for the experimental evidence of DM in the form of elementary particles. One such project - the PICASSO experiment (Project In CAnada to Search for Supersymmetric Objects) - is taking place in the deep underground facilities of SNOLAB at Sudbury, Ontario in Canada (at ~2km depth) (Fig. 1) [Leroy & Rancoita (2009)].

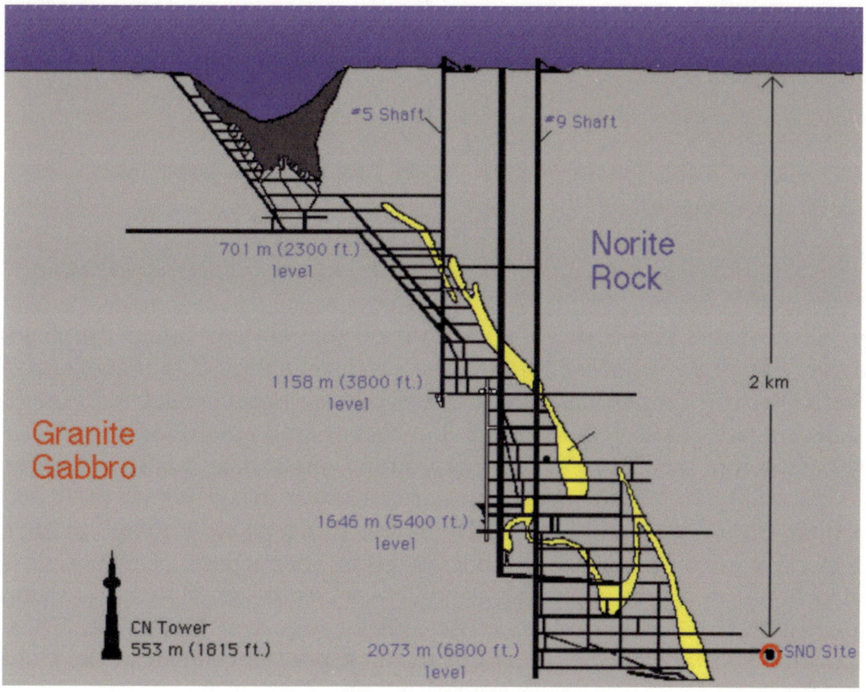

Fig. 1. Location of the PICASSO experiment at the SNOLAB cavity at the VALE-INCO coppernickel mine in Lively, Ontario, Canada.

It employs a phenomenon long used in bubble chamber detectors, where a superheated liquid starts to boil precisely along the tracks of charged particles. Although, all candidates for DM particles are considered to be electrically neutral, they nevertheless could react weakly with detector material creating detectable recoil nuclei. Historically bubble chambers were made of relatively large homogeneous volumes of superheated liquid. All such detectors were required to be re-pressurized immediately after each detected event in order to avoid dangerous and rapid pressure build-up. PICASSO detectors exploit this technique in a modified manner by using small droplets of superheated liquid dispersed and suspended in an elastic gel. Each superheated droplet acts as a small independent bubble chamber and will be contained in the gel. In order to trigger a phase transition possible, at least a minimum critical energy must be deposited by interacting particles within a critical volume along its track (Fig. 2).

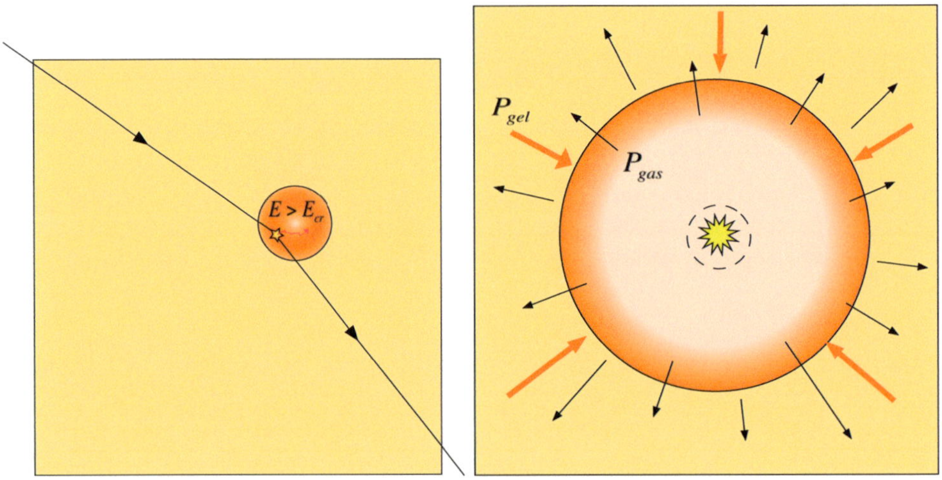

(a) Reaction inside the droplet can cause nuclear recoil;

(b) Liquid-to-gas phase transition;

Fig. 2. Illustration of a neutral particle reaction within the superheated droplet (a) followed by the transition into the gas bubble (b).

However, all detectors based on the principle of superheated liquid droplets must be repressurized eventually in order to keep the detector active. This brings expanded gas bubbles back into their droplet state and thus reverses the detector back to its original active state. If detectors are placed in a low radiation background environment, sufficiently long time may pass before the re-pressurising procedure will be needed. This specific detector type has the ability to effectively enhance the nuclear recoil signal over background radiation interactions (such as β and γ). Therefore, this type of detector could reveal the existence of dark matter by observing nuclear recoil interactions of DM particles in the superheated liquid droplets. Exploding gas bubbles create sound which is detected by a number of piezoelectric sensors located on the exterior surface of the detector. The PICASSO detectors need a special electronic platform that has been developed at the University of Montreal. This chapter describes only the general structure of the data acquisition system (DAQ) without dealing with details of the investigation of the signals and the sensors used in the PICASSO detector [Gornea et al. (2000), Gornea et al. (2001)].

2. History of the PICASSO experiment.

It is only natural to expect that larger physics experiments arrive from smaller scale trials. At the time of this publication the PICASSO experiment has already passed through several stages of its development with different detector technologies, a variety of sensory hardware and several data acquisition systems. The first detectors were relatively small. They were equipped only with one or two piezoelectric sensors. Each transducer channel had its own individual preamplifier box (Fig. 3).

(a) One of the earlier types of detectors;

(b) One of the earlier preamplifier boxes;

Fig. 3. A small size 1L PICASSO detector with only two sensors (a) and single channel preamplifier (b).

Acoustical signals were acquired independently from each sensor. Five channel analog-to-digital converter (ADC) VME boards were designed using ALTERA's FLEX10K family (Fig. 4). Besides difficulties of the firmware debugging, this FPGA platform had limitations concerning the recorded waveform length and scalability. Matching timing information obtained by different boards was difficult. At the end of the first phase of the experiment, it was clear that in order to accommodate many more of detector channels and longer waveforms, the experiment would need a new data acquisition hardware. The newer version of the DAQ system is detailed in this report while the description of the older system can be found in [Gornea et al. (2000), Gornea et al. (2001)].

Fig. 4. Previously used VME module for PICASSO data acquisition.

3. Detector and DAQ architecture.

The electronic system of the PICASSO detector includes several functionally independent subsystems. Each one is dedicated to control specific detector parameters (e.g. temperature and pressure regulation, on-line detector calibration, etc.) or to collect and process acoustical signals. Experimental data consist of waveforms from acoustical piezoelectric sensors simultaneously acquired from the entire detector. In its current stage, the detector layout consists of a set of 8 clusters, each containing 4 detector modules adding to a total of 32 detectors (Fig. 6 and 5). A group of 4 detectors is placed in an insulated metal box (Fig. 7) - Temperature-Pressure Control Sysytem (TPCS), where the temperature can be set to a pre-determined value with a precision of about ±0.5 °C. While the temperature can be set individually to each TPCS, the pressure can be set for all detectors simultaneously only.
Each detector has 9 piezoelectric sensors working as a group. There are three layers of sensors on the external surface of the acrylic container. Each layer contains three sensors distributed evenly along the detector's perimeter covering 120° sectors. Layers of sensors are rotated by 60° relative to each other. This is done for complete coverage of the active volume and acoustical triangulation of the event position. Sensors are made with cylindrical shape piezoelectric transducers mounted inside brass containers designed as Faraday cages in order to reduce electrical noise (Fig. 8). Electrical signals from piezoelectric sensors are sent over coaxial cables to be amplified and digitized. Each detector module is equipped with its own subset of electronics (preamplifiers and ADCs) in order to operate independently from the other units. These electronic boards are located in a metal enclosure placed outside and above the cluster of 4 detectors. The location of these board enclosures is chosen so as to keep the length of the coaxial cables to the practical minimum in order to minimize any induced electrical noise. Special care is taken to reduce the microphonic effect of the cable as

Fig. 5. View of the PICASSO set-up at the SNOLAB underground facility.

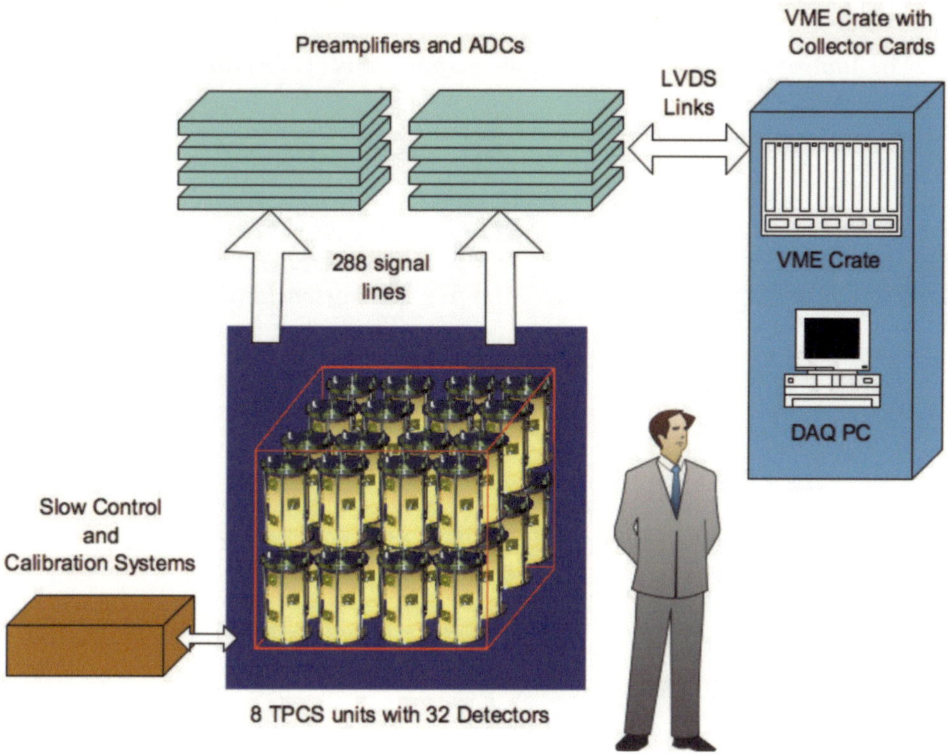

Fig. 6. PICASSO experiment from the DAQ perspective.

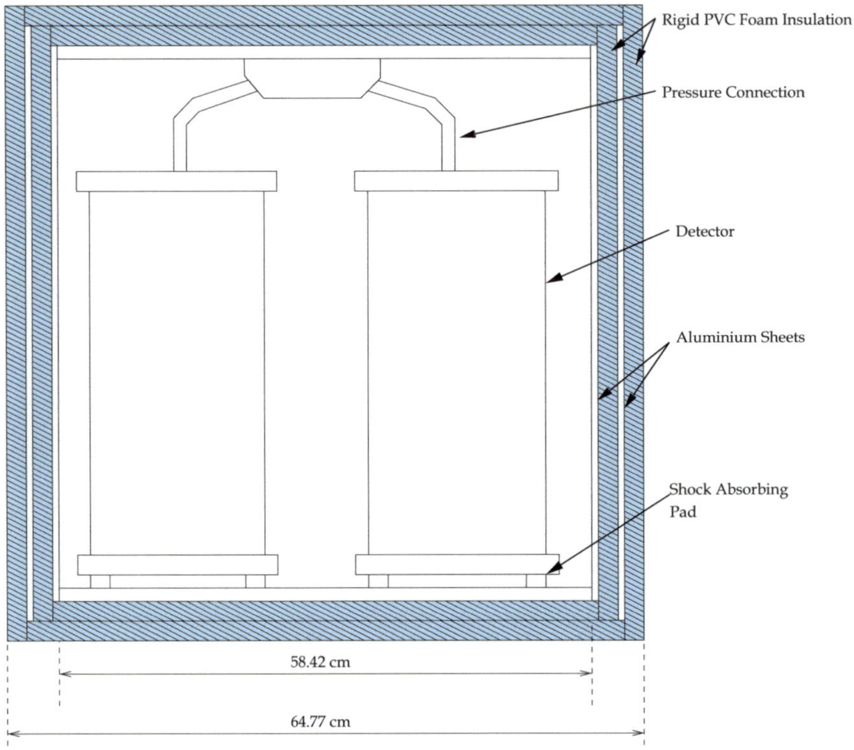

Fig. 7. The Temperature and Pressure Control System box (TPCS) (from [Clark (2008)].

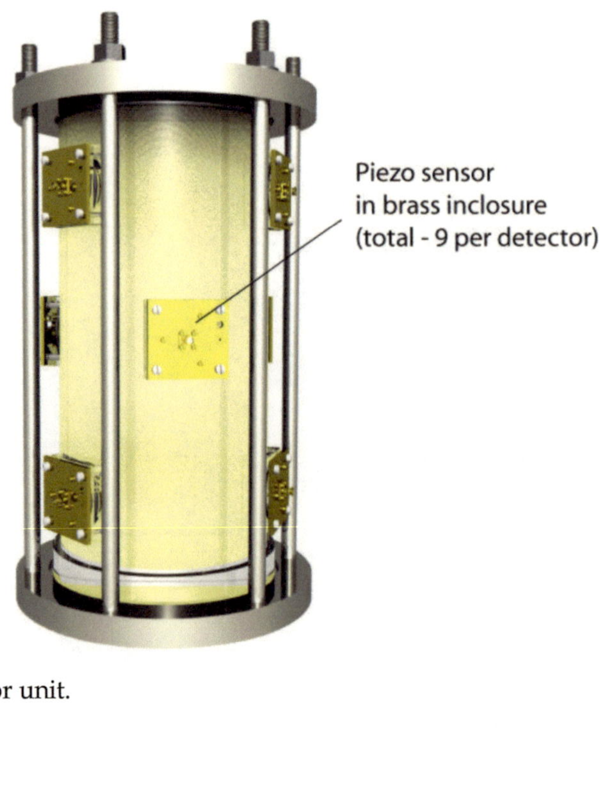

Fig. 8. Single detector unit.

well. In case of the piezoelectric sensors, this microphonic effect of the cable can be quite problematic due to the very high impedance of both - the sensors and the preamplifiers. Although, just one sensor is required per detector to provide a minimum of meaningful information for the data analysis, generally all 9 channels per detector module are required to make detectors most efficient and to perform off-line analysis of event localization [Aubin (2007)] within the detector volume. The most important step taken during the development of the second stage of the experiment was the design of a scalable data concentration scheme. In order to collect data from different modules and to be able to relate them in time, a special VME data collector card was designed. This card is a multi-purpose system able to concentrate data from 12 independent data sources (in the case of PICASSO, one source is one detector with 9 sensor waveforms). It has already been successfully used for the TIGRESS experiment [Martin (2007)]. For the purpose of the PICASSO application, special firmware logic has been developed and custom tailored to acquire and record a large number of acoustical signals from a multitude of detectors. Detailed description of the collector card operation is given later in this chapter. Fig. 9 demonstrates the relationship between different parts of the data acquisition and Fig. 10 presents the block-diagram for one detector channel.

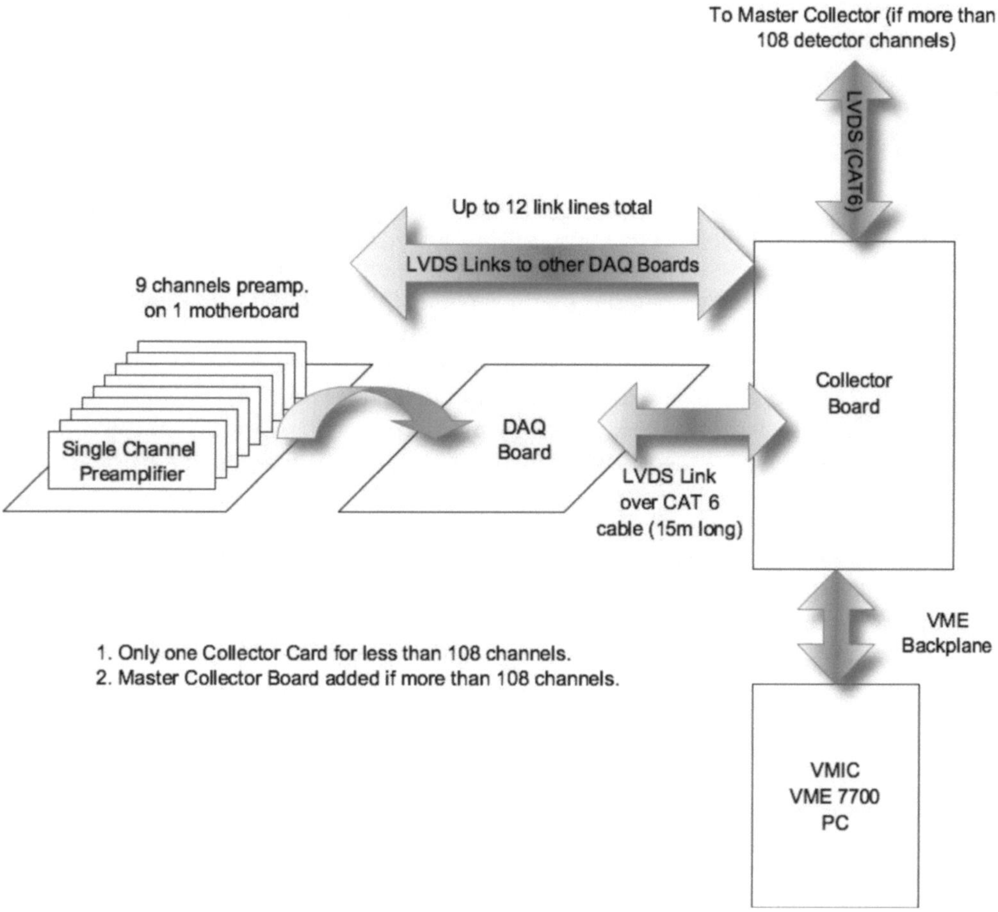

Fig. 9. Functional block-diagram of signal and data flow.

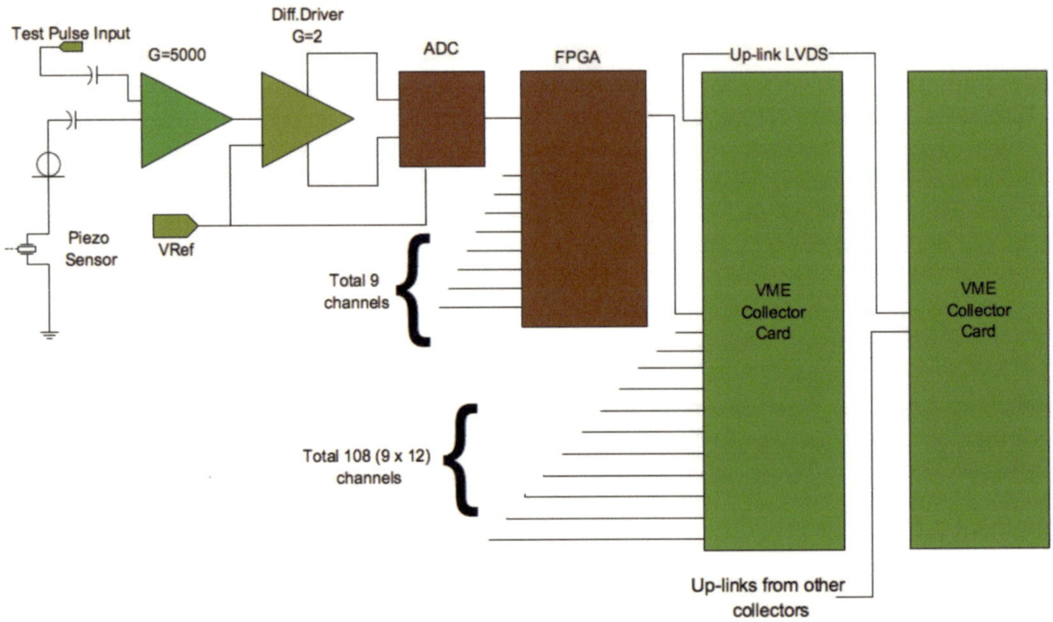

Fig. 10. Block-diagram for one detector channel.

4. Signal amplifier.

The amplifier design for piezoelectric sensors present several challenges. First of all, the bandwidth and the gain have to be chosen in order to preserve the information about the time evolution of the pressure build-up from the evaporation of the superheated droplet. Unfortunately, a piezoelectric material might have a very irregular non-linear response to the applied force. To better understand the difficulties arising here, the reader can be referred to the recent second edition of [Arnau (2008)]. For the purpose of the current work it is necessary to mention the lack of sufficient understanding of all details in the process of bubble creation and evolution triggered by nuclear reactions in superheated liquids. Different Dark Matter nuclear recoil experiments use slightly different methods of acoustical detection. The PICASSO group's study of acoustic signals shows that signals generated by rapid phase transition in the superheated liquid can be detected in the wide frequency region between ~1 KHz and ~200 KHz by different types of sensors. There is an indication that significant acoustic power is emitted in the low range of the frequency spectrum (Fig. 11). At the same time one can expect an external acoustical noise in the audio range at the low frequency end of the spectrum be quite significant and special care must be taken to reduce it.

The second challenge is a very high impedance of piezoelectric material. It gets even more complicated if the behaviour of the piezoceramic at different temperatures is taken into account.

Instead of individual preamplifier boxes used by PICASSO previously for each sensor, the new units combine 9 single channel boards carried on one motherboard. Each motherboard is assigned to one detector equipped with a full set of 9 sensors. This arrangement allows a considerable saving per channel on extra cables, connectors and enclosures. Overall view is presented in Fig. 12.

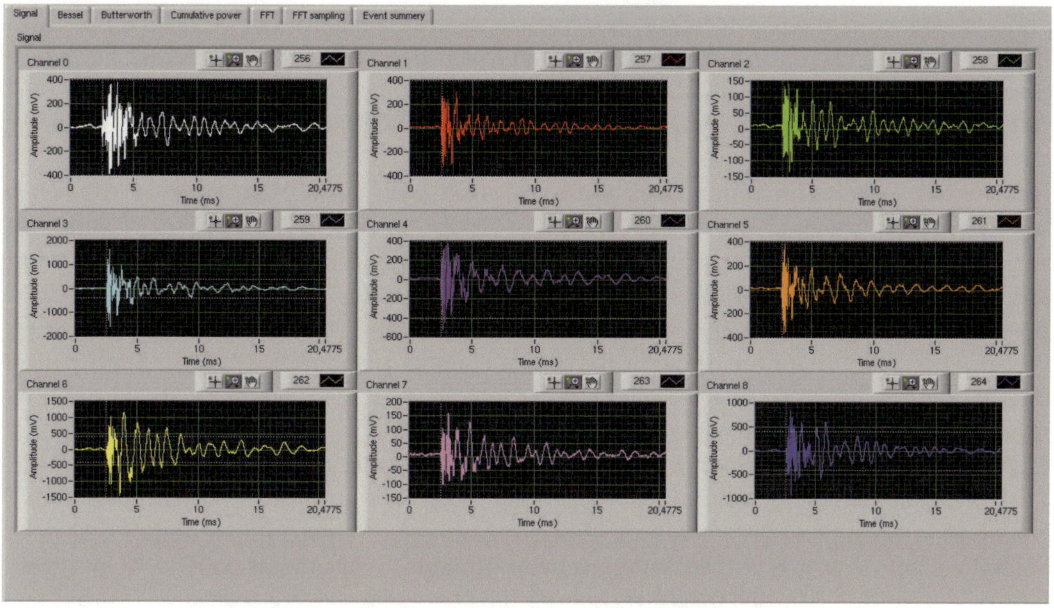

Fig. 11. Signal waveforms for one event obtained from a single detector.

Fig. 12. Electronics for one detector module (Front: Single channel boards on the carrier board; Back: Digitizing board; Small circuit left of digitizing board: 1-wire temperature sensor).

4.1 Single channel.

The single channel board carries a two-stage preamplifier with a DC coupled input and a band-pass filter. This board has a single ended output with a total gain of both stages between 1000 and 4000 depending on the requirements of the experiment. Due to the very high impedance of the piezoceramic, the first stage of the preamplifier is designed using n-JFET transistors. There were several versions of this board, each used at different periods of time of the experiment. The first version of the preamplifier had a pair of low noise n-JFET transistors connected in parallel, in order to cope with the large capacitance piezoelectric sensors (Fig. 13).

Later, when larger gain rather than ability to work with large capacitance of the signal source was requested, a second version of the preamplifier was built using an improved version of the microphone amplifier presented by A. Shichanov in 2002. Unfortunately, the original Internet link to his schematic is not active anymore. Therefore, we would like to present it here (Fig. 14) only with a minor modification. At the time of this writing, PICASSO is using this front stage in the single channel preamplifier boards. Each pair of JFET transistors has to be selected after closely matching by the value of saturated drain-to-source current and the pinch-off voltage.

Such a selection was performed with the help of specially built hardware controlled by USB-1408FS (Measurement Computing Corporation) - USB bus-powered DAQ module with 8 analog inputs, up to 14-bit resolution, 48 kS/s, 2 analog outputs, and 16 digital I/O lines. Software control was designed based on the National Instruments LabVIEW program. Nearly a thousand MMBFJ309LT1 n-channel JFET transistors were measured, sorted and grouped into closely matching pairs.

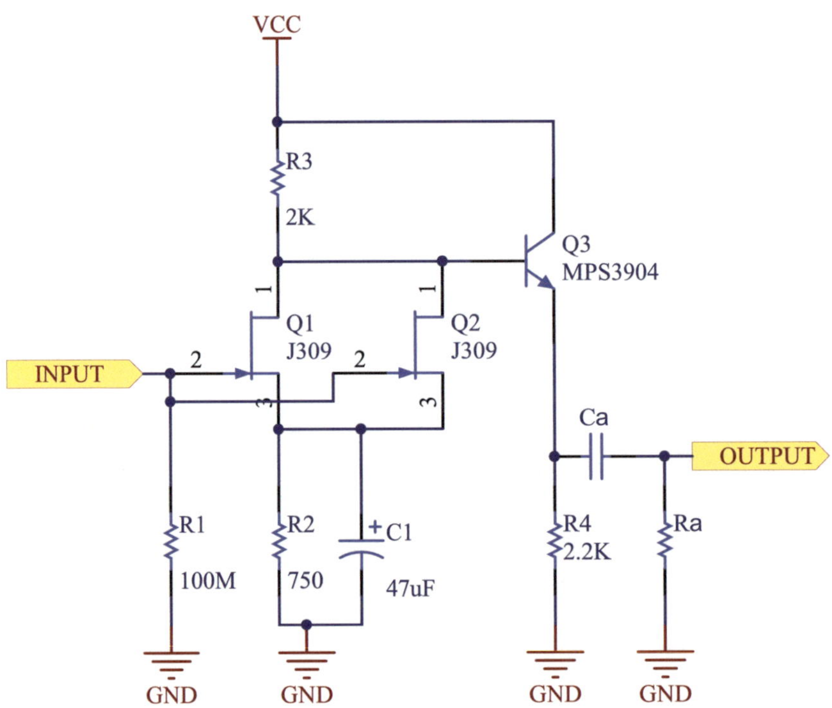

Fig. 13. First stage of the preamplifier in version 1.

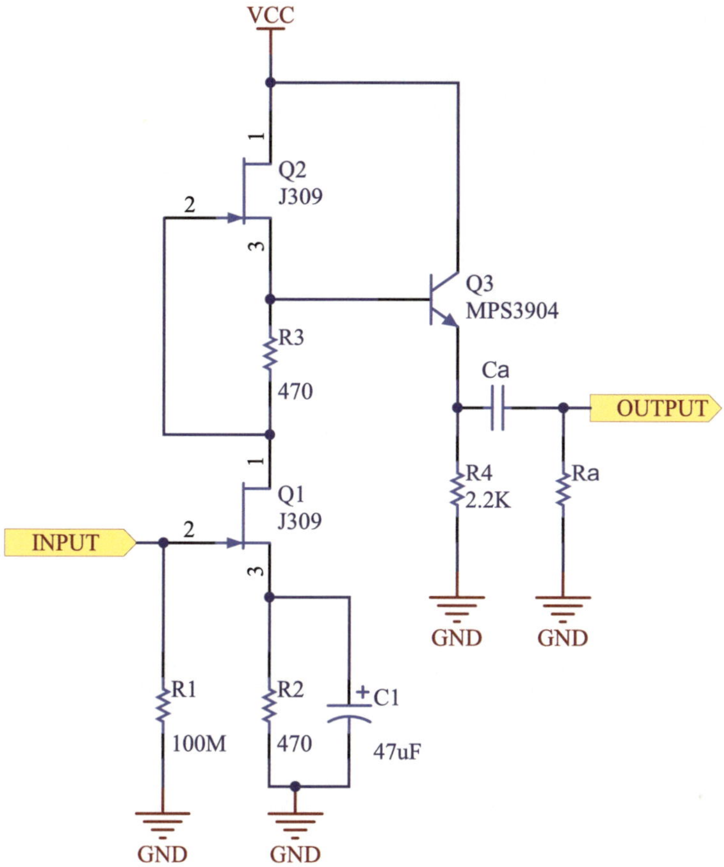

Fig. 14. Part of the microphone amplifier schematics used in the second version of the PICASSO preamplifier.

4.2 Preamplifier carrier board.

The preamplifier carrier board can hold up to 9 single channel boards. It also includes individual differential drivers for the next DAQ stage of digitizing circuitry as well as a reference source used by all of the differential drivers and the ADCs of the next stage. Differential drivers shift the bipolar range of acquired signals to a positive-only range of ADCs. Such a subdivision allows future trials of different amplifiers without changing the layout of the working detector modules. Any upgrade of the system in such a case will require less effort from the detector crew in the difficult underground working environment. The single channel preamplifier board can also be used separately from the current DAQ system with the same type of modules using the single ended data acquisition system which would not require a special data collection schema, i.e. in the stand-alone post-fabrication tests and calibration of the detector. Specifically for that purpose, the frequency range of the single channel amplifier is wider than required by described data acquisition system (Fig. 15). This allows it to be used with sensors which might have different ultrasound frequencies.

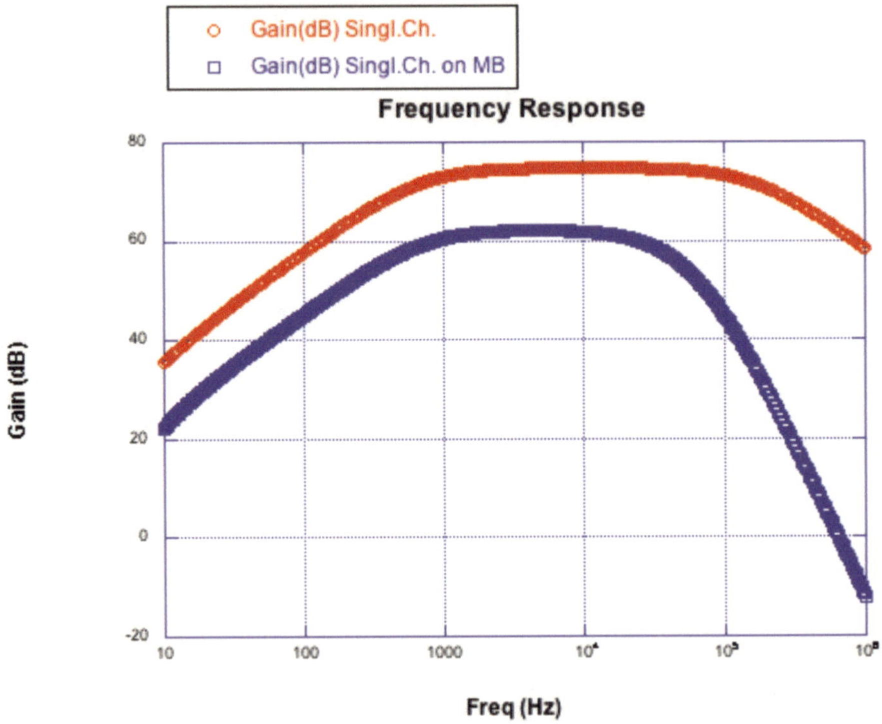

Fig. 15. System signal conditioning.

For additional signal conditioning flexibility, several layout implementations were introduced both on the single channel board and the carrier board. This allows both printed circuit boards (the single channel and its carrier board) to be assembled for different experimental needs:

- There is a choice between AC or DC coupling of the sensor signals. In the case of AC coupling, the high-pass filter frequency can be adjusted on the carrier board.
- In the first stage of the amplifier it is possible to employ either an active or a passive load. The passive load solution can accept sensors with high capacitance.
- Replacement of the preamplifiers is just a matter of unplugging the old board and inserting the new one and does not require re-soldering of any kind. Preamplifiers can have different gains on the same carrier board to investigate signals in different dynamic regions.

The carrier boards also include a calibration input used with an external pulse generator. It is coupled to each input via a small capacitor. The purpose of the calibration pulse is to monitor the gain of each channel and to investigate a possible degradation or even failing of the sensor itself.

5. Digitizer board.

Differential signals from the preamplifier carrier board are sent to the digitizer board through a short flat cable. Each digitizer board is equipped with 9 serial ADCs with 12-bit dynamic range (ANALOG DEVICES AD7450) controlled by one FPGA circuit (ALTERA Cyclone EPC6T144C8). The reference voltage on the preamplifier carrier board provides

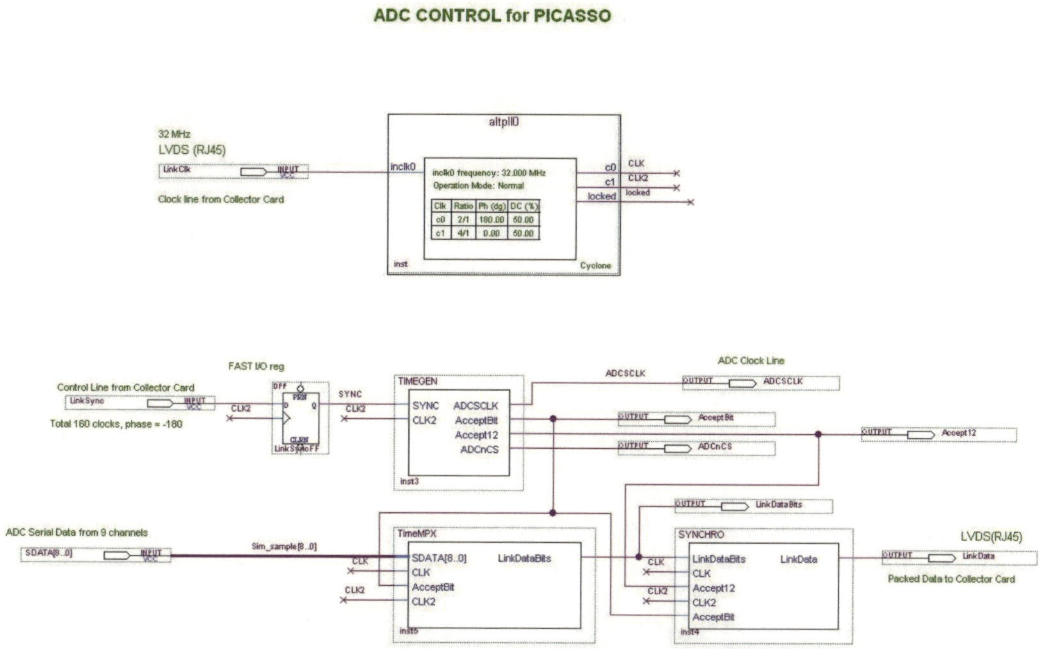

Fig. 16. Top page of the ALTERA Quartus II design software for the ADC controlling FPGA.

reference to all ADCs on the digitizer board as well. Due to the large number of digitizer boards required for PICASSO experiment their design includes only a bare minimum of hardware and firmware. The simplicity of the firmware design can be illustrated by Fig. 16. It shows the top level page of the FPGA design project for the ADC control.

5.1 Interface with the collector.

None of the digitizer boards carries an individual clock source. Instead these boards receive a 32 MHz clock from the collector board over a dedicated LVDS line. In addition to reducing the price of the digitizer board, such a scheme eliminates any run-away de-synchronization problem between different detector modules during long runs. An additional signal that indicates the beginning of the conversion comes from the collector card over a different LVDS line. After receiving the 32 MHz clock the FPGA uses its internal PLL block to create the 400 KHz clock needed by the ADCs as well as all other clocks needed for internal FPGA operation. Upon receiving the start signal for the conversion, the embedded control logic unit starts an acquisition cycle and polls samples from nine channels simultaneously. Each ADC sends one bit every 2.5 μsec to the FPGA until 16 bits are sent (12 bits of data and zero padding). Then the digitizer board transfers them to the collector through a custom made protocol with start and stop bits over CAT6 cables using LVDS levels. The mechanism to build a serial stream of data samples taken simultaneously works as follows: each simultaneously acquired set of 9 bits from each ADC is sorted to form a 9-bit word in serializer logic. Every additional set of 9 bits is attached to the previous word. After all 12 bits are acquired, the entire set is sent to the collector card as a serial stream.

A maximum of 12 DAQ boards can be connected to each collector. When all 108 channels are operational (at 400 Ks/sec), the collector card handles a data throughput of 518.4 Mbps.

Although the VME system can not process such a continuous data flow, the expected data rate in the normal mode of the detector will be much lower.

6. VME collector card.

The PICASSO DAQ system can have two different architectures. If the total amount of channels needed for the experiment is less than 108, only one collector can be used (Fig. 17). If the experiment requires more than 108 channels, it will need one collector for each group of 108 channels plus one extra collector board as the source of a synchronized clock for each downstream collector.

6.1 Single-collector system.

The structure of a single collector system is presented in the Fig. 18. As it was mentioned above, in the case of 108 channels they produce a data flow with a rate of 1296 bits for every 2.5 μsec (518.4 Mbps). These data are intended to be written in the on-board SDRAM. However, the samples are not recorded there immediately. There is a waiting cycle for 128 sets of such samples. Then every 320 μsec a burst-write process puts data into SDRAM for the entire set of 128 samples for every detector channel. The total amount of data samples recorded is 128 × 128 = 16384. In parallel with the continuous recording process, an embedded logic block checks the data flow. When the signal amplitude crosses over the user defined threshold level, then the corresponding channel is marked as active. Threshold comparison is performed on the processed stream of data. At first the raw waveform is digitally rectified. Then the rectified signal goes through the digital amplitude peak detector with constant decay. Such combined process create an envelope around the waveform. Finally only the envelope undergoes a test for threshold crossing. This process is illustrated on the Fig. 19.

Fig. 17. 6U VME collector card.

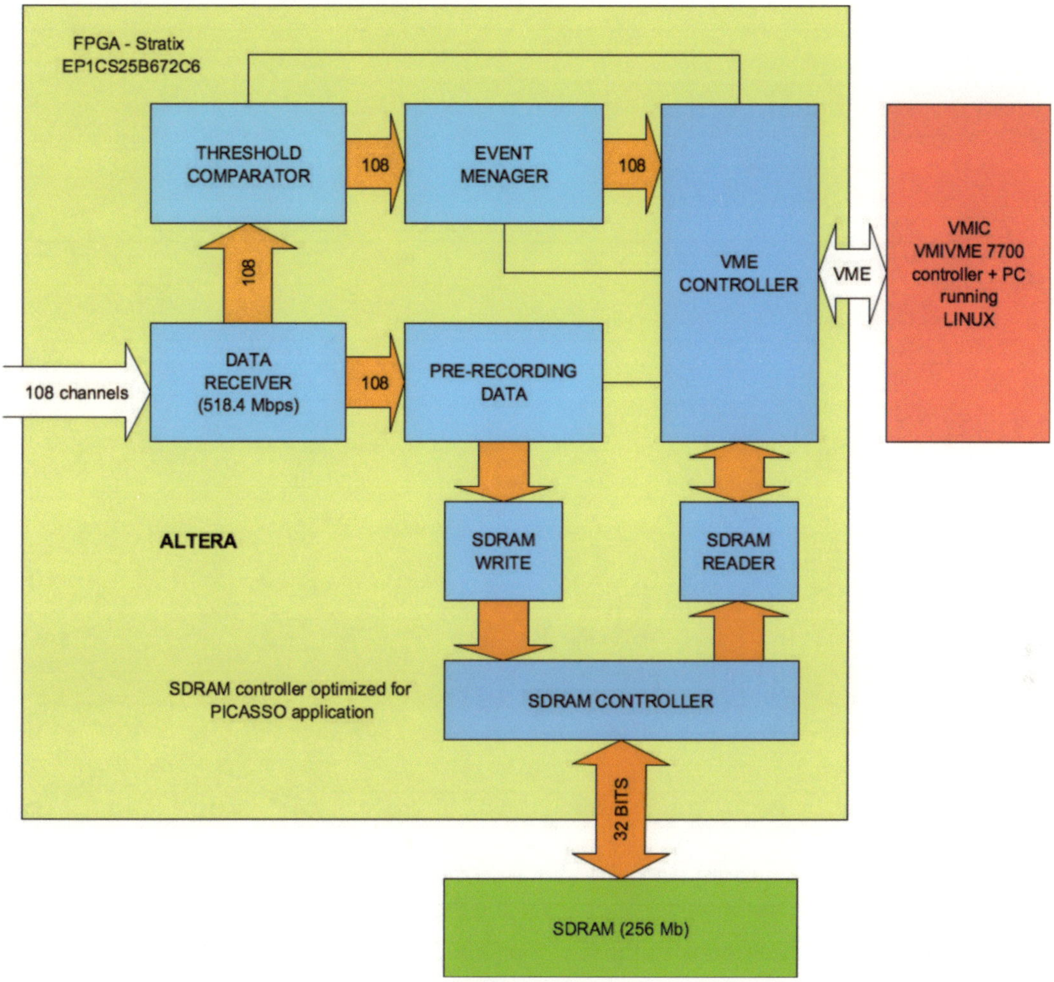

Fig. 18. Functional block-diagram of a collector board.

This trigger detection method was taken from the earlier version of the DAQ firmware and ensures consistency in the triggering technique across the different stages of the experiment. When a hit is detected, it is recorded in one of the eight segments contained in SDRAM and information about it is recorded in the event manager. After recording 16384 samples, the current event is locked. The software which runs on the VMIC (VME PC) controller is constantly pooling the event manager to see if there is any event that is locked. When it detects such a locked event, it checks the channel table to see if it corresponds to the user assigned group of channels which allow it to contribute to the event trigger. If it does, it sends a command to download the data desired. If it doesn't, the software unlocks the event to allow recording to continue. This communication of the VMIC controller with the collector card is implemented via the command and status register (CSR) in the collector's FPGA. If the VMIC is too slow, the SDRAM can become full with events locked in it. If this happens, the data would not be recorded anymore and a dead time counter would start to count the number of samples missed. The event manager block controls this logic.

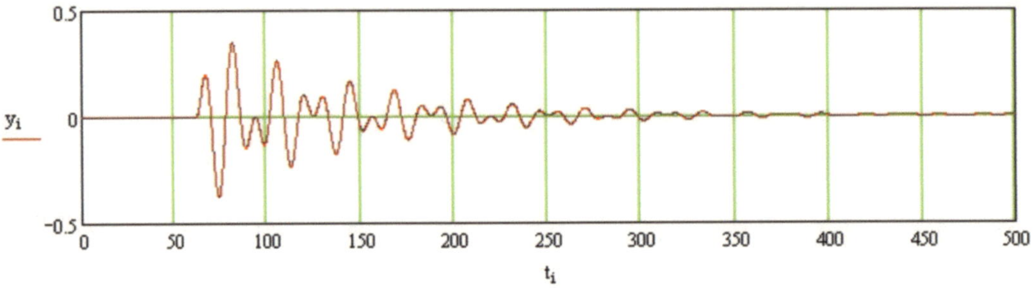

(a) Simulated waveform;

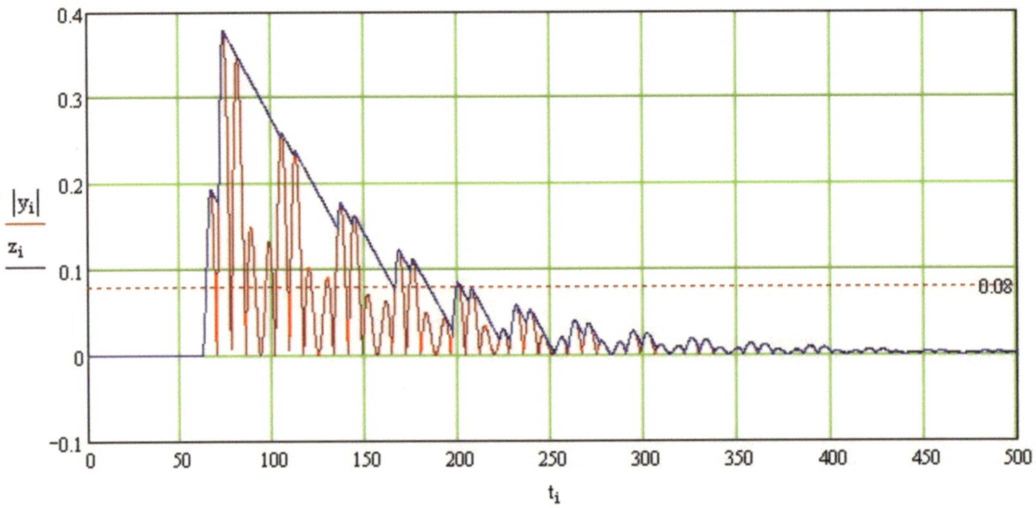

(b) Rectified signal (red graph) from the above plot with the calculated envelope around it (blue graph). Dashed horizontal line represents the threshold level;

Fig. 19. Mathematical illustration of the envelope building process.

6.2 DAQ software and global trigger.

The DAQ software runs on an embedded VME computer and implements various services. The experiment operator can dynamically map hardware resources to logical detection units. The event trigger is defined within each logical group which can be composed of multiple physical modules connected to the same collector board. The DAQ software polls the control and monitoring registers from every installed collector and searches for active acoustic channels. The trigger definition function uses operator defined connection maps and the information acquired from the collectors to compute the event trigger state in real time. The operator can configure the channel trigger thresholds and the multiplicity level. The task list generated by the trigger definition function is processed asynchronously by a transport function which fetches and stores the data on a local hard drive. The collector's firmware supports a parallel operation of trigger monitoring and data transfer services. In the current implementation using an off-the-shelf Linux distribution, the maximum data throughput allowed by the 32-bit block transfer mode has been easily reached. For physics runs, the detector is operated as a collection of logical detection units which are mapped to the 9-channel physical modules. Minimal bias runs using larger logical detection units allow precise determination of the electrical and acoustical correlations between channels. By stacking trigger definition functions, the full detector can be operated as a single logical unit although for physics objectives (e.g. identifying multiple fast neutron scattering) the offline event correlation algorithms are efficient and optimize data storage requirements. Using VME bus extenders, a single node system can acquire data from a 4000 channels detector. Very large scale implementations are possible when employing multiple VME nodes.

6.3 Multi-collector system.

Before the end of year 2007 the PICASSO experiment has crossed the threshold of 108 channels, therefore requiring more than one collector card. The setup has now three collector cards to hold all data samples and one extra card used as a master clock source.

7. Current state of research and future development.

The current phase of the PICASSO experiment has now all 32 detectors and electronics deployed. The data constantly flows to the data storage, and is being analyzed on the regular bases. There are plans at work for the third stage of the experiment where the total number of channels might rise significantly to about 4000 due to corresponding increase of the active mass of the detector. In this case the current scheme where the data stream goes via collector cards most likely will remain as the proven data acquisition technology. However, the analog part of the data acquisition system still has some potentials to be improved.

One of these potentially new tasks is the ability to greatly improve dynamic range of the DAQ by employing additional stage of logarithmic amplification. It is not clear yet if an equal amplitude resolution in the entire dynamic range of the piezoelectric sensor signals has significant implications on the quality of the data analysis. If only the general shape of the waveform spectrum is important, the implementation of a logarithmic amplification stage might still preserve the average threshold level for the detector while folding higher amplitudes back inside the range of the ADC. The latest tests with new preamplifiers indicates that it is possible to adjust the gain of each channel simply by adjusting the power level to the fist stage of the amplifier.

New development in advanced signal processing hardware platforms by the industry constantly offers to physicists ever more compact chips with combined functionalities and improved characteristics. Of special interest for the future of the PICASSO experiment could be multi-channel ADC chips with built-in programmable gain amplifiers. This technology can help to further reduce the per-channel cost of the data acquisition system.

Additional attention will be given to better power distribution system, when preference is given to the delivery of single low voltage AC power to the local units. Using such a solution can eliminate the use of long multi-wire cables with individual DC power lines. It also gives the opportunity to avoid unwanted ground loops in the system.

The future data flux may become to large to be acquired by a flat scheme where a new collector card is simply added to accommodate new channels. In this case the opportunity exists to use an hierarchical structure of collectors with new firmware where a suppression of the empty events is implemented. In such a scheme collectors in higher hierarchical positions can be used to concentrate non-empty waveforms.

Number of channels	288
Frequency range	1..80 KHz
Resolution	12 bit
ADC sampling rate	400 Ks/s

Table 1. PICASSO DAQ parameters

These plans will be better defined once the data analysis of the current experiment stage will be finished and the behaviour of superheated liquid detectors will be understood with much greater details. Some recent results can be found in [Archambault et al. (2009)].

8. References

Leroy, C. & Rancoita, P-G. (2009). Superheated Droplet (Bubble) Detectors and CDM Search, In: *Principles of Radiation Interaction in Matter and Detection, 2-nd Edition,* page numbers (721- 754), World Scientific Publishing Co. Pte. Ltd., ISBN-13 978-981-281-827-7, Singapore, 2009

Gornea, R., Boukhira, N., Boussaroque, I., Lessard, L., Di Marco, M., Martin, J.P., Vinet, J., Zacek, V., *A control and data acquisition system for a large volume superheated droplet detector,* IEEE Transactions in Nuclear Science, 2 (2000) 232

Gornea, R., Barnabe-Heider, M., Boukhira, N., Doane, P., Leroy, C., Lessard, L., Di Marco, M., Martin, J.-P., Zacek, V., Noulty, R.A., *The operation of large-mass room-temperature superheated droplet detectors,* IEEE Transactions in Nuclear Science, 2 (2001) 844

Aubin, F., *Caractérisation spatiale des événements dans les détecteurs PICASSO,* Mémoire de maîtrise, Universit´e de Montréal, 2007

Martin, J.-P., Mercier, C., Starinski, N., Pearson, C.J., Amaudruz, P.-A., *The TIGRESS DAQ/Trigger system,* 15th IEEE-NPSS Real-Time Conference, 2007

Arnau, A., (Editor), *Piezoelectric Transducers and Applications,* Second Edition, Springer, 2008

Clark, K.J., *A New and Improved Spin-Dependent Dark Matter Exclusion Limit Using the PICASSO Experiment,* Ph.D. Thesis, Queen's University, Kingston, Ontario, Canada, 2008

Archambault, S. et al., *Dark matter spin-dependent limits for WIMP interactions on ^{19}F by PICASSO,* Physics Letters B 682, page numbers (185 - 192), 2009

12

Data Acquisition Systems for Magnetic Shield Characterization

Leopoldo Angrisani[1], Mirko Marracci[2], Bernardo Tellini[2] and Nicola Pasquino[3]
[1]*University of Naples "Federico II", Department of Computer Science and Control Systems*
[2]*University of Pisa, Department of Electrical Systems and Automation*
[3]*University of Naples "Federico II", Department of Electrical Engineering*
Italy

1. Introduction

The purpose of an EM shield is to prevent undesired electromagnetic coupling between an EM source and a susceptible EM device. The mechanism of electromagnetic coupling is by radiation, inductive and capacitive coupling. The radiation of energy by electromagnetic waves characterizes the EM coupling in the far field region, while inductive (or low-impedance) and capacitive (or high-impedance) couplings are the driving mechanism of coupling in the near field region. In all the cases, a complete analysis of the shielding performances of an EM shield should require a full-wave solution of the electromagnetic problem. This means to solve a classical eddy current problem and in presence of magnetically permeable materials the analysis shall combine the Maxwell's equations with the magnetic properties of the shield.

Numerous studies of shielding problems can be found in the literature showing how this topic has been the subject of great interest to the scientific community for many years (Moser; 1988; Schelkunoff; 1943; Schulz et al.; 1988). Several analytical and numerical techniques have been developed during the years especially with the advent and proliferation of the electronic devices.

Different materials with a wide range of electrical and magnetic properties are used for shielding applications. As a matter of fact, an accurate knowledge of the electromagnetic properties of the material is an important task for a correct modeling and design phase. Further, shields have different shapes and contain apertures and all these parameters influence the shielding effectiveness, thus the electromagnetic susceptibility of the combined shield-electronic equipment system.

In a first part, this chapter reports on basic aspects of the shielding theory and standard measurement methods of shielding effectiveness in the frequency and time domain. Concepts and measurement techniques are discussed with reference to basic shield configurations and following the relevant standards (IEEE Std 299; 2006). A basic configuration of the experimental setup and instrumentation chain for shielding effectiveness measurements is reported.

In the second part, we focus on the magnetic shields that received most of the attention for shielding low-frequency magnetic fields (Celozzi & D'Amore; 1996; Hoburg; 1995; Sergeant et al.; 2006).
The case of a circular loop magnetically coupled to an indefinite conducting plate and that of a hollow ring shield placed coaxially around a circular loop are treated to support our discussion (Di Fraia et al.; 2009).
Then, we conclude with a discussion on the characterization of magnetic materials. As better discussed in the chapter, an accurate knowledge of the magnetic characteristics of a magnetic material is at the basis for an accurate study and measurement of the shielding effectiveness of a magnetic shield. Experimental setups and instrumentation chain commonly adopted for magnetic materials characterization are shown.

2. Shielding theory

The shielding effectiveness (SE) is defined as the ratio of the signal received (from a transmitter) without (*wo*) the shield, to the signal received inside the shield (*w*). Alternatively, SE is defined as the insertion loss when the shield is placed between the transmitting antenna and the receiving antenna (IEEE Std 299; 2006). Thus, SE can be defined as:

$$SE = 20\log\frac{|H_i|}{|H_t|} \tag{1}$$

where H_i and H_t are the incident and transmitted magnetic field.
Time-varying electromagnetic fields in conducting media are driven by diffusion (or diffusion-like) equations. The analysis of electromagnetic field diffusion in conducting media is, in practice, the analysis of eddy currents in those conductors. A basic knowledge and modeling of the skin effect and the eddy currents are necessary so that efficient measures are performed to characterize the EMC parameters of a shield.
Shielding problems are generally approached by the scientific community through the solution of the vector wave equation or through the application of the Schelkunoff's theory (Moser; 1988). The use of impedance concept for dealing with the theory of the electromagnetic shielding was first introduced by Schelkunoff and therefore it is known as the Schelkunoff's theory (Schelkunoff; 1943).
An extended analysis of various basic eddy current problems can be found in (Tegopoulos & Kriezis; 1985). Other treatments are reported in (Moser; 1988; Schulz et al.; 1988). In particular, an interesting study case is that of a loop antenna coupled to an indefinite conducting plate. A schematic representation of the problem is shown in Fig. 1.
The problem can be solved analytically and adopted as a benchmark for other analytical, numerical or experimental methods. As written in (IEEE Std 299; 2006) the shielding effectiveness can be related to the ratio of the voltage induced along the receiving loop without the shield, to that received in presence of the shield. Thus eq. (1) can be written as:

$$SE = 20\log\frac{|V_{wo}|}{|V_w|} \tag{2}$$

It is worth to say that in presence of nonuniform field distribution over the shield the SE parameter can vary significantly, depending on the adopted loop size. As a practical

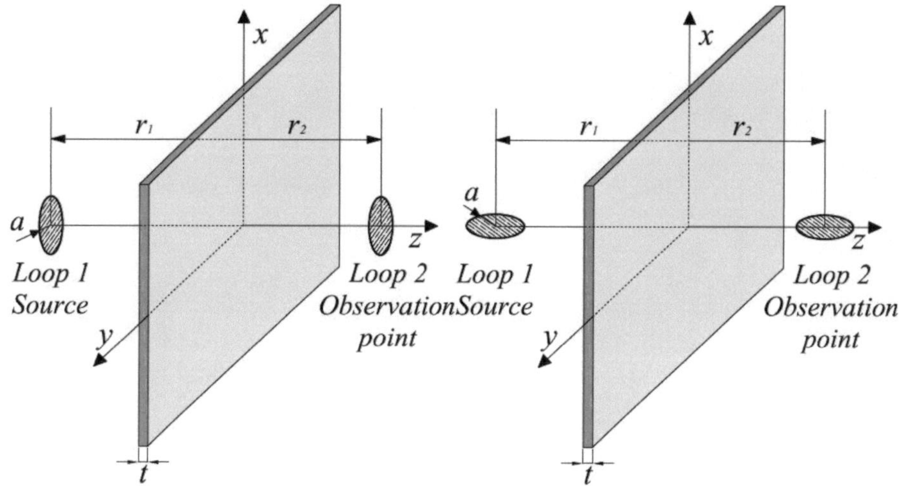

Fig. 1. Magnetic field loop source close to indefinite conducting plate.

consideration, it can be often the case that the geometry of the shield and the dimensions of the electronic device under test do not make it possible to place the chosen loop probe in the desired position and, as a consequence, to correctly perform the SE measurement. In some cases, this problem is solved by the use of smaller-size magnetic sensors. However, the averaging problem still stands and the estimation of the SE could be more properly defined by averaging the field over a spatial region better representative of the "victim".

As written in the previous text, an effective method for shielding problem consists in the application of the Schelkunoff's theory. Here, we limit to recall some basic aspects of this approach with reference to the case of a plane wave incident on an indefinite conducting lamination, and to the previous case of a loop coupled to an indefinite plate.

Due to the impedance discontinuity at the air-metal and metal-air boundaries and to the diffusion equation governing the field inside the shield, part of the energy is reflected at the two interfaces and part absorbed by the shield turning into heat energy. It is common notation to express the overall SE as the sum of three separate contributions:

$$SE = R + A + M \tag{3}$$

where all the terms are expressed in dB and R represents the reflection losses at the left and right interfaces, A is the term of the absorption losses, while M is an additional terms due to multiple reflection effects. In the case of Fig. 2, SE can be analytically evaluated and its expression is:

$$SE = 20\log_{10}\left|\frac{(\eta_0+\eta)^2}{4\eta_0\eta}\right| + 20\log_{10}|e^{t/\delta}| + 20\log_{10}\left|1-\left(\frac{\eta_0-\eta^2}{\eta_0+\eta}\right)e^{t/\delta}e^{-i2\beta t}\right| \tag{4}$$

where it is possible to recognize the reflection R, absorption A and mutual reflection M terms (Paul; 1992). η_0 and η represent the intrinsic air and shield impedance, respectively.

The Schelkunoff's theory can be extended to the case of shield in the near field region substituting the wave impedance of the magnetic field source in place of the impedance η_0 of the previous expressions. As well known from the theory, the wave impedance of a magnetic dipole can be expresses as:

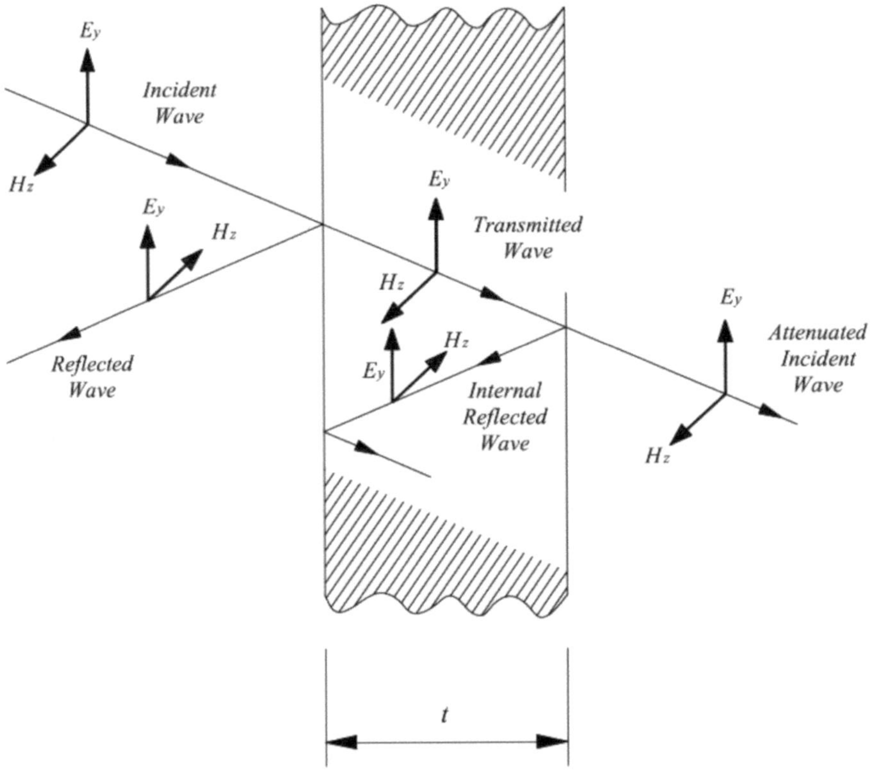

Fig. 2. Shielding effectiveness: plane wave incident on an indefinite conducting plate.

$$\eta_w = \frac{E_\phi}{H_\theta} - \eta_0 \frac{i/(\beta_0 r) + 1/(\beta_0 r^2)}{i/(\beta_0 r) + 1/(\beta_0 r^2) - i/(\beta_0 r^3)} \tag{5}$$

Thus, neglecting wave divergence in traversing our physically thin shield we can estimate the shielding effectiveness of the plate by replacing η_w for η_0 in eq. (4).

3. Shielding effectiveness measurement

According to the IEEE 299 standard the range measurement frequencies for shielding effectiveness evaluation are those reported in Table 1.

The measurements shall be made in accordance to specific relevant positions among the transmitting, receiving antennas and shield. In particular, performing measurement in the low frequency range, loops shall be spaced each one by 0.3 m from the respective shielding barrier and coplanar in a plane perpendicular to the wall, ceiling, or other surface being measured (IEEE Std 299; 2006). A typical configuration is shown in Fig. 3.

As a basic concern of the electromagnetic compatibilty, measurements should be oriented to detect the worste case in order to prevent as much as possible disturbances to electronic equipments from electromagnetic interferences (EMI). According to such a fundamental rule, one loop (typically the transmitting antenna) is kept in a fixed position, while the receiving loop is reoriented and physically swept searching for the worst condition. The maximum reading of the receiver is adopted for evaluating the SE.

ExtendedFrequencyRange	Antenna Type
50 Hz -16 MHz	Small loop
20 MHz -100 MHz	Biconical
100 MHz -300 MHz	Dipole
0.3 GHz -1 GHz	Dipole
1 GHz -100 GHz	Horn

Table 1. Range Measurement Frequencies for SE.

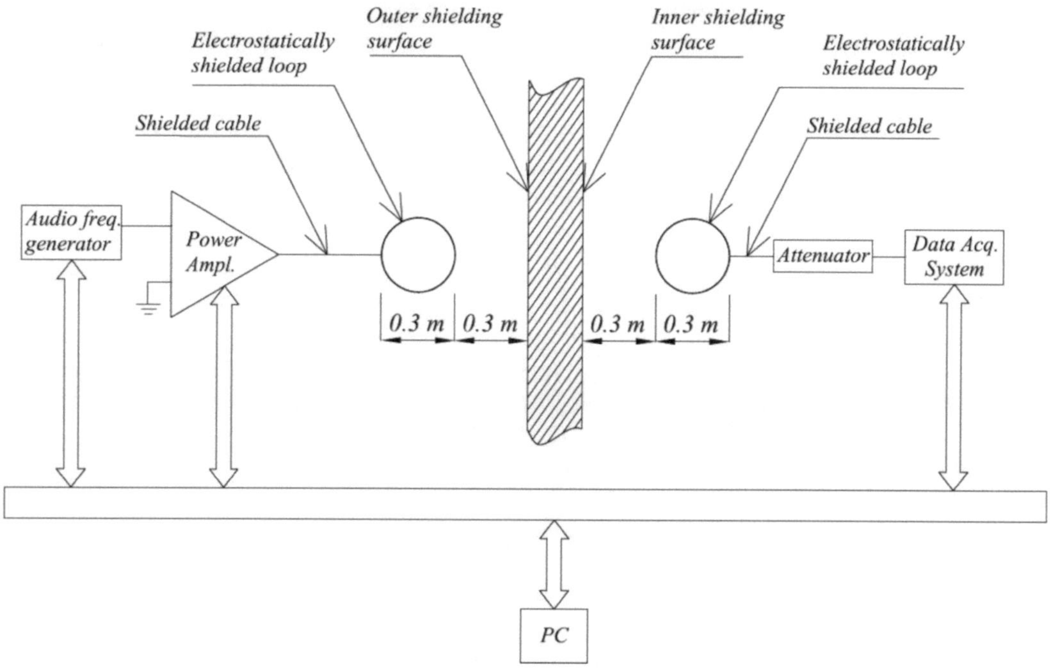

Fig. 3. Test configuration of SE measurements in the low frequency range.

Measurement data obtained following the previous procedure are converted in SE values through the following mathematical relations that vary vs. the operating frequency range:

$$SE_H = 20\log_{10}\left|\frac{H_1}{H_2}\right| \text{ or } SE_H = 20\log_{10}\left|\frac{V_1}{V_2}\right| \quad \text{(50Hz-20MHz)} \tag{6}$$

$$SE_E = 20\log_{10}\left|\frac{E_1}{E_2}\right| \quad \text{(20MHz-300MHz)} \tag{7}$$

$$SE_P = 20\log_{10}\left|\frac{P_1}{P_2}\right| \quad \text{(300MHz-100GHz)} \tag{8}$$

Many parameters such as the electromagnetic environment, the characteristics of the test site, the instrumentation chain itself, the positioning of the antennas participate at determining the measurement uncertainty of SE. The IEEE Std 299 reports that uncertainty in the measurement of SE is not required, even if *it is recommended that a measurement uncertainty analysis be performed on each set of measurements and discussed in the final report.* In addition, the IEEE Std 299 makes reference to the standards and technical notes relevant to the evaluation and expression of the uncertainty in measurement (NIST TN 1297; 1994).

3.1 SE time and frequency domain measurements: data acquisition systems

The procedure set in Standard IEEE Std 299 (2006) to test shielding effectiveness is basically a frequency domain technique, where a single tone within the test band is generated at a time and its amplitude is measured with and without the shield. A typical automated test and data acquisition procedure would therefore require repetitive execution of the following steps: firstly, the generator is set at a frequency and the signal is applied to the transmitting antenna; secondly, the receiver is tuned at the same frequency as the generator and the amplitude of the received signal is stored. Then the generator is set to the next frequency and the procedure goes on so to test all the frequency band. The time requirements for such a procedure to be run over the entire test band call for alternative methods and systems for shielding effectiveness measurement. In the following two proposals are presented.

3.1.1 Time-Frequency Representation

Time-Frequency Representations (TFR's) map a one-dimensional signal of time, $s(t)$, onto a two-dimensional function of time and frequency, $T_s(t, f)$ Hlawatsch et al (1992). A signal, as a function of time, may be considered as a representation with perfect time resolution. In contrast, the magnitude of the Fourier Transform (FT) of the signal may be considered as a representation with perfect spectral resolution but with no time information because the magnitude of the FT conveys frequency content but it fails to convey when, in time, different events occur in the signal. TFR's provide a bridge between these two representations in that they provide some temporal information and some spectral information simultaneously. In particular, most TFR's are "time-varying spectral representations," which are conceptually similar to a musical score with time running along one axis and frequency along the other. The values of the TFR surface above the time-frequency plane give an indication as to which spectral components are present at what times. Thus, TFR's are useful for the representation and analysis of signals containing one or more time-varying frequencies. One form of TFR (or TFD) can be formulated by the multiplicative comparison of a signal with itself, expanded in different directions about each point in time. Such representations and formulations are known as *quadratic TFR's* or TFD's because the representation is quadratic in the signal. One such representation is the Wigner-Ville Distribution:

$$T_s(t,f) = \int_{-\infty}^{+\infty} s(t-\tau/2)s^*(t+\tau/2)e^{-j2\pi f\tau}\,d\tau, \tag{9}$$

The cross-terms caused by their bilinear structure may be useful in some applications such as classification as the cross-terms provide extra detail for the recognition algorithm. However, in some other applications, as for example the shielding effectiveness measurement, these cross terms may produce misinterpretations and they would need to be reduced. One way to do this is obtained by comparing the signal with a different function. Such resulting representations are known as *linear TFR's* because the representation is linear in the signal. The windowed Fourier transform, also known as the Short-Time Fourier

Transform (STFT) localizes the signal by modulating it with a window function $h(\cdot)$, before performing the Fourier transform to obtain the frequency content of the signal in the region of the window. Its expression is:

$$T_s(t,f;h) = \int_{-\infty}^{+\infty} s(u)h^*(u-t)e^{-j2\pi fu}\,du. \tag{10}$$

In a digital implementation of a TFR, the obtained results are typically the squared values of the discrezited version of the aforementioned two-dimensional function, $T_s(n, v)$, the discrete variables, n and v, represent, respectively, the time and frequency. These values are collected in a matrix. Generally, row index is connected to frequency, while column index represents time. By visualizing the matrix along a time-frequency plane, it can directly be observed how the power spectral contents of the analyzed signal evolve versus time. So, shielding effectiveness measurements can automatically be carried out by simply manipulating the coefficients of the matrix.

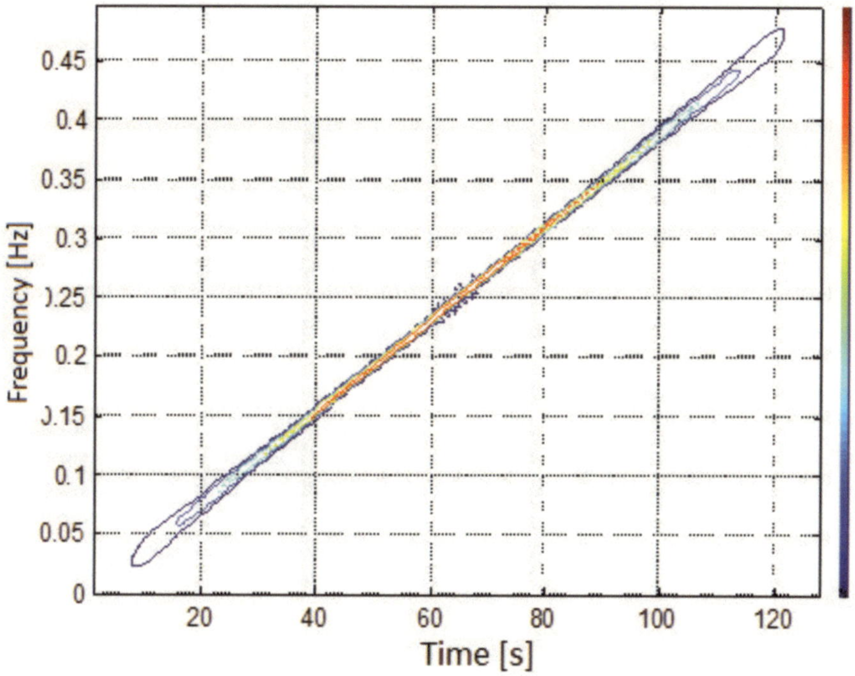

Fig. 4. Typical Time-Frequency Representation.

TFR's are often used for parameter's estimation Angrisani et al. (2002) and system testing Angrisani et al. (2000). Figure 4 shows a typical time-frequency representation for the response to an FM signal. This is what is expected to be seen when such techniques are applied to SE measurements: the whole frequency band in Table 1 is divided into sub-bands, then an FM spanning each sub-band is generated, and the response is first digitized by a data acquisition system with proper vertical resolution and sample rate, and then suitably processed in order to construct the desired time-frequency representation. The advantage over a frequency domain test is the capability of acquiring the response to more frequencies at the same time. Furthermore, unlike the classical approach such a methodology can be used even to characterize non-linear materials, as the analysis in the joint time-frequency domain can localize also harmonics and non-stationary components whereas a tone-by-tone investigation couldn't.

3.1.2 Pulsed signal characterization

Because of the wide frequency content of a pulse, it can be used to test the shielding properties of a material over an interval of frequencies. This is indeed quite a trivial task in terms of system requirements, given the excellent performance of both pulse generators and acquisition systems available on the market. The same envelope can be used to modulate different carriers so that the whole investigation band can be tested in different steps. With this approach, even a single pulse can be generated: due to the storing capability of modern digital oscilloscopes, by setting a pre-trigger acquisition mode with a one-shot trigger mode, the transient can be acquired and stored, and processed later (even off-line) by means of an FFT algorithm to detect the response of the shielding material to each frequency contained in the transmitted pulse. Again, unlike the direct frequency-domain analysis, this methodology can be used even in presence of dispersive or generally non-linear materials, given its nature of being a test for a packet of frequencies at the same time.

4. Magnetic shields

Magnetic field shielding at low and extremely low frequency (ELF) is a subject of particular interest for the industrial and scientific communities. Typical applications include medical instrumentation shielding, noise measurements, device characterizations. Magnetic materials with high magnetic permeability are commonly adopted for such cases. Two separate physical mechanism participate at determining the electromagnetic shielding in presence of magnetic materials: the "flux shunting" as a consequence of the high permeability of the shield material and the redirection of flux due to induced eddy currents (Hoburg; 1995). Both these phenomena together to the magnetic field source characteristics, the geometry of the shield and its relevant position with respect to the magnetic field itself contribute to determine the overall SE of a magnetic shield. Due to the highly nonlinear nature of the adopted magnetic materials, the shielding effectiveness vary with the field strength. Saturation effects as well as change of the equivalent magnetic permeability in presence of combined static and time-varying fields can cause inaccurate field analysis and measurements.

The IEEE Std 299, suggests to determine nonlinear effects by measuring the magnetic SE as a function of source strength. This should be done increasing in 10 dB steps, nominally 0.1Wto 1W and 10Wthe input power at the transmitting antenna. In particular the standard reports that: *If the magnetic SE decreases more than about 2 dB, then intermediate level measurements shall be made. The results shall then be plotted to determine the highest level permissible for linear performance (within ±1 dB).*

Recent hysteresis models have reached a high level of accuracy, as a consequence this makes possible to perform the SE analysis and measurement of a ferromagnetic shield through an accurate characterization of the magnetic behavior of the shielding material combined to a computational analysis (Bologna et al.; 2006; Celozzi & D'Amore; 1996; Di Fraia et al.; 2009; Sergeant et al.; 2006).

In particular, in (Di Fraia et al.; 2009) the authors studied an basic case of an iron hollow cylinder placed coaxially around a circular loop. The investigated geometry is shown in Fig. 5

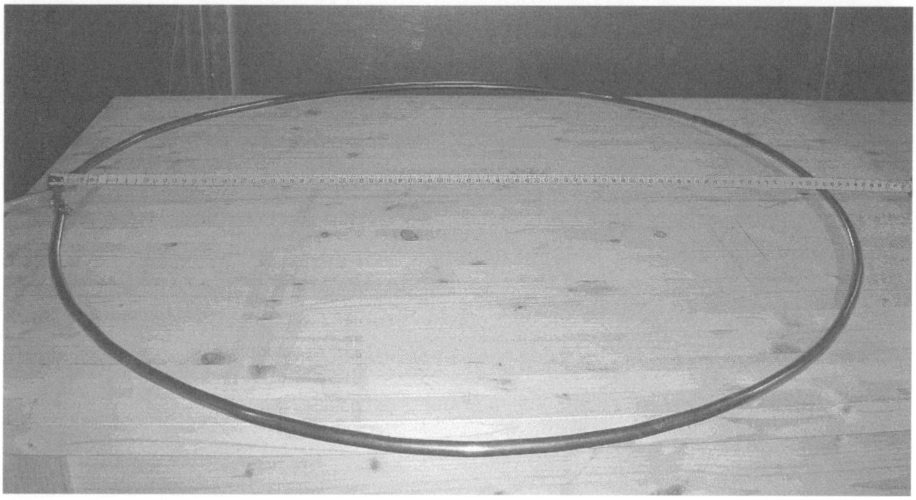

Fig. 5. Photograph of a basic setup for magnetic shield characterization.

The analysis was performed by combining magnetic characterization of the material with an analytical techniques and results were in good agreement with the measurements performed according to the standard procedure (Tellini et al.; 2005).

5. Magnetic material characterization: data acquisition systems

The expression "magnetic material characterization" commonly refers to experiments aimed at investigating the dependence of the macroscopic magnetization M vs. the effective magnetic field H in continuos media. In such a way the relationship $M(H)$ has a meaning at the macroscopic level, i.e., M represents the average magnetic moment over a representative spatial region of the material or over the whole test specimen.

Generally speaking an hysteresis loop is interpreted as a property of the material under test. On the other hand, many parameters among which the specimen geometry can influence the measurement and the resulting measured hysteresis cycle. The field H and $M$are vector quantities and, strictly speaking, any representation of hysteresis loops should be given in vector terms. However, many experiments and interpretations are based on a scalar representation, where the magnetization component along the field is given as a function of the field intensity. This description is useful and convenient when we can identify an "easy" direction of the fields along the magnetic sample and it is the approach used in this chapter. Of course, this method is not complete being neglected any consideration on the magnetization components perpendicular to the field. The use of vector hysteresis modeling and measurement should be otherwise mandatory for generic magnetic shield geometries.

One of the problems we have to face planning experiments of magnetic material characterization is the role of the demagnetizing fields. Such field occurs any time we have a discontinuity of the magnetization vector M ($\nabla \cdot M = 0$) and can influence the measuring methodology and accuracy of the results. Let us consider the basic example shown in Fig. 6.

A current $i_1(t)$ is driven through a primary coil generating a proportional magnetic field H_a. The voltage $v_2(t)$ induced along a secondary open circuit coil is proportional to the rate of change of the flux $\Phi = BS$, being S the cross-section area of the sample to which is linked the coil and B the average induction component perpendicular to the cross section).

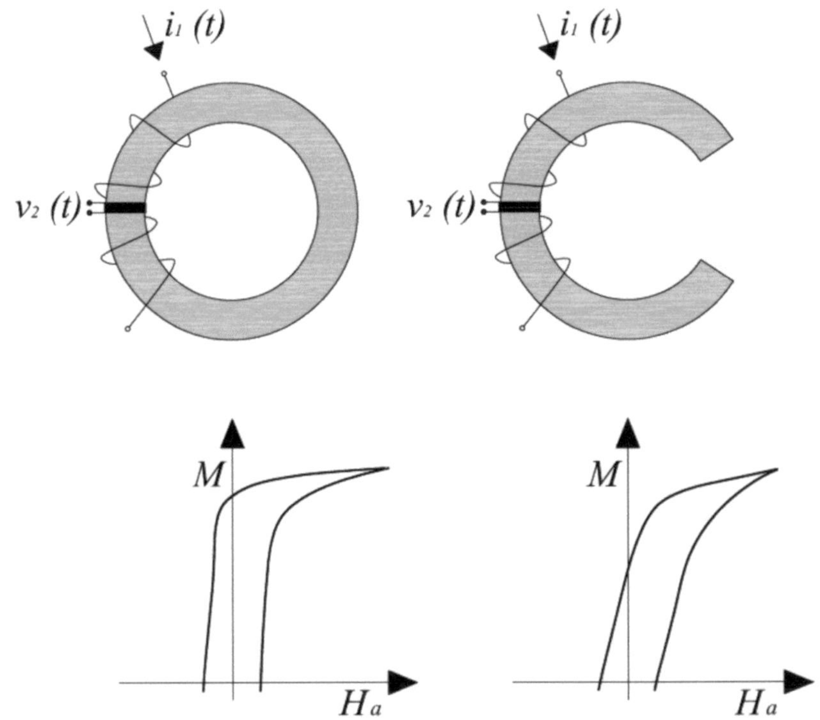

Fig. 6. Schematic representation of open and closed magnetic samples. The loop shape is affected by the specimen geometry.

The applied field H_a arising from the primary current $i_1(t)$ is the magnetic field that would be present inside the primary coil if magnetic materials were not inserted. In presence of the magnetic material, even driving the same current $i_1(t)$ the relationship between H and $i_1(t)$ obviously changes. This is easy to show, making two different experiments with the same magnetic material but adopting different specimen geometries, such as those shown in Fig. 6. As discussed in (Bertotti; 1998; Fiorillo; 2004) with the open sample configuration the effective field H acting in the material is not the applied field H_a related to the primary current and the demagnetizing field must be taken into account for the characterization of the magnetic material properties.

For such reasons often closed magnetic circuit are preferred to open samples in the measurements of magnetic hysteresis. The sample can be shaped in order to achieve flux closure with the material itself or with a yoke made of a high-permeability and high-section material. An intuitive closed magnetic circuit is represented by the toroidal configuration; some examples are reported in Fig. 7.

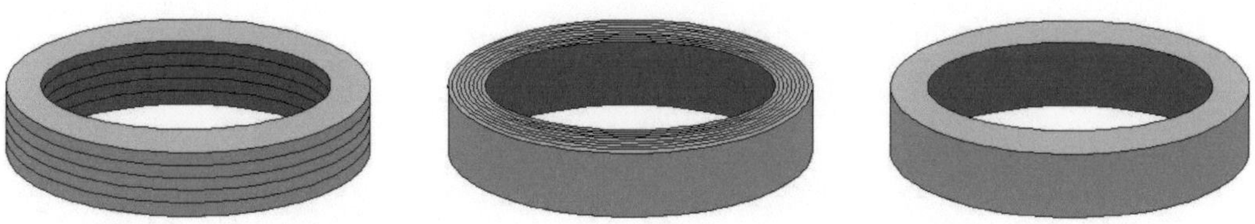

Fig. 7. Schematic representation of different made magnetic cores. Laminated (left one), wound ribbon (center), sintered powder (right one)

Cores can be obtained by stacking rings punched out of a lamination (left one), winding a ribbon-like sample (centre one) or sintering a magnetic powder (right one). The field inside the core can be generated by an uniformly primary winding ound around the core or, if an high intensity field is required, by means of an axial conductor of large cross-sectional area. The stacked specimen can be used in the case of isotropic (or with moderate anisotropy) materials like, for example, non-oriented electrical steels; in this case the magnetic properties measured are averaged over the lamination plane. Strip-wound cores, on the contrary, are used to provide magnetic properties over a definite direction in the plane of the sheet. In every case, using a toroidal core, some aspects must be taken into account:

- the preparation of the specimen and of the primary and secondary winding can be tedious;
- every next specimen requires the preparation of new windings;
- when we want to characterize a lamination along a definite direction a strip-wound core has to be built and this configuration implies the creation of bending stresses that can modify the results;
- the field strength available with the primary winding is limited and we can test only very soft magnets;
- the applied field decreases passing from the inside to the outside boundary of the toroid, being the field strength inversely proportional to the magnetic path length D (where D is the diameter of the considered circumferential field line). This leads to geometrical constraints among the internal and external diameter.

Such drawbacks typical of toroidal specimen brought to the development of a different closed magnetic circuit obtained by making a square assembly of strips cut along the desired testing direction, superimposed at the corners. The specimen is known as the Epstein test frame and such a magnetic configuration is a standard for measurements in steel sheets from DC to 10 kHz. A multiple number of four strips of width 30 mm and length variable from 280 to 305 mm are superposed at the corner to forma square. A weight of 1 N is placed on each corner in order to ensure a good and reproducible flux closure. Each side of the square is provided with a secondary and a primary winding wound on a rigid insulation support with rectangular section. The solenoids have all the same number of turns with a total of 700 primary and secondary turns in the frame used for DC and power frequency measurements and a total of 200 turns in the frame recommended for medium frequency range (0.4 - 10 kHz) (IEC 60404-2; 2008; IEC 60404-10; 1988). The mean magnetic path is fixed by the standard IEC 60404-2 in 0.94 m. In Figs. 8 and 9 a schematic drawing and a photograph of an Epstein frame are reported.

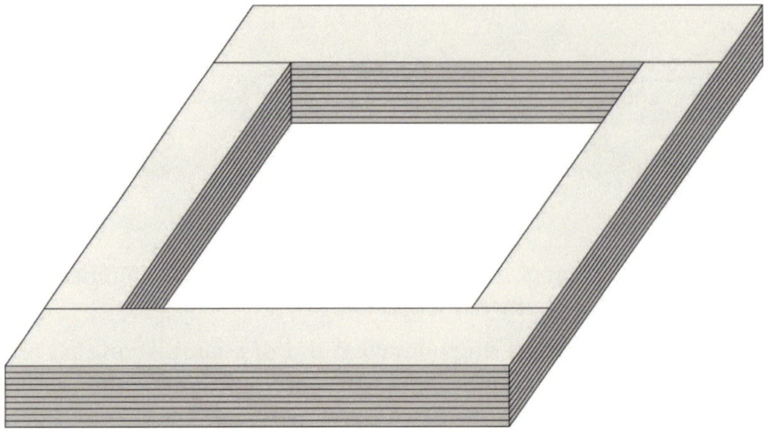

Fig. 8. Schematic drawing of the Epstein frame.

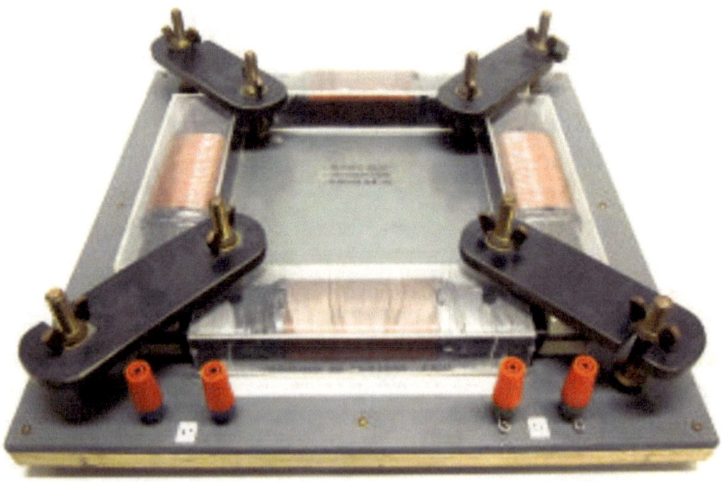

Fig. 9. Photograph of the Epstein frame.

A measurement technique commonly adopted for characterization of soft magnetic materials is the volt-amperometric method. This approach reconstructs the magnetic H and induction B fields via the measurement of the primary current i_1 and the secondary open circuit voltage v_2 through the Ampère and Lenz's laws:

$$H = \frac{N_1 i_1}{L_m} \qquad v_2 = N_2 S \frac{dB}{dt} \tag{11}$$

where N_1 and N_2 represent the number of turns in the primary and secondary winding (700 each one in the case of the Epstein frame used for DC and power frequency measurements); Lm is the mean magnetic path length (0.94 m in the case of the Epstein frame), and S is the cross section area of the magnetic circuit. The volt-amperometric method is generally applied for measuring of major loop or symmetric minor loops. Recently this techniques has been extended to the characterization of asymmetric minor loops and of magnetic materials under nonperiodic conditions (Tellini et al.; 2008, 2009).

In Fig. 10 a basic measurement scheme for characterization of soft magnetic materials is reported.

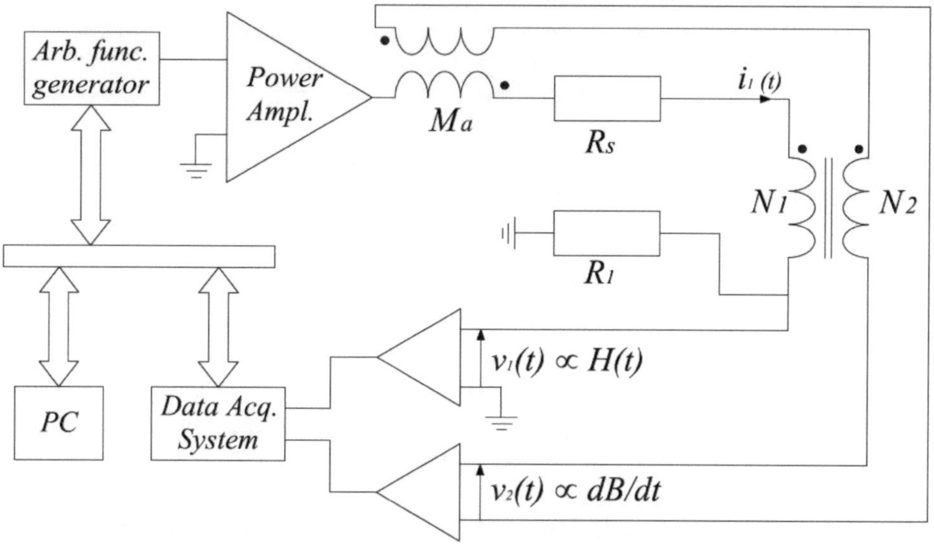

Fig. 10. Measurement scheme for characterization of soft magnetic materials.

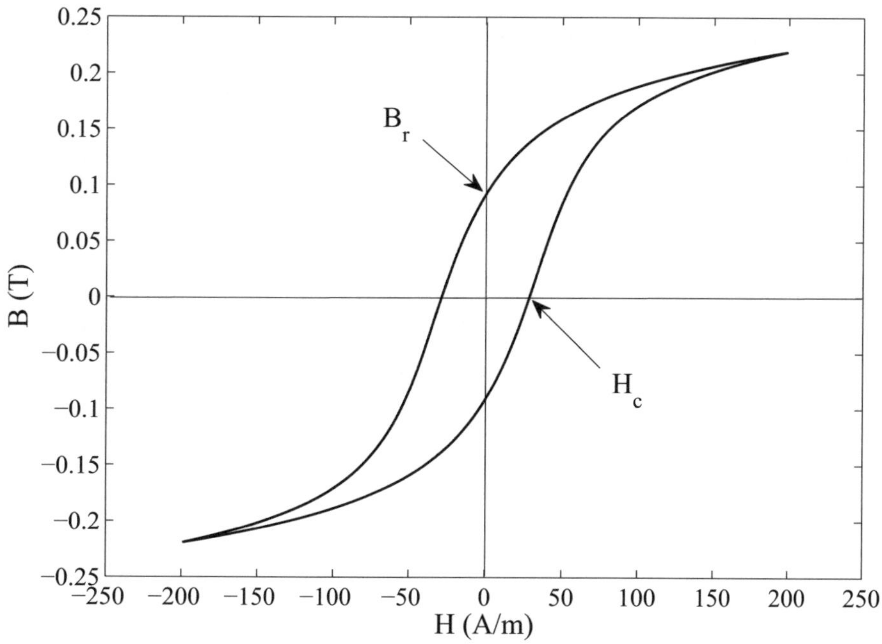

Fig. 11. Major loop obtained for a commercial soft ferrite. Coercive field *Hc* and induction remanence *Br* are indicated by arrows.

An arbitrary function generator is connected to the primary winding via a power amplifier. The primary current i_1 is measured via the voltage drop across a calibrated resistance R_H. The secondary open circuit voltage v_2 is measured by means of a high-impedance differential amplifier and a data acquisition system.

The data acquisition system must perform synchronous acquisitions between the two channels; a couple of identical DC-coupled variable-gain low-noise amplifiers is generally interposed between the $H(t)$ and dB/dt signal sources and the acquisition device (Fiorillo; 2004).

The mutual inductance M_a in the scheme of Fig. 10 is used to automatically compensate the air flux linked with the secondary winding. The presented scheme can be used to impose a prescribed time dependence (often sinusoidal) of the magnetization, i.e. the secondary voltage $v_2(t)$ for example by means of a digitally controlled recursive technique.

In Fig. 11, the hysteresis loop obtained measuring data on a commercial ferrite toroid is reported. Although a complete model of magnetic hysteresis is very complex, the coercive field H_c and the induction remanence B_r are two key paramaters that together to the saturation H_{sat}, B_{sat} values define in a first approximation the material magnetic behavior. The remanence B_r represents the induction value obtained after applying a large field to the specimen and then removing it, while the coercive field is the field needed to bring the induction field from B_r to zero. On the basis of H_c and B_r values, magnetic materials are commonly classified into soft and hardmagnetic materials. In Fig. 12 a typical major loop with a complete series of minor symmetric cycles is shown. Such data are a basic set for the identification of scalar hysteresis models such as the Preisach scalar model Cardelli et al. (2000). The magnetic sample under test was a commercial ferrite toroidal specimen.

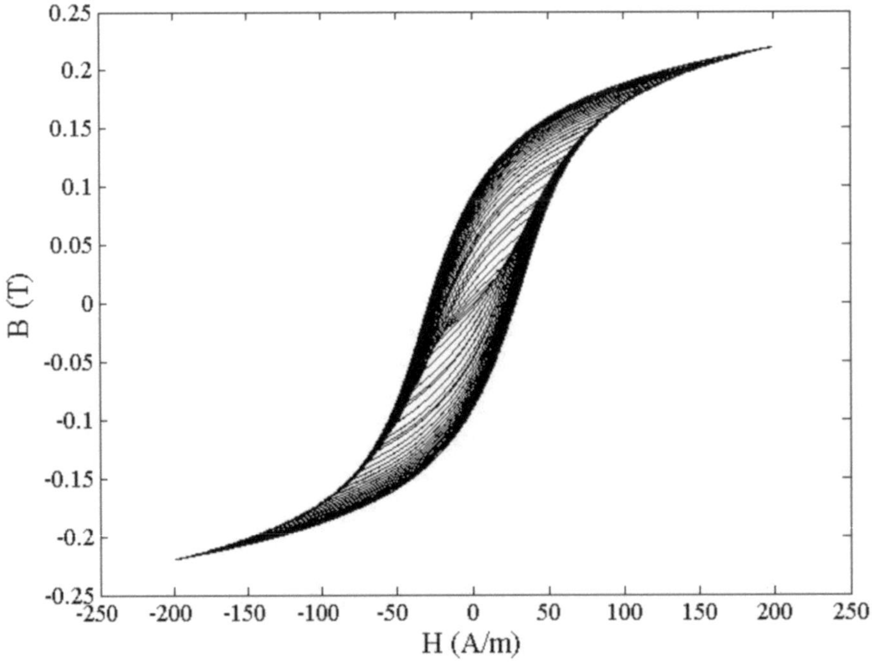

Fig. 12. Major loop and minor symmetric cycles obtained for a commercial soft ferrite.

6. Conclusions

The chapter presented basic aspects of the shielding theory and shielding effectiveness measurement. In a first part, some remarks were spent on the classical eddy current analysis and the impedance concept (Schelkunoff's theory) for approaching shielding problems. In a second part, the discussion was oriented towards common and alternative measurement procedures. In particular, time-frequency or pulsed signal based measurement techniques were described as possible effective tools for application to dispersive or non-linear shielding materials. The third and last part focused on the magnetic shields and on the characterization procedures of the magnetic materials. The discussion points out the importance of an accurate knowledge of the material magnetic behavior in order to improve the shielding design and to make more efficient the measurements of the shielding parameters.

7. References

Angrisani L.; Daponte P. & D'Apuzzo M. (2000) A measurement method based on time frequency representations for testing GSM equipment, *IEEE Trans. on Instr. and Meas.*, vol.49, No.5, October 2000, pp.1050-1055.

Angrisani L.; & D'Arco M. (2002) A measurement method based on an modified version of the chirplet transform for instantaneous frequency estimation, *IEEE Trans. on Instr. and Meas.*, vol.51, No.4, August 2002, pp.704-711.

Bertotti, G. (1998). *Hysteresis in Magnetism: For Physicists, Materials Scientists, and Engineers*, Academic Press.

Bologna, M.; Giannetti, R.; Marracci, M. & Tellini, B. (2006). Measuring the Magnetic Field Attenuation of Nonlinear Shields," IMTC Conference, (2006), 2200-2204.

Braun, S.; Donauer, T. & Russer, P. (2008). A Real-Time Time-Domain EMI Measurement System for Full-ComplianceMeasurements According to CISPR 16-1-1. *IEEE Trans. Electromag. Compat.*, Vol. 50, No. 2, (May 2008), 259-267.

Cardelli, E.; Della Torre, E.; Tellini, B. (2000). Direct and Inverse Preisach Modelling of Soft Materials. *IEEE Trans. Magn.*, Vol. 36, No. 4, (Jul. 2000), 1267-1271.

Celozzi, S. & D'Amore, M. (1996). Magnetic Field Attenuation of Nonlinear Shields. *IEEE Trans. Electromag. Compat.*, Vol. 38, No. 3, (Aug 1996), 318-326.

Di Fraia, S.;Marracci,M.; Tellini, B. & Zappacosta, C. (2009). Shielding EffectivenessMeasurements for Ferromagnetic Shields. *IEEE Trans. Instrum.Meas.*, Vol. 58, No. 1, (Jan 2009), 115-121.

Fiorillo, F. (2004). *Measurement and Characterization of Magnetic Materials*, Elsevier-Academic Press.

Hlawatsch, F. & Boudreaux-Bartels, G.F. (1992). Linear and Quadratic Time-Frequency Signal Representation, *IEEE Signal Processing Magazine*, April 1992.

Hoburg J. F. (1988). Principles of Quasistatic Magnetic Shielding with Cylindrical and Spherical Shields. *IEEE Trans. Electromag. Compat.*, Vol. 37, No. 4, (Nov 1995), 574-579.

IEC 60404-2 (2008). Magnetic materials - Part 2: Methods of measurement of the magnetic properties of electrical steel strip and sheet by means of an Epstein frame.

IEC 60404-10 (1988).Magneticmaterials - Part 10: Methods ofmeasurement ofmagnetic properties of magnetic sheet and strip at medium frequencies.

IEEE Std 299 (2006). IEEE Standard Method for Measuring the Effectiveness of Electromagnetic Shielding Enclosures.

IEEE Std 393-1991 (1992). IEEE Standard for Test Procedures for Magnetic Cores.

Krug, F. & Russer, P. (2005). Quasi-Peak Detector Model for a Time-Domain Measurement System. *IEEE Trans. Electromag. Compat.*, Vol. 47, No. 2, (May 2005), 320-326.

Moser J. R. (1988). Low-Frequency Low-Impedance Electromagnetic Shielding. *IEEE Trans. Electromag. Compat.*, Vol. 30, No. 3, (Aug 1988), 202-210.

NIST Technical Note 1297 (1994). Guidelines for Evaluating and Expressing the Uncertainty of NIST Measurement Results. Barry N. Taylor and Chris E. Kuyatt.

Paul, C. R. (1992). *Introduction to Electromagnetic Compatibility*,Wiley, NewYork.

Schelkunoff, S. A. (1943). *Electromagnetic Waves*, Princeton, NJ, Van Nostrand.

Schulz, R. B.; Plantz, V. C. & Brush D. R. (1988). Shielding Theory and Practice. *IEEE Trans. Electromag. Compat.*, Vol. 30, No. 3, (Aug 1988), 187-201.

Sergeant P.; Zucca, M.; Dupré, L. & Roccato, P. E. (2006). Magnetic shielding of a cylindrical shield in nonlinear hystereticmaterial. *IEEE Trans.Magn.*, Vol. 42, No. 10, (Oct. 2001), 3189-3191.

Tellini, B.; Bologna, M. & Pelliccia, D. (2005). A new analytic approach for dealing with hysteretic materials. *IEEE Trans.Magn.*, Vol. 41, No. 1, (Jan. 2005), 2-7.

Tellini, B.; Giannetti, R. & Lizón-Martínez, S. (2008). Sensorless Measurement Technique for Characterization of Magnetic Materials under Nonperiodic Conditions. *IEEE Trans. Instrum. Meas.*, Vol. 57, No. 7, (July 2008), 1465-1469.

Tellini, B.; Giannetti, R.; Lizón-Martínez, S. & Marracci, M. (2009). Characterization of the Accommodation Effect in Soft Hysteretic Materials via Sensorless Measurement Technique. *IEEE Trans. Instrum.Meas.*, Vol. 58, No. 10, (Aug. 2009), 2807-2814.

Tegopoulos, J. A. & Kriezis E. E. (1985). *Eddy Currents in Linear Conducting Media*, Elsevier, Amsterdam, Oxford, New York, Tokyo.

13

Microcontroller-based Biopotential Data Acquisition Systems: Practical Design Considerations

José Antonio Gutiérrez Gnecchi, Daniel Lorias Espinoza and Víctor Hugo Olivares Peregrino
Instituto Tecnológico de Morelia, Departamento de Ingeniería Electrónica Morelia, Michoacán, México

1. Introduction

Non-invasive bioimpedance measurements are an important part of routine diagnostic procedures. ECG (Electrocardiograph), EEG (Electroencephalograph), EMG (Electromyography) and EOG (Electrooculograph) measurements are amongst the most common non-invasive measurements used for diagnosis. The advances in microcontroller technology over the past 25 years have resulted in general-purpose, low-cost, low-power devices that can perform many of the operations involved in the measurement, and analysis process. Although the data acquisition system architecture is similar for the different non-invasive biopotential measurements, practical considerations have to be taken into account for each particular biopotential measurement: rate of amplification, filter bandpass frequency, overall bandwidth and Analogue-to-Digital conversion rate. This chapter presents an overview of the electrical characteristics of different biopotential measurements and general data acquisition architecture for portable biopotential measurement equipment. This chapter also addresses the importance of electrical isolation to ensure patient safety while using biopotential measurement equipment. Two case studies are presented: a microcontroller-based EEG data acquisition system for measurement of auditory evoked potentials for diagnosis of hypoacusis and a microcontroller-based ambulatory ECG data acquisition system.

2. Biopotential electrical characteristics

Non-invasive biopotential measurements rely on the fact that the activity of many body organs can be determined by measuring electrical signals in the vicinity of the organ to be studied. Amongst the most common biopotential measurements used for routine diagnosis are ECG (Electrocardiograph), EEG (Electroencephalograph), EMG (Electromyography) and EOG (Electrooculograph) measurements.

Electrocardiography refers to the registry of cardiac activity. A set of electrodes located non-invasively in the patient's thorax and extremities are used to capture small electrical signals resulting from the origin and propagation of electrical potentials through the cardiac tissues.

Thus, it is considered that the resulting signal record called electrocardiogram (ECG or EKG) represents cardiac physiology and is used for diagnostic of cardiopathies (Kilgfield et al., 2007; Berbari, 2000). Then, a thorough analysis of electrocardiogram patterns and cardiac frequency is used for evaluating the nature of hearth disease and detecting cardiac arrhythmias.

Electroencefalogram (EEG) signals reflect vital brain activities from fetus (Preissl, 2004) and newborns (Vanhatalo & Kaila, 2006), to adults (Cummins et al, 2007) in health and illness. In fact the EEG dynamics impact all levels of human life and their relationship with visual, auditory and somatosensory stimuli are of great importance (Klimesh et al., 2007). Brain activity is measured in a non-invasive manner by placing electrodes on the patient's scalp (Luck, 2005; Handy, 2004); the resulting data is known as encephalogram (Schaul, 1998).

Electromyography (EMG) refers to the registration and interpretation of the muscle action potentials. Electrical signals travel back and forth between the muscles and the peripheral and central nervous system control the movement and position of limbs (Hennenberg, 2000). Unlike ECG signals whose morphology and rhythm can be related to normal or abnormal cardiac activity, surface electromyography signals normally show random waveforms, because they represent a sum of action potentials from many independently activated motor units (Masuda et al, 1999). However, since the maximum frequency of EMG signals is within a couple of kilohertz, current analogue front-end instrumentation and microcontroller technologies can register muscle activity so that either time or frequency analysis methods can be used for neuromotor disorder diagnosis, functional electrical stimulation (FES) and rehabilitation.

Electrooculography (EOG) uses surface electrodes located around the eye cavity to measure potentials caused by change of illumination and/or movement of the eye. The retinal pigmented epithelium (RPE) is an electrically polarised pigmented epithelial monolayer that lies posterior to the photoreceptors and is responsible for the corneo-fundal standing potential (Arden & Constable, 2006). Thus EOG applications range from ophthalmologic analysis, diagnosis of pathology of retinal and RPE degenerations to brain-computer interfacing (Firoozabadi et al., 2008)

BIOPOTENTIAL MEASUREMENT	VOLTAGE RANGE	FREQUENCY RANGE (Hz)	VOLTAGE RANGE	FREQUENCY RANGE (Hz)
	Enderle J. 2000		Cohen A. 2000	
ECG, EKG, skin electrodes	0.5-4 mV	0.01-250	1 - 5mV	0.05-100
EEG, Scalp electrodes	5-200μV	DC-150	2-100μV	0.5-100
EMG				
needle electrodes	0.1-5mV	DC-10,000	100μV-10mV	5-10,000
surface electrodes	-	-	50μV-5mV	2 - 500
EOG, skin electrodes	50-3500μV	DC-50	10μV-5mV	DC-100

Table 1. Magnitude and frequency ranges of biopotential measurements as suggested by different authors.

Although different authors suggest different amplitudes and frequency ranges (Table 1) biopotential measurements share some common characteristics. First the potential magnitude is very small (from μVolts to miliVolts). Second, the frequency range of biopotential measurements is within a few hundred hertz to a few of Kilohertz.

3. General data acquisition system for biopotential measurements

Figure 1 shows a schematic diagram of a microcontroller-based, portable, battery operated biopotential measurement system.

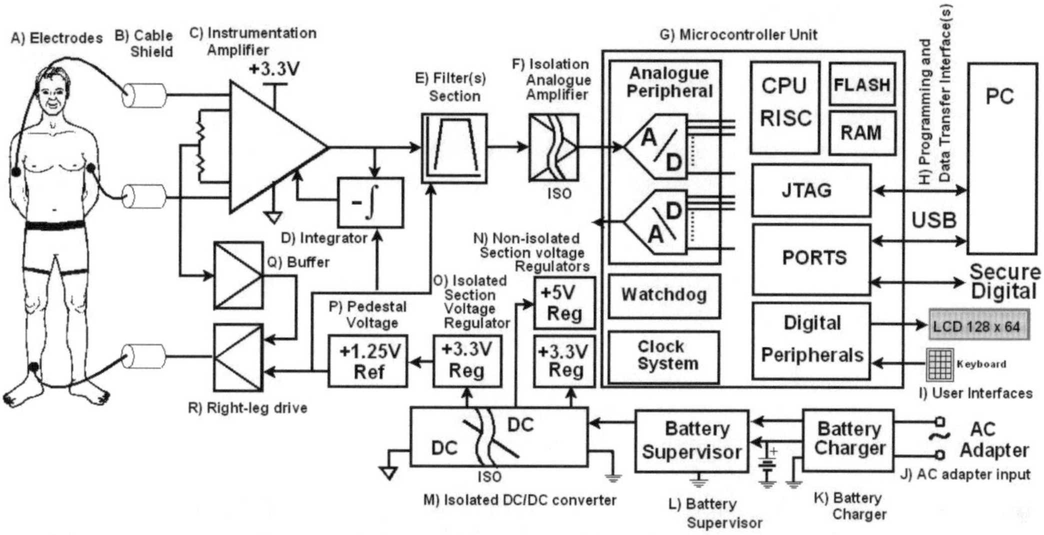

Fig. 1. Schematic diagram of a microcontroller-based portable biopotential data acquisition system (connections for ECG measurements).

3.1 Analog signal conditioning.

The manner in which a transducer interrogates the process, and the quality of information obtained, have a profound effect on the reliability and accuracy of the complete measurement system. Non-invasive measurement of bioelectrical signals is achieved by placing a set of surface electrodes on the skin (Figure 1A). Ionic charge carriers interact with the electrodes which serve as transducers, producing a current through the wires going into the instrumentation amplifier. A variety of electrodes exist for each particular biopotential measurement. For instance, the silver/silver-chloride (Ag/AgCl) electrode is a common choice for ECG measurements. For EEG measurements miniature gold cups of Ag/AgCl cups are commonly used. To reduce electromagnetic interference (EMI) the cable has to be shielded (Figure 1B). To increase the effectiveness against EMI, active shielding can be used, although it requires extra operational amplifiers and a few passive components to drive the shield. The de facto analogue circuit configuration for biopotential measurements uses an instrumentation amplifier as the first signal conditioning stage (Figure 1C). To reduce the effects of EMI, an instrumentation amplifier with CMRR (Common Mode Rejection Ratio) better than 100 dB must be used. The electrochemical cell produced by placing the electrode in contact with the skin results in a half-cell potential. For instance for a Ag/AgCl electrode in conjunction with the electrode gel used in ECG measurement, a 300 mV DC is produced that is also amplified by the instrumentation amplifier. DC offset correction can be accomplished by using an integrator circuit (Figure 1D) to restore the baseline potential. The resulting signal is fed to a bandpass and notch filter to reduce the EMI caused by the mains.
The common-mode is comprised mainly of two parts: 50 or 60Hz interference and DC electrode offset potential. Changes in the electrode surface contact due to patient movement

and other bioelectric signals such as EMG also contribute to measurement interference. Some of the noise is cancelled by the high CMRR of the instrumentation amplifier. Further CMRR noise rejection is achieved by deriving common-mode voltage to invert the common-mode signal and drive it back into the patient through the right leg using amplifier (right leg drive, Figures 1Q and 1R).

3.2 Patient safety considerations

It is worrying that there is a wide availability of biopotential measurement circuits over the internet that do not consider proper isolation. Many proposed circuits and/or project reports show that the user disregarded patient safety completely. In many cases, laboratory reports show the use of common power supplies and oscilloscopes connected directly to the mains. Other documents suggest the use of commercial data acquisition systems; although some consider the use of a portable computer, at some point it may be connected to the mains through the mains adaptor creating a serious risk condition. Connecting any type of device to the body at the same time as to the mains increases the risk of electric shock. If the designer of biopotential signal conditioning systems intends to connect the equipment to the mains and/or to the PC for on-line data transferring it is his/her responsibility to ensure that the leakage currents under the worst possible scenarios are within safety limits. The IEC 60601-1-1:2005 specifies the safety guidelines medical equipment and the manner in which testing should be conducted. In particular section 8.7 of the IEC 60601-1-1:2005 deals with leakage currents and patient auxiliary currents which limit the maximum leakage current to 10μAmps for ground intact tests and 50μAmps for ground fault tests. Similar guidelines are described in the FNPA 99 Standard for Health Care Facilities and the reader is advised to refer to those documents before testing the equipment on patients. There are various ways to isolate the circuitry connected to the patient from the mains. Figure 1 F and 1M show the use of analogue isolation amplifiers and isolating DC/DC converter in the signal and power trajectories respectively. Alternatively, the isolation can be accomplished by using an opto-coupler in the PC interface, although the power line has also to be isolated. The isolation amplifier can also be used for zero and span adjustment so that the measured signal occupies the entire analogue-to-digital (AD) input range.

3.3 Digitizing section

Current microcontrollers are powerful devices that can perform many of the operations necessary for data acquisition, signal processing, storage, display and transfer to a host computer. The analogue signal is fed to the microcontroller through the analogue-to digital converter (Figure 1G). Although a more powerful device such as a DSP (Digital Signal Processor) can perform faster and more complex calculations than a microcontroller, the frequency range of biopotential measurement (from DC to a few kilohertz) allows the execution of basic signal processing algorithms on-line and in real-time. For instance of FIR and IIR filter calculations, signal averaging and beat detection algorithms can be performed in between samples. More complex calculations such as arrhythmia detection using artificial intelligence methods and frequency-domain analysis would require a more powerful device. However, current microcontrollers are capable of interfacing with the user for operating the device (Figure 1I), transferring the data to a host PC for further analysis and allow in-system programming (Figure 1H) so that the equipment can be updated without altering the circuitry.

3.4 Power supply

Although portable measurement equipment can be effectively isolated by avoiding the use of an external AC adaptor and linking wirelessly to the host PC, the proposed scheme uses a battery charger to power up the device when the battery is depleted (Figure 1J and 1K). A battery supervisor selects the power source and feeds the isolating DC/DC converter to provide power to both sections of the circuit (Figure 1M). Two low dropout regulators provide the voltage for the digitizing and signal conditioning sections (Figure 1N and 1O). Since the analogue circuitry is powered by a unipolar voltage signal, the pedestal reference voltage is obtained from a voltage reference circuit with temperature variation coefficient better than 100ppm/°C. Alternatively a rail splitter circuit can be used. Thus bipolar input signals are measured using unipolar circuit polarization voltage. The non-isolated section uses two voltage regulators: a +3.3 V and +5V. The +3.3 regulator powers up the microcontroller whereas the +5V is used for supplying power to other devices such as the SD card.

3.5 Pre-competitive design

The great importance that biopotential measurements have for diagnostic, have led to a continuous scientific and technological effort to produce highly integrated data acquisition systems and powerful signal processing methods for eHealth applications. The current tendency in medical informatics in developed countries is directed towards three key issues (Maglogiannis et al., 2007): the widespread availability of software applications, availability of medical information anytime-anywhere and computation transparency. A typical application is telemedicine that involves measurement of physiological parameters for transmission to a remote location where specialists can provide diagnostic in real-time over a wireless connection. There are numerous commercial equipments available. However, in developing countries, as far as public health is concerned, the current eHealth needs are different, and the differences of technological capabilities of the public sector, compared to the private sector, are huge. Therefore, one of the main goals of university research and development activities must be the direct application of the results in the surroundings to impact health care positively.

Pre-competitive design for biomedical applications in developing countries involves identifying the current needs for instrumentation and deriving the appropriate solution according to those needs. Therefore, it can be considered as a middle-ground between university state-of-the-art research and commercial research performed by large corporations and/or public health institutions. It may is also be required that a third party, interested in advancing the state's own technology to promote the continuous development of technology, contributes funding and expertise to the development process. In the following sections two pre-competitive design case studies are presented: a microcontroller-based EEG data acquisition system for measurement of auditory evoked potentials for diagnosis of hypoacusis and a microcontroller-based ambulatory ECG data acquisition system auxiliary in the detection of cardiac arrhythmias.

4. Case study 1: Microcontroller-based EEG auditory evoked potentials measurement system auxiliary in the diagnosis of hypoacusis.

Although a great deal of research effort has been put into developing working Brain Machine Interfaces (BMI) (Sadja, 2008), still, development of EEG diagnostic equipment occupies an important place in research and development. Improvements and new devices are continually reported and registered for measuring Brain stem evoked potentials (Fadem, 2005; Kopke, 2007; Givens et al., 2005; DeCharms, 2007), as well as signal processing and analysis methods (Lam, 2007). Measurement of Event Evoked Potentials (AEP) due to external stimuli, allows the analysis of brain signal processing activities (Bonfis et al., 1988). Recent developments on signal processing and wireless technologies have also resulted in a number or commercial and experimental EEG devices. One particular application of EEG equipment is the diagnosis of hypoacusia by measuring auditory evoked potentials (AEP).

Hypoacusis (or hypocusya), refers to the level of hearing impairment of patients. One of the main factors that influence the recovery of patients suffering from hypoacusis is the early detection of auditory pathologies (National Institute of Health, 1993). For newborn patients, it is very important to obtain a diagnosis during the first three to six months after birth, so as to increase the chances of successful recovery and favor speech development. More than 90% of children suffering from moderate or acute hypoacusis are likely to go through correct hearing, intellectual and emotional development (Bielecki, 2004) if they are diagnosed during the first year after birth.

One of the reasons for continuous development of AEP measurement equipment is the noninvasive nature of the test: using a set of electrodes on the scalp, it is possible to register signals related to brain activity, in response to auditory stimuli. In addition, the objective nature of the test is suitable for screening newborns that cannot provide feedback information for diagnosis. The importance of AEP tests is recognized in Mexico's Health standard NOM-034-SSA2-2002, recommending its use for screening of hypoacusis risk cases during the first trimester after birth. However early diagnostic screening tests are not conducted regularly due to the lack of specialized equipment in public health hospitals. Thus there is little statistical information regarding hypoacusis information in Mexico. A sole study conducted in 16 states of Mexico reported that more than 20% of the population in rural areas of Michoacan, Mexico, suffer from some level of hypoacusia; 4.71% of the population suffer from moderate to severe hypoacusia (Rodriguez-Díaz et al., 2001). In rural areas in Mexico, where there is little or null access to diagnostic equipment, it is common to find patients suffering hypoacusia that are not diagnosed until much later in life precluding their integration to social and school life. There are a number of methods for diagnosis of hypoacusia; otoacoustic emission (EOAE) and impedance audiometry are amongst the most commonly used methods (White et al., 1993). Alternatively, assessing the hearing ability of patients can be achieved by measuring brain activity due to external acoustic stimuli. Thus, the use of EEG measurement equipment with Evoked Potentials analysis capabilities can be a cost-effective solution for the assessment of brain activity due to external auditory stimuli. In particular for newborn patients who can not provide feedback for diagnosis, the objective and non-invasive nature of the technique can provide useful information for early diagnosis of hypoacusia. This case study presents the design and construction of portable microcontroller EEG measurement equipment with auditory evoked potential analysis capabilities on request from the Michoacán State Public Health Secretariat (Spanish: Secretaría de Salud del Estado de Michoacán), Mexico. The aim is to produce equipment that can be used to asses the hearing capabilities of patients even if the study is carried out under non-controlled conditions (i.e noise proof facilities). Such equipment could then be used in locations where sound proof facilities are not available and a quiet room with ambient noise may suffice. The EEG equipment is initially intended for being used with a host PC for transferring the test results and keep patient records to aid statistical analysis and help establishing public health policies for the recovery of young patients. The software must be intuitive, provide the analysis functions commonly encountered in commercial equipment and permit registration of patient data.

4.1 EEG-ITM04 data acquisition system

Fig. 2 shows the schematic diagram of the EEG-ITM04 auditory evoked potential measurement system.

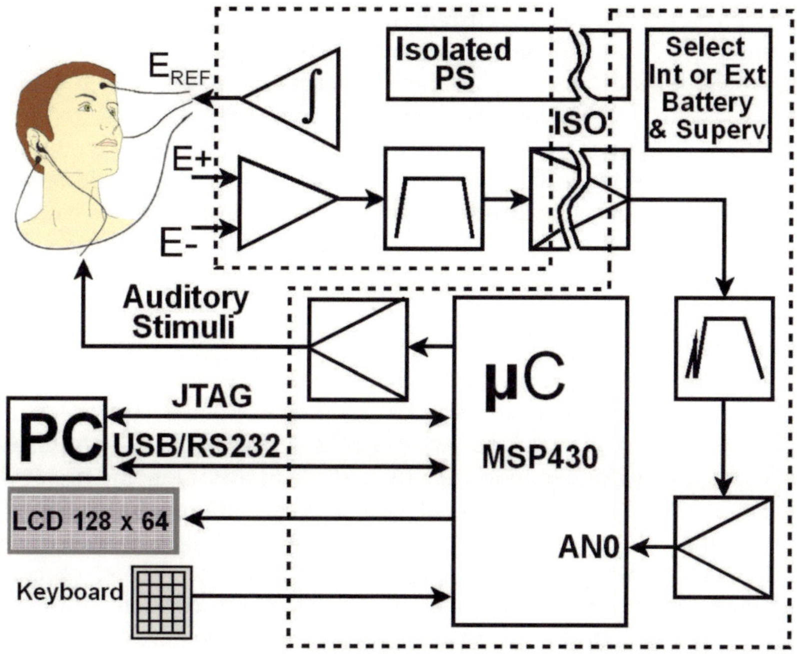

Fig. 2. Block diagram of the EEG-ITM04. A) Three-electrode scheme for measuring AEP, B) bandapass filter, C) analog isolation amplifier, D) notch and bandpass filter, E) signal scaling, F) microcontroller, G) auditory stimulus amplifier, H) user interface devices, I) power source selection and battery supervision, J) Isolated power supply.

One of the analogue to digital converter inputs of the microcontroller is used for digitizing the measured signals at a rate in excess of 40 KSPS (kilo samples per second) (Fig. 2F). The auditory stimulus consists of a 0.2 second duration pulse, (click). The microcontroller also synchronizes the data acquisition process with the auditory stimuli (Fig. 2G). The user operates the equipment through a keyboard, and LCD display. As well as its predecessor, the EEG-ITM04 includes a JTAG port for in-system programming and RS232 for data transfer to the host computer (Fig. 2H). An RS232-USB converter cable is used to interface the device with current personal computer systems.

4.2 Safety requirements

Although the circuitry uses an isolated power supply and isolation amplifiers, electrical safety is of great concern since the main purpose is directed towards evaluating hearing of newborns. Before the equipment is tested on patients, measurements were taken under different single-fault and normal operating conditions. The equipment was considered safe if, at least, minimal IEC60601-1 and NFPA 99 leakage current specifications are met:

A.- Patient to Ground (isolated): ≤10μA (GND intact)
B.- Patient to Ground (isolated): ≤50μA (GND open)
C.- Between Leads (isolated): ≤10μA (GND intact)
D.- Between Leads (isolated): ≤50μA (GND open)
E.- Between Leads (non-isolated): ≤50μA (GND intact or open).

The circuitry enclosure was placed on an isolated surface (rubber over wood) 3 meters away from any earthed surface. Leakage current measurement equipment was located 40 cm away from unscreened power cables. Measurements were carried out on all possible combinations (patient leads and AC adapter connections) using a 6 ½ digit meter. For ground-intact tests, the largest leakage current measured was 1.45 μA, between the reference electrode terminal and the mains ground. For ground-open tests the largest leakage current registered was 10.36 μA between the reference electrode terminal and the mains ground. Both measurements are within the safety specification values (10μA and 50μA respectively) and thus, pending corroboration from a certified laboratory, the equipment was considered safe.

4.3 Acoustic stimulus

One of the most commonly used methods for generating the auditory stimuli for auditory evoked potential tests consists of producing a sequence of pulses to drive a set of earphones, and record the resulting brain electrical activity over a period of a few milliseconds. Since the magnitude of the evoked response has a magnitude of just a few microvolts, the process is repeated 1000 to 2000 times and the results are averaged to improve the Signal-To-Noise Ratio. Assuming that the resulting data is a function, only, of the auditory stimuli, the averaged signal represents the hearing process. The data acquisition process has to be synchronized with the application of auditory stimuli, which consists of a 0.2 miliseconds pulse, which in turn drives the earphones. The pulse is generated 6.66 times per second. The output signal was calibrated using a TES1350 decibel meter, and a graduated scale is provided behind the amplitude control potentiometer in the frontal panel of the equipment.

4.4 Measurement of auditory evoked potentials

Auditory evoked potentials are characterized by three main parameters: polarity, latency (i. e. the moment of peak occurrence after stimulus presentation) and scalp distribution. Figure 3 shows a typical reference wave pattern for diagnosis of AEP.

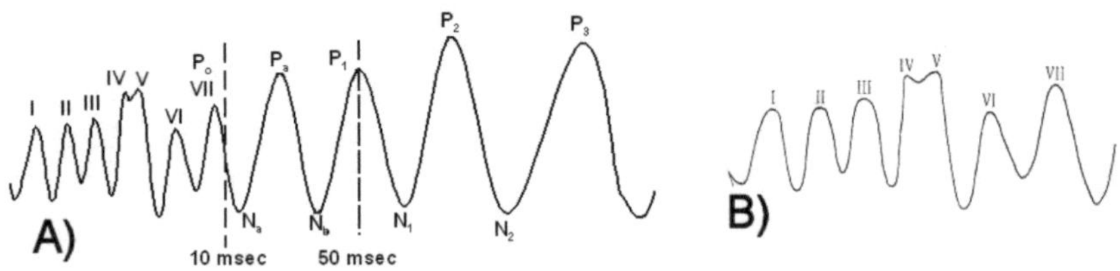

Wave	Ref. Values (ms)	
I	1.35	1.95
II	2.54	3.14
III	3.58	4.18
IV	5.00	5.60
V	5.32	6.12
VI	7.05	7.65
VII	8.70	9.40

Fig. 3. A) Typical AEP showing the three components and B) diagnostic reference values extracted from a test report sheet (Courtesy of Clinica de Especialidades de Morelia).

There are three types of components: early latencies or components (up to 10 miliseconds after the stimulus has been applied), middle components (from 10 miliseconds to 50 miliseconds) and late components (after 50 miliseconds). Although measurement of auditory evoked potentials does not constitute a hearing test per se, it can provide information about the hearing process. In addition, evoked potentials are not influenced by the state of consciousness (i. e. patient can be asleep) and result in objective data that do not require feedback from the patient. The occurrence of waves I - VII (Figure 3B) can be indicative of hearing whereas absence of some (or all) of them may indicate a hearing impairment. To produce the AEP graph it is necessary to apply the stimulus for 1000 to 2000 epochs (i.e. application of the stimulus and subsequently measure the resulting EEG signals) (1):

$$S_k = \mu + n_k \tag{1}$$

where S_k represents the kth epoch, μ is the deterministic evoked response and n_k represents zero-mean white noise uncorrelated to μ (Ropelman & Ros, 1986). For AEP measurements, is common to find that the early latencies (up to 10 ms) are used for diagnostic. However the magnitude of the measured signals is very small, and considering that the data acquisition process is synchronized with the stimulus, a signal analysis method consists of averaging the results of each epoch to improve the Signal-To-Noise ratio (SNR). Averaging over N data sets, Y_N, can then be written as (2):

$$Y_N = \frac{1}{N}\sum_{k-1}^{N} S_k = \mu + \frac{1}{N}\sum_{k-1}^{N} n_k \tag{2}$$

The advantage of this method is that it can easily be implemented on-line. The microcontroller chosen for this application is the MSP430F149IPAG from Texas Instruments. The MSP430 includes 2KB of RAM and 60 KB of flash memory. Each epoch begins by acquiring 2 miliseconds worth of data prior to producing the auditory stimulus; 15 miliseconds worth of data (after the stimulus is applied) are acquired by the microcontroller at a rate in excess of 40 KSPS, with 12 bit resolution. The data acquisition process results in a set of 800 12-bit values which are stored in RAM. During the following epoch, the microcontroller converts each sample and averages it with respect to the corresponding sample previously stored in RAM, replacing the old value. The process continues during the entire procedure until the test has concluded. The result is then stored in flash memory, occupying four 512 kb memory segments. It is common to find that additional digital filtering is required for enhancing the quality of the results. Once the test has finished and the resulting data is stored in flash memory, a digital filter, G(z), given by (3) can be implemented off-line.

$$G(z) = \frac{a_0 + a_1 z^{-1} + a_2 z^{-2} + \dots}{1 + b_1 z^{-1} + b_2 z^{-2} + \dots} \tag{3}$$

The state variable description of the filter (4):

$$\begin{aligned} \begin{bmatrix} x_1(k+1) \\ x_2(k+2) \end{bmatrix} &= \begin{bmatrix} 0 & 1 \\ -b_1 & -b_2 \end{bmatrix} \begin{bmatrix} x_1(k) \\ x_2(k) \end{bmatrix} + \begin{bmatrix} 0 \\ 1 \end{bmatrix} e(k) \\ u(k) &= \begin{bmatrix} a_1 & a_0 \end{bmatrix} \begin{bmatrix} x_1(x) \\ x_2(k) \end{bmatrix} \end{aligned} \tag{4}$$

can be implemented easily in canonical form as a subroutine of the microcontroller program (Figure 4). (Gutiérrez-Gnecchi, 2009).

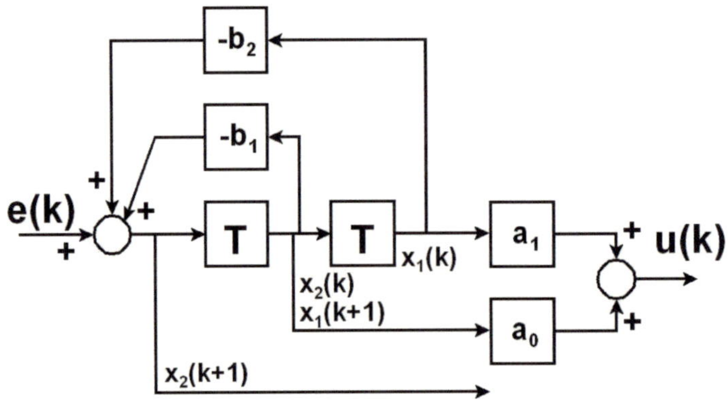

Fig. 4. Digital filter implementation

4.5 Software

A program, written in C++, was developed for transferring the test results to a host PC The program permits to register patient and test information (patient data, type of test, etc.). The program also shows on-line EEG data. Once the test has been completed, the program receives the data from the microcontroller. The EEG data can then be stored, plotted and subjected to further filtering and analysis. The program consists of three main windows. The first window registers the test and patient data (Figure 5A). The second window (Figure 5B) can be accessed by selecting the "CALIBRATE" button. Selecting the "GO ON-LINE" button displays on-line EEG data for the purpose of offset and gain adjustment of the measured signal. Activating the "GO TO TEST" initiates the test. The third window shows the test results (Figure 5C).

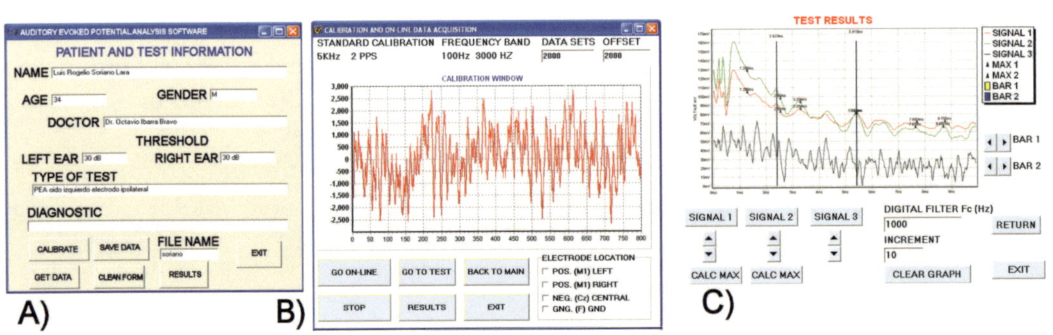

Fig. 5. A) Screen of the window first program used for registering patient information, B) calibration window and C) test results window. Results are shown for a healthy 34-years old male patient. The latencies are detected in agreement with expected values for healthy patients. C)

The test results window can display the results for both ears. In addition, to help the identification of the latencies (i.e. when the evoked potentials occur), there are buttons for calculating the local maximum values for both signals. A third unprocessed signal can be displayed for comparison. Additionally to the averaging function, a low-pass filter can be applied to the resulting evoked potential results. Horizontal displacement bars allow the exact identification of the time when the latencies occur.

4.6 Validation of the EEG-ITM04

Figure 6A shows the assembled EEG-ITM04.

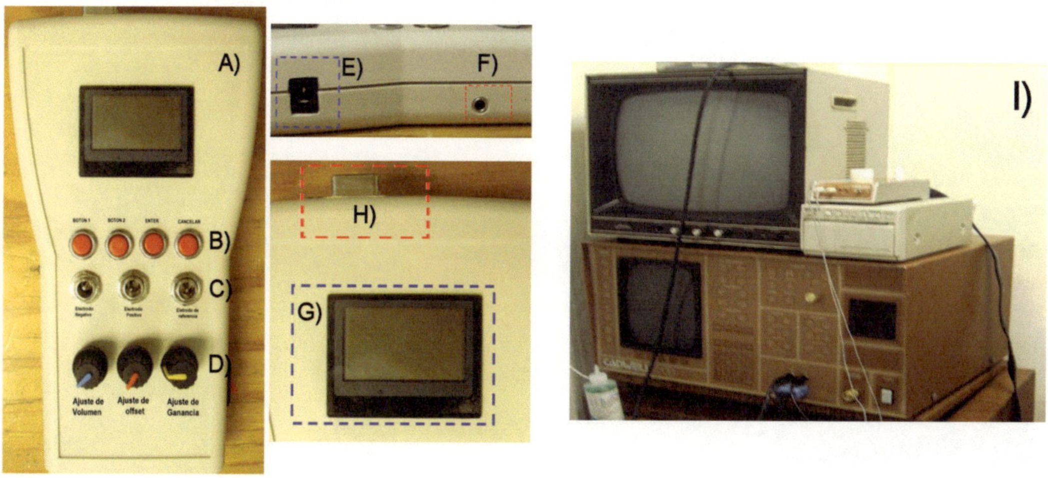

Fig. 6. The assembled EEG-IMT04 is a A) handheld device which includes B) menu navigation buttons, C) electrode connections, D) EEG signal adjustment knobs, E) AC adaptor connector, F) earphone plug connector, G) a 128 X 64 LCD and H) computer interface connector. I) Cadwell 7200 electroneurodiagnostic equipment.

In order to validate the performance the EEG-ITM04, a series of experiments were conducted at the Clinica De Especialidades de Morelia. Commercial equipment (CADWELL 7200, Figure 6I) was used for obtaining reference information. The EEG signals are measured using a three-electrode scheme. The positive and negative electrodes are connected over the ipsilateral (Figure 7A) and contralateral (Figure 7B) to the mastoid processes respectively. The reference electrode is located in the middle of the forehead (Figure 7C). The tests were conducted on 10 unmedicated young adults (average age of 25 years old. The test procedure was conducted in a quiet room, with the patients lying down, eyes closed, to avoid registering data from other types of sensory stimulation. Figure 8 shows the experimental set-up and the results of using the Cadwell 7200 and EEG-ITM04 on Patient 1.

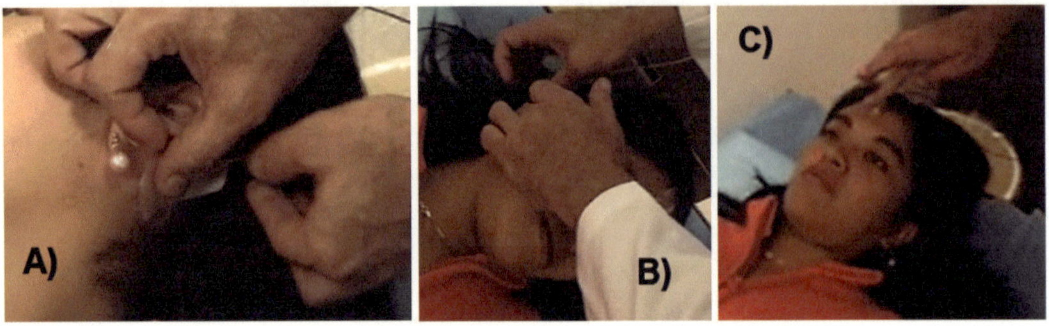

Fig. 7. Location of the electrodes for AEP measurements (testing the left ear). The positive and negative electrodes are connected A) ipsilateral and B) contralateral to the mastoid process. C) The reference electrode is located in the middle of the forehead.

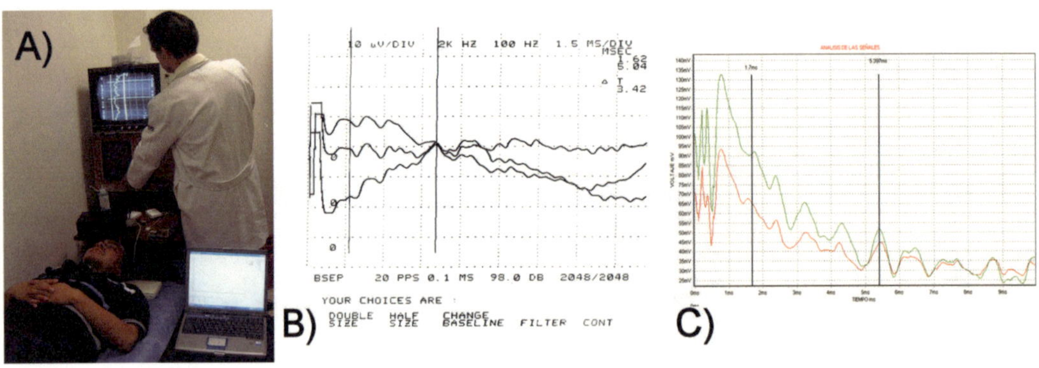

Fig. 8. A) Experimental set-up. Test results obtained for patient 1 using B) the Cadwell 7200 and C) EEG-ITM04.

In order to validate the performance of the EEG-ITM04, a series of tests using a 95 dB acoustic stimulus, at a rate of 6 pulses per second for 2048 epochs, were carried out using the Cadwell 7200 Electro-neurodiagnostic instrument (Figure 6I) for obtaining reference information (Figure 7B). Similar tests were conducted using the EEG-ITM04, using a 95 dB acoustic stimulus, at a rate of 6.66 pulses per second for 2048 epochs (Figure 7C).

4.7 Results and discussion

Table 2 shows a summary of the results for the 10 patients tested. The results show agreement between the CADWELL 7200 and EEG-ITM04 equipments, thus suggesting that the EEG-ITM04 can be used for diagnostic of some forms of hypoacusia, in non-ideal environments. Undoubtedly, there will be differences in the results between the CADWELL and EGG-ITM04. Different specifications for both devices and testing under slightly different conditions result in the differences shown. However, the results indicate that it is possible to detect the auditory evoked potentials even if the test is conducted on a non-ideal environment.

	CADWELL 7200 Latencies (miliseconds)					EEG-ITM04 Latencies (milisegundos)				
	I	II	III	IV	V	I	II	III	IV	V
Patient	1.62				5.04	1.720				5.390
1			3.64		5.56			3.528		5.631
2			3.68		5.44			3.571		5.652
3	1.44	2.88				1.445	3.121			
4		2.72			5.36		2.763			5.785
5			3.52		5.39			3.560		5.515
6	1.59				5.19	1.635				5.253
7		2.75			5.37		2.810			5.471
8	1.56	2.77				1.550	2.781			
9			3.69		5.58			3.692		5.921
10	1.49				5.16	1.510				5.180

Table 2. Summary of test results obtained from 10 patients using the Cadwell 7200 and EEG-ITM04 equipments

5. Case study 2: microcontroller-based ambulatory ECG data acquisition system auxiliary in the detection of cardiac arrhythmias.

Cardiovascular disease is of on the main causes of morbidity and mortality in Mexico (Velazquez-Monroy et al., 2007) and worldwide (Abegunde et al., 2007). The epidemic importance of chronic non-communicable diseases (CNCD) spread is currently overtaking infectious and parasitic diseases. In particular in emerging economy countries the rate of CNCD spread is greater than that in developed countries. In México ischemic hearth disease is the main cause of death and 15% to 30% of patients that have suffered an acute cardiac adverse event will die within the next 30 days (INEGI, 2002). In addition, current life habits such as sedentary life style, sodium, alcohol and tobacco consumption and poor diet habits increase the chances of suffering hearth disease early in life (Myers, 2003). Therefore, early arrhythmia detection by means of an electrocardiogram is a key factor in preventive treatment. A standard ECG uses 12 derivations or measurements of electric potential in different areas of the patient's body. A normal ECG consists of a repeated sequence of P, Q, R, S and T waves (Figure 9). The characteristics of a normal ECG sequence have been studied for over a century, and a set of normal conditions, usually described as a regular sinus rhythm (Ivanov, 2007), have been established for diagnostic purposes. When the rhythm, frequency or morphology of the ECG signal corresponding to the heartbeat sequence, are not consistent with those of the normal ECG, the condition is called arrhythmia. In general is considered that over 90% of arrhythmias can be detected by using a 3-derivation ECG (Figure 1B).

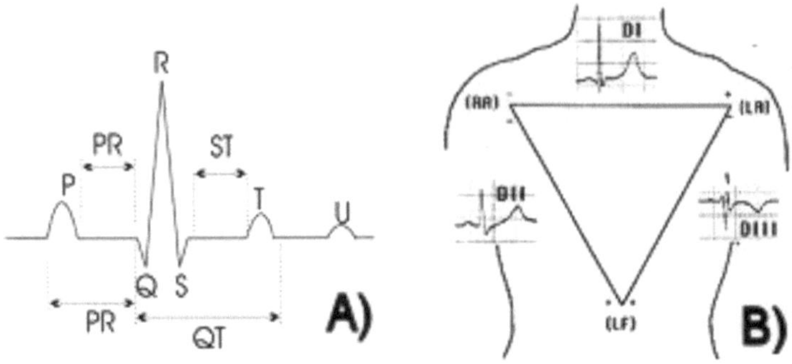

Fig. 9. A) Electric cardiac cycle and B) Three bipolar derivations (Einthoven Triangle)

There are two basic types of ECG monitors: continuous and intermittent recorders. Continuous ambulatory and recorders, also known as ambulatory electrocardiogram, ambulatory EKG, Holter monitoring, 24, 48, 72-hour EKG, or cardiac event monitoring continuously register on internal or external memory the cardiac activity. Intermittent recorders, either loop or event recorders, store data on request, generally by pressing a button. Since many cardiac events occur randomly and for a short period of time, it is desirable to store the ECG data continuously during the study.

The great importance that electrocardiography measurements have for diagnostic, have led to a continuous scientific and technological effort to produce signal processing methods for arrhythmia classification and ECG equipment. There are numerous commercial equipments and specialized software for arrhythmia detection. Although the advances in electronics have permitted that desktop or wearable ECG measurement systems are available for $1000 and $4000 UsDlls respectively, the added taxes and import costs result prohibitive for wide distribution in public health clinics in Mexico. Budget restrictions and the vast amount of patients and their medications impede the purchase of monitoring equipment and cardiac patients are referred to private clinics for biopotential measurements. Therefore it is necessary to dedicate research and development efforts in accordance with the current regional needs. The work presented in this case study is the result of a cooperation agreement between Morelia Institute of Technology and the Michoacán State Public Health Secretariat, financially supported by the Public Education Secretariat (SEP-DGEST) to develop royalty-free biomedical instrumentation equipment that facilitates routine diagnostic activities. The equipment ECG-ITM04 must have a number of specific characteristics. First the equipment must be able to allow ECG monitoring during routine diagnostic and during ambulatory activities for a period of 7 days. The instrument has to show on-line the ECG signals. The ECG-ITM04 has to be able to transfer the information on-line to a host computer during routine diagnostic. In case that the battery fades, a portable power supply has to be used to power up the device and charge the battery, while ensuring the safety of the patient. Finally it must be possible to upgrade the software to include further signal processing algorithms for arrhythmia detection and classification.

5.2 Hardware design

The schematic diagram of the ECG-IMT04 is actually shown in Figure 1. The equipment consists of 4 main sections: isolated power supply, analog signal conditioning and filtering, digitizing and signal processing, and data display and storage.

5.3 Isolated power supply

Since the ECG-ITM04 is intended for ambulatory measurements as well as for on-line transfer of ECG data to a host PC, it is essential to ensure patient safety from exposure to leakage currents. There are 3 main conditions of risk when operating the ECG: when the equipment is connected to the AC adapter, when the equipment is connected to the host PC or both. The power supply circuitry (Figure 1J - 1M) consists of an external input for a 9 Volt AC adapter, an RF input filter, a Nickel-Metal Hydride battery charger and supervisor, a 3-kV isolated DC-DC converter and two low dropout regulators (3.3V and 5V). Thus, the section dedicated for analog signal conditioning and filtering is effectively isolated from the digitizing section.

5.4 Analog signal conditioning

Measurement of cardiac signals is carried out by using a 3-wire scheme using a 110 dB CMMR instrumentation amplifier, right-leg drive signal, high- and low pass filters to provide a 200 Hz measurement bandwidth (0.02- 200 Hz), and gain adjustment (Figure 2E).

5.5 Digitizing and signal processing

The ECG_ITM04 is based on the MSP430F149 IPAG microcontroller from Texas Instruments©. The MSP430 is a 16-bit RISC, ultralow-power device with five power-saving modes, two built-in 16-bit timers, a fast 12-bit A/D converter, two universal serial synchronous/asynchronous communication interfaces (USART), 48 Input/Output pins, 60 kB of flash memory and 2 kB of RAM, which permits the implementation of all the functions required to build an ECG data acquisition system. Initially, it was considered that basic signal processing algorithms (digital filter and beat detection) are the main functions to be included. However, a JTAG interface implemented on the prototype allows in-system programming so that the equipment can be updated, and further signal processing algorithms can be included in the future, without changing the hardware.

5.6 ECG data display and storage

The ECG-IMT04 includes a 128 X 64 pixel resolution graphics displays the operation options (measure, store, transfer) and the ECG being recorded and/or monitored. The measured data can either be stored on a SD (secure digital) memory card or transferred to a host PC. The SD memory card and the graphics screen share the synchronization signal (UCLK) and the data output signal (SIMO). The second SPI communications port is used to transfer the data to a host computer a rate of 19200 baud through an RS-232 port if available. In order to maintain compatibility with current computer configurations and to save space in the PCB, the USB interface is fitted in the cable connector using a TUSB3410 RS232/IrDA Serial-to-USB Converter.

5.7 Patient safety considerations

Before the ECG-ITM04 was tested on volunteers, it was necessary to measure the leakage current for different risk conditions. The equipment was considered safe if, at least, minimal NFPA 99 leakage current specifications are met as described in section 4.2. The ECG data acquisition system was connected to the AC adaptor and placed on a wooden table, 4 feet from the floor and at least 15 feet away from any other source of interference. For ground-intact tests, the largest leakage current measured was 2.1 μA, between the reference electrode terminal and the mains ground. For ground-open tests the largest leakage current registered was 5.61μA between the reference electrode terminal and the mains ground. Both measurements are within the safety specification values (10μA and 50μA respectively) and thus, pending corroboration from a certified laboratory, the equipment was considered safe.

5.8 Experimental set-up

Figure 10A shows the assembled ECG-ITM04. The ECG sample rate is adjusted to take 500 sps (samples per second) and thus a 1 GB SD card can hold over 7 days of uncompressed continuous recordings. The device was connected 5 volunteers to wear for a period of 24-hours. Although the analog hardware includes two filter sections, including a 60 Hz notch filter, it is necessary to include a filtering operation in the microcontroller program.

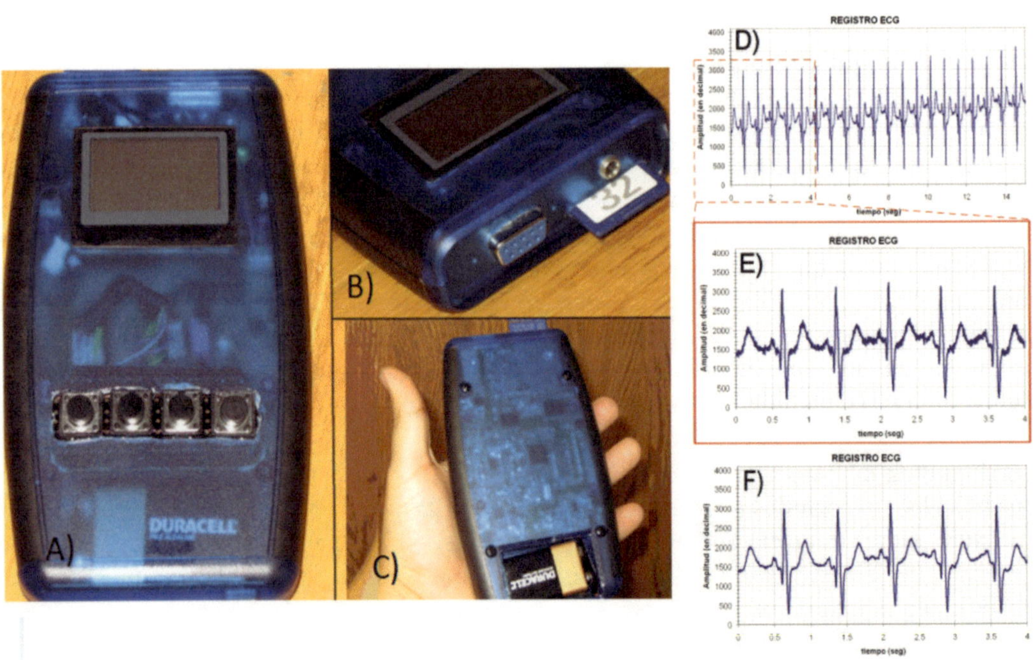

Fig. 10. A) Assembled ECG-ITM04, B) Serial port and SD card connections, C) Battery location. D) Typical EEG data exported into an Excel© spreadsheet. E) Close-up of a 4.5 seconds record and F) filtered signal (180Hz cut off frequency).

5.9 Results and discussion

Apart from the value that the ECG-ITM04 can have for diagnostic, it provides a unique opportunity to gather ECG information of the regional population for the purposes of statistical analysis and establishing public health policies. The value of an extensive database such as the MIT Arrhythmia Database has been widely recognized (Moody & Mark, 2001) and helped in the development of automatic arrhythmia recognition software. Therefore the authors consider that distribution of the ECG-ITM04 amongst the regional public health clinics can be an important step towards developing an ECG database.

6. Conclusions and future work

The design of portable data acquisition systems is a multidisciplinary task that involves many areas of knowledge. It is important that the finished equipment includes all the necessary features to ensure easy operation. When it comes to biomedical equipment it is essential to ensure patient safety.

The proposed general data acquisition scheme can be used with minimal modifications to perform different biopotential measurements. For instance the EEG-ITM04 does not include the SD memory interface because the results are stored in the microcontroller main memory, reducing the power consumption and processor computational time to perform signal processing operations. In contrast, at present, The ECG-IMT04 requires a mass storage device to record the cardiac signals over a large period of time. Moreover, differences are filter cut frequency and sample rate. Fixed analogue filter cut-frequencies are implemented instead of gain-programmable filters to save power and printed circuit board space. The designs presented in this work perform according to the specifications stated by the end user. However, the availability of analogue front ends such as the ADS1298 from Texas Instruments and the ADuC842 from analog Devices, and powerful low-power consumption processing devices imply that that the design has to be updated continuously. Current work is dedicated to reduce power consumption and size of the measurement equipment, increase the number of analogue channels processing power as well as including wireless data transfer to ensure patient safety and, overall, produce more versatile instrumentation.

7. Acknowledgements

The authors acknowledge the financial support from CONACYT under grant FOMIX-116062 that allowed the research to produce the EEG-ITM04. The authors also acknowledge the financial support from Dirección General de Educación SEP-DGEST) under grant 2317.09P that allowed the construction of the ECG-IMT04.

8. References

Abegunde D. O.; MathersC. D.; Adam T.; Ortegon M. & Strong K. (2007). The burden and costs of chronic diseases in low-income and middle-income countries, The Lancet, Volume 370, Issue 9603, 8 December 2007-14 December 2007, pp. 1929-1938

Arden G. B. & Constable P. A. (2006). The electro-oculogram, Progress in Retinal and Eye Research, Vol. 25, pp. 207–248

Berbari E. J. (2000). Principles of Electrocardiography, In: The biomedical Engineering Handbook, Volume I, 2nd Edition, J. D. Bronzino (Ed.), pp. 231-240, Boca Raton: CRC Press LLC.

Bielecki I.; Świetliński J;. Zygan L. & Horbulewicz A. (2004). Hearing assessment in infants from the hypoacusia risk group, Med Sci Monit, No. 10 (Suppl 2), pp. 115-117.

Bonfis P.; Uziel A. & Pujol R. (1988). Screening for auditory dysfunction n infants by evoked otoacustic emission. Arch. Otolaryngol. Head Neck Surg, Vol. 114, pp. 887-90.

Cohen A. (2000). Biomedical Signals: Origin and Dynamic Characteristics; Frequency-Domain Analysis, In: The biomedical Engineering Handbook", Volume I, 2nd Edition, J. D. Bronzino (Ed.), pp. 951-974, Boca Raton: CRC Press LLC.

Cummins T. D.; Finnigan S. & Ros J. (2007).Theta power is reduced in healthy cognitive aging, Int. J. Psychophysiol. Vol. 66, pp. 10–17

DeCharms R. C. (2007). Methods for Measurement and Analysis of Brain Activity. US Patent Applicacion. US 2007/0191704 A1.

Enderle J. (2000). Introduction to Biomedical Engineering. J Enderle (ED). pp. 549-626. San Diego, Calif.:Academic Press, 2000.

Fadem K. C. (2005). Evoked response testing system for neurological disorders. US Patent Application. US 11/570630.

Firoozabadi S. M. P.; Oskoei M. A. & Hu H. (2008). A Human- Computer Interface based on Forehead Multi-channel Bio-signals to control a virtual wheelchair, In: Proceedings of the 14th Iranian Conference on Biomedical Engineering (ICBME), Shahed University, Iran, pp. 272–277, Feb. 2008

Givens G.; Balch D. C.; Murphy T.; Blanarovich A. & Keller P. (2005). Systems, Methods and products For diagnostic Hearing Assesments Distributed Via the use of a Computer Network. US 6916291 B2.

Gutierrez Gnecchi J. A.; Doñan Ramirez R. & Esquivel Gordillo C. F. (2009). Design and Construction of a Portable EEG for Auditory Evoked Potential Measurements, In: Electronics, Robotics and Automotive Mechanics Conference (cerma 2009), pp.457-461

Handy T. C. (2004). Event-Related Potentials: A Methods Handbook, The MIT Press, Cambridge MA.

Henneberg K. A. (2000). Principles of Electromyography, In: The biomedical Engineering Handbook, Volume I, 2nd Edition, J. D. Bronzino (Ed.), pp. 242-251. Boca Raton: CRC Press LLC .

Instituto Nacional de Estadística, Geografía e Informática (INEGI). (2002). Estadísticas del Sector Salud y Seguridad Social. No.. 19, 2002. México, D.F., 2003. pp. 50-51.

Ivanov P. Ch. (2007). Scale-Invariant Aspects of Cardiac Dynamics Across Sleep Stages and Circadian Phases, IEEE Engineering in Medicine and Biology Magazine, Nov.-Dec.2007, Vol. 26, Issue 6 , pp. 33 - 37

Kligfield P.; Gettes L. S.; Bailey J. J.; Childers R.; Deal B. J. Hancock E. W.; van Herpen G.; Kors J. A. Macfarlane P.; Mirvis D. M. Pahlm O.; Rautaharju P.; & Wagner G. S. (2007). Recommendations for the Standardization and Interpretation of the Electrocardiogram: Part I: The Electrocardiogram and Its Technology A Scientific Statement From the American Heart Association Electrocardiography and

Arrhythmias Committee, Council on Clinical Cardiology; the American College of Cardiology Foundation; and the Heart Rhythm Society Endorsed by the International Society for Computerized Electrocardiology. Journal of the American College of Cardiology, Vol. 49, Issue 10, pp. 1109-1127.

Klimesch W.; Sauseng P.; Hanslmayr S.; Gruber W. & Freunberger R. (2007). Event-related phase reorganization may explain evoked neural dynamics, Neurosci. Biobehav. Rev. Vol. 31, No. 7, pp. 1003–1016.

Köpke W. (2007). Device for Determining Acoustically Evoked Brainstem Potentials. US Patent. US 7197350 B2.

Lam B. S. C; Hu Y.; Lu W. W.; Luk K.; Chang C.; Qui W. & Chan F. (2007). Multi-adaptive filtering technique for surface somatosensory evoked potentials processing, Med. Eng. Phys. Vol. 27, pp. 257-266, 2007.

Luck S. J. (2005). An Introduction to the event-related potential technique, pp. 27-33. The MIT Press, Cambridge MA. ISBN-10: 0-262-62196-7, ISBN-13: 978-0-262-62196-0

Maglogiannis I; Wallace M. & Karpouzis K. (2007). Image, signal and distributed data processing for networks of eHealth applications, IEEE Engineering in Medicine and Biology Magazine, Sept. Oct. 2007, Vol. 26, No. 5, pp. 14-17

Masuda K.; Masuda T.; Sadoyama T.; Inaki M. & Katsuta S. (1999). Changes in surface EMG parameters during static and dynamic fatiguing contractions, Journal of Electromyography and Kinesiology, Vol. 9, pp. 39–46.

Moody G. B. & Mark R. G. The Impact of the MIT-BIH Arrhythmia Database, IEEE Engineering in Medicine and Biology Magazine, May June 2001, Vol. 20, Issue 3, pp. 45-50.

Myers J. (2003). Exercise and Cardiovascular Health, Circulation 2003, Vol. 107, pp. e2-e5.

National Institute of Health: Early identification of Hearing impairment in infants and young children. (1993). NIH Consensus Statement, No. 11, pp. 1-24.

Preissl H.; LoweryC. L. & Eswaran H. (2004). Fetal magnetoencephalography: current progress and trends, Exp. Neurol. Vol. 190, pp. 28–36

Rodríguez-Díaz J. A.; Chavarria-Contreras C. L. & Montes de Oca Fernández E. (2001). Frecuencia De Defectos Auditivos En 16 Estados De México, Revista de la SMORL. Vol 46, No. 3, pp. 115-117

Rompelman O. & Ros H. H. (1986). Coherent averaging technique: A tutorial review. Part 1: Noise reduction and the equivalent filter. Part 2: Trigger Jitter, overlapping responses and nonperiodic stimulation, J. Biomed. Eng., Vol. 8, pp 24-35.

Sajda P.; Müller K. R. & and Shenoy K. V. (2008). From the Guest Editors. IEEE Signal Processing Magazine - Special Section - Brain Computer Interfaces. Vol 25, No. 1, Jan 2008, pp. 16-18.

Schaul N. (1998). The fundamental neural mechanisms of electroencephalography, Electroencephalography and clinical neurophysiology Vol. 106, pp. 101-107.

Vanhatalo S. & Kaila K.(2006). Development of neonatal EEG activity from phenomenology to physiology. Semin. Fetal Neonatal. Med. Vol. 11, pp. 471–478.

Velázquez Monroy O.; Barinagarrementería Aldatz F.; Rubio Guerra A. F.; Verdejo J.; Méndez Bello M. A.; Violante R.; Pavía A.; Alvarado-Ruiz R. & Lara Esqueda A. (2007). Morbilidad y mortalidad de la enfermedad isquémica corazón y cerebrovascular en México, Archivos de Cardiologiía de México. Vol. 77, No. 1, Enero-Marzo 2007. pp. 31-39.

White K. R.; Vohr B. R. & Behrens T. R. (1993). Universal newborn hearing screening using transient evoked otoacustic emission: Results from the Rhode Island hearing assessment project, Sem Hear, Vol. 14, pp. 18-29.

14

Data Acquisition for Interstitial Photodynamic Therapy

Emma Henderson, Benjamin Lai and Lothar Lilge
Department of Medical Biophysics (University of Toronto)
Canada

1. Introduction

Delivery of any medical therapy needs to aim at maximizing its dose and hence impact towards the target cells, tissues, or organs while minimizing normal tissue damage to reduce morbidity and mortality to the furthest extent possible. For most procedures, monitoring of physical, chemical or biological parameters known to correlate with the therapeutic dose, and hence treatment outcome, throughout the target and adjacent tissue is thus a central aim to improve predictions of an individual's clinical outcome. The medical intervention and physical, chemical, or biological parameters correlating or predicting dose will determine the desired spatial and temporal sampling frequencies required to make accurate inferences to treatment outcome. To illustrate this concept and the limitations imposed by data acquisition as it pertains to treatment monitoring of interstitial photodynamic therapy (IPDT), or the use of light activated drugs in oncology of solid tumors, is presented in this chapter.

2. Photodynamic Therapy

Photodynamic Therapy (PDT) is the use of a drug, called a photosensitizer (PS), activated by light to achieve spatially confined or tissue-specific cell death and tissue necrosis. In general, the PS in its administered form is non-toxic and is either applied topically or administered systemically by oral route or intravenous injection. A delay period is observed in order to achieve the desired biodistribution in the target versus adjacent normal tissue, and the target is exposed to light of a wavelength absorbed by the photosensitizer (Hamblin & Mroz (2008); Davidson et al. (2010); Dolmans & Dai Fukumura (2003); Plaetzer et al. (2009)). The absorption of light photons by the photosensitizer triggers a series of photochemical reactions which, in the presence of molecular ground state oxygen in the triplet state ($^3O_2$), result in the generation of reactive oxygen species (ROS), predominantly singlet oxygen ($^1O_2$), which in turn locally damage cellular components, or the vasculature, and cause the target cells and tissue to die by necrosis or apoptosis. Thus, the conversion of the photon quantum energy by the non-toxic PS into the toxic ROS requires spatial-temporal overlap of three physico-chemical parameters: namely light photons, photosensitizer and molecular oxygen. While photon/photosensitizer overlap is intrinsic to the light fluence rate [$mW \cdot cm^{-2}$] and its absorption coefficient [cm^{-1}], given by the photosensitizer's local concentration and molar extinction coefficient, the requirements on PS\$^3O_2$ spatial-temporal overlap are given by the photosensitizer's triplet state lifetime and the diffusion coefficient of oxygen in soft tissues and cells.

PDT finds a role in several stages in patient management in oncology. It is used prophylactically: in the treatment of Barrett's Esophagus, a metaplasia by stomach columnar epithelium in the squamous epithelium of the esophagus that significantly increases the probability to develop adenocarcinoma; actinic keratosis, which is associated with the development of skin cancer; or various forms of early cancer, such as of the skin, esophagus, bladder, and the oral cavity. These are excellent indications for PDT, and treatment planning or dose prescription is typically based on empirical models for administered drug concentrations [mg · kg^{-1}] and surface light exposure [J · cm^{-2}] of a given power density, or irradiance [mW · cm^{-2}]. Based on considerable empirical experience this is sufficient, as none of the three known physicochemical parameters governing treatment outcome - light, photosensitizer, and $^3O_2$- exhibit significant gradients across the thickness of the lesion (typically less than 3 mm). In malignant brain tumors, it is used as an adjuvant to surgery (Popovic et al. (1996)), where the resection cavity surface is the target, reducing the problem of PDT delivery to a 2D problem. Its use as a primary treatment in large tissue volume has been investigated in the prostate (Davidson et al. (2010)). Finally, PDT is used palliatively in cases of obstructive bronchial and esophageal cancers. These successes of PDT in oncology are driving research toward broadening its application to deep-seated, solid targets (such as the prostate, as mentioned above). Such targets, however, are not accessible for surface illumination and thus require an interstitial approach for light delivery. In an effort to develop PDT as a primary treatment modality also for large volumes of solid tumour, clinical trials targeting the prostate are underway, albeit often the target is the vasculature of the prostate. PDT is in principal also an attractive treatment option for head and neck tumors, where surgery or radiotherapy may be disfiguring, as surgical extraction of the tumor requires up to 2 cm of additional tissue margins to be removed, often including bone, teeth, skin and other structures.

While for surface targets it is safe to assume ubiquitous availability of oxygen as well as homogeneous photosensitizer distribution, the same can not be assumed in solid tumors. It is widely accepted that tumors of only 1-2mm^3 can survive in an avascular environment and angiogenesis is initiated if the tumor is to continue to grow (Folkman (1974)). The angiogenesis-derived neovasculature, however, is quite disorganized, exhibiting excessive branching and long tortuous vessels that are randomly fused with either arterioles or venules, resulting in an atypical microcirculation and often a hypoxic and acidic environment. This is significant for PDT, as the efficient delivery of PS and $^3O_2$ to the target is required for a therapeutic effect and these species are no longer homogeneously available across the tumor. Indeed, treatment failure is often attributed to insufficient oxygen or a heterogeneous drug distribution (Davidson et al. (2009)). In light of these heterogeneities in the distribution of PDT efficacy determining parameters within a tumor, the same concepts of empirically derived dose metrics cannot be maintained and the spatial-temporal distribution of these parameters becomes paramount to ensure that all volume elements of the tumor target have received a sufficient dose of light, photosensitizer and oxygen to produce sufficient ($^1O_2$) causing cell death. Thus, a continuous monitoring of the real time dose-rate throughout the target volume is cardinal in enabling the desired outcome, provided at least one of the treatment determining parameters is under the control of the surgeon and can be modulated locally. While various approaches for dose-rate monitoring are possible by optical fibers or electro-polarographic probes (Chen et al. (2008)), the majority of these techniques either feature probes that sample too large an area (Weersink et al. (2005)), or require a clinically ill-advised large number of invasive probes (Li et al. (2008), Johansson (2007)).

3. Dose definitions

Keeping in mind the action mechanism of PDT, one may be tempted to choose singlet oxygen ($^1O_2$) as the dose metric, since it is the agent that is causal to cellular or vascular damage for the large majority of photosensitizers, particularly as it emits phosphorescence at 1270 nm when returning into its $^3O_2$ ground state, which can be used to quantify its concentration in a temporally resolved manner. Indeed, $^1O_2$ has been shown to correlate with the biological outcome in vitro, and singlet oxygen luminescence detection (SOLD) is a useful technique for in vitro experiments (Jarvi et al. (2006), Li et al. (2010)). For in vivo work, however, SOLD is not a feasible technique: $^1O_2$ phosphorescence has a very low quantum yield and implantable detectors with sufficient sensitivity are lacking. Two principal alternative strategies exist. The first is to deduce $^1O_2$ deposition based on the physico-chemical parameters required for its generation in PDT: light, PS, and $^3O_2$. This is termed "explicit" dosimetry, since $^1O_2$ is calculated directly from the spatial-temporal co-localization of its precursors (Wilson et al. (1997)). The second approach, "implicit" dosimetry, chooses a surrogate for $^1O_2$ - such as an interim photoproduct whose production was shown to be directly related to $^1O_2$ production (Dysart & Patterson (2006), Finlay et al. (2004)). Thus the temporal-spatial dynamics of this photoproduct imply the production of $^1O_2$ and hence the cytotoxic dose. A possible candidate metric for this approach is the excited singlet state PS ($1PS^*$), quantified through its fluorescence intensity (Pogue et al. (2008)).
In the PS fluorescence studies the spatial-temporal rate of loss in one of the efficacy determining parameters is the dose metric, whereas in the oxygen consumption model developed by T. Foster and colleagues uses oxygen depletion as the metric (Foster et al. (1991)). One disadvantage of implicit dosimetry models compared to the explicit dosimetry models is the loss of the ability to identify the *origin* of temporal-spatial variations in PDT dose, which is clinically of importance as it can lead to treatment failure when there is no appropriate correction. In explicit dosimetry the general behavior of the light fluence rate field can be obtained from a small number of spatial location measurements as the general gradient of light extinction in biological tissue is low (1-10 cm^{-1}). Local $^3O_2$ and $1PS^*$rate changes are sufficient to identify the probable efficacy-limiting parameter. The desirable spatial and temporal sampling requirements are thus given by the physical light parameters of the tissue and the intrinsic biology determining the pharmacokinetics of photosensitizer and oxygen. Table 1 provides the desired temporal and spatial sampling rates and Table 2 provides the feasible sampling rates for the PDT efficacy determining parameters. The temporal sampling rates are easily attainable for stationary probes, while the spatial requirements are not attainable for the Photosensitizer and Oxygen quantification. Improvement in the spatial monitoring is feasible using scanning probes as proposed by Zhu (Zhu et al. (2005)), but this is at the cost of the temporal sampling rates.
Explicit dosimetry involves direct measurement of the treatment efficacy-determining factors: treatment light, photosensitizer and ground state oxygen. While implicit and explicit dosimetry (Wilson et al. (1997)) are equivalent dose measures at each interrogated point in the target, explicit dosimetry permits also a dose calculation at all points in the target, based on population averages or individual tissue optical properties and pharmacokinetic parameters, prior to therapy onset. Determination of spatial gradients of these dose determining parameters can guide the medical physicist and surgeon towards modifications in the treatment plan to overcome identified obstacles to successful treatment.

Parameter	Spatial	Temporal
Fluence rate Φ	~4 cm^{-1}	~0.03 Hz
Photosensitizer concentration [PS]	0.02 μm^{-1}	~0.05 Hz
Oxygen Concentration [$^3O_2$]	0.02 μm^{-1}	~0.07 Hz

Table 1. Desired sampling rates for each PDT parameter

Parameter	Spatial	Temporal
Fluence rate Φ	< 1 cm^{-1}	< 0.5 Hz
Photosensitizer concentration [PS]	single point	< 0.5 Hz
Oxygen Concentration [$^3O_2$]	< 1 cm^{-1}	~0.5-1 Hz

Table 2. Currently technically achievable sampling for stationary sensors

The gradients are determined by the physical properties of the tissues such as the photosensitizer pharmacokinetics, oxygen perfusion versus metabolic and PDT consumption, and light absorption μ_a [cm^{-1}] and scattering μ_s [cm^{-1}] coefficients. In the following sections, the techniques used to quantify the three parameters are presented and discussed.

4. Treatment light quantification

Prior to explaining the details regarding treatment light quantification, it is important to define two quantities, irradiance and fluence rate, and their differences relevant to biophotonic applications in turbid media such as biological tissues. Although both quantities have the same units, their meanings are in fact vastly different.

Irradiance, commonly denoted ***H***, describes the power density [$mW \cdot cm^{-2}$] at a point P(x,y,z) through a surface of unit area in the direction of a surface normal **r**. Shown in the Figure 1 is a surface of unit area within an environment containing diffuse light. Irradiance is calculated by integrating all optical power through the surface that travel in the same hemisphere of **r**. In terms of clinical PDT, irradiance is the quantity of interest when an external collimated treatment light is delivered to a tissue surface such as the skin, the esophagus (van Veen et al. (2002)) or the surface of the bladder (Star et al. (2008)). Fluence rate, commonly denoted as Φ, is the three-dimensional analogue of irradiance as it describes the power density [$mW \cdot cm^{-2}$] through a sphere of unit surface area, as shown in Figure 1b. Fluence rate can be derived from irradiance by integrating irradiance through a full solid angle of 4πsr. In PDT and other light-based therapies (Robinson et al. (1998); Amabile et al. (2006)), fluence rate is used to quantify treatment light when it is delivered to a tissue volume using devices such as isotropic diffusing tip fibers. Since this delivered light travels omnidirectionally, the power delivered in all directions must be accounted for (hence the integration over 4πsr). Its gradient in tissue is determined exclusively by the effective attenuation coefficient $\mu_{eff} = \sqrt{3\mu_a(\mu_a\mu_s(1-g))}$ where $g = cos(\alpha)$, is the average cosine of the scattering angle α.

4.1 Treatment light quantification on surfaces

Irradiance on tissue surfaces can be measured with a flat photodiode detector of known area placed on the surface. If a beam larger than the detector surface is used, the fluence rate is

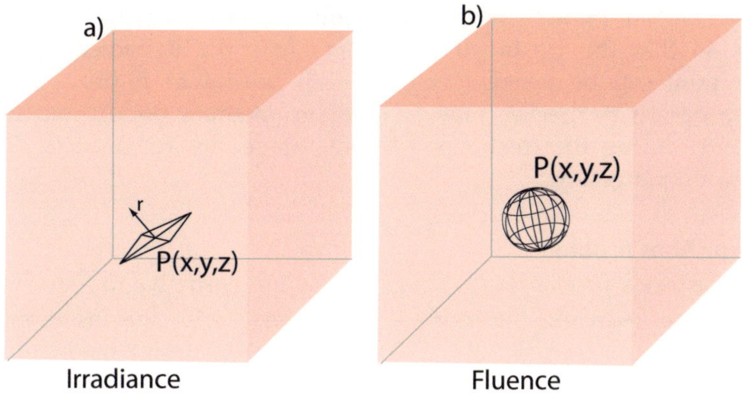

Fig. 1. The distinction between irradiance and fluence rate. The former considers optical power through a surface of unit area in a direction parallel to the surface normal (a). The latter considers the total optical power through though a sphere of unit surface area in all directions (b)

fluence rate is calculated by dividing the measured optical power by the surface area of the photodetector. Conversely, if the beam diameter is smaller, then the area of the beam is used to determine Irradiance.

4.2 Interstitial treatment light quantification

Interstitial PDT requires implanted optical fibers to deliver the treatment light to the tissue volume. These fibers may have cleaved ends (Johansson et al. (2007)), or specially designed ends with spherical or cylindrical emitting properties (Murrer et al. (1997); Vesselov et al. (2005)). Treatment light fluence rate quantification can be achieved via an additional set of embedded dedicated measurement fibers, typically cut-end (Johansson et al. (2007)), or by using the same delivery fibers reconnected to photo detectors if cut-end ((Svensson et al. (2007)) or isotropic diffusers (Yu et al. (2006); Trachtenberg et al. (2007)) are employed. The selection of the source fiber, emission and detector fiber acceptance properties and their physical separation determine the volume over which the tissue's optical properties are averaged. Thus, the use of closely spaced cut-end fibers provide the highest spatial resolution (Svensson et al. (2007; 2008)) whereas the use of a long emitter and detector (Davidson et al. (2009)) provides the lowest spatial resolution. Various existing techniques can be adapted to introduce the treatment light delivery fibers and detection fibers. For example, techniques similar to those used to implant radioactive seeds in prostate brachytherapy are employed to place the light delivery and detection fibers for prostate PDT (Weersink et al. (2005)). When using dedicated detection fibers they provide fluence rate measurements at single points, and several fibers are often necessary to obtain a useful coverage of the treatment volume (Zhu et al. (2006)).

Various approaches have been applied to reduce the number of detector fibers needed to adequately sample the target volume. One approach is to use the same delivery fibers as detection fibers, via sequential light delivery (Johansson (2007)). Another approach is to use a motorized system to translate the detector along an axis to quantify fluence rate at multiple locations, as described by Zhu et al (Zhu et al. (2005)). This technique also allows the investigators to measure the optical properties of the tissue volume in terms of the reduced scattering and absorption coefficients, since the changes in separation between light source and detectors are known. Such information can potentially be used to provide real-time feedback so that the treatment parameters (e.g. the delivered optical power, or treatment duration) can be personalized for each patient to improve its efficacy. The collected tissue optical properties may be used to generate population averaged tissue properties, which during the treatment planning stage, are required to determine light source and detector placement.

4.3 Multi-sensor fiber probes

Multi-sensor fiber-based probes (MSP) provide another alternative to reduce the number of detection fibers thus reducing the morbidity associated with the insertion of additional catheters (Pomerleau-Dalcourt & Lilge (2006)). These MSPs still maintain the ability to simultaneously sample multiple positions without the need for a translation system. The MSPs are comprised of highly fluorescent sensor materials, commonly dyes as used in the past for dye lasers, which have been pre-selected to minimize spectral overlap. The PDT treatment light acts as the excitation source for these dyes and hence, a sensor's emission intensity is proportional to the fluence rate. The MSP fabrication process involves removing the buffer and cladding layers of the fiber then applying the sensor material onto the exposed fiber core. This allows for detection of the fluorescence via a large solid angle, maximizing the sensors' responsivity. An optically clear epoxy is mixed with a solution of the sensor material, trapping the fluorescent molecules in the matrix which has an index of refraction similar to the cladding to increase the fluorescence captured into the fiber core. When inserted into the target tissue, the fluorescence intensity of each sensor on the MSP is proportional to the localized fluence rate. Spectrally-resolved detection is required to discriminate the contribution of each sensor and determine its fluorescence intensity. Once properly calibrated, such information provides absolute fluence rate values. The downside of this MSP approach is an increase in complexity of the data acquisition and pre-processing to extract the quantity of interest, here the fluence rate Φ. The techniques used for spectral discrimination of each fluorescent sensor is described in the following section, followed by results as the MSP is evaluated in an optical phantom.

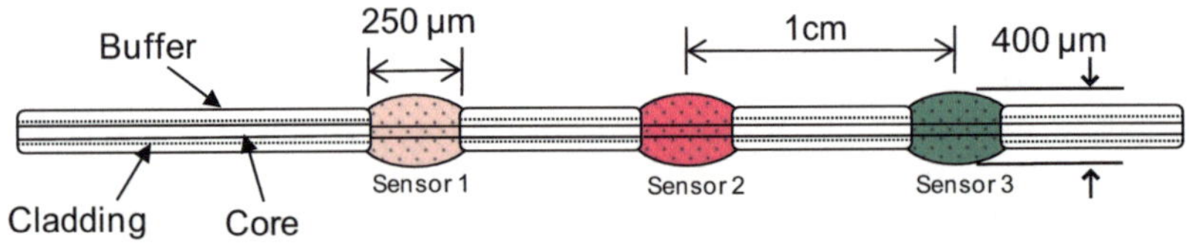

Fig. 2. Schematic of the multi-sensor probe (MSP) for spatially resolved fluence rate quantification. All sensors absorb the treatment light but emit with distinct spectra

4.4 Weighted least squares decomposition

The signal carried by the MSP fiber probe is a superposition of the individual fluorescent sensor emission. In order to obtain spatially resolved fluence rate quantification, spectrally-resolved detection is required. Since the fluorescent sensors are chosen to be spectrally distinct, a weighted least squares (WLS) algorithm is used to determine the contribution of each sensor.

Let the detected signal from the MSP be $S(\lambda)$. This quantity may be written as a sum of the contribution of each sensor with its own emission spectrum $F(\lambda)$, multiplied by a coefficient C which relates to the fluence rate of the excitation source. For simplicity, we do not consider noise due to the instrumentation, e.g. the charged coupled device (CCD) dark counts and read out noise, as well as measurement uncertainties of the data acquisition hardware. For N sensors embedded into a probe, the measured signal may be written as:

$$S(\lambda) = \sum_{i=1}^{N} C_i F_i(\lambda) \quad (1)$$

The goal is to determine C_i, which is correlated to the localized fluence rate, so that

$$S(\lambda) - \sum_{i=1}^{N} C_i F_i(\lambda) = J(C_1 ... C_N) \to 0 \quad (2)$$

Where $J(C_1...C_N)$ is the discrepancy function or error between the calculated and measured spectrum. Minimization of the square of this error across the entire spectral range of interest leads to a very good approximation of $S(\lambda)$:

$$\min \sum_{\lambda} \left[S(\lambda) - \sum_{i=1}^{N} C_i F_i(\lambda) \right]^2 \quad (3)$$

Minimization is typically achieved by differentiating the above equation with respect to each of the unknown values of C across the entire spectral range of interest λ. For example the jth component of the discrepancy function becomes

$$\frac{dJ}{dC_i} = 2 \sum_{\lambda} \left[S(\lambda) - \sum_{i=1}^{N} C_i F_i(\lambda) \right] F_j(\lambda) d\lambda = 0 \quad (4)$$

To simplify the expression, define the vectors **p** and Γ:

$$p_j = \sum_{\lambda} S(\lambda) \cdot F_j(\lambda) \quad (5)$$

$$\Gamma_{ij} = \sum_{\lambda} F_i(\lambda) \cdot F_j(\lambda) \quad (6)$$

Thus, the least squares expression can be simplified to become

$$\mathrm{p} - \Gamma \mathrm{c} = 0 \quad (7)$$

The amount of overlap between sensor spectra impacts significantly whether the least square approach derives an absolute or only local minimum as the least squares $\frac{dJ}{dC_i}$ becomes very flat across the planes of similar emitters . Therefore a modification to the least squares method is applied which introduces a weighting function to suppress areas where there is significant overlap, particularly when the slopes of two or more emission profiles over a specific wavelength range are similar.

The weighting function is based on the determinant of the matrix generated by taking the inner-products of every pair of fluorophore emission spectra for the specified wavelength range, say $\lambda \pm \frac{\delta}{2}$.
Recall that the inner-product of two vectors F and P is defined as

$$\cos(\mathbf{F}^\wedge\mathbf{P}) = \frac{<\mathbf{F}\cdot\mathbf{P}>}{|\mathbf{F}|\cdot|\mathbf{P}|} = \frac{\int F(x)\cdot P(x)\cdot dx}{\sqrt{\int F^2(x)\cdot dx\cdot \int P^2(x)\cdot dx}} \quad (8)$$

For a collection of fluorescent sensors, the determinant becomes

$$k(\lambda') = \det\left[\frac{\sum_{\lambda-\delta/2}^{\lambda+\delta/2} F_i(\lambda')\cdot F_j(\lambda')}{\sum_{\lambda-\delta/2}^{\lambda+\delta/2} F_i^2(\lambda')\cdot F_j^2(\lambda')}\right] \quad (9)$$

for i = 1...N and j = 1 ... N
The value of $k(\lambda')$ approaches zero at wavelength λ' when there is significant overlap between spectra, indicating that there is no solution to satisfy the system of equations. The determinant values calculated at different wavelengths make up the weighting function $w(\lambda)$, which is introduced into the least squares system of equations to suppress areas of spectral overlap and noise. The result is emphasised regions in all spectra that are favourable to increase the likelihood of obtaining a gradient of $\frac{dJ}{dC_i}$ in all dimensions and hence a unique and correct solution for:

$$p_i = \sum_{\lambda} w(\lambda)\cdot S(\lambda)\cdot F_j(\lambda) \quad (10)$$

$$\Gamma_i = \sum_{\lambda} w(\lambda)\cdot F_i(\lambda)\cdot F_j(\lambda) \quad (11)$$

4.5 Measurement accuracy

Tissue simulating optical phantoms consisting of Intralipid, a fatty emulsion normally used for intravenous feeding, as the scattering component and napthnol green as the absorbing component were prepared to assess the measurement accuracy of the MSP and fluence rate extraction system. The desired absorbing and reduced scattering coefficients (μ_a and μ_s', respectively) were obtained based on the dilutions as described by Martelli et al (Martelli & Zaccanti (1997)). The experimental setup involved submerging the MSP after calibration into the phantom at a fixed position. A spherical isotropic diffusing tip fiber connected to a 670 nm laser source was placed at different known distances from the sensors inside the phantom to evaluate the fluence rate sensitivity and accuracy of the probe. Since the optical properties of the phantom are known and uniform througout, the fluence rate at any distance away from the isotropic light source may be calculated using the diffusion approximation of the transport equation (Wilson & Patterson (1986)) and for comparison the detected fluence rate of the MSP.
For a spherical isotropic source in an optically homogenous medium delivering total power P, the approximate fluence rate as a function of radial distance r away from the source is:

$$\Phi(r) = P \times \frac{3\mu_s'}{4\pi r}\exp(-\mu_{eff} r) \tag{12}$$

It is highly desirable in the treatment volume targeted per light source to minimize light attenuation by tissue, which reduces light penetration, and thus to maximize treatment light delivery. Typically light sources in the red and far red regions of the optical spectrum are used (above 635 nm). In this region, tissue scattering dominates over absorption and the expression for μ_{eff} can be simplified to $\mu_{eff} = \sqrt{3\mu_a\mu_s'}$ (Pogue & Patterson (2006)).
An example of the calculated and measured fluence rates from the sensors are plotted together as a function of distance from the light source for a particular experiment. The measured fluence rate behaviour agrees well with the anticipated exponential decay as described by the diffusion approximation. The overall experimentally determined measurement accuracy for the MSP is better than 0.9 for fluence rates above 15 [mW · cm^{-2}] (Lai et al. (2009)). It is noteworthy to point out that this error includes errors in the initial probe calibration as well as uncertainties in the tissue simulating phantom's optical properties, which directly impacts the gradient of the measured fluence rate as a function of distance from the source. Figure 3 shows a comparison of the theoretical anticipated fluence rate attenuation and the experimental measurements.

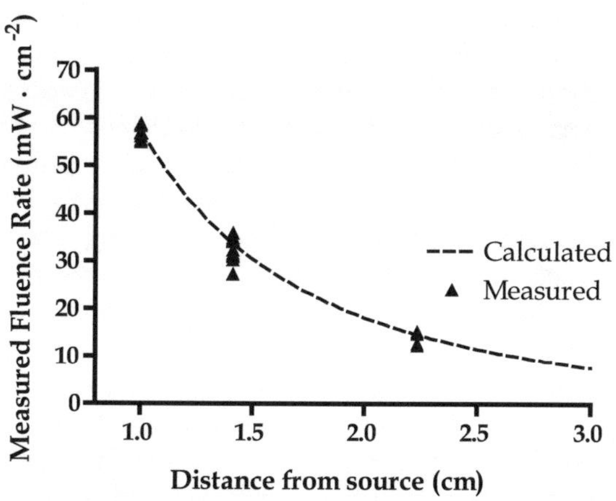

Fig. 3. Measurement of the characteristic drop in Φ(r) in a homogeneous optical phantom as a function of distance from the light source

5. Photosensitizer quantification

The first step in the activation of photosensitizer molecules upon absorption of a photon from the treatment light is its promotion to the singlet excited state. The photosensitizer is designed such that intersystem crossing to the triplet excited state is the preferred transition for deexcitation of the elevated singlet state. From the triplet excited state the photosensitizer is capable of interacting with ground state triplet oxygen, in an interaction which exchanges energy and electronspin thus producing singlet oxygen. However, the singlet excited photosensitizer may also return to the singlet ground state releasing a fluorescent photon with a wavelength proportional to the energy difference between the singlet ground and excited states. As a result, the fluorescence intensity may be used as an indicator of the amount of photosensitizer present in the treatment target if the excitation intensity, here the PDT fluence rate is known at this location. This photosensitizer fluorescence may be captured to track its depletion rate and to quantify the amount of photosensitizer present for the purpose of treatment monitoring.

Quantifying fluorescence on tissue surfaces require a photo detector or a detector array (for spatially resolved fluorescence imaging) with adequate sensitivity at the fluorescence wavelength. The detection system must be equipped with the necessary filters to remove the excitation light from saturating the sensor. Additionally, prior to administration of the photosensitizer, a baseline image or spectrum should be taken to account for any autofluorescence from tissue components such as elastin and collagen in the area of interest, to prevent overestimation of the quantified fluorescence. Previous studies (Van der Veen et al. (1994); Zaak et al. (2001)) have demonstrated that fluorescent photosensitizers like ALA-induced PPIX may be imaged with a standard CCD camera to observe fluorescence kinetics of the photosensitizer during PDT treatment.

Interstitial quantification of photosensitizer fluorescence requires interstitially implanted bare-end detection fibers for point measurements. An additional level of complexity is inherent to interstitial measurements, because the tissue optical properties (absorption, scattering and anisotropy), and source detector separation must be taken into account since these factors ultimately affect the attainable fluorescence due to variations of the excitation power (Canpolat & Mourant (2000)). Such systems have been described by several investigators Axelsson et al. (2009); Canpolat & Mourant (2000)). To determine the spatial photosensitizer distribution, multiple detection fibers are required to sample multiple spatial positions. Axelsson et al. has, based on the multiple fiber approach, presented a system to perform *in vivo* photosensitizer tomography for a targeted tissue volume, the prostate. A fiber switching mechanism permits the investigator to deliver light to each of the 18 implanted fibers sequentially while its six neighbouring fibers are used collect the photosensitizer fluorescence. A total of 108 measurements are made between 54 source detector pairs, to generate fluorescence data for tomographic reconstruction. As the optical sampling volume is a function of the tissue optical properties (Pomerleau-Dalcourt & Lilge (2006)) photosensitizer probe calibration in optical phantoms approximating the population average tissue optical properties for the organ of interest is desired.

Direct quantification of weakly fluorescing photosensitizers such as TOOKAD is performed via absorption spectroscopy. Weersink et al. demonstrated this technique *in situ* in the prostate with a light delivery fiber coupled to a broad spectrum source and a fiber-based isotropic detector. Both source and detector were directed to predetermined locations in the treatment volume using a brachytherapy template to maintain a known source-detector distance (Weersink et al. (2005)). The acquired spectrum from the isotropic detector was transformed to absorbance units and fitted to previously measured absorption spectra of the drug and its aggregate to quantify the PS concentration in tissue.

6. Oxygen quantification

The polarographic Clark-type electrode (Clark et al. (1953)) is the current standard tool for measuring partial oxygen pressure (pO_2) [kPa] of tissue (Cheema et al. (2008); Swartz (2007); Pogue et al. (2001)). Its mode of operation is based on the electrochemical reduction of ground state triplet oxygen ($^3O_2$) to generate a measurable electric current proportional to the concentration of $^3O_2$ around the probe. Absolute pO_2 quantification can be made after calibrating the electrode at a known pO_2 concentration and in the absence of oxygen. One

drawback of this technology is that oxygen is consumed to generate OH^- ions during the measurement process: $O_2 + 4e^{-1} + 2H_2O \rightarrow 4OH^-$ (Lee & Tsao (1979)). As a result, the sensitivity of Clark electrodes is directly related to the pO_2 of the environment it is measuring. To gain an appreciation of the impact that this may have within the context of PDT, it is worthwhile to note that the change in pO_2 from the atmosphere to tissue is a reduction of over 20 times (Ward (2008)). Consequently, the operation of the electrode behaves as an additional "oxygen sink" that further contributes to the depletion of $^3O_2$ in an environment that already contains low levels of oxygen, contributing further to the degradation of the measurable electrical signal.
An alternative to using an electrode is to optically measure $^3O_2$. This technique relies on the ability of $^3O_2$ to effectively quench the phosphorescence of molecules in the triplet excited (T1) state (Fitzgerald et al 2001). A phosphorescent molecule in the T1 state can return to the ground state via photon production (phosphorescence) or undergo a non-radiative energy exchange with $^3O_2$. In the event that an energy exchange takes place, the phosphorescence is said to be quenched and no photon is produced. This in effect reduces the exponential decay lifetime τ [s] of the compound, which is defined as the time required for the phosphorescence intensity to fall to $1/e$ or 37% of its initial peak value. Under constant temperature and atmospheric pressure, the variation between τ and pO_2 is linear and inversely related. An optical probe with embedded phosphorescent sensors, or an optode, can be fabricated to replace the electrode for oxygen quantification. This probe requires a short wavelength light source to promote the sensor material to the T1 state and hence induce phosphorescence which can be measured to derive the pO_2. The advantage compared to the electrode is that measurement sensitivity is inversely proportional to pO_2 and $^3O_2$ is consumed at a lower rate than the electrode. Commercially available oxygen measurement systems based on oxygen quenching have been made available from Oxford Optronics in the United Kingtom under the Oxylite brand, as well as from Ocean Optics sold under the NeoFox brand name. Both systems utilize a pulsed blue LED excitation source to generate the phosphor excitation and induce emissions from sensors embedded at the tip of fiber-based probes. Such systems, however, are capable of interrogating only one point at a time. Multiple fiber probes are thus required in order to perform spatially resolved pO_2 measurements, with the same limits to clinical acceptability as mentioned in previous sections.

6.1 Quantification techniques

There are two approaches to optically determine τ; in the time domain (TD), or in the frequency domain (FD). The TD method involves measuring the time needed for the phosphorescence to reach 37% of its initial intensity after induction of phosphorescence with a very short excitation pulse. The FD technique uses an amplitude modulated excitation source at a pre-selected frequency to induce a measurable shift in the phase and amplitude of the phosphorescence signal, as compared to the excitation signal. For a chosen modulation frequency ω [rad^{-1}], the relationship between τ and the phase (ϕ) and modulation index (m) are (Lakowicz & Masters (2008)):

$$\tan(\phi) = \omega\tau \tag{13}$$

and

$$m = \sqrt{1 + \omega^2\tau^2} \tag{14}$$

There are disadvantages for each approach in determining τ. For example, the FD technique requires higher computational resources as signal processing is performed to determine the phase offset and amplitude changes compared to the excitation. The TD technique does not need significant signal processing, at the expense of requiring significantly faster sampling hardware to ensure sufficient data points are collected to determine the decay time. Given the availability of high speed central processing units (CPUs) equipped with multiple processing cores, the cost of acquiring hardware for signal processing is drastically lower compared to the cost of acquiring a high-speed data acquisition device. Therefore the FD technique is preferred. For example, to measure a decay time of as low as 100 μs, the TD sampling hardware must have a sampling rate of at least 1 MHz to generate 100 or more time-resolved sampled points. For the FD system to accommodate this requirement, the modulation frequency needed to induce a phase offset to 90° is 10 kHz. Even with an oversampling factor of 10, the required sampling speed for the FD system is 100 kHz, which is still one order of magnitude slower than the TD system.

6.2 Frequency domain decay lifetime quantification

A block diagram of the FD system is presented in the figure 4. A 50:50, 2x2 optical coupler is used to direct excitation light to the oxygen sensor, and to guide captured sensor emissions to the photo-multiplier tubes (PMT). The excitation source is a 405nm laser diode, intensity modulated by a laser driver whose output is controlled by a programmable signal generator. The function generator is programmed to sweep through a frequency range from 100 Hz to 1 kHz. During operation, the optical coupler directs the excitation light captured at Port 1 to ports 3 and 4. The PMT at port 3 is equipped with a 405 nm bandpass filter to monitor the excitation source to be used as the reference signal. At port 4, phosphorescence induced by the delivered excitation light is captured by the coupler and re-directed to port 2 for detection by a second PMT equipped with a 650 nm long-pass filter, which generates the emission signal.

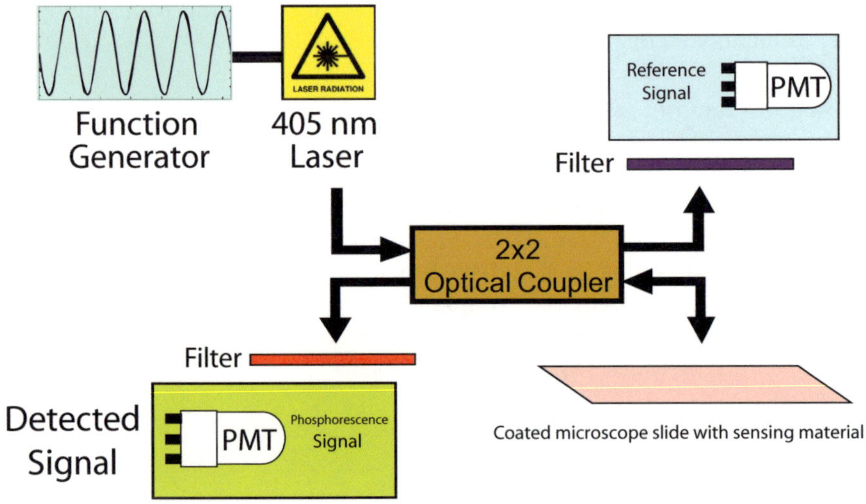

Fig. 4. Block diagram of the frequency domain system for pO^2 quantification

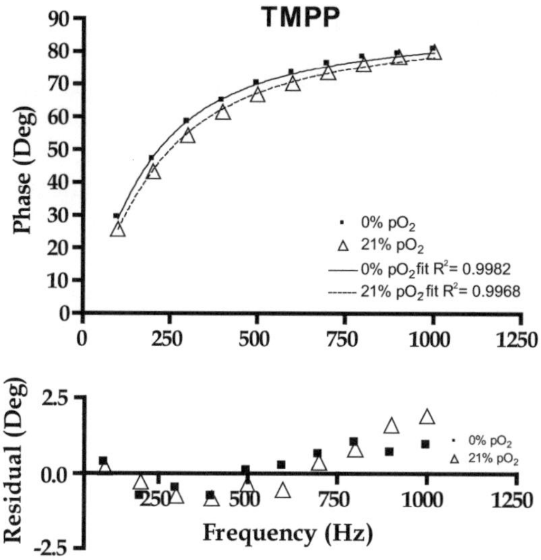

Fig. 5. Phase-frequency relationship of TMPP at 21 kPa and 0 kPa pO^2 demonstrating a change in decay lifetime

Phosphorescent palladium metalloporphyrin compound Pd-meso-Tetra(N-Methyl-4-Pyridyl) Porphine "TMPP" is used as the sensing material because of its long and measurable decay times in the μs range (Fitzgerald et al 2001). The compound is mixed into a compatible epoxy, spincoated onto a glass microscope slide, and allowed to cure. The decay lifetime of 760 μs at 21 kPa (atmospheric condition) and 903 μs at 0 kPa (anoxic) pO_2 is measured with the FD system. The value of τ should be constant for all modulation frequencies as long as the pO_2 does not change. Thus, the measured phase at different modulation frequencies follows the relationshiop described in Equation 13. Figure 5 shows a plot of the measured phase against modulation frequency at 21 kPa and 0 kPa. The solid and dotted lines represent the fitting used to determine τ based on the measured phase relationship for each oxygenation level, with a resulting R^2 greater than 0.99.

7. References

Amabile, G., Rotondi, M., Chiara, G., Silvestri, A., Filippo, B., Bellastella, A. & Chiovato, L. (2006). Low-energy interstitial laser photocoagulation for treatment of nonfunctioning thyroid nodules: therapeutic outcome in relation to pretreatment and treatment parameters, *Thyroid* 16(8): 749–755.

Axelsson, J., Swartling, J. & Andersson-Engels, S. (2009). In vivo photosensitizer tomography inside the human prostate, *Optics letters* 34(3): 232–234.

Canpolat, M. & Mourant, J. R. (2000). Monitoring photosensitizer concentration by use of a fiber-optic probe with a small source-detector separation, *Appl. Opt.* 39(34): 6508–6514.
URL: *http://ao.osa.org/abstract.cfm?URI=ao-39-34-6508*

Cheema, U., Brown, R., Alp, B. & MacRobert, A. (2008). Spatially defined oxygen gradients and vascular endothelial growth factor expression in an engineered 3D cell model, *Cellular and molecular life sciences* 65(1): 177–186.

Chen, Q., Chen, H. & Hetzel, F. (2008). Tumor oxygenation changes post-photodynamic therapy, *Photochemistry and photobiology* 63(1): 128–131.

Clark, L. et al. (1953). Continuous recording of blood oxygen tensions by polarography, *Journal of Applied Physiology* 6(3): 189.

Davidson, S., Weersink, R., Haider, M., Gertner, M., Bogaards, A., Giewercer, D., Scherz, A., Sherar, M., Elhilali, M., Chin, J. et al. (2009). Treatment planning and dose analysis for interstitial photodynamic therapy of prostate cancer, *Physics in Medicine and Biology* 54: 2293.

Dolmans, D. & Dai Fukumura, R. (2003). Photodynamic therapy for cancer, *Nature Reviews Cancer* 3(5): 380–387.

Dysart, J. & Patterson, M. (2006). Photobleaching kinetics, photoproduct formation, and dose estimation during ALA induced PpIX PDT of MLL cells under well oxygenated and hypoxic conditions, *Photochemical & Photobiological Sciences* 5(1): 73–81.

Finlay, J., Mitra, S., Patterson, M. & Foster, T. (2004). Photobleaching kinetics of Photofrin in vivo and in multicell tumour spheroids indicate two simultaneous bleaching mechanisms, *Physics in medicine and biology* 49(21): 4837–4860.

Folkman, J. (1974). Tumor angiogenesis factor, *Cancer Research* 34(8): 2109.

Foster, T., Murant, R., Bryant, R., Knox, R., Gibson, S. & Hilf, R. (1991). Oxygen consumption and diffusion effects in photodynamic therapy, *Radiation research* pp. 296–303.

Hamblin, M. & Mroz, P. (2008). *Advances in Photodynamic Therapy: Basic, Translational and Clinical*, Artech House Publishers.

Jarvi, M., Niedre, M., Patterson, M. & Wilson, B. (2006). Singlet oxygen luminescence dosimetry (SOLD) for photodynamic therapy: current status, challenges and future prospects, *Photochemistry and photobiology* 82(5): 1198–1210.

Johansson, A., Axelsson, J., Andersson-Engels, S. & Swartling, J. (2007a). Realtime light dosimetry software tools for interstitial photodynamic therapy of the human prostate, *Medical physics* 34: 4309.

Johansson, A., Axelsson, J., Swartling, J., Johansson, T., lsson, S. P., Stensson, J., Einarsdóttír, M., Svanberg, K., Bendsoe, N., Kälkner, K. M., Nilsson, S., Svanberg, S. & Andersson- Engels, S. (2007b). Interstitial photodynamic therapy for primary prostate cancer incorporating real-time treatment dosimetry, *Proceedings of SPIE*, Vol. 6427, p. 64270O.

Lai, B., Loshchenov, M., Douplik, A., Rusnov, R., Jimenez-Davila, M., Netchev, G. & Lilge, L. (2009). Three-dimensional fluence rate measurement and data acquisition system for minimally invasive light therapies, *Review of Scientific Instruments* 80(043104): 043104.

Lakowicz, J. & Masters, B. (2008). Principles of fluorescence spectroscopy, *Journal of Biomedical Optics* 13: 029901.

Lee, Y. & Tsao, G. (1979). Dissolved oxygen electrodes, *Advances in Biochemical Engineering, Volume 13* pp. 35–86.

Li, B., Lin, H., Chen, D., Wang, M. & Xie, S. (2010). Detection system for singlet oxygen luminescence in photodynamic therapy, *Chinese Optics Letters* 8(1): 86–88.

Li, J., Altschuler, M., Hahn, S. & Zhu, T. (2008). Optimization of light source parameters in the photodynamic therapy of heterogeneous prostate, *Physics in medicine and biology* 53(15): 4107–4122.

Martelli, F. & Zaccanti, G. (1997). Calibration of scattering and absorption properties of a liquid diffusive medium at NIR wavelengths. CW method, *Med. Biol* 42: 825–840.

M. Fitzgerald, DB Papovsky, MA Smiddy, JP Kerry, CK O'Sullivan, DJ Buckley and GG Guilbault, Non-destructive monitoring of oxygen profiles in packaged foods using a phase-fluorimetric oxygen sensor. Journal Food Science 66 (2001), pp. 105–110

Murrer, L., Marijnissen, J. & Star, W. (1997). Improvements in the design of linear diffusers for photodynamic therapy, *Physics in Medicine and Biology* 42: 1461–1464.

Plaetzer, K., Krammer, B., Berlanda, J., Berr, F. & Kiesslich, T. (2009). Photophysics and photochemistry of photodynamic therapy: fundamental aspects, *Lasers in Medical Science* 24(2): 259–268.

Pogue, B., Braun, R., Lanzen, J., Erickson, C. & Dewhirst, M. (2001). Analysis of the Heterogeneity of pO2 Dynamics During Photodynamic Therapy with Verteporfin, *Photochemistry and Photobiology* 74(5): 700–706.

Pogue, B. & Patterson, M. (2006). Review of tissue simulating phantoms for optical spectroscopy, imaging and dosimetry, *Journal of Biomedical optics* 11: 041102.

Pogue, B., Sheng, C., Benevides, J., Forcione, D., Puricelli, B., Nishioka, N. & Hasan, T. (2008). Protoporphyrin IX fluorescence photobleaching increases with the use of fractionated irradiation in the esophagus, *Journal of Biomedical Optics* 13: 034009.

Pomerleau-Dalcourt, N. & Lilge, L. (2006). Development and characterization of multisensory fluence rate probes, *Physics in Medicine and Biology* 51: 1929.

Popovic, E., Kaye, A. & Hill, J. (1996). Photodynamic therapy of brain tumors, *Journal of Clinical Laser Medicine & Surgery* 14(5): 251–261.

Robinson, M., David, S., Parel Ing, E. et al. (1998). Interstitial laser hyperthermia model development for minimally invasive therapy of breast carcinoma, *Journal of the American College of Surgeons* 186(3): 284–292.

Sean R H Davidson *et al* Treatment planning and dose analysis for interstitial photodynamic therapy of prostate cancer 2009 *Phys. Med. Biol.* 54 2293

Star, W., Marijnissen, H., Jansen, H., Keijzer, M. & Gemert, M. (2008). Light dosimetry for photodynamic therapy by whole bladder wall irradiation, *Photochemistry and Photobiology* 46(5): 619–624.

Svensson, T., Alerstam, E., Einarsdóttír, M., Svanberg, K. & Andersson-Engels, S. (2008). Towards accurate in vivo spectroscopy of the human prostate, *Journal of Biophotonics* 1(3): 200–203.

Svensson, T., Andersson-Engels, S., Einarsdóttír, M. & Svanberg, K. (2007). In vivo optical characterization of human prostate tissue using near-infrared time-resolved spectroscopy, *Journal of Biomedical Optics* 12: 014022.

Swartz, H. (2007). On tissue oxygen and hypoxia, *Antioxidants & Redox Signaling* 9(8): 1111–1114.

Trachtenberg, J., Bogaards, A., Weersink, R., Haider, M., Evans, A., McCluskey, S., Scherz, A., Gertner, M., Yue, C., Appu, S. et al. (2007). Vascular targeted photodynamic therapy with palladium-bacteriopheophorbide photosensitizer for recurrent prostate cancer following definitive radiation therapy: assessment of safety and treatment response, *The Journal of urology* 178(5): 1974–1979.

Van der Veen, N., Van Leengoed, H. & Star, W. (1994). In vivo fluorescence kinetics and photodynamic therapy using 5-aminolaevulinic acid-induced porphyrin: increased damage after multiple irradiations., *British journal of cancer* 70(5): 867.

van Veen, R., Aalders, M., Pasma, K., Siersema, P., Haringsma, J., van de Vrie, W., Gabeler, E., Robinson, D. & Sterenborg, H. (2002). In situ light dosimetry during photodynamic therapy of Barrett's esophagus with 5-aminolevulinic acid, *Lasers in surgery and medicine* 31(5): 299–304.

Vesselov, L., Whittington, W. & Lilge, L. (2005). Design and performance of thin cylindrical diffusers created in Ge-doped multimode optical fibers, *Applied optics* 44(14): 2754–2758.

Ward, J. (2008). Oxygen sensors in context, *Biochimica et Biophysica Acta (BBA)-Bioenergetics* 1777(1): 1–14.

Weersink, R., Bogaards, A., Gertner, M., Davidson, S., Zhang, K., Netchev, G., Trachtenberg, J. & Wilson, B. (2005). Techniques for delivery and monitoring of TOOKAD (WST09)-mediated photodynamic therapy of the prostate: clinical experience and practicalities, *Journal of Photochemistry and Photobiology B: Biology* 79(3): 211–222.

Wilson, B. (2008). Advanced Photodynamic Therapy, *Biophotonics* pp. 315–334.

Wilson, B. & Patterson, M. (1986). The physics of photodynamic therapy, *Physics in Medicine and Biology* 31: 327–360.

Wilson, B., Patterson, M. & Lilge, L. (1997). Implicit and explicit dosimetry in photodynamic therapy: a new paradigm, *Lasers in Medical Science* 12(3): 182–199.

Yu, G., Durduran, T., Zhou, C., Zhu, T., Finlay, J., Busch, T., Malkowicz, S., Hahn, S. & Yodh, A. (2006). Real-time in situ monitoring of human prostate photodynamic therapy with diffuse light, *Photochemistry and photobiology* 82(5): 1279–1284.

Zaak, D., Frimberger, D., Stepp, H.,Wagner, S., Baumgartner, R., Schneede, P., Siebels, M., KN "UCHEL, R., Kriegmair, M. & Hofstetter, A. (2001). Quantification of 5-aminolevulinic acid induced fluorescence improves the specificity of bladder cancer detection, *The Journal of urology* 166(5): 1665–1669.

Zhu, T., Finlay, J. & Hahn, S. (2005). Determination of the distribution of light, optical properties, drug concentration, and tissue oxygenation in-vivo in human prostate during motexafin lutetium-mediated photodynamic therapy, *Journal of Photochemistry and Photobiology B: Biology* 79(3): 231–241.

Zhu, T., Li, J., Finlay, J., Dimofte, A., Stripp, D., Malkowicz, B. & Hahn, S. (2006). In-vivo light dosimetry of interstitial PDT of human prostate, *Proceedings of SPIE*, Vol. 6139, p. 61390L.

Critical Appraisal of Data Acquisition in Body Composition: Evaluation of Methods, Techniques and Technologies on the Anatomical Tissue-System Level

Aldo Scafoglieri, Steven Provyn, Ivan Bautmans,
Joanne Wallace, Laura Sutton, Jonathan Tresignie,
Olivia Louis, Johan De Mey and Jan Pieter Clarys
Vrije Universiteit Brussel (VUB)
Belgium

1. Introduction

Human body composition (BC) could well be the only health-related discipline that allows both "simple indexes" e.g. the Body Mass Index, and "advanced technology" e.g. dual energy X-ray absorptiometry, to be used for the same purpose: the quantitative measurement of BC components for the prediction of health risk. Human BC probably is the most confusing health-related discipline also because of the mixture of apparent corresponding and analogue terminology. The major problems with quality control in BC are the large amount of different models and devices each with their own advantages and limitations, and their respective validation against other indirect data-acquisition methods or technologies. The validation of anthropometric techniques has generally been performed against two- or three-compartment models of BC such as hydrodensitometry or dual energy X-ray absorptiometry. These reference standards themselves are based on assumptions of a constant density, constant hydration and constant tissue distribution throughout the human body, without taking into account the biological variation of tissue composition. The quality control and validation of indirect *in vivo* measurements for BC against direct measurements is both scarce/almost un-edited and essential: it is known that there are wide variations in the indirect measurements currently used in practice, which makes any clinical decisions based on those measurements suspect. This chapter will give a critical appraisal of three frequently used data acquisition methods for measuring individual BC, in particular hydrodensitometry, body mass index and dual energy X-ray absorptiometry. In addition this chapter will provide a (renewed) critical appraisal of the most confusing terminology.

2. The hazards of hydrodensitometry

The human body composition can be considered according to different situations, within different disciplines and based on different theories, e.g. clinical versus biological approaches, chemical versus anatomical evaluations, *in vivo* versus *in vitro* research, direct data acquisition versus indirect prediction techniques, BC in ergonomics or BC in health sciences, etc…Most of these differentiations can be found in the respective 2-, 3-, 4- and 5-component (2C, 3C, 4C and 5C) models (Table 1) that have been described since the first model, e.g. the 4C model of Matiegka (1921).

Model 2C Siri (1956)	Fat	Fat Free Mass			
Model 2C Clarys & Martin (1985)	Adipose Tissue	Adipose Tissue Free Mass			
Model 3C Siri (1961)	Fat	Body Water		Density	
Model 3C Mazess et al. (1981)	Fat	Lean Body Mass or Lean		Bone Minerals	
Model 4C Widdowson et al. (1951)	Fat	Body Water		Proteins	Minerals
Model 4C Matiegka (1921)	Adipose Tissue	Skeletal Muscle		Bone	Residual Lean Mass
Model 4C Lohman & Going (1993)	Weight	Body Water		Bone Minerals	Density
Model 5C Clarys et al. (1984)	Adipose Tissue	Skin Tissue	Muscular Tissue	Bone Tissue	Organ Tissue
Model 5L Wang et al. (1992)	Atomic	Molecular	Cellular	Tissue/Organ	Whole Body
Model 5C Wang et al. (1992)	Fat	Extracellular Fluid	Intracellular Fluid	Extracellular Solids	Intracellular Solids

Table 1. Theoretical multi-components models used in body composition analysis
(C = Component, L = Level)

Partly in parallel and partly as a consequence of the development of these models, terminology and an associated confusion has installed itself over the years in particular within the (almost) colloquial use and mixing of the terms fat, adipose tissue (AT), lipids, fat free mass (FFM), lean and lean body mass (LBM) or adipose tissue free mass (ATFM). This multitude of related terminology has led to a proliferation of the confusion without reflecting on the absolute direct and indirect underlying values. This was already predicted in the sixties (Behnke, 1963) but confusion increased nevertheless. Chemical and anatomical analyses produce direct values and were originally applied in *in vitro* studies only (Brodie et al., 1998; Clarys et al., 1984, 1999; Forbes & Lewis, 1956; Forbes et al., 1953; Marfell-Jones et al., 2003; Roemmich et al., 1997). With the development of techniques, methods and equipment, magnetic resonance imaging (MRI) and computed tomography (CT) produce data that are closest to real data acquisition allowing comparison with what is considered as "direct" values (Janssen et al., 2002a; Mitsiopoulos et al., 1998).

2.1 Limitations and restrictions of hydrodensitometry

The term direct data acquisition is valid also for the volume measurements in plethysmography and water displacement. Hydrostatic weighing including the ad hoc density calculation is a direct value also but the next step allowing quantifying fat from it certainly is not a "direct" value. Apart from the direct underwater weighing, hydrodensitometry (HD) needs equally a direct measurement of residual lung and gastro-intestinal air, realizing that small errors in residual volume may create more important errors in the subsequent calculations. In addition, it needs to be reminded also that this measurement series is not evident with children, older individuals and persons (all ages) with aquaphobia. Hydrodensitometry is an essential part of the 2C model and has served as a direct "reference method" for many (if not most) BC techniques and methods (Brodie et al., 1998; Brozek et al., 1963; Ellis, 2000). This model is based on the assumption of a density constancy of 0.901 g/ml for fat and of 1.100 g/ml for FFM and, irrespective the technique or method it was used for, the background of constancy was projected to all tissues that compose FFM and irrespective the measurement of fat (Behnke et al., 1942; Siri, 1956). Although this knowledge, in part or as a whole, has been extensively described and discussed in the literature, one must ascertain that HD has not been abandoned as a reference and is used in various sport medical centers and sport science laboratories still (Brodie et al., 1998; Eston et al., 2005; Westerterp et al., 2008; Wouters-Adriaens & Westerterp, 2008). Readers are reminded that distinction needs to be made between HD for the purpose of %fat determination and for the purpose of single tissue density measurement. The first is a direct measure plus an indirect calculation, the latter remains direct to obtain density only, without associated problems. In general, the studies evaluating the quality of HD using an in vivo 4C model as the criterion have shown that estimation of body density accurately estimates the mean body composition of most groups of non-athletic adults e.g. black, elderly and obese subjects and its accuracy is not specifically related to race, age, gender or level of adiposity (Visser et al., 1997). However, various degrees of inaccuracy exist and systematic error is substantial for most individuals and groups of children, adolescents and athletes. In other words, the possibilities and limitations are or should be known and more definitive reviews and studies quantifying the inaccuracy of the method are available (Brodie et al., 1998; Clarys et al., 2010a; Ellis, 2000; Lohman, 1981; Modlesky et al., 1996; Roemmich et al., 1997; Visser et al., 1997). The cause of these inaccuracies is complex and not only a reflection of musculoskeletal development (Prior et al., 2001). Directly obtained data combined with known information could provide the missing links for this matter.

The purpose of this chapter section is to combine well known evidence with new direct data acquisition and analyses to accept or reject HD and the 2C model as a measure and as a reference.

2.2 Methodology

The bases for data collection is of an anthropological nature. Data sources are used from the 19th and 20th century and completed with the Brussels Cadaver Analysis Studies (BCAS) (Clarys et al., 1999). This data collection is partly projected on and combined with the basic plot of Siri's equation (Figure 1) theories to predict fat from whole body density within the 2C model (fat + FFM) (Siri, 1956).

Methodology varied across the different studies, depending on the objectives, but these differences would have little effect on the measured weights of the gross tissues.

Pooling of all Brussels data yielded a dataset of 34 cadavers (17 male and 17 female) with an age range 16-94 yrs. The 19th century data consisted of 12 subjects, age range 26-50 yrs (though four subjects were of unknown age). Adding the remaining five dissections of the mid 20th century yielded a total of 31 men (mean age ± sd; 56,6 ± 21,5y) and 20 women (mean age ± sd; 75,5 ± 15,4y) for whom the weights of skin, adipose tissue, muscle, and bone were known. Heights were not reported for three individuals. Detailed data are to be found in Clarys et al. (1999). In addition the *in vivo* HD literature was screened for biologically debatable data obtained within the 2C model, for example unrealistically low estimates of body fat (Adams et al., 1982; Katch & Michael, 1968; Pollock et al., 1977).

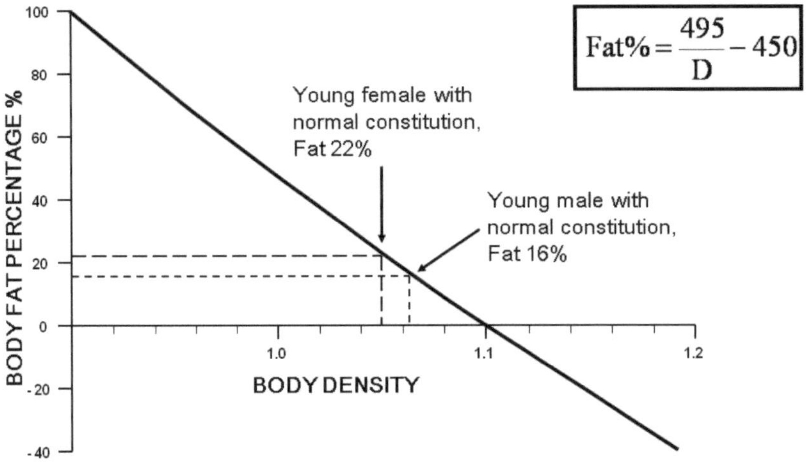

Fig. 1. Siri's plot (1956), the base of hydrodensitometry for the prediction of the percentage of body fat

2.3 Critical appraisal of body composition terminology

The densitometric analysis of BC has been limited in regard to its validity, by the absence of direct information of the fat content and densities of known bodies, segments and tissues. In attempts to identify the physiologically relevant tissues, the concept of the LBM was introduced more than half a century ago (Behnke et al., 1942). This consists of the FFM plus the essential lipids whose specification has varied from 2 to 10% for the FFM (Brodie et al., 1998; Keys & Brozek, 1953). Because of the imprecise definition of LBM, this term has led to much confusion in the literature and is often erroneously used as a synonym for FFM. The fat and FFM are chemical concepts without anatomical or physiological basis. It is composed of the fat-free tissues and fat-free fluids of the body. For its density to be constant requires that both the following conditions be satisfied simultaneously: 1) the proportions of all the fat-free tissues (FF muscle, FF bone, FF skin, FF organs, etc.) must be fixed and thus constant; and 2) the densities of these fat-free components must be constant.

In addition to FFM and LBM, the anatomical concept of ATFM (Table 1) was proposed as a normalizing approach for interpopulations comparisons (Clarys & Martin, 1985). With the confounding effect of the high variability of AT removed, the composition of the ATFM shows smaller deviations of its components and smaller differences between males and females than when body mass is used as a reference (Martin & Drinkwater, 1991). Changing from FFM to LBM and/or to ATFM is susceptible to significant error (Clarys et al., 2010a). As a result and within the 2C models fat + FFM and AT + ATFM we are dealing with two totally different models … a chemical 2C model and an anatomical 2C model (Figure 2). Pragmatic observers may recognize the 4C model of Widdowson et al. (1951) and the 4C or 5C models of Matiegka (1921) and Clarys et al. (1984) as respectively chemical and anatomical alternatives also.

To illustrate some of the problems caused by the failure of these assumptions and as a result of the terminology confusions Table 2 shows the results of so-called "chemical" %fat determinations on one single male subject on the same day. These results should have been identical or at least similar between methods and compared to the HD reference, but aren't. Some methods, indeed may suggest "chemical fat = lipids", e.g. dual energy X-ray absorptiometry, but other methods, e.g. Jackson and Pollock's formula (1978) with its anthropometrical parameters suggest the measurement of AT. Finally, bio-electrical impedance analysis (BIA) and HD are nor chemical nor anatomical techniques.

Chemical 2C model	**Anatomical 2C model**
Fat **(= lipids)** **+** **Fat Free Mass (FFM)** **(= fluids + proteins + body minerals)**	**Adipose tissue** **(= subcutaneous + intramuscular + internal)** **+** **Adipose Tissue Free Mass (ATFM)** **(= skin + muscles + bone + organs)**

Fig. 2. Two-component models … two different worlds

Method	Predicted whole body %fat
Anthropometry (Deurenberg et al., 1991)	25.1
(Jackson and Pollock, 1978)	12.1
Dual energy X-ray absorptiometry	17.5
Bio-electrical Impedance Analysis	21.5
Hydrodensitometry (Siri formula)	26.8

Table 2. Predicted %fat by 4 different methods on one single male subject on the same day

2.4 Variation of bone density and water content of body tissues

It needs repeating that HD does not take into account density differences and water content variations of its lean tissues (fat-free or adipose-free). Bone is the tissue with the highest density and varies physiologically with age and exercising habits, while water is the element fluctuating most within the lean tissue component (Clarys et al., 1999, 2005, 2010a; Johansson et al., 1993).

In HD, but also in newer technologies, e.g. DXA body fat is calculated on the constancy assumption that ≈73% of LBM is water (Brommage, 2003; Clasey et al., 1999; Eston et al., 2005; Prior et al., 1997). This assumed constancy of hydration e.g. the observed ratio of total body water to FFM was confirmed by Wang et al. (1999). However, this assumption is subject to some questions that highlight the need for more research on the matter. Viewing Tissue Water Content (TWC) obtained by lyophilisation (Table 4) in several studies, one can make two observations: 1) assuming a constant % of water in FFM may be jeopardized by the variable TWC within and between the tissues that compose FFM; and 2) water content in AT is highly variable e.g. ranging from ±17% to ±84%. The studies of Wang et al. (1995, 1999) did indeed raise the question "Does body adiposity influence hydration?". The data in Table 3 and 4 clearly suggest that whatever constancy claimed it cannot be maintained. Component models should allow for hydration variability. According to Fogelholm et al.

(1997) knowledge of the hydration household is recommended when assessing changes in BC during substantial weight reduction.

	Muscle	Skin	Viscera	Bone	AT
Forbes & Lewis (1956) (n=2)	1) 67.5 2) 68.2	53.7 51.8	73.4 72.0	26.8 31.6	26.2 18.3
Mitchell et al. (1945) (n=1)	79.5	64.7	76.6	31.8	50.1
Cooper et al. (1956) (n=2)	1) 68.9 2) 77.3	53.5 72.5	73.7 77.8	30.2 39.5	16.8 83.9
Forbes et al. (1953) (n=1)	70.1	57.7	73.3	28.2	23.0
Clarys et al. (1999) (n=6)	70.8	63.2	79.1	---	21.6

Table 3. Water content (%) of lean and adipose tissue masses in humans (lyophilisation)

Table 4 on the other hand, lists direct mean densities of separate bones of the body. Different bone dimensions, a maximum difference between bones of 0.406 g/ml and all densities superior to 1.100 g/ml will influence the density of the LBM. No doubt that the amount of variance shown will lead equally to serious error in the densitometric prediction of body fat (Clarys et al., 2010a).

Bone	Density (g/ml) mean ± sd
Pelvis	1.164 ± 0.037
Tibia	1.242 ± 0.055
Humerus	1.262 ± 0.054
Femur	1.267 ± 0.053
Clavicula	1.315 ± 0.058
Radius	1.353 ± 0.070
Ulna	1.395 ± 0.078
Cranium	1.403 ± 0.061
Mandibula	1.570 ± 0.100
Mean separate bones	1.330 ± 0.053
Whole skeleton	1.236 ± 0.039

Table 4. Mean densities (g/ml) of separate bones and of the whole skeleton (n=25)

The step from "error" to "hazard" is not too difficult and for the purpose we have reproduced the basic plot of Siri's equation (Figure 1) allowing for the prediction of fat. Applying the values ρ_{FFM} = 1,100 g/ml and ρ_{Fat} = 0,901 g/ml, one recognizes the well-known equation of Siri (1956). The plot of this equation shown in Figure 1 is projected beyond the normal range (0,901-1,100) for whole body density. Typical fat values for young males (16%) and young females (22%) are illustrated. The negative region indicates clearly that if whole body densities greater than 1,100 g/ml are observed then negative values of body fat will be predicted. The occurrence of such values would be a clear indication of violation of the assumption of constant density for the FFM. Negative values of body fat presumably have been omitted as erroneous in the past and one can assume that many of these data never were published. A review of the literature, however, reveals a few studies showing these anomalous fat estimations. Repeating these data will complete the whole picture as stated in the purpose. In a study of 20 elite middle-distance and marathon runners, Pollock et al. (1977) found that 5 had predicted body fat less than 2%. The leanest of these had a total estimated fat content of 120 g, less than the amount typically found in the brain or vertebral column alone. In addition, this subject displayed measurable subcutaneous AT since the sum of the 7 skinfolds taken was 31,5 mm, an average of 4,5 mm per skinfold. This average corresponds with the absolute maximum skin thickness to be found in the shoulder region (Clarys et al., 2005). In young males, body densities of 1,102 g/ml and 1,104 g/ml have been measured, corresponding to -0,8% and -1,6% fat, respectively (Behnke et al., 1942; Katch & Michael, 1968). However, it is for lean mesomorphs that the most anomalous results have been found. In a study of 29 Canadian professional football players, Adams et al. (1982) found that 12 had predicted fat (from density) less than 2%. Of these, nine had an estimated amount of fat ranging from zero% fat to -12% fat. Table 5 shows whole-body density, predicted fat percentage and the sum of 10 skinfolds for each of these 9 subjects.

Subject number	Body density (g/ml)	%fat (Siri's equation)	Sum of 10 skinfolds (mm)
22	1.100	0.0	63
16	1.101	-0.4	74
24	1.102	-0.8	57
2	1.103	-1.2	55
5	1.103	-1.2	97
9	1.105	-2.0	69
26	1.105	-2.0	87
28	1.129	-11.6	64
25	1.130	-12.0	88

Table 5. Negative body fat predictions for 9 professional football players (Adams et al., 1982)

Evidence was presented that the variations in bone density and H_2O content of tissues in the composition of the FFM are considerably greater than suggested by previous researchers. For a lean male of whole body density 1,100 g/ml, a measurement deviation as small as ±0,020 g/ml leads to percent fat predictions ranging from +8,3% to -8,0%. This variability explains the inaccuracy of body fat predictions observed by some researchers when applying conventional HD.

2.5 Validity of hydrodensitometry

In combination with the subject's cooperation dependence, its related error allowance, whole body density and the derived %fat is affected with a serious violation of its basic assumptions and can no longer be considered as valid, not to mention as a criterion measure. Whole body density may not be confounded with single tissue density, which remains a useful biological parameter since it produces indication of changing tissue proportions and ad hoc density patterns within the body. Consideration should be given to the undeniable fact that many if not most *in vivo* whole body fat and AT determination methods have been validated with HD. For the practitioner or the research laboratory that does not have the resources to have higher order models or imaging possibilities such as MRI or CT, the acceptance and enforcement of the hypothesis that HD and the 2C model are not appropriate and that consequently it should be banned from operation is a too strong message that may not be extrapolated to predictive survey research and may not suggest that all methods and techniques derived or validated against HD are also invalid and obsolete (Clarys et al., 2010a).

3. Controversial use of body mass index in longevity

The body mass index (BMI) and waist circumference (WC) are parameters used in the screening for and classification of overweight and obesity in adult individuals, based on their respective (apparent) correlation with total body and visceral adiposity (NHLBI, 1998; WHO Obesity, 2000). These relationships, however, are based on indirect estimations of adiposity and/or other prediction values (Baumgartner et al., 1995; Clarys et al., 1999; Scafoglieri et al., 2009). In fact, the validation of BMI and WC as indicators of adiposity has principally been performed against 2C or 3C models of BC such as HD, BIA or DXA. These reference standards are based on predictive equations that assume constancy and/or homogeneity of the compartments without taking into account the human biological variation of tissue composition (Clarys et al., 2009, 2010b; Deurenberg, 2003; Heymsfield et al., 1997; Scafoglieri et al., 2009, 2010). Ideally, validation as markers of adiposity should be performed against multi-compartment models of BC as provided by three-dimensional imaging techniques such as CT and MRI or against direct measurements of AT such as total body carbon assessment and whole-body dissection (Heymsfield et al., 1997; Kvist et al., 1988; Ludesher et al., 2009). Even though CT and MRI are often cited as in vivo reference standards for the quantification of tissue-system level components, publications describing validation of these techniques with human cadavers remain scarce (Abate et al., 1994; Foster et al., 1984; Janssens et al., 1994; Mitsiopoulos et al., 1998; Rossner et al., 1990; Scafoglieri et al., 2010).

Emerging evidence indicates that health-related assessment of BC in the elderly is more appropriate if muscle mass and adiposity are considered jointly, instead of separately (Rolland et al., 2009; Zamboni et al., 2008). In this context, BMI has been suggested as a powerful indicator of muscle mass in elderly persons (as determined by DXA) (Iannuzzi-Sucich et al., 2002). Sarcopenia, defined as age-related loss of skeletal muscle mass, creates a major BC change that contributes to a large percentage of disability with increasing age (Bautmans et al., 2009; Janssen et al., 2002b). In parallel, ageing is accompanied by an increase in visceral adiposity, which is a known risk factor for morbidity and mortality, even when the total amount of AT remains constant (Zamboni et al., 1997). Because AT replaces lean tissue with increasing age, older subjects tend to present a greater proportion of AT compared to younger individuals with the same BMI (Baumgartner et al., 1995; Elia, 2001).

It remains unclear how BMI and WC relate to BC measures in the elderly. Therefore the aim of this chapter section is to explore the relationship of BMI and WC with important metabolic tissues masses, in particular with muscle tissue mass, with adipose tissue mass, with muscle/AT mass ratios and with trunk adipose tissue distribution, based on an anatomical 5C model obtained by dissection of cadavers of elderly persons.

3.1 Methodology

By means of a will system, adult Belgian citizens can donate their bodies for medical and scientific research purposes to the university of their choice. All data were collected in the Department of Anatomy at the Vrije Universiteit Brussel (Brussels, Belgium) during separate whole-body dissection projects known as the BCAS (Clarys et al., 1984, 1999; Janssens et al., 1994). The most common cause of death of the subjects was heart disease (Table 6).

	Female (n = 17)	Male (n = 12)
Natural	5	6
Heart attack	6	4
Stroke	1	0
Accident	1	0
Cancer	2	1
Renal insufficiency	1	0
Respiratory insufficiency	0	1
Leukemia	1	0

Table 6. Causes of Death of the Subjects (official diagnose on death certificate)

Data from 29 well-preserved white Caucasian cadavers of subjects aged 65 years and over (17 female and 12 male) are reported here. Out of one BCAS project 14 female and 9 male cadavers were included, with a mean age of 77,5 ± 6,9 years (Clarys et al., 1984, 1999). Data from three male and three female additional cadavers with a mean age of 80,7 ± 6,8 years were obtained from another BCAS dissection project (Clarys et al., 1999; Janssens et al., 1994). All cadavers were embalmed within 48 hours after death. All applicable institutional, governmental and legal regulations concerning the ethical approval of human volunteers were followed during the study.

The BCAS projects provided anthropometric measures allowing for the calculation of BMI and WC. Supine length was measured with the cadaver on a horizontal surface, using a custom-made anthropometer. Body mass index was calculated as weight divided by height squared (kg/m^2). For ease of measurement, the cadaver was suspended by an adapted orthopaedic head harness, and manipulated by a pulley attached to the ceiling. Waist circumference (the smallest girth between the iliac crest and the costal border) was measured with a flexible plastic tape ruler to the nearest 0.1 cm. All measurements were performed with the cadaver warmed to ambient temperature (24°C) in order to limit temperature-related differences in texture and mobility of the skin and AT.

The cadavers were weighed immediately before dissection, which started in the early morning and continued until completion (± 14-20h later). All cadavers were dissected into their various components expressed on the tissue-system level i.e. skin, muscle, adipose tissue, viscera and bones; which were weighed to the nearest 0.001kg with dehydration reduced to a minimum (Wang et al., 1992). Detailed methodology of dissection procedures has been reported elsewhere (Clarys et al., 1984, 1999; Martin et al., 2003a). The evaporative loss of body fluid during the dissection was calculated as the difference between total body weight before dissection and total tissue weight after dissection. The individual loss in each cadaver was allocated back to the different tissues in proportion to their respective masses. After this correction, the sum of the weights of all dissected tissues was equal to the cadaver's whole body weight prior to dissection.

Six body segments were defined: the four limbs, trunk and head. Weights of all tissues were recorded as total body adipose tissue mass (AT), trunk subcutaneous adipose tissue mass

(SAT) and trunk internal adipose tissue mass (IAT, the sum of intra-abdominal AT (i.e. visceral and retroperitoneal AT) and intra-thoracic AT), muscle tissue mass, bone tissue mass, skin tissue mass and visceral tissue mass.

Three measures of muscle to adipose tissue proportions were considered: the ratio of muscle mass to AT, the ratio of muscle mass to IAT and the ratio of muscle mass to SAT. Two measures of regional trunk adipose tissue proportion were calculated also: the ratio of IAT to AT and the ratio of IAT to SAT.

Statistical Package for Social Sciences (version 17.0.1 for Windows, SPSS Inc, Chicago, USA) was used for the data analysis. Data are reported as mean ± standard deviation. Normality of data distributions was verified using Kolmogorov-Smirnov Goodness of Fit test (p>0.05). Gender differences in BC were calculated using unpaired t-tests. The relationships of BMI and WC with BC constituents were assessed using Pearson correlation coefficients. Subjects were classified according to BMI based on the International Classification of adult underweight (BMI ≤ 18,5 kg/m^2), overweight (BMI ≥ 25 kg/m^2) and obesity (BMI ≥ 30 kg/m2) as defined by the WHO (2000). Females and males were also classified in low-risk (females, < 80 cm; males, < 94 cm), moderate-risk (females, ranging from 80 cm to 88 cm; males, ranging from 94 cm to 102 cm) and high-risk (females, ≥ 88 cm; males, ≥ 102 cm) WC categories as proposed by Lean and colleagues (1995).

3.2 Direct relationship of body mass index with body tissue distribution

Total body weight (BW) for the whole sample before dissection was 60,0 ± 12,9 kg. Evaporative loss of fluid (ELF) during dissection was 2,0 ± 0,6 kg and the accuracy of the whole-body dissection method (ELF/BW) ranged from 0,6% to 6,8% (mean = 3,3 ± 1,3%).

Compared to female, male were significantly taller (p<0.01) and showed lower AT (p<0.05), higher muscle (p<0.01), bone (p<0.001) and visceral tissue masses (p<0.05); higher muscle to AT ratio and muscle to SAT ratio (p<0.01), and higher proportions of IAT (p<0.01) (Table 7). No significant gender differences were found for age, weight, BMI and WC.

BMI and WC were significantly and positively related to various tissue masses in both sexes (Table 8). Muscle tissue, AT and IAT correlated better with BMI (r-values between 0.68 and 0.89) than with WC (r-values between 0.49 and 0.71). SAT correlated equally well with BMI (r-values between 0.61 and 0.78) and with WC (r-values between 0.62 and 0.83).

Both in females and in males BMI was significantly and inversely related with ratios of muscle mass to AT masses (Table 8). Both muscle tissue mass and AT masses increase with BMI in a quasi-linear manner; their ratio, however, decreases with increasing BMI. Visual inspection of BC graphs revealed major differences in muscle tissue mass proportions according to gender and WHO cutoff-values for BMI. For example, the ratio of muscle mass to AT mass ranged from 0,5 to 2,5 in males with normal BMI-values, and the ratio of muscle mass to IAT mass was not significantly different in subjects with normal BMI compared to those presenting an elevated BMI (Figure 3).

Waist circumference correlated significantly and inversely with ratios of muscle mass to AT masses in females, but not in males (Table 8). Visual inspection of BC graphs revealed important differences in muscle tissue mass proportions based on WC categories, similar to those found based on BMI-classification. This is not surprising given the fact that BMI and WC are highly correlated both in females (r=0.77; p<0.001) and in males (r=0.91; p<0.001).

	Female (n = 17) Mean ± sd (range)	Male (n = 12) Mean ± sd (range)
Physical characteristics		
Age (years)	79,9 ± 7,1 (68-94)	75,6 ± 6,1 (65-87)
Weight (kg)	58,8 ± 11,6 (32,0-75,4)	61,7 ± 14,9 (38,5-85,7)
Height (m)	1,59 ± 0,07 (1,46-1,73)	1,67 ± 0,06 (1,60-1,80)†
BMI (kg/m²)	23,4 ± 4,6 (12,9-30,9)	21,9 ± 4,3 (14,7-28,4)
Underweight (n)	2	2
Normal weight (n)	9	7
Overweight (n)	4	4
Obese (n)	1	0
WC (cm)	80,4 ± 7,3 (69,7-94,0)	83,4 ± 7,0 (73,1-94,3)
Low-risk (n)	9	10
Moderate-risk (n)	6	1
High-risk (n)	2	1
Body composition		
Total body adipose tissue (kg)	23,2± 8,9 (4,6-40,1)	16,4 ± 6,8 (5,7-25,7)*
Trunk Subcutaneous AT (kg)	7,6 ± 3,1 (2,5-13,4)	5,4 ± 2,7 (2,6-10,4)
Trunk Internal AT (kg)	3,1 ± 1,7 (0,3-5,8)	3,0 ± 1,6 (0,5-5,3)
Skin (kg)	3,2 ± 0,6 (1,7-4,1)	3,5 ± 0,7 (2,5-4,7)
Muscle (kg)	17,1 ± 3,2 (12,2-23,4)	22,5 ± 6,2 (14,0-34,8)†
Bone (kg)	7,7 ± 0,8 (6,7-10,0)	9,6 ± 1,5 (7,4-12,6)‡
Viscera (kg)	7,5 ± 1,4 (5,8-10,7)	9,8 ± 3,2 (6,3-18,9*
Muscle/AT	0,90 ± 0,53 (0,36-2,70)	1,56 ± 0,57 (0,65-2,46)†
Muscle/IAT	9,4 ± 10,8 (2,4-46,2)	10,7 ± 7,7 (3,1-26,9)
Muscle/SAT	2,7 ± 1,2 (1,0-5,0)	4,9 ± 1,8 (2,0-9,1)†
IAT/AT (%)	12,6 ± 3,5 (5,3-17,6)	17,6 ± 5,3 (9,1-24,8)†
IAT/SAT (%)	40,5 ± 15,5 (10,9-73,9)	58,9 ± 27,9 (18,8-116,9)*

Table 7. Physical Characteristics and Body Composition of the Subjects (sd = standard deviation, BMI=body mass index, n=total number of subjects, WC=waist circumference, AT=total body adipose tissue, IAT=trunk internal adipose tissue, SAT=trunk subcutaneous adipose tissue.*p<0,05,†p<0,01,‡p<0,001)

	BMI		WC	
	Female	Male	Female	Male
Muscle	0.68†	0.89‡	0.50*	0.71†
AT	0.80‡	0.84†	0.67†	0.70*
IAT	0.72†	0.68*	0.49*	0.44
SAT	0.61†	0.78†	0.62†	0.83†
Muscle/AT	-0.67†	-0.62*	-0.64†	-0.49
Muscle/IAT	-0.63†	-0.68*	-0.55*	-0.36
Muscle/SAT	-0.54*	-0.42	-0.55*	-0.57
IAT/AT	0.54*	0.40	0.23	0.07
IAT/SAT	0.50*	0.18	0.16	-0.09

Table 8. Pearson correlation coefficients for the relationships of BMI and WC with BC in 17 female and 12 male cadavers by dissection (BMI=body mass index, WC=waist circumference, AT=total body adipose tissue, IAT=trunk internal AT, SAT=trunk subcutaneous AT. *p<0,05,†p<0,01,‡p<0,001)

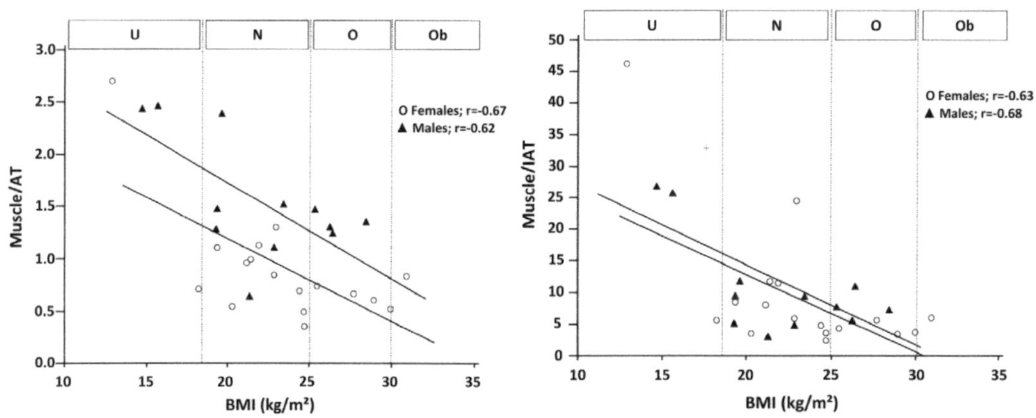

Fig. 3. Relationship of BMI with muscle tissue mass proportions in 29 elderly cadavers (U=underweight, BMI<18,5; N=normal weight, 18,5≤BMI<25; O=overweight, 25≤BMI<30; Ob=obese, BMI≥30)

Body mass index correlated significantly to measures of trunk adipose tissue proportions in females, but not in males (p<0.05; Table 3). Waist circumference was not significantly related to the ratio of IAT to AT nor to the ratio of IAT to SAT in our sample (p>0.05; see Table 3). Visual inspection of the graphs shows that trunk AT distribution varies considerably between sexes and within categories. For example, the ratio of IAT to SAT was not different between low-risk and moderate-risk females (Figure 4).

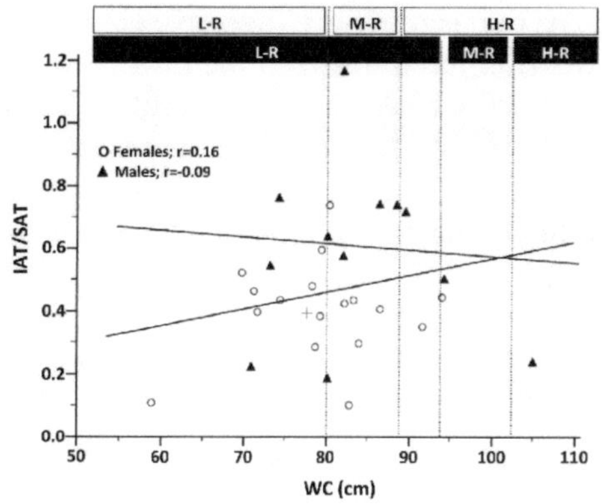

Fig. 4. Relationship of WC with trunk adipose tissue distribution in 29 elderly cadavers (□ = Female categories: L-R=low-risk, WC<80cm; M-R=moderate-risk, 80cm≤WC<88cm; H-R=high-risk, WC≥88cm; ■ = Male categories:. L-R=low-risk, WC<94cm; M-R=moderate-risk, 94cm≤WC<102cm; H-R=high-risk, WC≥102cm).

3.3 Inter-individual and sex specific differences in body composition

Understanding the relationship between BMI, WC and BC in the elderly may provide better interpretation of these measures in clinical practice (Bedogni et al., 2001). The exact determination of the muscle and adipose tissue compartments is difficult in living humans, and mainly based on 'reference' BC methods such as CT or MRI (Abate et al., 1994; Mitsiopoulos et al., 1998). It needs consideration that this is the first report relating BMI and WC to directly obtained measurements of the muscle and adipose tissue compartments in elderly subjects (Martin et al., 2003a; Scafoglieri et al., 2010).

The present design is unique in the sense that it requires no assumptions regarding the measurement and the calculation of the BC constituents. It shows that moderate to strong relationships of BMI and WC with absolute tissue masses and with muscle tissue mass proportions in elderly subjects exist. These results confirm the findings of previous validation work using CT and MRI on living subjects (Ferrannini et al., 2008; Kvist et al., 1988; Lee et al., 2000; Ludesher et al., 2009). However cautious clinical interpretation is warranted since important inter-individual differences in tissue proportions were found in subjects with similar BMI and/or WC values.

Sarcopenic-obesity has been defined as a condition in elderly persons reflected by low muscle mass (sarcopenia) in combination with high AT mass (obesity) (Zamboni et al., 2008). Although it is unclear which clinical condition, sarcopenia or obesity, may precede in the development of sarcopenic-obesity, it is suggested that the age-related increase in adipose tissue mass generally precedes the loss of skeletal muscle mass (Rolland et al., 2009). The BMI and WC may offer the clinician a practical anthropometric measurement for assessing a subject's whole body and visceral AT content. In our sample sex specific differences in BC were found, elderly females proportionally having more adipose tissue than males of similar age and BMI, who in turn are more muscular. Consequently the ratio of muscle mass to total body AT mass was found to be significantly higher in males compared to females. The observation that BMI is significantly and inversely related to the ratio of muscle to total body AT mass for both sexes in the present study, might validate the association of BMI with the lean/fat ratio as determined by BIA (Ozenoglu et al., 2009). It has to be pointed out that the significant inverse relationship between BMI and the measures of muscle mass distribution in this sample may result from the high muscle tissue proportions of the individuals classified as underweight. It has been suggested previously that regional muscle/AT ratio is closely related to aging and to visceral AT accumulation (Kitajima et al., 2010). Interestingly and in contrast to the sex specific differences in total body adiposity and muscularity, internal AT mass was not different between females and males in our sample. Since the latter represents a major metabolic compartment within the body, this observation might be of great importance. Although BMI is related to IAT in the present study, it has to be pointed out that important inter-individual differences within and between adjacent WHO-classifications do exist. Elderly individuals with similar BMI-values do not necessarily present similar levels of internal adiposity. This observation might jeopardize the clinical interpretation of the association between BMI and BC compartments based on BMI alone. These results suggest that additional assessment (such as imaging methods) may be indicated in order to quantify this important metabolic compartment. In this context, it has been suggested that ultrasound is able to account for visceral adiposity although this may be debatable (Martin et al., 2003b).

Besides the determination of absolute AT quantities, its distribution within the body is an important health consideration (Baumgartner et al., 1995). It is well known that visceral AT concentration carries greater cardiovascular health risk compared to subcutaneous AT accumulation (Larsson et al., 1992). Visceral AT and subcutaneous AT can predict different health-risks, based on their own morphological and functional features, even for a given level of abdominal adiposity (Sniderman et al., 2007). Visceral AT has been repeatedly linked to an increased risk of dyslipidemia, dysglycemia and vascular disease. By contrast, subcutaneous AT has been associated with better metabolic outcomes. This study observed sex specific differences in trunk adipose tissue distribution. Elderly males showed lower AT mass but higher proportions of internal AT compared to females of similar age and similar BMI. This observation supports previous findings as determined by MRI (Ferrannini et al., 2008). In our sample BMI was positively related to regional AT distribution in females only, suggesting that BMI-values do not allow distinction between internal and subcutaneous AT accumulation in elderly males. This is partly in agreement with the findings of Seidell et al. (1987) who found no significant correlations between BMI and the ratio of visceral to subcutaneous AT area using CT in a younger population (Seidell et al., 1987). Waist circumference is generally accepted as a practical measurement for assessing a subjects visceral AT content. However, since WC is a composite measure of visceral and subcutaneous AT, it might not distinguish visceral from subcutaneous AT. To our knowledge, no recent studies are available reporting the relationship of WC with trunk AT distribution (as defined in this chapter). In the present study, WC was not significantly correlated to measures of trunk AT distribution, such as the ratio of IAT to SAT. It should also be observed that WC was a better correlate of SAT than of IAT in both sexes, suggesting that WC might be a more appropriate indicator of subcutaneous than of internal adiposity, in particular in elderly males. This observation supports previous findings using MRI in vivo (Ferrannini et al., 2008). These results indicate that inter-individual differences in trunk adipose tissue composition might not be detected by simple anthropometric measures such as BMI or WC, in particular in elderly persons.

3.4 Limitations of post mortem cadaver dissections

The 'reference' method for the determination of BC presented here was cadaver dissection. Although this method has limitations including tissue dehydration, an age matched in vivo and post mortem constitutional and anthropometric comparison has shown an overall similarity of macroscopic characteristics between subjects (Clarys et al., 2006). Since no data are available on the duration of the clinical-pathologic status of the subjects, it remains unclear to which extent body composition might have been affected in the chronically ill subjects (n=6). On the other hand, it has to be pointed out that adiposity indices such as BMI and WC are regularly used in the evaluation and follow-up of the nutritional status both in healthy elderly and in patients. The precision of our method to determine BC averaged 3,3%, which indicates that dehydration and/or losses of material during the dissection procedures were negligible. It is therefore unlikely that the method of choice biased the results presented here. Moreover the mean difference between actual weight and CT derived or MRI estimated weight reaches 5,6% to 6,0%, the latter being considered as a gold standard method in BC (Baumgartner et al., 1995; Clarys et al., 1999). An inevitable restriction proper to a whole-body dissection is the relatively limited number of individuals whose BC can be determined. This is due to the work-related intensity of the dissection procedures combined with the limited availability of subjects. Results of the nature as presented here should preferably be confirmed in a larger sample, but one must realize that such opportunities and possibilities will remain very cumbersome, difficult and scarce.

3.5 Critical appraisal of the Body Mass Index as a body composition tool

This post mortem *in vitro* evaluation suggests that BMI and WC are significantly related with adipose tissue mass and with several ratio's of muscle to adipose tissue in elderly subjects. However elderly persons with similar BMI and/or WC values do not necessarily present similar tissue mass proportions, limiting their use when comparing individual BC within and between adjacent classification systems. Since BMI and WC are composite measures of BC, assessment of important metabolic body compartments themselves is warranted in elderly persons (Scafoglieri et al., 2010).

4. Dual energy X-ray absorptiometry: What are we measuring?

Although BC data acquisition and ad hoc analysis are both popular and important, selecting an appropriate method or technique for accurate and/or precise assessment of individuals and/or groups remains a challenging task within various sectors of public health. Since the fifties and sixties, with the pioneer work of Keys & Brozek (1953), Forbes et al. (1956), Siri (1956), Brozek et al. (1963), Behnke (1963), Durnin & Rahaman (1967), body composition almost became a scientific discipline profiling itself with the development of many methods, techniques and equipment. Popular approaches have been criticized over the years because they are subject to measurement errors and/or violation of basic assumptions underlying their use such as HD (Clasey et al., 1999; Elowsson et al., 1998; Heyward, 1996; Johansson et al., 1993; Prior et al., 1997) or anthropometry e.g. skinfolds (Beddoe, 1998; Clarys et al., 1987, 2005; Martin et al., 1985, 1992) and the universally accepted new method of choice, the dual energy X-ray absorptiometry or DXA (Bolotin, 1998, 2007; Bolotin & Sievanen, 2001; Bolotin et al., 2001; Clarys et al., 2010b; Provyn et al., 2008).

4.1 Validation of dual energy X-ray absorptiometry

Curiously, after reviewing the literature of DXA application, one cannot avoid obtaining a very controversial impression of this new method. On the other hand, we find an important number of validation and application studies that support the DXA technique as convenient, as the criterion for %fat, for lean body mass (LBM), and as a criterion for bone mineral content (BMC) (Clasey et al., 1999; Haarbo et al., 1991; Johansson et al., 1993; Prior et al., 1997; Pritchard et al., 1993). A number of authors as mentioned in Provyn et al. (2008) suggest DXA as the gold standard for validation of other techniques essential for the measurement of BC (Eston et al., 2005; Poortmans et al., 2005; Salamone et al., 2000). In addition to the violation of basic assumptions as referred to earlier, one needs to repeat and underline that DXA, hydrodensitometry, anthropometry, air-, gas- and water displacement methods, bioelectrical impedance (BIA) are all indirect *in vivo* techniques for measuring BC. Validation or even cross-validation in between indirect methods cannot guarantee both accuracy and reality precision. Perfect correlations and low coefficients of variation allow for good predictions and assumptions only (Bolotin & Sievanen, 2001; Provyn et al., 2008). Possibly the greatest problems with accuracy/precision in DXA are found with fat and lean tissue estimates (Prentice, 1995), with its projected areal bone density (Bolotin, 2007; Bolotin et al., 2001; Clarys et al., 2008) and with the basic confusion between overall BC terminology e.g. fat, adipose tissue (AT), fat free mass (FFM), LBM, lean, adipose tissue free mass (ATFM), bone mineral density (BMD), surface and volume density, bone mineral content (BMC), ash weight, actual mineral content and BMC, with or without soft tissue covering (Clarys et al., 2010b; Martin et al., 1985; Provyn et al., 2008; Wadden & Didie, 2003).

These issues give rise to concern, but the accuracy of absorptiometry can be affected by the choice of calibrating materials. As a consequence, both absolute and relative values can differ substantially between manufacturers, between instruments and the ad hoc software used (Clasey et al., 1999; Prentice, 1995). Despite the multitude of DXA validation studies and despite the related controversy of its measuring quality, it is being reaffirmed that there have been comparatively few validation experiments of accuracy and precision of either bone or body composition measurements by cadaver and/or carcass analysis. More of these validations against direct values are necessary before we can be confident about the accuracy of absorptiometry (Prentice, 1995). A review of the state of the art of carcass studies related to DXA (Clarys et al., 2008) reveals validation attempts with rhesus monkeys (Black et al., 2001), mice (Brommage, 2003; Nagy & Clair, 2000), piglets (Chauhan et al., 2003; Elowsson et al., 1998; Koo et al., 2002, 2004; Picaud et al., 1996; Pintauro et al., 1996), pigs (Lukaski et al., 1999; Mitchell et al., 1996, 1998), pig hind legs (Provyn et al., 2008), chickens (Mitchell et al., 1997; Swennen et al., 2004) and with dogs and cats (Speakman et al., 2001). The majority of these validation studies were based on chemical analysis and only a few on direct dissection comparison. Almost all studies indicated perfect correlations for all variables with DXA, but approximately half of the results of the various variables were found to be significantly different ($p<0.001$ and $p<0.05$). In approximately a third of these studies, DXA was suggested to be valid and accurate for all its variables, while two studies indicated significant differences and/or erroneous data at all levels and for all variables. However, two important statements resulting from these studies are retained: a) dissection and direct comparison combined with bone ashing is considered the most accurate and direct validation technique (Elowsson et al., 1998) and b) further research with direct dissection and ashing is needed (Prentice, 1995), in particular, with focus on the influence of abdominal and thoracic organs associated with dispersed gas/air pockets and internal panniculus adiposus (Provyn et al., 2008). Since BC measurements by DXA are increasingly used in clinical practice and because dissection is the best possible direct measure, no study has been giving clarity yet about the content and meaning of "lean" as produced by DXA, different intra-tissue combinations, e.g., skin, muscle, viscera and bone will be related to the DXA-lean variable. Exact knowledge of what is the content of the meaning of "lean" as measured by DXA is mandatory. In this chapter section we will compare DXA fan beam data, with both dissection and CT scanning data.

4.2 Methodology

Twelve, 6-18 month-old "Belgian Native" pigs were prepared for human consumption and were acquired within 2 days intervals, immediately after electroshock slaughter (6 female and 6 castrated males, mean weight ± standard deviation (sd), 39.509 ± 4.335 kg). Special permission was obtained from the Belgian Directorate General of Public Health, Safety of the Food Chain and Environment, for the transport of the carcasses and for the non-removal of abdominal and thoracic content which is a normal procedure in consumption matters. The carcasses were exsanguinated and decapitated between the atlas and the occipital bone. To minimize further dissection error, front and hind legs were disarticulated distal from humeri and femora e.g., on elbow and knee level, respectively. The mean weight ± sd of the remaining carcass plus viscera was 33.051 ± 3.324 kg (whole carcass weights being taken with a digital hang scale (KERN-HUS-150K50) accurate to 50g. The composition of the carcasses was studied in the following order.

A QDR 4500A upgraded to Discovery HOLOGIC DXA device (Hologic, Waltham, MA, USA) utilizes a constant X-ray source producing fan beam dual energy radiation with effective dose equivalents (EDE) of 5 μSv (Prentice, 1995).

The estimations of fat and lean mass are based on extrapolation of the ratio of soft tissue attenuation of two X-ray energies in non-bone-containing pixels. The two X-ray energies are produced by a tungsten stationary anode X-ray tube pulsed alternately as 70 kVp and 140 kVp. The software (for Windows XP version 12.4.3) performs calculations of the differential attenuations of the two photon energies and presents data for each carcass of percentage of fat, fat mass (g), lean mass (g), bone mineral mass (g), BMD in g/cm^2 and total weight. According to the manufacturer, a coefficient of variation (CV) for human BMD of 0.5% can be expected during repeated measurements.

To determine the reliability of DXA measurements, each pig carcass was scanned three times consecutively without (2x) and with (1x) repositioning. From these data, the CV for the different tissue types was calculated.

The DXA equipment was calibrated daily with a spine phantom (supplied by the manufacturers) to assess stability of the measurements, but also calibrated weekly using a step phantom to allow for correction of sources of error related to e.g. skin thickness.

Whole body scans of the pigs were taken with a CT scanner (type Philips Brilliance BZC 16, Koninklijke Philips Electronics NV, Eindhoven, The Netherlands) using the following settings: 120 kVp, 200 mAs, pitch 0.641, slice collimation 64 x 0.625 mm, reconstructed slice width 0.75 mm and using the Brilliance™ V2.3.0.16060 software. Tissues (Adipose tissue = AT, soft tissue = ST and bone = B) were classified based on Hounsfield Units (HU) and their respective volumes were calculated using a maximum likelihood Gaussian mixture estimator implemented in Matlab (The Mathworks Inc., Natick, United States). The following optimal classification scale was employed to determine each tissue: AT: -180..-7 HU; ST: -6..+142 HU and B: +143..+3010 HU (McEvoy et al., 2008; Vester-Christensen et al., 2009). Tissue volumes were multiplied by their reference densities with AT=0.923 g/cm^3, ST=1.040 g/cm^3 and B=1.720 g/cm^3 to obtain tissue weight estimates.

After the DXA measurements, the carcasses were dissected into their various components as expressed on the tissue-level system: skin, muscle, adipose tissue, viscera and bones (Wang et al., 1992). Muscle included tendon, blood vessels and nerves belonging to the ad hoc muscle. The subcutaneous, intramuscular (mostly intra-tendon) and intra-visceral AT was combined as one tissue. Again blood vessels and nerves within AT were attributed to AT. Bones were carefully scraped, ligaments were added with muscle tendons to muscle tissue, and cartilage remained part of the bone tissue.

Seven expert pro-sectors and anatomists worked simultaneously and each dissected particle was collected under cling film and kept in color-labeled, continuously covered plastic containers (12x10x10 cm) of known weight in order to minimize or eliminate evaporation (Clarys et al., 1999, 2010b; Provyn et al., 2008). Full containers mass was measured during the dissection by 2 researchers using Mettler-Toledo digital scales (Excellence XS precision balance Model 40025) accurate to 0.01g. Once a bone was fully prepared, the same procedure was followed but completed with its hydrostatic weight whilst placed in a wire cradle suspended to the same scale allowing for the volume-based bone density (g/cm^3) calculation.

After the dissection and multiple weighing procedures, samples of all tissues of approximately 100g to 150g (min-max) were deep-frozen. Small parts were cut off and weighed in recipients of known weight before lyophilisation overnight. With dried samples, the water content was measured after storing into metal cells, and fat (lipids) extracted with technical Hexane using a Dionex accelerated solvent extractor. After the hexane evaporation of the extraction, total (final) lipid content was determined (weighed).

Part of the dissection protocol of the twelve porcine carcasses was the total defleshing of the skeleton, including the removal of extra-osseous soft tendon and ligament tissue by scraping. Cartilage and intra-osseous tissue (e.g. intervertebral discs) remained intact. The whole skeleton was diamond-cut into pieces in order to fit in the ashing furnace (type Nabertherm, Liliental, Germany). After incineration, each sample was heated using a ramped temperature protocol of two hours to 800°C and ashed for eight hours, as determined by prior pilot work. Before weighing on the Mettler Toledo precision scale (accurate to 0.01g) the ash was cooled undercover and collected in a main container. The ashing of one full porcine skeleton took between 50 to 60 hours.

Data are reported as mean(x) ± standard deviation(sd). Normality of all variables was verified with a Kolmogorov-Smirnov test and all DXA, CT and dissection data were (matrix) compared with Pearson correlation coefficients, while differences were verified with one-way analysis of variance repeated measures (Anova). Reliability and consistency of these results were verified with intra-class correlations (ICC) and Bland-Altman plots were used to access agreement of the direct carcass dissection data with the indirect DXA and CT estimates. All statistical tests were performed using SPSS 16.0 for windows and p values of <0.05 indicated significant differences.

4.3 Definition, quantification and comparison of DXA variables

Comparing directly and indirectly obtained data of masses and densities (e.g. of whole body bone-, adipose- and non adipose tissue) using 3 different techniques yields information on the ad hoc terminology used in the respective methodologies. Table 9 shows an overview of terminology used per technique as applied and the assumed measure of the same values.

Dissection	DXA	CT	Biological background
Total mass (g)	Total mass (g)	Total mass (g)	-
Total tissue mass (g)	Total mass (g)	Total mass (g)	The Σ of all dissected tissue masses
Adipose tissue (g)	Fat (g)	Adipose tissue(g)	AT is an anatomical issue Fat is a chemical issue (e.g. lipids)
Adipose tissue free mass (ATFM) (g)	Lean or lean body mass (LBM)(g)	Fat free mass (FFM) (g)	ATFM is an anatomical concept LBM = FFM plus essential lipids
Skeleton mass (g)	Bone mineral content (BMC)(g)	Bone mass (g)	Skeleton and bone mass are morphological issues; BMC suggests the Σ of all mineral constituents of the skeleton
Skeleton density (g/cm^3)	Bone mineral density(g/cm^2)	Bone density (g/cm^3)	Volume (g/cm^3) based versus surface (g/cm^2) based density

Table 9. Different terminologies assumed to measure a similar outcome (DXA=dual energy X-ray absorptiometry, CT=computed tomography)

Although the basic assumption of equality of outcome and despite the different terminology used, knowledge of the ad hoc mass and density names will create a better understanding of the respective data acquisitions (e.g. Table 10). Table 10 combines the data acquisition of all directly obtained measures and the complete set of indirect estimates made by DXA and CT. The purpose of this Table 10 is to evaluate the predictive quality of both DXA and CT, but also to evaluate precision and accuracy between direct and indirect values. For a good understanding and despite the significance of a correlation found, this study considers $r \geq 0.90$ as a good, $r \geq 0.80$ as a medium, and $r \geq 0.70$ an average (mediocre) indicator of prediction confirmed or rejected by the ICC. The Anova statistics are considered as an indicator of precision or accuracy. Significant differences are set at $p<0.05$. If not significantly different with the dissection reference, one can assume an acceptable level of measurement precision. A non-significant result between DXA and CT indicates similarity between data only, since DXA nor CT is considered to be a reference in this study.

Table 10 confirms that for almost all soft tissue comparisons, including total masses, a majority of good correlations ($r \geq 0.90$), two medium correlations ($r \geq 0.80$) and two average ($r \geq 0.70$), adiposity prediction expressed in % seems to be problematic for the CT. Despite the majority of good prognoses for prediction related to the dissection reference, we do find significant differences in accuracy for total masses (DXA), adiposity (g and %)(DXA and CT) for all non-adipose soft tissue combinations (DXA and CT) and for all bony comparisons. Except for the ashing, there are indications of acceptable precision and comparability with DXA-BMC. The ICC and the Bland-Altman plots confirm the findings as shown in Table 10.

Variables	Dissection x ± sd	DXA x ± sd	CT x ± sd	r	Anova F	ICC
Total mass(g)	33051.3 ± 3323.8	33192.3 ± 3336.6	--	1.00	17.903†	1.00‡
	33051.3 ± 3323.8	--	33041.7 ± 3337.8	0.99	0.006	0.99‡
	--	33192.3 ± 3336.6	33041.7 ± 3337.8	0.99	1.463	0.99‡
Total tissue mass(g)	32723.4 ± 3427.0	33192.3 ± 3336.6	--	1.00	24.061‡	0.99‡
	32723.4 ± 3427.0	--	33041.7 ± 3337.8	0.98	2.689	0.98‡
Adipose tissue/Fat(g)	3571.6 ± 632.8	5653.1 ± 934.1	--	0.91	268.516‡	0.85‡
Adipose tissue/Adipose tissue(g)	3571.6 ± 632.8	--	5508.3 ± 844.7	0.72	131.446‡	0.69†
Fat/Adipose tissue(g)	--	5653.1 ± 934.1	5508.3 ± 844.7	0.80	0.777	0.80†
Adipose tissue/Fat (%)	10.8 ± 1.27	17.0 ± 1.87	--	0.81	370.409‡	0.76†
Adipose tissue/Adipose tissue(%)	10.8 ± 1.27	--	16.6 ± 1.19	0.31	195.514‡	0.31
Fat/Adipose tissue(%)	--	17.0 ± 1.87	16.6 ± 1.19	0.46	0.594	0.41
ATFM/Lean+BMC(g)	29479.7 ± 2874.7	27544.7 ± 2681.5	--	0.99	227.140‡	0.99‡
ATFM/Soft Tissue+Bone(g)	29479.7 ± 2874.7	--	27525.0 ± 2559.9	0.98	142.665‡	0.98‡
Lean+BMC/Soft Tissue+Bone(g)	--	27544.7 ± 2681.5	27525.0 ± 2559.9	0.97	0.012	0.97‡
Muscle/Lean(g)	17684.3 ± 1908.8	27103.1 ± 2647.3	--	0.95	1012.029‡	0.90‡
Muscle/Soft Tissue(g)	17684.3 ± 1908.8	--	24166.7 ± 2270.1	0.94	790.922‡	0.93‡
Lean/Soft Tissue(g)	--	27103.1 ± 2647.3	24166.7 ± 2270.1	0.97	196.183‡	0.96‡
Skin	1326.7 ± 244.0	--	--	--	--	--
Muscle+skin/Lean(g)	19011.1 ± 2092.3	27103.1 ± 2647.3	--	0.95	960.440‡	0.93‡
Muscle+skin/Soft Tissue(g)	19011.1 ± 2092.3	--	24166.7 ± 2270.1	0.95	642.421‡	0.95‡
Viscera	7465.3 ± 803.8	--	--	--	--	--

Variables	Dissection x ± sd	DXA x ± sd	CT x ± sd	r	Anova F	ICC
Muscle+skin+viscera/Lean(g)	26476.4 ± 2593.8	27103.1 ± 2647.3	--	0.99	61.326‡	0.99‡
Muscle+ skin+viscera/Soft Tissue(g)	26476.4 ± 2593.8	--	24166.7 ± 2270.1	0.97	162.206‡	0.97‡
Skeleton mass/BMC(g)	2505.3 ± 317.5	441.6 ± 64.6	--	0.62	641.302‡	0.24
Skeleton mass/Bone mass(g)	2505.3 ± 317.5	--	3358.3 ± 446.1	0.59	65.404‡	0.55*
BMC/Bone mass(g)	--	441.6 ± 64.6	3358.3 ± 446.1	0.40	566.598‡	0.11
Ash weight/BMC(g)	445.6 ± 66.2	441.6 ± 64.6	--	0.73	0.086	0.73†
Skeleton Density(g/cm^3)/BMD(g/cm^2)	1.201 ± 0.02	0.782 ± 0.09	--	0.68	370.144‡	0.24
Skeleton Density/Bone density(g/cm^3)	1.201 ± 0.02	--	1.720 ± ND	ND	ND	ND
BMD(g/cm^2)/Bone density(g/cm^3)	--	0.782 ± 0.09	1.720 ± ND	ND	ND	ND

Table 10. Comparison between direct dissection data values with the corresponding DXA and CT values (DXA=dual energy X-ray absorptiometry, CT=computed tomography, x=mean, sd=standard deviation, r=Pearson correlation coefficient, ICC=intra-class correlation coefficient, ATFM=adipose tissue free mass, BMC=bone mineral content, $^*p<0.05$, †$p<0.01$, ‡$p<0.001$, ND=not determined, CT considers bone density as a constant value)

4.4 Variation of hydration status and lipid content of tissues

The dissection tissue masses were subdivided according to anatomic segmentation into upper limb, lower limb and trunk (e.g. for skin, muscle and bone). For adipose tissue, additional differentiation was made for subcutaneous (e.g. external) and visceral (e.g. internal) trunk AT. For each segment, the water content and the fat (e.g. lipid) content was determined for the respective tissues and presented as % of the studied mass per tissue in Table 11.

Body fat (BF) is defined as the ether-extractable constituent of body tissues, (Table 11) and must be considered as a chemical component of the body. This is already known since Keys & Brozek (1953). The interchangeable use of the terms BF and AT has led and is leading still to ambiguities and serious error. Amongst all DXA validation studies, only a few (Elowsson et al., 1998; Nagy & Clair, 2000) have defined the meaning of its adiposity variables mentioning or precising as DXA fat and lean against chemical (CHEM Fat and CHEM Lean). Table 1 indicates other discrepancies e.g., for the non-adipose terminology. Adipose tissue free mass is an anatomical concept and lays in the continuation of the AT versus FM. DXA pretends to measure Lean or Lean Body Mass as opposed to FFM, which could be expected since manufacturers claim to measure chemical components.

If we look at the mean value level of the respective variables in Table 10, there cannot be any doubt that both DXA and CT are producing anatomical-morphological quantities, evidently at all adipose and non-adipose combinations. In addition DXA and CT do not take into

Tissue	Segment	Water content (%) x ± sd	Lipid content (%) x ± sd	r
Skin	Upper limb	61.0 ± 8.6	4.6 ± 6.0	- 0.73
	Lower limb	60.7 ± 4.9	4.3 ± 1.4	- 0.55
	Trunk	50.1 ± 9.3	10.2 ± 7.4	- 0.20
Adipose	Subcutaneous Upper limb	47.2 ± 7.0	15.0 ± 7.0	- 0.72
	Subcutaneous Lower limb	47.2 ± 6.6	15.6 ± 6.9	- 0.84†
	Subcutaneous Trunk	21.0 ± 5.3	29.0 ± 7.3	- 0.16
	Visceral Trunk	50.1 ± 10.6	19.0 ± 6.7	- 0.70
Muscle	Upper limb	75.4 ± 1.4	1.4 ± 1.0	- 0.86†
	Lower limb	74.5 ± 2.7	3.1 ± 3.2	0.16
	Trunk	73.8 ± 3.9	3.7 ± 2.3	- 0.70
Bone	Upper limb	39.0 ± 8.2	10.9 ± 2.7	- 0.84†
	Lower limb	39.5 ± 8.1	9.8 ± 1.9	- 0.71
	Trunk	49.4 ± 2.4	7.7 ± 3.3	- 0.20

Table 11. Water (lyophilisation) and lipid (ether extraction) content of different tissues and relationship (x=mean, sd=standard deviation, r=Pearson correlation coefficient, †$p<0.01$)

account the water content and lipid content variations (Table 11) of both its adipose and non adipose constituents. Small variation of tissue hydration may explain important differences of ad hoc estimates (Prior et al., 1997; Wang et al., 1999, 1995).

Both in CT, DXA and other newer technologies (Muller et al., 2003) body fat is calculated on the constancy assumption that ≈73% of LBM (e.g. Lean or Lean + BMC) is water. This assumed constancy of hydration e.g., the observed ratio of total body water to FFM was confirmed in humans by Wang et al. (1999). However, this assumption is subject to some questions that highlight the need for more research on the matter. Viewing Tissue Water Content (TWC) obtained by lyophylisation in several human tissue studies one can make two observations: 1) assuming a constant % of water in FFM may be jeopardized by the variable TWC within and between the tissues that compose FFM; and 2) water content in AT is highly variable e.g. ranging from ±17% to ±84% in humans (Provyn et al., 2008; Clarys et al., 2010a).

This is confirmed in our study on animal corpses with % whole body water content ranging from ±20 to ±50% (Table 11) repeating that the constancies claimed by DXA and CT cannot be maintained (e.g. with fluid ranging between ±50 to ±61% for skin, between ±39 to ±49% for bone but little variability for muscle.

Since no total tissue lipid extraction was carried out because technical circumstances allowed sample fractionation only, lipid content is expressed as % of the measured sample mass. Sample masses being identical for hydration and lipid fractionation (Table 11) one learns that lipid content of tissues is variably related to its ad hoc fluid content, but if the extremities are considered separately one notices an apparent constancy both in hydration and lipid fractionation. The fact that all trunk tissue data (e.g. in skin AT, muscle and bone) deviate both, but non systematically in hydration and lipid content from the upper and lower extremities indicate the importance of the trunk as discriminating segment and the associated abdominal/metabolic syndrome theories. As Elowsson et al. (1998) and Provyn et al. (2008) were previously evaluating the accuracy of DXA with dissection in animals, both studies motivated the choice of using plain carcasses (decapitated pigs without abdominal

and thoracic organs) or just hind legs to minimize various errors. According to Elowsson et al. (1998) with DXA this would marginally increase DXA's underestimation. This can no longer be supported; on the contrary, not measuring the internal trunk will just increase the error because of an assumption of segment constancy of hydration and ad hoc lipid fractionation. Wang et al. (1999) examined *in vitro* and *in vivo* studies allowing a review and critical appraisal of the importance of hydration of FFM and confirming the findings of Provyn et al. (2008). They conclude that, even though methodological limitations preclude a highly accurate analysis, adult mammals, including humans, share in common, a relatively constant hydration of FFM. The segmental data presented in Table 11 within a 4C dissection model dismisses the idea of constant hydration of FFM. In addition, the assumed ad hoc constancy of 0.73 cannot be retained.
The question whether the hydration status of FFM or LBM or ATFM reflects physiologic regulatory mechanisms (Going et al., 1993; Wang et al., 2005) cannot be answered, but it seems that trunk non-adipose tissues may affect hydration differently than the lean tissues of the extremities or vice-versa (Table 11).

4.5 Critical appraisal of DXA variables

Regardless of the existing mechanisms and regardless of the hydration and lipid (fat) content of non-adipose tissue, this macro quality evaluation has not been able to detect what the content is of the DXA non-adipose variables, e.g., "lean" and/or "lean + BMC". We still do not know what DXA is exactly measuring under these ad hoc headings. "Lean" compared with muscle tissue, with muscle plus skin tissue and with muscle plus skin plus viscera (dissection and CT) resulted in equally high correlations (r-values between 0.94 and 0.99) assuming a good prediction estimate but with systematic significant difference confirming its imprecision "lean + BMC" is certainly not measuring ATFM (e.g. skin + muscle + viscera + bone) although its high r=0.99, but again with a significant difference ($p<0.001$) indicating a lack of precision and accuracy. Contrarily to Bloebaum et al. (2006), but in agreement with Louis et al. (1992), BMC seems a good estimate (r=0.73) with no significant difference of its ash weight. The impression is given however, that DXA non-adipose values are expressed as anatomical-morphological values combined with chemical elements. We cannot confirm what the non-adipose component of DXA is measuring, but we do confirm that all the DXA components and the CT bone components are subject not only to measurement error but also to terminology error and violation of basic assumptions.
It is known since many decennia that density in its weight/volume quantification (g/cm^3) can be considered as an additional and separate dimension of BC. The DXA-derived BMD, however, is a weight/surface quantification (g/cm^2) and therefore not a true density, nor the density based on which indication of osteoporosis classifications were studied in the past (Bolotin, 1998, 2007; Bolotin & Sievanen, 2001; Bolotin et al., 2001; Lochmuller et al., 2000). In a pilot (dissection) study using porcine hind legs in which DXA BMD was compared with bone covered with muscle, AT and skin tissue and compared with scraped bones only (Clarys et al., 2008; Provyn et al., 2008) it was found that DXA BMD underestimates true density with more than 40%. In the present sample (Table 10), under whole body conditions, one notices a similar level of high underestimation of DXA but with a better correlation, e.g. r=0.68 for the whole body value against r=0.39 for the hind leg study. The extensive work done by Bolotin (2007) shows DXA measured BMD methodology (*in vivo*) to be an intrinsically flawed and misleading indicator of bone mineral status and an

erroneous gauge of relative fracture risk. The transfer of their findings to the in situ carcass situation of the present evaluation confirms that the DXA methodology cannot provide accurate, quantitative precise, meaningful determinations of true bone densities and proper bone mass because of the contamination of independent soft tissue, e.g., fluid and lipid content contributions.

The majority of present consensual acceptance and understanding of the DXA estimate quality rests solely upon a number of well-established, multiconfirmed, *in vivo* and in situ significant high correlations. This is confirmed. In terms of true "reality precision" measures, DXA produces inaccurate and misleading values at all levels of output. Both the adipose and non adipose components of DXA ignore the ad hoc lipid content and the non adipose variables do not take into account the true composing tissues. "Lean" and "lean + BMC" of DXA do not correspond to anatomical/morphological tissue combinations, nor to chemical values. It cannot be determined what DXA really measures. BMC versus ash weight is the only variable with a close reality and non significant difference output. DXA and CT are based on a series of constancies within tissues, regardless of segments, hydration and lipid content variability. The hypothesis that DXA methodology provides accurate, precise and relevant BC determinations are proven to be unwarranted and misplaced (Clarys et al., 2010b).

5. Conclusion

Accurate and precise measurement of human biological variation of tissue composition is both important and imperative in BC data acquisition. Together with the proliferation and abundance of different BC models, methods, techniques and equipment used in nutrition and health assessment, it is imperative that the BC data collector realizes that: a) all indirect models, techniques and devices are based upon assumptions and combined errors, b) different techniques for the same purpose may yield significant varying results… and c) at all times the assumption based prediction is a substantial different matter from accurate precision that is needed on the individual medical or other check-up. Within a clinical context, the borderline between prediction and accuracy has become vague and may need re-newed attention.

A closer collaboration between different scientific disciplines and stakeholders (nutritionists, clinicians, engineers and high technology companies) will contribute to increase the excellence of health-oriented BC research.

6. References

Abate, N.; Burns, D.; Peshock, R.M.; Garg, A. & Grundy, S.M. (1994). Estimation of adipose tissue mass by magnetic resonance imaging: validation against dissection in human cadavers. *J Lipid Res,* 35(8), 1490-1496.

Adams, J.; Mottola, M.; Bagnall, K.M. & McFadden, K.D. (1982). Total body fat content in a group of professional football players. *Can J Appl Sport Sci,* 7(1), 36-40.

Baumgartner, R.N.; Heymsfield, S.B. & Roche, A.F. (1995). Human body composition and the epidemiology of chronic disease. *Obes Res,* 3(1), 73-95.

Bautmans, I.; Van Puyvelde, K. & Mets, T. (2009). Sarcopenia and functional decline: pathophysiology, prevention and therapy. *Acta Clin Belg,* 64(4), 303-316.

Beddoe, A.H. (1998). Body fat: estimation or guesstimation? *Appl Radiat Isot,* 49(5-6), 461-463.

Bedogni, G.; Pietrobelli, A.; Heymsfield, S.B.; Borghi, A.; Manzieri, A.M.; Morini, P.; Battistini, N. & Salvioli, G. (2001). Is body mass index a measure of adiposity in elderly women? *Obes Res,* 9(1), 17-20.

Behnke, A.J.; Feen, B. & Welham, W. (1942). The specific gravity of healthy men. Body weight divided by volume as an index of obesity. *J Am Med Assoc,* 118, 495-498.

Behnke, A.R. (1963). Anthropometric evaluation of body composition throughout life. *Ann N Y Acad Sci,* 110, 450-464.

Black, A.; Tilmont, E.M.; Baer, D.J.; Rumpler, W.V.; Ingram, D.K.; Roth, G.S. & Lane, M.A. (2001). Accuracy and precision of dual-energy X-ray absorptiometry for body composition measurements in rhesus monkeys. *J Med Primatol,* 30(2), 94-99.

Bloebaum, R.D.; Liau, D.W.; Lester, D.K. & Rosenbaum, T.G. (2006). Dual-energy x-ray absorptiometry measurement and accuracy of bone mineral after unilateral total hip arthroplasty. *J Arthroplasty,* 21(4), 612-622.

Bolotin, H.H. (1998). A new perspective on the causal influence of soft tissue composition on DXA-measured in vivo bone mineral density. *J Bone Miner Res,* 13(11), 1739-1746.

Bolotin, H.H. (2007). DXA in vivo BMD methodology: an erroneous and misleading research and clinical gauge of bone mineral status, bone fragility, and bone remodelling. *Bone,* 41(1), 138-154.

Bolotin, H.H. & Sievanen, H. (2001). Inaccuracies inherent in dual-energy X-ray absorptiometry in vivo bone mineral density can seriously mislead diagnostic/prognostic interpretations of patient-specific bone fragility. *J Bone Miner Res,* 16(5), 799-805.

Bolotin, H.H.; Sievanen, H.; Grashuis, J.L.; Kuiper, J.W. & Jarvinen, T.L. (2001). Inaccuracies inherent in patient-specific dual-energy X-ray absorptiometry bone mineral density measurements: comprehensive phantom-based evaluation. *J Bone Miner Res,* 16(2), 417-426.

Brodie, D.; Moscrip, V. & Hutcheon, R. (1998). Body composition measurement: a review of hydrodensitometry, anthropometry, and impedance methods. *Nutrition,* 14(3), 296-310.

Brommage, R. (2003). Validation and calibration of DEXA body composition in mice. *Am J Physiol Endocrinol Metab,* 285(3), E454-459.

Brozek, J.; Grande, F.; Anderson, J.T. & Keys, A. (1963). Densitometric analysis of body composition: Revision of some quantitative assumptions. *Ann N Y Acad Sci,* 110, 113-140.

Chauhan, S.; Koo, W.W.; Hammami, M. & Hockman, E.M. (2003). Fan beam dual energy X-ray absorptiometry body composition measurements in piglets. *J Am Coll Nutr,* 22(5), 408-414.

Clarys, J. & Martin, A. (1985). The concept of the adipose tissue-free mass. In Norgan, N. (Ed.), *Human body composition and fat distribution.,* pp. 49-61, Wageningen: Wageningen Agricultural University.

Clarys, J.P.; Martin, A.D. & Drinkwater, D.T. (1984). Gross tissue weights in the human body by cadaver dissection. *Hum Biol,* 56(3), 459-473.

Clarys, J.P.; Martin, A.D.; Drinkwater, D.T. & Marfell-Jones, M.J. (1987). The skinfold: myth and reality. *J Sports Sci,* 5(1), 3-33.

Clarys, J.P.; Martin, A.D.; Marfell-Jones, M.J.; Janssens, V.; Caboor, D. & Drinkwater, D.T. (1999). Human body composition: A review of adult dissection data. *Am J Hum Biol,* 11(2), 167-174.

Clarys, J.P.; Provyn, S.; Marfell-Jones, M. & Van Roy, P. (2006). Morphological and constitutional comparison of age-matched in-vivo and post-mortem populations. *Morphologie,* 90(291), 189-196.

Clarys, J.P.; Provyn, S. & Marfell-Jones, M.J. (2005). Cadaver studies and their impact on the understanding of human adiposity. *Ergonomics,* 48(11-14), 1445-1461.

Clarys, J.P.; Provyn, S.; Wallace, J.; Scafoglieri, A. & Reilly, T. (2008, 8-11 December). *Quality control of fan beam scanning data processing with in vitro material.*, Singapore.

Clarys, J.P.; Scafoglieri, A.; Provyn, S. & Sesboüé, B. (2009). The hazards of hydrodensitometry. *Biom Hum et Anthropol,* 27(1-2), 69-78.

Clarys, J.P.; Scafoglieri, A.; Provyn, S.; Sesboüé, B. & Van Roy, P. (2010a). The hazards of hydrodensitometry. *The Journal of Sports Medicine and Physical Fitness,* 0(0), 000-000.

Clarys, J.P.; Scafoglieri, A.; Provyn, S.; Louis, O.; Wallace, J.A. & De Mey, J. (2010b). A Macro-quality Evaluation of DXA Variables Using Whole Dissection, Ashing, and Computer Tomography in Pigs. *Obesity (Silver Spring),* 0(0), 000-000.

Clasey, J.L.; Kanaley, J.A.; Wideman, L.; Heymsfield, S.B.; Teates, C.D.; Gutgesell, M.E.; Thorner, M.O.; Hartman, M.L. & Weltman, A. (1999). Validity of methods of body composition assessment in young and older men and women. *J Appl Physiol,* 86(5), 1728-1738.

Cooper, A.R.; Forbes, R.M. & Mitchell, H.H. (1956). Further studies on the gross composition and mineral elements of the adult human body. *J Biol Chem,* 223(2), 969-975.

Deurenberg, P.; van der Kooy, K.; Leenen, R.; Weststrate, J.A. & Seidell, J.C. (1991). Sex and age specific prediction formulas for estimating body composition from bioelectrical impedance: a cross-validation study. *Int J Obes,* 15, 17-25.

Deurenberg, P. (2003). Validation of body composition methods and assumptions. *Br J Nutr,* 90(3), 485-486.

Durnin, J.V. & Rahaman, M.M. (1967). The assessment of the amount of fat in the human body from measurements of skinfold thickness. *Br J Nutr,* 21(3), 681-689.

Elia, M. (2001). Obesity in the elderly. *Obes Res,* 9 Suppl 4, 244S-248S.

Ellis, K.J. (2000). Human body composition: in vivo methods. *Physiol Rev,* 80(2), 649-680.

Elowsson, P.; Forslund, A.H.; Mallmin, H.; Feuk, U.; Hansson, I. & Carlsten, J. (1998). An evaluation of dual-energy X-Ray absorptiometry and underwater weighing to estimate body composition by means of carcass analysis in piglets. *J Nutr,* 128(9), 1543-1549.

Eston, R.G.; Rowlands, A.V.; Charlesworth, S.; Davies, A. & Hoppitt, T. (2005). Prediction of DXA-determined whole body fat from skinfolds: importance of including skinfolds from the thigh and calf in young, healthy men and women. *Eur J Clin Nutr,* 59(5), 695-702.

Ferrannini, E.; Sironi, A.M.; Lozzo, P. & Gastaldelli, A. (2008). Intra-abdominal adiposity, abdominal obesity, and cardiometabolic risk. *European Heart Journal Supplements,* 10(B), B4-B10.

Fogelholm, G.M.; Sievanen, H.T.; van Marken Lichtenbelt, W.D. & Westerterp, K.R. (1997). Assessment of fat-mass loss during weight reduction in obese women. *Metabolism,* 46(8), 968-975.

Forbes, G.B. & Lewis, A.M. (1956). Total sodium, potassium and chloride in adult man. *J Clin Invest,* 35(6), 596-600.

Forbes, R.M.; Cooper, A.R. & Mitchell, H.H. (1953). The composition of the adult human body as determined by chemical analysis. *J Biol Chem,* 203(1), 359-366.

Forbes, R.M.; Mitchell, H.H. & Cooper, A.R. (1956). Further studies on the gross composition and mineral elements of the adult human body. *J Biol Chem,* 223(2), 969-975.

Foster, M.A.; Hutchison, J.M.; Mallard, J.R. & Fuller, M. (1984). Nuclear magnetic resonance pulse sequence and discrimination of high- and low-fat tissues. *Magn Reson Imaging,* 2(3), 187-192.

Going, S.B.; Massett, M.P.; Hall, M.C.; Bare, L.A.; Root, P.A.; Williams, D.P. & Lohman, T.G. (1993). Detection of small changes in body composition by dual-energy x-ray absorptiometry. *Am J Clin Nutr,* 57(6), 845-850.

Haarbo, J.; Gotfredsen, A.; Hassager, C. & Christiansen, C. (1991). Validation of body composition by dual energy X-ray absorptiometry (DEXA). *Clin Physiol,* 11(4), 331-341.

Heymsfield, S.B.; Wang, Z.; Baumgartner, R.N. & Ross, R. (1997). Human body composition: advances in models and methods. *Annu Rev Nutr,* 17, 527-558.

Heyward, V.H. (1996). Evaluation of body composition. Current issues. *Sports Med,* 22(3), 146-156.

Iannuzzi-Sucich, M.; Prestwood, K.M. & Kenny, A.M. (2002). Prevalence of sarcopenia and predictors of skeletal muscle mass in healthy, older men and women. *J Gerontol A Biol Sci Med Sci,* 57(12), M772-777.

Jackson, A.S. & Pollock, M.L. (1978). Generalized equations for predicting body density of men. *Br J Nutr,* 40(3), 497-504.

Janssen, I.; Heymsfield, S.B.; Allison, D.B.; Kotler, D.P. & Ross, R. (2002a). Body mass index and waist circumference independently contribute to the prediction of nonabdominal, abdominal subcutaneous, and visceral fat. *Am J Clin Nutr,* 75(4), 683-688.

Janssen, I.; Heymsfield, S.B. & Ross, R. (2002b). Low relative skeletal muscle mass (sarcopenia) in older persons is associated with functional impairment and physical disability. *J Am Geriatr Soc,* 50(5), 889-896.

Janssens, V.; Thys, P.; Clarys, J.P.; Kvis, H.; Chowdhury, B.; Zinzen, E. & Cabri, J. (1994). Post-mortem limitations of body composition analysis by computed tomography. *Ergonomics,* 37(1), 207-216.

Johansson, A.G.; Forslund, A.; Sjodin, A.; Mallmin, H.; Hambraeus, L. & Ljunghall, S. (1993). Determination of body composition--a comparison of dual-energy x-ray absorptiometry and hydrodensitometry. *Am J Clin Nutr,* 57(3), 323-326.

Katch, F.I. & Michael, E.D., Jr. (1968). Prediction of body density from skin-fold and girth measurements of college females. *J Appl Physiol,* 25(1), 92-94.

Keys, A. & Brozek, J. (1953). Body fat in adult man. *Physiol Rev,* 33(3), 245-325.

Kitajima, Y.; Eguchi, Y.; Ishibashi, E.; Nakashita, S.; Aoki, S.; Toda, S.; Mizuta, T.; Ozaki, I.; Ono, N.; Eguchi, T.; Arai, K.; Iwakiri, R. & Fujimoto, K. (2010). Age-related fat deposition in multifidus muscle could be a marker for nonalcoholic fatty liver disease. *J Gastroenterol,* 45(2), 218-224.

Koo, W.W.; Hammami, M. & Hockman, E.M. (2002). Use of fan beam dual energy x-ray absorptiometry to measure body composition of piglets. *J Nutr,* 132(6), 1380-1383.

Koo, W.W.; Hammami, M. & Hockman, E.M. (2004). Validation of bone mass and body composition measurements in small subjects with pencil beam dual energy X-ray absorptiometry. *J Am Coll Nutr,* 23(1), 79-84.

Kvist, H.; Chowdhury, B.; Grangard, U.; Tylen, U. & Sjostrom, L. (1988). Total and visceral adipose-tissue volumes derived from measurements with computed tomography in adult men and women: predictive equations. *Am J Clin Nutr,* 48(6), 1351-1361.

Larsson, B.; Bengtsson, C.; Björntorp, P.; Lapidus, L.; Sjöström, L.; Svärdsudd, K.; Tibblin, G.; Wedel, H.; Welin, L. & Wilhelmsen, L. (1992). Is abdominal body fat distribution a major explanation for the sex difference in the incidence of myocardial infarction? The study of men born in 1913 and the study of women, Göteborg, Sweden. *Am J Epidemiol,* 135(3), 266-273.

Lean, M.E.; Han, T.S. & Morrison, C.E. (1995). Waist circumference as a measure for indicating need for weight management. *Bmj,* 311(6998), 158-161.

Lee, R.C.; Wang, Z.; Heo, M.; Ross, R.; Janssen, I. & Heymsfield, S.B. (2000). Total-body skeletal muscle mass: development and cross-validation of anthropometric prediction models. *Am J Clin Nutr,* 72(3), 796-803.

Lochmuller, E.M.; Miller, P.; Burklein, D.; Wehr, U.; Rambeck, W. & Eckstein, F. (2000). In situ femoral dual-energy X-ray absorptiometry related to ash weight, bone size and density, and its relationship with mechanical failure loads of the proximal femur. *Osteoporos Int,* 11(4), 361-367.

Lohman, T.G. (1981). Skinfolds and body density and their relation to body fatness: a review. *Hum Biol,* 53(2), 181-225.

Lohman, T.G. & Going, S.B. (1993). Multicomponent models in body composition research: opportunities and pitfalls. *Basic Life Sci,* 60, 53-58.

Louis, O.; Van den Winkel, P.; Covens, P.; Schoutens, A. & Osteaux, M. (1992). Dual-energy X-ray absorptiometry of lumbar vertebrae: relative contribution of body and posterior elements and accuracy in relation with neutron activation analysis. *Bone,* 13(4), 317-320.

Ludesher, B.; Machann, J.; Eschweiler, G.; Vanhöfen, S.; Maenz, C.; Thamer, C.; Claussen, C. & Schick, F. (2009). Correlation of fat distribution in whole body MRI with generally used anthropometric data. *Invest Radiol,* 44(11), 712-719.

Lukaski, H.C.; Marchello, M.J.; Hall, C.B.; Schafer, D.M. & Siders, W.A. (1999). Soft tissue composition of pigs measured with dual x-ray absorptiometry: comparison with chemical analyses and effects of carcass thicknesses. *Nutrition,* 15(9), 697-703.

Marfell-Jones, M.; Clarys, J.P.; Alewaeters, K. & Martin, A.D. (2003). The hazards of whole body adiposity prediction in men and women. *Biom Hum et Anthropol,* 21(1-2), 103-117.

Martin, A.D.; Daniel, M.; Clarys, J.P. & Marfell-Jones, M.J. (2003a). Cadaver-assessed validity of anthropometric indicators of adipose tissue distribution. *Int J Obes Relat Metab Disord,* 27(9), 1052-1058.

Martin, A.D. & Drinkwater, D.T. (1991). Variability in the measures of body fat. Assumptions or technique? *Sports Med,* 11(5), 277-288.

Martin, A.D.; Drinkwater, D.T.; Clarys, J.P.; Daniel, M. & Ross, W.D. (1992). Effects of skin thickness and skinfold compressibility on skinfold thickness measurement. *Am J Hum Biol,* 4, 453-460.

Martin, A.D.; Janssens, V.; Caboor, D.; Clarys, J.P. & Marfell-Jones, M.J. (2003b). Relationships between visceral, trunk and whole-body adipose tissue weights by cadaver dissection. *Ann Hum Biol,* 30(6), 668-677.

Martin, A.D.; Ross, W.D.; Drinkwater, D.T. & Clarys, J.P. (1985). Prediction of body fat by skinfold caliper: assumptions and cadaver evidence. *Int J Obes,* 9 Suppl 1, 31-39.

Matiegka, J. (1921). The testing of physical efficiency. *American Journal of Physical Anthropology,* 4, 223-230.

Mazess, R.B.; Peppler, W.W.; Chesnut, C.H., 3rd; Nelp, W.B.; Cohn, S.H. & Zanzi, I. (1981). Total body bone mineral and lean body mass by dual-photon absorptiometry. II. Comparison with total body calcium by neutron activation analysis. *Calcif Tissue Int,* 33(4), 361-363.

McEvoy, F.J.; Madsen, M.T.; Strathe, A.B. & Svalastoga, E. (2008). Hounsfield Unit dynamics of adipose tissue and non-adipose soft tissues in growing pigs. *Res Vet Sci,* 84(2), 300-304.

Mitchell, A.D.; Conway, J.M. & Potts, W.J. (1996). Body composition analysis of pigs by dual-energy x-ray absorptiometry. *J Anim Sci,* 74(11), 2663-2671.

Mitchell, A.D.; Rosebrough, R.W. & Conway, J.M. (1997). Body composition analysis of chickens by dual energy x-ray absorptiometry. *Poult Sci,* 76(12), 1746-1752.

Mitchell, A.D.; Scholz, A.M.; Pursel, V.G. & Evock-Clover, C.M. (1998). Composition analysis of pork carcasses by dual-energy x-ray absorptiometry. *J Anim Sci,* 76(8), 2104-2114.

Mitchell, H.H.; Hamilton, T.S.; Steggerda, F.R. & Bean, H.W. (1945). The chemical composition of the adult body and its bearing on the biochemistry of growth *Journal of Biology and Chemistry,* 158, 625-637.

Mitsiopoulos, N.; Baumgartner, R.N.; Heymsfield, S.B.; Lyons, W.; Gallagher, D. & Ross, R. (1998). Cadaver validation of skeletal muscle measurement by magnetic resonance imaging and computerized tomography. *J Appl Physiol,* 85(1), 115-122.

Modlesky, C.M.; Cureton, K.J.; Lewis, R.D.; Prior, B.M.; Sloniger, M.A. & Rowe, D.A. (1996). Density of the fat-free mass and estimates of body composition in male weight trainers. *J Appl Physiol,* 80(6), 2085-2096.

Muller, M.J.; Bosy-Westphal, A.; Kutzner, D. & Heller, M. (2003). Metabolically active components of fat free mass (FFM) and resting energy expenditure (REE) in humans. *Forum Nutr,* 56, 301-303.

Nagy, T.R. & Clair, A.L. (2000). Precision and accuracy of dual-energy X-ray absorptiometry for determining in vivo body composition of mice. *Obes Res,* 8(5), 392-398.

NHLBI. (1998). Clinical Guidelines on the Identification, Evaluation, and Treatment of Overweight and Obesity in Adults--The Evidence Report. National Institutes of Health. *Obes Res,* 6 Suppl 2, 51S-209S.

Ozenoglu, A.; Ugurlu, S.; Can, G. & Hatemi, H. (2009). Reference values of body composition for adult females who are classified as normal weight, overweight or obese according to body mass index. *Endocr Regul,* 43(1), 29-37.

Picaud, J.C.; Rigo, J.; Nyamugabo, K.; Milet, J. & Senterre, J. (1996). Evaluation of dual-energy X-ray absorptiometry for body-composition assessment in piglets and term human neonates. *Am J Clin Nutr,* 63(2), 157-163.

Pintauro, S.J.; Nagy, T.R.; Duthie, C.M. & Goran, M.I. (1996). Cross-calibration of fat and lean measurements by dual-energy X-ray absorptiometry to pig carcass analysis in the pediatric body weight range. *Am J Clin Nutr,* 63(3), 293-298.

Pollock, M.L.; Gettman, L.R.; Jackson, A.; Ayres, J.; Ward, A. & Linnerud, A.C. (1977). Body composition of elite class distance runners. *Ann N Y Acad Sci,* 301, 361-370.

Poortmans, J.R.; Boisseau, N.; Moraine, J.J.; Moreno-Reyes, R. & Goldman, S. (2005). Estimation of total-body skeletal muscle mass in children and adolescents. *Med Sci Sports Exerc,* 37(2), 316-322.

Prentice, A. (1995). Application of dual-energy X-ray absorptiometry and related techniques to the assessment of bone and body composition. In Davis, P.S.W. & Cole, T.J. (Eds.), *Body composition techniques in health and disease.*, pp. 1-13, New York: Cambridge University Press.

Prior, B.M.; Cureton, K.J.; Modlesky, C.M.; Evans, E.M.; Sloniger, M.A.; Saunders, M. & Lewis, R.D. (1997). In vivo validation of whole body composition estimates from dual-energy X-ray absorptiometry. *J Appl Physiol,* 83(2), 623-630.

Prior, B.M.; Modlesky, C.M.; Evans, E.M.; Sloniger, M.A.; Saunders, M.J.; Lewis, R.D. & Cureton, K.J. (2001). Muscularity and the density of the fat-free mass in athletes. *J Appl Physiol,* 90(4), 1523-1531.

Pritchard, J.E.; Nowson, C.A.; Strauss, B.J.; Carlson, J.S.; Kaymakci, B. & Wark, J.D. (1993). Evaluation of dual energy X-ray absorptiometry as a method of measurement of body fat. *Eur J Clin Nutr,* 47(3), 216-228.

Provyn, S.; Clarys, J.P.; Wallace, J.; Scafoglieri, A. & Reilly, T. (2008). Quality control, accuracy, and prediction capacity of dual energy X-ray absorptiometry variables and data acquisition. *J Physiol Anthropol,* 27(6), 317-323.

Roemmich, J.N.; Clark, P.A.; Weltman, A. & Rogol, A.D. (1997). Alterations in growth and body composition during puberty. I. Comparing multicompartment body composition models. *J Appl Physiol,* 83(3), 927-935.

Rolland, Y.; Lauwers-Cances, V.; Cristini, C.; Abellan van Kan, G.; Janssen, I.; Morley, J.E. & Vellas, B. (2009). Difficulties with physical function associated with obesity, sarcopenia, and sarcopenic-obesity in community-dwelling elderly women: the EPIDOS (EPIDemiologie de l'OSteoporose) Study. *Am J Clin Nutr,* 89(6), 1895-1900.

Rossner, S.; Bo, W.J.; Hiltbrandt, E.; Hinson, W.; Karstaedt, N.; Santago, P.; Sobol, W.T. & Crouse, J.R. (1990). Adipose tissue determinations in cadavers--a comparison between cross-sectional planimetry and computed tomography. *Int J Obes,* 14(10), 893-902.

Salamone, L.M.; Fuerst, T.; Visser, M.; Kern, M.; Lang, T.; Dockrell, M.; Cauley, J.A.; Nevitt, M.; Tylavsky, F. & Lohman, T.G. (2000). Measurement of fat mass using DEXA: a validation study in elderly adults. *J Appl Physiol,* 89(1), 345-352.

Scafoglieri, A.; Provyn, S. & Clarys J.P. (2009). Validation in vitro de l'indice de masse corporelle et autres variables anthropométriques dans la prédiction de la composition corporelle de la personne âgée. *Biom Hum et Anthropol,* 27, 43-55.

Scafoglieri, A.; Provyn, S.; Bautmans, I.; Van Roy, P. & Clarys, J.P. (2010). Direct relationship of body mass index and waist circumference with body tissue distribution in elderly persons. *Journal of Nutrition, Health and Aging,* 0(0), 000-000.

Seidell, J.C.; Oosterlee, A.; Thijssen, M.A.; Burema, J.; Deurenberg, P.; Hautvast, J.G. & Ruijs, J.H. (1987). Assessment of intra-abdominal and subcutaneous abdominal fat: relation between anthropometry and computed tomography. *Am J Clin Nutr,* 45(1), 7-13.

Siri, W.E. (1956). The gross composition of the body. *Adv Biol Med Phys,* 4, 239-280.

Siri, W.E. (1961). Body composition from fluid spaces and density; analysis of methods. In Brozek, J. & Henschel, A. (Eds.), *Techniques for measuring body composition*, pp. 223-244, Washington, DC: National Academy of Science.

Sniderman, A.D.; Bhopal, R.; Prabhakaran, D.; Sarrafzadegan, N. & Tchernof, A. (2007). Why might South Asians be so susceptible to central obesity and its atherogenic consequences? The adipose tissue overflow hypothesis. *Int J Epidemiol,* 36(1), 220-225.

Speakman, J.R.; Booles, D. & Butterwick, R. (2001). Validation of dual energy X-ray absorptiometry (DXA) by comparison with chemical analysis of dogs and cats. *Int J Obes Relat Metab Disord,* 25(3), 439-447.

Swennen, Q.; Janssens, G.P.; Geers, R.; Decuypere, E. & Buyse, J. (2004). Validation of dual-energy x-ray absorptiometry for determining in vivo body composition of chickens. *Poult Sci,* 83(8), 1348-1357.

Vester-Christensen, M.; Erbou, S.G.H.; Hansen, M.F.; Olsen, E.V.; Christensen, L.B.; Hviid, M.; Ersboll, B.K. & Larsen, R. (2009). Virtual dissection of pig carcasses. *Meat Science,* 81(4), 699-704.

Visser, M.; Gallagher, D.; Deurenberg, P.; Wang, J.; Pierson, R.N., Jr. & Heymsfield, S.B. (1997). Density of fat-free body mass: relationship with race, age, and level of body fatness. *Am J Physiol,* 272(5 Pt 1), E781-787.

Wadden, T.A. & Didie, E. (2003). What's in a name? Patients' preferred terms for describing obesity. *Obes Res,* 11(9), 1140-1146.

Wang, M.C.; Bachrach, L.K.; Van Loan, M.; Hudes, M.; Flegal, K.M. & Crawford, P.B. (2005). The relative contributions of lean tissue mass and fat mass to bone density in young women. *Bone,* 37(4), 474-481.

Wang, Z.; Deurenberg, P.; Wang, W.; Pietrobelli, A.; Baumgartner, R.N. & Heymsfield, S.B. (1999). Hydration of fat-free body mass: review and critique of a classic body-composition constant. *Am J Clin Nutr,* 69(5), 833-841.

Wang, Z.M.; Heshka, S.; Pierson, R.N., Jr. & Heymsfield, S.B. (1995). Systematic organization of body-composition methodology: an overview with emphasis on component-based methods. *Am J Clin Nutr,* 61(3), 457-465.

Wang, Z.M.; Pierson, R.N., Jr. & Heymsfield, S.B. (1992). The five-level model: a new approach to organizing body-composition research. *Am J Clin Nutr,* 56(1), 19-28.

Westerterp, K.R.; Smeets, A.; Lejeune, M.P.; Wouters-Adriaens, M.P. & Westerterp-Plantenga, M.S. (2008). Dietary fat oxidation as a function of body fat. *Am J Clin Nutr,* 87(1), 132-135.

WHO Obesity. (2000). *Preventing and managing the global epidemic.* Geneva: World Health Organization.

Widdowson, E.; McCance, R. & Spray, C. (1951). The chemical composition of the human body. *Clin Sci,* 10, 113-125.

Wouters-Adriaens, M.P. & Westerterp, K.R. (2008). Low resting energy expenditure in Asians can be attributed to body composition. *Obesity (Silver Spring),* 16(10), 2212-2216.

Zamboni, M.; Armellini, F.; Harris, T.; Turcato, E.; Micciolo, R.; Bergamo-Andreis, I.A. & Bosello, O. (1997). Effects of age on body fat distribution and cardiovascular risk factors in women. *Am J Clin Nutr,* 66(1), 111-115.

Zamboni, M.; Mazzali, G.; Fantin, F.; Rossi, A. & Di Francesco, V. (2008). Sarcopenic obesity: a new category of obesity in the elderly. *Nutr Metab Cardiovasc Dis,* 18(5), 388-395.

16

High-Efficiency Digital Readout Systems for Fast Pixel-Based Vertex Detectors

Alessandro Gabrielli, Filippo Maria Giorgi and Mauro Villa
University of Bologna and INFN Bologna
Italy

1. Introduction

Particle physics is one of the science branches which heavily relies on most advanced technologies due to the increasing complexity of the problems it has to face. In future colliders, luminosities and beam energies are scaling upwards. These are necessary conditions for the discovery of new physics which both result in a larger amount of data that need to be brought out of the detector. That's why one of the crucial points for new experiments is the evolution of data acquisition systems. Data acquisition systems employed in particle physics experiments followed the global technology trend and moved towards digital electronics and transmission lines, in this chapter we will describe how the effort of our work has been applied in this direction trying to extend digital processing on the very front-end of the detector. We will show how digital elaboration on the very front-end can help coping with new stringent requirements.

One possible scenario for the discovery of new physics is the chance to investigate with high-precision some apparently known processes instead of brutally scaling the $\sqrt{s}$ energy foreseeing to achieve the threshold for new heavy particle discovery. High luminosity e^+e^- accelerators can provide clean signals at very fast rates in order to provide in a reasonable amount of time the required statistics for high-precision new physics investigations. The next-generation flavour factories are aiming at luminosities up to $10^{36}cm^{-2}s^{-1}$ (refer to SuperB Collaboration (2007)) which imply a very high particle rate especially in the first layer of the innermost detector: the vertex tracker.

This perspective opened new challenging researches for the realization of very fast and efficient sensors and readout electronics capable to take advantage of these super-luminous facilities. In this chapter we would like to present our works on data acquisition chains, which is focused on the front-end side of the detector but involves also external DAQ boards. We will show how we have expanded digital signal processing of a classical DAQ systems outside the walls of the counting rooms to the front-end chips. What we present is far from being a complete and definitive DAQ for a tracker design, but it provides viable solutions and technicalities for what concern the readout electronics world.

The front-ends targeted by our data acquisition system are silicon sensors and, in particular, wide matrices of pixels. The huge improvements of the last decade in the world of the silicon industries, and the new technology processes that emerged recently, have stimulated the curiosity of the scientific community. Several types of pixel sensors for particle physics

applications have been produced and integrated on large particle detectors, and some other are still under investigation or produced as prototypes. Hybrid pixel sensors for example, consisting of a sensitive layer bump-bonded to a standard CMOS layer, have been employed on the two major experiments operating at LHC:[1] The ATLAS silicon pixel detector [R. Klingenberg for the ATLAS pixel collaboration (year 2007)] integrates 80 million channels on a total active surface of 1.8 m^2, while CMS [S. Schnetzer for the CMS Pixel Collaboration (year 2003)] has a total pixel active area of 1 m^2 and 66 millions of channels.
Other kind of silicon pixel sensors exploit the deep N-well sub-micron technologies, that allow, with a standard CMOS process, the integration of the sensor with the analog front-end and the digital readout electronics on the same substrate. This monolithic sensors are very promising in terms of granularity and material budget (down to 50 microns of pitch and thickness); this pixel variant is known as DNW MAPS (Deep N-Well Monolithic Active Pixel Sensors). [A. Gabrielli for the SLIM5 Collaboration (year 2009)],[G. Rizzo for the SLIM5 collaboration (year 2007)].
Furthermore, a lot of attention is being dedicated to the possibility of exploiting new 3D integration technologies. In this perspective the aim is to stack many ultra-thin (15 μm) silicon layers with a high interconnection density given by 1 μm-wide through-silicon via. L. Gaioni et Al. (year 2009), R. Lipton (year 2007).
It is clear that the new frontier is then the possibility to exploit to the maximum level the integration of sensor, analog front-end and the digital logic on the same sensor chip. Our work proceeded in this direction, and proposes a series of digital sparsification and readout digital architectures that can be paired with several kinds of pixel technologies. These digital circuits are highly speed optimized, we aimed at sustaining a hit flux of 100 MHz/cm^2 which is, by order of magnitude, the value foreseen on the innermost detector layer of a flavor factory like SuperB.
Our goal is to read the hits from the matrix as soon as they form, in order to promptly reset the pixels and then reducing the sensor dead time. In this context we present different readout architectures comparing the achievements in terms efficiencies and time resolutions. We also give a brief description of the developing process consisting of conceptual design, VHDL description model, model validation, estimation of the efficiencies and finally digital ASIC design.
Silicon sensors that implement nontrivial sparsification circuits and a digital data interface can provide a more robust interconnection with the data acquisition system. In addition the chance of having a data-push event-formatted stream directly out of the front-end chip, can simplify the processing algorithm on the data acquisition boards. This can be translated into wider margins on triggering latencies and less stringent computational power requirements on the DAQ boards. We present for example a data-push front-end architecture that sends out encoded events where hits are already time sorted & space aligned (divided on the base of their spatial origin on the matrix). This allowed to remove the hit sorting algorithms on the DAQ firmware, resulting in a smoother data flow.
It is evident that the possibility to exploit more and more complex digital architectures in direct contact with the sensor readout opens a new field of research: how can be improved the DAQ performance by preprocessing data on the very front-end? We are investigating

[1] Large Hadron Collider, a proton/ions accelerator built at CERN (Geneva, CH).

these opportunities working both on the digital front-end architectures, and DAQ counterpart electronics.
Several chip submissions, within fruitful collaborations like SLIM5 and VIPIX, adopted the architectures that we have developed and allowed us to test them on an accelerated particle beam. In this occasions we could also test the interaction between these digital front-end architectures with a powerful DAQ system. We present here also the external DAQ infrastructure used to test the pixel detectors, a multi-FPGA VME board called EDRO (Event Dispatch and Readout) capable of an integrated I/O of 30 Gbps. It features also an associative memory interface, in order to exploit fast triggers (< $1\mu s$) coming from an external board that compare the incoming hits to a bank of predefined patterns.
In summary, we think that now the silicon technologies allow the data acquisition to expand inside the walls of pure sensors world, increasing the synergy between these two elements that for long have been considered different fields of research.

2. Silicon vertex trackers

In a high energy collider experiment, the innermost detector is appointed to perform an accurate reconstruction of the particle tracks coming out of the interaction vertices, from which the name "tracker". Several coaxial layers of sensors are displaced around the beam pipe in the interaction region, with the detected crossing points it is possible to track a particle trajectory. Resolution and efficiency are the two main parameters to optimize but typically one has to trade off between these two. A higher number of channels and a smaller radius around the interaction point can improve the resolution at the cost of an increasing rate that worsen the efficiency.
Another crucial point is the total amount of material that we use for the construction of a tracker since the particles we want to measure actually interact with the detector itself. Depending on its momentum, a particle can be deflected at a non negligible angle each time it crosses a layer of the detector, making difficult to reconstruct the original trajectory. This undesired effect is known as multiple-scattering. In order to reduce the probability for a particle to scatter at large angles, it is very important to keep low the material budget of the entire detector.
Nowadays silicon detectors are widely used for this kind of application since the integrated circuit technology allows the integration of high-density micron-scale electrodes on large wafers providing an excellent position resolution. A silicon sensor grants also an easy integration with the semi-conductor-based readout electronics and, as we will discuss later, they can be fitted also on the same silicon substrate. This is a great advantage in terms of material budget if we consider that we can thin the silicon substrate roughly down to a hundred of microns. That is made possible because the density of silicon and its small ionization energy[2] can produce an adequate signal with a sensitive layer of that scale.
A typical silicon detector is composed by:

- **The Sensor:** It is the sensitive part of the detector. It is a capacitive element appointed to collect the charge that forms in the silicon substrate translating it into a tension signal (for minimum ionizing particles the most probable charge deposition in a 300 micronthick silicon detector is about 3.5 fC (22000 electrons) [W-M Yao et Al. (year

[2] It is the minimum energy required to extract a bounded electron

2006)]. It is typically implemented as a reverse-biased *p-n* junction which forms a region depleted of mobile charge carriers and sets up an electric field that sweeps the charge generated by radiation and diffusing in the substrate.

- **The Analog Front-end:** It is the analog electronics directly connected to the sensor, its task is to amplify, adapt and discriminate the sensor signal with a voltage threshold. Keeping the front-end noise low is a critical issue either to improve the energy resolution (which depends on the collected charge) and to allow a low detection threshold. For certain energy values, particles are more reluctant to ionize and release less charge, the electronics *ENC* (Equivalent Noise Charge) should be below this value. A scheme of a typical front-end circuit is presented in Fig. 1.
- **The Latch:** It is the memory element that keeps track of a threshold crossing. It is reset after the channel has been read out. The longer it takes to read and reset the latch, the longer the sensor is "blind" to new incoming particles.
- **The Readout:** It is the electronics appointed to extract the hit information from each pixel latch. It can be implemented in very different ways depending on the optimization targets. This is the element on which we focused our work.

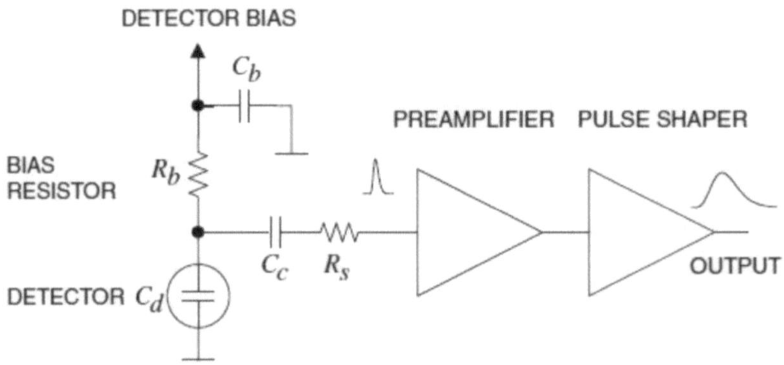

Fig. 1. Typical detector front-end circuit.

The silicon sensors can be implemented with different granularities and form factors, for example the *Silicon Strip Sensors* are long and thin *p-n* junctions that extends for several centimeters and they are about 50 microns wide. The longer the *p-n* junction is, the higher the capacitive load C_d, which means slower signals and higher power consumption. Pixel devices instead, are matrices of square-shaped sensors that improve granularity and provide faster signals. In this way the same area is covered by a greater number of channels, giving a more precise spatial information.

In a particle tracker, the error on the reconstructed position of the vertex is dominated by the spatial resolution of the innermost layers, therefore they are typically instrumented with pixel sensors due to their higher resolution. Moreover, since the area to be instrumented increases with radii, and since pixels sensors present a higher cost-per-area, the outer layers of the tracker are typically instrumented with silicon strips.

3. Pixel detectors

In the digital era the word "pixel" is very diffused, since it embodies the concept of digital quantization in the field of *imaging*. Nowadays a large variety of electronic devices based on silicon incorporate "pixel sensors". The most common and diffused semiconductor pixel sensors are those employed in modern digital cameras, mobile phones and, more generally, in almost every portable device. This kind of silicon sensor detects visible-light photons and it is designed to have a wide and optimized dynamic range in order to exalt, for example, the brightness and contrast of the subject. A statistical number of photons is collected in the sensor array making some pixels "brighter" than others. The whole matrix has to be read out in order to provide the final image.

The pixel sensors adopted in particle physics experiments instead, should detect traversing charged particles or photons. These detectors should be sensitive even to the crossing of single particles. By means of this, and due to the high flux of particles nearby the interaction point of a collider (our goal is to sustain 100 MHit s^{-1} cm^{-2}), tracker sensors are optimized in terms of readout speed rather than dynamic range. Moreover, in some cases the readout phase is continuous, overlapped to the acquisition phase, and concentrated only on the hit regions, since what the physicist are looking for is not a *photo* of the event but the spatial position of a trace produced by an impinging particle. The superimposition of several layers gives the spatial information to reconstruct a particle trajectory as it was discussed in section 2. The information about the quantity of charge collected in a fired pixel can be read out. It is useful to enhance the sensor resolution in case of clustered events where the reconstructed crossing point of the particle can be evaluated with a centre of mass algorithm (a spatial weighted average where the charge acts as a weight). This information is also useful to reconstruct the amount of energy lost by the particle in the detector. This would give a calorimetric information dE/dx, that can be used for particle identification. Though, the extraction of this information is not for free, it can be rather very time consuming especially for pixels since the density of channels is very high (400 channels/mm^2 with a 50-micron pitch). When a pixel get fired by a crossing particle, it is unable to detect any other impinging particle until it is read out and reset. This time laps, during which the pixel is latched, is called *dead time*. In our specific case-study, the dead-time introduced by charge extraction wold be unaffordable, consequently the readout we developed extracts only the hit/not hit information from the pixels.

A very simple readout structure for a CMOS APS - *Active Pixel Sensor* - is shown in Fig. 2, and it is know as the 3T (three transistor) configuration.

A 3T APS matrix is read out with the so called *rolling shutter* procedure. Each row is read out one after the other driving a column bus. A the other end of the column bus the front-end electronics processes the pixel signals. The advantage of this method is that the sensor matrix can collect charge during a continuous acquisition process.

A pixel detector can be implemented with different fabrication technologies. The most common and diffused at the moment foresees the interconnection of a sensor silicon layer to a standard CMOS-process integrated circuit (that hosts the front-end electronics) by means of an array of micro solder bumps. This kind of sensors are known as hybrid pixel sensors. They are employed in both the major experiments taking place at CERN: ATLAS and CMS (ref. R. Klingenberg for the ATLAS pixel collaboration (year 2007) and S. Schnetzer for the CMS Pixel Collaboration (year 2003)).

It is possible to get rid of the delicate bump-bonding procedure integrating both sensor and readout on the same substrate processed in standard CMOS technology: this kind of device are known as MAPS (*Monolithic APS*). The *p-n* sensitive junction can be obtained by an n well implanted in the p substrate. The use of this technology for the detection of charged particles is challenging since only the very thin epitaxial layer (10-20 microns) of the silicon

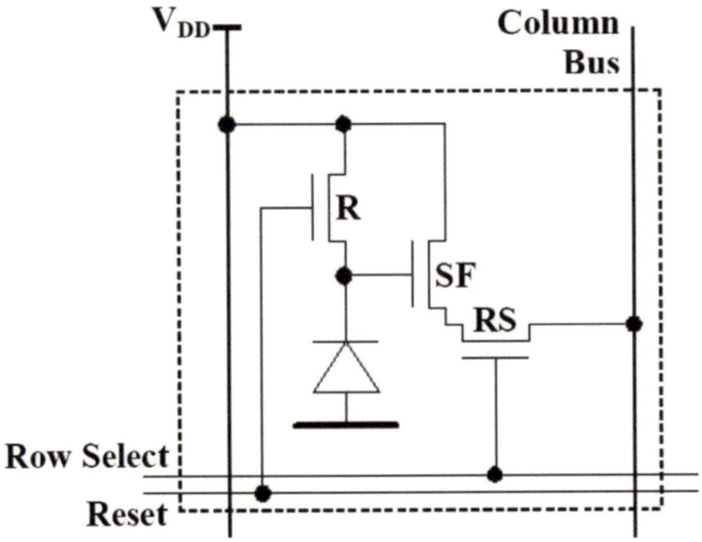

Fig. 2. Three transistor readout for a matrix of pixels. *Reset* transistor **R** clears the pixel of integrated charge, *Source Follow* transistor **SF** amplifies/buffers the signal and *Row Select* transistor **RS** selects the row for readout.

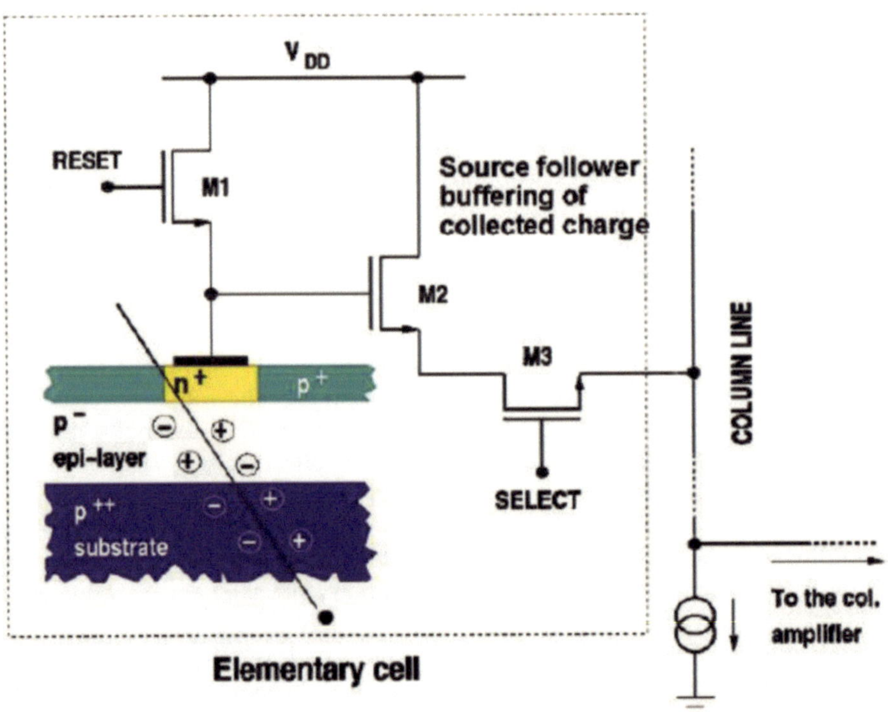

Fig. 3. Schematic view of a CMOS MAPS device with typical 3T readout structure. G. Rizzo for the SLIM5 collaboration (year 2007)

is available as sensitive volume. On the other hand, this allows to thin down the substrate to its mechanical limits and to build vertex detectors with an extremely low material budget.
Modern CMOS processes allow triple well structures, a feature that has been explored to increase the collection efficiency and to implement in-pixel front-end electronics S. Bettarini et Al. (year 2007). A deep and extended N-well is used as the collecting electrode, wherein a p layer is deposited to host the NMOS transistors of the front-end electronics. The large electrode area improves the collection efficiency, and the charge to voltage conversion, which generally decreases with the capacitive area, is enhanced by the in-pixel active amplifier. The front-end PMOS transistors are enclosed in additional N-wells, that actually steal charge to the main collecting electrode, therefore the in-pixel analog and digital electronics is quite limited in order to keep a high collection efficiency. The enclosure of the analog front-end at pixel level in the deep N-well brings a significant noise improvement, N. Neri et Al. (year 2010) report a measured ENC of $75e^-$. Moreover, the possibility to include also digital components at pixel level allows to develop faster readout, improving the speed limits of the typical rolling shutter architecture used for 3T APS structures.
Another promising processing technology, that captured the attention also of the physics community, allows the integration of several ultra-thin silicon layers (~15 μm thick) in a 3D structure, interconnected by micron-scale through-silicon vias L. Gaioni et Al. (year 2009)R. Lipton (year 2007). This means in principle that a silicon detector could stuff the sensor layer, the analog front-end electronics and dense digital logics at pixel level for enhanced readout capabilities, all on independent substrates (low noise, almost 100% active area) within a silicon stack only few hundreds of microns thick (very low material budget).
There are also ongoing researches that aim to integrate deep N-well MAPS structures in 3D vertically integrated IC [V. Re et Al. (year 2010)] represented in Fig. 4.
Our work is intended to exploit the new opportunities brought by these technological innovations, in order to provide readout architectures characterized by higher efficiencies. The main aspect we are trying to optimize, is the reduction of the average pixel dead-time. We are investigating different ways to extract the hits as fast as possible from the sensor matrix, in order grant a high detector efficiency. In second place we want to compress the large amount of data produced in high luminosity experiments, in order to reduce the on-chip memory and the output data bandwidth, with a consequent improvement of the static and dynamic power consumption.

4. Tools and procedures

In this section we want to present the working procedures, the typical project flow and also the tools that we use for the design and implementation of an embedded readout in a sensor chip.
In first place we start a new project taking into account the structural parameters, like pixel resolution and the total sensitive area, and considering the typical working conditions in terms of hit rate, time resolution and so on. We deal with our partners that provide the sensor matrix in order to find a routable structure that can improve the hit extraction algorithms but, at the same time, that can be scaled up to the desired dimensions. This step was found to be crucial since it requires to be quite forward-looking. The point is to establish the demarcation line between the full-custom design of the matrix and the world of standard-cells. The pinout of the whole matrix is then defined. In addition, a precise and sharp edge between these two blocks is fundamental for an accurate set up of the logical test benches that are performed along the implementation phase.

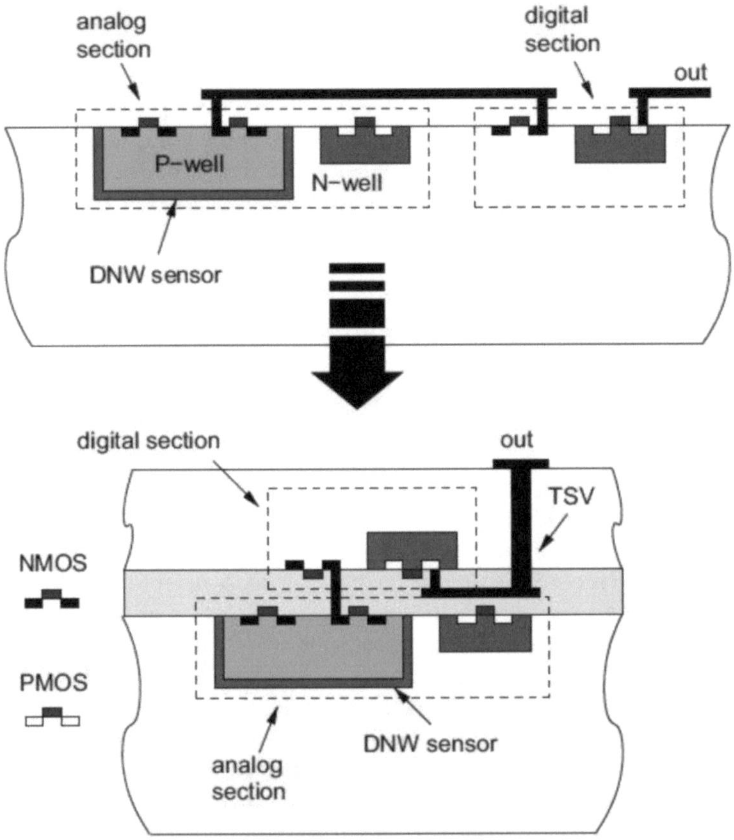

Fig. 4. Section view of a 2-TIER 3D MAPS structure.

Thereafter we try to project the readout architecture that fits at best in these requirements, and that optimizes the average pixel dead-time. We want to get as closer as possible to the pixel physical limit, mainly due to the front-end shaping-time (ref. to section 2). The architecture is developed in blocks, each one with specific and dedicated tasks. Once we have the complete conceptual design of each block, and of its task, we start to code the architecture with a specific hardware description language called VHDL (Very high speed Hardware Description Language).

VHDL can look like a sequential compiled language like C at first sight: it has a defined syntax, statements, functions and so on. But, at a closer look, it reveals the differences: since VHDL is used to describe digital architectures, the code has not a sequential flow from the beginning to the end, but it is divided in concurrent statements. Each of them is parallel, and it represents the equivalent of an independent circuit. Only the statements that are included inside special code blocks like *processes, functions* or *procedures* are sequential. The sequential execution of the statements inside a process is a high-level logical representation of the behaviour of the corresponding gates net. VHDL syntax is suitable both for a high-level behavioural modeling of electronic devices, and also for a gate-level net-list description. Moreover, in VHDL it is possible to give a hierarchical structure to the code, describing small components to be incorporated and interconnected into a higher level entity; this simplifies the maintenance and re-use of code. We took also a great advantage of VHDL by describing the architectures in a parameterized way, so that it could be easily adjusted to fit with different matrix dimensions and granularities.

A high-level hardware description in VHDL (or in any other HDL language like Verilog) can be translated into a net-list by specific EDA tools (Electronic Design Automation) that compile the code and implement the desired functions with the physical components found in a library. These libraries must be provided by the foundry where the designer wants to submit the IC. For our applications we used the *Synopsys Design Compiler* tool, a high-end product synthesizer for ASIC design (Application Specific Design Circuit).

But VHDL is intended also for circuit simulation, providing the designers with a set of non-synthesizable functions that can be used to build powerful test benches: for example text file I/O capability has been extensively used to load matrix patterns, and store simulation results. This constructs can be included in a top-level hierarchical entity that describes the stimuli and interconnects them to the top-level entity of sythesizable logic. We compiled and run our test benches with Mentor Graphics ModelSim, another EDA application that perform a logical simulation of the architecture giving the designers a plenty of tools for architecture debug and optimization.

Several steps of simulations take place during the implementation of the readout, a first logical model of the matrix sensor is connected to a hit file loader and integrated in the readout test benches. This is the starting point for every logical simulation of the high-level VHDL code since it allowed us to stimulate the components of readout as we pleased. Once each readout block has been coded and interconnected in the top hierarchical entity, we start a a dedicated simulation campaign in order to evaluate the efficiencies of that architecture. For this purpose a VHDL Monte Carlo hit generator stimulate the matrix and several millisecond of system working are simulated and analysed.

The top readout entity is then synthesized by the EDA tool. The produced net-list can be simulated in turn exploiting the cell models library furnished by the foundry within their design kit. This models includes the timing characterization of each component so that the post synthesis simulation can take into account also the propagation delay of signals as they go through the standard cells.

The following step is the physical implementation: in this phase the produced net-list of standard components should be placed on a predisposed area and routed. We adopted SoC (System on Chip) Cadence Encounter tool, a CAD developed for IC floor-planning, standard-cells placement/routing, and timing analysis. The floor-plan of an IC typically starts with the geometrical definition of the IC area, then we define the disposition of I/O pads. At this point we can import the matrix layout as an independent block and we define the readout core area as shown in Fig. 5.

The design placement and routing are performed by semi-automatic algorithms that leave to the designers the possibility to set a wide set of parameters and constraint. A delicate constraint is that on core interconnection to the matrix block.

The production flow foresee several iterations of implementation followed by timing extraction and analysis in order to find an optimal configuration. When an optimum is reached a DRC (Design Rule Check) is run on the design in search of constraint and rule violations. The final step is the extraction of the GDSII file, that contains the graphic layout of the IC to be sent to the foundry.

Now we will describe the main features of some of the matrix and peripheral architectures that we have developed, in conjunction with the efficiency evaluation studies that we have performed on them, focussing on those that have been implemented on silicon.

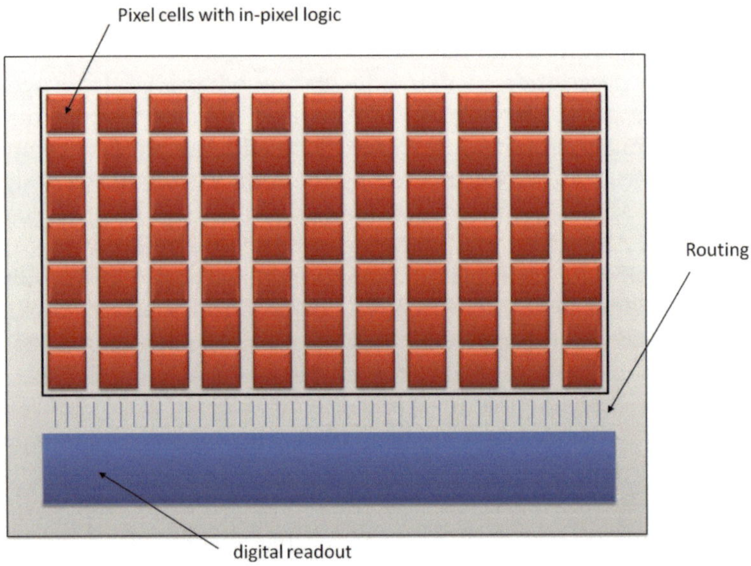

Fig. 5. Top schematic view of the peripheral readout and sensor matrix. Figure not in scale.

5. A sparsified readout matrix

The main goal of a sparsified readout architecture is the association of a spatial and temporal coordinate to each fired pixel. The term *sparsified* means that hit extraction and encoding is focussed on sparse randomly-accessible regions of the matrix, where it is known the presence of fired pixels. This method is in opposition to a full matrix sequential readout, and it is meant to achieve a faster readout and reset of fired pixels. In this architecture, these sparse and randomly accessible regions are the pixels themselves.

The idea is to incorporate few digital logic within pixels, exploiting for example a DNwell MAPS sensor technology, and realize in a dedicated portion of the chip area a complex digital readout system. The key concept is to use only inter-pixel global wires and not point-to-point wires from the border of the matrix to single pixels or groups of pixels. In Fig. 6.a is presented a pixel interconnection scheme exploiting global wires only. This approach allows to reduce wire density, that does not depend on the size of the matrix (number of pixels), in order to grant a higher scalability of the architecture.

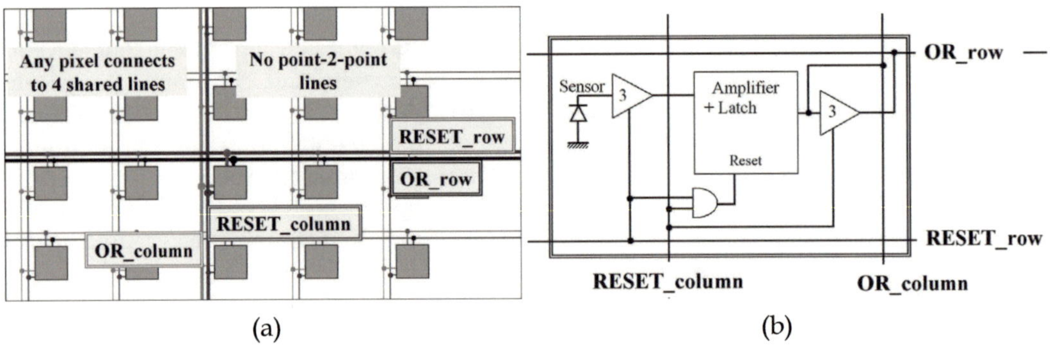

Fig. 6. In (a): The wired-or matrix layout. In (b): The 4 wire in-pixel logic.

Let us now discuss in details the functions of each line:

- *OR_row* is a 3-state buffered horizontal output wire to read the pixel status. When the buffer is enabled through the RESET column vertical line, pixel output is read via the OR row wire. This line is shared with all pixels in the same row by creating a wired-or condition. As only one pixel at a time is allowed to be read, the OR row coincides with the pixel output value.
- *RESET_row* is a horizontal input wire to freeze the pixel by disconnecting it from the sensor. Moreover if RESET row is asserted along with the RESET column line, it resets the pixel. This line is shared with all pixels in the same row.
- *OR_column* is a vertical output line that is always connected to pixel output. This is shared with all pixels in the column by creating a wired-or condition. If at least one pixel of the column is fired, this global wire activates, independently of the number of hits and their location.
- *RESET_column* is a vertical input line to enable the connection to the sensor via a 3-state buffer. It is used to mask an entire column of pixels. Again, if used with the RESET row, it resets the pixel.

In Fig. 7 we present an example in the situation of a 5 hit cluster. The active wired-or conditions cause the activation of three OR column wires. This corresponds to the *Sample Phase* of Tab. 1.

Phase	RESET row	RESET column	OR row	OR column
Sample	1	0	Z	*pixel*
Hold-Mask	0	0	Z	*pixel*
Hold-Read	0	1	*pixel*	*pixel*
Reset	1	1	0	0

Table 1. Pixels readout phases.

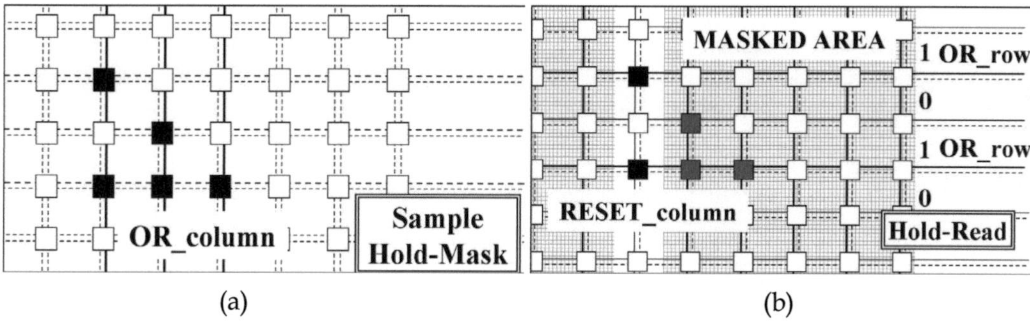

Fig. 7. In (a): Columns and rows of the hits. In (b): Readout starts for the first enabled column.

During *Hold-Mask phase* the matrix is frozen by de-asserting all the RESET row signals, no more hits can be accepted by the matrix. This determines the time granularity of the events. Pixels are then read out column by column during the *Hold-Read phase* by masking all matrix but the desired column with the RESET column signal. The pixel content is put on the OR row bus and can be read out. Afterwards, the column is reset by re-asserting the RESET row signal in conjunction with RESET column.

The readout process moves on to all the columns that presents an active OR column signal, and skipping the empty regions of the matrix. The two Hold-Read and Reset phases are the only two cycles needed to enable and read out an entire column of pixels, thus the entire readout phase takes twice as many clock periods as the number of activated columns.
During the readout process, the whole matrix is frozen in order to avoid event overlaps. This is done to individuate and delimit precise time windows to which hits belong. The time period is beaten synchronously in the whole detector, in order to allow the off-line reconstruction of tracks from the space-time coordinates of the associated hits.

6. The AREO readout architecture

6.1 APSEL3D

Next step of this chapter is the presentation of the peripheral readout logics that perform the hit extraction from the matrix, encode the space-time coordinates, and form the digital hit-stream to be sent out of the sensor chip. One of the first architectures that we have developed, has been realized on silicon within a sensor chip called APSEL that was realized by the SLIM5 collaboration [A. Gabrielli for the SLIM5 Collaboration (year 2008)]. The architecture involved took the name AREO because it is the APSEL chip REad Out. The IC is a planar MAPS sensor that exploits the triple well technology described in section 3 and provided by ST Microelectronics in a 130 nm process. The AREO architecture was developed to be coupled with a matrix that presents dedicated in pixel digital logic and global connection lines shared among regions of pixels. The sensor matrix is 256 pixels wide (32 columns by 8 rows) divided into 16 regions of 4 × 4 single pixels called *Macro Pixels* (MPs) (see Fig. 8). The pixel pitch is 50 microns.

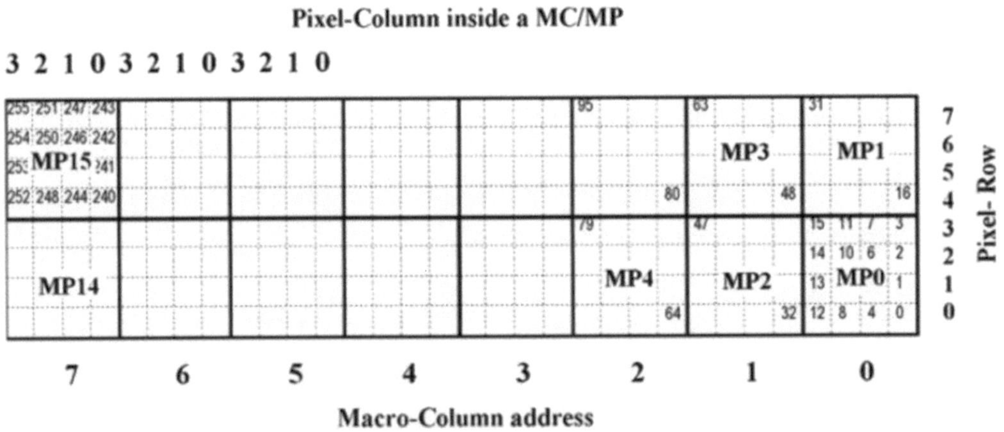

Fig. 8. The matrix divided into Macro Pixels

Each MP has two private lines that interconnect it to the peripheral readout: a *fast-or* and a *latch-enable* signal. When a pixel in a clear MP gets fired, the fast-or line get activated and, when the latch-enable is set to low, all the pixels within the MP are frozen and cannot accept new incoming hits any more.
Internally to the peripheral readout a time counter increments on the rising edge of a *bunch crossing* clock (BC). When the counter increments, all the new MPs that present an active fast or are frozen and they are associated to the precedent time counter value. In this way all the

fired pixels within a frozen MP are univocally associated to the common *time-stamp* (TS) stored in the peripheral readout.
The hit extraction takes place by means of an 8-bit wide *pixel data bus* shared among all the pixel rows. Each pixel is provided with a tri-state buffer activated by a *column enable* signal shared by the pixel column, as it is shown in Fig. 9.

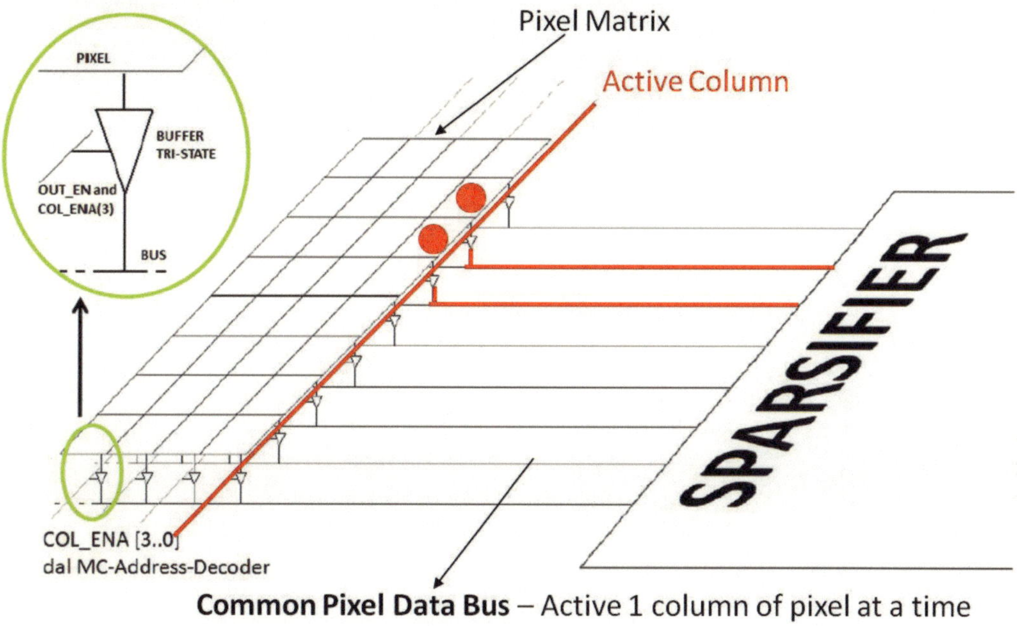

Fig. 9. Common data bus and pixel drivers

The vertical pile of 2 MPs is called *Macro Column* (MC). Only the MCs that present at least one frozen MP are scanned. If there are no frozen MPs in a MC, its four columns are skipped from the readout sweep in order to speed up the hit-extraction process.
To scan a MC means to activate in sequence its four columns since it is not know a-priori which is the one that contains the hit. Each pixel column is readout in one clock cycle, so the whole MC readout takes place in 4 read clock periods. After the readout phase of a MC, the reset condition is sent to the pixel logic by enabling contemporaneously the first and the last column of the MC (MC col. ena = 1001). Since the column enable signals are shared among all the pixels of a column, in order to prevent the resetting of a MP on that MC, which was not frozen, a *Macro Row* enable is routed to the matrix and taken into account during the output-enable and reset phase of the pixels. In this way only the desired MP of a MC can be read out and reset, while the other keeps collecting hits. The typical MP life-cycle is shown in Fig. 10.
All the hits found on the active column can be read out in one clock cycle, independently of the pixel occupancy, thanks to a component called *sparsifier*. This component is appointed to encode each hit with the corresponding x and y spatial coordinates and with the corresponding time stamp.
Next to the sparsifier there is a buffering element called *barrel*, which is basically an asymmetric FIFO memory with dynamic input width based on rolling read/write

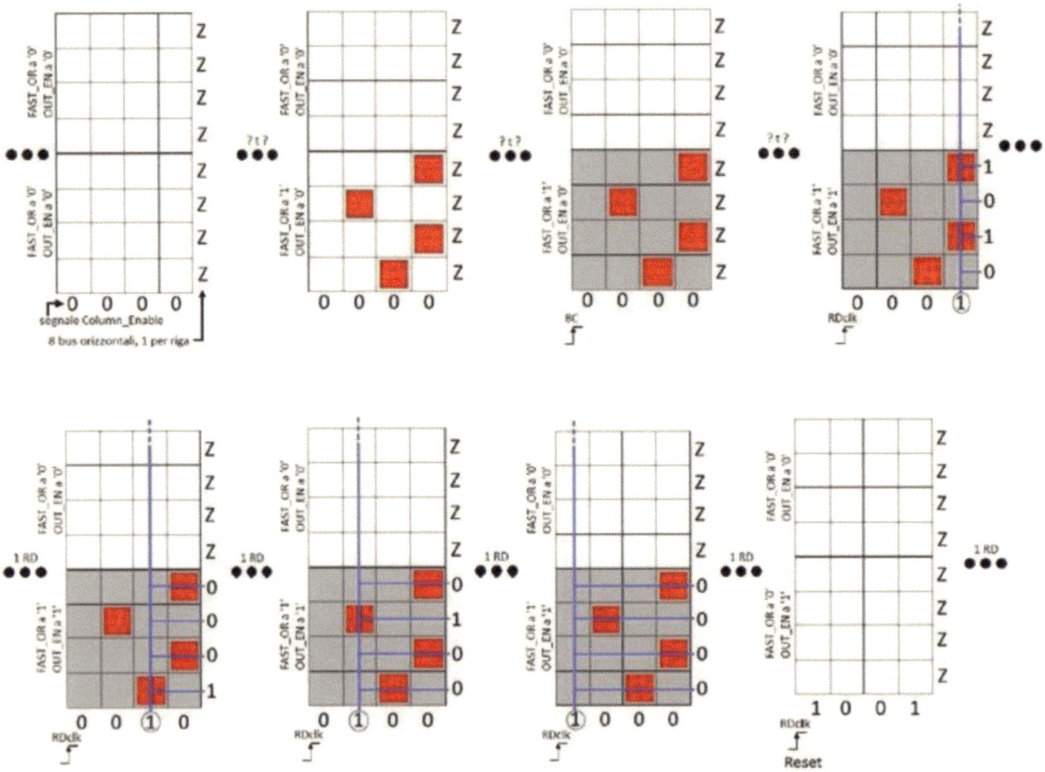

Fig. 10. MP life cycle. The hits populate the MP. A BC edge freezes the MP. The MP columns are read out one by one. A final reset condition is applied.

addresses. It can store up to 8 encoded hits per clock cycle which means that it has 8 independent write address pointers that can be enabled or not depending on how many hits are found on the current active column. Due to the reduced dimensions of the connected matrix, the barrel depth was of only 16 hit-words. The barrel output throughput is 1 hit per clock cycle. The hits are encoded with the format described in Tab. 2:

hit field	length	name	function
hit[11:9]	3 bits	pxRow	pixel row address
hit[8:7]	2 bits	pxCol	pixel column within MC
hit[6:4]	3 bits	MC	Macro Column address
hit[3:0]	4 bits	TS	time stamp field

Table 2. Hit encoding in APSEL3D readout. The global *x* address must be reconstructed by the MC and pxlCol fields. The algorithm is $4MC + pxCol$. A *data valid* bit is added to the coded hits when they are sent on the output bus.

Since the developed architecture is data-push, which means that no external trigger is required, the hits are automatically popped out of the barrel and sent out on the synchronous *output data bus*. The readout architecture is synchronous on the external *read clock*. While a different clock is used to feed the slow control interface, for the chip control.

Slow control (SC) is based on a source synchronous bus of three *SC mode* bits and on 8 bits of *SC data*. Depending on the value of the SC mode bus sampled at the rising edge of the *SC clock*, different slow control operations can be performed. One of the main task of the slow control interface is to load the mask patterns that can exclude sets of MPs from the acquisition process.

The AREO architecture is also provided with a digital matrix, which is a copy of the full-custom sensors array but realized in standard-cells and residing in the chip periphery with the readout itself. It has been implemented for digital test purposes. With the slow control interface it is possible to select the operating mode from digital to custom: in *digital mode* the readout is connected to the register-based matrix, while in *custom mode* it is connected to the sensor matrix. Through SC it is possible to load a predetermined pattern on the digital matrix, in this way we can verify the correspondence between the loaded hits and those observed on the chip data bus.

The readout efficiencies will be presented in the next subsection, where the application of this architecture on a bigger matrix is described.

6.2 APSEL4D

Thanks to the fruitful SLIM5 collaboration, it was possible to implement the AREO architecture even on a wider 4096-pixel matrix, in the chip that was named APSEL4D. Scalability is one of the major issues when using non-global lines. The number of private connections scales with number of pixels and thus with area, which is a quadratic growth respect to linear matrix dimensions. The contact side between the matrix and the readout, where the routing signal shall pass through, increases linearly which means that whatever is the finite dimension of a wire, exists always an upper limit in matrix size. In our case the fast-or and latch-enable signals are non-global lines but they are shared among groups of pixels; this allows to push the limit further.

In this chip the readout is connected to a 128×32-pixel matrix with the same characteristics of the 3D parent. The subdivision into MPs follows the same rules of the APSEL3D version, a schematic view of the matrix of MPs is shown on Fig. 11.

Also the readout architecture kept the same original idea, but it has been scaled to the larger matrix with the replication of some basic components. Since the matrix readout takes place by columns, the enlarging in the horizontal direction led only to a longer column sweeping time and a longer x address field in data. The extension in the vertical direction was achieved by paralleling 4 couples sparsifier-barrel. A scheme of the AREO v.4D readout is presented in Fig. 12.

The parallel data coming out of the barrels are stored in the *barrel final* by the *sparsifier out*. In this way hits are sent one by one on the *formatted data out bus*. The barrels and the barrel final have a depth of 32 hit words. If a rate burst fills up the barrels, a feedback circuit stops the matrix readout in order to flush data out of the barrels. This increase the pixels dead-time but it grants that no data is lost. The hit format of the AREO v.4D architecture is reported in table Tab. 3.

Due to the higher number of channels, the encoded pixel address has increased in length. The time counter was raised from a modulo 16 to a modulo 256, thus the time stamp field is now 8-bit wide.

The implementation went through and the final layout of the readout is shown in Fig. 13.

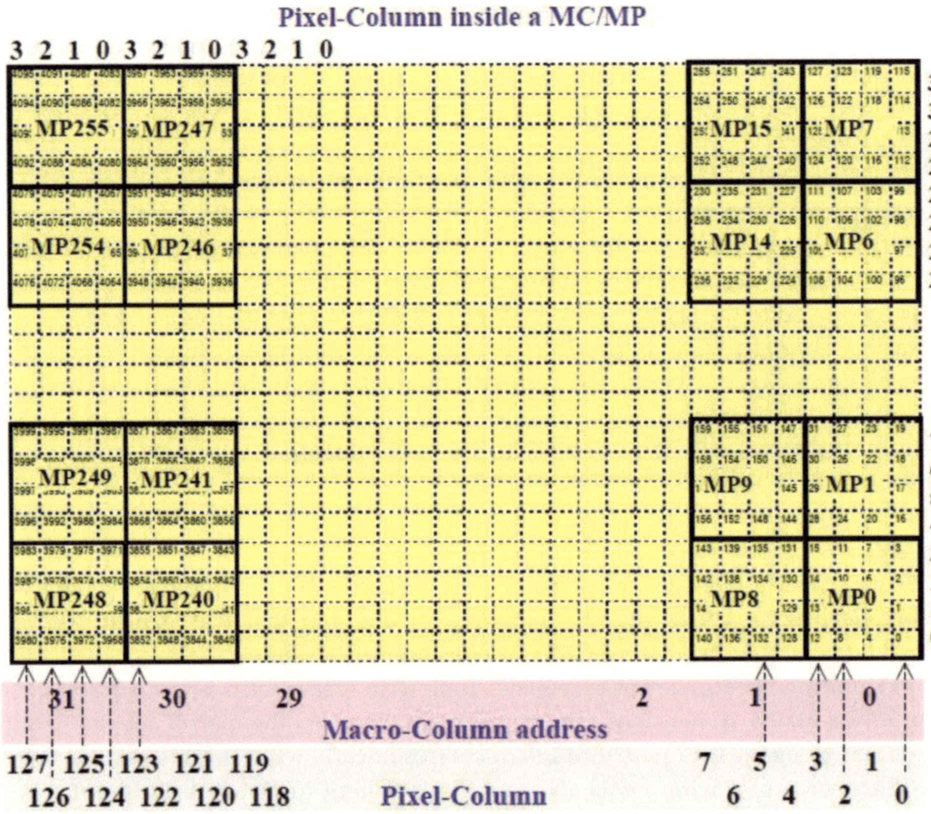

Fig. 11. APSEL4D matrix and MPs.

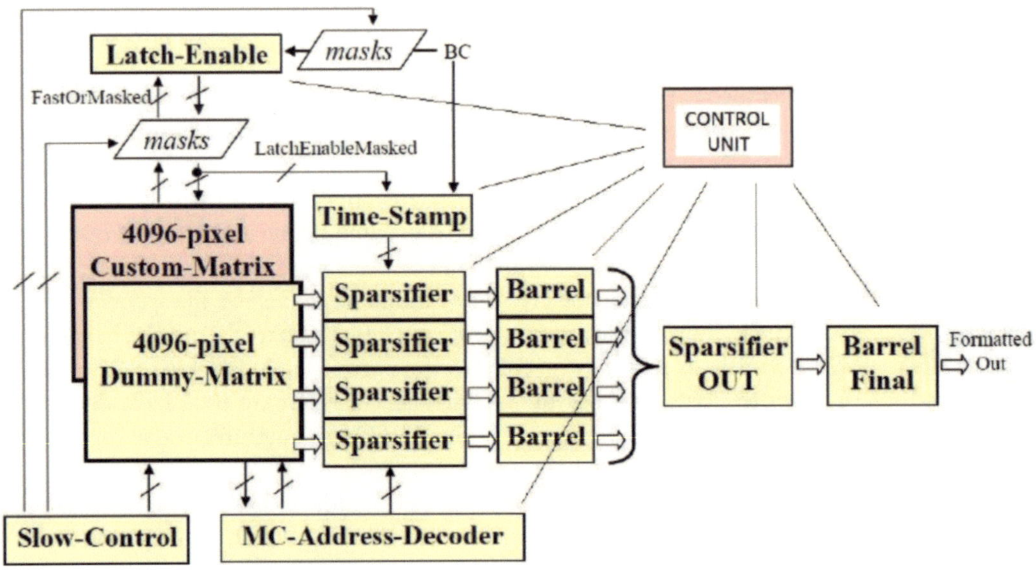

Fig. 12. APSEL4D schematic readout

hit field	length	name	function
hit[19:15]	5 bits	pxRow	pixel row address
hit[14:13]	2 bits	pxCol	pixel column within MC
hit[12:8]	5 bits	MC	Macro Column address
hit[7:0]	8 bits	TS	time stamp field

Table 3. Hit encoding in APSEL4D readout. The global x address must be reconstructed by the MC and pxlCol fields. The algorithm is $4MC + pxCol$. A *data valid* bit is added to the coded hits when they are sent on the output bus.

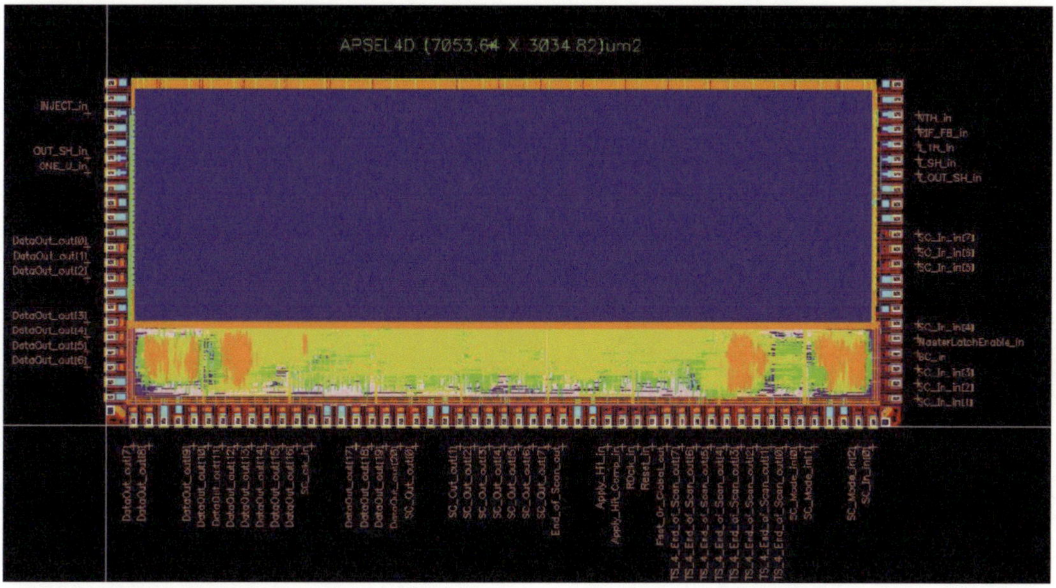

Fig. 13. APSEL4D layout

Several logical simulations were run with the source code of this architecture during the implementation phase. These simulations have generally two main objectives: formerly to verify the correct operation of the logic described and in second place to evaluate the efficiency of the architecture with a statistical sample of randomly generated hits. We present the results of the efficiency studies.

Several behaviours were observed by varying the flux of incoming particles and the readout clock speed. In Fig. 14 we plot the readout efficiency against the average hit rate. It is important to clarify what is the inefficiency, where it comes from and how we measure it. The inefficiency is the quantification of how much information we are loosing, being it of physical relevance or not. A part of it is proportional to the average pixel dead-time, being it due to front-end shaping time or to the readout hit-extraction speed. The longer the pixel is blind, the more information is lost. The readout scheme implemented and the readout clock, determine the hit extraction speed. Another origin of inefficiency is the hit congestion in the readout de-queuing system. For example, in this particular architecture, a hit congestion causes the hit extraction to stop, thus resulting in further increasing dead-time. Anyhow, it is important to understand that this origin of inefficiency is unrelated to previous one: if we could could count on an infinite output bandwidth, or a infinite buffer, then we would have no inefficiency due to hit congestion, but the same inefficiency due to hit-extraction algorithms.

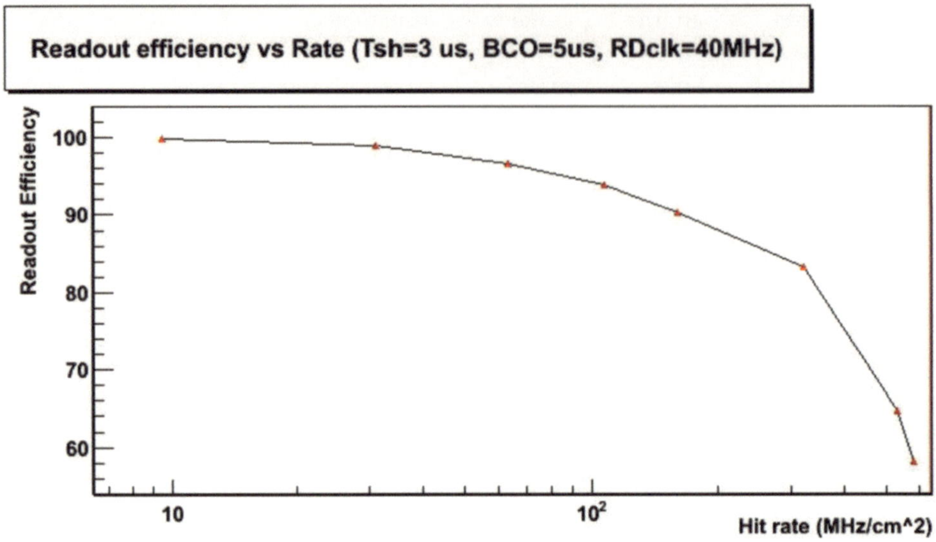

Fig. 14. Readout efficiency of the AREO v.4D architecture VS hit rate. 40 MHz of read clock and 5 μs of BC clock.

We measure the efficiency as

$$\epsilon = 1 - \frac{\nu_{blind}}{\nu_{TOT}} \quad (1)$$

where ν_{blind} is the number of hits generated on a blind pixel and ν_{TOT} is the total number of generated hits. In this case a pixel is considered blind if it is already latched or if it belongs to a frozen MP. For this particular architecture, this measure includes the hit-extraction and the hit-congestion inefficiencies.

For what concerns the results presented in Fig. 14, the inefficiency up to 300 MHz/cm^2 is dominated by the hit-extraction delay, thereafter, for higher rates, we start to observe hit-congestions that stop the matrix scan, with a resulting abrupt steepening of the curve.

In Fig. 15 we plot the efficiencies measured while varying the BC clock period. We recall that the BC clock increments the time counter and it makes start a new scan of the matrix.

In this case we see that there is a plateau extending up to about 3 microseconds, then a drastic fall in the efficiency occurs. This happens because it is more convenient to have a continuous sweeping of the matrix rather than long periods of scan inactivity. Remember that the readout is waiting for the next BC to start a new matrix scan. Thus, if the matrix scan is much faster than the BC period, then for the the most of the time hits accumulates in the matrix without being extracted. The points in the plateau (BC < 3 μs) correspond instead to a situation where the sweep is almost continuous, and then the efficiency is roughly constant. The average time that takes to the readout to perform a complete scan of the matrix is what we call the *Mean Sweeping Time* (MST). It depends on the architecture, the hit flux, the matrix dimensions and the read clock frequency. The point here is that a 5 μs-BC clock is for sure not the optimal working point for this configuration since the MST is much lower than BC period (MST $\ll$ BC).

For thoroughness we report also the readout efficiency plotted against the read clock frequency in Fig. 16.

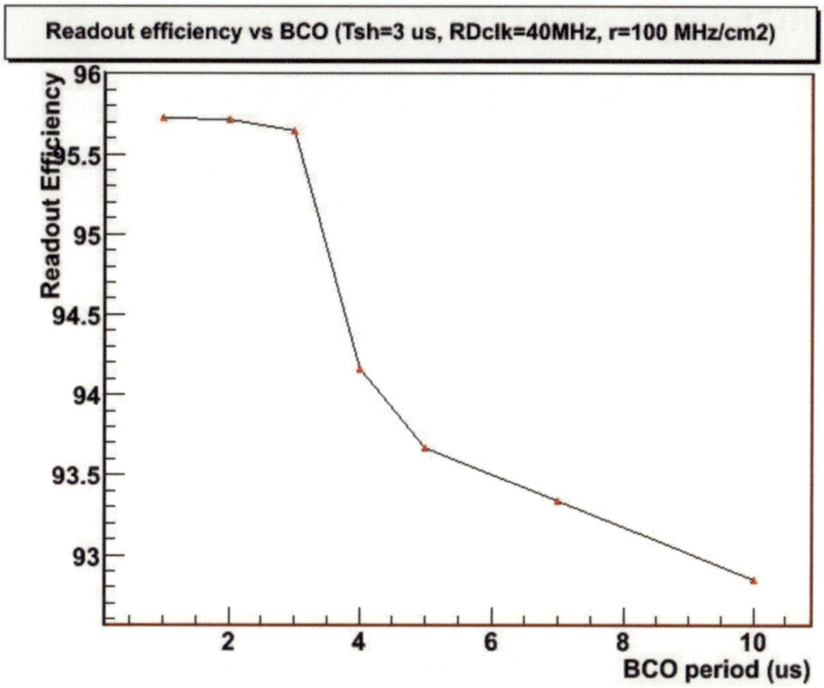

Fig. 15. Readout efficiency of the AREO v.4D architecture vs BC clock period. 40 MHz of read clock and 100 MHz/cm² of hit rate. The plateau within 3 μs is characterized by a continuous matrix scan operation. The efficiency drop as the mean sweeping time becomes negligible respect to the BC clock period.

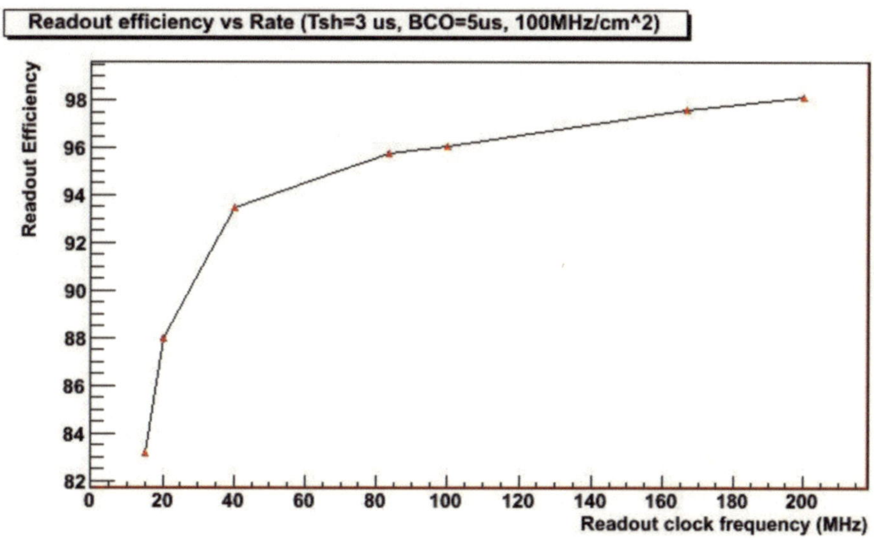

Fig. 16. Readout efficiency of the AREO v.4D architecture VS read clock frequency. 100 MHz/cm² of hit rate and 5 μs of BC period.

7. The SORTEX readout architecture

The experience matured during the AREO development and simulation, and then its integration in a DAQ chain (described in section 8), highlighted new possibilities of optimization.
In first place we developed a toy Monte Carlo in C++ that emulated the behavior of the matrix and readout. It was useful to run parametric scans, for example we could evaluate the dependency of the efficiency against the MP dimensions. The plot in Fig. 17 shows the efficiency against the MP x dimension (in pixels), the MP total area is preserved.

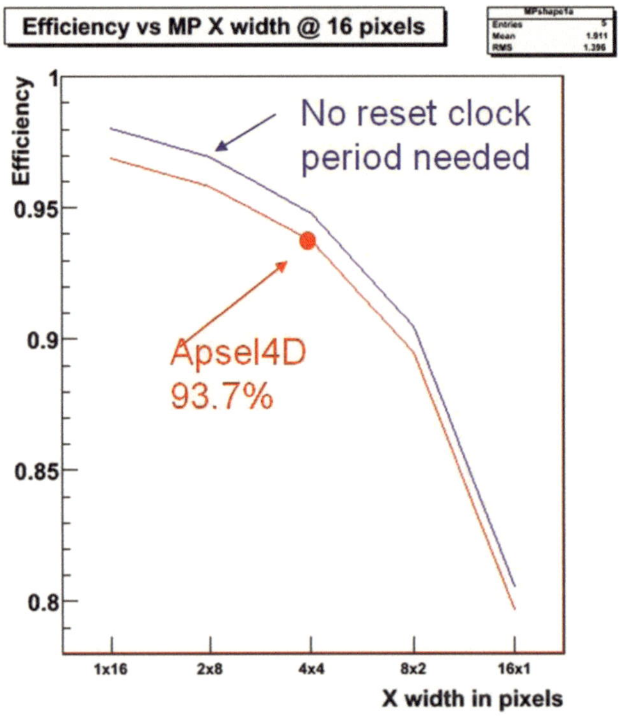

Fig. 17. Readout efficiency of the AREO v.4D architecture vs MP x dimension. 100 MHz/cm² of hit rate and 5 μs of BC period. The APSEL4D configuration is highlighted. The blue line doesn't take into account the clock period dedicated to the reset of the MP. Random and uniform pattern generated.

From this plot it is clear that a higher efficiency is obtained if we decrease the x dimension of the MP. This is due to the freezing of MPs and the high vertical parallelization of the architecture. Since the total MP dimension is conserved in these simulations, the dead-area induced by a single hit is the same, but it can be read out faster: A frozen 4×4 MP requires 4 clock cycles to be read out, a 2×8 MP only 2 cycles. Moreover, if we manage to remove the required reset clock cycle, we can further improve the readout efficiency.
These were the starting points for the development of a new architecture. Other consideration where done about adding extra parallelization to the architecture. We have yet a powerful vertical parallelization for the hit extraction then, foreseeing to scale towards bigger matrices, we decided to add also a horizontal parallelization.

The plot in Fig. 18 shows the efficiencies of 4 readouts running in parallel on different portions of the matrix area. The best results are achieved with the subdivision of the scanned area along the x dimension. It is clear that the shorter is the scan, the better is the efficiency. Thus we added the extra parallelization in this direction, by implementing 4 shorter readout scans, working on different vertical portions of the matrix area that we called *sub-matrices*. When we designed this architecture we had in mind to optimize it for a big matrix, suitable for the installation on a tracker module. The targeted final matrix dimension was 320×256 pixels with a pitch of 40 microns and a total area of about 1.3 cm^2. Each sub-matrix is then 80×256 pixel wide and covers an area of about 0.3 cm^2.
For what concern the optimization of the MP x size, since the expected hits on a tracker sensor can have a spatial correlation (which means that a single particle can fire two or more adjacent pixels) we decided for the 2×8 shape rather than 1×16. The Monte Carlo simulations, in fact, generated uncorrelated hits and then advantaged the thinnest configuration possible 1×16.

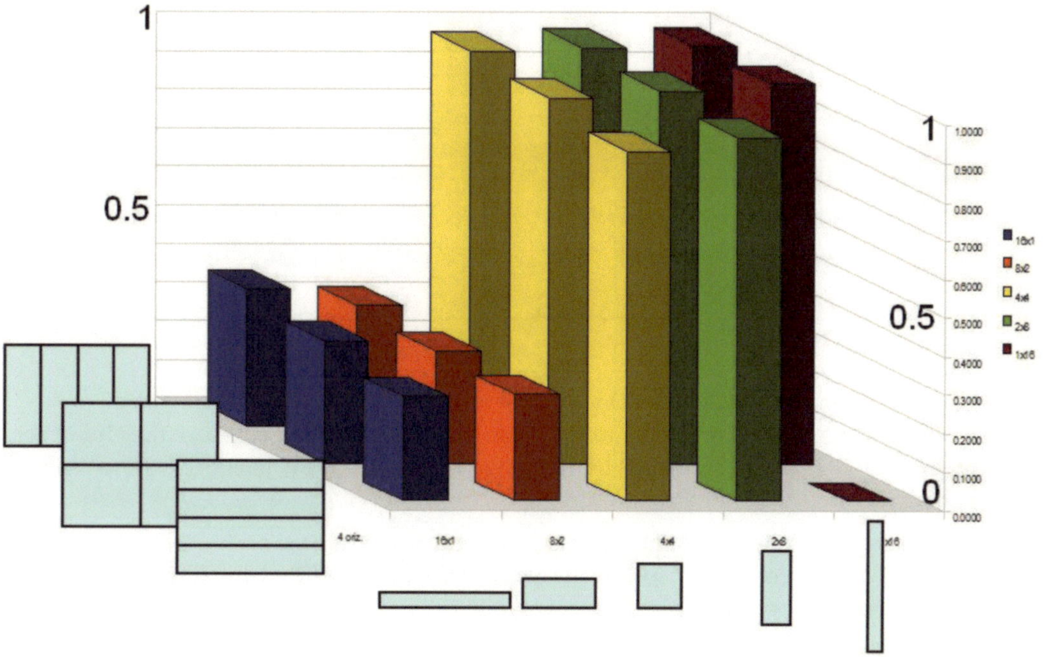

Fig. 18. Readout efficiency of 4 parallel AREO v.4D architectures VS MP x dimension and geometrical subdivision of the matrix area. 100 MHz/cm^2 of hit rate and 1 μs of BC period. Values are reported in Tab. 4

4×1	0.36	0.31	0.97	0.98	0.99
2×2	0.32	0.30	0.95	0.97	0.99
1×4	0.27	0.28	0.91	0.94	/
	16×1	8×2	4×4	2×8	1×16

Table 4. Table of values plotted in Fig. 18

During the integration of the AREO v.4D architecture in a DAQ system, we realized that was more difficult to re-order externally the flux of the time-unordered hits coming from the AREO architecture. This architecture in fact, doesn't grant that hits are sent out ordered respect to their time stamp. The hit flux on output is time sorted only in the $MST \ll BC$ region, where to each time stamp (BC edge) corresponds an independent matrix scan, andwhere the hit queues have time to be fully emptied before the arrival of a new BC. Unfortunately this is the region where the architecture is less efficient, and therefore where we don't want to make it work. We saw in fact that better efficiencies are achieved when we get close to the $MST \lesssim BC$ region. Since MST is a *mean* sweeping time, it means that its distribution can have tails above the BC period. In these tails we can have the mixing-up of time stamps in the AREO architecture. This situation is presented in Fig. 19.

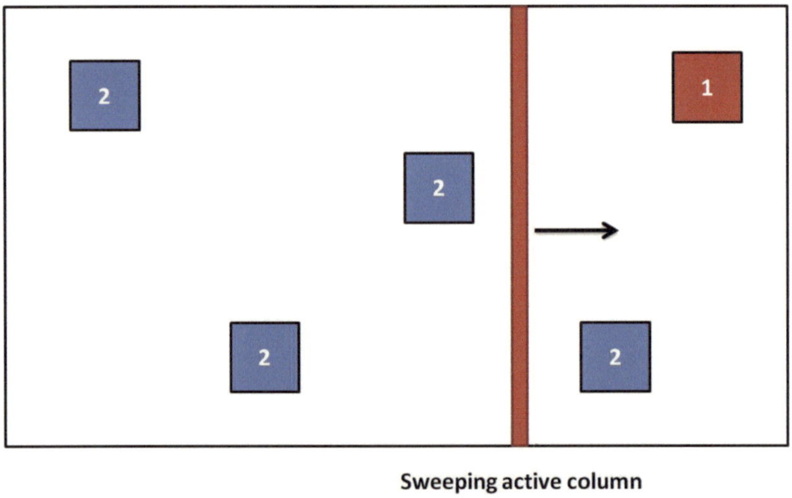

Fig. 19. Case of hit mixing in the AREO v.4D architecture. Tails of the *sweeping time distribution* allow a matrix scan to take longer than a BC period. Hence, before the end of the scan triggered by BC edge 1, a new set of MPs, tagged by BC edge 2, gets frozen and read out together.

The idea is to prevent tails to mix-up the hits in order to have a time sorted extraction of hits from the matrix. This concept inspired the name *SORTEX* (SORted hit EXtraction) of the new architecture developed.

For this purpose we introduced in this architecture the *scan buffer* element. It is a formatted FIFO memory that stores a new list of frozen MPs with its associated time stamp at each BC. The active column sweep logic pops a list out of this FIFO before starting a new scan. In this way the blue MPs drawn in Fig. 19 would not be considered during the scan number 1 since they belong to a different list.

These are tail effects and we will show through the results of simulations that the efficiency is not afflicted by this feature. It is worth to say that in this way we obtained a sorted hit extraction without any modification of the matrix logic.

Anyway, a sorted hit-extraction from the matrix is not sufficient to grant the time sorting on the output bus of the chip. It is important to avoid also the time stamp mixing in the hit dequeuing system. Till now, the *sparsifier out* component, that was shown in Fig. 12, did not consider the TS of the hits before writing them into the next *barrel out*. Therefore, in the

SORTEX architecture the *sparsifier out* is substituted by a new component called *concentrator* which takes care of preserving the time sorting of the hits before writing them into the next barrel.

Now that hits are ordered inside the barrels, we thought to exploit this feature in order to optimize the on-chip required memory and the total output bandwidth. The 8-bit TS field was removed from the hit word format, and it was replaced by a dedicated header word.

We wanted to improve the dynamic readout performances also by taking into account the spatial hit correlation that one would expect due to the physical nature of the signal. A cluster optimization algorithm was then introduced in the SORTEX architecture. The active column has been subdivided into 8-bit wide *zones*. Each sparsifier, that in the AREO architecture encoded a column of 8 pixels simultaneously, now encodes 8 zones per clock cycle, which means a column of 64 pixels. Thus 4 sparsifiers only can encode the whole of the active column.

The hit word now encodes the hit y coordinate by the zone address and the zone pattern itself. This technique is advantageous in case of clustered events. Respect to a classical direct xy encoding, the zone encoding technique increases the length of an encoded hit but in case of clustered events it reduces the total number of required hit words. In the AREO architecture the width of the y address is given by $\log_2 H$ where H is the height in pixels of the matrix (binary encoding). With a zone sparsification algorithm, the y pixel address is given by the zone pattern, which is W bit wide, and by the zone address which is only $\log_2 (H/W)$ bit wide. Then the hit word is incremented by the quantity Δ given by:

$$\Delta = \log_2 H / W + W - \log_2 H = W - \log_2 W \quad (2)$$

The increment Δ is small for small W, and the hit word can transport the information of up to W hits. An example of the application of the zone encoding algorithm is shown in Fig. 20.

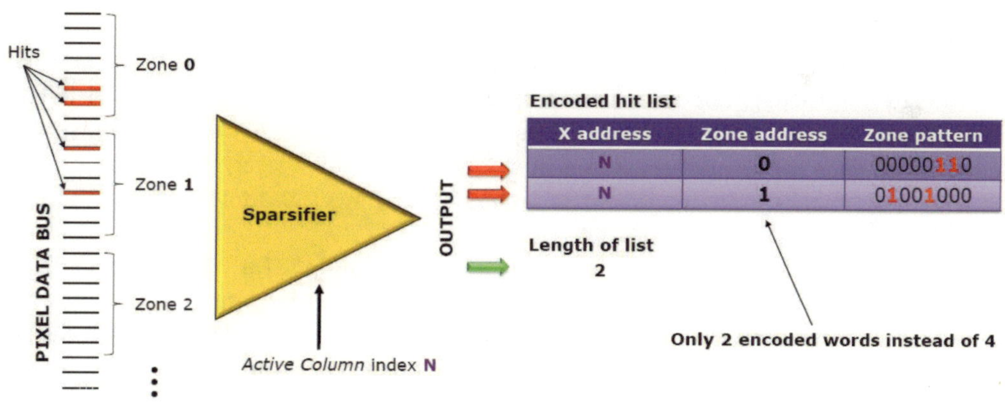

Fig. 20. Example of zone sparsification algorithm.

We want to show now, with the help a concrete example, the benefits brought by the time sorting and the zone sparsification algorithms. Let us apply to the 320×256 matrix the hit encoding scheme adopted in the AREO architecture. Then the hit-word length L is:

$$L = X_{addr} + Y_{addr} + TS = \log_2 320 + \log_2 256 + 8 = 9 + 8 + 8 = 25\text{bits} \quad (3)$$

and the produced data rate R is:

$$R = L \cdot C_f \cdot \Phi \cdot A = 25\text{bits} \times 4 \times 25\text{Mtracks}^{-1}\text{cm}^{-2} \times 1.3\text{cm}^2 = 3.2\text{Gbps} \quad (4)$$

where C_f is an hypothetic cluster factor of 4, Φ is the particle flux and A is the sensor area. Now if we introduce the time sorting of the hits, and assuming that each leading TS word is followed by about 10 hits[3] we have

$$L = X_{addr} + Y_{addr} = 9 + 8 = 17\text{bits} \quad (5)$$

and

$$R = L \cdot C_f \cdot \Phi \cdot A \cdot 1.1 = 2.4\text{Gbps} \quad (6)$$

The 1.1 factor is the rate increment due to the presence of the TS words. Now let us introduce also the zone sparsification algorithm. In order to simplify calculations we assume that the cluster factor has a fixed shape of 2×2 pixels. The number of hit words that need to be sent depends on the overlapping of the cluster shape on the zones grid. There are 8 possible geometrical configurations, only in 1 of them the cluster overlaps 4 different zones. In the remainder 7 configurations only 2 hit-words are produced. It is possible then to evaluate the data rate R with a weighted average over the possible configurations.

$$R = [2(L + \Delta) \times \frac{7}{8} + 4(L + \Delta) \times \frac{1}{8}] \cdot \Phi \cdot A \cdot 1.1 = 1.8\text{Gbps} \quad (7)$$

where $\Delta = 5$ is the increase in word length due to the zone sparsification, considering that the SORTEX architecture adopted $W = 8$. (ref. to eq. 2).
1.8 Gbps vs 3.2 Gbps corresponds to a considerable 45% reduction of the output bandwidth. The reduction of the produced data rate, can bring significant improvement also in the on-chip required memory. The SORTEX architecture, as well as the AREO one, is data-push which means that there is not an extensive memory that buffers the hits during the latency of an external trigger. Though buffering is useful in other situations, for example in case of rate-bursts. In these cases, that represent fluctuations over the average hit rate, for a short period of time the hits are produced at a higher rate respect to the output data bus bandwidth.
We realized a brief study on the optimal barrel depths. In Fig. 21.a we plotted the barrel output rate against the input rate. In ideal conditions, where no hits are lost, the two values should be equivalent until the maximum output rate of the barrel is reached. We recall that the barrel can store more than 1 hit-word per clock cycle. The saturation limit at 40 MHz corresponds to the output bandwidth of a barrel driven with a 40 MHz clock. In these non-ideal conditions instead, we observe hit losses even when the mean input rate is below the 40 MHz. This losses are due to the statistical fluctuations above the mean, it is possible to observe how they decrease as the barrel gets deeper.

[3] value not far from that expected with Φ=100 Mhit s^{-1} cm^{-2}, A=1.3 cm^2 and 1 μs of BC.

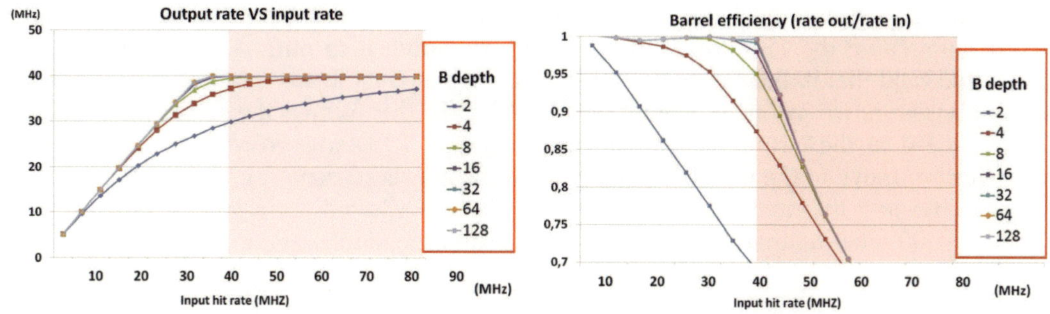

(a) (b)

Fig. 21. In (a): Output rate vs input rate of a barrel. In (b): barrel efficiency vs input rate. 40 MHz read clock, in the pink region the input rate is grater than the output bandwidth of the barrel.

We divided the barrels into 2 categories: the 2nd layer barrels or *B2*, which are connected to the spasrifiers and which receive data from a 16th of the matrix (4 barrels for each sub-matrix). And the 1st layer barrels that gathers data from the 4 B2s of a sub-matrix (refer to Fig. 22). A B2 must sustain a hit rate of 130 MHz/16 = 8.2 MHz, and a B1 8.2 MHz × 4 ≈ 32 MHz. Looking at those values on the *x* axis in Fig. 21.b, we opted for a depth of 8 for the B2s and a depth of 64 for the B1s. In this plot we expressed the efficiency as the ratio between the output and the input rate. A zoom in the knee region of the efficiency plot highlights the performance of different barrel depths.
Since we have now 4 independent readout units, and thus 4 *barrel out* equivalents (B1s), we introduced a new component called *final concentrator* that drives the output data bus. It performs a round robin cycle over the 4 B1s in order to extract all their data relative to a certain TS.

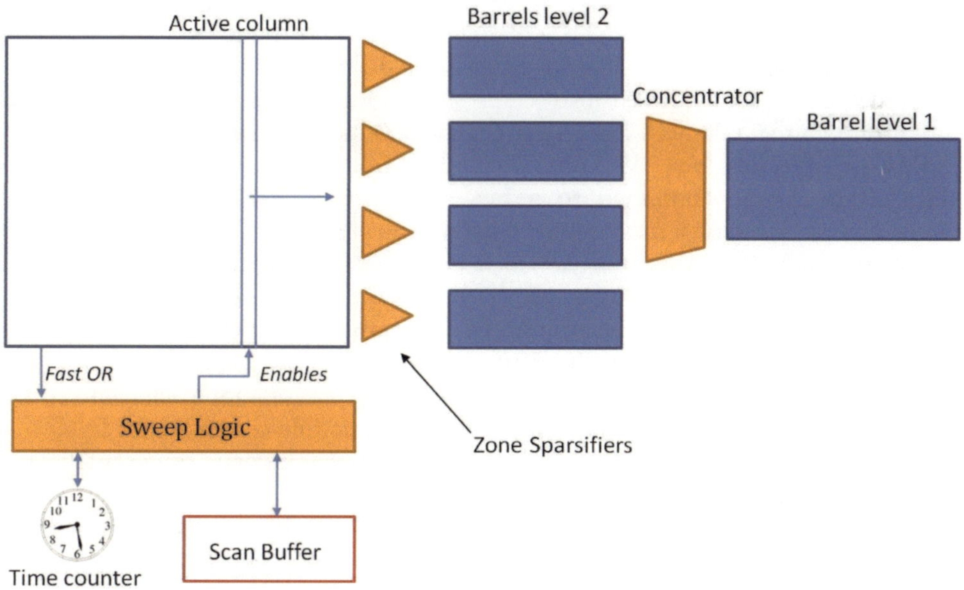

Fig. 22. SORTEX readout for a single sub-matrix

The final concentrator then, empties one B1 at a time, extracting first the leading header words containing the TS information. Before forwarding it to output bus, it adds a 2-bit formatted field that individuates the sub-matrix origin. The format of a header word on the output bus is shown in Tab. 5. The whole bunch of hits that follows the TS header in that B1 is forwarded to the output bus. When the following TS header-word is found, the final concentrator move to the next B1. The hit-word formats is presented in Tab. 6. We mention that the B1s and the final concentrator are fed by a dedicated clock-tree net, so that they could run at higher frequencies respect to all the rest of readout.

hit field	length	name	function
hit[21]	1 bit	DV	1 = data valid
hit[20]	1 bit	Header bit	1 = header word
hit[19:10]	10 bits	/	unused
hit[9:8]	2 bits	SM addr	sub-matrix address
hit[7:0]	8 bits	TS	time stamp

Table 5. Header word format. SORTEX architecture divided into 4 sub-matrices.

hit field	length	name	function
hit[21]	1 bit	DV	1 = data valid
hit[20]	1 bit	Header bit	0 = hit word
hit[19:18]	2 bits	Sp addr	sparsifier address
hit[17:15]	3 bits	Z addr	zone address
hit[14:8]	7 bits	X addr	x address (sub-mat. relative)
hit[7:0]	8 bits	TS	time stamp

Table 6. Hit word format. SORTEX architecture on 320×256 pixel matrix.

The SORTEX architecture is controlled by an I^2C-like interface that allows to read and write two sets of 16-bit registers, one can be accessed in read/write mode (RW) and the other set is read-only (RO). This interface was developed to reduce the footprint of slow control I/O pads foreseeing to mount several sensor chips on a module. In the AREO v.4D architecture, slow control required a dedicated clock, an SC mode 3-bit bus, then an 8-bit input data bus and an 8-bit output data bus. With an I^2C standard interface only 2 bidirectional pins are required. They can be connected to a bus shared by several sensor chips. The I^2C communication is based on a master that imparts clock and orders, and a slave that executes and answers. Only the master entity, which for us is the module controller, can start a communication by addressing a chip on the bus. Each chip is able to recognize its own address embedded in the transmission protocol. We implemented only few characteristic of the I^2C standard and that is why we use the "like" suffix. For example this communication protocol foresee a multi master initial negotiation, in case that several masters are connected on the same bus. In our case the master is always the module controller (or DAQ master) and the sensor chips are always the slave counterparts. A schematic representation of the foreseen I^2C interconnection scheme is shown in Fig. 23.

All the slow control operations are implemented through register R/W operations. Acquisition parameters and settings are mapped on the RWregisters, while acquisition monitors and flags can be read in the RO registers. A special RW register is the command register, a special slow control unit execute the instructions written in this registers. For example a testing routine that stimulates in sequence all the inputs of the sparsifiers has been implemented. It is possible to check if the outgoing pattern matches with that produced by the stimulus.

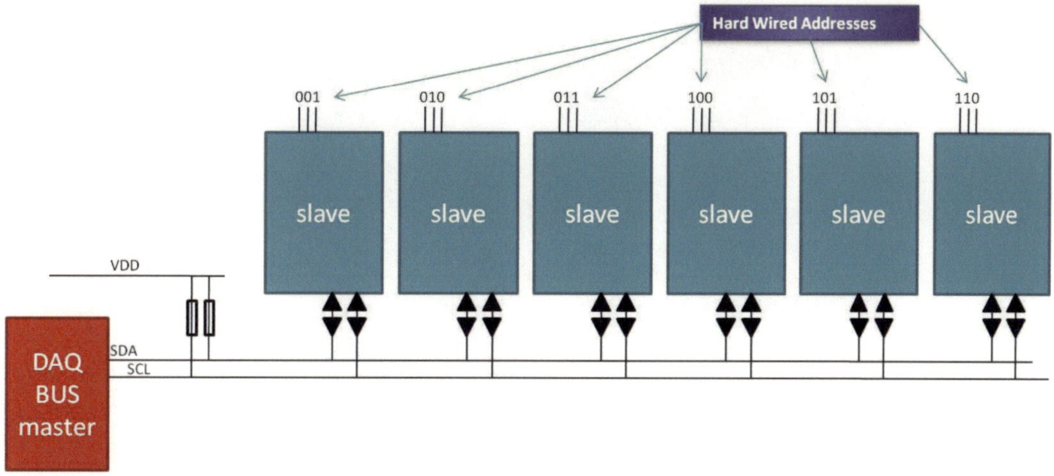

Fig. 23. I^2C bus scheme.

For SORTEX architecture verification and for efficiency evaluation purposes, we realized a full VHDL test bench with integrated Monte Carlo generator. We simulated several milliseconds of acquisition that corresponds to about 500k events. Three main reports are produced by these simulations. The first is the Monte Carlo generation report, that includes all the generated events. Then we produced a pixel latch report, reporting all the hits that were latched on the matrix. The third one is the output report, a list of the hits sent out on the data bus. The hits lost between the MC generation report and the pixel latch report are considered as hit-extraction inefficiency. They were lost due to a frozen MP or an already hit pixel. Hits lost by readout are considered as an acquisition fault. In Fig. 24 we report the hit extraction efficiency of 1 sub-matrix SORTEX readout plotted against read clock frequency and BC clock. In these simulations we never observed faulty hit losses deriving from a misbehaviour of the architecture.

The efficiency drop observed at point BC=250 ns and RDclk=60 MHz was due to repetitive scan buffer overflows. In that point the MST ≈ BC and the scan buffer depth is not sufficient to absorb the statistical fluctuations. It is important to state that a scan buffer overflow does not imply a loss of hits. When no space is available in the scan buffer, if there are new MPs that need to be frozen they are left active for the next BC period until an empty memory location is available. If the readout "loose" one BC, the event tagged with the successive time stamp will include also the hits belonging to the previous time window. In this case no hit information is lost, the only inconvenient is a worse time resolution and a drop in the efficiency. The efficiency drop is due to slower scans since, in these situations, it happens often that a MP list refers to a longer acquisition time. Anyhow, the readout is not intended to work in this conditions, the results presented wanted to point out the performance limits of this architecture.

In Fig. 25 we plotted the efficiencies obtained with the full SORTEX architecture on the 4 sub-matrices. The same reverse trend under 200ns of BC is observed due to scan buffer overflows.

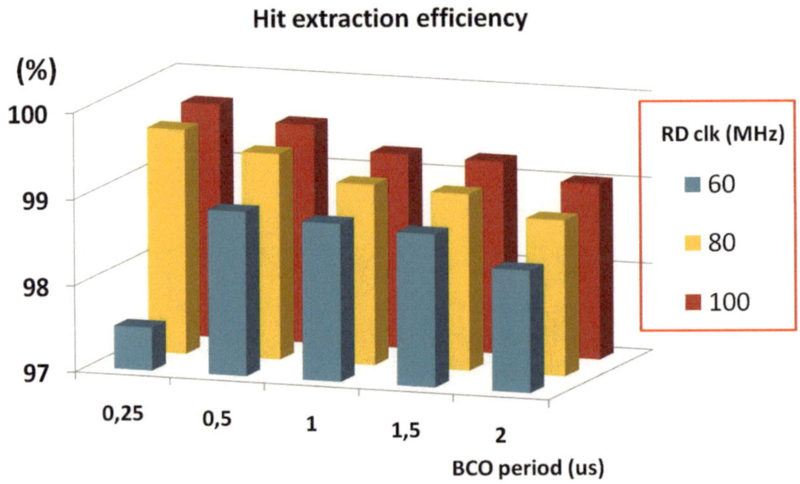

Fig. 24. Hit extraction efficiency of SORTEX architecture vs BC clock and read clock. 1 submatrix simulated only. Hit rate 100 MHz/cm[2].

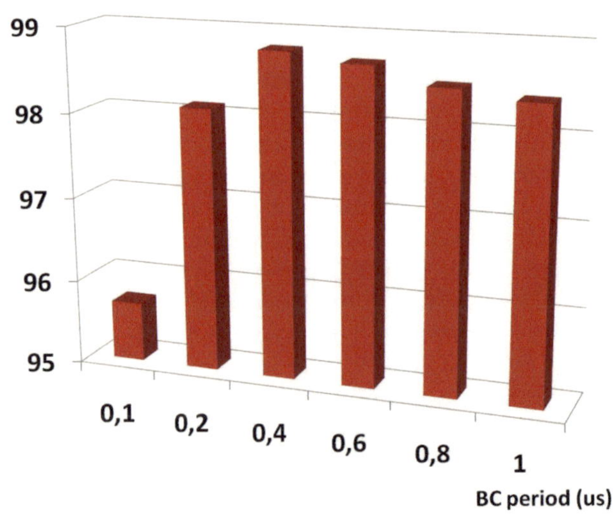

Fig. 25. Hit extraction efficiency of full SORTEX architecture vs BC clock. Read clock 67MHz, output stage clock 200 MHz. Hit rate 100 MHz/cm[2].

8. DAQ integration

The data-push architectures described, are designed to sustain intense hit fluxes, then producing high data rates (order of 2 Gbps per chip). A robust and powerful DAQ system then must be provided in order to handle the considerable amount of data received by the front end chips.

We present a high data rate acquisition system that was involved also for the beam tests of the APSEL4D chip [M. Villa for the SLIM5 Collaboration (year 2009)]. The data acquisition was done by means of two high bandwidth, fully programmable 9U VME board (EDRO)

that have been designed to stand a 12 Gbit/s input rate, 1.2 Gbit/s output rate and have the possibility to perform different types of trigger strategies on data. The most important one was the on-line track identification performed with the help of an Associative Memory board [G. Batingani et Al. (year 2008)], which demonstrated the capability of the setup to trigger on identified tracks with a minimal latency (< $1\mu s$).
The EDRO board is based on FPGAs (Field Programmable Gate Arrays), a picture is presented in Fig. 26. The acronym stands for Event Dispatch and Read Out. It is a 9U VME master board holding 5 mezzanine boards mounted on piggy-back. It is capable of an integrated input/output of 30 Gbps.

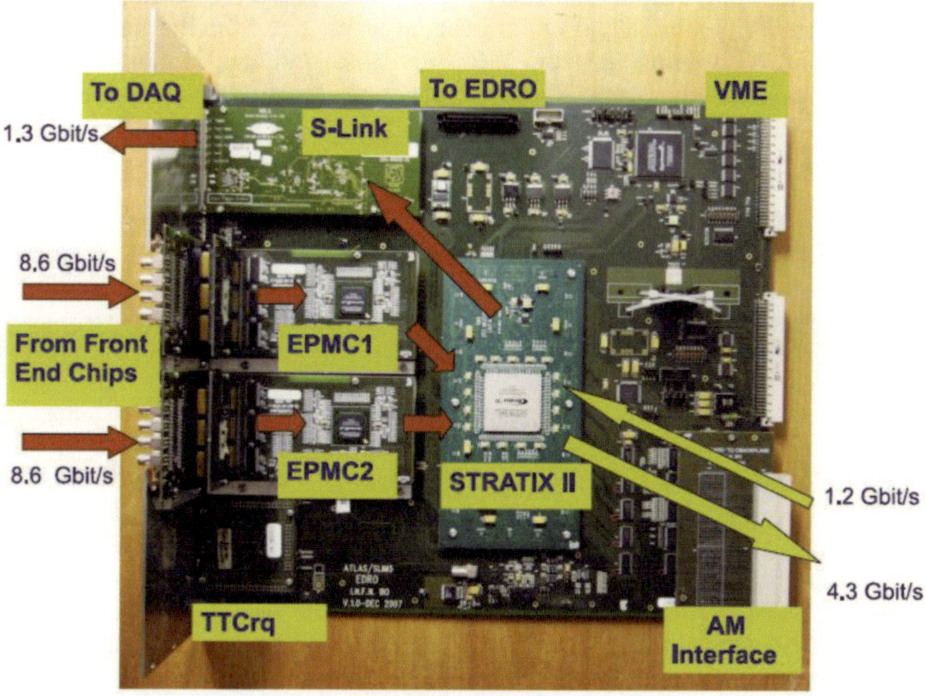

Fig. 26. EDRO board picture. (Event Dispatch and ReadOut).

A TTCrq mezzanine card [G.B. Taylor (2005)] developed for LHC experiments has been used as a 40 MHz clock source. Two Programmable Mezzanine Cards (EPMC) are responsible for the communication to/from the front-end chips. They host an Altera Cyclone II FPGA in a BGA package and several LVTTL/LVDS converters for the communication to/from the front-end chips.[4] Each EPMC can handle 2 Apsel4D chips. The limit is imposed by the high number of I/O required by the AREO architecture rather than the front-end data rate, since each EPMC can handle up to 8.6 Gbps.
Internal logic and most of the on-board data transfer run at 120 MHz clock, ensuring a data input/output of the order of 12.4 GBit/s. The hits collected from the EPMCs are forwarded

[4] Differential signaling is used on the 30 m cable that connect the EDRO board to the electronics in the experimental area. There, the signals are converted back to single ended CMOS to be connected to the APSEL4D digital I/O

to the main mezzanine of the EDRO board: an 18 layers board holding an Altera Stratix II FPGA with 1508 pins, developed for the CMS muon finder [J. Ero et Al. (year 2008)]. The large number of logical elements (> 100k) and memory (> 6Mbits) of the FPGA have been exploited to implement the event building and triggering process running at 120 MHz with minimal inefficiencies. Hits from the EPMCs can be forwarded to the external associative memory board by using LVDS serializer/deserializers. Triggered events are first stored on long local buffers and then forwarded to the last piggy back board, called S-Link LSC (Link Source Card) [H.C. van der Bij et Al. (year 1997)], developed at CERN for the data sending to the final DAQ PC. A set of connectors for EDRO-EDRO communication, EDROAM communication and input/outputs from LEMO signals completes the board.
These boards have been intensively used for the data acquisition from the chips featuring an AREO architecture. We are now developing few hardware and firmware upgrades to these boards, foreseeing to test other devices based on newer readout architectures like SORTEX.

9. Conclusions

The next generation of particle accelerators, that are being designed for new discoveries in the world of high energy physics, opened new challenges in the design of appropriate detectors. The high particle fluxes that are expected in proximity of the interaction region, require extensive researches in the field of silicon tracker detectors. We presented an introduction on silicon sensors and, in more details, on silicon pixel detectors. New opportunities are given by the technological improvement of the silicon industry, the 3D, or vertical integration for example is a promising process for hyper-integrated systems.
In this context we described our approach in the design of innovative digital readout architectures. We presented mainly two proven readout architectures, AREO and SORTEX. AREO architecture has been implemented on several chips thanks to the SLIM5 collaboration. We have mentioned the APSEL chip family, in particular the 3D and 4D versions characterized by different matrix dimensions (256 and 4096 pixels respectively) but same sensor technology (planar CMOS MAPS sensor). The AREO architecture has been adopted, within the same collaboration framework, also to build a vertically integrated MAPS sensor. At the moment, the 32×8 sensor matrix and the readout layers are still in production. An efficiency study on the 4D version of the architecture was presented, and it showed an efficiency of about 96% with a flux of 100 Mhit $cm^{-2} s^{-1}$. We have put this target since it seems to be the most probable value at 1÷2 cm of radii from the interaction point of the next generation, highest-luminosity B-factories like SuperB (10^{36} $cm^{-2} s^{-1}$).
We described then the SORTEX architecture designed for wider matrices (320×256 pixels) and born on the experience matured with the APSEL chip family based on AREO. The new architecture is characterized by several innovations suggested also by a more exhaustive simulation campaign. A higher parallelization and a higher optimization of the sparsification algorithms allowed to raise the efficiency over 98% with an increased area (read as global rate) increased of a factor greater than 10. The SORTEX architecture has been adopted on a reduced 32x128 matrix sensor realized as a hybrid pixel sensor by the VIPIX collaboration. The CMOS layer implementing the front-end electronics and digital readout has just come out of foundry.
We are planning the design of a new architecture based on a different matrix logic. Preliminary simulations showed a very promising hit-extraction efficiency above 99% and

an improved time resolution capability, this architecture plans to take great advantage from the new vertical integration technology.
A powerful DAQ board has also been presented, a high bandwidth 9U VME board based on high-performance FPGAs for event building and triggering. It was developed to handle a front-end rate of more than 16 Gbps, and it was provided with a 4.3 Gbps associative-memory interface for a high-speed track identification support. A couple of this boards, called EDRO, have been integrated in the data acquisition system for the beam test set up of the APSEL4D chip. We intend to go further with the innovation of pixel readout circuits and with their integration in high performance DAQ systems, giving the scientific community our little contribution for a chance of new discoveries.

10. References

A. Gabrielli for the SLIM5 Collaboration (year 2008). Proposal of a sparsification circuit for mixed-mode MAPS detectors, *Nuc. Instr. and Meth. in Phys. Res. A* 596: 93–95.

A. Gabrielli for the SLIM5 Collaboration (year 2009). A 4096-pixel MAPS device with on-chip data sparsification, *Nuc. Instr. and Meth. in Phys. Res. A* 604: 408-411.

G. Batingani et Al. (year 2008). The associative memory for the self-triggered slim5 silicon telescope, *IEEE Nucl. Sci. Symp. Conf. Record 2008* pp. 2765 - 2769.

G. Rizzo for the SLIM5 collaboration (year 2007). Recent development on CMOS monolithic active pixel sensors, *Nuc. Instr. and Meth. in Phys. Res. A* 576: 103–108.

G.B. Taylor (2005). *Timing, Trigger and Control (TTC) System for the LHC Detectors,* http:// www.cern.ch/TTC/intro.html.

H.C. van der Bij et Al. (year 1997). S-link, a data link interface specification for the lhc era, *Nuc. Sci. IEEE Trans.* 44-3: 398–402.

J. Ero et Al. (year 2008). The CMS drift tube track finder, *J. Inst. 3 P08006* .

L. Gaioni et Al. (year 2009). A 3d deep n-well cmos maps for the ilc vertex detector, *Nuc. Instr. and Meth. in Phys. Res. A* doi:10.1016/j.nima.2009.09.041.

M. Villa for the SLIM5 Collaboration (year 2009). The l1 track trigger and high data rate acquisition system for the SLIM5 beam test, *IEEE Nucl. Sci. Symp. Conf. Record 2009.*

N. Neri et Al. (year 2010). Deep N-well MAPS in a 130 nm CMOS technology: beam test results, *Nuc. Instr. and Meth. in Phys. Res. A* doi:10.1016/j.nima.2010.02.193.

R. Klingenberg for the ATLAS pixel collaboration (year 2007). The ATLAS pixel detector, *Nuc. Instr. and Meth. in Phys. Res. A* 579: 664–668.

R. Lipton (year 2007). 3D-vertical integration of sensors and electronics, *Nuc. Instr. and Meth. in Phys. Res. A* 579: 690–694.

S. Bettarini et Al. (year 2007). Development of deep N-well monolithic active pixel sensors in a 0.13 μm CMOS technology, *Nuc. Instr. and Meth. in Phys. Res. A* 572: 277–280.

S. Schnetzer for the CMS Pixel Collaboration (year 2003). The CMS pixel detector, *Nuc. Instr. and Meth. in Phys. Res. A* 501: 100–105.

SuperB Collaboration (2007). *SuperB Conceptual Design Report,* http://arxiv.org/abs/ 0709.0451v2. V.

Re et Al. (year 2010). Vertically integrated deep N-well CMOS MAPS with sparsification and time stamping capabilities for thin charged particle trackers, *Nuc. Instr. And Meth. in Phys. Res. A* doi:10.1016/j.nima.2010.05.039.

W-M Yao et Al. (year 2006). *J. Phys G: Nucl. Part. Phys.* 33: 284–285.